THE Architects AND THE City

CHICAGO ARCHITECTURE AND URBANISM

A series edited by   Robert Bruegmann
                      Joan Draper
                      Wim de Wit
                      David Van Zanten

THE Architects

HOLABIRD & ROCHE OF

City

AND THE

CHICAGO, 1880–1918

ROBERT BRUEGMANN

IN ASSOCIATION WITH

THE CHICAGO HISTORICAL SOCIETY

THE UNIVERSITY OF CHICAGO PRESS

CHICAGO AND LONDON

Works in Chicago Architecture and Urbanism are supported in part by funds given in memory of Ann Lorenz Van Zanten and administered by the Chicago Historical Society.

This work was aided by a grant from the Graham Foundation for Advanced Studies in the Visual Arts.

Robert Bruegmann is professor of architectural history at the University of Illinois at Chicago. He is the author of *Holabird & Roche/Holabird & Root: An Illustrated Catalog of Works, 1880–1940.*

The University of Chicago Press, Chicago 60637
The University of Chicago Press, Ltd., London
©1997 by The University of Chicago
All rights reserved. Published 1997
Printed in the United States of America
06 05 04 03 02 01 00 99 98 97   1 2 3 4 5
ISBN: 0-226-07695-4 (cloth)

Library of Congress Cataloging-in-Publication Data
Bruegmann, Robert.
    The architects and the city: Holabird & Roche of Chicago, 1880–1918 / Robert Bruegmann.
      p. cm.—(Chicago architecture and urbanism)
    "In cooperation with the Chicago Historical Society."
    Includes bibliographical references and index.
    ISBN 0-226-07695-4 (cloth: alk. paper)
    1. Holabird & Roche (Chicago, Ill.) 2. Chicago school of architecture
(Movement) 3. Architecture—Buildings, structures, etc. I. Title. II. Series.
NA737.H558B78 1997
720′.92′277311—dc20
                                          96-22151
                                        CIP

This book is printed on acid-free paper.

CONTENTS

v

During the nearly fifteen years I have been doing research on the firm of Holabird & Roche/Holabird & Root, I have received an enormous amount of help from many individuals and institutions. I have thanked many of them in the acknowledgments section of the Holabird & Root catalog volumes published by Garland Publishing Company in 1991. If I do not repeat this voluminous list of names here, it is not for want of continued gratitude. What I shall do below is acknowledge those individuals and groups who aided me specifically on this narrative volume.

I am once again deeply indebted to the Chicago Historical Society. Without the continuing cooperation of many individuals at this admirable institution this volume would never have appeared. I thank Harold Skramstad and Ellsworth Brown, former directors, and Douglas Greenberg, director; Larry Viskochil, until recently curator of prints and photographs; Eileen Flanagan of prints and drawings; and Janice McNeill, the Society's librarian. For their staunch support of this project for many years I am especially indebted to Wim de Wit, formerly curator of the Society's architectural collections and a strong supporter of this work; Scott LaFrance, curator of the Charles F. Murphy Architectural Study Center until his recent and tragically early death; Margaret Kelly, acting curator of the collection; and Russell Lewis, assistant director for research and curatorial affairs, who has been involved with this project virtually from the start and who has been unfailingly enthusiastic and helpful. I am also extremely grateful to the Society for playing host to the Chicago Urban History seminar. Over the years the dedicated efforts and intellectual hospitality of stalwarts like Russell Lewis, Michael Ebner, and Ann Durkin Keating resulted in a series of meetings that have done much to expand my urban horizons.

Parts of the manuscript, or all of it, were read by Peter Hales, my colleague in the Department of Art History at the University of Illinois at Chicago, Perry Duis of the Department of History at the same institution, Sally Chappell, recently retired from the Art Department at De Paul University, Mark Burnette of the Evanston Historical Society, and Michael Ebner of the History Department at Lake Forest College. All these people offered excellent counsel. I am also grateful to my fellow editors in the series Chicago Architecture and Urbanism—David Van Zanten of Northwestern University, Joan Draper of the University of Colorado, and Wim de Wit, formerly of the Chicago Historical Society and now of the Getty Trust in Santa Monica—for their willingness to include this book in the series.

For sharing information and insights with me or challenging my thinking about some of the issues I raise in this book I thank Daniel Bluestone, Thomas Hines, Scott Jorgenson, Katherine Solomonson, Mitchell Schwarzer, Eric Monkennen, Carol Willis, Eric Sandweis, and Gwendolyn Wright. I also thank Dennis McClendon of Chicago Cartographics, who not only provided the maps for both the catalog volumes and this project, but also played a major role in shaping the content and served as the proverbial tireless fact checker.

Finally, I thank several people at the University of Chicago Press, notably acquisitions editors Karen Wilson, who stood by this project for ten years, and Susan Bielstein, who saw this volume to completion, manuscript editor Alice Bennett, who performed wonders in pulling together a manuscript produced in phases over many years and making it coherent, and designer Marianne Jankowski, who created the elegant format.

This book grew out of an effort to understand the vast and varied man-made landscape that constitutes the Chicago metropolitan area and its hinterland. I set out to explore aspects of this story by carefully examining the enormous body of records available for one of America's largest and most prominent architectural firms, the organization that started as Holabird & Simonds in 1880 and has continued to the present under successive partnership agreements as Holabird, Simonds & Roche; Holabird & Root; Holabird, Root & Burgee; and finally, once again, Holabird & Root.

My work on this topic started when I arrived in Chicago in 1978 to teach at the University of Illinois at Chicago. Like many other newcomers I was at once attracted and repelled by the city, exhilarated by its sheer size and diversity but dismayed by the rawness and apparent disorder. I soon became aware that my reactions were typical. For over a century newcomers have had to come to terms with a place where huge industrial buildings jostle against modest single-family houses and miles of commercial strips and rail yards all but overwhelm the occasional park or public building. In a search for the order behind this landscape, I started to look for a topic that could serve as a point of departure for investigation.

At the time, Chicago was known in architectural history primarily as the place that had created the great commercial structures of the "Chicago School" of the 1880s and 1890s, the reform domestic work of Frank Lloyd Wright and his followers in the "Prairie School" in the early twentieth century, and the modernist work of Ludwig Mies van der Rohe and his American followers in the postwar "second Chicago School." For reasons I did not then fully understand, these buildings and their treatment in standard histories left me unmoved, so I looked elsewhere. What caught my eye was the set of spectacular stepped-back office buildings of the 1920s, among them the Chicago Tribune, Palmolive, Board of Trade, and Civic Opera Buildings. To my amazement I could find very little serious writing about them, even though when they were built they were among the best known and most discussed structures in America. It turned out that one after another of the most compelling examples were by the same firm: Holabird & Root. On further inquiry I discovered that the firm still existed and that in 1979 it had donated to the Chicago Historical Society almost all of its drawings and other records created before 1945. I went to look.

Thus began a project that has occupied me more or less continuously for over fifteen years. The first step, even before the monumental task of processing all the drawings at the Chicago Historical Society was completed, was an exhibition I curated there in 1980, with an accompanying essay on the firm in *Chicago History*. In this exhibition and essay I tried to create a framework for discussing the work of the firm outside the traditional plot of the two "Chicago schools" and to deal with the work not as part of the evolution of "progressive" styles but as a record of intervention by the architects into the built fabric of the city. Once the show was over, I had intended to move on to other work, but in 1982 Ann Van Zanten, then curator of the Society's architectural collections, proposed transforming the manuscript catalog of the firm's drawings into a small published catalog introduced by a series of short essays we would write. Shortly after I agreed to collaborate on this effort but before any substantial work was started, Ann's life was tragically cut short, and the project continued under my direction. The more I studied the drawings and other records, and the more I searched for information about the firm in the other collections of the Society, the more I realized how important these documents could be in revealing unexplored aspects of the city's history. Both the entries and the essays mushroomed as I found the materials necessary to flesh out the historical context of the firm's work.

Soon it became apparent that the project could no longer be shoehorned into a single volume, let alone the small-format book originally envisioned. At about that time an editor at Garland Publishing Company proposed publishing the catalog separately in a multivolume edition. After years of labor by me and by students and volunteers at the Society under my direction, the three-volume catalog *Holabird & Roche/ Holabird & Root: An Illustrated Catalog of Works, 1880–1940* finally appeared in 1991. It documents over fifteen hundred projects for new buildings, substantial remodelings, interiors, and furniture designed by the firm between 1880 and 1940. In these volumes I attempted to collect and summarize as much information as could be found on the firm's commissions, using the Holabird & Root archives at the Chicago Historical Society as well as a broad array of other materials. This work, primarily documentary rather than interpretive, forms the basic underpinnings of the present project. Although this book is intended as a self-contained narrative and has its own abridged catalog, anyone interested in the full documentation for any of the firm's buildings should consult the catalog volumes. To make this easier, throughout this book I have supplied the entry number from the catalog after the initial reference to a Holabird & Roche project.

This book is the first of a projected two-volume set whose goal is to examine the work of the firm from an interpretive historical perspective. This volume deals with 1880 to 1918, tracing the origins of the firm, its early work, its maturation in the boom years of the 1880s and early 1890s, and the slow but steady growth of expertise in many building types in the first two decades of the twentieth century, all under the leadership of the founding partners, William Holabird and Martin Roche. The second volume will cover the years from 1919 to the early 1940s, including the work of the firm during the boom period of the 1920s, the lean years of the depression, and the war years. During the period covered in the second volume, the firm was dominated by a second generation of partners, including John A. Holabird and John Wellborn Root Jr.

At first glance some of these dates may seem arbitrary. Ending this volume at the end of World War I, for example, might seem illogical, since the founding partners both lived into the 1920s, John Holabird until 1923 and Martin Roche until 1927, and it was not until 1927 that the firm name changed from Holabird & Roche to Holabird & Root. But the name change only made official a transition that had been in progress since the mid-1910s, when the next generation first entered the office, so I have chosen to end this volume with World War I and start the second volume with the return to the office, immediately after the war, of the young men who would lead the second generation. Likewise I have used 1945, the date of John Holabird's death, as the cutoff for the second generation, even though John Root lived until 1965. This reflects the fundamental changes that appeared in the firm and in the city in the postwar period and the cutoff date of the Holabird & Root donation to the Chicago Historical Society.

Organization and Goals of the Book

I have tried to link two fields of study that I feel ought to be close cousins but in practice have been distant relatives. As I became increasingly aware in preparing this book, the rift between architectural history and urban history runs deep and presents a formidable challenge to any project of this kind.

Much of the "urban history" of the past several decades has grown in response to the crisis of the central cities in the post–World War II years. Historians of the city have been especially keen on identifying and exploring what is specifically "urban" in the development of our metropolitan regions. They have concerned themselves with what they felt were the most fundamental elements that generated America's great cities in the late nineteenth and early twentieth centuries, then left them vulnerable in the postwar years. Because of this interest, their focus was largely on the city center and on the elements in it that survived from the traditional industrial city. They have been less interested in what happened at the periphery of the metropolitan area. In addition, because the training of historians focuses primarily on social, political, and economic forces, on the printed word and the statistical table, they have often given short shrift to the fabric of the built environment. Buildings, whether the apartment blocks along Haussmann's boulevards or the early office buildings of late nineteenth-century Chicago, are usually presented as illustrations of the effects of more basic historical forces. With a few notable exceptions, historians have tended not to see the design and construction of buildings as integral parts of the city's development.

Modern architectural history, on the other hand, grew out of a completely different set of concerns. Heavily influenced by the theoretical ideas of nineteenth-century art history, one branch of architectural history has been concerned with categorizing buildings according to either their aesthetic merit or how they fit into a great chain of stylistic development running from the pyramids to Versailles to the Villa Savoye. Another strain exhibits a strong impulse to see buildings in moral terms. Does a given building honestly express its function, its structure, the age in which it was built? Out of the effort to reconcile these often conflicting goals, much of recent architectural history has tried to correlate "progress" in programmatic and technical means with a succession of "progressive" styles, usually the creations of single, heroic designers. Once the canon of approved works was established, the architectural historian could go back to recover some of the social and economic factors that led to the production of a given building. But these factors, it was clearly implied, could never get to the heart of the design, since the role of art is to transcend the specific circumstances that led to it. Because what was important and less important was already determined, moreover, the architectural historian's task was to flesh out the details of a story whose main lines were presumed to be known.

The result has been a dramatic split between the city as seen by a historian and the city as seen by an architectural historian. Many of the biggest or most prominent structures in any American city barely appear in architectural history, and many of the major monuments of architectural history are extremely marginal in the tale told by the urban historian. The Holabird & Roche buildings most discussed in modernist architectural history were usually relatively inexpensive speculative structures at the fringes of the Loop that could be classified as belonging to the Chicago School. Although these buildings were not unknown to discerning viewers at the turn of the century, they did not for the most part elicit much comment, even in the architectural journals. Many other Holabird & Roche buildings from these years that are barely mentioned in modernist architectural history, on the other hand, loomed large on the cityscape. Few Chicagoans were unaware of the LaSalle Hotel, the Boston Store, or the Cook County Courthouse and Chicago City Hall.

In trying to place the buildings of Holabird & Roche more firmly within the realm of urban history, I have paid little attention to many of the matters that have most engaged architectural historians. For example, I have made relatively little attempt to attribute designs to individual designers. Except in a few cases, this practice does not seem particularly fruitful. To say that Martin Roche "designed" the Tacoma Building is fundamentally misleading. Holabird & Roche, like many large twentieth-century commercial architectural firms, was organized more like a business office than an artist's studio, and almost all projects were the product of many hands. Although Martin Roche himself undoubtedly drew much of the ornamental detail for the Tacoma, evidence makes it clear that his partner William Holabird, as well as the client, Wirt D. Walker, the contractor, George A. Fuller, an elevator manufacturer, and a terra cotta salesman all played large roles in its creation. I hope that these essays will suggest something of the daily operation of the firm and how its members engaged with all the other players involved in creating the built environment.

This book is meant to be a set of interlocking explorations into the operation of the architects in the city. The Holabird & Roche material is ideal for this purpose because it covers so many building types with such extensive documentation. Although the high office building must be part of this discussion, many of the most illuminating building types have rarely appeared in architectural histories. The telephone switching station and automobile showroom provide fascinating evidence on the search for an appropriate expression for new pieces of the urban fabric. The design of a major military installation or a large city hotel illustrates the process of city building in miniature, since each constituted its own small world. The work at the Glen View Golf and Polo Club or the Coleman Lake Club in northern Wisconsin provides a rare glimpse of the architects at the intersection of work and recreation.

Writing this work presented substantial conceptual and organizational problems, in part the result of the immense scale of the enterprise. Between 1880 and 1940 Holabird & Roche was responsible for thousands of commissions, some built, others remaining on paper, ranging from tombstones and boiler room alterations to entire industrial and institutional complexes. Holabird & Roche worked on programs as diverse as racetrack grandstands and public housing projects, for sites all over the country and abroad, often making it difficult to imagine that the projects were all the work of the same architectural office. Yet there was clearly a kind of unity. After some acquaintance with the firm's work, it is often not hard to pick out its other buildings, even when the buildings seem at first glance quite different.

The great challenge was to convey some sense of this unity and at the same time to point out the particulars that best illuminate a specific time or place and shed light on the city building process. To deal with this problem, within each of the four major divisions of the book a chronological chapter on the organization, personnel, and business practices of the firm is followed by a set of detailed explorations of particular issues. Thus the chronological chapters (1, 3, 9, and 15), form a self-contained narrative. Each of the other chapters is organized around one or more specific topics. Some deal with the development of a given building type: for example, the department store on State Street in the years 1890–1910; others explore the workings of the real estate market, as in the creation of the speculative office building; still others trace the role of clients like the Chicago Telephone Company; the changing character of specific areas of the city like the corner of Monroe and Michigan; or the importance in Chicago history of a single landmark structure such as the Cook County Courthouse and Chicago City Hall. I hope by this method to balance the need for narrative unity with the possibility of extended exploration into topics that cannot fit within any single plot line.

Another problem sprang directly from the nature of commercial architecture. Commercial architects, like all architects, functioned in part as artists. They tried to make their buildings beautiful as well as useful. But if they wanted to stay in business, they also functioned as businessmen. Like many businessmen, members of the Holabird & Roche firm did not feel it was in their best interest to indulge publicly in speculative musings or make known their aesthetic reactions to the work of their own firm and others. There are only a few scraps of evidence on what anyone in the firm thought about the important architectural issues of the day—or about any subject, for that matter. I have tried to piece together what fragments I could find to give some sense of these men, but in the end access to them must be primarily through a close reading of their buildings. My desire to discover something of the point of view of the authors behind the works has reinforced the decision to talk about minor as well as major buildings in the firm's oeuvre. Sometimes a tiny bank in a rural area can reveal more about its creators than a skyscraper in the Loop.

This, then, is a book about how the partners and employees at Holabird & Roche operated in the urban realm, how they used Chicago, its central business district, its neighborhoods, its suburbs, and its vast hinterlands as a place to build a career and make a living, to engage in civic and cultural activities, and to find relaxation and relief from urban pressures. It is about how their work shaped the city and how it reflected some of the most important forces in urban life during the years between the late nineteenth century and the end of World War I. It is a study of the architects and their city.

One final point. I have tried to present the work of the architects from the standpoint of their own time and, whenever possible, to describe how their buildings were seen and judged at that time. I attempt to show, for example, that the fixation by modernist historians on the few relatively undecorated loft and office buildings of the 1880s has led to an unbalanced picture of the work of the firm and the way it was received in its own day. But it is useless to suggest that I have achieved objectivity, a goal as futile as it is naive. The past is a shifting landscape that is seen anew by each successive era, and it is obvious that few scholars would engage in a study of this magnitude without a definite point of view. In case my own program is not immediately clear, let me state at the outset that I greatly admire both the work of the firm and the city it helped create. I believe, moreover, that the kind of architectural history that elevates the reputations of single iconoclastic creators over those of firms like Holabird & Roche, which were responsible for substantial portions of our cities, in the end demeans both profession and city and alienates the public.

A book like this might be seen as a defense of the existing order of the city. It is true that the kinds of buildings designed by Holabird & Roche and presented here were commissioned by a relatively small segment of the American population, the segment that actively controlled day to day much of the production and wealth of the country. But I hope no one will read this work as an unthinking apology for the firm or for the American upper middle class it served, or as a call to return to some former golden age.

The changes in Chicago during the years covered by this book were enormous, and they were often achieved at great cost. Although there is now a certain nostalgia for the city in the late nineteenth and early twentieth centuries, it was far from being a golden age. Even more than most American cities, Chicago was often harsh and turbulent in its social and political environments as well as in its physical and climatic ones. It cannot be denied that the attitudes of just such upper-middle-class citizens as William Holabird and Martin Roche, by upholding the status quo, could be considered partly responsible for the class dissension, labor unrest, and environmental problems of these years.

I do not want to downplay these problems. In this book the labor trouble that in part led to the creation of Fort Sheridan, the invasion by commercial buildings of South Michigan Avenue, one of Chicago's most prestigious residential areas, the widespread fear and resentment aroused by big buildings put up in the speculative frenzy of the 1880s and 1890s, and even the deforestation of the landscape of northern Wisconsin by Chicago lumber interests are all episodes connected in one way or another with the commissions of the firm.

And yet for all these problems, Holabird & Roche and its clients were engaged in an optimistic enterprise. They felt that the problems of change were temporary and were more than offset by the great increase in opportunities for all citizens. Certainly the architects and their clients created buildings that most citizens from that day to this have found both useful and aesthetically pleasing. For all its faults, the American political and economic context they worked in made possible, if not a golden age, at least a remarkable variety of living, working, and recreational environments. No previous society in history boasted more choices and chances for the population at large. Thus readers should feel free to see this book as a reminder of how design professionals and other citizens can operate in what appear to be chaotic and disturbing times yet create a built environment that can serve the needs of the present and future with dignity and grace.

Part

One

THE FOUNDING OF
THE FIRM

In 1880 William Holabird and Ossian C. Simonds founded the firm of Holabird &
Simonds.[1] The two men could not have picked a more auspicious time. The country
was finally recovering from a major economic panic in the early 1870s and was on the
brink of a boom that would last through the 1880s. The nation's population was rapidly expanding, with large cities getting the lion's share of the growth.

Among all the big cities, however, Chicago experienced the most extraordinary
rise. By 1880 the city's early history had already become legend.[2] From its beginning
in 1830 on an inhospitable stretch of marshy terrain that smelled of onions, Chicago
had grown into a city of over 300,000 in less than four decades. Then, rebounding
after the Great Fire of 1871, one of the most destructive in recorded history, Chicago
rebuilt and expanded even faster, jumping to over 500,000 in population by 1880.

Chicago's commercial development had proceeded apace. By 1880 the city had
become the trading center of America's vast heartland. First the rivers and canals, then
the railroads, brought in farm produce and carried manufactured products to its markets. To Chicago came grain and cattle from across the Midwest, to be traded, pro-
cessed, and shipped to the rest of the world. After the Civil War, the city's development as one of the world's great railroad centers led to its dominance in the lumber,
coal, and steel industries and the manufacture of farm implements, railroad cars, machinery, and household goods of all kinds.[3]

Indeed, it seemed to many Chicagoans that their city was well on the way to
overtaking New York. Nor was this simply more of the inflated rhetoric that had
earned it the nickname "Windy City." Given contemporary conditions, this was a rea-

sonable prediction, shared by many impartial observers. The pioneer of American urban statistics, Adna Weber, writing in 1899 in his authoritative *Growth of the Cities in the Nineteenth Century,* put it this way:

> New York's primacy depends on the location at the junction of the land and water transportation; in New York occurs the change of ownership and transfer of goods in the commerce between Europe and the United States. If the water route could be extended inland to Chicago by means of a ship canal, Chicago would become the terminus of European commerce, and with scarcely any doubt, take from New York the rank of commercial and financial center of the New World, and prospectively, of the globe.[4]

Chicago was experiencing changes of all kinds faster than the more established cities in the East or in Europe. It was a tumultuous place, building and rebuilding itself so fast that at times it must have seemed the entire city was under construction. It was the "Shock City" of the 1870s and 1880s, where travelers went to view the future. Descriptions of the journey into Chicago by train quickly became a standard feature in American literature.[5] From them we can get some sense of the place where the firm of Holabird & Simonds was established and of the urban environment in which they started to work.

Virtually all these descriptions begin with the train rushing through the productive countryside beyond the city. Of course the train itself plays a powerful role in suggesting the intricate but uneasy relationship between the rich agricultural hinterlands through which the tracks ran and the great city beyond to which both passengers and products flowed. Long before the train reaches the city there are portents of what is to come. The characters in the novels see clouds of industrial smoke hovering on the horizon. This sight triggers conflicting feelings—excitement about the dynamic energy of the city but at the same time fear of its forbidding scale, congestion, and anonymity.[6]

Dotting the countryside beyond the continuously built up Chicago area are small towns and villages, some centers of agricultural production, some hives of industry, still others primarily bedroom communities for the great city. On the railway maps these suburbs seem strung out along the lines like beads on a necklace.

As the train draws closer to the Loop, the density of settlement quickly increases. Except for the large system of parks and boulevards laid out in the 1860s and encircling the city's built-up area from Lincoln Park on the north to Jackson Park on the south, all the land has been covered by a grid of streets and new houses as soon as it has become accessible by horsecar and cable car.

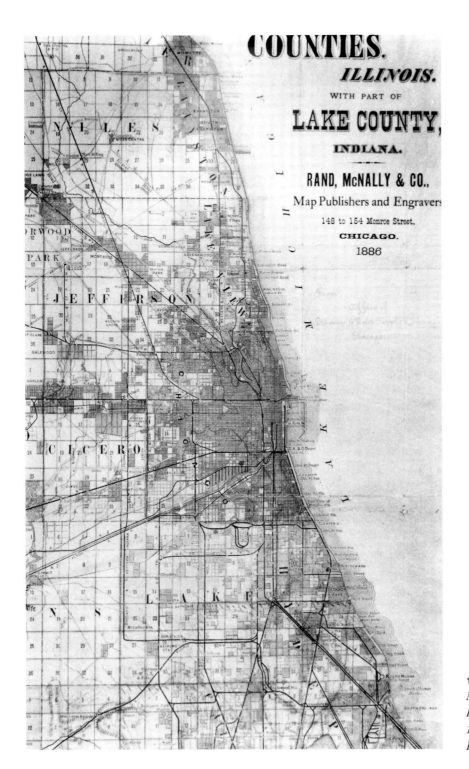

COUNTIES.
ILLINOIS.
WITH PART OF
LAKE COUNTY,
INDIANA.

RAND, McNALLY & CO.,
Map Publishers and Engravers
148 to 154 Monroe Street,
CHICAGO.
1886

1.1

*Map of Chicago and its region.
Rand, McNally and Company,
1886. University of Chicago
Library.*

The rapidity of Chicago's growth is apparent from the window of the railcar. Entire neighborhoods are under construction as development leapfrogs outward, rushing forward in some places while bypassing other areas altogether, thus sparing their rural character. Even in neighborhoods built up all at the same time, development is uneven. In some neighborhoods single-family houses sitting behind large or small front yards adjoin apartment buildings and shops that come all the way out to the lot line. Some houses have bridges from the sidewalk to a raised first floor, reflecting the city's decision in the 1850s to raise the street level above Chicago's mud. In the finer neighborhoods, deed covenants and neighborhood pressure have led to more coherent rows of masonry houses, lining the streets in a display of ample means and love of comfort.[7] The most remarkable characteristic of Chicago to many easterners was the large number of single-family detached houses. Although many were modest one-story flat-front cottages on small lots, they represented a momentous American social revolution. They signaled the development of an urban pattern in which a high percentage of the middle class could aspire to a single-family house, an option that had until recently been almost exclusively the domain of the wealthy.

Extending in fingers from the business district are dense areas crisscrossed by railroad lines and filled with factories, warehouses, and other industrial establishments. These almost always inspire awe. "Huge, misshapen buildings appeared in flat spaces, amid hundreds of cars. Webs of railway tracks spread out dangerously in acres of marvelous intricacy, amid which men moved, sooty, grimy, sullen, and sickly," is Hamlin Garland's description in *Rose of Dutcher's Coolly*.[8] Interspersed with the industrial areas are the famous ethnic working-class neighborhoods such as Bridgeport and Back of the Yards that provide the workforce for Chicago's immense industrial machine. Then there are the slums, areas crowded with brick and frame tenements, devoid of amenities, housing thousands of the city's poorest residents.

Finally, the train crosses the no-man's-land of rail yards and freight houses to reach the edge of the central business district and railroad terminals. Leaving the train, the traveler joins the crush of people surging out of the cavernous train sheds onto the street. Near the station are hotels, warehouses, and other buildings catering to arriving and departing travelers and freight. Closer to the center of the Loop are loft districts where five- and six-story utilitarian brick warehouses form a tight semicircle to the north, west, and south of the central business district. A few blocks, and the traveler is at the very center of the Loop, the tight core of the business district created by the cable car circuit and later defined by the elevated railway lines. Here there are government buildings with stone facades along Clark and Dearborn, office buildings, department stores, and hotels farther east along State, Wabash, and Michigan.

The overwhelming impression is of movement and activity. In the Loop everything is congested. Pedestrians pack the sidewalks. The streets are filled with horse-drawn carriages, freight wagons, street railway cars, cable cars, and people everywhere, all in a hurry. "America is energetic, but Chicago is in a fever. It does not rest one moment, but goes on, on—ever ceaselessly ahead—to buying and selling and getting gain. Everything is rapid, everything is keen. There are hardly any idlers on the streets. Everyone has an object in immediate view—and is walking fast to reach it," Englishman C. B. Berry wrote in 1879.[9]

Chicago in 1880 was a noisy, exciting place, where anything seemed possible except to find time to reflect on the rush of events, their causes, or their consequences. In this tumultuous young city was founded, in 1880, the architectural firm of Holabird & Simonds.

William Holabird

William Holabird, the elder of the founding partners, was born in Amenia Union, Duchess County, New York, in September 1854, one of three children of Samuel Beckley Holabird, an officer in the United States Army, and Mary Theodosta Grant Holabird.[10] Young William apparently spent his childhood in St. Paul, Minnesota, while his father occupied posts around the country as he rose through the army ranks.[11]

1.2
Holabird family tree. Drawn by John A. Holabird Jr.; detail redrawn by Dennis McClendon, 1996.

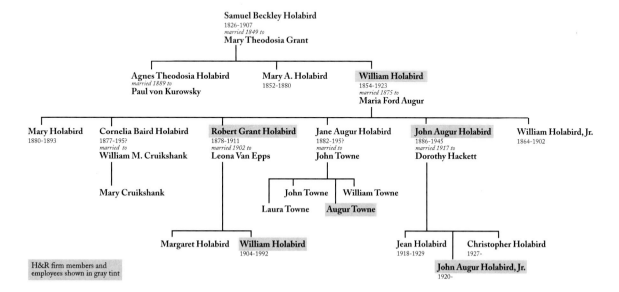

Samuel Beckley Holabird's career was eventually capped in 1883 by his appointment as quartermaster general of the army with a rank of brigadier general. In this position he would secure his place in military history by inventing the pup tent and the canvas fatigue uniform. Despite a modest army salary, by the 1870s Samuel Beckley Holabird was quite affluent, if not wealthy, perhaps the result of trading in the New Orleans cotton futures market.[12]

William graduated from St. Paul High School in 1871. In 1873 he entered West Point, probably with some help from his father. His career at the Academy was far from smooth, judging from the scanty evidence available. He was expelled once, according to Holabird family legend, for rowing across the Hudson to Garrison, New York, the prototypical saloon town that seems to be found near all military installations.[13] He was reinstated, apparently again with his father's help, only to resign in 1875 in the wake of another disciplinary action. According to a much later account, William resigned because he had been "angered by being disciplined for breaking a camp rule to aid a sick comrade." It is likely that this version of the story was obtained from the Holabird clan and represented the accepted, if perhaps selectively remembered, family oral tradition. A second, unauthorized version has William resigning "in order to get married."[14] This appears more likely. It is known that William met Maria Ford Augur, known as "Molly," in New Orleans during a visit to his father, who was by then a lieutenant colonel and quartermaster general of the Louisiana Department. William and Molly, who was herself the daughter of an army officer, apparently had a short and tumultuous courtship. The were married on 29 December 1875.[15]

After his marriage William immediately moved to Chicago, possibly because his father was being sent there as chief of the Military Division of the Missouri, a job he held until 1878.[16] William undoubtedly already knew Chicago, however, since he would have changed trains there on trips from St. Paul to the south and east of the country as his father moved from place to place. He was also influenced, no doubt, by the reputation that post-Fire Chicago enjoyed as a splendid place for ambitious young engineers.

William promptly applied for and, on the basis of his engineering training, got a job with William Le Baron Jenney.[17] By choosing to work for Jenney, he threw in his lot with a man who was still in his forties but already provided a serious challenge to the established order in the Chicago building world. Schooled at the Ecole Centrale des Arts et Manufactures in Paris, and with extensive experience as an engineer in the United States Army, Jenney was much more highly trained than pioneer designers like W. W. Boyington and John van Osdel, who had dominated practice in the city before and just after the Chicago Fire.[18] Although there is considerable debate about his personal sophistication and artistic ability, Jenney was undoubtedly a highly competent

William Holabird at West Point (seated on right). Photograph ca. 1874. Chicago Historical Society Architectural Collections.

engineer and architect. He became a kind of father figure to a whole generation of prominent architects that flourished in the city in the last two decades of the nineteenth century.[19]

By the time Holabird arrived at the office in 1875, Jenney had finished his first two major Chicago buildings, the Portland Block of 1872 and the Lakeside Building of 1873. Although neither was among the most prestigious buildings of the day, the Portland did achieve a kind of notoriety for its use of ordinary brick instead of the cut stone that had been customary. About the Portland Block, the author of *Industrial Chicago* observed: "To the surprise of architects and builders, pressed brick was used for the front in preference to stone, and this being its first introduction to Chicago as a facade material for a massive building, the innovation was usually coldly received." Within four years, however, the author continued, "this material had won first place, and stone was excluded for the great majority of the modern office buildings."[20] Jenney was obviously in sympathy with the hard-nosed developers of his day and perfectly willing to provide sound but inexpensive structures rather than elaborate works of art, a characteristic shared by most of the famous alumni of his office.[21] The energetic

Holabird supplemented his earnings at Jenney's office by moonlighting as a clerk for the Chicago quartermaster's department, a job he undoubtedly secured through his father.[22]

Ossian Simonds

At Jenney's office, Holabird met the two men he would later have as partners—Ossian Cole Simonds and Martin Roche. Simonds, who arrived at the office in 1878, three years after Holabird, was born in 1855 near Grand Rapids, Michigan, and brought up on the family farm. He had entered the University of Michigan in 1874 to study civil engineering, but he switched briefly to architecture when Jenney taught there in 1876. Simonds graduated in 1878 and moved to Chicago.[23]

One of Simonds's first jobs in Jenney's office was to survey land owned by the Graceland Cemetery Association. This apparently mundane assignment had major consequences. It brought Simonds into contact with Bryan Lathrop, president of the Cemetery Association, a prominent figure in the Chicago real estate world and, in the years to come, a major source of architectural commissions, not only because of work on his own account but through out-of-town investors he represented.[24] Lathrop "discovered" Simonds, according to a later chronicler, presumably meaning that Lathrop first recognized his talent for landscape design. This discovery apparently led directly to the formation of the firm of Holabird & Simonds. The reason Simonds was able to quit his job with Jenney and start practice with Holabird was, it seems, an agreement with Lathrop that allowed Simonds to set up his new firm while designing a major enlargement of the cemetery.[25] Whether this landscape work was done on his own or through his new partnership is not known, but Simonds's Graceland work proved very influential. Already by 1880 he had started to use wild native trees and shrubs in apparently natural, uncontrived ways. This work later came to be cited as an important early example of the "prairie spirit" in landscape.[26]

It seems likely, then, that Simonds was somewhat more important than Holabird in creating the firm and securing work that attracted attention. Twenty-five years old at the time the firm was founded, he was a year younger than Holabird, but he had completed his university education, whereas Holabird had not, and his Graceland Cemetery connection provided the partners with important potential commissions and valuable contacts.

Holabird & Simonds opened its offices in a sixteen-by-twenty-foot room in the Major Block, an opulent seven-story structure at the southeast corner of LaSalle and Madison in the heart of the Loop (fig. 5.10). By 1880 the ornate cut stone ornamenta-

1.4

Graceland Cemetery, view of entrance showing landscape work by Ossian Coles Simonds and gates (246), 1896, and office building (244), 1896, by Holabird & Roche. From Simonds, Landscape Gardening, *1920.*

tion of this structure, erected soon after the Chicago Fire, probably looked slightly out of date compared with the newer, more straightforward buildings of architects like Jenney. Its great virtue undoubtedly was relatively low rent.[27] Holabird apparently worked a full day in the quartermaster's department, where he had become chief clerk, allowing him time for his own office early in the morning and late in the afternoon. Simonds was busy at Graceland. No commissions have been definitely identified from the firm of Holabird & Simonds, which lasted only months.

In 1881, a year after the founding of the firm, Simonds was made superintendent of the cemetery, and the press of business forced him to withdraw increasingly from the day-to-day work of the partnership. With neither partner able to devote full time to the office, Holabird & Simonds decided to take on a third member of the firm. The two partners, according to later testimony, recognizing that they were "long on engineering and short on architecture," picked Martin Roche for his design ability and because he told them he could live on a salary of forty dollars a month.[28]

Martin Roche

Surprisingly little is known about Martin Roche's early years or, for that matter, about any period in his life. He was born in 1855 in Cleveland, Ohio, moving to Chicago with his family in 1857, where he attended public schools. He was first apprenticed with a cabinetmaker at age fourteen, but by 1872, at seventeen, he found work in Jenney's office. It was here that he met Holabird and Simonds when they joined the firm in 1875 and 1878, respectively.[29] Roche was present in the office when Jenney was erecting some of his most interesting loft buildings, notably the Holmes Estate Building on Washington Street and a building for Levy Leiter (dubbed Leiter 1 by historians) at Wells and Monroe Streets. By the time of the latter building Roche had become head draftsman in the office.[30] He was also called on to draw up decorative schemes for other kinds of building. There is, for example, a record of a Persian room commissioned by the president of a railroad company.[31]

City directories show that the reorganized Holabird, Simonds & Roche partnership soon moved about a block south and east, to the new First National Bank Building on Monroe Street.[32] Designed by Chicago architects Burling and Whitehouse, its sober rows of mostly rectangular windows and nearly even cornice line, like the work of Jenney, signaled a marked shift away from the heavier, more ornate post-Fire blocks like the Major toward the simpler massing and profiles that would become common in many of the business buildings of the 1880s. It is likely that the firm moved into this building when it opened in 1882.[33]

The firm took on its first employee in October 1882 when the partners hired Edward A. Renwick. Renwick, born in 1860 in Grand Rapids, had come to Chicago earlier in the year to work for Simonds, a friend of his family. Because he was so busy on cemetery work and therefore unable to devote as much time to the firm as his partners did, Simonds donated Renwick's services as his contribution to the partnership in lieu of money.[34] Renwick has left an account of his first day in the office. Judging from quite a few similar accounts by other Chicago architects, the kind of sink-or-swim initiation he experienced was standard practice in architectural offices of the day. According to Renwick, "My first morning in the office, Mr. Roche, although he knew I knew nothing about architectural drawing handed me a tracing and said, 'color this. I have an errand and am going out of the office.' I asked in bewildered manner how he meant to color it and he said, 'Why brick, red, stone, blue, wood, yellow' the method used in those days—and closed the door. That was his way of tutoring."[35]

For the firm of Holabird, Simonds & Roche there is only the most fragmentary documentation. It appears that the first years were tenuous ones, and that Martin Roche continued designing furniture to supplement the firm's income from architectural work. None of Roche's furniture is known to survive, but there is a record of some work for the office of Bryan Lathrop (cat. no. 3) and mention of a set of pieces for the Chicago Library Society, one item a table with fourteen sides and thirty-two legs.[36] According to Renwick, the first real job the firm had was commissioned by a man named Isaac Wolf (cat. no. 4). "When the wolf came to the door, I took him in," Roche was reportedly fond of recalling in later years.[37]

Only slightly more is known about two other commissions. The first was an office and railroad station for Graceland Cemetery (cat. no. 2). A photograph published in 1883 confirms that this structure, documented in a set of drawings at the Chicago Historical Society, was ultimately built, but it disappeared long ago. A microfilm copy of a lost set of drawings, also signed Holabird, Simonds & Roche, shows a three-story apartment building called the Hickmott Flats, to be constructed near what is now the corner of Clark and Fullerton (cat. no. 5). It is not known whether this structure was built.

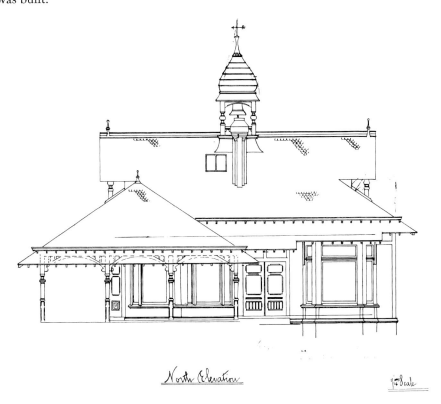

North Elevation

1.5
Graceland Cemetery, cemetery office and station (2), ca. 1880–83, probably at Chicago and Evanston Railroad (later Milwaukee Road, now CTA elevated line) at Seminary and Buena Streets, front elevation. Chicago Historical Society Architectural Collections.

1.6

Hickmott Flats (5), ca. 1883, probably 2200 or 2300 block
of N. Clark Street, front elevation. Print from microfilm.
Art Institute of Chicago–University of Illinois microfilm project.

Even if both these commissions were executed, neither of them would likely have aroused much attention. The apartment building was a standard three-flat—a three-story brick structure with one apartment per floor—like hundreds of others on Chicago streets. The office-station was likewise entirely typical, although its somewhat irregular massing and knobby appearance recall the 1870s more than the 1880s.

If these initial designs provide no dramatic opening chapter in what would become a remarkable success story by the end of the decade, they do give some clues to the work of the firm throughout its subsequent history. They are both relatively simple, straightforward buildings that appear to follow closely the program laid down for them by the client, an attitude that characterizes most commercial architects of any period. Also as in most commercial architecture, there was a certain conservatism about artistic expression. Despite the demands new building types would impose and the innovations technology would make possible, the works of the firm were almost always well within what was considered appropriate for a given building type at a particular time.

Holabird, Simonds, and Roche remained together for only two years. In 1883 O. C. Simonds left the firm, presumably to devote himself full time to landscape gardening and the work at Graceland Cemetery. About then the two remaining partners moved once again, this time about a block east to room 55 of the Montauk Block at 64–70 W. Monroe Street, between Dearborn and Clark.[38] Edward Renwick later recalled that the office consisted of a drafting room twenty by thirty-five feet and a private office, all at the rear of the top floor. The Montauk was not just another Chicago office building. Completed the year before, in 1882, this ten-story "skyscraper" was the first in Chicago to rise substantially above the five- or six-story plateau created by the city's largest commercial structures.[39] (See fig. 5.1.)

The Montauk marked an epoch in other ways. It was the first major commission of architects Burnham and Root, a firm founded in 1873 that would soon become Chicago's largest, and it was also the largest development to date by Boston businessmen Peter and Shepherd Brooks, who would soon become the most conspicuous developers in Chicago's Loop.[40] The fate of the young firm of Holabird & Roche would be intimately bound up with the subsequent history of both the developers and the slightly older architectural firm.

From the front steps of the Montauk the young partners could witness the results of Chicago's post-Fire building boom. Every building in sight had been put up since flames had swept the Loop twelve years before, and many rebuilt structures had already been demolished again so the property could be redeveloped, often on a vastly expanded scale. They would eventually get a good deal of this work for themselves, but for the first year or two after their installation in Chicago's newest and tallest building the partners had to wait, contenting themselves with commissions for work on a very modest scale.

THE PARTNERS:
WILLIAM HOLABIRD
AND MARTIN ROCHE

All observers seemed to agree that William Holabird and Martin Roche, dissimilar as they were, formed a well-matched pair. Holabird was a commanding presence. Standing six feet, five inches tall, he maintained a military bearing throughout his life. As he became older he put on a great deal of weight, by his later years reaching more than 260 pounds. Photographs confirm that his height, girth, and distinguished appearance made him the very image of the nineteenth-century patriarch, and he played the part perfectly. Holabird had not only the physical presence but also the intellectual capacity to impress friends and clients. Edward A. Renwick later recalled:

> Holabird was a man of quick decisions, he was apt to decide almost instantly whether or not a thing interested him. He was very forceful. He was a great reader and had the gift which his father and grandfather before him had, of being able to grasp the whole contents of a page at a glance, and also the memory to retain it for years. He could take a book, a complicated work on engineering, home in the evening, and bring it back the next morning. Five years later a dispute might come up and Holabird would say, "Here, give me that book," and turning almost instantly to the page he would point out the quotation which he had remembered.[1]

Renwick also recalled that Holabird was "a man who could be very charming [but] could also be very much the other way."[2] Renwick went on to record Holabird's social deftness and his hearty sense of humor, but he also chronicled occasions when the latter overcame the former. He recalled one client who wrote to the partners complaining about water appearing on his plate glass window and suggesting the architects

2.1
William Holabird. Photograph ca. 1910. Chicago Historical Society Architectural Collections.

install a tin eave along the top. Either inadvertently or because of poor spelling, the client left the *a* out of "eave." Holabird wrote back explaining that the problem was not a leak but condensation, and that the "tin Eve wouldn't be worth A-dam." This humor at the expense of a client lost the firm a commission, according to Renwick, but it appears it was an aberration.

One measure of the impact of Holabird's larger-than-life persona was that his grandson John Holabird Jr., then only a young boy, after nearly six decades remembered his grandfather distinctly:

> I remember he had a Pierce Arrow . . . and a chauffeur named Harry who picked us up . . . and drove us out for Sunday dinner. . . . He was just a huge presence at the table for a little boy of two or three. All I can remember is this absolutely monster image with a very bristly white beard that hurt when you kissed. He was gruff, with a deep voice. He could scare the daylights out of any of his draftsmen. He did pretty well with his small grandson too.[3]

William and Molly Holabird had six children: Cornelia Baird in 1877, Robert Grant in 1878, Mary Swift in 1880, Jane Augur in 1882, William Jr. in 1884, and John Augur in 1886. The family apparently lived in Chicago while William worked for Jenney, but in 1882 they moved to Evanston. From 1884 until his death they occupied a substantial house at 1500 Oak Street, which may have been owned by Samuel Beckley Holabird when he lived in the Chicago area during the 1870s. It was from this house that William commuted into the city every day (fig. 8.5).[4]

Holabird seems to have played much the same role in his firm as did Daniel Burnham at Burnham and Root and to a lesser extent Dankmar Adler at Adler and Sullivan, the two firms that in the 1880s and 1890s most closely resembled Holabird & Roche in age of partners, type of commissions, and office setup. Holabird, clearly the "front man" who took charge of the business aspects of the firm, was very much at home in the rough-and-tumble world of Chicago business. Constantly on the train to cities across the Midwest and the East, he was the one who brought in most of the commissions. Conservative, middle-class, and Republican, he was a substantial propertied citizen. He was also widely considered scrupulously honest, earning the firm a reputation for absolute reliability. Like many of his successful architect friends, Holabird was a joiner. He belonged to numerous clubs, among them the Evanston Club and the Evanston Country Club in his hometown; the University, Chicago, City, Union League, and Mid-Day Clubs in Chicago; the Glen View Golf and Polo Club in Golf, Illinois; and the Coleman Lake Club in northern Wisconsin where he fished. In part these clubs served as places for recreation, but it is conspicuous how many of these organizations were lodged in buildings by the firm and how often clients' names appear on the membership rosters. Even at play, work was never far from his mind.[5]

From the early days of the partnership, William Holabird seems to have enjoyed considerable financial ease, probably in good part because of his father's readiness to help. Soon he was making a good deal of money on his own. He invested over the years in parcels of land in Chicago for which the firm did innumerable development schemes, and he invested in several of the developments for which the firm served as architect. For Holabird, personal life and business, though separate, had many points of overlap. His son John Holabird, writing after his father's death in 1929, probably echoed the way his father would have spoken about his life in business: "Mr. Holabird was not interested in becoming a very wealthy man, but found satisfaction in the consciousness of a life well lived. . . . He was a member of many clubs, found time to serve on Committees and Boards, a man of great purposes and vision for extending the usefulness of his profession and for those causes that he believed vitally affected the life of the community in which he lived."[6]

In the office, by all accounts, Holabird left the day-to-day supervision of design mostly to Roche, although he certainly helped work out the overall program, configuration, and materials of most of the firm's important buildings. In the early years he also did a good deal of the engineering and specification work, but it is obvious that by the late 1880s, when he could delegate some of these tasks, he gladly did so. He did keep up with all the latest trade information, however, and with the work that was going on in the office. Edward Renwick recalled: "Holabird had a brilliant mind, exceptional in its grasp of the problems which came up, and there were many of them. . . . Holabird's judgment was excellent, and he had ideas on all subjects, but the details had to be worked out by someone else. I don't know whether he could have worked them out, but I know he wouldn't."[7]

Renwick stated, for example, that although Holabird never made drawings and did little engineering, he more than any other Chicago architect worked with manufacturers to turn out new products useful for the building industry. Renwick also testified to Holabird's role in making design decisions: "He was an excellent critic; he knew the styles, and he had good taste. He could make remarks which would completely spoil a design for you, for instance, one time Roche had a design made and Holabird looking at it said, 'It looks just like a Saratoga trunk.' From that time on that was all you could see in it."[8]

At the time of his death in 1923, Holabird's career was summarized in an unsigned piece in the *Economist* that in spite of, or perhaps because of, the usual hyperbole and conventional language expected in this kind of writing, probably captures the way Holabird himself would have described the ideal commercial architect:

William Holabird . . . achieved the ultimate in architecture. . . . Mr. Holabird was not only a success in his profession as an architect but he was a success as a business man as his buildings were always successful buildings, that is, they were always profitable for their owners. Some architects will say that it is their function to design a beautiful or a perfect structure from the viewpoint of design and construction but it seems that the big buildings that Holabird & Roche designed always had those qualities worked out well to the complete satisfaction of the investor. This was the result of talent and clear thinking directed seriously along the lines of beauty and utility. Aside from his talent as an architect and organizer, Mr. Holabird was rich in affection for his fellow men and it is the good fortune for few men to have as many credit marks for untold kind acts as had Mr. Holabird. There was nothing he would not do for his friends, and for that matter, for those whom he could help even though he might not

Martin Roche. Photograph by Arlington Studios, ca. 1900.
Chicago Historical Society Architectural Collections.

know them. It seemed his duty always to be helpful. Many of the younger
men, notably real estate men in Chicago who came to know him addressed and referred to him affectionately as "Uncle Bill," and his loss to
them will be very great.[9]

Anyone familiar with Chicago architecture in the late nineteenth century will recog-
nize the parallels with "Uncle Dan" Burnham, who clearly served as a role model for
the slightly younger William Holabird.

Martin Roche

Holabird's partner, Martin Roche, was a very different kind of man. Shy and retiring
and a lifelong bachelor, he joined a number of clubs but did not seem at home in the
vigorous world of business affairs. This may have been due in part to physical problems: Roche suffered from curvature of the spine, causing a stoop.[10] Edward Renwick
wrote of him:

> his affliction made him appear rather below medium height, though his
> big frame, large head, hands and feet indicated that he should have been

a very tall man. He was very retiring and modest, unassertive. He was a great student in his particular field, but didn't reach much beyond it. In all the years that I knew Mr. Roche intimately, going to the opera, theatre, lunching and camping with him, I never heard him mention his deformity but once. One evening we were waiting for our sketching class which met in the office, and I read an item about a young bully who had kicked a younger boy in the back and the boy would suffer permanent injury. Roche said, with a look of the greatest bitterness I ever saw on his face, "He ought to be hung," in a moment he added, "That's what happened to me, a boy kicked me." I think this deformity changed his nature a good deal, instead of being self assertive as he would naturally have been, he became retiring, shy.[11]

Renwick stated that Roche was in many ways completely the opposite of Holabird in character, illustrating this remark by a story that took place in Naples during a trip to Europe:

It was in '96 and Naples was considered rather rough, it was even thought there was some danger in foreigners going around the city alone. Roche and Holabird . . . wanted to go out and walk around the city. As soon as they started out a cabby hailed them but Holabird told him they wanted to walk. Roche, in walking along the street if he was looking at anything, would always lag behind you, perhaps twenty or thirty feet. This was particularly true when he was with Holabird, whose mind took in sights simultaneously and instantly, he could glance at a window and know everything that was in it, while Roche whose mind worked much more slowly, would stand in front of it for sometime. Well, they were dragging along in this way up the street when suddenly Holabird heard Roche's voice rip out, the cabby had jumped out and bundled Roche bodily into his cab. Holabird had to rush back and rescue him. It was impossible to imagine anyone treating Holabird thus unceremoniously.

In his early years in Chicago Roche lived on the South Side. In the late 1870s city directories listed him at 3200 S. Dearborn, a small frame dwelling set amid tightly packed rows of similar houses.[12] He shared the house with his sister and his brother-in-law, John Tait, a stone contractor and later a real estate dealer.

Increasing prosperity for Roche or Tait or both allowed them to move about 1888. Although they only moved a few blocks south and east to 3614 S. Grand Boulevard (now Martin Luther King Jr. Drive), the change was dramatic. The new house was a substantial three-story brownstone designed by Holabird & Roche costing $12,000 (cat. no. 53), on one of Chicago's finest residential streets. At the time Roche moved in, the block was just filling in with houses similar to one another in size, configuration, and facade materials, the latter most often "graystone," creating a unified wall of dignified stone fronts along the wide, landscaped boulevard.

There exist only a few other scraps of information about Roche's character. All touch on his unassuming demeanor and his quiet kindness. Mrs. John A. Holabird Sr., daughter-in-law of William Holabird, recalls that he was the "fairy godfather of the Holabird family" and that much of the fine art the Holabirds owned was the gift of Martin Roche.[13]

Seven volumes of Roche's diaries have survived, each covering a single year between 1888 and 1917.[14] Almost all the entries are confined to observations about work or the daily routine. On Sunday, 8 January 1888, he noted that the weather was fair, with light snow, the thermometer at thirty degrees: "Visited Renwick, examined house the firm are building at Buena Park. To bed at 11:25." This was a typical entry for that year. Every now and again a personal comment did creep in. He noted the day in 1895 when he went skating for the first time in twenty years. During 1888 he learned to play cribbage, went to the theater a good deal, and took several trips out of town. In New York he enjoyed the theater but decided Coney Island was the "worst place I ever visited." At Niagara Falls he "examined all points of interest. Got swindled as usual." When Benjamin Harrison was elected on 6 November Roche declared that he was "elected upon wrong principles," free whiskey and high tariffs.

On 20 December 1899 he ordered his first pair of glasses. On 19 February 1916 he noted that an Italian banker's home at 3710 S. Grand Boulevard, in the block south of his home, was blown up by the Italian Black Hand Society. Over the years even these kinds of comments become rarer. By 1917 the typical entry was reduced to "Office all day. Home all evening. Up at 6, To bed at 10:45."

Because Roche's diaries tell so little about his emotional life, one is obliged to look closely for those rare occasions when he does reveal himself. One telltale sign is an obsession with recording birthdays and death days. Every year for decades after she died in 1884, for example, Roche wrote himself a reminder of his mother's birthday. On 6 January 1916 the diary notes: "100th anniversary of my Mother's birth." This obsession with family anniversaries probably arose in part because Roche never married and raised a family of his own. His sister's family seems to have functioned as a surrogate. The diaries show that Roche became an integral part of the Tait household. They reveal, for example, that Tait and Roche, besides sharing a house for over thirty years, invested a good deal of money in real estate together, and they commissioned several buildings from Holabird & Roche. A typical entry written on 10 April 1899: "Bought 20 shares of Federal Steel and Wire stock today. 1/2 belongs to Tait. Cost $1265."

Roche seems to have treated the Taits' children almost as if they were his own. The diaries betray his anguish when, in rapid succession between 1915 and 1917, Tait died, then Tait's son David, and Roche's sister fell ill. In 1917, the year David died, Roche spent hours at the hospital every day for weeks. He finally recorded on 23 January, "Dave was almost unconscious and lingered until 9:20 when he died. Dear Dave. His life just filtered out to the last breath without any pain." Roche was deeply aware of the passing of his extended family. The last notation of the day reads, "Only three left now."

The impression given by the diaries, that Roche was a solitary, lonely figure, seems to be confirmed by other sources. Edward Renwick commented on a pattern in Roche's friendships:

> There was a strange thing about Roche, he would be extremely intimate with someone for a period of time, but if that person, as invariably must happen, ever once fell below what was his very high and inflexible standard of conduct, Roche would never have anything more to do with him. It was so with many others, Hermon MacNeil the sculptor, O'Connor the designer of the Lincoln Memorial down at Springfield. They were more than brothers for a long time, but suddenly Roche would announce, "I'm through with so and so, never want to see him again." And he never would. Or perhaps he wouldn't announce it at all, but the friend who up to that time had been in the office every day would just never come again. The same thing happened with his own nephew, who said to me once, "I don't know what is the matter with Uncle Martin, he won't even let me in his office. I don't know of anything I have done." It didn't matter whether he knew of it or not, Roche did and that was enough.[15]

It is tempting, from the viewpoint of the late twentieth century, to raise an eyebrow at Renwick's phrase "more than brothers," particularly in light of some of the voluptuous male sculptural figures of Hermon MacNeil, but there is not enough evidence to know how telling this stock phrase may be.[16]

If Roche's personal life remains shrouded, his role in the office is somewhat clearer. Edward Renwick, writing in 1932, had this view of Roche's role: "Roche during all this period was the sole designer, he made not only the sketches but the smaller scale sketches in design and supervised the large scale ones. Holabird was obtaining the business. We had a well organized office, each having his particular part to do. We each had the part that we were best fitted for."[17]

This description of the artist-creator sheltered by a carefully organized office bureaucracy and an assertive and socially active partner seems to characterize a number of the important late nineteenth-century architecture firms. "Art-architects" such as Harvey Ellis in Minneapolis and Louis Sullivan, John Root, and Charles Atwood in Chicago were relieved by their partners of much of the burden of dealing with clients and construction problems so that they could concentrate on the "artistic" aspects of design.

It is important to remember that when architects or writers of this era used the words "artist" or "designer" the words did not mean the same thing as they have meant since the European modernists came to dominate architectural education. Most architects of the late nineteenth century believed art was the ornament that was added to construction. The elaborate foliage executed in terra cotta and metal on the Tacoma Building, for example, was art, and it was almost certainly the work of Martin Roche. The plan, overall configuration, and structure of the building, on the other hand, were thought to belong more to the realm of business and were not exclusively, usually not even primarily, the concern of the "designer." In the case of the Tacoma these larger considerations were determined in great part by the client and contractor in consultation with both partners, the engineers, and cost estimators. Certainly Martin Roche would not have been excluded from these concerns, but they were not considered to be matters that would naturally fall to him.

Roche was a demanding presence in the office, requiring care and diligence but he was considered generous to those who applied themselves. His kindness to draftsmen and his interest in their education were frequently noted.[18] In the Chicago architectural community he never took a conspicuous role in the way Holabird did, but he was a conscientious member of the city's professional organizations.[19]

In short, we know a good deal and almost nothing about William Holabird and Martin Roche. The descriptions of them that have survived were made by people who attempted to portray the partners as they probably would have wished to be seen. They come across clearly as professionals committed to their architectural practice, but it is difficult to penetrate beyond this. Most of what we know about Holabird and Roche we can find out only by looking at their buildings.

Part

TWO

THREE

THE   FIRM

1884–1886

During the first few years of practice, William Holabird and Martin Roche, like most architects just starting out, got by with modest commissions, usually for building renovations. They had every reason to be optimistic about their future prospects, however. During the decades after the Civil War, construction volume in Chicago had a sharp upward trend, although it was always subject to the periodic slumps that accompanied the boom and bust cycles of nineteenth-century Chicago business. From a low point of about $500,000 of total new construction in the city in 1861, during the war years, the figure climbed to an average of over $30 million a year just before and after the Great Fire. Construction volume did go into a sharp but short downturn in the mid-1870s, reaching a trough of $6 million in 1874, but by the late 1870s it was definitely on the upswing again, reaching $22 million by the end of 1883, the year Holabird & Roche was organized.[1] It would remain near this level for several years, then rise sharply in the last years of the decade. The firm of Holabird & Roche was launched on this rising tide (see chart on Chicago construction at end of volume).

The decades after the Civil War were marked by a significant shift in the way buildings were designed. Traditionally all but the largest buildings in Chicago had been designed by master builders—that is, craftsmen trained in the traditional building trades. The two most prominent of these, John Van Osdel and W. W. Boyington, became the first really successful designers of large buildings in Chicago. By the 1850s they and some of the other more ambitious builders had started to call themselves architects, a term whose use would not be legally regulated until the end of the century.

Until the Fire there were few professionally trained architects or engineers in Chicago to dispute their claim to the title. Augustus Bauer, for example, trained at the Darmstadt Polytechnic, had practiced in Chicago since the 1850s. William Le Baron

Jenney, who had studied at the Ecole Centrale des Arts et Manufactures in Paris, had come to the city in 1867. By the time of the Fire neither of these men had yet developed a practice that could rival that of Van Osdel or Boyington in size or number of commissions.[2] Builders continued to dominate the field in the design of all kinds of small and inexpensive buildings. In the 1880s, however, as Chicago's economy expanded and the city's businessmen became more ambitious, they increasingly turned to trained architects and engineers who could give them sophisticated, up-to-date engineering and design expertise. The list included Daniel Burnham, John Root, Peter Bonnett Wight, Henry Ives Cobb, Solon Spencer Beman, and Louis Sullivan. By the late 1870s these men were in a position to challenge Van Osdel and Boyington for major commissions in the city and for leadership in the architectural profession.[3]

Among the new breed of architects the firm of Holabird & Roche found itself admirably positioned. With Holabird's engineering degree, Roche's design sense, and both partners' experience in Jenney's office, they were as well prepared as anyone in the city to take on whatever challenges their clients could offer. Growth of the Holabird & Roche office was rapid. Although financial records for the firm before the turn of the century are sketchy, it is possible to get some idea of the volume of business by adding up the totals for the known pieces of construction built to designs by the office each year. In the first three years Holabird & Roche is known to have obtained at least a few substantial commissions, including a $15,000 factory, a $60,000 retail building, and a $40,000 structure for Northwestern University, for an average of nearly $40,000 a year. Assuming an average fee of 6 percent, the firm would have earned $6,900 on these buildings over the three years, or just over $3,000 a year. Even with no operating expenses, this would have translated into no more than $1,500 per partner. By comparison, a female stenographer-typist at that time might have expected to earn $600 a year and a senior executive's salary would have started at about $4,000.[4] The documentation for the Holabird & Roche office is obviously very inexact. On the one hand, it represents only new buildings on which contract figures have survived. The firm almost certainly worked on other commissions that supplied further income. It is probable, in fact, that a high percentage of its income in the earliest years came from building inspections, renovations, and remodelings of which no trace remains. On the other hand, Holabird & Roche was not always willing or able to charge a 6 percent fee. Still, the figures give some idea of the volume of work and income compared with later years, and they certainly suggest that there would have been very little profit once office expenses were paid.[5]

There is also little evidence concerning office practice in the earliest years except a few entries in the surviving diaries of Martin Roche. Although these notes are laconic, they do give some hints of the routine the partners followed in getting the jobs, designing the buildings, supervising construction, and carrying out all the other tasks involved in running an architecture office. On a given day Roche might leave home at 7:00 in the morning, stop by the office, visit two or three building sites in Chicago and Evanston, call on a client, and return to the office before returning home for dinner and then going out to a play in the evening.

As brief as the references are, the large number of trips around the city during the day suggests the amount and variety of work involved in running a small office. It also provides eloquent testimony to Chicago's extraordinary transportation system. This system of railroads, cable cars, and streetcars allowed Holabird and Roche to start their day some fifteen miles apart—Holabird in Evanston and Roche on the South Side— do business over the entire metropolitan area, eat out or go to the theater in the evening, and then return home.

As the work increased, the office expanded and became more departmentalized. When he started in 1882, for example, Edward Renwick, the firm's first employee, did everything from drafting to fetching coffee. As the firm hired additional draftsmen, Renwick gave up many of these tasks and became foreman of the drafting room. For a few years, though, he continued as bookkeeper, construction supervisor, and specifications writer.[6] From the very first, commercial commissions dominated the work of Holabird & Roche. Among its earliest substantial buildings were the Webster Building, a four-story retail structure for the burgeoning business center at Madison Street and Ogden Avenue on the city's Near West Side (cat. no. 11), and the three-story Wheeler factory building on the South Side (cat. no. 24). More significantly, in late 1884 or early 1885 Holabird & Roche came into contact with several individuals intimately involved in the construction of major buildings in the Loop. The initial contact was apparently Bryan Lathrop. Lathrop, who met Holabird and Roche through Ossian Simonds at Graceland Cemetery, occupied offices immediately across the hall from the architects in the Montauk Block. Lathrop represented Francis Bartlett of Boston, who, almost certainly on Lathrop's advice, came to the firm in 1884 for a "taxpayer," a small one-story commercial building with large areas of plate glass (cat. no. 7).[7]

It was again almost certainly Lathrop who provided the contact with his brother-in-law, Owen Aldis. Aldis had arrived in Chicago in 1875, where he got his start as a title lawyer. He soon became an important real estate agent and developer.[8] Although nothing is known about the project, Aldis commissioned from Holabird & Roche an addition to a building at Wabash Avenue and the Chicago River.[9] It must have gone well, because in October 1884 the firm received a commission from the Brooks brothers of Boston, whom Aldis represented. The contract, signed by Peter C. Brooks, was for a building on the corner of Dearborn and Harrison (cat. no. 14). Although the

Brookses did nothing on this site immediately,[10] Holabird & Roche could now claim clients who were well on their way to becoming the largest developers in the Loop.

In addition to large commercial buildings, Holabird & Roche continued to work on numerous small-scale commissions, mostly houses and apartments in the middle-class neighborhoods mushrooming at the periphery of Chicago's built-up area, both within the city limits and outside them. These included places like Douglas, Oakwood, and Hyde Park to the south, Buena Park, Ravenswood, and Evanston to the north, and Austin and Oak Park to the west.

The largest commission to come into the office in 1883–86 was for a proposed military installation north of Chicago although actual construction on the permanent buildings would not get under way for several years. (cat. no. 13, figs. 4.2–4.11). Holabird & Roche also received a commission from Northwestern University for a building to house the university's chemistry and physics departments (cat. no. 29).

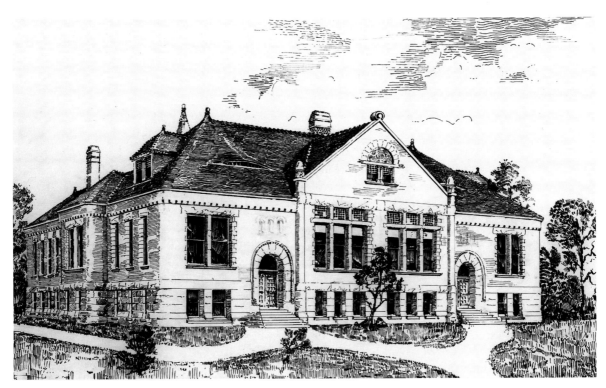

3.1

Northwestern University, Evanston, Illinois, Science Hall (29), 1886–87, perspective.
Chicago Historical Society Architectural Collections.

1887–1889

The years 1887 to 1889 were prosperous ones for Chicago and for the firm of Holabird & Roche. Construction figures for Chicago ranged from just under $20 million
in 1887 to over $25 million in 1889. Although the known commissions on which
Holabird & Roche collected fees in 1887 and 1888 remained below $50,000, the figure
jumped to over $584,000 in 1889, largely the result of the $484,000 cost of the firm's
first really large commercial building, the Tacoma. At a fee of 6 percent this would
translate into $30,000 income for the firm from this building alone, a tenfold increase
over the figures for the mid-1880s. In addition to the size of commissions, the number
of jobs started to multiply. Whereas only seventeen commissions are known from the
first half of the 1880s, there are over a hundred for the second half. By this time the
firm had joined the ranks of the major players among Chicago's commercial architects
and had gained an enviable reputation for technical expertise and compete reliability.

Edward Renwick has left an account of the way the office was run during this
period:

> I think that part of our success was due to the fact that we were fairly well
> balanced. Holabird made the business contacts with clients and had much
> to do with bringing in the business, from there on his part was more that
> of critic than active participator. Roche took up the designing and fol-
> lowed that through. Then it was up to me to write the specifications, take
> bids, award the contracts and erect the building. . . . It made a good
> strong team.[11]

As the commissions grew in size and complexity, the firm started to expand rapidly, taking on dozens of new draftsmen in the late 1880s. Although the partners kept
a tight control of design, it is obvious that by the mid-1880s different hands in the
office were responsible for different kinds of projects. For Graceland Cemetery, for
example, the firm designed a solid, almost primeval granite-walled chapel and crypt
(cat. no. 49). By contrast, the First Congregational Church at Lake Linden in Michigan's Upper Peninsula, finished in 1887 (cat. no. 27), with its frame construction, tall,
somewhat awkward proportions and massing, large overhanging eaves, variegated surfaces of shingles, sticklike framing elements, and diagonal boarding, looks as if it came
from a completely different set of hands.[12]

There are several possible explanations. It may be that the firm had distinct city
and country modes. It is also possible that the differences reflect the clients' wishes.

3.2
*Graceland Chapel and
mortuary crypt (49),
1888, view of exterior.
Photograph by Ralph
D. Cleveland.
Courtesy of Graceland
Cemetery and
Crematorium.*

The Michigan congregation, for example, may have wanted a building that would have seemed slightly old-fashioned in the city by the late 1880s. It is also possible that the commissions were obtained and monitored by individuals in the office with different aesthetic tastes. For example, it is quite possible that Edward Renwick, who came from Grand Rapids and spent considerable time traveling in Michigan and Wisconsin, may have had something to do with the work in small towns in these states.

Different stylistic preferences in the office appear even in the drafting styles. Whereas most of the drawings were done with a simple, even-weighted line and plain hand lettering that became the office standard for decades, there is a set of somewhat more labored drawings made in the mid-1880s with larger, more ornamental lettering, usually forcefully underlined. A good example can be found in the sheets prepared for a building on Van Buren Street for Thomas Coughlan (cat. no. 34), in which the slightly fussy design seems to mirror the drafting style perfectly. In any case, this diversity in drawing techniques would diminish markedly in the 1890s, although the diversity in architectural style continued for several more decades.

First Congregational Church, Lake Linden, Michigan (25), 1886–87, view of exterior. Photograph ca. 1975 by Kevin Harrington.

One of the minor commissions of 1886 led to Holabird & Roche's first really important completed structure. Early in that year a Chicago developer named Wirt Walker came to the firm with a relatively minor remodeling job on an old building he owned on LaSalle Street. Through a very circuitous path this minor project turned into the commission for a first-class office building (figs. 5.3–5.14). Called the Tacoma

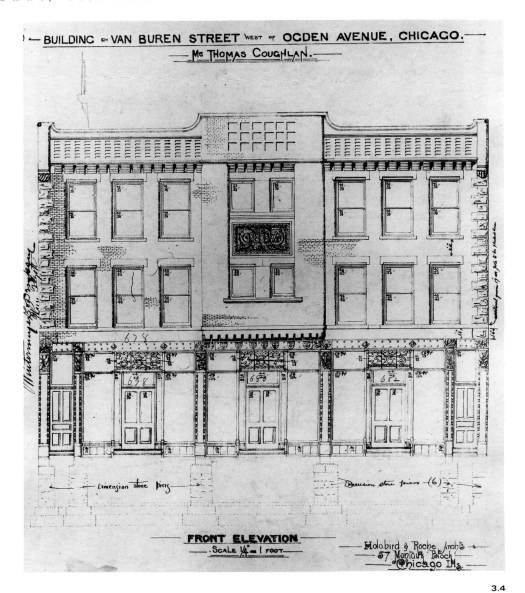

) — BUILDING on VAN BUREN STREET WEST of OGDEN AVENUE, CHICAGO. —

— Mr THOMAS COUGHLAN. —

FRONT ELEVATION
SCALE ¼" = 1 FOOT

Holabird & Roche Arch's
57 Montauk Block
Chicago Ill.

3.4

Thomas Coughlan store and apartment building (34), 1887, probably Van Buren Street
west of Ogden Avenue, elevation. Chicago Historical Society Architectural Collections.

(cat. no. 22), this twelve-story structure was one of the most prominent new office buildings in the Loop and the first conspicuous demonstration anywhere of the possibilities of metal skeletal framing on a large office building (figs. 5.3–5.14). The firm also designed for Walker a large factory building at Dearborn and Harrison Streets (cat. no. 54). Finally, in addition to the big business buildings, it continued to do a substantial number of houses, institutional structures, and government buildings, particularly in Evanston.

1890–1893

The Chicago building boom of the late 1880s peaked in the early 1890s. Total construction volume in the city reached a new high in 1890 of $47 million, surpassing for the first time the record set in 1872 during the rush to rebuild after the Fire. In 1891 the figure reached $54 million and in 1892, $63 million. After this it dropped substantially because of the nationwide business downturn of the 1890s, falling back to $28 million in 1893.

At Holabird & Roche the figures mounted even faster than those for the city itself, largely because of a few large buildings. Because construction took a good deal of time and the firm entered the buildings in its books at the time of completion, figures for the firm tend to lag up to two years behind the city figures, which were based on building permits. The Monadnock addition (cat. no. 150) came in at $636,000 in 1893, the Old Colony Building (cat. no. 201) at $929,000 in 1894, and the Marquette (cat. no. 200) at $1,357,000 in 1895.

In addition to the large office buildings, there were an increasing number of smaller commissions, a number of them larger than anything the firm had done in its early years. Figures for work completed by Holabird & Roche averaged about $700,000 from 1890 through 1892, then jumped to $961,000 in 1893, $1,551,000 in 1894, and $2,272,000 in 1895. Comparing figures for the best Holabird & Roche year with the best year for the city as a whole suggests that by this time Holabird & Roche was responsible for something like 3.5 percent of all new construction in the city, and this estimate probably considerably understates the case, since it is likely that Holabird & Roche had more commissions than those for which records have survived. The kind of practice Holabird & Roche had grown into in the late 1880s was a new phenomenon in architectural history. There had been large architectural offices in the past. The architects of major public commissions like the Houses of Parliament in London in the early nineteenth century or the Paris Opera House at midcentury had been obliged to manage large budgets and oversee the work of a great many individuals. Not until the post–Civil War period in the United States, however, did the the idea of a permanent large office run on the lines of a major business concern emerge. Not surprisingly, the earliest such offices developed in Boston and New York. Then, virtually overnight, Chicago's building boom of the 1880s lifted a handful of Chicago offices into the front rank nationally. By the early 1890s Holabird & Roche had become one of the largest offices in the country, probably surpassed only by the firm of Burnham and Root in Chicago and a few other firms nationwide, notably the office of McKim, Mead and White in New York.[13]

To handle this growing volume of work, the Holabird & Roche office continued to expand. By the early 1890s it employed up to forty draftsman. The office routine also became more complex. Edward Renwick later recalled:

> We also finally hired a bookkeeper, and we even put on airs and hired a stenographer. Up to this point all our specifications and our correspondence had been done in long hand, first I did them myself then later got a copyist so that when I scribbled them off they could be copied in a good flowing hand. While we were in the Montauk Block we had acquired a telephone. Holabird thought it was perfectly useless, that it was much better to send a boy. We had a swarm of office boys waiting for errands, but when we installed the telephone we found we could do without several of the boys.[14]

At some point in the late 1880s or early 1890s the firm appears to have moved back temporarily into the First National Bank Building at the northwest corner of Monroe and Dearborn,[15] but in spring 1892 it moved again, this time to the Monadnock Building, presumably in connection with a commission received by the firm for the addition to the south end of this building (cat. no. 150).[16] The Holabird & Roche office occupied part of the top floor. Edward Renwick in later years recalled the office: "The layout of our offices in the Monadnock was, at the south end Roche's private office, then a large library, on the north side of the library Holabird's office then the bookkeeper's office with a space where drawings could be spread out for contractor's figuring, then at the north end my office, with switchboard in the lobby between." According to Renwick, who by this time had relinquished his role as foreman of the drafting room to devote more time to estimating and specifications writing, the firm created a drafting room by building an L-shaped penthouse on the north and east sides of the building's roof.[17] Of this drafting room he wrote:

> It was extremely light and a perfect drafting room, the only drawback being that to get there from our offices you had to go up through the attic and on to the roof. This made, necessarily, some lost motion, and resulted in the fact that we didn't get up there as often as we should have. Therefore it depended pretty much on the superintendent of the drafting room

whether or not the work was efficiently and speedily done. We made several changes in superintendents trying to find one who could accomplish this.[18]

The move of the firm coincided with a major expansion and reorganization of the practice. The partners hired a construction engineer, Henry J. Burt, and set up a new electrical department. To provide more regular structural engineering services they entered into an agreement with Corydon T. Purdy. Purdy, first on his own, later as Purdy and Phillips, and finally as Purdy and Henderson, provided structural engineering services for the firm from 1892 through 1911.[19]

By far the largest concentration of Holabird & Roche's work in the early 1890s was located in the south part of the Loop within steps of the Monadnock Building. In

3.5

Pontiac Building (61), 1884–91, 542 S. Dearborn Street, northwest corner of W. Harrison Street, view showing the building under construction. Photograph from Brooks Family Papers. Chicago Historical Society Architectural Collections.

this immediate area the firm had no fewer than five major projects going on almost simultaneously along Dearborn Street, two south of the Loop elevated tracks and three to the north. To the south were the fourteen-story Pontiac (cat. no. 61), originally intended as a loft building but changed to office use as the area became more intensively developed, and the twelve-story Caxton (cat. no. 75), an office building. To the north were the sixteen-story Monadnock addition (cat. no. 150), Marquette (cat. no. 200), and Old Colony (cat. no. 201), all three high-class office buildings. In addition to the office buildings on Dearborn, the firm completed the Venetian Building, a twelve-story structure just off State Street that housed professional offices, and a six-story building in Kansas City, Missouri (cat no. 111), a commission from Boston developer Francis Bartlett, the man who built the Old Colony Building. The Kansas City building appears to have been the firm's first major out-of-town commission. (For the Monadnock addition see fig. 6.4; for the Marquette, figs. 7.2–7.14; for the Venetian, figs. 10.4–10.6.)

This set of buildings secured the reputation of the firm. Among the largest architectural commissions in Chicago, they received very good press. All but one of the buildings, moreover, was a commission from the Brooks brothers. The very public switch of these developers from Burnham and Root, whom they had used on most of their earlier buildings, to Holabird & Roche completed the process by which Holabird & Roche entered the ranks of America's largest and most successful architectural practices.[20]

Even after it had become one of Chicago's most successful commercial architects, Holabird & Roche continued to do designs for houses and small apartment buildings as well as many other building types throughout the metropolitan area. A good example of a surviving Holabird & Roche house for an affluent but probably not wealthy client is the turreted "graystone" residence for Frederick H. Prince (cat. no. 94) at 1845 N. Orleans Street on Chicago's North Side. Holabird & Roche's involvement with a house for Bryan Lathrop, on the other hand, seems to mark a turning point in the firm's residential designs. When Lathrop decided to build a new home for himself (cat. no. 165) in what was then emerging as the city's new Gold Coast on the Near North Side, he turned not to Holabird & Roche, who had done so much commercial work for him,[21] but to the famous New York firm of McKim, Mead and White. That he would do this, even though the house was much less expensive than the large office buildings he commissioned from Holabird & Roche, clearly shows that Holabird & Roche, like many of its Chicago colleagues, was considered a commercial and not a residential or institutional architectural firm. For really prestigious work, including expensive houses, institutional structures, and government buildings, many Chicagoans did the same thing they did when they wanted really high-style clothes or furniture.

THE · OLD · COLONY · BUILDING · CHICAGO · ILL ·

3.7
Old Colony Building (201), 1893–94,
401 S. Dearborn Street, southeast corner
of Van Buren Street, perspective. From
American Architect and Building
News, *11 March 1893.*

SECTION

SCALE ¼ = ONE FOOT

FRONT ELEVATION
RESIDENCE OF BRYAN LATHROP ESQ.

M⁽K⁾IM, MEAD & WHITE, ARCHTS. NEW YORK
HOLABIRD & ROCHE, SUP⁽T⁾S, CHICAGO.

3.10

Bryan Lathrop house (Fortnightly Club) (165), 1892, 120 E. Bellevue Place, McKim, Mead and White architects,
Holabird & Roche associated architects, front elevation and wall section. Chicago Historical Society Architectural Collections.

The Lathrop house, with its elegant classical exterior and highly developed plan, undoubtedly made the Romanesque houses of the day, including those by Holabird & Roche, look heavy and old-fashioned. Although it is unclear exactly what design role Holabird & Roche may have played on this commission, it seems that the Chicago firm was responsible for many of the interior details. The importance of this house to Holabird & Roche can be judged by the later residential work of the firm, which is markedly more sophisticated in its use of classical conventions in plan and elevation.

A brief look at the list of other commissions from the years 1890 to 1893 provides striking testimony to the range of the firm. In addition to the remodeling of a Roman bath and hotel in Chicago (cat. no. 96) and a new bank building in Duluth (cat. no. 107), the firm designed for the Catholic order of Servite Sisters a mortuary vault, a barrel-shaped structure with a curious, grottolike front (cat. no. 100), and for a site just west of Chicago in Cicero, the Corrigan and Burke racetrack (cat. no. 156), a mostly utilitarian metal-and-wood grandstand.

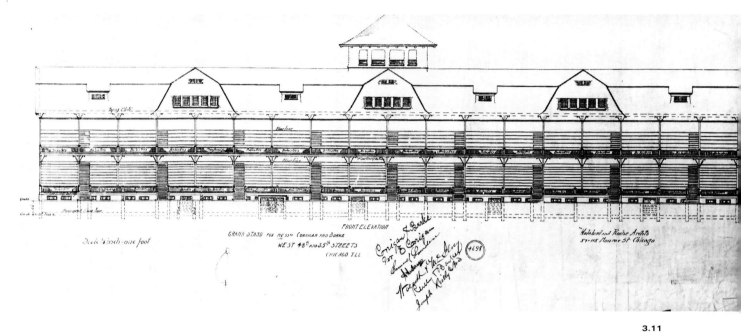

3.11

Grandstand, Corrigan and Burke Racetrack (156), 1902, Cicero, Illinois, front elevation. Chicago Historical Society Architectural Collections.

World's Fair

The role Holabird & Roche played at the 1893 World's Columbian Exposition probably accurately reflects the firm's place in the Chicago architectural firmament at the time the Fair was being planned in the late 1880s or early 1890s. Although Holabird & Roche had finished some large buildings in the Loop by 1890, notably the Tacoma, it was not yet in a class with the largest Chicago firms either in the importance of the commissions or in the dollar volume of its total output. Thus it is not surprising that its contribution to the Fair, which included a small building for New South Wales, a larger but utilitarian livestock pavilion (cat. no. 178), and several smaller structures, did not have major visibility.[22]

Visibility they certainly would have had if the firm's project for an 1,110 foot steel tower designed for David Proctor and the Columbian Tower Company (cat. no. 182) had been built. It is unclear exactly how serious this proposal ever was, but Holabird & Roche was not in the habit of indulging in idle speculation. It is probably just as well the Proctor Tower was never built. As a rather ungainly variant on the tower Alexandre-Gustave Eiffel had produced for Paris in 1889, its design would probably have earned more notoriety for its lack of art than respect for its engineering.[23]

3.12

*World's Columbian Exposition, New South Wales Building (179), ca. 1892–93, view of exterior. Photograph ca.
1893. Chicago Historical Society Prints and Photographs Department, ICHi-14389.*

3.13

*World's Columbian Exposition,
Boone and Crockett Club (172),
1892–93, view of exterior.
Photograph, ca. 1893. Chicago
Historical Society Prints and
Photographs Department,
ICHi-02397.*

PROCTOR STEEL TOWER
ADOPTED BY
WORLD'S COLUMBIAN EXPOSITION
CHICAGO

CORYDON T. PURDY
CHIEF ENG'R.

HOLABIRD AND ROCHE
ARCHITECTS.

SCALE 1 INCH–30 FEET

3.14
World's Columbian Exposition,
Proctor steel tower (183),
ca. 1892, elevation.
Chicago Historical Society
Architectural Collections.

If Holabird & Roche's participation at the Fair was limited, the prospects it opened up were not. The experience of collaborating with famous architects from New York and Boston at the Lathrop house and at the Fair worked to the advantage of both easterners and westerners. By the end of the Fair, the easterners had learned a good deal about the organization and administration of large commercial practices like those of Holabird & Roche. Chicago architects like William Holabird and Martin Roche, on the other hand, had gained the recognition they sought from the nation's architectural establishment and had seen firsthand the work of designers much more experienced than they in dealing with a wide range of building types and stylistic possibilities.

FOUR

At the turn of the century a visitor to Fort Sheridan wishing to take the fastest route from Chicago's Loop would have boarded a train on the lakefront line at the Chicago and North Western Railway's depot just north of the Chicago River.[1] Alighting one hour later at the Fort Sheridan station, twenty-five miles north of the Loop, our visitor would have had a short walk to the gates of the fort. Arriving at the central part of the complex, he would have seen unfolding a fifty-four-acre central parade ground, dominated to the south by a great range of buildings with a huge tower in the center. To the north he would have seen some smaller buildings, and to the east, glimpsed through the abundant foliage above the lake bluffs, a few residences. The landscape scheme for the fort had been done by Ossian Simonds and the buildings, erected between 1889 and 1893, by Holabird & Roche. Together, with the aid of a beautiful lakeside site, they created one of the most impressive military installations of the late nineteenth century.[2]

A pervasive attitude of Americans throughout history has been suspicion of a large standing military, and it is characteristic that the imagery of Fort Sheridan was oddly equivocal. There was no fortified boundary wall, no display of heavy artillery, not even much martial symbolism in the decoration of the buildings. When the parade ground was not being used for organized activities, it could easily have been mistaken for the central quadrangle of a university campus. Even the word "fort" would have seemed innocent enough, a quaint anachronism from the days when the United States Army and General Philip Sheridan, for whom the installation was named, battled Indians on the frontier. Certainly nothing in the name, the setting, or the appearance of the fort would have suggested the turbulent urban conflicts in Chicago, miles to the south, that had called it into being.

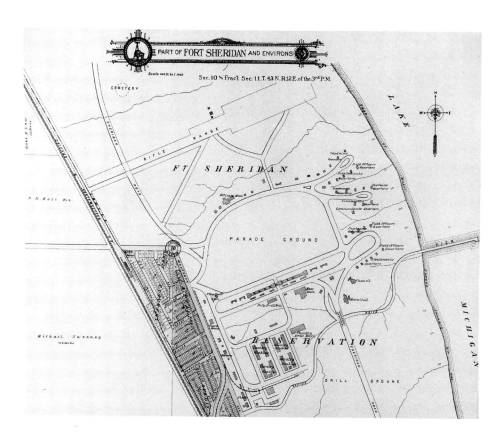

4.1

Fort Sheridan, site plan. From Standard Atlas of Lake County, *1907.*

4.2

Fort Sheridan (142), water tower, cavalry barracks (left), and infantry barracks (right), all completed ca. 1892. Courtesy of National Archives.

Fort Sheridan
captains' quarters
(131) completed 1890,
showing loop roads
along bluffs. Courtesy
of National Archives.

Fort Sheridan was, in fact, a direct response to the sometimes bloody Chicago labor strife of the 1870s and 1880s. As the country's industry boomed in the post–Civil War years, the prosperity was not shared equally. In Chicago, while the foundations were being laid for some of the city's great fortunes, many citizens were obliged to work long hours at tedious and sometimes dangerous jobs to feed their families, often living in crowded, ramshackle quarters. Those who had work feared losing their jobs during business downturns, frequent and jarring events in this era of boom and bust.

In this dynamic but often brutal business atmosphere, American labor started to flex its muscles. Following the business downturn and resulting unemployment caused by the panic of 1873, labor riots and street brawls became increasingly common. In 1877 labor unrest that started as a relatively minor affair in the East soon spread to Chicago, where freight trains were stopped and factories closed. Although the actual fighting was confined to skirmishes, it was necessary to mobilize a large armed contingent to keep the peace. In addition to 450 city national guard reservists, federal troops were called in from the Dakota Territory and Rock Island. In all, some 20,000 men were in arms.[3]

The 1877 railroad strike was profoundly unsettling to Chicagoans. The threat to the unity and stability of the country was greater than that caused by any event except the Civil War. To many of Chicago's middle class it seemed a fundamental challenge to the American economy, for they fervently believed that any collectivization of labor sabotaged the free market system and that tolerating violence undermined the very basis of the country.

Chicago's industrialists also felt personally vulnerable. In the 1880s most of the owners of the steel mills, packing yards, and lumber mills were still individual entrepreneurs. The great consolidated corporations of the twentieth century were for the most part in the future. The factory owner more often than not worked in an office at the plant, a stone's throw from the mass of laborers in the workshops and mills.[4] The houses of Chicago's wealthiest citizens, lining Prairie Avenue and the nearby boulevards to the south on Chicago's Gold Coast, moreover, lay immediately adjacent to some of the city's poorest neighborhoods. Within five blocks lay the Federal Street slum, and one mile beyond was Halsted Street, where Irish butchers had brandished their cleavers during demonstrations in 1877. More often than not the company owner and his chief lieutenants drove to the factory each day through working-class neighborhoods and tenement districts.

The massive masonry walls, castellations, towers, and heavy wrought-iron gates of the industrialists' châteaus were more than mere decorative evocations of medieval and early Renaissance Italy and France. At the house Holabird & Roche built for James R. Walker on Prairie Avenue in 1891–93, for example, the thick stone walls and heavy corner turret crushing down on the entrance arch may have been primarily symbolic, meant to evoke an image of impregnable security, but the architects were careful to provide a raised basement, a deep-set exterior front door, and beyond that a vestibule and another door, all creating a formidable physical as well as psychological barrier between the residents and the world outside. In contrast to the lighter, more open forms of many Holabird & Roche houses for sites farther from the business center, the Walker house looked as if it could actually withstand a siege.

Among the responses of Chicago's "solid citizenry" to the unrest of 1877 was pressure for a federal garrison close to Chicago, so troops could enter the city quickly in an emergency. Spearheading this drive was the Chicago Commercial Club. Although it was a private and highly exclusive organization, in typical nineteenth-century fashion the club played a quite public role in planning for the Chicago area. This was considered by many observers to be perfectly natural, since neither the city of Chicago nor most of its sister cities across the country would have anything resembling an official planning body until well into the twentieth century. In response to the labor unrest, the Commercial Club became keenly interested in the role of the military in keeping order in the volatile city. A monthly meeting in February 1879 had as its topic "The Military, as Protectors of Property, Local and National." Army generals figured prominently as speakers at the club in these years.[5] It appears that the idea

4.4

James Walker house (154), 1891–93, 1726 S. Prairie Avenue, perspective. Chicago Historical Society Architectural Collections.

of a military base on the North Shore was already under discussion in the early 1880s, and further meetings related to this topic occurred in May 1885 and March 1886.

The violent Haymarket riot of 1886 provided the final compelling argument, if any was needed. Club members stepped up their campaign to convince the government to station troops near Chicago by offering six hundred acres of land if the army would establish a post there. Whether the tract was chosen because it was already owned by club members or whether they purchased the land at that time in a deliberate attempt to place the military garrison next to affluent suburban communities is hard to say. Certainly locating a military base between Highland Park and Lake Forest would have had both advantages and disadvantages. It might have been a reassuring daily presence for many wealthy residents of the area, but a military base is often not the most genteel of neighbors, and the donation precluded the future development potential of a magnificent lakefront site. In March 1887 the federal government accepted the deed to the land and established the fort. It was named Fort Sheridan after General Philip Sheridan, a Civil War general who had intervened in Chicago's affairs at crucial moments in the past: to quell unrest following the Great Fire of 1871 and to keep order during strikes in 1874–77.

The early involvement of Holabird & Roche at Fort Sheridan is difficult to assess. The firm began work on designs for the fort in 1884, three years before the post was officially established.[6] Did the government engage them even before the land was accepted from the Commercial Club, or were they working for the club? The first task would naturally have been to carefully survey the site and make a master plan, but it is not clear to what extent the master plan was the work of army engineers, of Holabird & Roche, or of the architects' former partner Ossian Simonds. Firm records suggest that the architects did lay out at least the sewage and water systems, perhaps with the help of Simonds, who was later hired to do the landscaping, but it is hard to know exactly whom to credit with overall site design.[7]

Finally, and most intriguing, there is the question of the role of Samuel Beckley Holabird, William Holabird's father. S. B. Holabird had become by this time quartermaster general of the army, living in Washington, D.C. Since he was responsible for the lodging and equipment of the army, as a matter of course he would have been involved with the design and construction of the fort. No one in the late nineteenth century would have been surprised to see relatives of highly placed officials receiving contracts, but so far no records have tied S. B. Holabird directly to the awarding of the architectural commission to his son's firm.

The firm first planned a set of temporary buildings and then the permanent establishment. Because of the distance of the fort from Chicago, the poor roads, uncooperative weather, and labor problems, construction of the first permanent buildings was difficult. There was also bureaucratic bumbling. Firm records preserve many comments about the ineptitude of Post Commander MacCauley, for example. The firm seems to have learned to get along with bureaucracies at a very early date, however, and by 1893 the original sixty-seven buildings, all but one designed by Holabird & Roche, were completed.[8]

It is likely that here, as at other installations, the army itself played a major role in the design. According to standard practice, army officers in Washington, D.C., would send sample drawings for the fort's officers and the architectural firm to use as guidelines for new construction. When the architects finished their plans they sent them to Washington, where army personnel tried to rationalize and standardize them, often demanding significant modifications before giving final approval. An anonymous employee later described the process:

> I worked for some time under Bagley [Holabird & Roche employee J. W. Bagley] in the drafting room on Fort Sheridan work. The work was re-

duced to standards and reproduced in hectograph [a method of making prints from drawings] form. The regular routine was followed: sketches of proposed buildings were submitted to Washington and often disallowed, then other sketches prepared, and finally an approved working drawing and specifications completed, bids taken, contracts let and buildings erected.[9]

The general plan of Fort Sheridan, with its vast parade ground surrounded by buildings, was a common one, especially in the forts established in the American West during the pioneer years. The setting was much more picturesque than at most military installations, however, and Simonds attempted to enhance it. Instead of an absolutely regular plan, for example, the fort has sinuous roads that run along the contours of the land. The large industrial buildings were placed well away from the lake and hidden from the parade ground by more pretentious structures. The houses were sited on cul-de-sacs carefully threaded between the lakefront ravines, to provide the best views and disturb the lakefront as little as possible. As one reviewer later reported: "Nature did much, and Mr. Simonds has shown that rare thoughtfulness so unusual in his profession of merely helping nature, and not attempting to obliterate it."[10]

The Holabird & Roche buildings at the fort were nothing like the flimsy wooden structures of the Indian outposts that were the most common installations the army constructed in the West. Instead they were of masonry and resembled the more established arsenals and bases of the East.[11] Fort Sheridan was like a small city in both function and appearance. In fact one might argue that the fort, at the very outset of the architects' careers, foreshadowed the kinds of work they would do later in the city itself. Unlike most cities, however, Holabird & Roche's buildings at Fort Sheridan had a family likeness because the architects were able to specify a limited palette of materials for them all—notably a buff-colored brick made on the site for walls, limestone for foundations and some decorative trim, and slate for roofs—and a common vocabulary of flat walls, simple massing, and regular fenestration. This unified a set of buildings that ranged from utilitarian warehouses—rectangular blocks with severe hipped roofs, simple rectangular openings, and no decoration—to the more fanciful turreted and dormered houses of the commanding officers. The style of the buildings, adapted from the Romanesque mode so popular at the time, was rationalized and simplified to satisfy the military's penchant for real and apparent economy.

Like any city, the fort had public, residential, and industrial areas. At the very center of the "public" part, where the town square would have been, was the parade ground, a large, slightly irregular rectangular open space. This area was dominated to the south by two massive ranges of barracks, one for infantry and the other for cavalry

4.5
Fort Sheridan water tower (142),
view of tower base from
Architectural Reviewer, *June 1897.*

(cat. nos. 141, 143) flanking the fort's central feature, the enormous water tower (cat. no. 142). Rising from the south side of the parade ground, the 167 foot structure loomed above the surrounding landscape like the tower of a midwestern courthouse, unmistakably signaling the presence of the fort.

The tower was a common feature in late nineteenth-century army posts. This one was unusually thin and tall for a military building. In its original condition, with a high pyramidal peak above an open loggia overlooking the surrounding countryside, it was also surprisingly delicate at the top. It was designed, no doubt, with the fort's elegant suburban neighbors in mind. Although every citizen of adjoining Lake Forest or Highland Park would have known exactly what institution the tower represented, they may well have appreciated the way it evoked a Tuscan campanile or some other European landmark, providing a comfortable, picturesque backdrop to their semirural estates. The army has never been known for extended flights of fancy, however, and the tower also housed a 94,000 gallon tank for maintaining the post's water pressure.

The view close up within the fort was quite different from that seen by suburban neighbors. At close range the lower part of the brick shaft, with its bulbous projecting corners and slit windows, recalls a medieval fortification more than a church tower. At the bottom the brick tower flares outward to meet an impressive stone base dramatically opened by a great arch to provide a carriageway. The enormous rusticated stones forming the wedge-shaped voussoirs of the arch reinforce the impression of ponderous weight above the narrow opening and bring to mind a medieval sally port. Creating such an opening in the base of a massive tower was expensive and completely superfluous, of course, since there was ample space for passages on either side of the tower or through the adjacent barracks buildings, but the architects and the army apparently felt it necessary to create at least one impressive set piece that was unmistakably martial, perhaps to counteract the somewhat fanciful crowning element visible from the surrounding suburbs.

The adjacent barracks, one for the infantry, another for the cavalry, each housing four hundred men, were placed directly against the tower on each side. They provided

4.6

Fort Sheridan, quartermaster's stables area (137), completed 1890, view with workshop (right foreground), veterinary hospital (right center), stables (right background), and quartermaster's stables (left). Courtesy of National Archives.

an unbroken wall over a thousand feet long, punctuated only by a regular sequence of doors, windows, dormers, and chimneys. Just behind this massive public facade to the south was the working part of the post, including the army mess hall and central heating plant (cat. no. 164), the fire station (cat. no. 209) and the infantry drill hall (cat. no. 208). Farther south, across an iron bridge spanning one of the narrow ravines that extended into the fort, were five long, low, barnlike stable buildings with many chimneys and outbuildings (cat. nos. 139, 194). These constituted the first eight of a planned symmetrical group of twelve structures. Farther along were storehouses (cat. no. 135), workshops (cat. no. 136), and bakery (cat. no. 134). With their simple rectangular massing, sober brick facades, and profusion of stacks, these buildings looked like a collection of railroad shop structures.

Conspicuous at the entrance side of the fort was the post's guardhouse (cat. no. 133), which could hold fifty prisoners. This building, with its symmetrical plan and colonnaded porch, was one of the most prominent of all the post structures, and it was made even more impressive by wings added in 1905–6. At the time it was designed, it had to fulfill functions proper to two different eras that, for the moment, continued to coexist at the fort. Its chief function was to confine unruly soldiers, but it was also used on occasion to house Indians who still roamed the prairie to the West, more often because of drunkenness than actual attacks. It could also have been used in case of labor violence in Chicago.

4.8
*Fort Sheridan
guardhouse (133),
completed 1890.
Courtesy of National
Archives.*

The final area of the fort, on the eastern edge of the property along the wooded lakefront, contained the officers' quarters. Laid out along four loop roads between the parade ground and the ravines on the edge of the lake, this whole area looked remarkably like some of the neighborhoods in the adjoining suburbs. In fact the houses were a simplified version of the ones Holabird & Roche built in outlying city and suburban neighborhoods during these years.[12] The sixteen houses for officers, designated lieutenants' quarters (cat. no. 128), and captains' quarters (cat. no. 131), were all basically similar: simple two-and-a-half-story structures, notable primarily for the large arched entrances in their gabled fronts and inset entry porches. "Most charming little houses they are," wrote one contemporary critic, "although built of common light-colored brick with stone trimming and little or no pretense. The location and surroundings are so picturesque that their simplicity is forgotten, or if thought of, only adds charm to the effect."[13]

If the lieutenants' and captains' houses were modest, the adjoining field officers' quarters (cat. no. 129), with their large entrance porches, corner turrets, elaborate dormer windows, and terra cotta trim, would have been perfectly at home on the most elegant streets of the suburbs adjoining the base. All the officers' quarters were apparently rather grand by the standards of contemporary army forts in the West. One observer later recalled: "The 15th infantry was stationed at the post while I was there and the officers' quarters was something of a revelation to men that had been fighting Indi-

4.9
Fort Sheridan lieutenants' quarters (left, 128) and field officers' quarters (right, 130), completed 1890. Courtesy of National Archives.

4.10
Fort Sheridan field officers' quarters, interior view. From Attention and at Rest, *1897.*

ans for several years on the Western plains. The furniture of the captains' houses rattled around like one pea in a pod, sliding door keys were a curiosity as were some of the other equipment. The commandant's residence was a palace."[14]

In addition to the three major zones at the fort, there were several buildings isolated from the rest for safety or convenience. Notable among these were the post's pumping station (cat. no. 132), under the bluffs along the lake, and the tiny dead house (cat. no. 210) and magazine (cat. no. 191), both placed alongside the southernmost ravine.

Contemporary reactions were largely favorable. Samuel Beckley Holabird's comments on the fort have been preserved. Not surprisingly, he was pleased. In his diaries is this entry: "2 September: Visited Fort Sheridan. Called on Col. Crafton and saw several of his officers . . . The tower of the waterworks is a beautiful and original structure. It is remarkably well built. The barracks are good, as buildings for the purpose

4.11
Fort Sheridan, pumping station (132), completed 1890. Courtesy of National Archives.

designated. The officers' quarters are plain and in good taste."[15] A writer for the *Architectural Reviewer* agreed with Holabird's assessment of the architecture: "Altogether the effect is that of a little city built by one mind, and while . . . there is a similarity of material used, there is sufficient variation in the architecture and such good taste in the landscape effects that the result is most pleasing."[16]

Let the last appraisal be from the florid pen of a railroad promotional writer early in the century. This writer, consciously overlooking all the inconvenient realities of a military installation, probably describes the fondest hopes of the men who lobbied so hard to bring the fort to this location. Fort Sheridan, he wrote,

> is the last word in a modern military post, and one of the most beautiful in the United States. . . . Fort Sheridan's daily life and routine with the underlying current of waiting—always waiting for the call to boots and saddles—is an inspiration worth a longer journey than the hour's ride from the heart of Chicago. All the beauty and poetry of a protected nation is symbolized in the picture of the wooded military reservation, the perfectly ordered post with its flying flags and silent waiting guns; the quick-moving pictures of khaki clad men in drill parade and guard mounting; and in the background old Lake Michigan, calm and powerful as a great army at rest, throwing a soft gray haze over the foliage of ravines and parade ground, like the atmosphere of a Corot picture.
>
> The thrill of military music is punctuated by the sharp commands of officers, and the echoing shots from the rifle range. The inspiring strains of the band come from all directions at once and a man's blood bounds quicker in his veins, and his heart beats faster for love of his country and flag.[17]

Over the succeeding years, the landscape and buildings at Fort Sheridan have stood up well to hard use, as the base has served its intended functions, first as a potent military presence in the continuing labor disputes in the 1890s, then in preparation for the major wars of the twentieth century.[18] Some of the original buildings, notably the water tower, have been altered somewhat; but whether because of the army's recognition of their architectural importance or the basic conservatism of the vast federal bureaucracy, the additions are relatively few and remarkably sympathetic. After the Holabird & Roche buildings were finished, some new structures, completed about 1905–10 from plans prepared by the quartermaster general's office, still fit in reasonably well. It was only in the most recent buildings, many of them intended to be temporary, that the original spirit of the place was lost. They were mostly built out of sight of the central parade ground, however. Even with the departure of the army in the 1980s the fort has remained remarkably intact.[19]

No one has ever suggested that Fort Sheridan was an artistic masterpiece. Apart from the water tower, few of the buildings can be credited with great originality or subtlety of design, but the overall effect was unified and substantial, perfectly appropriate for the military and its largely utilitarian purposes. Apparently everyone was pleased. The completion of such a large and conspicuous project must have brought the young architectural firm great satisfaction, not to mention needed revenue. As for the Commercial Club, it is hard to imagine a more reassuring and solid symbol of order and discipline for the wealthy North Shore and the entire Chicago region.

FIVE

CAPITAL, TECHNOLOGY,
AND THE TALL OFFICE
BUILDING: THE TACOMA

If Fort Sheridan, Holabird & Roche's first substantial commission, could be counted as a solid success, the Tacoma Building, the firm's first really large commercial project, was a triumph. What had started out as minor remodeling became a very large new building. Its story provides a striking demonstration of new development and construction practices in a new building type, the speculative tall office building. What makes the story of the Tacoma and Holabird & Roche's subsequent office buildings particularly interesting is that they went up during a brief moment of major transformation in the real estate industry in which Chicago led the country.[1]

The Speculative Office Building

In Chicago in the 1880s the idea of a building devoted entirely to offices was quite new. In the early nineteenth century, most companies' offices occupied space immediately adjacent to the places where goods were produced or traded. A New York or London banker's office, for example, might be on a mezzanine above the banking floor. In the mid-nineteenth century, with the enormous jump in the scale of businesses, a new managerial class developed. These office workers did not actually make or sell products. Their work was paperwork, controlling the operations of the increasingly complex business systems.[2] As their numbers grew, so did the size of buildings. Businesses like banks, newspapers, and insurance companies led in this development because they employed large numbers of highly trained professionals. The change was visible in London in the early nineteenth century and then in New York and other cities of the eastern United States.[3] Chicago was somewhat slower, but by the early 1880s it could count quite a few companies that built themselves large structures housing small armies of managerial employees.[4]

Soon other kinds of business followed suit. The offices of most early manufacturing companies had been adjacent to the factories. These companies, particularly when they ceased to be run day to day by the company founders and became large corporations, found it convenient to build offices downtown. Although these offices were far from the factories, the telephone allowed easy communication, and the central location made interaction easier between the companies and the growing number of accountants, lawyers, brokers, and other urban professionals who served them.[5]

Not every company could afford to build its own building, however, leading to a sharp rise in demand for speculative office space—that is, space built by developers and leased to anyone who could afford the rent. In the early nineteenth century most speculative buildings were designed to accommodate a wide mixture of uses. They might house storage space or showrooms or have any number of other uses. By mid-century the idea of the speculative building solely for office occupancy had gained acceptance in the larger, older cities of Europe and the eastern United States.[6] It appears that it was not until the late 1860s that Chicago first had business blocks devoted almost entirely to first-class office use.[7] The typical large office building at that time was a four- to six-story structure erected by an individual or a small, tightly controlled partnership and would have cost $50,000 to $100,000 to build. With land prices added, the cost would have run $100,000 to $200,000. The most expensive buildings of this type still cost less than $500,000.[8] A good example was the Honore Block at the northwest corner of Adams and Dearborn. Constructed in 1873, the Honore was a massive pile with a grand twenty-three-bay stone facade in the style of the great Venetian Renaissance architect Michele Sanmicheli. Originally crowned by an elaborate mansard roof with numerous dormers and metal crestings, it looked more like a public building than a mere business block. Although the walls were skeletal, perforated by enormous windows, the freestanding columns supporting cornices at every story, and pilasters behind the columns supporting the window arches created an effect of dignity and permanence even after the mansarded roof was removed so another story could be added. This was one of the premier Chicago business blocks of the immediate post-Fire years.[9] Entire streets were lined with similar buildings. (For a good example of post-Fire buildings see fig. 5.10.)

With the Montauk, which, as we have seen, briefly housed the young firm of Holabird & Roche, the height of the office block jumped. Designed by Burnham and Root in 1881, the Montauk was Chicago's first "skyscraper," the first office building to break significantly from the plateau of five- and six-story buildings that were standard in big commercial structures of the day.[10] With the Montauk, Chicago followed in the

5.1

Montauk Block, 1881, 64–70 W. Monroe, Burnham and Root architects. Photograph by J. W. Taylor. Chicago Historical Society Prints and Photographs Department, ICHi-01035.

path of New York, where the first very high buildings had been built as early as the 1870s. The Montauk was financed by the Brooks brothers of Boston, who became the single largest developers in the Chicago boom of the late 1880s. To wealthy eastern merchants the prospect of sharing in the enormous profits generated by Chicago's economic boom was a powerful incentive, overcoming the problems and risks inherent in dealing with investments made in far-off places.[11]

This was the case with the Montauk's sponsors. The Brookses' family fortune had been already established by the beginning of the nineteenth century by their grandfather, Peter Chardon Brooks (1767–1849), reportedly Boston's first millionaire, through marine insurance. His friends characterized him as a sedate and conservative investor; his detractors called him downright stingy. His heirs earned the same kind of reputation.[12]

Tracing the Brookses' involvement in Chicago real estate is difficult. They rarely divulged any more information than was absolutely necessary. In fact Peter Brooks apparently made a considerable effort to hide his real estate dealings from Boston friends and acquaintances so he could play the role of gentleman farmer on his Medford estate. The brothers seem to have become involved in Chicago real estate before the Fire in the 1860s, when they bought an existing building, the four-story Portland Block, which had gone into foreclosure. After the Fire they commissioned William Le Baron Jenney to design a new eight-story Portland Block with a passenger elevator. Although in the end the building was built only to five stories, the idea for a tall elevator building was not forgotten.[13] It resurfaced with the Montauk.[14]

In much of the architectural history of the past several decades, the appearance of the Montauk and the other early skyscrapers has been explained largely in terms of the development of new building technologies, notably new structural means. This explanation seems inadequate for several reasons. The technology that made possible the first skyscrapers had been available for some time. The passenger elevator was first used in Chicago in the 1860s.[15] The problem of building large buildings on the relatively soft clay underlying Chicago had been addressed by the development of scientifically calculated isolated footings in the early 1870s.[16] Extensive use of interior metal framing went back to at least the late eighteenth century.[17] Fireproofing of some sort, finally, had long been practiced, and by the early 1870s it had already come to the form it would take throughout the rest of the century.[18] Had advances in structural technology been the dominant factor in the creation of the skyscraper, we might have expected the first skyscraper in Chicago to have appeared more than a decade earlier.

In fact, within the area of technology the advent of the telegraph and the telephone and new methods in lighting, heating, and sanitation probably did at least as much to make the high office building feasible. Until the new means of communication permitted exchange of information between offices and new means of servicing these offices made it possible to stack huge numbers of people vertically without discomfort or risk to health, the tall building could not have emerged. At least as important, moreover, were new market forces put into motion by the enormous growth in the number of well-paid managerial employees and their desire to be close to the center of the city, the resulting rise in land values, and a revolution in the way capital could be amassed for building purposes. All these things were necessary to make tall buildings profitable. It was in great part the prospect of profit that finally spurred the architects and engineers to develop and exploit new and existing technologies.[19]

Aesthetically, the Montauk was one of the new no-nonsense commercial buildings of the kind Jenney had pioneered and his former employees Burnham and Root developed much further. Ten floors of flat brick walls, regular, segmentally arched windows, and very little trim followed one another relentlessly from the narrow entranceway upward floor after floor to the corbelled cornice. This facade probably reminded citizens more of industrial structures of the day than of downtown commercial buildings. How different this was from the Honore Block. Compared with the Honore, the Montauk seemed to many Chicagoans brutally plain, pinched, and ill proportioned.[20]

The Home Insurance and Rookery

Only a few years after it was built the Montauk was all but eclipsed by larger and more amply proportioned structures. Two of these, both on LaSalle Street, are critical for understanding the subsequent story of the Tacoma. The first was the Home Insurance Building of 1884–85 (fig. 5.2).[21] Insurance companies not only boasted more liquid capital than almost any other American business enterprise, but they had more need for an extensive managerial labor force. It is not surprising that they were among the earliest and grandest builders of large office buildings.[22] For this building William Le Baron Jenney continued his experiments at reducing and simplifying the exterior surfaces that he had started at the Portland Block and the structural innovations that he had pioneered at a loft building that building historians have dubbed the Leiter I, completed in 1879 (fig. 11.1). At the Leiter I Jenney had started with a typical midcentury loft-building formula in which a masonry bearing wall enclosed an interior structure of metal columns and beams. In this system the interior framing held up most of the interior of the building. The exterior wall held up only itself and one end of the last beam. What Jenney did at the Leiter I was to move the last column of the interior framing out to the very edge of the space. This meant that almost all the weight was carried on the interior frame and very little on the exterior walls. This allowed Jenney to reduce the exterior walls to a minimum and to introduce the largest possible windows, a feature very welcome to the owners of companies that operated in loft buildings and depended on natural light for their operations.[23]

At the Home Insurance Building Jenney went one step further. He took the outermost interior metal column and moved it all the way out to the exterior masonry pier, embedding it in the pier. It has often been claimed that the Home Insurance was the first fully skeletal building, but informed observers have always realized this was not entirely correct, since the masonry wall still carried some load. Jenney's own descriptions of the building, moreover, make it clear that his intentions had nothing to do with creating a new skeletal structural system. He was merely reinforcing a stone wall so he could open it up more.[24] Because the Home Insurance was a prestigious building for a prime site on LaSalle Street, Jenney could not leave it as bald as the

5.2

Rookery Building, 1886, 209 S. LaSalle Street,
Burnham and Root architects. Home Insurance Building by
William Le Baron Jenney, 1884, visible at left.
Photograph by Barnes-Crosby. Chicago Historical Society
Prints and Photographs Department, ICHi-19186.

Leiter I, so he grafted onto the loftlike block a heavy three-story base and arcaded top, a set of belt courses and pilasters, and a frontispiece, all of which made it clear that this was a building of some pretensions but also gave it a decidedly choppy appearance.

The other building, one that would exert a much greater influence on the Tacoma, was the Rookery. Like the Montauk, this was a product of the team of Burnham and Root and the Brooks brothers and their agent Owen Aldis. Erected on a scale unprecedented for Chicago, the Rookery Building, at LaSalle and Adams Streets, covered a full quarter block and rose eleven stories.[25] The Rookery did not follow in the line of the Montauk and the Home Insurance Building. In the Rookery, undoubtedly because of the unequaled site and the rents it would command, Burnham and Root were able to convince their client to sacrifice some degree of practicality in order to create a major monument. Because the building occupied a full quarter block, it was necessary to cut into the block in some way to allow light and air into every office space. It is likely that the greatest amount of office space would have been created by using some version of an H or E plan or perhaps a series of small interior light courts. Burnham and Root and their clients opted instead for a simpler but far grander effect. They threw a band of offices around the perimeter of the site, leaving the entire interior open as a huge light court above the second floor and, below the metal-and-glass roof structure at the second floor, an enormous interior atrium. The exterior walls, likewise, seem to have been designed at least as much for artistic effect as for utility. Floor-to-ceiling heights changed constantly, not for any programmatic reason, but as a device for composing the facade, and the use of arched rather than flat-headed windows blocked light. It appears that Burnham had wanted to use the same structural system on the outer walls of the Rookery as Jenney had done at the Home Insurance, thus creating much larger windows, but he abandoned the idea when Root convinced the Brooks brothers not to sacrifice the aesthetic effect of his weighty Romanesque exterior. Skeletal construction was used in the light court, however, presumably because the aesthetic aspects were less important.[26] In its monumentality and in its equipment the Rookery set a new standard for office buildings in the city. It was the point of departure for the most ambitious Chicago office buildings of the next generation.

The Rookery also illustrates changes in the way large office buildings were developed. Unlike the Home Insurance, the Rookery was a speculative building. It was financed through the mechanism of the safety-deposit company, one of the most curious legal fictions of the age. In the nineteenth century, as it became necessary to raise ever larger sums of money for enterprises of unprecedented scale—for example, for building railroads or steel mills—any number of new ways to raise capital were explored. The most important by far was the limited liability corporation. This form of business enterprise, a blending of features found earlier in the joint stock company and the corporation, a kind of organization long seen in guilds, universities, and other civic entities, was first used extensively in Britain in the early nineteenth century. It came to be widely used in the United States only in the second half of the nineteenth century. [27] The use of the corporate organization and the issuance of stocks and bonds made possible much larger capital pools than those available to any individual or private partnership.[28] In part this was due to one of the corporation's key features, limited liability. An individual investor or member of a partnership was personally liable for all the losses incurred by the business he had invested in. For this reason even a minor business investment could be disastrous, resulting in loss of all the investor's personal assets including the family home. With limited liability any investor stood to lose only the equity actually invested.[29]

The problem was that the use of the corporation to construct speculative real estate was at best legally questionable. Corporations could, of course, construct buildings in which to carry out the business for which they were chartered, but the state of Illinois, in the General Corporations Act of 1872, forbade corporations from developing more space than they needed for their own use and strictly prohibited corporations devoted to real estate development. With these prohibitions lawmakers aimed at protecting small businesses and curbing speculation. As the capital needs of developers grew, canny businessmen found various ways around these laws. Corporate officers, for example, soon realized that their right to build buildings for themselves opened a window of opportunity. Some simply built a much larger structure than they needed, arguing that this space was needed for future expansion. In such a case, lawyers for the companies contended, they should be allowed to rent out the space in the interim. At the Rookery an even more audacious ploy was used. The purpose of a safety-deposit company was ostensibly to create large safes. The company would, of course, need to build a structure to house them. What if they then built an entire office building around a few safes?[30]

This was the fiction that permitted the Brooks brothers and their associates to build the Rookery. In the case of the two slightly later Holabird & Roche buildings, the Venetian and the Champlain, the brothers turned to the "Massachusetts Trust," another device to circumvent restrictions on corporate real estate development.[31] The legality of both operations was challenged several times over the next decades, and it was not until well into the twentieth century that the right of corporations to build speculative space was firmly established in Illinois. The lack of strict enforcement was due in part to difficulties in interpreting the law. It was also due, almost certainly, to the growing realization that only corporations could raise enough capital to build on the scale that had come to characterize the new American city. Amazing as it now seems, many of the largest buildings in Chicago in the late nineteenth century, including virtually all of those best known in architectural history, were developed using financial methods of dubious legality.

One final feature of the Rookery that is important to understand in charting the rapid development of the speculative office building was the practice of building on long-term leaseholds. Until the Fire much of Chicago development was done on land held by the landowners in fee simple. The increasing use of fifty- and ninety-nine-year leases after the Civil War meant that developers did not have to buy the land to control the site. Banks were understandably reluctant at first to lend for projects not secured by landownership, but given the enormous profits to be made, insurance companies and wealthy individuals could be found who were willing to take the risk.[32] Using a long-term lease and a corporate structure, plus loans and proceeds from the sale of stocks and bonds, a developer could put up a very large building using relatively little of his own money. As long as he could fill it with paying tenants he would be able to pay the ground rent, pay off loans and bonds, issue generous dividends to stockholders, and still leave a large profit for himself. This was normally done with large buildings in Chicago during boom periods like those of the late 1880s.[33] As a consequence much more intensive building was possible, driving up land prices sharply. For example, the average value of Loop land rose 29 percent in the brief period 1886–92, in great part because larger buildings allowed a much greater exploitation of the land.[34]

In a business downturn, of course, all the financial devices that allowed the developer to build with relatively little money of his own started to work against him as the income failed to cover the ground lease and debt service. In the process real estate empires came crashing down. The Brookses, because they were extremely conservative in their business practices, rarely faced this problem, but many others did. The turbulence in the real estate market and the danger of unscrupulous speculators led in the 1880s to the founding of a number of organizations that attempted to regulate practices and bring order to the real estate profession.[35]

The Birth of the Tacoma

In 1885, while the Rookery was still under construction, Chicago lawyer and businessman Wirt D. Walker entered Holabird & Roche's offices with a project for a building on LaSalle Street just two blocks north of the Rookery. Only twenty-five years old, Walker came from an affluent family and was already accustomed to dealing with big real estate projects. After graduating from Yale in 1880, he studied law at the Union College of Law in Chicago and in the office of Dexter, Herrick and Allen. Although he was admitted to the bar in 1882, the death of his father thrust him into the role of manager of the family's extensive real estate holdings. He would be instrumental, among other things, in the construction of the Auditorium Building, Chicago's most conspicuous civic real estate venture of the late 1880s and the most public of all corporate ventures in real estate in late nineteenth-century Chicago.[36]

Walker had a shrewd eye for development possibilities in the Chicago Loop. Early in the 1880s he invested heavily on Dearborn Street, especially in the area south of what was then the core of the business district. By the late 1880s this part of Dearborn, close to the Dearborn Street Station, rivaled the stretch of LaSalle Street just north of the LaSalle Street Station, as the center of Chicago business.[37] On one of his properties, the southeast corner of Dearborn and Harrison, he commissioned from the fledgling firm of Holabird & Roche a six-story building that was finished in 1888. With its interior mill construction, arched brick street walls, and large cast iron and plate glass shop windows on the ground floor, this was a typical loft structure of the time. In the mid-1880s he also had the firm design a low building at the southwest corner of Wabash Avenue and Van Buren Street, a "taxpayer"—that is, an inexpensive structure with large plate glass shopfronts that would at least pay the taxes while waiting for the land to appreciate to the point where a much larger building could be profitably developed (fig. 18.3).[38]

The Tacoma Building started off even more modestly. It appears that Walker's

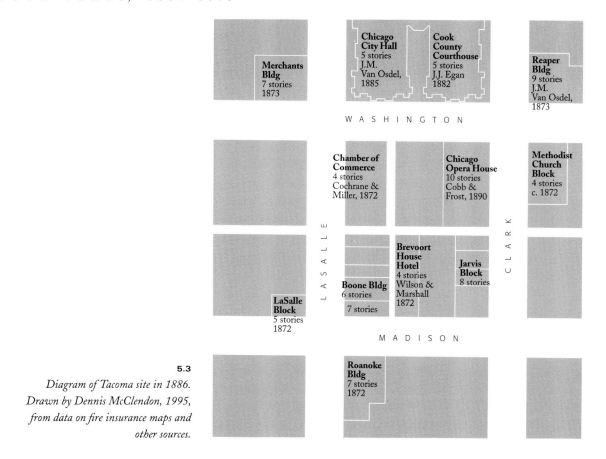

5.3

Diagram of Tacoma site in 1886.
Drawn by Dennis McClendon, 1995,
from data on fire insurance maps and
other sources.

original scheme involved remodeling an existing building he owned on the northwest corner of LaSalle and Madison Streets.[39] This structure, a typical modest post-Fire building, occupied a single city lot with a frontage of only 25 feet along LaSalle, where the frontage was valuable, but 110 feet of less valuable frontage along Madison. It had heavy masonry walls that took up a great deal of space and an "English basement," an arrangement in which there were two shops levels, one a half-story below grade, the other a half-story above. This configuration, presumably intended to double the street-level commercial space, had been common in post-Fire Chicago but was fast being abandoned, probably because it made both spaces inconvenient. Although the building was only fourteen years old, so much work had been done in Chicago since that time that it seemed old-fashioned. Walker consulted five architects to see which could devise the most economical remodeling scheme.[40]

Holabird & Roche made an interesting proposal. The firm suggested removing the exterior walls and substituting a new framework of metal, covering this with a thin

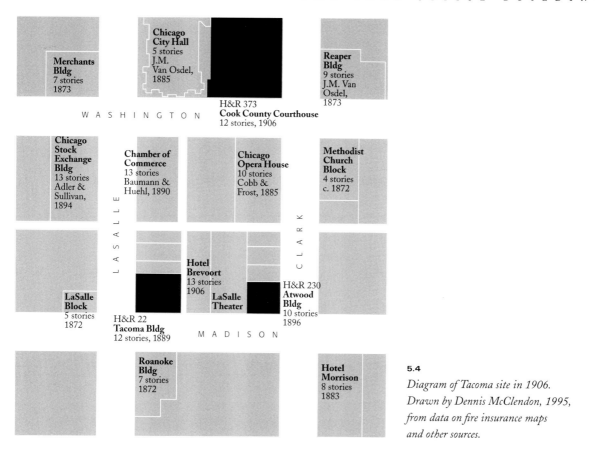

Merchants Bldg
7 stories
1873

Chicago City Hall
5 stories
J.M. Van Osdel, 1885

H&R 373
Cook County Courthouse
12 stories, 1906

Reaper Bldg
9 stories
J.M. Van Osdel, 1873

WASHINGTON

Chicago Stock Exchange Bldg
13 stories
Adler & Sullivan, 1894

Chamber of Commerce
13 stories
Baumann & Huehl, 1890

Chicago Opera House
10 stories
Cobb & Frost, 1885

Methodist Church Block
4 stories
c. 1872

LASALLE

Hotel Brevoort
13 stories
1906

LaSalle Theater

H&R 230
Atwood Bldg
10 stories
1896

CLARK

LaSalle Block
5 stories
1872

H&R 22
Tacoma Bldg
12 stories, 1889

MADISON

Roanoke Bldg
7 stories
1872

Hotel Morrison
8 stories
1883

5.4

Diagram of Tacoma site in 1906. Drawn by Dennis McClendon, 1995, from data on fire insurance maps and other sources.

terra cotta cladding. Holabird & Roche had gotten this idea from Sanford Loring of the Chicago Terra Cotta Company.[41] Loring, who had worked extensively with a number of architects in an attempt to find uses for his patents, undoubtedly had previous experience with remodelings of the kind Walker was proposing, and it is known that he had suggested the idea to other architects.[42] It had become common for owners of commercial buildings to remove the heavy walls at the base of old buildings and install large new windows to increase the area of the grade-level shops, providing them with more light on the interior and increasing their presence from the sidewalk. This could be done, even at considerable expense, because of the sharply rising rents commanded by well-located street-level shopfronts. To do this kind of renovation, the heavy masonry walls were replaced with relatively thin metal columns and beams. Large windows could then be inserted in front of the columns to create nearly continuous plate glass surfaces interrupted only by narrow metal or terra cotta frames.[43] The idea of using lightweight metal or terra cotta panels bolted back to the frame behind them was probably inspired by the example of the cast iron fronts that had been used on thousands of loft and other buildings in New York, Chicago, and elsewhere in the preceding decades.[44]

In addition to facade remodelings, Loring and the architects were also undoubtedly aware of a number of recent uses of terra cotta panels applied to a metal frame on new buildings. One of the best known was to be found in the light court of the Produce Exchange in New York City of 1882–83, designed by one of New York's most important commercial architects, George B. Post. A similar arrangement was found on the interior of the Rookery Building, where the interior court was constructed using a metal framework with glazed terra cotta as a facing.[45] On the twelve-story Mallers Building, started in 1884, a partial skeleton system with terra cotta cladding was used to create projecting bays on the street front of the building.[46]

It seems that in all these examples, far from being the positive advance that many modernist historians have claimed, skeletal construction was considered by many architects, at least in the 1880s and early 1890s, to be merely expedient. It was used to increase rental area and bring sunlight into buildings, but the less substantial appearance it created was considered a liability. The use of thin sheets of terra cotta as a cladding made the problem even worse, so it is no surprise that Burnham and Root confined this system to the courtyard of the Rookery and used palpably heavy masonry for the facades.[47] When Holabird & Roche proposed, undoubtedly with the approval of both the client and the contractor, to use the system seen in the Rookery court for the entire facade of Walker's building, it was clearly not in the name of art. The proposal was strictly an economic proposition: it would have saved a strip of space two feet wide on the street side of each floor, increasing the rentable space by 240 square feet per floor. At $1 rent per square foot per year, the 240 square feet multiplied by seven stories would have yielded an additional $1,680 per year.[48]

In the end, Walker apparently decided this was too much money just to remodel an old building. Instead he asked the firm to design a new twelve-story building for the site. This the architects did, first trying the scheme suggested by Loring. The result would have been an entirely skeletal structure except for the existing party walls. But the architects and client were clearly worried about the effect of wind loads on such a tall building. Although engineers knew theoretically that wind bracing was an issue, the bulk of masonry needed to hold up almost all previous structures in the city was easily greater than necessary to withstand wind pressure. When buildings started to become much higher and lighter, however, wind pressure started to be an important consideration.[49] The architects sent their drawings to Professor John B. Johnson, dean of engineering at Washington University. Johnson reported that the wind-bracing would not be adequate.[50]

Professor Johnson's findings were sufficiently troubling that the architects abandoned their project and returned to a scheme that had masonry side and rear walls but incorporated the skeletal construction on the front. At this point the *Economist* of 15 January 1888, using words that undoubtedly came directly from the architects, reported:

> To erect a high building with the usual bulky walls was to sacrifice much needed space. Messrs. Holabird and Roche, the architects, determined therefore to adopt the following method of treatment: "A heavy brick wall 3 feet in thickness will be built on the north side of the lot. . . . The whole facade of the building, however, will be constructed of wrought iron and steel, terra cotta and plate glass. The exterior supporting columns will be of steel, of 'I' and lattice section, running from the basement to the roof and firmly riveted together. From these heavy cross plate steel girders extend to and are firmly anchored in the massive brick wall on the north lot line. Upon these girders the iron beams rest. Each floor is treated as a horizontal truss, diagonal steel tie rods being inserted. This gives great lateral stiffness. The result of this construction will be on absolutely rigid building from foundation to roof. The floors throughout and the roof will be of hollow terra cotta arches, and all iron and steel work in the building will be fire-proofed with terra cotta. . . . The exterior of the fire-proofing will be covered with ornamental cast-iron or terra cotta."

In other words, the building would be a hybrid of bearing-wall construction and the newer skeleton construction like the Rookery, but it would reverse the two types. The skeletal construction would go on the outside.

A week later the *Tribune* repeated the startling information that the building would rise twelve stories on a parcel measuring 25 by 100 feet—in other words, the typical Chicago city lot on which most houses were constructed. The writer further reported that "some of the builders have claimed that these structures might be made 20 stories just as well as two or twelve" but concluded, "this appears to be an unwarranted flight of fancy." He offered the following opinion: "The office building of this period has probably about reached the limit of height. It is high enough now in all conscience." This last sentence is revealing. The *Chicago Tribune* has always been a conservative paper, siding more often than not with business and against those who would place onerous restrictions on its development. The *Tribune*'s reaction is a good indication of how ambivalent even conservative Chicagoans were about the sudden explosion in scale of their city. Events would prove how strong the negative feelings had grown in the 1880s.[51]

Walker gave the order to start construction on his new building. The old building was demolished, and work started on the foundations. Then, to the amazement of sidewalk superintendents and of Holabird & Roche as well, construction abruptly stopped. Walker had apparently gone ahead with his plans only as a bluff to get possession of the adjacent lot at a lower price. The owners of the other lot, the Parmly brothers, were major Chicago landowners and, no doubt, experienced in these hard-nosed negotiations. Apparently thinking that Walker needed their site to build a tall building, they had held out for a high price. When Walker refused to buy and started work on a twelve-story building without the adjacent property, the startled owners must have realized that the new construction methods allowed him to reduce the walls to the point where he could erect an economically feasible structure without having to secure their lot, leaving them with a less valuable property that would now be lost in the shadow of the giant to the south. They quickly capitulated, selling the 55 by 100 lot for $200,000.[52]

Back to the Drawing Board

Now Walker had a really prime site measuring 80 feet by 110 on one of the most valuable corners in town. The first job was to determine the general configuration of the building, since even the expanded site was too small to adapt the Rookery's square-doughnut plan. Fortunately, two entries in the diaries of Martin Roche—entries all the more extraordinary since these diaries hardly ever reveal anything about the design process—provide a very good record of the moment when the most critical decision about the building was made. On 8 March 1888 Roche wrote: "Mr. Walker called at the office. . . . Mr. W. E. Hale suggested a new plan for the Walker Buildings as per sketch." William Ellery Hale was originally a manufacturer of elevators, but he became an important figure in Chicago real estate, developing in the 1890s, among other buildings, the Reliance Building.[53] It is possible that Hale was in the office trying to sell elevators for the new building and while there offered some free advice. It is also possible that he was interested in investing in Walker's new building. The sketch showed an L-shaped building filling the street sides but creating a court in the angle of the L that would admit light and air to the interior offices. Running through the center of the L-shaped building was a set of parallel lines indicating a corridor. This corridor would have given access to the offices, each of which would have gotten light from windows either on the street or on the court. No matter how high adjacent build-

5.5

Tacoma Building (22), 1886–89, northeast corner of LaSalle and Madison Streets. Sketch plan by Martin Roche, in Roche diary, 8 March 1888. Chicago Historical Society Architectural Collections.

ings might reach, every office in Walker's building would be assured access to at least some light and air.

The walls in this sketch were presumably of load-bearing masonry. It is likely that the architects, when confronted by the new site, were under fewer space restrictions and went back to standard masonry wall construction.[54] But soon they decided to study whether Loring's terra cotta skeleton wall might prove useful on the enlarged site. They calculated that although the cost would be $10,000 greater, the building would yield $4,500 more in rents each year. On 23 March 1888, Roche recorded in his diary: "Started sketches for Mr. Walker's cast-iron and masonry building design. Mr. Walker suggests walls as per sketch." The sketch that followed showed a configuration similar to the earlier one but with two changes. Now the street walls were no longer shown as a solid line but appeared as a series of dots, representing the metal columns of the facade. Apparently in an effort to counteract the lightening of the front of the building two heavy lines were added through each side of the L, representing new masonry walls. They clearly indicate that Holabird & Roche was cautious in its approach to a

5.6
Tacoma Building.
Sketch plan by Martin Roche,
in Roche diary, 23 March 1888.
Chicago Historical Society
Architectural Collections.

technique that had never before been used on such a scale. The final structural scheme was apparently drawn up by an engineer named Karl Seiffert, who reportedly had previously worked for Burnham and Root on the Rookery. It may be that Seiffert, who is otherwise unknown, was actually working for the consulting firm of Wade and Purdy, but the evidence is strangely inconclusive.[55]

Walker named his building the Tacoma, an Indian word meaning "the highest," but also a name commonly used in the late nineteenth century for Mount Rainier in Washington State.[56] Walker's choice of this name marked an important step in the process by which owners of Chicago office buildings, who earlier had named buildings after themselves (the McCormick Building or Farwell Block) or used general references to geography and history (Lakeside Building, Richelieu Hotel), added an entire repertory of romantic allusions to the history of Chicago, the American West, and the American Indian and drew explicit parallels between skyscrapers and mountains.[57]

By the time he was ready to start construction Walker had organized a corporation, the Tacoma Safety Deposit Company, to sell bonds. These were placed by the private banking firm of Arthur O. Slaughter.[58] The use of the safety-deposit corporation to finance the building must have seemed an even more transparent maneuver to get around the prohibition on corporations building speculative space than the one the Brookses used at the Rookery. At least at the Rookery the great safe in the basement and the numerous safes on upper floors gave some evidence that this was an important part of the building's purpose. Neither the plans nor the advertising for the Tacoma gave much evidence that Walker had any interest in safes.[59]

To build the Tacoma, Walker commissioned as contractor another transplanted easterner, George A. Fuller. In this building Fuller took a major step in transforming both the Chicago and the American building world. The Tacoma was perhaps the earliest large-scale demonstration of the use of the single-contract general contractor, a business practice that revolutionized large-scale construction throughout the country. Before the development of Fuller's system, contracts were usually let separately by the building's owner or architects. The demolition companies, masons, carpenters, plumbers, and cabinetmakers all negotiated contracts with, then worked directly under the supervision of, the client or the architect. In the Holabird & Roche ledgers all the early buildings have a large roster of individual contractors, each responsible for one aspect of construction. As buildings grew larger and more complicated and the parts of buildings increasingly were purchased ready-made from factories rather than fabricated or finished on site, this arrangement became impractical.

At the Tacoma separate bids were solicited, but when Fuller offered the lowest price on the two biggest pieces of work, masonry and the metal skeleton, he was awarded a contract that included all the trades except the elevator installation, which was contracted separately.[60] The contracts for the Tacoma do not survive, but the Chicago Historical Society does own a slightly earlier set of contracts between Shepherd Brooks and architects Holabird & Roche and between Brooks and contractor George A. Fuller for the Pontiac Building. The contracts date to 1886 although the building was not started until several years later. In these contracts Fuller was engaged to do excavation work, foundations, masonry, and steel and iron work. Although this represented a substantial advance over earlier practice in which all of these contracts would have been let separately, many other parts of the building, including carpentry and utilities, all of which were added at the Tacoma, were not yet included. Interestingly, these contracts, which are undoubtedly similar to the lost set for the Tacoma, are strictly between individuals, not between business entities. This was perhaps due to legal restrictions, perhaps to the Brookses' conservatism. The architects' fee was set at 4 percent, a figure that probably represents some hard bargaining by Brooks. Fuller, on the other hand, got 10 percent on the total cost of excavation and masonry and 5 percent on the cost of the steel and iron work.[61]

By the time of the Tacoma, Fuller had nearly completed the fully developed single-bid, single-contract system in which one firm was charged with responsibility for all the work, either directly or by subcontracting.[62] In this system Fuller offered, in a single firm, expertise in financing, engineering, and ordering materials as well as in construction itself. This control over the whole building process allowed him to build more quickly, with more control over the quality of construction and budget than his competition. By ensuring that materials were delivered to the site only at the time they were actually needed, for example, he was able to avoid tying up large amounts of capital while supplies sat unused at the building site. He became immensely successful by following his two guiding principles: "Do it right" and "Do it on schedule time."[63]

In the late 1880s his advice was already taken very seriously, and his suggestions often helped shape the final appearance of many Chicago buildings.[64] It is not known what role he played in the design of the Tacoma, but he was very likely consulted early on about the feasibility of the proposed structural system. It was reportedly Fuller who suggested using rivets instead of bolted connections for many of the joints.[65] This process, highly unusual at the time, was used to speed up construction and to provide more rigid connections on a structure whose stability was an issue.

Construction was pushed forward with remarkable speed. The foundations, like those in earlier tall buildings, consisted of a "floating raft," a series of flat stones or concrete slabs reinforced by metal members that spread the load of the walls over a wide area, allowing it to "float" on Chicago's spongy clay subsoil. In place of the iron rails used at the Montauk, Holabird & Roche specified iron I-beams. These resisted even better the force of the weight they carried and so allowed smaller footings. This became the common practice in footings during the next decade until concrete caissons became common.[66] The structure of the building consisted of cast iron columns supporting wrought iron and steel beams. This would be the last of the large iron frame buildings as, over the next few years, steel gradually replaced iron. As the building went up it attracted a great deal of attention. According to one account written during construction: "The Tacoma is the object of a great deal of comment, and much of it is unfavorable. Many people have an idea that it is a mere shell set up on pins and that if two wide-awake blizzards should ever happen to meet in Chicago, it would come down with a great flop."[67] The paper went on to assure its readers that a well-known New York engineer had deemed it perfectly sound, however. Edward A. Renwick, in the 1930s, recalled: "It is hard to realize now the sensation it made. . . . New York papers sent representatives out to see it and report on it. A corps of policemen was needed on Madison street to clear away the crowd. Not just for a day or two only, but week after week."[68]

This reception suggests that it was the Tacoma, not any of the previous experiments, which were usually on a small scale or on an interior or rear wall, that marked the first clear demonstration of the potential of metal skeletal framing on a large scale. One of the most interesting aspects of this story is the total absence of any contemporary commentary linking the development of the metal frame of the Tacoma's front wall with William Le Baron Jenney's Home Insurance Building, even though the Home Insurance was only two blocks south of the Tacoma, was finished the same year Holabird & Roche started work on the Tacoma, and had been designed by the man in whose office both Holabird and Roche had worked. Although the claim that the Home Insurance had the first metal skeleton has always been contested and is clearly inaccurate, many historians have assumed that the building, which did have a nearly complete metal skeleton, at least marked a major step in the development of this technology and had a major influence on the buildings that followed.[69] The story of the Tacoma suggests otherwise.

Holabird & Roche, although it undoubtedly knew all about the advances at the Home Insurance Building, was exploring the use of a skeleton from a completely different point of view. The architects were not interested in lightening a masonry wall. They had created heavy masonry rear and interior walls to carry as much of the building's load and wind load as possible. In the front wall they were concerned primarily with cladding. They intended to create a frame on which to hang the thin panels that would enclose the building with minimum weight and bulk. The result is that where the Home Insurance had relatively thick walls and was constructed in a way that attracted little attention, the Tacoma's cladding was obviously much thinner and did not need to be applied one story at a time. In fact the cladding at the Tacoma was started simultaneously at the second, sixth, and tenth floors.[70] This demonstration drew the crowds to the sidewalks in front of the construction site and offered the first major public evidence of the possibilities of metal framing. According to Thomas Tallmadge, quoting Mark Twain, "'After Columbus discovered America it stayed discovered.' In that sense the Tacoma was the Columbus of skeletal construction."[71]

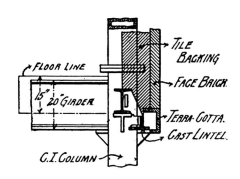

5.7

Tacoma Building, diagram of cladding showing the cast iron column, wrought iron beam, and brick and terra cotta facing. From Freitag, Architectural Engineering, *1901.*

After the Tacoma skeletal construction soon became commonplace, but the process was a halting one.[72] The first building by Holabird & Roche that could be said to have a complete metal skeleton both front and rear is the Caxton of 1889–90. It is likely that Holabird & Roche was willing to use the system there only because it was a relatively small building with party walls to the north and the south. On more pretentious buildings the firm continued to experiment with combinations of masonry bearing walls and the new structural system well after the demonstration of complete metal framing in the street walls of the Tacoma. The Pontiac Building, which was apparently designed in 1889 and finished in the first days of 1891, again had a mixed system. Holabird & Roche's addition to the Monadnock Building, probably designed about 1891 and completed by 1893, used bearing-wall construction similar to Burnham and Root's original portion in one half of the structure and skeleton construction in the other. It was only with the Marquette Building, whose final design emerged in 1893 and whose construction ended in 1895, that skeleton construction became standard for all of Holabird & Roche's major office buildings.

The use of a complete metal frame was often called "Chicago construction" because it was most conspicuous in Chicago, but it appears that similar kinds of experimentation were undertaken by architects in Chicago and elsewhere in the same years. The best contemporary summary of this process came from Montgomery Schuyler, who wrote that the "steel frame, skeleton or so-called 'Chicago' construction . . . seems to have been introduced independently and almost simultaneously in more than one city about 1889."[73] There were a number of other Chicago buildings constructed at just about this time that had partial or full metal skeletal frames.[74] The same was true in New York. At Bradford Gilbert's Tower Building, built in 1888–89, for example, a fully skeletal lower section was surmounted by a mixed masonry and skeletal frame.[75] New York's first really important all skeletal structures, the Manhattan Life Insurance Building and Bruce Price's American Surety Buildings, were completed about the same time as Holabird & Roche's Marquette.[76]

At the time of the erection of the Tacoma its metal framing, though highly noteworthy, was not considered epoch making. It was only in the light of later events, including the erection of much higher buildings in the twentieth century and particularly a fascination with this technology by the leaders of the new European avant-garde architecture, that the invention of the metal skeleton frame became a major historical moment and was considered the chief factor in the rise of the skyscraper. This was possible only because by that time most of the tall buildings of the 1880s had faded into oblivion. A debate started on the "origins of the skyscraper" and the identity of the first skeletal building. The two main contenders were the Home Insurance and the Tacoma. About 1930 both buildings were demolished and extensive studies were

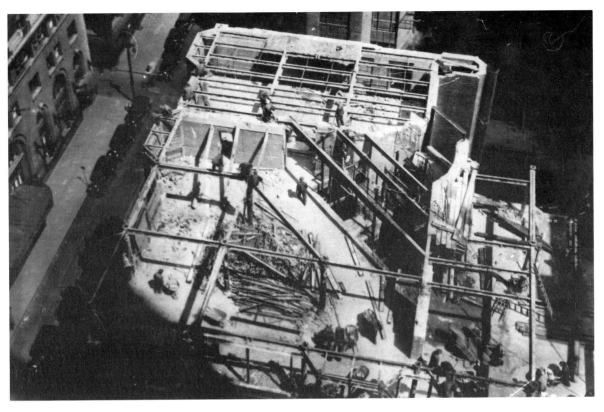

5.8

Tacoma Building, view of building during demolition. Photograph taken from sixteenth floor of Roanoke Building (across Madison Street) by William B. Mundie, 29 May 1929, showing two interior masonry walls, cast iron columns, and wrought iron beams. From Art Institute of Chicago–University of Illinois microfilm project.

undertaken on their framing. In one of the most startling twists in architectural historiography, a combination of partisanship by those commissioning the studies, national pride, and the polemics of the emerging European modern movement somehow led to the conclusion that Jenney had provided the conclusive demonstration of skeletal construction.[77] As we have seen, nothing could be further from the truth. If any building should be credited with this step it is probably the Tacoma; but merely to substitute the Tacoma for the Home Insurance Building in the history of metal framing would be just as misleading. The Tacoma represented a jump in scale and sophistication of a process that had been under way for many years and that would be pushed further by others almost immediately afterward.

The reason many European modernists were so interested in metal skeletal construction was that they wanted to create a new architecture based on new materials.

The metal skeleton seemed an ideal starting point and the relatively sparsely decorated Chicago office buildings of architects like Holabird & Roche a harbinger of things to come. This led to a powerful polemic but poor history. Holabird & Roche clearly did not share the obsession with "structural expression" that can be found in the work of certain theorists and critics of the nineteenth century and even more dogmatically in the writings of the European modernists of the 1920s.[78] Since they considered the structural system of the Tacoma primarily a practical problem, Holabird and Roche were highly unlikely to have assigned great symbolic value to the steel frame. The architects undoubtedly would have agreed that a building's structure should be expressed. This was no more than the common academic wisdom of their day, and there is no evidence that they felt that expressing the steel frame presented any particular problem.

The ornamental systems used on the Tacoma and later high buildings were derived primarily from stone architecture—not surprisingly, since columns, capitals, entablatures, and arches had long been seen as metaphors for expressing structure even when they were not in fact carrying anything more than themselves. This device had been highly developed in classical architecture, where, for example, the nonstructural stone pilasters at the Colosseum in Rome were used to articulate a monolithic concrete structure. In even the most severe buildings designed by Holabird & Roche the orders usually survive at least in a vestigial form as a reminder of the metaphor for the actual structure, which was often hidden from view.

If this story of the development of skeletal framing, halting and discontinuous, seems less heroic than the usual version in which Jenney invented the system in a single leap of imagination, it does seem to mirror more accurately the way many basic changes occur and how American cities have been built.

Finishing Construction and Raising the Flag

In addition to the reactions to its structural system, comments about the building's appearance started to appear while it was still being built. On 20 October 1888 the *Economist* noted that construction was under way and predicted that the structure would be one of the most beautiful in the city because it would be light and airy and devoid of the "pretense of superficial ornamentation." A *Tribune* writer, in a review of Chicago's architecture published on 13 January 1899, had a somewhat different opinion. The building "makes no pretensions whatever to picturesque or architectural effects," he wrote. "It looks to be just what it is—a large collection of offices for the money-makers of Chicago." These two opinions probably convey quite accurately the range of responses of many Chicagoans, architects and nonarchitects alike, to the Tacoma.

What Holabird & Roche had done at the Tacoma was to follow the path Jenney and Burnham and Root had been traveling and to push well beyond them. Much more than Jenney at the Home Insurance, the partners were willing to take the loft tradition they had learned in Jenney's office and apply it to an office building. Jenney's building used classical ornament where Holabird & Roche's used a kind of Romanesque, but this was not important. What was important was that whereas Jenney's facades had at least nominally been composed as balanced, symmetrical compositions, at the Tacoma, as at Burnham and Root's Montauk, Holabird & Roche was content to extrude bay after bay with no attempt to order them into a recognizable composition. The Tacoma's elevations were not framed by heavier end pavilions, and though the architects did provide a distinct, if not very convincing top, they provided no base at all. In fact, with its enormous sheets of glass at ground level supporting projecting bays, the Tacoma appeared to defy gravity. With the Tacoma as with Burnham and Root's slightly earlier Montauk and slightly later Monadnock, the high-class office building on a principal banking street came as close to looking like a loft building as could be seen anywhere in the late nineteenth century.

Early in May 1889, on schedule, the building was completed. It had cost $484,165, or forty cents per cubic foot.[79] The *Tribune* reported on 12 May:

> It is now something more than a week since the flag waving at the top of the Tacoma flagstaff, 200 feet above the street, indicated the occupancy of the new building which has excited so much comment. Since that time, tens of thousands of people have passed through its halls, the universal opinion being that the building stands almost unequaled. In this opinion experts unite, conceding that for light, cheerfulness, comfort, beauty and accessibility it can not be excelled.

An even better idea of the novelty of the building was conveyed in a Chicago guidebook published in 1892, three years after its opening:

> Tacoma Building—towering above its surroundings to the dizzy height of twelve clear stories. This was among the first of the modern sky-scrapers erected in Chicago. The corner which it occupied was for years covered by a tumble down brick building put up in haste after the Fire. It was wiped out to make room for the "Tacoma." We must spend an hour in this building going to the top by elevator and walking down. From the twelfth story we are able to obtain a splendid bird's eye view of the city,

and we can see far out on Lake Michigan if the smoke isn't too dense. This is a colony of offices. What all the people who occupy the offices do will be a source of wonder to the visitor throughout this and several other trips, but as they are all compelled to pay high rentals it is presumed that they are doing something to coax the almighty dollar in their direction. Otherwise they would seek cheaper quarters or establish themselves on the curbstone in front.[80]

What would a Chicagoan have seen while visiting the building at the time of its completion? As one approached it from the east along Madison Street, the first im-

5.9 (opposite)

Tacoma Building, view to northeast. Photograph by Barnes-Crosby. Chicago Historical Society Prints and Photographs Department, ICHi-19223.

5.10

Tacoma Building, view looking north on LaSalle Street with (from right), Republic Building, 1872, Andrews Building, 1872, Major Block, 1872, then Tacoma Building with the Chamber of Commerce Building, 1890, in the background. Photograph by Barnes-Crosby. Chicago Historical Society Prints and Photographs Department, ICHi-19223.

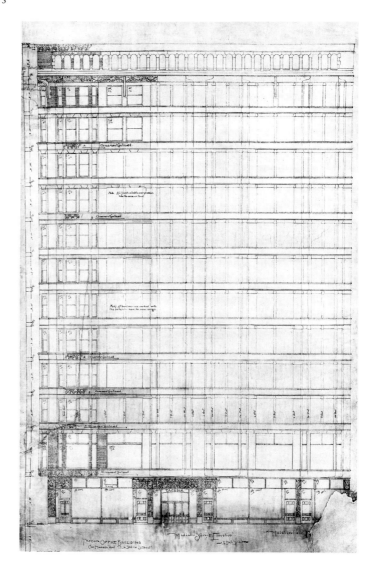

5.11
Tacoma Building, Madison Street elevation.
Chicago Historical Society Architectural Collections.

pression would have been of its sheer height. Next to it to the east along Madison, separated by a narrow alley, was the opulent five-story stone-fronted Brevoort Hotel, one of Chicago's prominent post-Fire buildings. The Brevoort's arched windows and great ornamental cornice would have been completely overwhelmed visually by the gigantic east wall of the Tacoma, a solid cliff of brick extending straight up twelve stories, interrupted only by the rectangular window openings. This was clearly one of the Tacoma's masonry bearing "back" walls, one that, the architects and the owners imagined, would soon be hidden by another tall building beside it. (See fig. 9.1.)

By comparison the Tacoma's fronts on LaSalle and Madison were very open. At sidewalk level six shops opened to the sidewalk through enormous plate glass show windows. Above the shops the street wall formed a great undulating surface as the ample bays filled with glass projected over the sidewalk. The bay window was another remarkable real estate ploy. It allowed the building owner to rent space over the public sidewalk, making a profit on land that wasn't even his own. It also increased the light and air entering the offices. On the other hand, the added space was often not really very useful because it was only a narrow strip somewhat detached from the major volume of space, and the extra income was at least partly offset by the substantial cost of the additional steel framing necessary to cantilever the bay out over the sidewalk. The city's building laws had long permitted this kind of projection over the public right-of-way or over land within required setback areas for houses and small buildings, but it was never contemplated that anyone would use it on a building of this size. From the point of view of city officials and the public, the bays projecting over the sidewalk provided no advantages and were safety hazards. The practice was soon stopped.[81]

Almost the entire surface of the Tacoma's swelling wall was glass. In the 1880s windows on office buildings had become larger and larger. By the time of the Tacoma they had reached enormous proportions and were interrupted only by the narrowest of brick frames. Although some commentators have suggested that these huge windows were necessary to ensure adequate light, it appears that by then any possible utilitarian purposes had long been left behind.[82] The huge windows were part of a new business aesthetic. In fact windows of this size presented substantial difficulties: the heat gain in summer and the drafts in winter must have been formidable. To remedy this problem, building owners often resorted to awnings.[83] Photographs of the Tacoma and other early skyscrapers show hundreds of blinds and awnings adjusted to various positions either to allow maximum light into the rooms on gray days or to keep the full rays of the sun from roasting those seated behind the immense sheets of glass.

A further problem was aesthetic. The use of enormous sheets of glass could give very large buildings a disconcertingly insubstantial appearance. This was a major concern to owners during the early years of the high building, particularly those whose buildings had the new, relatively light metal frames and extravagantly open street level as did the Tacoma. At the sidewalk level all but the corner pier disappeared, and the entire building appeared to float above a nearly continuous band of plate glass shopfronts. The columns were visible behind the glass, but even covered with their terra cotta fire protection they probably looked totally inadequate to support the cliff of masonry overhanging the ground floor. Perhaps to counteract the impression of flimsiness, the corner pier at the Tacoma, much heavier than structural needs would have demanded, proceeded decisively from the flag mast at the top directly down to the

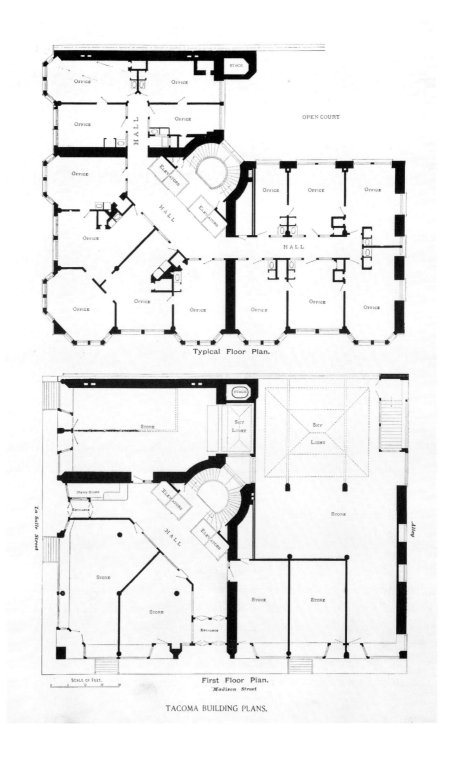

5.12
*Tacoma Building,
plan of first floor and
typical floors from
"The Tacoma" rental
brochure. Chicago
Historical Society Library.*

Typical Floor Plan.

First Floor Plan.
Madison Street

TACOMA BUILDING PLANS.

sidewalk level, where it plunged into the ground as if to anchor the building deep in the earth.

At the top of the Tacoma street facades the windows in the flat part of the wall were arched, and the walls of the projecting bays opened in a series of columns, creating little balconies and giving the appearance of an open loggia at the top of the building. The loggia was in turn crowned by a cornice that, seen from below, made a bold silhouette against the sky. The facade as a whole was undeniably austere, but this austerity was counteracted by several features. One was the luxuriant bands of floral ornamentation between and above the shop windows and above the first, second, third, fourth, eighth, tenth, and twelfth floors as well as in the upper cornice. Moreover, the windows were filled with signs painted on the glass in black and gold announcing the companies lodged within.

The visitor could enter the shops directly from the street. The most notable was Swatek's, called by a writer in the *Tribune* "one of the most artistically furnished and decorated cigar stores to be found in Chicago." An "ornament to the building," the writer called the shop, and went on to describe it:

> The interior finishing is of the highest grade and reflects great credit for the firm of Stotz, Woltz and Co., who executed the work. The ceiling is decorated in imitation of old silver and blends with the mural decorations. This is the work of Peter Emmel, and shows that when Mr. Swatek undertakes anything money is a second consideration. The label of Flor de Tacoma, illustrating the building, is appended to the brands of cigars imported exclusively for this firm.[84]

The visitor could enter the building itself either from LaSalle or from Madison Street. In either case a marble-floored corridor led back to four elevators, two on each side of a narrow passage. What the Tacoma did not have was anything even resembling a lobby. Walker undoubtedly rejected this feature after seeing how much space it would have subtracted from the street-level stores, given the building's small floor plate. The elevators and almost all the other accessories were decorated with foliage similar to that on the building's exterior. From the small elevator hall, a passage led back to the great circular staircase. Standing at the center of the staircase well and looking up, the visitor would have seen a marble-sided shaft twelve stories high as the staircase circled up continuously to a skylight on the roof. Using the staircase or one of the elevators, the visitor could ascend to the office floors. The elevators aroused much excitement. Even after half a century, architect William Gray Purcell still remembered them:

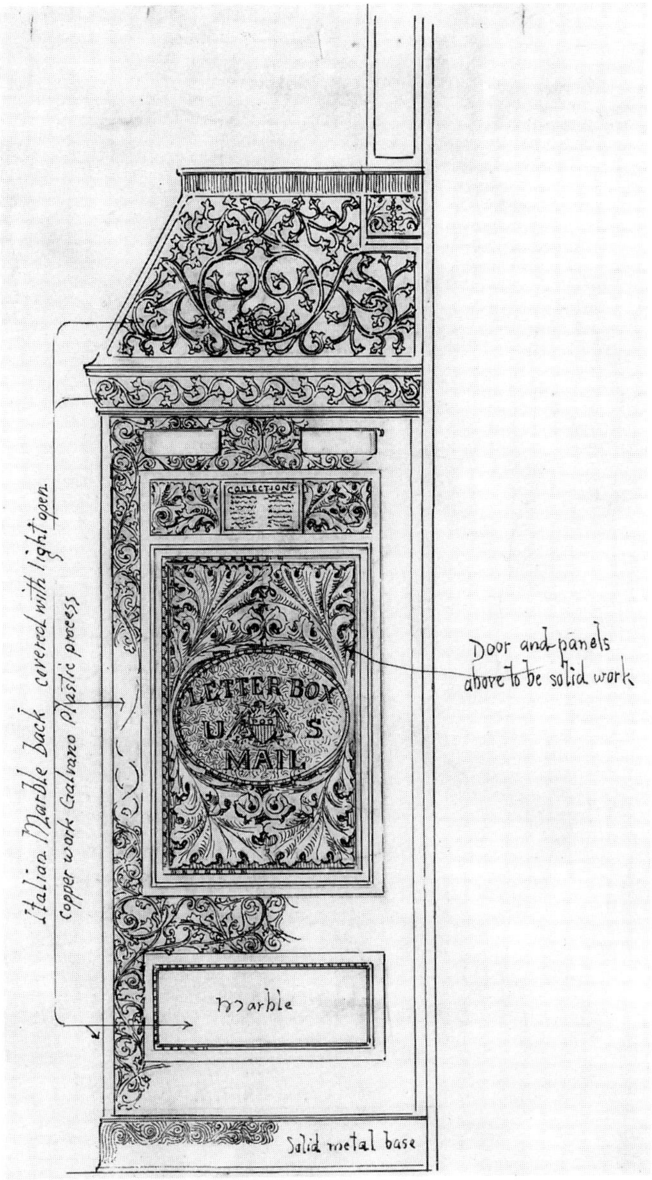
Italian Marble back covered with light open
copper work Galvano Plastic process
COLLECTIONS
LETTER BOX
U S
MAIL
Door and panels
above to be solid work
Marble
Solid metal base

5.13

Tacoma Building, mailbox, elevation drawing. Chicago Historical Society Architectural Collections.

In 1902 . . . I went "in town" from Oak Park every Saturday noon to take the week's drafting work of Oak Park architects E. E. Roberts up to the sunny 13th floor for blue prints. . . . Those fancy Tacoma elevators, with open work iron grille cabs and open shafts so you could see cars scooting

past, down and up, provided a vivid sense of their new high speed. To
start the car, elevator "boys" no longer dragged down on speeding, oily,
wire control-cables grabbed with a square of leather. Instead, in blue
broadcloth and gold braid, professional operators gentled a temperamen-
tal nickel plated shovel-handled affair, wigwagging out of the car floor.
Expert—and proud of it—they hit the floor level every time.[85]

The elevators at the Tacoma were hydraulic Hales elevators of the vertical cylinder
variety.[86]

Julian Ralph, a British visitor to Chicago, also penned a description that gives a
good idea of the impression elevators like those at the Tacoma made on visitors:

> In the tall buildings are the modern and rapid elevators, machines that fly
> up through the towers like glass balls from a trap at a shooting contest.
> The slow-going stranger, who is conscious of having been "kneaded"
> along the streets, like a lump of dough among a million bakers, feels him-
> self loaded into one of those frail-looking baskets of steel netting, and the
> next instant the elevator-boy touches the trigger, and up goes the whole
> load as a feather is caught up by a gale. The descent is more simple. Some-
> thing lets go, and you fall from ten to twenty stories as it happens. There
> is sometimes a jolt, which makes the passenger seem to feel his stomach
> pass into his shoes, but, as a rule, the mechanism and management both
> work marvelously toward ease and gentleness.[87]

Above the first floor the Tacoma was L-shaped to provide light and air either
from the court or from the street front to a veritable warren of offices. On each floor
the tile-floored, marble-wainscoted corridor led past a series of glass partition walls
that separated the corridor from the front offices. The front offices usually contained
several desks, a closet, a washbasin, and a vault. This would have been occupied by
secretaries, clerks, and other lesser employees who controlled access to the "private
office" occupied by the boss, with its huge window to the street or courtyard. Because
the partitions between offices and between corridor and office were glazed at the top,
natural light reached all the way from the street or courtyard to the corridor whose
marble and plaster surfaces were all white to reflect the light.[88] This was important
because although offices in the Tacoma were equipped with both electricity and gas,
artificial lighting levels were considered insufficient.[89] The offices were heated in the
standard way, with steam radiators.

5.14

Tacoma Building, view of New York Mutual Life Insurance Company offices.
From Flinn, Standard Guide to Chicago, *1892. Chicago Historical Society Library.*

Although most of the office layouts were standard and the walls and fixtures apparently built along with the rest of the building, some of the floors were rearranged to suit the particular needs of clients. The *Tribune,* for example, published a description of the law firm of Cratty Brothers and Ashcroft:

> No finer suite of law offices can be found in America than those occupied by the well known law firm on the eighth floor. Entering from the hall the visitor is ushered into the general office which covers an area of over 1500 square feet extending clear across the building and to the east front. It is lighted from three sides of the building. Off this room in the southwest corner are the private apartments of Thomas Cratty, the senior member of the firm. In the southeast corner is that of Edwin M. Ashcroft. All of these private apartments are elegantly furnished and provided with signal buttons and other appurtenances of a complete law office. In the northwest corner are the cloak rooms and private apartments for ladies. It would delight the heart of any lawyer to see this suite of offices.[90]

Guidebooks of the day advised that a good view could be obtained by taking the elevator to the top floor and looking out the stairwell window to the northeast. But even better was the view to the west from the men's toilet on the twelfth floor. The sanitary facilities were concentrated here, apparently to keep plumbing to a minimum. They were reportedly as grand as anything in the building. Purcell, as late as 1953, remembered the toilets vividly:

> Men's toilets for the entire building were constructed five steps down above the 13th floor level over in the northeast roof area. They were indeed astonishing, the subject of much codgery humor. They had all marble stalls and walls, with large plate glass mirrors, even larger than the Palmer House Barber Shop. The women were convenienced on the 12th floor directly below, but in 1890–96, there were not many women in offices.[91]

A visitor really interested in the working of the building might have asked the manager to show him the spaces not seen by the public, the machinery for the four Hales elevators, the three horizontal tubular boilers supplying the "overhead" system of steam heat, the Worthington pumps, and the Durham system of sanitary waste disposal with ample provisions for avoiding flooding.[92]

The building was rented out at the substantial sum of $1.45 a square foot on the average. The rent levels at the Tacoma apparently reflected a transition between the earlier, lower office buildings and the new skyscrapers. In preelevator buildings the rent levels were highest at the bottom of the building, since offices there required climbing fewer stairs. At the Tacoma this was apparently still true, since the most prestigious offices were on the mezzanine and lower floors. The American Surety Company of New York, with $1 million in capital, occupied rooms 311–14, for example. Atwater, Derwend and Company, real estate brokers, moneylenders, and rental agents who had moved from the Adams Express Building, occupied another suite of rooms on the third floor.

By the time of the Tacoma it had become clear that the upper floors provided space that was farther removed from the dirt and noise of the street, and the elevator solved the problem of access. The result was that rents on the upper floors were also high. On the eleventh floor, for example, were the Drury Brothers, real estate dealers and compilers of tax abstracts. The part of the building that tended to lag was the middle section.[93] A list published by the *Tribune* in 1889 shows that the vast majority of tenants were lawyers and insurance and real estate dealers, but there also many other trades represented, including a crushed stone dealer and roads contractor in 207 and a representative of the Illinois Terra Cotta Lumber Company in 605–6.[94]

In short, the Tacoma was a small city in itself. It may well have been the model for the famous description of the Clifton, the great building that served as the backdrop to Henry B. Fuller's celebrated novel of Chicago life, *The Cliff-Dwellers,* published in 1893:

> From the beer-hall in its basement to the barber-shop just under its roof, the Clifton stands full eighteen stories tall. Its hundreds of windows glitter with multitudinous letterings in gold and in silver, and on summer afternoons its awnings flutter score on score in the tepid breezes that sometimes come up from Indiana.

After a description of the elevators, Fuller continued:

> The tribe inhabiting the Clifton is large and rather heterogeneous. All told it numbers about four thousand souls. It includes bankers, capitalists, lawyers, "promoters"; brokers in bonds, stocks, pork, oil, mortgages; real-estate people and railroad people and insurance people—life, fire, marine, accident; a host of principals, agents, middlemen, clerks, cashiers, stenographers, and errand-boys; and the necessary force of engineers, janitors, scrub-women, and elevator hands.
>
> All these thousands gather daily around their own great camp fire. This fire heats the four big boilers under the pavement of the court which lies just behind, and it sends aloft a vast plume of smoke to mingle with those of other like communities that are settled round about. These same thousands may also gather—in installments—at their tribal feast, for the Clifton has its own lunch-counter just off one corner of the grand court, as well as a restaurant several floors higher up. The members of the tribe may also smoke the pipe of peace among themselves whenever so minded, for the Clifton has its own cigar-stand just within the principal entrance. Newspapers and periodicals, too, are sold at the same place. The warriors may also communicate their messages, hostile or friendly, to chiefs more or less remote; for there is a telegraph office in the corridor and a squad of messenger-boys in wait close by. In a word, the Clifton aims to be complete within itself.[95]

This description suggests a profoundly ambivalent relationship between the building and the city. On the one hand, the building contributes to and is a distillation of the vitality of the city outside. On the other hand, it was a reaction against the noisy incoherence and uncertainty of the street. Many of the functions of the city outside were gathered together within the carefully controlled private spaces of the miniature city that was the Clifton or the Tacoma.[96]

The Tacoma was an instant success for all involved. For Wirt D. Walker, the owner, it was a complete success, but at a high price. One biographer put it in almost Faustian terms: "The Tacoma building is the building on which Mr. Walker prides himself. . . . He watched carefully every detail in the construction of the Tacoma. So assiduously did he apply himself to study and business affairs night and day that his health gave way, and he felt the necessity of retiring from active business."[97] In fact Walker died shortly after the steel work had been completed, leaving no one in charge of the building. The rental agent oversaw completion.

For George A. Fuller, the Tacoma provided a successful test for his system of general contracting. Within the next decade Fuller and a group of competitors who adopted his methods created a new industry and came to dominate all really large-scale construction in Chicago, New York, and other cities. By 1910 his firm would be counted the largest construction company in the world. For the career of Holabird & Roche, the Tacoma proved equally important. Although very few people at the time or subsequently have claimed that the Tacoma was an important work of art,[98] it gave the architects the experience and the reputation to compete for the largest jobs in the boom years of the late 1880s, years when Chicago developers and architects vied with each other to apply the lessons of the Tacoma in a bid to create ever taller, more profitable buildings.

SIX

THE SKYSCRAPER
AND THE CITY:
THE MARQUETTE I

No design from the office of Holabird & Roche appears more resolved and less conflicted than that of the Marquette Building. The simple massing as seen from the street sides, the rich but unobtrusive terra cotta cladding, the regular window rhythms, the underscoring of the bottom, top, and sides by a more heavily textured cladding all give the building an air of classical solidity, permanence, and repose. The apparent inevitability of the design stands in striking contrast to the context it sprang from, however. The four years between the completion of the Tacoma and the final design of the Marquette witnessed an intense, often turbulent debate as architects, developers, and the general public tried to come to terms with a cityscape that was transforming itself.

Reactions to the High Building

The sheer volume of new building in the boom years of the late 1880s made Chicago the most dramatic example anywhere of the effect of tall buildings on the cityscape. At the time of the Fire, real estate professionals estimated that there was something under 300,000 square feet of first-class office space in the Loop. By 1882, the year the Montauk Block joined the city's church steeples and grain elevators in rising above the approximately six-story limit that characterized almost all preelevator business buildings, the total amount of office space in Chicago's Loop had grown to 500,000 square feet. By 1892 the figure stood at nearly 2,000,000.[1] The skyscraper played a key role in this dramatic development. Between 1882 and 1890 the average height of a major business building at the center of the Loop jumped from six to ten stories, with at least eleven buildings rising over ten stories, culminating in the highest of them, the Manhattan, which reached sixteen.[2]

The impact of these new buildings was immense. Visitors from all over the world came to view Chicago's new skyscrapers and get some insight into what the future of the modern city might hold. For many, the result defied all conventional terms of reference. Here, for example, is the reaction of a Boston architect:

> We well remember our sensations on emerging from the Rock Island Railway Station one frosty morning. The sun had not yet penetrated the depths of the cavernous streets, and, walking up the avenue towards the Grand Pacific, with the huge buildings to the right and left and the great hotel looming up ahead, with its numerous chimneys and gables, the first turn bringing us face to face with the enormous Russian-like tower of the Exchange, the effect was overpowering, and completely annihilated criticism. Such structures seemed more than human, especially under the dim veil of the morning light, which revealed only their immense forms and shrouded their defects of detail. . . . It forms a picture such as can be found nowhere else in the world, and one feels very small indeed when undertaking to grasp the whole of such structures and weigh them and consider them in mind.[3]

In the vast literature on the new skyscrapers it is remarkable how many passages, like this one, neither condemn nor condone the new structures but present them as some kind of immense and uncontrollable force of nature.[4] Perhaps the most spectacular description of this kind appeared in the opening lines of Henry Blake Fuller's novel *The Cliff-Dwellers*. Here Fuller wrote:

> Between the former site of old Fort Dearborn and the present site of our newest Board of Trade there lies a restricted yet tumultuous territory through which, during the course of the last fifty years, the rushing streams of commerce have worn many a deep and rugged chasm. These great canyons—conduits, in fact, for the leaping volume of an ever increasing prosperity—cross each other with a sort of systematic rectangularity, and in deference to the practical directness of local requirements they are in general called simply—streets. Each of these canyons is closed in by a long frontage of towering cliffs, and these soaring walls of brick and limestone and granite rise higher and higher with each succeeding year, ac-

cording as the work of erosion at their bases goes onward—the work of that seething flood of carts, carriages, omnibuses, cabs, cars, messengers, shoppers, clerks, and capitalists, which surges with increasing violence for every passing day. This erosion, proceeding with a sort of fateful regularity, has come to be a matter of constant and growing interest. Means have been found to measure its progress—just as a scale has been arranged to measure the rising of the Nile or to gauge the draught of an ocean liner. In this case the unit of measurement is called the "story." Ten years ago the most rushing and irrepressible of the torrents which devastate Chicago had not worn its bed to a greater depth than that indicated by seven of these "stories." This depth has since increased to eight—to ten—to fourteen—to sixteen, until some of the leading avenues of activity promise soon to become little more than mere obscure trails half lost between the bases of perpendicular precipices.[5]

This kind of description, in which the cityscape is compared to a natural landscape, became a kind of literary formula.[6] It betrays a profoundly ambivalent relationship with the high building. For Fuller it represented all that was bold and new but also all that was crass and reprehensible about America in general and Chicago in particular. At once engaged in and alienated from his own city, Fuller alternated in his work between celebration and condemnation.[7] For Fuller, as for many observers, traditional standards about the appearance of a building or a city were rendered useless by the vast scale changes of the late nineteenth century. Because the new buildings were the result of new economic forces, moreover, any assessments concerning buildings were necessarily dependent on judgments about the function of the buildings, the real estate market, and the nature of the city and a society caught in the throes of rapid modernization.

No one doubted that the tall building had been successful from a financial point of view. Throughout the late 1880s developers were able to fill their new buildings almost as fast as they could construct them. As a consequence, the price of land in the central district soared, further encouraging high construction. For much of the business community this was a blessing. Not only the developers but most landowners in the Loop profited greatly. The new buildings, moreover, not only maintained the character of the Loop as a conveniently compact business district, but in many cases provided dramatically improved working conditions by raising the offices above the dirt and noise of the street and assuring every office light and air from huge window openings. The positive reactions were not just motivated by practical business concerns. For many Chicagoans the new buildings were tangible manifestations of new, larger-scale business ventures, new technologies, and a new age. They constituted a powerful symbol of the aspirations and civic pride of the city.

There were, of course, observers who realized how much suffering the new economic forces creating the city's skyscrapers could cause for individuals. Many of these authors, even while decrying the injustice, still believed they were inevitable. Consider this extraordinary passage by the Kirklands, writing in 1894 in the *Story of Chicago*. Describing one of the great new skyscrapers in the Loop, they wrote:

> The building is permeated with the atmosphere of concentrated energy, hurry and intensity of purpose which are the component parts of the latter-day drama known as American business life. A mighty Juggernaut, this impulse rolls on, unmindful of the disappointments and sorrows of the unfortunate; equally unmindful of the triumphs and joys of success; and the mighty car carries this nation at the head of the industrial procession of the world.[8]

A writer in the British journal the *Builder* came to a similar conclusion about the logic that led to the tall building.

> Chicago architecture must be estimated by the Chicago standard. Whatever opinion may be held as to the characteristics of Chicago life, its rush and turmoil and business proclivities, it should be remembered that these elements are as much part of the city as a more staid and regular existence is of older communities.[9]

Negative Reactions

Not everyone saw as inevitable either the skyscrapers or the economic and social system that created them. The most immediate criticisms of the skyscraper concerned health and safety. As we observed in the case of the Tacoma, there was considerable public mistrust of the new structural systems that were coming into being in the 1880s. Although tensions would subside after new buildings were completed and safely tenanted, the fear that they were too flimsy and impermanent and might prove unstable under certain conditions never entirely disappeared.

The fear of fire was an even more potent concern. The memory of the Great Fire made Chicagoans suspect the reliability of construction described as "fireproof." This concern intensified in the 1880s with the increasing scale of buildings. If a major fire broke out at the top of one of the skyscrapers, it would be well beyond the reach of the firefighters' hoses and ladders. Couldn't the fire spread as it had in 1871, this time leaping from building to building ten stories above the street level? Both municipal authorities and fire insurers were concerned about this possibility. If any such disaster struck, moreover, what would happen to the people pouring out of the tall buildings? Some reckoned there would be no room on the sidewalks for the fleeing occupants. How many might be trampled in the ensuing chaos? Although expert opinion more often than not discounted these fears, there is ample evidence that in the public mind, and even in the minds of some architects and engineers, they remained strong.[10]

For some citizens negative reactions to the tall structures reflected a growing concern about the effects of American big business generally.[11] Because the skyscraper was such a conspicuous symbol of the growing power of business in the late nineteenth century, it provided a nearly irresistible target for the increasingly militant reformers in the trust-busting years of the 1880s.[12] As we have seen, the possibility of limited liability real estate investment lured investors from around the world. These were often men with little personal stake in the actual building or in the city where it was built. According to the reformers, the skyscrapers proved how a powerful few could alter the center of the city virtually at will, destroying cherished landmarks, banishing civility from the streets, cutting off light and air to the sidewalks, and creating a streetscape whose abrupt changes of scale and texture were totally unfamiliar. The privately owned tall buildings loomed over the city's churches and government buildings, defying a visual hierarchy that had characterized Western cities for millennia.[13] In a well-known essay novelist Henry Blake Fuller captured the revulsion felt by many: "Nowhere is the naif belief that a man may do as he likes with his own held more contentiously than in our astounding and repelling region of 'skyscrapers,' where the abuse of private initiative, the peculiar evil of the place and the time, has reached its most monumental development."[14]

Even for those accepting the new requirements of capital formation, there were issues of fairness. Although in many cases tall buildings greatly enhanced the value of the land they occupied and also that of adjacent parcels that might be redeveloped, in other cases owners were afraid the huge new structures might dwarf their own buildings, drain them of renters, and leave them in perpetual shadow. Others believed, with considerable justification, that the concentration in certain parts of the central district would depress values in the areas just beyond, where development otherwise might have been channeled.[15] On these issues architects, engineers, and the business community itself were divided. Increasingly even the most ardent advocates of laissez-faire came to realize something needed to be done, if only to ensure the competition necessary in a free market.

Finally, there were the aesthetic considerations. The cityscape created during the great building boom of the post–Civil War era was widely considered to violate all existing standards of beauty. Descriptions of Chicago's business district were often biting. In his novel *Rose of Dutcher's Coolly*, Hamlin Garland used the same kind of geological and biological metaphors as Fuller did to describe the view from a Chicago window, but his imagery stressed the more violent side of Nature. From the window was visible

> a stretch of roofs, heaped and humped into mountainous masses, blurred and bent and made appalling by smoke and plumes of steam. A scene as desolate as a volcano—a jumble of hot bricks, jagged eaves-spouts, gas-vomiting chimneys, spiked railings, glass skylights, and lofty spires, a hideous and horrible stretch of stone and mortar, cracked and seamed into streets. It had no limits and it palpitated under the hot September sun, boundless and savage. At the bottom of the crevasses men and women speckled the pavement like minute larvae.[16]

Particularly galling to many Chicagoans were the unflattering comparisons between Chicago and other cities, particularly the monumental capitals of Europe. Although these comparisons had already become a fixture in descriptions of Chicago by the mid-nineteenth century, for decades Chicagoans had been able to defend their city by arguing that it was still unformed, young and growing. By the late nineteenth century, as the Chicago economy started to mature and citizens' aspirations had risen, this explanation no longer satisfied.[17]

Aesthetic objections united with health and safety issues to create a heady mix. Agitation in Chicago to tame some of the more hostile aspects of the skyscrapers, to make them more appealing and compatible neighbors in the cityscape, seems to have jelled in the mid-1880s. A proposal to limit building heights to one hundred feet failed in the City Council in 1884, but a fire that broke out in 1885 at the up-to-the-moment Grannis Block, designed by Burnham and Root and owned by the Brookses, brought the issue back to the fore.[18] After the question had simmered for the next few years, action was precipitated by the spring 1890 announcement of the Masonic Temple Building on State Street, constructed to designs by Burnham and Root. Not only was this building huge—at twenty-one stories it was briefly the highest in the world—but the fourteen almost identical stories in its midsection deeply offended the aesthetic sensibilities even of many observers who were generally sympathetic to the tall building.[19]

The Marquette Team

Ironically, it was the negative reaction to high buildings that occasioned the birth of the Marquette. The site was owned by William E. Slater of Norwich, Connecticut, but controlled through a ninety-nine-year lease by a safety-deposit company called the Marquette Building Company, which included Owen Aldis, George A. Fuller, and Brooks brothers, who had a controlling interest. A prime site, it commanded an annual rental of $40,000.[20] As we have seen, in the mid-1880s the Brooks brothers had increasingly turned from the slightly older firm of Burnham and Root to the younger and less established firm of Holabird & Roche. The reasons for this shift can only be surmised. It is possible that by this time Burnham's firm had become so large and successful that the partners were less able to devote as much personal attention to the Brookses' commissions as the brothers desired. It is also likely that as they became successful Burnham and Root were less inclined to accept the developers' architectural fee structure or to agree with the design implications of their cost-cutting suggestions. Being partners in a younger and smaller firm, Holabird & Roche might well have been more eager to make the necessary accommodations. It is also possible, finally, that either the Brookses or Owen Aldis, their agent, simply preferred the Holabird & Roche designs.[21]

By the end of the 1880s the Brookses had assembled their team, which consisted of Holabird & Roche, George A. Fuller, and Owen Aldis. Aldis, as always, was indispensable. A Chicago agent was an important asset for any out-of-town investor, but for the Brooks brothers it was especially true since they operated entirely through their agent. As far as it is known, they never visited Chicago to see their investments. Aldis, in addition to representing the Brookses, also started investing on his own, becoming by the end of the century one of the most important owners and managers of real estate in Chicago.[22] Various combinations of the Marquette team, including the Brookses, Aldis, Fuller, and Holabird & Roche, would go on to do quite a few buildings together over the next decades, sometimes as designers and managers, sometimes as equity holders in the enterprise. The profitability and consistent aesthetic expression of these buildings have earned their creators a place in history as one of the most successful development teams in the field of commercial architecture.[23]

Designing the Marquette

The site for the Marquette was a very auspicious one in the heart of the Loop at Adams and Dearborn Streets. According to a writer in the *Economist:*

The land on which the Marquette is to stand is unquestionably the best site for a great office building in Chicago. It is at a point which can, under no conceivable circumstances, ever be far from the business center of the city. It is on one of the two most important banking streets of the city, one block from the busiest part of the great retail street, a stone's throw from the government building and a convenient distance from the transportation lines running in every direction. The south and east exposures insure an abundance of direct sunlight in the offices on the street fronts, which will rent at the highest rates ever paid for offices in this city. The ample area of the lot also admits of the lowest costs per square foot in the management of the building.[24]

Occupying the land at the time it was purchased by the Brooks brothers was the grand old Honore Building, with its heavy masonry facade and elaborate arched windows—a relic of the immediate post-Fire days.[25] Although it was not clear at first whether the Brookses would continue to operate this structure for a while or immediately erect a new building on the site, events forced their hand.

As we have seen, the agitation against high buildings that had surfaced periodically in the 1880s suddenly reached a critical point in the spring of 1890 with the announcement of the Masonic Temple Building. Agitation mounted as the new structure started rising. When Holabird & Roche learned in November 1891, probably through George A. Fuller, that the City Council was debating and was about to pass an ordinance that would severely restrict building heights, the firm advised a number of its best clients to take out permits for high buildings quickly even if they had no immediate plans to build, so they would ensure themselves the right to build to any height they wished. Edward A. Renwick later wrote an account of this episode:

The first intimation of this move came to our office one Thursday morning at eleven o'clock. A friend of mine called and told me that the Council would pass an ordinance Monday night limiting the height to 130 feet, the ordinance would be signed the next morning by the mayor and would go into immediate effect. I advised Mr. Holabird of this information, which was naturally of prime importance to us. We decided to make an offer to some of our clients to make the necessary permit drawings at our own expense for several sixteen story buildings, providing the owners would pay for the taking out of the permits. If our clients could be persuaded to act quickly enough we could get the permits out before Monday night and insure to them and to us the erection of several more buildings in excess of the proposed 130 feet.[26]

According to Renwick he and Holabird visited clients and between them collected orders for five buildings. After returning to the office and comparing notes, Renwick continues, Holabird exclaimed:

> "And now we've got 'em, what in Hell are we going to do with 'em?" We had eight draftsmen in the office, the problem was how to get the drawings made and the permits taken out for these five buildings before Monday night. Mr. Roche started making the designs, working at top speed. The entire force was put on the development of the designs, but still we didn't have enough men. It was my job that afternoon to increase the force to the point where we could handle the work. I got enough men by night so we could make a relay organization, twelve hours through the day and twelve hours through the night, time out for meals of course. By Friday morning I had forty draftsmen at work. Monday at ten o'clock the sets of drawings, basement, first and second stories, typical floor plan, roof plan, elevation, sections, steel diagram, plumbing diagram, for all five buildings were complete. I took them to the City Hall to take out the permits. . . . By four o'clock the permits were obtained and paid for, and I left for home and bed.[27]

The result was a successful coup by the architects and the development interests. By applying their much vaunted organizational efficiency, they had outmaneuvered the slower-moving reform efforts in the city government. Yet this flurry of efficient responses exacerbated the already hostile relations between the development community and the public. The *Economist,* reporting on this event, noted:

> The most noticeable effect of the agitation in favor of limiting the height of buildings so far is to stimulate their construction, and it no doubt occasioned some consternation in the ranks of those in favor of the measure when they discovered Monday afternoon that the city building department had given permission to erect five structures not one of which is less than sixteen stories high and which represent an expenditure of $3,100,000. That was probably the most interesting day in the history of the city building department.[28]

The measure at hand had been a move to prohibit buildings taller than twelve stories until the council could act on a major revision of the building code. The measure was defeated, as were several subsequent attempts, but the wave of new permits in November 1891 undoubtedly strengthened the hand of the anti-skyscraper forces, and after several attempts, in 1893 the city council finally passed a stringent 130 foot height limit.[29] This measure marked a major turning point. Although it was constantly attacked and later liberalized somewhat, the law remained on the books until the

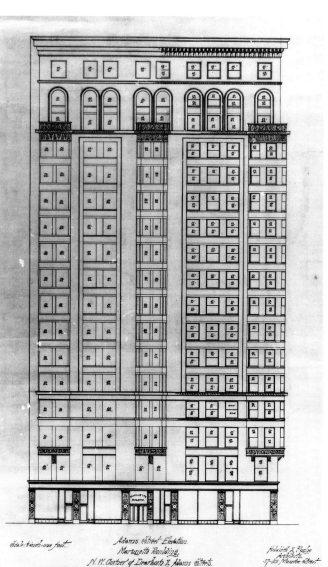

6.1
Marquette Building (200), 1891–95, 140 S. Dearborn, northwest corner of Adams Street, preliminary scheme, elevation. Chicago Historical Society Architectural Collections.

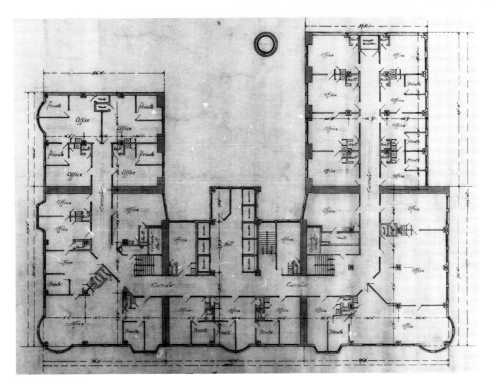

6.2
*Marquette Building,
preliminary scheme,
typical floor plan.
Chicago Historical
Society Architectural
Collections.*

1920s. It had a profound effect on the Chicago skyline and was believed by some real estate figures to have put Chicago at a severe disadvantage compared with New York. This latter contention is highly dubious.[30]

Although the great haste had turned out to be unnecessary from the point of view of the developers, for Holabird & Roche it had the highly beneficial effect of making it much easier for these clients to use its services when they were finally ready to build. It is likely that a set of drawings preserved primarily on microfilm documents the design of the Marquette as submitted to the building department in 1891. These drawings show a structure similar in many ways to the Tacoma with interior load-bearing walls but entirely skeletal exterior walls opened in large projecting bay windows. The resulting elevation was curiously unresolved and tenuous. This might have been a result of the haste with which the design was put together. It might also reflect a lessening of interest in the kind of design the Tacoma represented.

The right to build having been obtained, Holabird & Roche's plans sat on a shelf for over a year until the Brooks brothers were ready to proceed. By the time planning for the building resumed in 1892, Holabird & Roche was ready to abandon the first scheme in favor of a quite different design in which the firm would resolve some of the tension surrounding the speculative office building.

The Skyscraper as Design Problem

The tall speculative office building raised major design problems not only because of its sheer size, but because it did not fit in easily within the traditional hierarchy of building types in the city. In the decades before the Marquette, two distinct types of buildings housed office space. On the one hand there was the loft, a simple rectangular building usually at the edges of the central business district, with large open floors and row after row of windows. These buildings usually accommodated many kinds of activity in addition to offices, especially offices for individuals who needed to be adjacent to wholesaling, warehousing, and light manufacturing activities. The other kind of office was in the great four- and five-story palazzo-style omnibus blocks like the Honore that occupied the heart of the city. These buildings housed mainly lawyers, brokers, and others whose main dealings were with other white-collar workers but also stores and occasionally other uses.

As we have seen, Burnham and Root's Montauk and Holabird & Roche's Tacoma, finished in 1889, were both part of the new wave of buildings destined strictly for office use, but in many ways they looked more like loft buildings. In both the architects dispensed with the pavilions and corners, the sculptural features and great overhanging cornices that had been used to bring office buildings into line with the traditions of classical architecture and raise them from merely utilitarian status to the level of what most architects thought of as architecture.

The drive toward simplicity was abetted by powerful new economic forces. As long as office buildings had been erected by companies for their own use, they were considered monuments to their owners even if much of the space was rented out. As we have seen, the relationship between those commissioning buildings and the resulting real estate changed dramatically in the late nineteenth century as the scale of speculative office buildings grew, financing was channeled through trusts and limited liability corporations, and management was taken over by professional managers. The result was a growing distance between investors and the real estate itself. A correspondent for the British architectural journal the *Builder* perhaps exaggerated the situation for the benefit of his London readers, but he succinctly summarized a trend when he wrote that "the great office buildings of Chicago are looked upon by their owners simply as sources of revenue, not as architectural monuments."[31]

The need to attract passive investors, those who would not necessarily take a day-to-day interest, and to assure them the project could achieve a secure and constant cash flow, led in turn to more precise and complex accounting procedures reflecting not just current interest payments, construction costs, and rental income but the possible effects of future changes in these cash flows. All these factors were well known by the late nineteenth century. What was still somewhat novel was the calculation necessary to determine the rate at which the building would become obsolete. In previous eras most substantial buildings were considered permanent improvements. Well built and adequately maintained, masonry buildings would last, if not indefinitely, at least well beyond the lifetimes of the owners and their immediate heirs.

In the late nineteenth century several factors together made this assumption untenable. In this era sharp rises in downtown land prices and the rate of new construction created a situation in which old buildings ceased to be financially competitive. The case of the Honore Block, demolished less than twenty years after it was built to make way for the new Marquette Building, was not uncommon. It simply could not generate the kind of income promised by new construction. In other cases a developer erecting a building for one type of use found the entire industry had disappeared. In still others a building erected on prime commercial land could soon find itself bypassed as that kind of commercial activity moved from the core to a peripheral location.[32]

Another factor was the length of ground leases. Although ninety-nine years was a standard lease for downtown Chicago real estate, by the late nineteenth century many of the leaseholds had been subleased for considerably less time. Any investor had to make sure he could earn an adequate rate of return before the property reverted to the owner of the land.

Just as important as the advent of new building materials and technologies was their short life expectancy. The elevator, for example, one of the most expensive parts of any tall building, wore out much faster than the building itself. The same was true of the complicated new heating and lighting systems. There was also uncertainty about the new structural systems. When architects and engineers started using large amounts of metal encased in concrete or terra cotta blocks in foundations and walls, they did not know how long this metal would last. When the Montauk Building was demolished in 1902, for example, engineers were surprised that the steel was nearly intact, with no sign of major corrosion because they had not expected it to last long. Well into the early twentieth century engineers were still unsure how metal in walls and foundations deteriorated over time.[33] The recognition that buildings had finite lives led to an entire new branch of real estate accounting: depreciation, the calculation of the amount of money needed to replace a building at the end of its useful life.[34]

All these factors meant that for many investors building came to mean ensuring a given cash flow rather than creating permanent improvements to the city. Buildings increasingly became standardized investment commodities as had happened with corn or hogs earlier in the century. It probably seemed logical to many investors that the new economic realities encouraged simplicity, standardization, and efficiency.[35] There was also a moral dimension to this progression toward simplicity. As the speculative office building came to be viewed as an instrument for making money, it was likewise viewed as a mere place of work by the companies that rented space. As the managerial force grew, so did the space that was devoted to internal operations and not on public view. Many architects and other observers of the late nineteenth century would have agreed with critics like the nineteenth-century British writer John Ruskin that a strictly utilitarian building, for reasons of decorum as well as economy, should be plain and inexpensive.

The Skyscraper as Public Building

Although the forces pushing toward simple, unadorned structures in Chicago were formidable, there were compelling countervailing pressures. Some of these pressures came from the marketplace itself. In a very competitive speculative office building market, it was not enough to offer mere space. Smart developers of prime pieces of real estate realized they could secure more leases and charge higher rents by incorporating interesting new architectural features as long as they did not actually cost too much. We have seen how the Brooks brothers were willing to sacrifice considerable utility and square footage at the Rookery because they knew a building at that location could support rents high enough to cover the added costs.

Developers also realized that totally unregulated development threatened their own economic interests. If the developer of a parcel in a prime office district could build anything he chose, for example, he could put up a very inexpensive building that housed undesirable users or could erect one so large it would dwarf elegant older neighbors. Actions like these could damage all the surrounding properties. For reasons of this kind many important real estate developers threw their weight on the side of regulatory measures, both internal to the profession and external, to protect their own interests.[36]

No less important was a widespread feeling about decorum and the hierarchy of building types in the city, which considerably complicated ideas like those of Ruskin. A building like the Tacoma or the Marquette was not just a place of work. As we have seen in the case of the Tacoma, it was a small city in itself, where thousands of Chicagoans met daily and where they ate, made purchases, and carried out other everyday routines. In this way it functioned as a public building in the same way as did the city's hotels, railroad stations, or theaters, all privately owned. Although some hotels and theaters started to look a good deal like commercial buildings in the mid-1880s, for the most part they maintained a decidedly public character with elaborate architectural treatments and monumental interior spaces. Decorum suggested that the office building, as a kind of public structure, should have a similar architectural character.

Finally, there was civic pride. By the late nineteenth century many Chicagoans believed the city had reached economic maturity but had a great deal of catching up to do on other fronts. George W. Steevens, writing in his *Land of the Dollar,* published in 1897, observed: "Chicago is conscious that there is something in the world, some sense of form, of elegance, of refinement that with all her corn and railways, her hogs and by-products and dollars, she lacks. She does not quite know what it is, but she is determined to have it, cost what it may."[37]

The question of the appropriate form and decoration of the speculative office building was considerably more than a mere aesthetic question for the architects and developers. How could they blunt the mounting public criticism of these enormous money-making machines that suddenly upset all received ideas about scale and threw public streets, sidewalks, even whole buildings into permanent shade? How were they to reconcile the private, mercantile character of the building with the increasingly public character that was inevitable in a structure that had become like a small city? How were they to balance the client's demand for the strictest economy with a need to enhance and embellish the appearance of the city? How, finally, could they create a set of simple, standardized spaces that could be rented easily to any business and that incorporated all the latest technological advances but at the same time provide a specific, memorable imagery for the building and some kind of symbolic connection with the site, the city, and its history?

World's Fair

To understand the final designs for the Marquette it is useful to look more closely at several events that took place between its initial and final designs. The first was the planning for the 1893 World's Fair. As we have seen, Holabird & Roche had only a minor role in the preparations for the Fair. In fact, Chicagoans as a whole played a secondary role as pride of place around the Court of Honor at the Fair was given to a small group of eastern architects including McKim, Mead and White, Richard Morris Hunt, and Carrere and Hastings. Historians have tended to believe that this division of labor represented a capitulation to the easterners and that the Fair marked an about-face for Chicagoans. In the 1880s, so this line of reasoning goes, Chicago architects had been innovators, creating new structural systems and a simpler stylistic expression not dependent on historical styles and the influence of Europe and the eastern United States, especially New York. The creation in 1884 of the Western Association of Architects as a rival to the eastern-dominated American Institute of Architects is cited as an expression of the profound split in ideals. Then, to continue this plot line, came the World's Fair. Suddenly a wave of conservative classical architecture overwhelmed the indigenous Chicago tradition.

Actually the relationship between practitioners in the two cities appears to have been considerably less adversarial and more productive for both. First of all, as we have seen in the case of the Lathrop house, it was not at all uncommon for Chicagoans to hire New York architects for specialized work on highly prominent residential or monumental public designs, and it probably seemed an entirely natural division of labor to most observers at the time. All the members of the New York group had designed major public buildings and had practices that extended far beyond New York. Few of the Chicago architects could be identified with conspicuous public commissions, and most of them worked primarily in the Chicago area.[38]

Certainly architectural practice was perceived to be somewhat different in Chicago than it was in New York, but this does not appear to have resulted from any fundamental differences in opinion on the art of architecture. Rather, it appears the differences were due to divergent ideas about the business of architecture. For a number of the most prominent New York architects, individuals who had an immense influence in the American Institute of Architects, architecture at the level they aspired to was a profession akin to that practiced by the painter or sculptor. The highest goal for many of the most prominent New York architects, as it had been for their teachers at the Ecole des Beaux-Arts in Paris, was to secure monumental religious and public commissions. Only in these commissions could they express what they felt were the loftiest ideals of architecture and of society. Even though many of the New York architects did commercial work, they rarely considered these buildings prime opportunities for the art of architecture. Further, even with commercial buildings the goal was to find patrons who would defer to the artist's judgment in matters of taste so that the necessary engineering and practical concerns could be subordinated to more aesthetic matters.

The demands of commercial practice in Chicago led to a quite different situation. Montgomery Schuyler observed, "There is no atmosphere in the world that less resembles the still air of delightful studies than that of the heart of Chicago. And so, the successful practitioner of architecture in Chicago is primarily an administrator."[39] In Chicago the profession, and the Western Association of Architects, was dominated not by purveyors of monumental buildings but by commercial firms like Burnham and Root and Holabird & Roche. Unlike their New York counterparts, they tended to combine architecture and engineering within the same organization, and even though the Chicago firms never took the ultimate step of transforming themselves from partnerships into corporations as several Detroit firms would do in the early twentieth century, they were definitely run more like large businesses than like artists' ateliers.[40]

The Chicago firms had few patrons but many clients, and these clients were quite ready to overrule their architects if aesthetic demands interfered with commercial considerations.[41]

The rise of the Western Association of Architects was a symptom of these differences. Its founding made apparent a split between two models for the practice of architecture, one based on the artist's studio and the other on the large company. It signaled the desire of the large commercial firms practicing in the latter mode to gain recognition in a profession that had been dominated by the former.[42] At the time of the merger of the WAA and AIA in 1887, and certainly by the time of the 1893 Fair, many of these issues had been resolved. The cooperation of Chicago and eastern architects at the Fair suggests some of the ways this resolution worked in practice.

Far from being a capitulation by Chicagoans, this cooperation represented a mutual agreement. The easterners, aware of the way architecture was developing in the country, were willing to accept the western commercial architects as peers and to learn from their prodigious business and organizational abilities. The westerners welcomed the chance to learn from their distinguished colleagues from New York. What they learned was not primarily the correct use of classical styles, although some of the Chicagoans did learn that, but the enormous range of expressive potential in architecture.[43] For architects like Daniel Burnham or William Holabird, engineers by training and without an extensive exposure to the high art of architecture, their profession was primarily about problem solving. The encounter with elegant and highly sophisticated artists like McKim must have been dazzling. It considerably expanded the horizons of Chicago architects by suggesting the vast array of stylistic choices that could be made, how far any style could be manipulated for expressive effect, and the possibilities of collaboration with painters, sculptors, and other artists.

Two Chicago Skyscrapers

In explaining the differences between the first and second schemes for the Marquette and the way William Holabird and Martin Roche may have been influenced by their participation in the World's Fair, it is useful to look at two major Chicago buildings that were being designed and built during these years and whose designs represented extreme positions in regard to the speculative office building. At one extreme was Burnham and Root's Women's Temple Building of 1891–92 on LaSalle Street. This was not a mere speculative building like the Rookery. Because it was commissioned by an important and high-minded Chicago organization, the Women's Christian Temperance Union, it, like the Auditorium Building, was considered a civic venture. Burnham

117

6.3
*Women's Temple Building, 1892,
102–16 S. LaSalle, northwest corner
of Monroe Street, Burnham and Root, architects,
exterior view. Photograph by Barnes-Crosby.
Chicago Historical Society Prints and
Photographs Department, ICHi-19133.*

and Root felt they needed to create a building that was more monumental than the Rookery. At the Women's Temple the massive rusticated base, the great arched openings, the heavy indentations in the wall plane, the central court in front, the swelling corner bays, and, above all, the great pitched roof with its rows of dormers, all suggested an important public monument. These features were undoubtedly very expensive, but presumably the Women's Christian Temperance Union and its investors were willing to put up the money for two reasons. The first was that the building was a shrine to a cause. The second, somewhat ironically, was that because the building was a shrine and because the WCTU was not a commercial organization, it could command premium rents.[44]

The other building, the original north end of the Monadnock Building, was commissioned by the Brooks brothers, designed by Burnham and Root, and finished in 1891. The Monadnock represents the extreme example of the drive toward unornamented simplicity. To the amazement of many Chicagoans, the Monadnock was even

6.4

Monadnock Building (150), 1891–93, 54 W. Van Buren between Dearborn and South Federal Streets, exterior view from southeast showing Holabird & Roche addition in foreground, Burnham and Root original north half in background, finished 1891. Photograph by Barnes-Crosby. Chicago Historical Society Prints and Photographs Department, ICHi-19191.

less ornamented than the Montauk. According to legend, John Root, exasperated by the clients' constant demand for ever greater simplicity and less ornament, responded by designing a structure so plain that it almost represented a dare. His design defied all the canons of good taste by eschewing traditional means of articulation and rising nearly sheer from the sidewalk in a single towering shape, inflected only slightly by a very gentle inward tapering of the building as it rose and a slight outward corbelling of the masonry at the very top.[45]

Some of the plainness of the Monadnock could be excused by its location on the extreme southern edge of the city's office district, adjacent to many loft buildings. Still, at the time of its completion Burnham and Root's Monadnock was widely considered just too extreme.[46] Although decades later it became the building of its day most admired by European modernists, at the time it was built, even the author of the architectural sections of *Industrial Chicago,* a consistent and vigorous defender of Chicago's commercial architecture, could not approve of its appearance: "The commercial style, if structurally ornamental becomes architectural. . . . Thus there is a distinction between the Woman's Temple and the Monadnock building. The first is an architectural house, the second an engineer's. The distinctions might be continued ad infinitum; but the one given shows where architects draw the line between architecture and civil engineering."[47]

It seems likely that even the Brooks brothers and Owen Aldis felt they had gone too far in the Monadnock Building. This was probably one reason they turned to Holabird & Roche to do the south addition built in 1892–93. The Holabird & Roche addition, in part because it used more skeletal construction, was cheaper and lighter and contained more floor space than the original building.[48] The Brookses and Aldis undoubtedly urged Holabird & Roche to follow the original building in its main lines. In fact, even though the structural system was modified, Holabird & Roche preserved the major lines of the original structure's exterior configuration but in key places "corrected" it to make it more compatible with received artistic norms.[49]

The major change Holabird & Roche made was to articulate the building into more readily discernible parts. The Holabird & Roche portion of the building, unlike the Burnham and Root section, was given a base. The lower three stories were faced in large blocks of ashlar masonry and grouped together under a cornice with each bay defined by a pilaster. Large arched openings were created to mark the location of the building's entrances. This resolved one of the most unsuccessful aspects of the Burnham and Root building, the greatly underscaled entranceway in the narrow north end of the building. The Holabird & Roche base treatment, especially the large arches, gives the building a kind of Roman scale and grandeur.

Although Holabird & Roche could not do much with the central portion of the addition, which was simply too high and bulky to be treated in accord with classical proportions, some of the parts, especially those most conspicuous to the viewer, could at least be given classical ornament. The flat portions of the central section of the building were separated more distinctly from the projecting bays by moldings, making them read as pilasters. The central mullion of each bay window was treated as a pilaster surmounted by a composite capital. At the top the upward lines were resolved in a series of arched windows, and the whole was capped with a gigantic cornice, providing a pronounced termination to the structure. All these things brought the exterior of the building a little more into line with classical ideals, even if its bulk and general configuration defied really classical solutions. The experience of Holabird & Roche and the Brooks brothers on the Monadnock was apparently the necessary catalyst for resolving the conflicting demands of the 1880s and early 1890s in the final design for the Marquette.

SEVEN

THE   SKYSCRAPER

AND   THE   CITY:

THE   MARQUETTE   II

At some point in 1892 the Brooks brothers decided to revive their plans to build at Dearborn and Adams, and Holabird & Roche went back to the drafting board. In February 1893 the plans were made public when the *Economist* noted that the Marquette Building Company would definitely demolish the Honore Block at the expiration of its current lease. The magazine reported that the new design called for a sixteen-story steel frame building of "brown obsidian brick embellished with terra cotta," entirely fireproofed, finished with the best materials and equipment. The plan would be completely up-to-date, "a second Rookery."

Perhaps in reaction to this article, a letter of 1 March 1893 from S. B. Holabird in Washington to his son recorded the elder Holabird's reaction to the news. It conveys admirably something of the approach of both father and son:

> I see that in all human probability you are to build the Marquette Block. I congratulate you for it is the well deserved fruit of good honest hard work with the judgment and skill that succeeds where thoroughly applied. . . . I suppose you are sensible enough to keep your satisfaction out of sight and so appear to take it as a matter of course—an every day affair—one that you expect to be repeated right along. I have no doubt that you will make it your magnum opus, your great work and that it will stand a monument of what can be done in Chicago this year.[1]

The last sentence with its odd pairing of the phrase "magnum opus" and the highly qualified "in Chicago this year" suggests both the workmanlike, no-nonsense business approach and aspirations for high artistic achievement.

The Marquette Company borrowed $800,000 from the Scottish Provident Institution, and demolition of the Honore Block started.[2] Construction was started in late 1893, and the building was finally finished in 1895 at a cost of $1,367,201, or 33 cents per cubic foot. That the building cost less per cubic foot than the Tacoma while all the appointments and finishes were of higher quality may reflect economies of scale, or it may have been a result of lower construction costs during the economic downturn of the 1890s. It may also have been due to the superior efficiency of the Brooks brothers' development team. At the time of its completion the Marquette was almost universally counted a success. D. Everett Waid, writing in the *Brickbuilder,* called it "the finest office building in Chicago."[3] The author of the article "Chicago" in the *Encyclopaedia Britannica,* eleventh edition, published in 1910, mentioned eight commercial buildings but singled out the Marquette for its architectural value. "Consistently and handsomely decorated with works of art," the author wrote, it is "one of the finest office

7.2 (opposite)
Marquette Building,
view of exterior from
southeast. Photograph
by Barnes-Crosby.
Chicago Historical
Society Prints
and Photographs
Department,
ICHi-19052.

7.1
Marquette Building,
view of the building under construction.
Courtesy of Commission on Chicago Landmarks.

buildings in the country." The judgment of this author was typical of the reception the Marquette received. It was certainly the best known and most praised Holabird & Roche building of its day.

This praise reflected an appreciation that the finished building, as successfully as any office building of the time, was able to reconcile the seemingly impossible conflict between demands for economy and simplicity and demands for a marketable image and artistic distinction. The final design for the Marquette also reflects the experience of Holabird & Roche since the completion of the Tacoma, advances in technology, reactions to the debates that had swirled around the high office building, and the firm's acquaintance with the plans for the 1893 Fair.

Looking at the finished building, it is immediately apparent that Holabird & Roche had made major changes since its initial design. One major revision was the removal of the bearing walls and the substitution of a complete metal skeleton. This reflects Chicago architects' and clients' rapidly increasing confidence in the new structural system.[4] Another major change was the abandonment of the bay windows and Romanesque details of the earlier scheme for a much simplified massing and a nominally classical style.

In its general lines the Marquette was about as simple as any building in the Loop could be. On both street frontages it rose straight from the sidewalk to the cornice with hardly a projection of any kind except a relatively small portico at the entrance and a cornice at the top. The walls came all the way out to the lot line. Ornamental belt courses were allowed to extend a few inches beyond the lot line, but otherwise only the cornice projected from the sheer walls. The large horizontal three-part "Chicago windows," which had a fixed central pane and movable side sashes, lined up from bottom to top and side to side with hardly any variation. No arches or other deviations from the underlying structural steel added to the cost of the building. In fact, nothing about the general configuration of the Marquette would have given a clue that it was anything more than a loft building.

Neither Holabird & Roche nor the Brooks brothers wanted the public or potential clients to think it was only that, however. The trick was to give it solidity and dignity without sacrificing economy to art.[5] The architects used two strategies to make sure no one would read the building as a simple loft structure. The first was to manipulate the facade even further toward classical ideas of proportion, symmetry, and regularity than they had done in the Monadnock addition. Economy dictated that except for a few surfaces at the base of the building that were seen close up by pedestrians, virtually the entire decorative scheme be done in brick and terra cotta, which were much cheaper than stone. Although the relatively thin cladding necessarily followed closely the structural frame of the building, the architects organized the facades into

7.3

Marquette Building, view to the northwest along Dearborn Street with Monadnock Building in left foreground, Federal Building filling block beyond, and Marquette Building in distance. Great Northern Hotel by Burnham and Root in right foreground. Photograph by Barnes-Crosby. Chicago Historical Society Prints and Photographs Department, ICHi-19257.

balanced, classical compositions by manipulating the terra cotta surfaces in an attempt to disguise the thinness of the cladding and to alleviate the monotony of the absolutely regular window openings. Horizontally each facade was articulated into three parts in the classical fashion, with a central, nearly unornamented block framed by wider, slightly projecting end bays whose visual weight was reinforced by heavy rustication. The architects also created a classical three-part composition vertically. At the bottom of the building they created a three-story base by grouping the lower two floors under one cornice and treating the entire third floor with its own cornice as a classical attic story. Again heavily rusticated, the cladding on this base became more elaborate the closer it came to the ground and the entryway. Above the base stretched the slightly recessed and relatively smooth middle section of the building. This in turn was capped by a crowning feature consisting of three floors, two of them grouped under a cornice, and finally a third with its own lavish projecting final cornice. Architects and clients may have believed this cornice had some value in keeping water off the facades, but it served primarily as a visual element.[6]

This scheme seemed to resolve an impossible contradiction. When most earlier designers of office buildings had tried to order the facades of their office buildings and distinguish them from mere lofts, they had used traditional classical means, deploying projecting pavilions, heavy belt courses, frontispieces, colonnades, arcades, and other sculptural elements. In the Marquette the ordering was done in much the same way but with materials so thin that the result, as substantial as it appeared, was actually more like painting than sculpture. This scheme allowed the building to be as simple and repetitious as any loft building but at the same time maintained as much of the classical tradition as possible given the scale and the unrelenting programmatic demands of a new building type. Not only did classical architecture seem much more flexible than the older Romanesque and Italianate forms, whose arched windows, turrets, and other features were expensive to construct and blocked light, but the use of classical architecture promised to control the wild proliferation of stylistic elements that had characterized the third quarter of the nineteenth century.[7] This was, of course, the most important lesson of the Court of Honor at the World's Fair.

Another reason the Marquette seemed to work better than the Tacoma was that the detailing at a small scale was completely consistent with the larger ordering devices. At the Tacoma the wall surfaces were covered with a Romanesque ornament that seemed to have little relation to the rigid verticals and horizontals of the loftlike bulk of the facade. At the Marquette it was the cumulative effect of the small elements that created the ordering pattern for the entire facade, and the classical ordering of the overall composition was reinforced by the detailing of even the smallest element.

To maintain the classical effect, Holabird & Roche designed the terra cotta so it looked like heavy cut stone. To simulate rusticated blocks the architects specified deeply recessed joints and a classical guilloche pattern, giving the substance a weighty materiality. They even designed the edges of these fictive stone blocks with a smooth band and light parallel lines that unmistakably recalled the chisel marks, or "marginal drafting," on ashlar, though terra cotta is molded and fired, not sculpted. For the pedestrian walking along the side of the building the illusion is nearly complete. The Marquette Building masonry looks much more like the heavy stone used in an Italian Renaissance palazzo than like thin terra cotta cladding.

The other strategy the architects used to make sure visitors read this structure as a high-class office building was to concentrate sculptural decoration on the one very

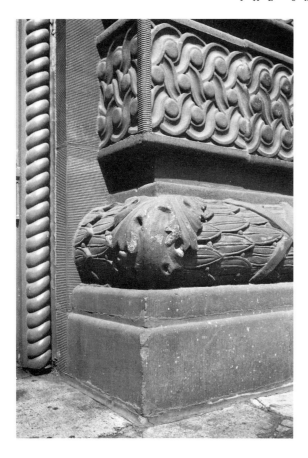

7.4
Marquette Building, detail of terra cotta cladding by doorway.
Photograph by Robert Bruegmann, 1995.

small area that was most in view—the entry sequence. The main entrance to the build-ing was signaled by the polished granite columns of a projecting portico placed in the middle of the Dearborn Street facade. This, the only significant projection from the body of the building, was allowed under a provision in the building code in the 1890s. City officials undoubtedly had added this provision, like the one permitting bay win-dows to project over the lot lines, because they wanted to encourage architectural rich-ness and variety. If building owners knew that every inch of decoration was at the expense of rentable floor area, they reasoned, the owners would probably not approve any. The officials undoubtedly felt that allowing an ornamental balcony, portico, or cornice to project a few feet over the right-of-way was an incentive to improve archi-tecture at no cost to the city. Unfortunately, as in the case of the bay windows, these projecting features were soon found to be troublesome. Cornices could fall, and proj-ecting porticoes blocked pedestrian traffic. The ordinances were amended, and the Marquette's portico was removed.[8] The Marquette's reputation has benefited from this

7.5

Marquette Building, view of portico. Photograph from Inland Architect, May 1896.

alteration, since the portico clearly betrayed a lack of familiarity with classical composition and the Greek orders. The use of three columns rather than four contravened classical ideas and resulted in the placement of a solid on the axis of the entrance where one might have expected a void. The columns, moreover, displayed altogether too much entasis, the slight but characteristic bulge on classical columns as they taper upward, giving an awkwardly overweight appearance.[9] Finally, in the frieze above the door, below a panel inscribed with the name Marquette, the architects saw fit to put the little peglike pieces called guttae that in classical buildings usually were placed directly beneath the three-grooved part of the cornice called the triglyph. The problem at the Marquette was that there were no triglyphs and worse, the guttae were not even positioned above the columns. It is likely that this foray into more academically correct classical architecture was prompted by the architects' experience at the Fair, but it turned out to be too much of a stretch for the designers at Holabird & Roche, who were just not familiar enough with the conventions of the genre. Fortunately, the portico was removed so skillfully that only early photographs offer convincing proof it was ever there.

7.6

Marquette Building, detail of panther-head push panels on doors by sculptor Edward Kemeys. Photograph by Robert Bruegmann, 1995.

Another lesson probably learned from the Fair was the potential for collaborating with sculptors, painters, and other artists on the embellishment of the building. The bronze doors at the front of the Marquette were decorated with ornamental patterns, plaques, and push plates with panther heads, all executed by Edward Kemeys, a sculptor who had done considerable work at the Fair and who became famous for his lions in front of the Art Institute of Chicago. Above the doors were bronze plaques executed by another well-known sculptor, Hermon MacNeil, depicting scenes from the journey of Jacques Marquette and Louis Jolliet and from Marquette's second trip to Chicago. These were the first in a sequence of works that constituted a memorial to the French explorer and made the entry spaces a miniature art gallery.[10]

7.7

Marquette Building,
view of panels above
front doors by sculptor
Hermon MacNeil.
Photograph by Robert
Bruegmann, 1995.

From the front doors and vestibule a short but broad passage led to the lobby. Although few Chicago commercial buildings dispensed with lobbies altogether, as had the Tacoma, most were meant to be crossed rapidly. People might meet and talk there, but they were not encouraged to linger. These lobbies, like those of the major business hotels, were public places in that anyone could enter them, but they were also clearly private. Anyone who threatened to disrupt the business atmosphere or who did not conform to accepted standards of dress or behavior would have been rapidly ejected by the management. More than any other area, the lobby set the tone. It was the place to provide a distinctive image, a sense of place and, if possible, a touch of artistic grace that would raise the building above the general run of commercial structures.

This the Marquette lobby certainly did.[11] Hexagonal in plan and two stories high, it was floored with ceramic tiles, and the walls were sheathed in creamy white marble. Along the rear of the space the open cages of the building's elevators allowed light to filter in from windows in the outer wall past the grillwork of the elevator enclosures to illuminate the extensive decorations.[12] These decorations, all based on the explorations of Père Jacques Marquette and the founding of Chicago, formed the most coherent and ambitious cycle found in any Chicago commercial building of the day. Above the elevator doors were bronze portraits of Indian chiefs and white explorers. These were mostly from the hand of Kemeys, but two of them were listed in publicity materials as being the work of A. A. Bradley of Boston. Only later was it discovered that these

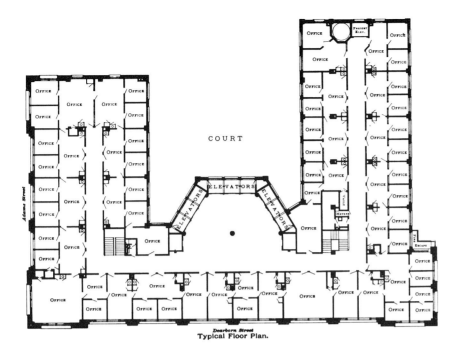

COURT

Adams Street

Dearborn Street
Typical Floor Plan.

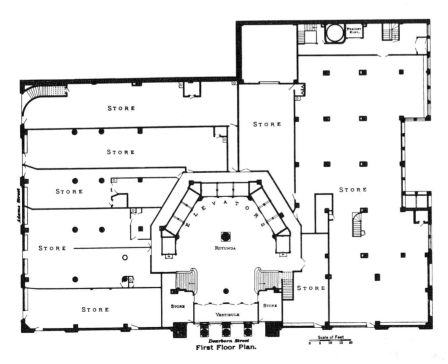

STORE

STORE

STORE

STORE

STORE

STORE

STORE

STORE

STORE

STORE

STORE

STORE

ELEVATORS

ROTUNDA

Adams Street

VESTIBULE

Dearborn Street
First Floor Plan.

Scale of Feet

7.8

*Marquette Building,
plan of first floor and
typical floor, from
"The Legend and
Legacy of Père
Marquette," rental
brochure, 1895.
Chicago Historical
Society Library.*

7.9
*Marquette Building,
view of lobby,
photograph from "The
Legend and Legacy of
Père Marquette,"
rental brochure, 1895.
Chicago Historical
Society Library.*

7.10
*Marquette Building, view of mosaics in lobby designed by J. A. Holzer of Tiffany Studios,
photograph from "The Legend and Legacy of Père Marquette," rental brochure, 1895.
Chicago Historical Society Library.*

were done by Amis Aldis Bradley, Owen Aldis's sister.[13] At the edges of the central space fluted Corinthian columns of Carrara marble supported a balcony whose parapet walls were faced with mosaic panels designed by J. A. Holzer and executed by the Tiffany Glass and Decorating Company. Three of these depicted the building's namesake among the Indians of Illinois and were accompanied by quotations from Marquette's diaries. Between the narrative panels were other panels containing trophies, artfully composed of European and Indian motifs: a belt of wampum balancing an ecclesiastical vestment, for example, or an Indian headdress set against a European helmet. In the center of the rotunda stood a single column of polished Carrara marble that extended to a vaulted ceiling filled with more mosaics from the Tiffany Company.

The decoration of the lobby, though undeniably impressive, did not really bear much relation to the exterior of the building. There is some evidence that it was the special project of Owen Aldis, who did the translations from Marquette's diaries used on the parapet walls. It is easy to see why the themes of the discovery of a new land, the development of commerce, and the transformation of wilderness into a wealth-producing city would have appealed to Aldis or to the Chicago businessmen who used this space. Nettlesome details like the prior claim of the Indians to the land were glossed over by romantic allusions to a once glorious culture of the distant past. Even for those tenants who paid little heed to the details, the mosaics and sculpture provided a daily reminder of the remarkable history of Chicago and the high-class character of their place of work. The lobby was widely considered the most "artistic" in late nineteenth-century Chicago. In contemporary reports on the building it was almost universally singled out for attention, being described as elegant in effect and as eminently appropriate for a distinguished office building.

Although rich in decoration and larger than most lobbies of the day, the Marquette lobby took up only a small part of the ground floor. This was not surprising, since it generated no revenue. The ground floor was occupied largely by shops, which generated a great deal, and by the Marquette Buffet. From the lobby a sweeping flight of marble stairs led to the second or "banking" floor, another rental space that was highly lucrative, in part because it was so easily accessible either by the stairs or by the elevator. An early rental brochure shows that this space housed the bond and securities firm of N. W. Harris and Company and the Bankers National Bank. The Harris offices, with their mosaic floor, mahogany woodwork, and copper grilles, were considered among the most elegant in Chicago.[14]

After visitors walked back to the rotunda, the elevators would take them to the office floors, three through sixteen. As at the Tacoma, the presence of elevators had started the trend toward higher rentals for the upper floors, but this change had still not yet played itself out.[15] On most upper floors offices were divided by partitions in the usual manner. Most suites contained a "general office" opening off the corridor and communicating with one or more private offices on the perimeter of the building, each with a window looking out over the street, an alley, or the interior court. The general offices, usually housing secretarial and clerical staff, were provided with telephones, coat closets, and washbasins. The wings to the west were shown as undivided on some published plans, with a notation that they could be subdivided as desired by the tenants.[16] It appears that the practice of leaving floor plans open to be subdivided at will by the tenants was just beginning to take hold. Earlier buildings were usually designed with all the offices fully laid out. This arrangement was logical because the partition walls, although nonstructural, were the obvious place to hide water supply and waste water return lines to supply the washbasins in each office.[17] It appears that at some point during the 1880s and 1890s the demand for larger, more flexible spaces started to outweigh the desire for basins.

The building, like Henry B. Fuller's Clifton, was a small city in itself. The rental brochure divided its list of tenants into sixty-three categories ranging in size from the lawyers, with seventy-three entries, to barbers, bicycle suppliers, soap makers, and writers of business literature, which boasted only one each. Even this comprehensive set of categories was not inclusive enough to contain the Harson Tree Trans-

7.11
Marquette Building,
view of buffet,
photograph from "The
Legend and Legacy of
Père Marquette,"
rental brochure, 1895.
Chicago Historical
Society Library.

7.12
*Marquette Building,
view of office of N. W.
Harris and Company,
photograph from "The
Legend and Legacy of
Père Marquette,"
rental brochure, 1895.
Chicago Historical
Society Library.*

planter, King's Collecting Agency, Taxpayer's Defense League, and thirty other entries grouped under "miscellaneous." In addition there were the services provided in the building. On the seventh floor were the women's toilets and on the sixteenth floor the men's, grouped, as they had been at the Tacoma, to save space and minimize expensive plumbing. Also on the sixteenth floor was the barbershop, elaborately decorated with ceramic tile floors, marble wainscoting, seven mahogany barber chairs, French plate glass mirrors, and a suspended ceiling of Venetian glass.

Behind the scenes, hidden from casual visitors, was the complicated machinery that allowed the building to function. In the attic were the janitors' quarters, storage space, 20,000 gallon water tanks, and, surprisingly enough, artists' studios, probably occupying space that was otherwise difficult to rent because there was no direct elevator access. In the basement were the elevator pumps, the boilers, and a large refrigeration plant for Grommes and Ullrich, who sold expensive wines in one of the ground floor shops. All floors were accessible by hydraulic passenger elevators and one freight elevator. The building was both piped for gas and wired for Edison service electricity, with all wires encased in bronze conduit. The building was heated by steam, the heat regulated in each office by an automatic temperature regulator.[18]

At the very top of the building was another area not usually accessible to visitors—the roof. It was an excellent vantage point from which to look down along the canyons Fuller described and measure the progress of the first generation of skyscrapers, standing out above the old plateau of post-Fire business blocks.

7.13

View from roof of Marquette Building looking north on Dearborn Street. The tall structure east of Dearborn is the Unity Building (Clinton J. Warren, 1892). To the west is the Hartford Building (Henry Ives Cobb, 1893). Photograph from "The Legend and Legacy of Père Marquette," rental brochure, 1895. Chicago Historical Society Library.

The Marquette and Contemporary Office Buildings

I have tried to suggest that the success of Holabird & Roche at the Marquette stemmed from the way the architects balanced conflicting demands by fusing two older and quite distinct building types, the loft and the post-Fire mercantile palace. Although the Marquette Building represents one of the most successful attempts to achieve this synthesis, this quest seems to characterize much of the most important commercial work by Holabird & Roche's colleagues in Chicago and elsewhere in the country. Although they are quite different in details, buildings by other Chicago commercial architects, such as William Le Baron Jenney's Leiter II Building of 1889–91, Louis Sullivan's Wainwright Building of 1890–91 in St. Louis, and the D. H. Burnham Company's Frick Building in Pittsburgh of 1901, all exemplify the same attempt to order immense facades by overlaying a rational gridlike pattern of windows with a decorative system derived from classical antiquity that visually strengthens the two sides, top, and bottom.

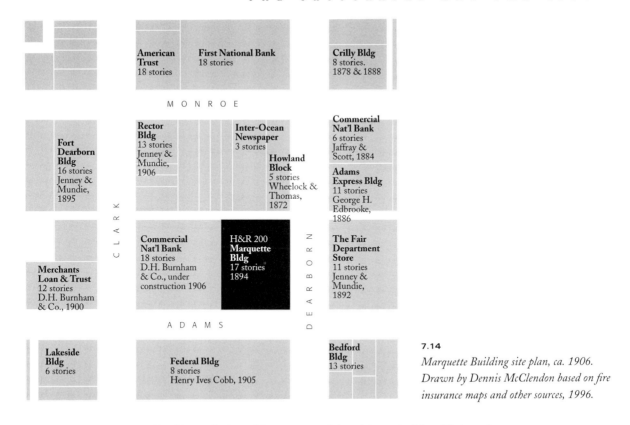

7.14

Marquette Building site plan, ca. 1906. Drawn by Dennis McClendon based on fire insurance maps and other sources, 1996.

This is also true of buildings designed by commercial architects in New York and on the East Coast. As many contemporary observers noted, the business buildings on Chicago's Dearborn Street or LaSalle Street were somewhat different from their counterparts on New York's Broadway. What accounts for this difference? As I tried to prove in an earlier chapter, it was not a dramatic divergence in the artistic philosophies of architects in the two cities. It was more a matter of the way commercial architecture was produced.

The clients for the largest Chicago office buildings were unlike those in New York, a city whose economy had evolved over the previous century into one based primarily on trading and services. Not surprisingly, its major commercial monuments, like Bruce Price's American Surety Building of 1894–95, housed the headquarters of well-established newspapers, banks, and insurance companies. Chicago, on the other hand, was a very new city, built on recently established manufacturing operations. The major Chicago entrepreneurs of the day—the McCormicks, the Armours, and their fellow industrialists—were for the most part still actively building up their manufac-

137

turing capacity. It is conspicuous how many of these Chicago men worked in offices at or near their factories. They had neither the time nor the inclination to build lavish monuments to themselves downtown. Instead Chicago's Loop was dominated by speculative office buildings like the Marquette, usually erected by out-of-town developers like the Brooks brothers who had a major economic stake but little personal or emotional investment in the city.

The site context was also quite different. Whereas New York's downtown had grown up over centuries, leading to a somewhat irrational network of streets and an extremely heterogeneous collection of building sites, Chicago's central district had been laid out relatively recently with a regular grid of wide streets and a systematic use of alleys. This allowed larger, more regular buildings.[19]

All these factors contributed to the difference in appearance between the Marquette and the more pretentious buildings on Broadway. It was not that there were no buildings in New York that looked like the Marquette. Quite a few bore a fairly strong resemblance. It was just that they were loft structures devoted to manufacturing, retailing, and wholesaling.[20] In fact one of the best analyses of the spirit of Chicago office buildings like the Marquette that can be found in the turn of the century architectural press was actually written about loft buildings on Fourth Avenue in New York.[21] Even many of the less pretentious New York office buildings are in many ways not so different from the Marquette.[22] Many of these came from big commercial firms: George B. Post's Mills Building of 1881–85 and Clinton and Russell's Broad Exchange Building of 1896 or Atlantic Building of 1901 at 49 Wall Street are fairly similar to buildings designed by Holabird & Roche. This picture will probably become much clearer when more is known about the New York commercial architects who were more Holabird & Roche's equivalents than firms like McKim, Mead, which have been to date the focus of most writing on New York architecture.[23]

A good indication that architects in both cities held many of the same basic beliefs can be found in the best contemporary analysis of Chicago's commercial buildings, the section on architecture in the great compendium *Industrial Chicago.* Even as vigorous a proponent of Chicago architecture as the anonymous author of this 1891 text clearly saw the history of the "commercial style" as a joint New York–Chicago venture. In his most extended definition of this term he wrote:

> Commercial architecture is the just title to be applied to the great airy buildings of the present. They are truly American architecture in conception and utility. The style is a monument to the advance of Chicago in commerce and commercial greatness and to the prevailing penchant of casting out art when it interferes with the useful. It is a commanding style

without being venerable, and after straining necks and eyes to catch a glimpse of the cornice and count the number of floors, the height, proportion and capacity are all that afford delight. Later the feeling of delight merges into one of novelty, and patriotism coming to the rescue, lets the new style down easily, by instilling into the mind the gigantic quantities of material used in one of those monuments, its great capacity, its magnificent systems of lighting, heating and transportation, its great strength and men learn to look upon it with the same wonder and admiration which the big elephant in Lincoln Park wins from children. This style began with the Western Union Building, New York, in 1873, and was extended to Chicago in 1876 in the Portland, reached its childhood in 1882 in the Montauk and its boyhood with the Manhattan and Fair and Masonic Temple in 1890–91.[24]

If this passage had been written in 1895 or later the author might well have used the Marquette to represent the culmination of the process.

It seems quite likely that Holabird & Roche and most of its Chicago colleagues, although they may have disputed details, would have agreed with the spirit of the *Industrial Chicago* account. It also seems unlikely that any of them would have suggested the stripped-down style seen at the Marquette was suitable for a more expensive or prestigious owner-occupied business structure. It is clear that when the budget and the program allowed, Holabird & Roche and its Chicago contemporaries were perfectly happy to provide elaborately ornamented Romanesque or classical structures, as John Root proved at the Women's Temple Building and elsewhere. The problem was that there was little market for such buildings in late nineteenth-century Chicago.

Given this situation, members of the Chicago architectural profession undoubtedly felt it wiser to acquiesce in clients' demands for simplicity rather than fight them on the grounds of art and, rather than decrying the situation, to make a virtue of necessity in their public announcements by professing a preference for simpler forms. Louis Sullivan, for example, spoke eloquently about the desirability of architects' refraining from ornament for a time so that they could concentrate on designing buildings that would be "comely in the nude."[25] This has been taken by later historians as a call by a Chicagoan for unornamented buildings. What is interesting is not that this remark reflects some inherently reductive character of Chicago, but how clearly it springs from Sullivan's own eastern and European training. It is exactly what any French Beaux-Arts atelier leader would have told his painting students, to make their studies and even preliminary drawings with nude figures as a way to understand the underlying structures of the bodies, but these painters would no more have painted a nude coronation scene than Sullivan would have designed a public building with no ornamentation.

It is not surprising that the most discerning and sympathetic critic of the Chicago buildings of the late nineteenth century was Montgomery Schuyler of New York. Schuyler, when he lauded Chicago's big commercial blocks, did not do so because he wished to overturn architectural traditions. It was because he believed that the most important architectural tradition was the moral tradition that ran through the works of the great English critic John Ruskin, and that it had been lost in some of the most conspicuous work in the East by an excessive adherence to the details of the classical style rather than to the principle of decorum that dictated that the character of a building should match its status and use.

Whether Chicago invented the new model for the speculative office block or whether it was developing simultaneously in a number of cities, it became the new standard for office buildings in most of the major commercial cities in the American West. From Duluth to Denver, great sober rectangular blocks with regular windows lined the streets that were the local equivalents of LaSalle or Dearborn in Chicago's Loop.[26] The type so clearly represented by the Marquette thus became a national vernacular. It was this vernacular, schematized and extended across the whole city, that formed the basis for the illustrations in the 1909 *Plan of Chicago* by Daniel Burnham and Edward Bennett. It was in this way that Holabird & Roche and the Chicago architects made their contribution to the efforts at the turn of the century to tame some of the wildest excesses of American business and the American urban fabric.

The Marquette in Architectural History

The completion of a building does not end its history, of course. The way the Marquette was viewed in subsequent architectural history is an integral part of its story and suggests quite a bit about qualities inherent in its design. Although the building elicited high praise at the time of its completion, it usually did not merit a mention in art history texts because the speculative office building was not considered a major artistic problem. By the mid-1920s the Marquette, like the vast majority of late nineteenth-century commercial buildings in Chicago, had been largely forgotten as a new crop of dramatically taller skyscrapers went up around the Loop.

As we have already seen in the case of the Tacoma, Chicago commercial buildings of the 1880s and 1890s reappeared in architectural history rather unexpectedly in the late 1920s. As the American economy boomed and American influence in world affairs increased, many Americans became obsessed by the question of what was peculiarly

7.15
*Detail from plate 122,
Burnham and
Bennett,* Plan of
Chicago, *1909.*

American in American culture. In architecture one of the most obvious answers was
the steel framed skyscraper. This in turn led to an inquiry into the development of the
skeletal frame construction. A number of the most influential architectural historians
of the late 1920s and early 1930s considered the metal skeleton the most important
innovation of the period.[27] As noted earlier, Holabird & Roche's Tacoma and William
Le Baron Jenney's Home Insurance Building were extensively discussed at this time.[28]
Because the Marquette was built at the moment when the skeleton had already started
to become standard, it was not usually mentioned.

The Marquette came to the fore with the rise of the term "Chicago school" in the
early 1930s. Although this term had been used earlier, in the 1900s and 1910s, it appears to have been coined in New York, and in any case, at that time it referred primarily to literature and by extension to the residential work of architects like Louis Sullivan and Frank Lloyd Wright. In the 1920s a new definition came into use through the
polemics of European avant-garde architects and their American followers. The most
important players on this side of the Atlantic were Philip Johnson and Henry-Russell
Hitchcock, who in the 1930s first used the term "Chicago school" in the way it would
be used for decades afterward.[29] For Hitchcock and Johnson the "Chicago school" was

a loose group of Chicago architects who attempted to create an architecture that turned its back on historical precedents, defied contemporary trends in Europe and the eastern United States, and attempted to use a straightforward expression of program and structure as the basis for design. The "school," according to this view of history, flourished in the 1880s and early 1890s but was cut short by a wave of classical architecture following in the wake of the 1893 World's Fair.

The Marquette soon came to be central to this thesis. In his enormously influential *Space, Time and Architecture,* first published in 1941, Sigfried Giedion described the building as a typical example of the "Chicago school."[30] Giedion was followed by Carl Condit, who provided the most fully developed elaboration of the "Chicago school" in his book *The Chicago School of Architecture,* published in 1964. In that book Condit stressed the gridlike character of the Marquette's exterior as an expression of the underlying steel frame. For example, he described the exterior in the following way: "The wide, smooth expanse of glass transforms the big elevations in graceful patterns of light; the openings are perfectly scaled and proportioned; the deep reveals give a powerful statement to the steel cage on which the walls are carried."[31] This description, which emphasizes the abstract elements of the building's facades, says nothing about the terra cotta cladding and classical detail. Indeed, it could have been a description of any number of modernist skyscrapers of his own day, which is precisely why it was so admired by the historians of the era. The "Chicago school" view of the Marquette was very persuasive in the postwar years. It accorded perfectly with qualities most highly prized by contemporary modernist architects and artists, and the claim that American buildings could at last be added to the pantheon of great works of architectural history satisfied postwar patriotism and Chicagoans' civic pride. It was so effective that it inspired contemporary architects to design buildings consciously in what they felt was the spirit of the "Chicago school."[32]

I hope it is obvious from the descriptions and illustrations in this chapter that this reading does not correspond with the evidence we have about the intentions of William Holabird and Martin Roche or the Marquette's reception by Chicagoans of the day. Nothing suggests that the architects had any intention of creating an ahistorical, undecorated building. The rich classical decoration in terra cotta should be enough to dispel that idea. Likewise the chapter on the Tacoma should have made it clear that the architects were not likely to have been interested in creating a gridlike building to celebrate an underlying skeletal structure, since they saw this structural system more as an expedient than as a virtue.

This is not to say that Condit and Giedion were wrong, however. Although I believe my reading of the Marquette comes closer to explaining how the building was viewed by most observers in its own day, that was not Giedion's or Condit's intention. From the vantage point of their own era, through the lens of European avant-garde modernism, they saw a different building than observers in 1893 saw and a different one than we see today. What is probably most interesting about this tale is not who is right or wrong in the interpretation but that the Marquette, like relatively few buildings or works of art, has been read in ways that seem almost diametrically opposed. This might be the mark of a fundamentally ambiguous design. More probable in this case, it might be a feature of a building whose architects successfully reconciled demands that seemed almost impossibly contradictory.

EIGHT

ALONG   LEAFY   AVENUES:

WILLIAM   HOLABIRD'S

EVANSTON

Chicago in the late nineteenth and early twentieth centuries aroused powerful but mixed emotions. As we have seen, the first impression was often discordant and cacophonous. Leaving one of the train stations in the Loop, visitors would be assaulted by the heavy smoke that clung to the city, the press of foot traffic, the din of passing vehicles, the massive buildings blocking the sun and funneling the stiff Chicago breezes directly into their faces. What they would not see was greenery. As the density in the central area increased, the green spaces that had inspired Chicago's motto *urbs in horto*—"city in a garden"—had retreated farther and farther from the Loop. In fact visitors who saw only the central area, frantically rebuilding itself in an effort to wrest every square foot of rentable space from the site, may well have found this motto laughable.

For those who traveled farther afield, however, the residential neighborhoods of the city and suburbs revealed a quite different face of the metropolis.[1] The comments of William Archer, writing about 1900, were not atypical: "Walking in Dearborn-street or Adams-street of a cloudy afternoon, you think yourself in a frowning and fuliginous city of Dis, piled up by superhuman and apparently sinister powers. Cycling around the boulevards of a sunny morning, you rejoice in the airy and spacious greenery of the Garden City."[2]

This quotation betrays certain characteristic enthusiasms of the last decade of the nineteenth century. During this decade a cycling craze heightened interest in city streets, their pavement, and the scenery along them. In Chicago many cyclists would have followed the same path chosen by the owners of elegant carriages and their less affluent neighbors who walked along the course of the great ring of parks and boulevards that had been planned in the 1860s.[3] The idea of sightseeing in residential neighborhoods was likewise a prominent feature of the decade, fostered in great part by a tremendous increase in the production of city guidebooks.[4] Although the boulevards provided a constant reminder of *urbs in horto*, this motto did not refer just to publicly owned open space. The residential settlement pattern of Chicago was different from that of older American cities. In contrast to New York, Boston, or Philadelphia, cities that had grown up when high density was unavoidable since almost all workers had to walk to their jobs, Chicago was the first great city in the world to develop during the era of commuter transportation.

For the affluent the steam railroad provided an efficient means of commuting into town from far-flung city neighborhoods and communities that already in the nineteenth century extended far out into the hinterlands. For Chicagoans of more moderate means the quick succession of improvements in mass transit, from the horse-drawn omnibus to the horse-drawn street railway, then the cable car, the electric street railroad, and finally, starting in the 1890s, the steam-powered elevated railways, made it possible to break out of the old patterns. Neighborhoods no longer had to cluster tightly around the downtown and outlying factories. The greatly expanded territory easily accessible by transportation systems made it possible for the residential units to be spread farther apart and for neighborhoods to sprawl over the landscape in a much looser pattern than had previously been possible. Tightly packed row houses and multifamily homes built up to the lot lines on the front and sharing party walls on the sides, a pattern common in eastern American cities, had also been common in Chicago earlier in the century. After the Fire, Chicago's residential neighborhoods became looser, more heterogeneous landscapes in which single-family detached houses, two-flats, and three-flats shared the block. Typically, the two- and three-flats were all but indistinguishable from the single-family houses. This was not surprising, given the appeal of the single-family house. Although houses might be only a few feet apart, that few feet made all the difference. It gave the middle-class family what had usually been reserved for the wealthy: a building and a surrounding landscape that was entirely theirs. As the American economy grew, ownership of a single-family home, even in the great city, became possible for middle-class Americans, and the fact that it was much easier to attain in the new, sprawling cities of what was then the American West than in the more tightly built up cities of the East was a major attraction in the great westward migration.

In its first years Holabird & Roche designed residences for a fairly wide spectrum of the people of the Chicago area, from small speculative units in the central city like the Gage Cottages (cat. no. 79) to the large summer house built for banker Byron Smith in Lake Forest (cat. no. 203). It is likely that the Gage Cottages were so inexpensive that Holabird & Roche's fees would not have covered the costs of designing

8.1

Byron Smith house, Briar Lodge, Lake Forest (203), view of exterior. Photograph from Brickbuilder, *May 1900.*

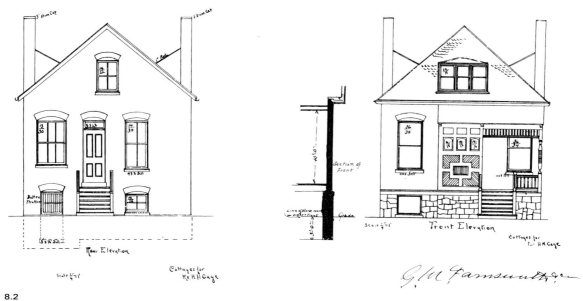

8.2

H. H. Gage Cottages (79), ca. 1890, 900 W. Lake Street, elevations. Chicago Historical Society Architectural Collections.

them and supervising their construction. They were probably done as a favor to a client who either was personally acquainted with the partners at Holabird & Roche or had commissioned them to do more substantial work. Normally such buildings were designed by speculative builders or contractors. Although Holabird & Roche undoubtedly made money on the Smith commission, it too was exceptional in the firm's oeuvre. It is likely that this commission also came because the firm was doing commercial work in which Smith had an interest. Like other large-scale commercial architects of the day, William Holabird and Martin Roche did not have the time or inclination to engage in all of the delicate and often emotionally charged consultations that clients for large houses often demanded. This kind of work typically went to specialists who could spend a month or two in extensive interviews with the clients, even accompanying them to Europe to study historic houses and to buy woodwork, furnishings, or whole rooms to ship back to Chicago.

Between these extremes were the neighborhoods that housed the great bulk of Chicago's middle class. As in nearly all nineteenth-century American cities, the city's middle-class neighborhoods constituted a broad band beyond the crazy quilt of land uses immediately adjacent to the downtown area. It was in these neighborhoods, typically some three to eight miles from the Loop, that Holabird & Roche did most of its late nineteenth-century residential work.

Evanston

A good place to study early Holabird & Roche single-family detached houses, along with the schools, churches, clubs, and other neighborhood buildings that accompanied them, is Evanston, the community where William Holabird lived. Like the residential areas closer to Chicago that were opened up by the arrival of the cable car, streetcar, and elevated lines, Evanston grew rapidly in the last decades of the nineteenth century. Between 1870 and 1890, for example, the town grew from some 3,000 people to 13,000. By 1910 there were 25,000.[5]

Unlike some of the newer streetcar suburbs around Chicago, Evanston had been a railroad suburb since the middle of the nineteenth century. Also unlike many of these communities, Evanston was no mere bedroom community or collection of speculative subdivisions. It had grown up around Northwestern University and several related educational institutions. By the time William Holabird and his family arrived in the early 1880s, the town was already a long-established community with a proud history and an impressive collection of social and cultural institutions. Along with Hyde Park on the South Side, it was considered one of the most civilized, genteel places in the Chi-

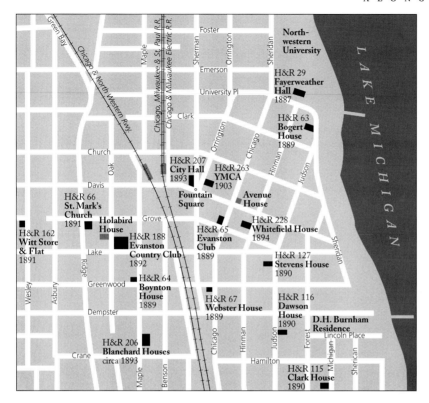

8.3

William Holabird's Evanston, Illinois, ca. 1900. Map by Dennis McClendon, adapted from maps at the Evanston Historical Society and other sources, 1995.

cago metropolitan area. According to the *Standard Guide to Chicago:* "A drive through the principal streets of Evanston will reveal the attractiveness of the place by every side and continually the eye is greeted with a sight of beautiful lawns, tasteful flower gardens and ornamental grounds. They form a pretty foreground for the elegant residences that are almost always built a good distance from the street."[6]

Evanston was home to a disproportionate number of Chicago's more prominent architects, notably Daniel Burnham, who established himself at a lakefront estate in the manner of the captains of industry who were his clients (lower right in fig. 8.3).[7] Founder of a firm that eventually became Burnham's chief rival in commercial work in Chicago, fellow member with Burnham of numerous clubs in Chicago and Evanston, and neighbor, William Holabird must certainly have thought often about Burnham's career and domestic surroundings. Holabird was apparently not comfortable living in such a conspicuous way. Even when he was in a financial position to emulate Burnham, he chose to remain in the fairly modest house at 1500 Oak Street where the family had lived ever since 1884. It was in a solidly middle-class area close to but not among the really large houses to the west on Ridge Avenue or the mansions east of Sheridan

8.4

View of the corner of Maple Avenue and Grove Street, Evanston. From Hesler's Photo Art Gallery: Photographic Views of Picturesque Evanston, *1887. Courtesy of Evanston Historical Society.*

Road on the lakefront. It is not known whether William Holabird bought the house or whether he received it from his father, who had lived in Evanston during the years he was quartermaster of the Missouri territory. It appears that the major change William Holabird made was to add a separate but connected library in 1907 to house the books bequeathed by his father.[8]

The house William Holabird lived in lay just west of Evanston's downtown, across the tracks of the Chicago and North Western and the Chicago, Milwaukee & St. Paul Railroads. Their stations, near the point where the lines diverged at Davis Street, marked the nucleus of the town and constituted the point from which the daily tide of workers flowed into Chicago in the morning and to which they returned in the evening. From his front door Holabird would have had a three-block walk to the North Western depot. From there a thirty-minute ride would have taken him to the North Western Station just north of the Loop. His office was ten minutes away by foot.

The area immediately around the Holabird house constituted a virtual catalog of neighborhood building types designed by Holabird & Roche. About two blocks to the south of the Holabirds, the Boynton house, set on a generous lot at 1007 Greenwood (cat. no. 64), was a substantial upper-middle-class suburban residence. Boynton, a manager of the Washburn and Moen Manufacturing Company, was one of the firm's typical residential clients. Judging from the $25,000 he spent on his house, he was certainly relatively affluent, but he was not by any means one of the major captains of industry. His house, built in 1889, was ample but not pretentious, with an uncomplicated and commodious plan. On the ground floor a central hallway ran down the middle of the public space, with the parlor, sitting room, and library on one side balanced by the reception room, dining room, and main stairway on the other. These interior spaces flowed into one another through large sliding doors and from the interior out onto the extensive veranda.

The house presented its front to the street in a forthright manner, set back behind a wide lawn. By contrast, trees shaded the other elevations. The flowing interior spaces and simple swelling masses covered with horizontal boarding and shingles are reminis-

8.6

C. T. Boynton house,
Evanston (64), ca.
1889, exterior view.
Photograph 1898.
Courtesy of Evanston
Historical Society.

cent of the prevailing modes of the 1880s, but the classical ornamentation of the three-part window in the gable and the bilateral symmetries in the plan betray the increasing influence of the classical revival that was starting to become a major force in Chicago domestic design. With its ponderous overhanging gable, a side bay swelling out to contain the dining room, and its porch wrapping from the front along one side, the house sat very solidly along the wide, tree-lined street, comfortable and respectable among similar neighbors. Holabird & Roche designed a number of houses like the Boyntons', contributing to the stately rhythm of the panorama that unfolded from the windows of a horse-drawn carriage at the turn of the century. Much of this feel still survives on streets like Judson and Forest Avenues, although unhappily without the great elms that once lined most of Evanston's roadways.

Complementing the houses were religious, government, and club structures also designed by Holabird & Roche. It is interesting to compare these buildings with similar ones the firm designed for sites in Chicago. The Evanston buildings, though obviously institutional in character, had a scale and texture that was more villagelike than citylike. They tended to occupy larger lots, often on street corners, and presented simple, straightforward facades and domestic-scale foundation plantings to the street just like large suburban houses.

One of the most prominent of Holabird & Roche's Evanston commissions was St. Mark's Episcopal Church (cat. no. 66). Situated on Ridge Avenue almost immediately behind the Holabird house, this was the congregation the Holabird family attended until William had a falling-out with the minister. Finished in 1891, St. Mark's was a remarkably blunt building. Constructed of rusticated stone and almost devoid of ornament, its massive corner tower seems to outweigh the rest of the church. Although the interior was lavishly polychromed and fitted out with sumptuous furnishings, the exterior looks like a modest medieval British parish church dropped on an Evanston corner.

8.7

Saint Mark's Episcopal Church, Evanston (66), 1889–91, exterior view looking southeast. Courtesy of Evanston Historical Society.

It is conspicuous, however, that the church, though probably similar in size to a British country church, has a completely different relation to the houses around it. Rather than dominating the center of a tightly packed village, the Evanston church occupies a corner lot in the middle of acres of houses. The houses, moreover, are much larger than those in a medieval town, rivaling the church in size.

Deprived of the difference in scale that marked the church in the medieval village, the architects turned to other means to set off the house of God from the houses of men. Although the church shared some of the characteristics of the domestic designs, notably the gable form along the street, the thick masonry walls and narrow vertical windows created a striking contrast with the large windows and beckoning porches of the houses to each side. It was a secure place, well separated from the bustle of everyday life. It may have been that Holabird and his partner were still thinking about their work at Fort Sheridan. In any event, it appears they may have gone a little too far for the tastes of the day. It is conspicuous how all the later additions, the first by Holabird & Roche but later ones by other architects, attempted to soften the bluntness of this original structure by introducing lighter materials and less heavy proportions.

Clubs

The same attempt to fit into the neighborhood yet signal an institutional character can be found in two clubs designed by the firm. William Holabird belonged to both. The Evanston Club (cat. no. 65), finished in 1889, was a men's club housing dining rooms and lounges, a bowling alley and billiard room, music room, and library. It was on the northwest corner of Grove Street and Chicago Avenue, just across downtown Evanston from the Holabird house. Given its modest program and its location in the heart of a residential neighborhood, it is no surprise that the building had a large shingled gable and a modest domestic image similar to the Boynton house. In fact it cost some $4,000 less to build. Its larger lot, wider setback, greater building length, and multiple entrances all bespoke its institutional character, however, and it must have reminded many Evanstonians of similar though grander places they had visited on the East Coast.[9]

The Evanston Country Club of 1892 (cat. no. 188), on the other hand, with its great two-story classical porch and heavy cornice, appears to have been the product of a more ambitious membership. This club was almost immediately across the street from the Holabird house. Little is known about its appearance except what is visible in photographs of the exterior, but these photographs unmistakably suggest that the intention was to have a grander, more public image, perhaps recalling one of the pavil-

8.8
Evanston Club,
Evanston (65), 1889,
view of exterior. From
Architectural
Review, *June 1897.*

ions with plantation house imagery built for a southern state at the 1893 Fair. It seems fitting that this building later housed Evanston's municipal offices.

Before leaving Evanston, we might take a quick look at Evanston's original village hall (cat. no. 207), a building designed by Holabird & Roche about 1891. The site was at the northwest corner of Fountain Square, the triangular open space created by the intersection of two grid systems in the heart of the town's central district. By 1890 the square was surrounded by neat but hardly remarkable brick shop buildings. The village of Evanston, after doubling in population during the preceding decade, decided it needed a permanent place for its trustees to meet instead of the rented quarters they had been using, as well as a new home for the police and fire departments. The new building broke dramatically with the surrounding buildings in scale and texture and dominated the square. It must have been envisioned as the first structure of the new, vastly expanded commercial center many Evanstonians expected to develop. When Evanston changed its legal status from village to city in the year after the building was erected, however, the imagery may have seemed wrong. Whereas the clubs betray the

8.9

Evanston Country Club (188), 1892, view of exterior. From Inland Architect, *December 1892.*

gradual transition from Romanesque and other mid-nineteenth century modes toward the classical styles that dominated civic architecture at the turn of the century, the inspiration for the Evanston village hall is clearly not classical. Like St. Mark's Church, it looks as though it could have been plucked directly from some medieval village, although in this case it appears that Germany rather than England was the model.

Imagery turned out to be the least of the building's problems. Owing to budget problems only part of the original design was completed, and even then only the exterior. From photographs it looks as if the building had been cut in half by a giant knife. It was probably intended that a future addition to the rear would mirror the part that was built and complete the original design. If so, it would have created a very impressive foursquare block whose four towers would have even more clearly dominated the city's business center. Had it been finished, this would have been one of the firm's most noteworthy buildings, and it might have secured for it a reputation for civic and institutional commissions.

8.10
*Evanston City Hall
(207), 1891–93,
view of exterior.
Courtesy of Evanston
Historical Society.*

This was not to be, however. Just before the building was put into service Evanston annexed South Evanston, and the uncompleted building was found to be too small. The city started thinking about a new structure, but nothing happened, and the city offices stayed in the new but badly overcrowded quarters. Complaints about the inadequacy of the structure were loud and sustained, but because the city government always intended to move, the full design of the Holabird & Roche building was never completed. Somehow the village made do until 1946, when the government offices moved into the Holabird & Roche–designed old Evanston Country Club, which not only had more space but probably seemed to many to have a more appropriate city imagery.

Despite all of the problems associated with the building, mostly not of the architects' making, and the fact that it has been all but unknown in architectural history, this must have been one of the most impressive buildings in the Chicago suburbs. The arched windows, dormers, and polychrome patterns gave it a lively surface, allowing it to fit in with the animated commercial buildings on each side. On the other hand, though it counted no more stories than most of them, its great pitched roof and corner towers crowned with conical caps gave it a distinctly public appearance. Even half complete, it must have dominated its neighbors much as the combination markets and village halls of European villages did. Unfortunately the building was demolished in 1946 as soon as the city government was transferred away from it, and there appears to be remarkably little evidence of what daily commuters to the Loop via the railroads thought as they passed this structure every evening on their return home.

The city hall and the other commissions of the firm in Evanston have a number of similarities, but what is most surprising is how much they differ. These buildings, all designed within the span of ten years and for sites only a few blocks from each other, testify to the architects' skill at fitting into various contexts. They also demonstrate how eclectic the firm's production was. No single stylistic trend dominated. As was the case throughout Holabird & Roche's history, different situations called forth different responses.

Part

Three

NINE

THE FIRM

1894–1896

The 1893 World's Columbian Exposition coincided with a severe national business downturn. In Chicago the volume of new construction fell from over $63 million recorded in 1892 to under $29 million in 1893. It inched up to over $30 million for the next two years but then fell almost to $22 million for 1896 and remained at this level for several years. Holabird & Roche witnessed a similar decline in commissions, although, as usual, the consequences of the downturn were delayed, since the firm continued to receive fees for the big buildings designed at the tail end of the boom period and that were still under construction well into the first years of the recession. The result was that the firm's account books, which recorded work when it was finished rather than when the permit was taken out, showed construction totaling over $1.5 million in 1894 and over $2 million in 1895, primarily owing to work designed in 1891 and 1892. But by 1896 the figure was only $236,000. The following years saw something of a rebound as the totals for 1897 came to $617,000 and those for 1898 to $464,000, but this was still far less than the cost of a single large office building like the Marquette.[1]

William Holabird and Martin Roche, like most Chicago businessmen, seem to have taken the boom and bust cycle as a matter of course. They seized the opportunity of the business downturn to go to Europe in 1896, the first time for both of the partners. There is little record of what they saw or did, but the firm's ledgers disclose that their trip cost $1,500. By this time the office had been reduced from over forty employees to three: Renwick, Charles E. Fox, and Frank B. Long.[2] Probably in anticipation of the trip, in 1896 Renwick was taken in as a general partner with a one-fifth interest in the firm.[3] Thereafter there would be no change in the partnership structure until after World War I.

9.1

Atwood Building (230),
1895, 6 N. Clark Street,
northwest corner of Madison Street,
view of exterior with Hotel
Brevoort and Tacoma Building
(Holabird & Roche) farther west
(left) along Madison. Photograph by
Barnes-Crosby. Chicago Historical
Society Prints and Photographs
Department, ICHi-19046.

During the lean years of the late 1890s Holabird & Roche continued to do much the same kind of work it had done during the boom of the late 1880s. There was just less of it. The mainstay of the practice continued to be the large commercial building. During the mid-1890s the firm worked on several substantial commercial structures, including the Atwood Building (cat. no. 230) on Clark Street in the Chicago Loop, the metal and glass clad Champlain Building (cat. no. 215, fig. 10.10), also in the Loop, and the D. S. Morgan Building (cat. no. 222) of 1894, in Buffalo, New York. The partners were listed as consulting architects to the Buffalo firm of Green and

9.2

*D. S. Morgan Building, Buffalo, New York (222), 1894;
Green and Wicks, architects, Holabird & Roche,
consulting architects, view of exterior. Photograph from*
Prominent Buildings Erected by the George A. Fuller
Company, *1904. Chicago Historical Society Library.*

Wicks for the last of these, but it is likely that Holabird & Roche was primarily responsible for the design. This commission provides ample testimony that by the 1890s
Holabird & Roche had joined Burnham and Root and, to a lesser extent a number of
other Chicago firms, as national authorities on the design of the tall building.

As usual, beside the large-scale commercial work, during these years the firm
received a good many residential commissions. The eight-unit Naughton Apartment
Building (cat. no. 248), erected in 1896 in a substantial middle-class neighborhood
on Chicago's mid-North Side, reflects a tendency for larger apartment buildings in
the 1880s and 1890s to be so simple in massing and so devoid of ornament that they
converged in appearance with commercial buildings.[4] The shadowy commission for
the University Apartments (cat. no. 237), a scheme involving thirty-eight similar

9.3

University Apartments (237), 1895–96, Cottage Grove Avenue and Thirty-fourth Street, perspective. From Economist, *28 December 1895. Chicago Historical Society Library.*

buildings grouped into superblocks on the South Side, in contrast, provides fascinating evidence of what the firm might have done when confronted with the task of designing an entire residential district. This complex, which would have occupied a site on what had been the grounds of the original University of Chicago, was reportedly the largest such development in Chicago to that date.[5] Construction was apparently started and some of the buildings were completed, but postwar redevelopment has wiped out whatever evidence remained of this grandiose but mysterious scheme.

One of the most interesting things about the work of Holabird & Roche from the late 1880s through the late 1890s is the contrast between the continuities in approach for the commercial work and large apartment buildings and a fairly major change in the appearance of the single-family houses it designed. This change might be attributed to the firm's work with McKim, Mead and White on the Lathrop house (cat. no. 165) in 1892. It is just as likely that it could have been the result of hiring a new draftsman. In any event, where the single-family houses of the earlier period had been straightforward in both plan and elevation, by the mid-1890s Holabird & Roche's houses became considerably more sophisticated studies in plan, massing, and detail.

A good example of the new tendencies is the house for Arthur O. Slaughter (cat. no. 221), a broker, a member of the Chicago Board of Trade, and the individual who placed the bonds for the Marquette Building. Situated in the elegant Kenwood district of Chicago's South Side, this house, at a cost of some $73,000, was the most substantial city house the firm had done. Its ambition to do sophisticated design like that seen

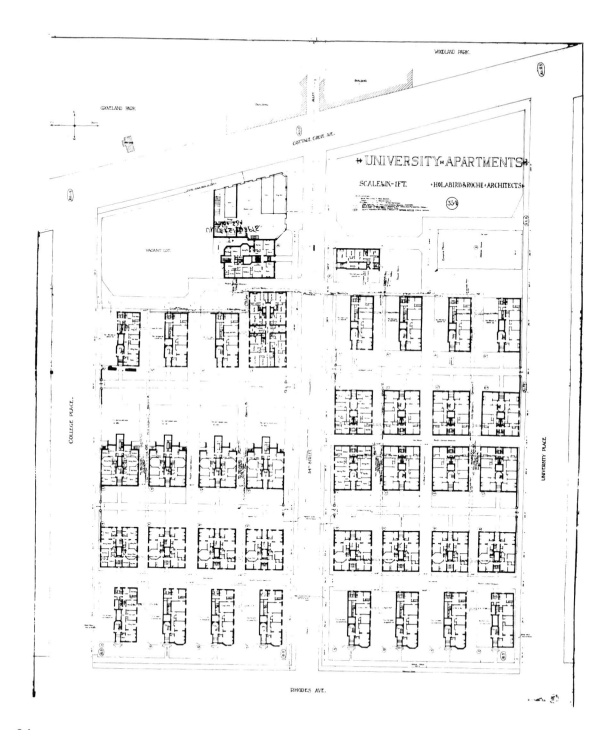

9.4

University Apartments, site plan. Chicago Historical Society Architectural Collections.

9.5

Arthur O. Slaughter house (221), 1894–96, 4548 S. Drexel Avenue, northwest corner of Forty-sixth Street, elevation and wall section. Chicago Historical Society Architectural Collections.

in the work of the eastern architects is immediately visible in the elaborate plan, with its axes and cross axes.

The contrast between Holabird & Roche's residential and commercial work is nowhere more evident than in another residential commission of these years, the house for Arthur Aldis (cat. no. 243), the younger brother of Owen Aldis and founder, with him, of the real estate firm of Aldis, Aldis and Northcote in 1888. The Aldis house, miraculously still standing on Lake Shore Drive, with its polychromed surfaces, exotic Islamic arches, and tile roof, looks like stage scenery for an opera set in Venice. To some observers today this apparition is even more surprising when it is compared with

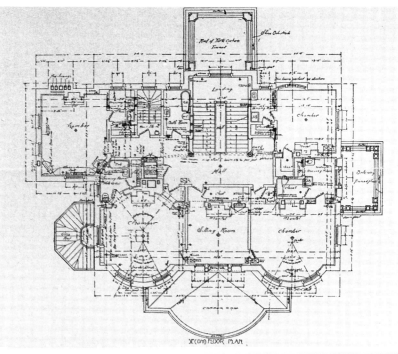

SECOND FLOOR PLAN

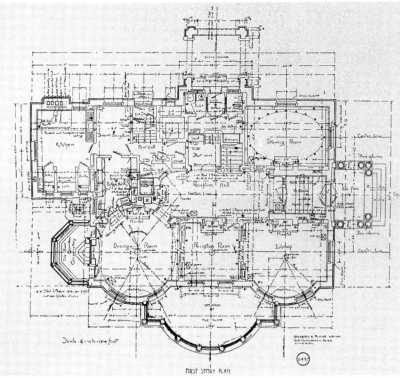

FIRST STORY PLAN

9.6
*Arthur O. Slaughter
house, plans. Chicago
Historical Society
Architectural
Collections.*

the austerity of the Loop buildings for which Aldis and his brother were responsible, notably the Montauk, Monadnock, and Marquette. If this seemed paradoxical to anyone in Chicago at the time there is no record of it. Business life and home life were different things entirely, and it is unlikely that either architects or clients thought a house modeled on a Venetian palazzo was incongruous or that the firm needed to worry about stylistic consistency among its products.

1897–1900

The last years of the century remained relatively slow ones for the city and for the firm. Construction volume in Chicago continued to decline, reaching a trough at $19 million in 1900. Holabird & Roche's recorded construction volume was listed at $464,000 in 1898, $1,144,000 in 1899, $204,000 for 1900, and $605,000 for 1901. Although this was not a great deal of work by previous standards, it still constituted as much as 5 percent of the total construction recorded in the city in certain years. Although most of the buildings from these years were relatively inexpensive, often loft structures, several of them count among the most satisfying products of the firm. One further event of these years that may have had little short-term effect but was undoubtedly important in the long run was the publication, in 1897, of the first major retrospective review of the firm's work.[6] Written by Charles E. Jenkins, the heavily illustrated article was very positive in its assessment, particularly of Fort Sheridan and the Marquette Building.

Commercial work continued to dominate the firm's output. During the last three years of the century the drafting room at Holabird & Roche must have been awash in drawings for loft buildings. These included the Hart, Schaffner & Marx (cat. no. 255), Williams (cat. no. 260), Ayer (cat. no. 264), Bailey (cat. no. 265), and McCormick (cat. no. 266). Despite a similar program, these buildings display a dazzling variety of surface treatments (figs. 11.1–11.14). In addition the firm did two related but more specialized commercial structures. The LeMoyne warehouse (cat. no. 294) on N. Clark Street on the city's Near North Side, because its most important program requirements were easy access and resistance to fires, was built with very few windows. To compensate for the loss of windows on the facade, it became a study in brick colors and textures. At the Central Trading Company (cat. no. 291), a large annex to the Mandel Brothers department store, on the other hand, the architects created a particularly rich ornamental patterning in white glazed terra cotta (figs. 10.11–10.12).

The firm's most conspicuous apartment building at the turn of the century was the McConnell Apartments (cat. no. 257) on prestigious Astor Street. Seven stories

9.8

McConnell Apartment Building (257), 1897, 1210 N. Astor Street, northwest corner of Division Street, perspective.
Chicago Historical Society Architectural Collections.

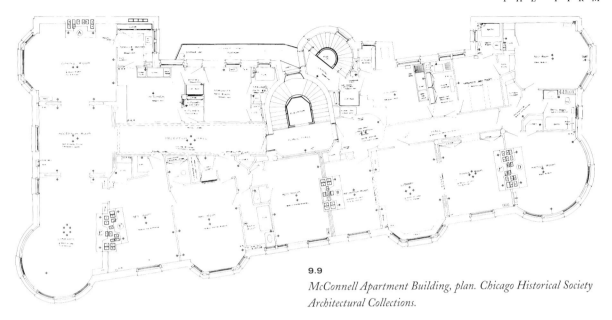

9.9
McConnell Apartment Building, plan. Chicago Historical Society Architectural Collections.

high, it must have created a stir on a street that was otherwise almost entirely lined with single-family houses.[7] The exterior, moreover, with its projecting bay windows and almost unornamented brick surfaces, must have looked to many neighbors like a Loop office building. Prefigured already in Holabird & Roche's earlier apartment buildings such as the Naughton, this short-lived trend, visible in a number of the city's most prominent hotels and apartment buildings of the 1890s, raises interesting questions. Was this plainness the result of economic demands, as was clearly the case with many of the Loop office buildings? This explanation does not satisfy, since most descriptions of the building emphasized its aesthetic desirability, and no public complaints appear to have surfaced. It seems more likely that the brief convergence of residential structures and office buildings sprang from the association of the new office buildings with efficiency and modernity.

In addition to its work in the city, the firm also continued to work in the outlying communities and suburbs. A prominent commission of this era is the clubhouse for the Glen View Golf and Polo Club (cat. no. 261) in the countryside west of Evanston, in what is now Golf, Illinois (figs. 13.2–13.4).

1901–1903

By the early years of the century prosperity had returned to the Chicago building industry. A damaging strike in 1900 by a newly created and militant group of construction workers had been quashed by the united action of the city's leading business-men, contractors, and architects, and the next few years were prosperous ones.[8] Chicago recorded a steady growth in new construction, rising from $19 million in 1900 to $63 million by 1905. Holabird & Roche's ledgers show construction totaling some $3,526,000 in 1902, $1,106,000 in 1903, and $2,986,000 in 1904, meaning that the firm continued to capture between 5 and 10 percent of all new construction in the city. This volume of work started to bring it abreast of the largest firms in the country.[9] The increasing business soon made it necessary to organize the firm's files better. In 1902 the partners instituted a new method of keeping track of commissions using a logbook in which employees recorded all commissions in a continuous numerical sequence. This system is still in use today.

Although William Holabird was never as prominent in civic affairs as his colleague and rival Daniel Burnham, he and his firm did play important roles in the Chicago architectural community. A drawing of a "taproom" shown in the Chicago Architectural Club's annual exhibition and published in its *Annual* reminds us of the large numbers of young draftsmen and designers who came through the Holabird & Roche offices. Not known to be connected with any of the firm's actual commissions, this drawing was most likely the work of one of the younger employees of the office, an exercise in rendering technique. The Holabird & Roche office, like that of Jenney, operated both as a place of business and as a kind of educational institution.

During the first years of the new century the firm continued to design office buildings similar to those it had completed in the boom years of the late 1890s. The Chicago Savings Bank Building (cat. no. 359), which continued in the mode Holabird & Roche had established for office buildings in the previous decade, is today perhaps the most nearly intact of all Holabird & Roche structures from the turn of the century. The new home for the Chicago Tribune Company, one of Chicago's most venerable and important business enterprises (cat. no. 308), was the most important commission the firm had yet received. Given a prominent central Loop site and a generous budget, the firm produced a building whose highly articulated facades and elegantly furnished lobby were obviously intended to create a more monumental effect than the firm's earlier speculative office structures.[10] Unfortunately, most observers felt that Holabird & Roche failed in this effort, producing instead an uneven design with none of the clarity of the firm's less expensive buildings.

Successful or not, this design undoubtedly testifies to changing aesthetic ideals. Although it was not apparent to many observers at the time, Chicago's great post–Civil War boom years were over. There seems to have been a feeling that the city had matured. The old individual entrepreneurs had given way to vast corporations, and the city, through the 1893 Fair, had convinced itself that it was finally a great world me-

9.10
*Chicago Savings Bank
Building (359),
1903–4, 7 W.
Madison, southwest
corner of State Street,
view of exterior.
Photograph by Jim
Norris. Courtesy of
Holabird & Root.*

9.12
Chicago Tribune Building, view of stair hall. From Inland Architect, *September 1902.*

tropolis. The following observations by Henry Hyde in *Harper's Weekly* in 1901 probably reflect the viewpoint of many of Chicago's architects as well as businessmen:

> Heretofore the congested business centre of the city, the birthplace of the steel-ribbed skyscraper, has been remarkable only for the number of these commercial towers of Babel, which spring up like exclamation points against the sky-line, and make of such streets as Dearborn and LaSalle artificial box canyons, in the narrow bottoms of which cable trains, trucks, and crowds of busy men hurry about in noisy confusion. . . . The building of sky-scrapers still goes on in Chicago, though more slowly, and with an idea of combining utility and some degree of dignity, if not beauty. And in the natural evolution of business the time has been reached when a considerable number of large commercial enterprises, grown great in wealth and influence, have found it desirable to erect for their housing monumental buildings, which give to Chicago streets an entirely new touch of dignity and attractiveness.[11]

9.11 (opposite)
Chicago Tribune Building (308), 1901–2, 7 S. Dearborn Street, southeast corner of Madison Street, exterior view. Photograph by Barnes-Crosby. Chicago Historical Society Prints and Photographs Department, ICHi-19251.

Despite its somewhat conservative exterior appearance, the Tribune Building did embody several important advances in technology. The most important was the deep basement and the concrete construction that made it possible. To house the huge presses in such a way that they would not create vibrations in the rest of the building, it was necessary to put them in a subbasement of unprecedented depth, extending thirty-three feet below the sidewalk level and thus penetrating the stratum of hard clay on which most of the city's earlier foundations had rested. This required elaborate precautions in shoring up the walls of the adjoining properties and making the exterior walls of the Tribune basement water and pressure resistant.[12]

This construction was the occasion of one of the most revealing statements made by either partner during their careers. William Holabird, writing in *Inland Architect*, suggested that the firm's use of reinforced concrete in the Tribune basement might prove to be part of a "logical development of a new style of building indigenous to this country, for it is here only that we are likely to find architects broad enough to depart from ancient forms and to attempt a new development."[13] This appears to be the only time either Holabird or Roche has been recorded as making any direct statement on the possible future of architecture. This reticence is not surprising. Unlike Louis Sullivan or John Root, who had formal architectural training and had studied at the Ecole des Beaux-Arts in Paris where theoretical speculation about architecture was common, Holabird and Roche had not had such training and were plain-speaking commercial architects, preoccupied with day-to-day concerns. It is characteristic that this comment was made about a technical feature invisible to the public eye on a highly conservative building. The quotation strongly reinforces the notion that Holabird did not condone novel expression for its own sake. Instead, economic or programmatic requirements would call forth new solutions. The successful commercial architect was one who would push fearlessly into the new aesthetic territory these developments might lead to without being paralyzed by traditional forms. It is quite likely that this statement would have been considered a sober, mainstream position by most commercial architects in Chicago or anywhere else in the first years of the twentieth century.

In addition to the office buildings, the firm continued to do a series of loft buildings, for example, one each for the George Hill Company (cat. no. 306), the Liquid Carbonic Company (cat. no. 336), the Clow Company (cat. no. 310), and the Ryerson Company (cat. no. 366). It also completed a conspicuous high-rise commercial building for State Street, the twelve-story white terra cotta Republic Building (cat. no. 344), an elevator version of the traditional shops building (figs. 12.11–12.16). Perhaps the most spectacular new direction for the firm came with the commission for an expansion of the Auditorium Annex (Congress) Hotel (cat. no. 355). This project, carried out in two steps between 1900 and 1906, launched a practice in hotel design that would became one of the largest in the country by the end of the first decade of the century (figs. 16.2–16.9).

During the first years of the century the firm was also able to expand its range of institutional work. In the years 1902–4 Holabird & Roche started a long association with Children's Memorial Hospital (cat. no. 333), drawing up a master plan for the institution and designing the Maurice Porter Pavilion, the first of many commissions for the hospital, nearly all of them classical pavilions of brick with stone trim. These years also witnessed the start of what would be another decades-long association, this time with the American Medical Association (cat. no. 328). The first work for the Association was a structure of three stories plus raised basement in brick with stone

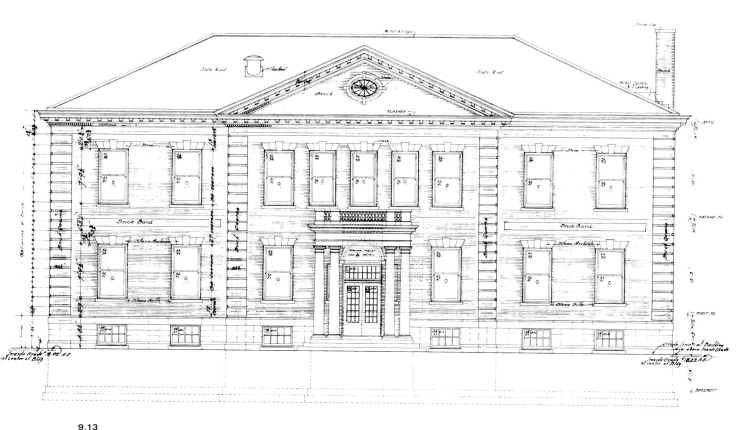

9.13
Children's Memorial Hospital, Maurice Porter Pavilion (333), 1902–8, Fullerton Street west of Orchard, north (Fullerton Street) elevation. Chicago Historical Society Architectural Collections.

trim that occupied the site of two row houses along Dearborn Street on the city's Near North Side.

Another conspicuous category of commissions that came to the firm in the early years of the twentieth century was summer houses and resorts. Although some of these were quite grand—for example, the Wells house at Lake Geneva (cat. no. 352)—others, like the clubhouse and a series of cottages at the Coleman Lake Club in Wisconsin (figs. 14.2–14.7) and the Huron Mountain Club in Michigan, were very modest. The firm also produced, usually with the help of local associated architects, houses for Chicagoans vacationing elsewhere in the country: for example, Green Gables—the Henry Dibblee residence at Rye Beach, New Hampshire (cat. no. 275)—and the Bryan Lathrop "cottage" at York Harbor, Maine (cat. no. 325). These were both shingled buildings with informal, asymmetrical plans quite different from anything the firm produced in the Midwest.

Finally, during these years the firm had occasion to design unusual structures for two sporting organizations. For the Chicago Jockey Club it produced the grandstand at Hawthorne Racetrack (cat. no. 349), just west of the city in the suburb of Cicero. This structure, with its rather lacy metal roof, replaced an earlier, heavier Holabird & Roche–designed building (cat. no. 156), mostly of frame construction, that had burned. The other building, designed in association with Jarvis Hunt for the Chicago Yacht Club (cat. no. 309), was a spreading, almost boatlike structure of heavy timbers and wide verandas that sat along the lake embankment immediately in front of the Chicago Loop.

1904–1907

The amount of construction in Chicago jumped from nearly $45 million in 1904 to $68 million in 1908. At Holabird & Roche the figures, delayed as usual because of the lag in the completion of construction, were $651,000 in 1905, $332,000 in 1906, $3,017,000 in 1907, and $6,641,000 in 1908, bringing its share of the total work in the city up to about 10 percent in the latter year.

In addition to the growth in volume, there was a change in the kinds of commissions. It might well be argued that 1904–7 witnessed the final coming of age of the firm. Although by 1904 Holabird & Roche was firmly established and had done an enormous amount of work of all kinds, most of it had involved commercial structures for private clients. During the next few years Holabird & Roche finally received its first really large-scale public commission, the Cook County Courthouse (cat. no. 373),

SCALE ¼ INCH = 1 FT.

· EAST ELEVATION ·

CLUB HOUSE FOR THE CHICAGO YACHT CLUB.

SHEET (3243)

HOLABIRD AND ROCHE
JARVIS HUNT   ASSOCIATE ARCHITECTS

9.14
Chicago Yacht Club (309), 1901–2, at lakefront near Monroe Street, architects Holabird & Roche and Jarvis Hunt, east elevation. Chicago Historical Society Architectural Collections.

the largest and most visible public commission of its day in Chicago. The firm also received a series of commissions for important hotels, notably the LaSalle (cat. no. 418) and the Sherman House (cat. no. 410). On State Street Holabird & Roche started work on the Boston Store (cat. no. 384), the first of the firm's large department stores. Finally, there was the commission for the University Club (cat. no. 383), which many critics felt was Martin Roche's most accomplished work. These commissions mark the point where Holabird & Roche finally followed D. H. Burnham and Company into the national spotlight as a major force in both the business and the art of building the American city. (On the Cook County Courthouse see figs. 17.8–17.12; on the LaSalle and Sherman House hotels, figs. 16.10–16.14; on the Boston Store, figs. 12.2–12.8; and on the University Club, figs. 19.3–19.10.)

TEN

STATE STREET
IN THE NINETIES

One of the most interesting challenges the firm tackled in the 1890s was how to design for State Street, Chicago's preeminent shopping thoroughfare. The street had been built up with large and opulent department stores, hotels, and other commercial buildings just before the Great Fire and rebuilt along the same lines after it. These businesses were hugely successful, driving up land prices along State Street to the highest levels in Chicago and the highest anywhere outside Manhattan.[1]

By the early 1890s, despite later, more up-to-date buildings like Jenney's Portland Block, State Street still maintained much of its bombastic post-Fire era glory. Marshall Field's, for example, with its high mansarded pavilions, and the Palmer House with its corner turret, gables, and dormers, set the tone for many lesser edifices, their imagery likewise borrowed from Renaissance and baroque palaces, filtered through midcentury London and Second Empire Paris. According to one observer, the effect was especially startling after a snowfall, when fresh white drifts built up on the grimy projecting surfaces of sills, dormers, pediments, and turrets.[2]

If there is one constant in retail merchandising, it is change. One year's most desirable commodity becomes the following year's white elephant. So it was with the buildings along State Street. By the early 1890s, when Holabird & Roche got its first large commissions there, this streetscape had come to look dark, heavy, and old-fashioned. The firm was among the small group of architects who started to explore how the street might be made lighter, less ponderous, and more up-to-date. The pioneer, in this as in so many other ways, was William Le Baron Jenney. With the Siegel, Cooper and Company store building (later dubbed the Leiter II) and the Fair Store, both finished about 1891, Jenney took a decisive step in the creation of the turn-of-the-century Chicago department store. Both were large, simple masses whose

10.1

State Street, view looking north from Madison Street in 1890s with Columbus Memorial Building (tall structure with tower on east side of State Street) and side wall of Reliance Building (on west side of street). Photograph by Barnes-Crosby. Chicago Historical Society Prints and Photographs Department, ICHi-19294.

spacious, open floors and large windows brought them more into line with the speculative office buildings and loft structures in the Loop.[3] The only concession Jenney made to the department store's elevated status was a very thin veneer of classical detailing. At the Leiter II Building, for example, he manipulated his white Maine granite cladding to produce slightly strengthened corners, classical pilasters running across several floors, and a projecting cornice, all in such low relief that they were relatively inexpensive, did not take up valuable floor space, and were barely visible from a distance. The result, a set of flat walls, light in color, with huge windows allowing passersby a glimpse of the merchandise inside, must have been quite novel.

The two Jenney buildings set the stage for the golden age of State Street department store construction when, in a sustained surge of building between 1890 and 1915, seven of the great State Street department stores reached their ultimate size.[4] In addition to the department stores there were a host of other buildings, created to provide every amenity for the shopping crowds. In the 1890s Holabird & Roche's principal contribution was twofold. First, it was the most important office in the continuation of Jenney's search for new materials and a new image for State Street shopping. It also led the way in the creation of a new building type, the vertically organized tall professional and shops building on the "arcade" principle.

10.2

Leiter II (Siegel Cooper and Company) Building, 1891, southeast corner of State and Van Buren Streets, Jenney and Mundie architects, view of exterior from southwest with Holabird & Roche's State Safety Building beyond the elevated tracks on Van Buren Street in the background. Photograph by Barnes-Crosby. Chicago Historical Society Prints and Photographs Department, ICHi-19297.

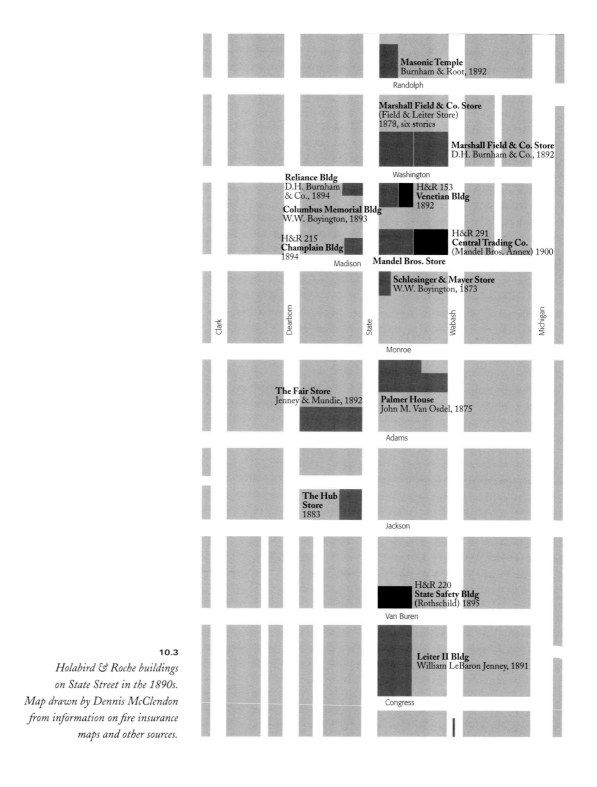

Masonic Temple
Burnham & Root, 1892

Randolph

Marshall Field & Co. Store
(Field & Leiter Store)
1878, six stories

Marshall Field & Co. Store
D.H. Burnham & Co., 1892

Washington

Reliance Bldg
D.H. Burnham
& Co., 1894

H&R 153
Venetian Bldg
1892

Columbus Memorial Bldg
W.W. Boyington, 1893

H&R 215
Champlain Bldg
1894

H&R 291
Central Trading Co.
(Mandel Bros. Annex) 1900

Madison

Mandel Bros. Store

Schlesinger & Mayer Store
W.W. Boyington, 1873

Clark

Dearborn

State

Wabash

Michigan

Monroe

The Fair Store
Jenney & Mundie, 1892

Palmer House
John M. Van Osdel, 1875

Adams

**The Hub
Store**
1883

Jackson

H&R 220
State Safety Bldg
(Rothschild) 1895

Van Buren

Leiter II Bldg
William LeBaron Jenney, 1891

Congress

10.3
*Holabird & Roche buildings
on State Street in the 1890s.
Map drawn by Dennis McClendon
from information on fire insurance
maps and other sources.*

The Venetian Building

The Venetian Building (cat. no. 153) of 1891–92, just east of State Street at 15 E. Washington, was a twelve-story steel frame building. It was developed by the Chicago Real Estate Trustees, a trust set up by Owen Aldis in 1890 that included himself, Bryan Lathrop, the Brooks brothers, and others. Set up on the Massachusetts Trust model because of Aldis's fears about the legality of the safety deposit company, this was apparently Chicago's first real estate trust.[5] The Venetian Building was designed specifically for medical offices, and they occupied almost all the space except the lower floors, which were maintained for retail.[6] The largest building of its type in Chicago, it was situated just off State Street for the convenience of individuals who worked in the Loop or who wanted to combine a trip to the doctor or dentist with shopping and other errands in the Loop.

Because this was not a standard office building on Dearborn or store on State Street, the developers and architects apparently felt it should have a unique image. An early announcement stated that the building, which had not yet been named, would be executed in St. Louis granite bricks with terra cotta trim, sport a red pitched roof, and be in the early French Renaissance style of François I.[7] By the time the rental brochures had gone out, the building had become known as the Venetian. It is possible the architects had changed their minds about the design and had incorporated new design elements they considered to be more Venetian Renaissance than François I. It is just as likely that the design inspiration did not change but that someone on the developer's side decided that the name Venetian, with its exotic overtones and its desirable associations with commerce and art, would help lease space. Chicago, like Venice, was a commercial city by the water. Why shouldn't it have palaces like those on the Grand Canal? As for any obligation to use correct stylistic labels in the business of real estate, this was considered no more binding in the 1890s than it is today. The idea was to convey desirable associations, not to satisfy the historian's trained eye.

When the building was finished visitors could see that the dark brick or terra cotta cladding common in most buildings of the 1870s and 1880s had been replaced by long Roman bricks of a warm buff color and terra cotta trim of the same hue, producing a lighter than usual effect. The central section of the building, like that of the Marquette, was remarkably straightforward. Huge three-part windows took up most of the elevation. Only the narrowest wall surfaces, virtually unornamented, remained between them, giving the building a light, modern appearance. The windows let large quantities of natural light into the shops and medical offices. This was obviously crucial for the exacting work performed by the physicians and dentists, but particularly in a building like the Venetian, light was also important for other reasons. Well into the

187

10.4
Venetian Building (153), 1891–92, 15 E. Washington Street, exterior view with Columbus Memorial Building under construction to the right. Chicago Historical Society Prints and Photographs Department, ICHi-14372.

10.5

Venetian Building, perspective. From Inland Architect, *August 1891.*

twentieth century, until the germ theory of disease gained nearly universal acceptance, many people believed that the various mysterious disease agents were harbored in dirt or darkness. Clean, light colored, impervious surfaces and a flood of sunlight were virtually synonymous with health.[8]

The large windows at the Venetian also provided a prominent location for what was really a huge signboard. Vast amounts of lettering and a variety of other graphic devices painted in black and gold on the windows advertised jewelers and druggists as well as doctors and dentists. Glowing brilliantly against the darker surface of the glass during the daytime, they were equally effective when backlit at night. The signs were crucial in luring the customer off the sidewalk and up the elevator.

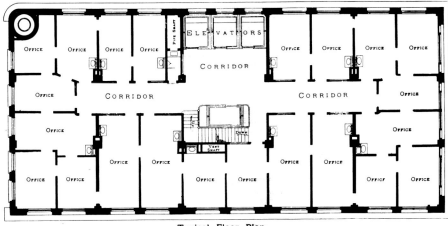

Typical Floor Plan.

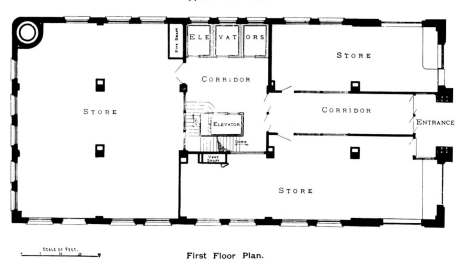

First Floor Plan.

10.6

Venetian Building, plan of first floor and typical floor. From Prominent Buildings Erected by the George A. Fuller Construction Company *(New York, 1894).*

At the top of the building the sober fenestration of the middle section gave way to a complicated and playful proliferation of decorative patterning, arched windows, and—most remarkable in a commercial building—a pitched roof. Except for the last, all the ornamental features were merely skin deep. The pitched roof, on the other hand, involved constructing an elaborate frame that enclosed a large cubic footage that could not be rented. This extravagant gesture by the Brooks brothers was almost surely a considered response to a real estate problem. In this case it was probably considered necessary to distinguish the building from simple office or retail structures and justify the premium rents that the doctors and dentists surely paid. The Venetian was well received and a financial success, and it spawned a number of similar buildings for professional offices and for retail use over the next several decades.

State Safety

Holabird & Roche's first large structure actually on State Street, the State Safety Building (A. M. Rothschild Store), 1894, at the northeast corner of State and Van Buren (cat. no. 220), is curiously obscure. Except for some notices in the *Economist*, a photograph or two, and the drawings in Holabird & Roche collection, there is little evidence that this building ever existed. This is difficult to understand, since the seven-story building with its flamboyant illuminated corner tower must have attracted a great deal of attention in its day. It is likely that neither the architects nor the critics were

The Store
that stands
for Absolute
Dependability

Courtesy,
Accuracy,
Completeness,
foundation stones
of this store

Rothschild's a Store of Progress

Progress in every direction. Rapid, continuous increase of business, improvement of methods and details of organization, quickly adopting new ideas and installing new devices which have proved practical—constantly aiming to do business better and to be of greater service to the public, each year, each season, each day.

That this store is the center of supply for thousands of Chicago families is best evidenced by the fact that this immense block is inadequate to the fulfillment of our ideals; such is our progress that this great building is now only temporary.

The Home
of the
Famous
Meister
Piano

Rothschild & Company

All El. Trains
Stop Here.
Direct Bridge
Entrance

State and Van Buren Streets and Wabash Avenue

10.7
*State Safety Building
(A. M. Rothschild Store) (220),
1894–95, 337 S. State Street,
northeast corner of Van Buren Street,
advertisement. From Jones,* A Half
Century of Chicago Building, *1910.*

191

10.8

*State Safety Building (A. M. Rothschild Store), view from the southwest with Leiter II Building in foreground.
Photograph by Barnes-Crosby. Chicago Historical Society Prints and Photographs Department, ICHi-19214.*

much pleased with it. Still, it marks a very interesting stage in the search for cladding material on State Street. The building was constructed for Abram M. Rothschild, a German émigré, who with his brothers had moved to Chicago after the Fire and had started a clothing store on W. Madison Street. Business prospered greatly, and by the early 1890s Rothschild was attempting to secure a block-long frontage on State Street for a major new department store just north of the huge edifice occupied by the Siegel, Cooper and Company store (Leiter II).

As was often the case with the assemblage of large Loop properties, the site acquisition process was clandestine and complicated. Either on its own or on behalf of Rothschild, a syndicate called the State Safety Company, undoubtedly a safety deposit company, got control of the desired property through a ninety-nine-year lease. By the time news of the land deal broke in the newspapers in 1894, the old building on the site had been demolished and the new one designed by Holabird & Roche was already under construction. At this point Rothschild controlled all but the northernmost forty feet of the block front. The seven-story building was built in "semimill" construction, that is, a system with metal columns, in this case round, and heavy wood joists and floor construction. The front wall, however, like the Tacoma's, was entirely framed in metal and was designed to accommodate a thin, nonbearing cladding that would cover the minimal wall surfaces left between the huge three-part windows. This was done for the same reason Holabird & Roche's clients had agreed to this method at the Ta-

10.9
State Safety Building (A. M. Rothschild Store), elevations with cast iron cladding. Chicago Historical Society Architectural Collections.

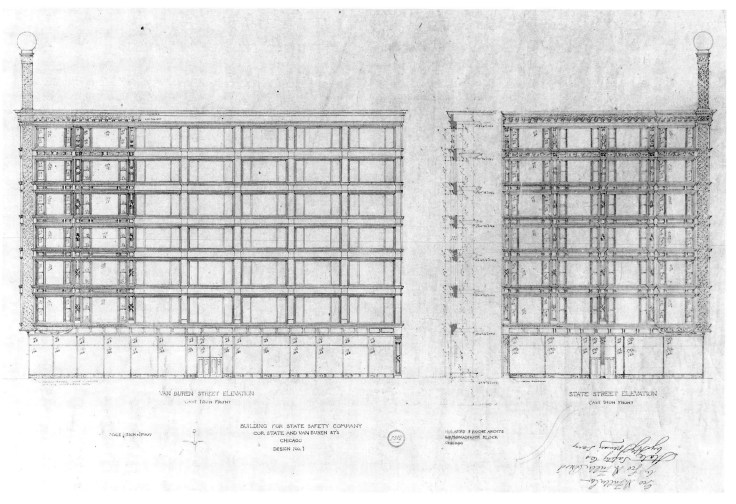

VAN BUREN STREET ELEVATION
CAST IRON FRONT

BUILDING FOR STATE SAFETY COMPANY
COR. STATE AND VAN BUREN STS
CHICAGO
DESIGN No. 1

STATE STREET ELEVATION
CAST IRON FRONT

coma—to allow them to cut down on the thickness of the wall and to let in maximum light and air. Nowhere was this logic followed more systematically than in the State Street department stores, where natural light was essential for viewing the merchandise. To get natural light all the way to the back of the very deep floors, the architects attempted to provide the largest windows possible.

Existing elevation drawings show that two facing materials, one cast iron, the other brick and terra cotta, were proposed and a set of drawings was made for each. The presence of the cast iron set is somewhat surprising. Cast iron had been extensively used in the 1860s and 1870s because it was much cheaper than cut stone but could be easily molded into the shape of the high relief pilasters, attached columns, and voussoirs so popular in stone architecture in these years. When painted, these metal pieces looked remarkably like their lithic prototypes, particularly after a few years in Chicago's sooty air. By 1890, however, the fashion for the material had passed, along with the fashion for lavish stone facades. One of the major controlling factors was the increasing production and declining cost of terra cotta. Why, then, did Holabird & Roche choose to use the cast iron system? It is unlikely that the iron front could be made more cheaply than the terra cotta. It seems more likely that the decision was aesthetic, that all the more ornament was desired because there was so little space remaining for it, and that for high relief ornament cast iron was clearly a better material than the more fragile terra cotta. Perhaps Rothschild, though he wanted the huge windows he saw on the neighboring Siegel, Cooper store, rejected any treatment that might have resembled Jenney's relatively sparse classical scheme of pilasters, colonnettes, and entablatures.

The Holabird & Roche cast iron design, on the other hand, created an effect almost closer to millinery than to masonry. Virtually every square inch of available wall surface was covered with pilasters, moldings, and panels. The exuberant effect was heightened still further by the decorative treatment of the building's corner turret, which held aloft an eagle perched on a ball, wings outspread. Covering the shaft of this turret, each elaborate diamond-shaped indentation shone with the light of an electric light bulb, creating a decorative effect akin to those on theaters.

The State Safety Building again suggests how independent the structural system was from the cladding. Structure was chosen primarily for its solidity and economy. The cladding, on the other hand, was the client's primary method of alerting pedestrians to the nature of the building. With masonry bearing walls the structural system and exterior surface had been the same thing. One of the side effects of the increasing use of machine-made lightweight cladding materials like cast iron and terra cotta was that it allowed the architect maximum freedom to depart from the lines of the interior structure in the facade design.

The brick and terra cotta design that was not used but that the architects reportedly preferred was much simpler. Except for the pilasters at the base and the intricate frieze of interlocking circles at the cornice, the wall surfaces here were almost completely flat. Only the corner tower and the rope moldings of the windows provided relief on the facades. Unlike earlier State Street "palaces," notably the recently completed Marshall Field Annex at Wabash and Washington, designed by the D. H. Burnham Company, or even Holabird & Roche's own Venetian Building, the terra cotta and brick facade was apparently not intended to look like stone. In its simplicity and very low relief this scheme seems to serve as an important link between the heavy cast iron facades of midcentury and the kind of light, elegant facades that would come to the fore in designs by Holabird & Roche and by Louis Sullivan at the turn of the century.

Champlain

The curious case of a third Holabird & Roche building, the Champlain (cat. no. 215), 1892–95, provides an even more vivid glimpse into the search for a new image for the shopping street. A ninety-nine-year leasehold for this site was obtained about 1890 by the Chicago Leasehold Trustees, another Massachusetts trust again set up by Owen Aldis and including the Brookses and Bryan Lathrop. This time, in addition to the developers, William Holabird and Martin Roche both invested in the scheme.[9] The architects had secured a permit in 1891 during the scramble to obtain permits before the city passed its height restrictions. The *Economist* of 10 September 1892 carried a report on the intended structure. It was to be sixteen stories high, of fully fireproofed steel frame construction with all the latest features. But in one aspect it would be extraordinary. According to the paper,

> The most important innovation will be the use of thin plates of aluminum
> for both the State Street and the Madison Street front, the metal to have
> a slight alloy which will give it a pleasant gold color. The material is
> called aluminum bronze, although it is different from any aluminum
> bronze heretofore produced. The architectural conception of the facade is
> that of a metallic construction representing the metal construction within.
> It has never heretofore been practicable to carry out this idea of representing on the front of a "modern" building what the building was, that is
> to say a structure of metal. This will be the first time in the history of architecture that aluminum is used for the exterior of a building, and it is

sure to command great attention all over the world. The metal has been used to a considerable extent in the Monadnock Block and the Woman's Temple in this city for interior work, such as railings, elevator cabs, letter boxes, etc., but never has it been used, save in some petty way, on the outside. Very careful study has been made of this subject by Holabird & Roche, architects of the Trustees' Building, Aldis, Aldis & Northcote, the agents, and the George A. Fuller Company, the well known builders, and it is found that the metal meets all the requirements of the case. It will not oxidize, it is easy to keep clean, provision has been made for any contraction or expansion by changes in temperature, and of the beauty of the metal as it will appear in the structure there can be no question.

The article went on to state that the building would have as much glass as possible. Each window was to consist of two sheets of plate glass eleven feet long, joined at the center with a thin strip of aluminum. To each side would be a smaller operable window two to three feet wide. This would have created "Chicago windows" twenty-five feet wide. The writer continued:

> The two fronts of this building will present a beautiful surface of aluminum bronze and plate glass. There will be three columns on the State Street front and four on Madison Street, running up the entire height of the building, the metal of these columns being in ornate and pleasing forms, developing at the cornice into interlacing palm leaves. A few difficulties of minor consequence were encountered in elaborating these plans, but it is believed that they have all been overcome. Provision has been made for convenient access to these large windows for the purpose of washing and also for keeping the metal surface clear of soot. The window frames will be covered with gold leaf and the radiators within the building, which, owing to the large amount of glass, will be visible from the outside, will be gilded and present a pleasing appearance. One of the great advantages of this lavish use of plate glass will be in the fact that merchants can have immense signs on the window if they choose. One pane of glass will take a sign twenty-two feet long and as broad as may be desired.

It is not surprising that this announcement created considerable controversy. The building as described, with its enormous windows and gold metal frame, would have been astonishing in a city still dominated by heavy masonry piles. The writer of the

10.10 (opposite) *Champlain Building (215), 1894–95, northwest corner of State and Madison Streets, exterior view looking northwest with buildings of the Boston Store visible on both sides. Photograph by Barnes-Crosby. Chicago Historical Society Prints and Photographs Department, ICHi-19240.*

197

article, realizing that the project might not be taken seriously, reminded his readers that the developers, architects, and contractors were all among the most sober and serious men of affairs in the city. It was taken seriously by the professional community. Criticism arrived from as far away as London, where the scheme was attacked by a writer in the London-based magazine the *Builder*. The well-known American critic Barr Ferree responded in the pages of the American journal *Engineering Magazine* defending the scheme. It is not clear why this project was dropped, but by March 1893 the *Inland Architect* reported that the building had been redesigned and would have terra cotta fronts. It is not clear how much else in the design was changed, but the move away from the gold metal frame removed the most arresting aspect of the scheme. The later, more conventional design was carried out, and the building, which, like the Venetian, housed professional offices and shops, was finished in 1895.

The Champlain Building was still far from ordinary. The use of flat white terra cotta for the exterior surfaces above the first two floors was considered quite a novelty. In the Rookery and Tacoma Buildings exterior terra cotta was always a dark color resembling brownstone or granite. In the Venetian it had been buff, probably resembling sandstone or limestone. White tiles and brick, often with a glazed finish, were not unknown. They were common in kitchens and bathrooms and were used extensively in hospitals and other institutional buildings, which needed smooth, shiny surfaces that were easily cleaned. Thus they had long been associated with cleanliness and health. They also were used in the courtyards of large office buildings such as the Rookery, to increase the light entering the offices. To use a flat white material on a large scale on the exterior of a building, however, was startling. Perhaps the influence of the 1893 World's Fair made architects eager to try white facades in the city.

The experience of the Champlain proved that white unglazed terra cotta was not the answer. Although there were some positive comments, it seems the general reaction to the Champlain's cladding was highly negative. Witness the remarks in the *Brickbuilder* of June 1895:

> On State Street, nearly opposite the "Columbus," stands the "Cham-
> plain." . . . Above the first two (black iron on brown terra cotta) stories
> the fronts are a dead white terra cotta, with such an effect that the first syl-
> lable of "Champlain" has been replaced with a word usually represented
> by a blank. The building is offensively plain to incite such profanity.[10]

None of the three buildings mentioned so far—the Venetian, the State Safety, and the Champlain—survived to become a landmark structure along State Street. Each of the three suffered an early demise, a fate not uncommon for retail buildings.

The Champlain, finished in 1905, went down in 1915, and the State Safety—finished the same year—disappeared in 1911, both so their sites could be reused for larger retail structures. The Venetian survived World War II but came down not long after. Even though these buildings have not loomed large in architectural histories, however, they did play a crucial role in crystallizing a number of ideas about the type and appearance of buildings that would dominate State Street for the next several decades. The primary idea, that a building devoted to retail sales or professional offices needed large, open floors flooded with light, could no longer be expressed on the exterior by heavy walls of dark masonry and by arched, gabled, turreted, and mansarded fronts. The three Holabird & Roche buildings and the three facade materials used on them demonstrate the architects' and owners' search for a new formula. In each case a new, manufactured product with low relief ornament was used in a way that started to negate the classical idea of the facade as an expression of the vertical columns carrying horizontal entablatures. Instead, in each case thin, nearly flat panels seemed to form a series of "picture frames" for the building's windows, focusing attention on the merchandise inside or the lettering on the windows. All that was missing now was an ideal material for these panels.

Reliance Building

It was in the upper portion of the Reliance Building, constructed in 1895 at State Street, that the firm of D. H. Burnham introduced for the first time on the exterior of a major building the material that seemed to provide just the qualities Holabird & Roche had been looking for. That material was again terra cotta, but this time it had a marvelously lustrous creamy white glaze.[11] The program of the Reliance, similar to that of Holabird & Roche's Venetian and Champlain, was to house shops and professional offices. The building was originally designed by John Root, but only the lower floors were constructed. When the project was revived after a hiatus, Charles Atwood of the Burnham Company redesigned the building's upper floors with huge rippling bays of windows, only the smallest unglazed area remaining between them. What little wall surface remained was almost entirely covered with a very low relief ornament loosely based on motifs from the Gothic era executed in the new terra cotta produced by the Northwestern Terra Cotta Company.

Despite the reputation the building has gained through the work of modernist historians, it probably did not impress many architects of the day. It was not particularly large or dramatic, and its upper stories rested somewhat incongruously on a base of quite different character that had been designed by John Root and constructed in the earlier building campaign. Charles E. Jenkins, writing about the building in the *Architectural Record,* probably echoed the judgment of many observers at the time. "It is hardly to be supposed that even the designer will consider it a masterpiece," Jenkins wrote. The cladding material, on the other hand, Jenkins believed, would make it "stand out as a conspicuous mark in the history of architecture in America." He believed the material might lead to a successful new architectural streetscape.[12]

A shining white surface had long been associated with the glistening marble of antique monuments, as the 1893 World's Fair had reminded every Chicagoan. The possibility of white walls in a very dark and dirty downtown must have been especially appealing. The most extravagant claims were made for the material, moreover. It was thought to be extremely durable, impervious to moisture and stains, and easily washed to remove any sooty buildup. Unfortunately, as it turned out, these claims were not justified, but this was not known at the turn of the century.[13] About 1900 white glazed terra cotta seemed to be the material of the future. When building resumed after the downturn of the mid-1890s, Holabird & Roche and its clients specified it again and again in buildings all around the city.

The Mandel Annex

The firm made its first really large-scale use of white glazed terra cotta at the Central Trading Company Building (cat. no. 291), constructed in 1900–1901 just off State Street at the northwest corner of Wabash Avenue and Madison Street. This building was occupied at its completion by the Mandel Brothers store, an important State Street retail operation. The building, even though it was larger than the Mandels' existing buildings to the west along Madison and to the north along Wabash, was used as an annex with the anticipation that the State Street frontage would eventually be rebuilt.

The Mandel Annex initially occupied a relatively small lot measuring 64 feet by 150. Nine stories in height, it consisted of three bays on Wabash and seven on Madison. In 1905 the building was enlarged by a three-bay expansion to the north, eleven stories high, that matched the old structure exactly. At the same time Holabird & Roche removed the cornice of the old structure, added two stories, and replaced the cornice at the top to create a uniform structure eleven stories high, extending six bays along Wabash and seven along Madison. This kind of staged construction, sometimes anticipated, often not, was extremely common in Holabird & Roche's retail buildings. It involved some ingenious maneuvering. On the level of functional demands it usually involved keeping part of a building operating, with all of the heating plant and elevators functioning, while the new work was being done. On an aesthetic level, it required

10.11

Central Trading Company Building (Mandel Brothers Annex) (291), 1900–1901, northwest corner of Wabash Avenue and Madison Street, advertisement showing Holabird & Roche building at right in 1901 and 1905 views. From Jones, A Half Century of Chicago Building, *1910.*

that both the original facade and one stretched to totally different proportions look balanced and finished. One of the major reasons Holabird & Roche preferred simple, repetitive facade treatments on its commercial buildings was to simplify this process as much as possible.

At the Mandel Annex the steel columns and beams at the exterior of the building were clad, as they had been in the Reliance, in a thin covering of creamy white terra cotta. Between the columns, each of the wide, horizontal bays was almost entirely filled with glass. On the typical floor the windows were of the "Chicago window" type with a fixed central panel flanked on each side by an operable double-hung sash window.

The upper floors were recessed slightly behind the lower two floors. At first glance this is surprising, since it sacrificed floor space in the upper floors and produced an awkward disjunction between the bottom and top of the building. It is likely that it was done to allow for a novel feature. By cantilevering the building's outer enclosure

10.12
*Central Trading Company
Building (Mandel Brothers
Annex), detail of exterior.
Photograph by Robert
Bruegmann, 1995.*

several feet out from the structural columns at the lower two floors, Holabird & Roche was able to go even further than it had gone at the Tacoma in creating a nearly complete glass wall. At the Mandel Annex the nearly continuous strip of glass rose a full two stories, uninterrupted by columns and divided by only the narrowest mullions. This created the most extensive display windows in the city, not only at the sidewalk level but on the second floor, where they would have been highly visible to the thousands of riders of the trains on the Union Loop Elevated tracks that had been constructed along Wabash Avenue just a few years earlier in 1897.[14]

At the same time the Mandel Annex was under construction, another department store structure immediately across Madison Street was going up with a similar terra cotta cladding. This was the first unit of Louis Sullivan's celebrated Schlesinger and Mayer store (Carson Pirie Scott).[15] The two buildings, both standing and in good condition today, provide an interesting comparison. Their upper floors are surprisingly similar. Both are clad in creamy white glazed terra cotta framing huge rectangular windows. Both employ intricate patterns of low relief ornament to give life to the surface. In many ways both are the logical culmination of the experiments of Holabird & Roche and others over the preceding decade.

But the buildings also clearly betray different aspirations. The Mandel Annex is more straightforward. Here the window frames are surrounded by hundreds of tiny dentil- like moldings that, though in low relief, cast sharp shadows, giving the wall

10.13
Carson Pirie Scott store, 1900, 1903, southeast corner
of Madison and State Streets, architect Louis Sullivan,
detail of exterior. Photograph by Robert Bruegmann,
1995.

considerable texture. These moldings create elaborate frames for the windows, separating them from the smooth wall surfaces, a distinction emphasized by a rope molding just at the point where the wall plane meets the window reveal. At the top of the first two floors and again at the main cornice, the ornament becomes most concentrated, with a frieze of interlocking bands creating circle and quatrefoil motifs, the whole capped by a richly bracketed cornice. Energetic lions on baroque shields anchor the upper corners. The thickening of the ornamental treatment at the edge is minimal, however. The result is that the entire building looks like an extrusion of a single unit, the window bay. It could have been made higher or lower, wider or less wide by adding more units, as indeed it was.

Sullivan, on the other hand, followed a more idiosyncratic and personal path. Recent research has shown that he actually started with the idea of using white marble for his facades but, probably for reasons of economy, replaced the marble with terra cotta.[16] Despite the substitution, Sullivan took care to detail the terra cotta pieces so they resembled finely cut ashlar. The idea that Sullivan was creating a marble palace also accounts for the pronounced division into base, main body, and entablature. At the top of his building he recessed the top floor and cantilevered the main cornice over it in a dramatic way, making of this floor a kind of loggia. At the base the creamy terra cotta abruptly gives way to a spectacular tangle of decorative iron foliage painted in lush greens and reds to imitate old bronze. In the middle, in the main body of the building, Sullivan created a very flat wall with the ornament concentrated at a few key points. Instead of surrounding the windows with frames as Holabird & Roche had done, Sullivan made his ornament shallower in relief and concentrated it in narrow strips on the wall and in bands in the window reveals, emphasizing their depth, again suggesting that Sullivan was unwilling to lose the bulk of a masonry wall. Although treating the wall as if it were masonry was perhaps more conventional than the treatment by Holabird & Roche, the ornament itself is much less conventional, with tight, intricate tendrils in a kinetic, almost syncopated pattern, looking from the ground somewhat like a series of starbursts in a darker field.

The two buildings reflect profoundly different points of view. Sullivan here, as elsewhere, was concerned above all with expressing himself through the art of architecture. Although he needed to provide properly functioning buildings for his clients, he

10.14
Central Trading Company (Mandel Brothers Annex),
detail of terra cotta cornice. From Brickbuilder, *May 1901.*

204

seems to have been personally more interested in fusing a traditional, noble building type like the palazzo with a new decorative style appropriate to America and the modern era and, not incidentally, instantly recognizable as his own. To this end he attempted to embellish buildings like the Schlesinger and Mayer with a new, highly stylized ornament, derived not from conventional historical models but from nature, although nature transformed by the human hand into repetitive forms suitable for execution in modern materials.

Holabird & Roche, on the other hand, as commercial architects, thought first and foremost about creating useful buildings. Certainly they did aspire to making these buildings beautiful, and Martin Roche was a highly sensitive and talented designer of ornament, but his approach in achieving beautiful buildings was more conventional than Sullivan's. The irony is that in many ways Holabird & Roche's more traditional decorative vocabularies applied to buildings of an entirely new scale often produced results at least as novel as Sullivan's. Roche's approach ended up giving the Mandel Brothers store a system of ornament that was less expensive, less personal, and more applicable to the problem of cladding buildings of unprecedented size. What he may have lost in spontaneity he gained in consistency and legibility by the public.

By 1900 Holabird & Roche had found a formula for the State Street commercial building. Together, the steel frame, the large plate glass window, and white glazed terra cotta proved to be a potent combination. Over the next decade and a half Holabird & Roche would use it to build thousands of square feet of retail space along State Street.

ELEVEN

THEME AND VARIATION:
THE LOFT BUILDING

A photograph made about 1900, showing the intersection of Wells Street and Monroe, forcefully conveys the character of Chicago's west Loop loft district at the turn of the century. The clarity of this print, made with a large negative and long exposure time, seems to capture with almost uncanny precision the undeviating grid of orthogonal streets, the relentless blocks of building walls rising sheer from the sidewalk, and the elevated tracks encroaching on what little open space remained in the public right-of-way.

Also called the "warehouse" or "heavy wholesaling" district, this area of the central business district, roughly between Wells Street and the south branch of the Chicago River, contained hundreds of lofts, all-purpose commercial structures with large, open floors devoted to wholesaling, warehousing, and light manufacturing operations such as clothes making or printing. Areas of this kind constituted a major part of the central business district of almost every large American city in the late nineteenth century.

The photographer probably took the shot very early in the morning so that the bases of the buildings would not be obscured by a crush of traffic and people on the streets. The photo does give a hint, in a slight blurring visible on the sidewalks and around the vehicles parked on the street, of a few early morning pedestrians and vehicles moving too quickly to leave their image on the plate but foreshadowing the frenetic activity that would soon fill the area. By the beginning of the workday thousands of employees would jostle each other on the sidewalks and the streets, joining the throng of pedestrians and dodging all manner of horse-drawn vehicles.

The photograph, made by the Barnes-Crosby Company, one of Chicago's most important architectural photographers, was probably commissioned by Holabird &

Roche to document the Williams Building (cat. no. 260), built in 1897, which occupies the center of the photograph.[1] The Williams provides an excellent example of a typical loft building at the turn of the century. Commissioned in 1897 by J. M. Williams, who had made some money in Wisconsin land, the building replaced a five-story post-Fire loft structure, occupied by wholesale jobbers of clothing and woolen goods. The old building, which had burned, probably looked very similar to the ones that survived it and are visible to the right and left of the new Holabird & Roche structure in the photograph.

The new Williams Building housed the same kind of tenants as the old structure on the site, presumably more efficiently and at higher rents. Ten stories high, this building had a complete steel frame clad in pressed brick. Above the ground level, which was suitable either for offices of the concerns occupying the floors above or for shops that catered to workers in the area, the building consisted of open floors, each containing a single large space interrupted only by the column grid, staircases, elevators, and small offices. Built at a cost of $182,822, or 10.6 cents per cubic foot, one-third of the Marquette's 33.1 cents per cubic foot, the Williams was about as simple and inexpensive as a large building in the Loop could be.

To fill in some of the action and color that are not conveyed by the photograph, one can turn to several evocative passages of Theodore Dreiser's *Sister Carrie*. In the opening pages of this novel, set in 1889, the young heroine searches for work in the "big manufacturing houses along Franklin Street and just the other side of the river."[2] Carrie finds herself walking among immense and impressive wholesale houses. "The large plates of window glass, now so common, were then rapidly coming into use," Dreiser writes, "and gave to the ground floor offices a distinguished and prosperous look. The casual wanderer could see as he passed a polished array of office fixtures, much frosted glass, clerks hard at work, and genteel business men in 'nobby' suits and clean linen lounging about or sitting in groups. Polished brass or nickel signs at the square stone entrances announced the firm and the nature of the business in rather neat and reserved terms."[3] Dreiser completes his picture by describing some of the inhabitants of the front offices and the hundreds of workers toiling above, a vast hive of human activity.

As impressive as the loft district was to Carrie, it had another side. For many of the workers in the huge upper floors, operating machinery in the close atmosphere of a stifling summer day, far from the windows, these buildings were anything but pleasant. Not only were their jobs tedious, but they were also dangerous. In textile buildings, for example, fires were frequent because of the presence of tons of flammable material, and workers were not always able to escape. As deplorable as these losses were, they seem to have been accepted as a necessary evil in the production of essential goods.

11.1

Williams Building (260), 1897–98, 205 W. Monroe Street, southwest corner of Wells Street, view to the southwest, with Leiter I Building by William Le Baron Jenney visible on the right and the tracks of the Loop elevated running along Wells Street in the foreground. Photograph by Barnes-Crosby. Chicago Historical Society Prints and Photographs Department, ICHi-19006.

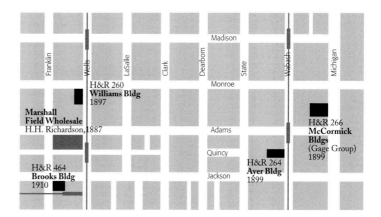

Franklin · Wells · LaSalle · Clark · Dearborn · State · Wabash · Michigan

Madison

Monroe

H&R 260
Williams Bldg
1897

**Marshall
Field Wholesale**
H.H. Richardson, 1887

Adams

H&R 266
**McCormick
Bldgs**
(Gage Group)
1899

Quincy

H&R 464
Brooks Bldg
1910

H&R 264
Ayer Bldg
1899

Jackson

11.2

Some Holabird & Roche loft buildings at the turn of the century. Map drawn by Dennis McClendon from information on fire insurance maps and other sources.

The loft building was not a place for delicate sensibilities. It was a place where necessary tasks were performed for the minimum pay per hour. It was a machine to make money.

Because they provided inexpensive space for work that needed to be performed near the center of the city but that brought very little return per square foot, little money was wasted on landscaping, open spaces, civic amenities, architectural effects, or even cleaning once the buildings were erected. In fact, if there is a single building type that might satisfy the Marxist urge to find direct translations of laissez-faire economics into metal and brick, it would be the loft building.[4] The workhorse of the nineteenth-century city, the loft building was subject to such stringent program and budget restraints that the architects had little room to experiment with design. Virtually every building rose directly from the sidewalk to precisely the height allowed by law or determined by calculations to ensure maximum return on investment. Virtually every one consisted of almost uninterrupted interior spaces lit by numerous large windows arranged in a regular pattern in the enclosing brick or terra cotta walls.[5] To view these buildings as strictly determined by function and economics, however, fails to take into account the complex and dynamic interplay between economic constraints, the vagaries of the real estate market and of architectural tastes, and the personalities of clients and architects in the late nineteenth-century city.[6] This is confirmed by even a cursory examination of the work of Holabird & Roche, Chicago's premier designer of high-quality loft structures at the end of the century. However constricting the program and budget, Holabird & Roche found it could use slight variations in window heights and spacing, window trim, stringcourses, cornices, and cladding materials to give surprising variety to the streetscape. In fact it appears that for architects like Holabird & Roche, the restrictions were congenial. The firm's loft buildings have con-

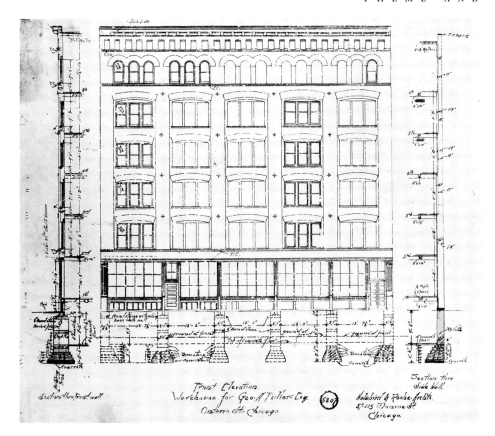

11.3
*George A. Fuller
warehouse (147),
1891, Ontario Street,
elevation and wall
sections showing "mill
construction." Chicago
Historical Society
Architectural
Collections.*

sistently been ranked with the best of its work, and within a very narrow range they provide a staggering wealth of inventive design.

Development of the Chicago Loft

Loft districts were a result of the increasing segregation of the country's central business districts into zones. In the early years of Chicago a jumble of buildings by the edge of the main branch of the Chicago River accommodated virtually all of the city's commercial functions as well as civic and government activities. With the growing size and complexity of the city's economy around midcentury, the central business district grew and segregated itself out. By the time of the Fire, retail uses occupied State Street and the streets adjacent to it, while the most prestigious office buildings and govern-

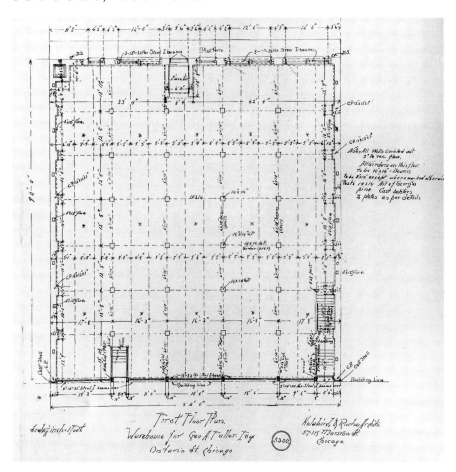

11.4
George A. Fuller
warehouse, plan.
Chicago Historical Society
Architectural Collections.

ment buildings were found along Dearborn and LaSalle a few blocks to the west.[7] Light manufacturing, wholesaling, and warehousing were relegated to the periphery of the central business district where cheaper land was available, especially the heavy wholesaling district west of Wells Street.

The basic idea of the loft was that it was cheap, generic space. The drive for economy produced an interesting succession of structural innovations. The earliest lofts were usually constructed with brick walls on the exterior and on the interior a system of slow burning heavy wood columns and beams called mill construction. This proved to be a very efficient way of building, and it continued to be used well into the twentieth century. A building designed by Holabird & Roche for the George A. Fuller Company provides a good example. Drawings show fourteen by fourteen inch yellow pine posts holding up six by fourteen inch pine beams, anchored at their ends by the exterior walls of load-bearing brick. For structural reasons and for fire safety, metal

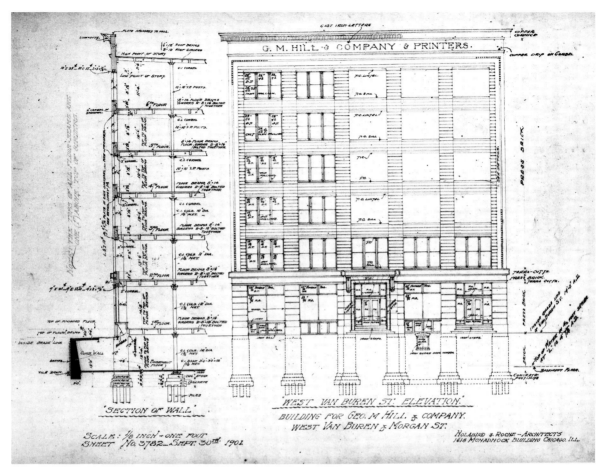

11.5

Hill Company Building (306), 1901–2, southwest corner of Morgan and Van Buren Streets, elevation and partial section showing "mill construction." Chicago Historical Society Architectural Collections.

started to replace wood for the interior framing system at midcentury. First wood posts were replaced by cast iron columns. The result was a system called semimill construction. This kind of building technique, which we encountered in the State Safety Building on State Street, is visible in drawings showing the lower floors of the George M. Hill Company in 1901 (cat. no. 306), where cast iron columns between ten and twelve inches in diameter held up pairs of eight by sixteen or eight by eighteen inch wood beams. Eventually, with prices for iron dropping, the wood beams were replaced by wrought iron ones, producing an entire interior framing system of iron. Shortly thereafter steel started to replace the iron. In all these cases the exterior walls continued to be bearing walls of masonry.

BORN BUILDING
Erected by

Alling Construction Co.
General Contractors
72 Madison Street   Chicago

11.6

Born Building (432), 1908, 540 S. Wells Street, advertisement for Alling Construction Company. From Jones, A Half Century of Chicago Building, *1910.*

From the 1890s onward, architects of more expensive lofts increasingly turned to the new all-steel skeleton framing system developed for office buildings in which both the interior loads and the exterior walls were carried on a cage of steel and a complete system of fireproofing protected the metal from fires.[8] Holabird & Roche was quick to turn to this system for its loft buildings on expensive land because it reduced the amount of valuable floor space eaten up by walls. Metal skeletal framing was the system the firm used in the Williams Building and most prominent central business district

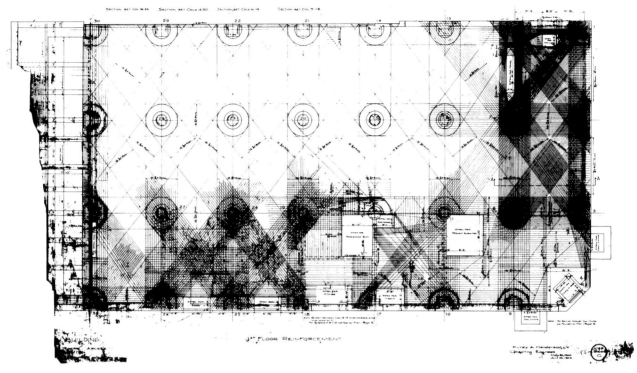

11.7
Born Building, plan of first floor concrete reinforcement. Chicago Historical Society Architectural Collections.

loft buildings thereafter, although earlier systems continued to be more practical for outlying buildings of this kind for several decades.

Finally, starting in the early twentieth century, reinforced concrete frames started to come into use. The Born Building of 1908 (cat. no. 432) constituted Holabird & Roche's first use of the material in this way.[9] Contrary to what one might expect and what modernist historians have tried to suggest actually did occur, all of these changes in structural systems seem to have had little effect on the appearance of the buildings. It is all but impossible to know whether wood, metal, or concrete lies behind the walls of a Holabird & Roche loft building. As we saw in the case of the proposal for a metal facade for the Champlain Building, Holabird & Roche was not averse to expressing on the exterior of the building the framing system within, but it appears that in the case of the Champlain it was an attempt to give a prominent building on State Street a specific marketable imagery. It appears that for most building types the course of action seen at the Born Building, in which the structural system was quite independent of the facade treatment, was more typical.

The Barnes-Crosby photograph gives a good idea of the changes in exterior appearance of the Chicago loft from the Fire to the end of the century. The structures visible on each side of the Williams Building in the photo were almost certainly constructed immediately after the Fire and illustrate the type that was common throughout the 1860s and early 1870s. Five or six stories high, they range in style from the relatively simple brick wall of the building to the immediate left of the Williams to the much more opulent facade, probably cast iron, immediately to its right.

At the extreme right of the photograph is the slightly blurred image of the first Leiter Building designed by William Le Baron Jenney and constructed in 1879 while all three of the original Holabird & Roche partners were still in his employ. As we have seen, this building was an early example of a nearly complete skeleton.[10] In exterior appearance the Leiter Building, with its very large double-hung sash windows set between relatively narrow mullions, is both simpler and more open than the immediate post-Fire lofts in the photograph. What little ornament the Leiter I has consists of highly simplified, lightly incised panels that generally reinforce visually the building's rectilinear structure. The brick corner columns, for example, are interrupted at every floor level by pieces of cut stone that mark the level at which, behind the masonry envelope, the horizontal beams tie into the exterior walls. The cast iron mullions protrude slightly at the base and top, which again emphasizes structure, this time by producing a visual compression at the critical juncture of horizontal and vertical elements. Jenney's building was almost a diagram of an efficient structural system.[11]

Jenney's was not the only model Holabird & Roche could have used for its loft buildings, however. Throughout the history of the building type, there were attempts to introduce more pretentious stylistic elements. These were usually short-lived. In the 1880s many loft buildings sported adaptations of the Romanesque style introduced by the Boston architect H. H. Richardson. Architects in Chicago needed only to travel to the west Loop warehouse district to see the wholesale store Richardson designed in 1885 for Marshall Field. Perhaps the most magnificent loft building ever constructed, it inspired countless imitations.[12] Holabird & Roche, for example, used this mode for a six-story commercial building on Harrison Street between Dearborn and Plymouth Court that it designed for Chicago businessman Wirt D. Walker (cat. no. 54) about 1888. For most loft buildings the expense of using large stones, elaborate cornices, and arched windows—which not only were more expensive to build but admitted less light than simple rectangular windows of the same height—could not be justified. For this reason the Romanesque tended to be used only on the more conspicuous loft buildings of the 1880s and soon went out of fashion.

By the end of the nineteenth century most large loft buildings in the central business district designed by Holabird & Roche or any other architect consisted of eight to twelve floors with large, open interior spaces wrapped in minimal exterior walls with huge sheets of plate glass set between panels of brick or terra cotta. The facades had minimal detailing, usually concentrated around the doorway and at the top of the building, although they were enlivened in a more ephemeral manner by a profusion of lettered signs in the windows advertising the businesses within.

Once a solution to the problem of the loft building was found, few architects felt it necessary to alter the formula, at least until World War I, when the program for industrial spaces started to change dramatically. Holabird & Roche turned out dozens of buildings like the Williams, with small and highly interesting variations. Although they were conceived as "background buildings," these structures were almost without exception carefully composed and in a few cases really inspired pieces of work. Three sets of Holabird & Roche loft structures demonstrate the diversity that was possible within the narrow constraints imposed by the building program.

The McCormick Buildings

Besides the heavy wholesale district in the west part of Chicago's central business district, there was a loft district in the south Loop around "Printers' Row" on Dearborn Street and another on the Near North Side west of Wells Street reaching from just north of the Chicago River to Chicago Avenue.[13] The exact boundaries of these districts were never precise, since loft buildings were often built in areas that were otherwise devoted to retail or office uses, and other building types were often found in the loft districts. The loft building itself was so versatile, moreover, that it could be used for virtually any purpose, so that the distinctions could blur between the loft building and modest structures designed specifically for office or retail use.

In fact these distinctions often were deliberately blurred, as with a set of Holabird & Roche loft buildings on Michigan Avenue. The McCormick Buildings (cat. no. 266; known today as the Gage Group) at Michigan Avenue north of Monroe Street were developed in 1898–99 by various members of the McCormick family for three wholesale millinery businesses, all previously on Wabash Avenue. All three business concerns—Theodore Ascher and Company, the Edson Keith Company, and Gage Brothers and Company—intended to use the ground floor to exhibit goods and the upper floors for their manufacture. It might seem strange today that manufacturing was considered an appropriate use of land on what is today an elegant boulevard with magnificent views out to Grant Park, but at the turn of the century the major improvements that would transform the area east of Michigan Avenue from railroad yards and raw landfill into Grant Park had barely started, and the stretch of Michigan Avenue just south of the river was anything but a high-rent district.

11.8

McCormick Buildings (Gage Group) (266), 1898–99, 18–28 S. Michigan Avenue, Holabird & Roche, architects, Louis Sullivan designer of facade for 18 S. Michigan (twelve stories at right). At far right, Chicago Athletic Club (Henry Ives Cobb, 1893). At left, McCormick Building (ca. 1885) and adjacent low structure are future site of University Club. Detail of photograph, ca. 1902–5, Chicago Historical Society Prints and Photographs Department, ICHi-00986.

In the original Holabird & Roche design, all three McCormick Buildings were to have had extremely simple elevations with huge windows and nearly unornamented brick piers and spandrels. This design was carried out and can still be seen today on the southern two buildings on the site. These are among the most deceptively simple facades ever produced in Chicago. At first glance they appear to be nothing more than the unadorned construction itself, but it is only necessary to go around to the rear, alley elevation to see what actual unadorned construction would look like. Here a wall of Chicago common brick is opened by large, standard double-hung windows in a somewhat irregular pattern that accommodates the stairs, toilets, and other functions behind the wall. This was the most direct and least expensive way to enclose a building.

Holabird & Roche's front facade, on the other hand, could have been accomplished only with considerable artifice. What at first appears to be a flat wall with large window openings turns out to be a highly modulated surface. Framed in elaborate surrounds composed of multiple moldings, the vertical tiers of windows become the most prominent feature of the facade. Because these frames spill over onto the area of the vertical piers, they tend to lock pier and window together in an accelerated vertical pattern, but by cutting across the horizontal spandrel panels and window sills, they produce a tight, interlocking system and a dynamic visual play of light and shadow across the entire surface.

The seemingly simple Holabird & Roche facade was not enough for the Gage brothers, who were to occupy the northernmost of the buildings. They wanted something more obviously "artistic." They convinced the McCormicks to engage Louis Sullivan to design their facade. The magazine *Brickbuilder* of December 1899 explained: "The firm of Gage Bros. and Co. . . . offered to pay additional rent at the same percentage on the increased cost of employing Mr. Sullivan and erecting such a front as he should design. They did so because they thought it would benefit their business in an equal degree. They put an exact commercial value on Mr. Sullivan's art, otherwise he would not have been called in." The exact commercial value of Sullivan's art was apparently $2,500—the amount subtracted from Holabird & Roche's architectural fees to pay Sullivan—plus the added cost of construction, which would probably have been minimal.

This quotation provides excellent testimony about the role of architecture, art, and business in turn of the century Chicago. It is apparent that for the Gage brothers art was something extra, something that could literally be added to mere construction, in this case onto a building that had already been designed. The needs of the program had to be met first. After that, a certain amount of art could be applied because art had a commercial value. Although few Chicago architects of the era would have totally accepted this proposition, they were loath to contradict their clients on the matter because they knew this was a way they could place their own work firmly within the context of the principles that businessmen believed regulated the marketing of any product or service. It was this willingness to stress the compatibility of art and business rather than their points of conflict that perhaps most clearly distinguished Chicago commercial architects from the most famous of their East Coast colleagues.

At the McCormick Buildings Louis Sullivan explored a route quite different from that taken by Holabird & Roche in reconciling art and business. Existing drawings of the northernmost of the McCormick structures suggest that Sullivan worked directly over elevations prepared by the Holabird & Roche draftsmen. This, together with the record of Holabird & Roche's payment to Sullivan for the work, suggests he must

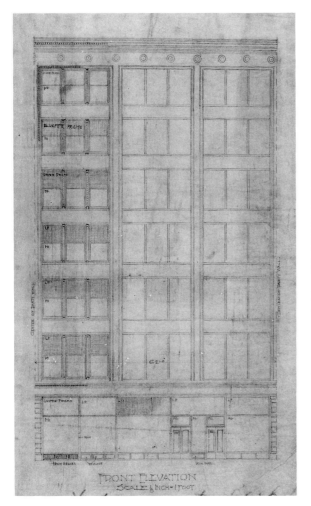

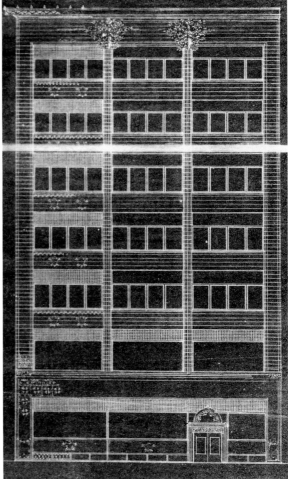

11.9

McCormick Buildings (Gage Group), elevation of 18 S. Michigan as drawn by Holabird & Roche. Chicago Historical Society Architectural Collections.

11.10

McCormick Buildings (Gage Group), print of drawing by Louis Sullivan over elevation by Holabird & Roche for 18 S. Michigan. Chicago Historical Society Architectural Collections.

have worked very closely with the Holabird & Roche organization, probably in the Holabird & Roche office itself, as what would today be called a "design consultant." There is every indication that Sullivan's additions were done with the firm's full cooperation and approval, and it is almost certain that Holabird & Roche prepared the actual working drawings and supervised construction of the entire project.

In his drawings Sullivan transformed the facade. Where Holabird & Roche had specified red brick and terra cotta, the ordinary materials of loft buildings, Sullivan

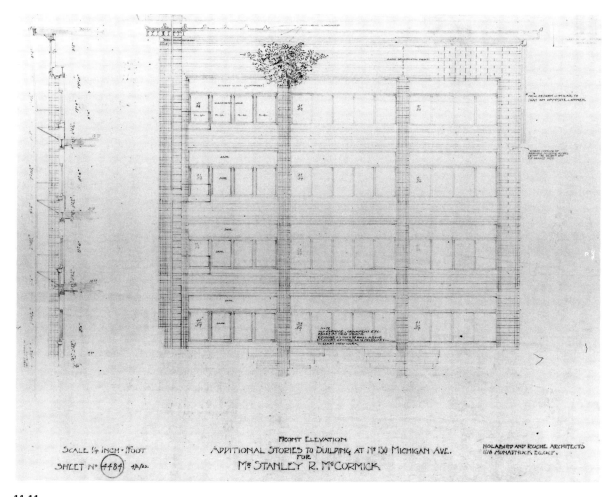

11.11

McCormick Buildings (Gage Group), pencil drawing by Louis Sullivan over elevation by Holabird & Roche for 18 S. Michigan.
Chicago Historical Society Architectural Collections.

specified a pale terra cotta that he probably thought of as akin to marble.[14] Where Holabird & Roche's facade was composed of flat wall planes articulated by relatively simple moldings, Sullivan seems to have been driven to ornament every surface and to enrich every element. What had been sills with simple dentil moldings in the Holabird & Roche facade become a composition of blind arches. Where Holabird & Roche used simple terra cotta blocks to define the window heads, Sullivan created an elaborate latticework in low relief.

The greatest transformation came in the area of the piers. Left as flat surfaces between the window frames in the Holabird & Roche elevations, in the Sullivan facade they were converted into a sharply profiled strip that looks a little like the clustered colonnettes in the nave arcade of Gothic churches. Here this added to the piers' vertical rush to their termination above the top windows in an explosion of swirling foliage that pushed out over both the columns and the parapet wall at the top of the building, contrasting dramatically with the regularity and rectilinearity of the rest of the elevation. Sullivan's ornament, barely indicated on drawings with a few strokes of a hard pencil, looks almost like a sketch of a tree or plant rather than part of the underlying elevation drawing that had been laid out with precise, hard-edged, evenly weighted lines by Holabird & Roche draftsmen. The Sullivan additions are obviously freehand, suggesting the lines of the ornament by a nervous calligraphy. It seems that Sullivan's goal was to emphasize the hand-wrought character of the terra cotta rather than the repetitive, mass-produced impression so apparent in the Holabird & Roche drawings.

The Holabird & Roche and Sullivan facades at the McCormick Buildings provide an even more direct example of the complex relation between commercial architecture and art architecture than the comparison of the Mandel Annex and the Schlesinger and Mayer store discussed in the previous chapter. In the Holabird & Roche facades the art is disguised as utility. It appears to be nothing more than the bare minimum, although it actually entailed a lot of artifice. Sullivan's artistic version, on the other hand, like the work of many contemporary designers of the aesthetic movement in Britain or art nouveau in continental Europe, sets up patterns deliberately in opposition to what appear to be the functional elements of the building. Some observers believed, in fact, that Sullivan had compromised the utility of the structure with his interventions.[15] It seems unlikely that he was actually protesting utility or business. It is more probable that for him, as for the owners, art just represented a higher kind of utility. Art, whether for its advertising value or as a civilizing element in the city, simply had different purposes, he might have said. For the owners, this utility could be measured in increased rents. It is harder to gauge how Sullivan would have judged success. It appears that, whatever its public function, it also had a private function. It is likely that this wild and irregular tangle of ornament represented for him a therapeutic act, freeing him, the viewer, or the occupant from the constraining regularity of business and life and allowing the usually repressed emotional side to burst through. Perhaps the most curious thing about the McCormick Buildings is the way each of the two facade treatments maintains an integrity of its own while coexisting surprisingly well with the other part of the complex. It also provides an excellent side-by-side comparison between two quite different approaches to design in Chicago at the turn of the century.

The Ayer (McClurg) Building

At the same time Holabird & Roche was engaged with the McCormick Buildings, the firm was also doing designs for a site two blocks south and one block west on Wabash Avenue for Boston developer Frederick Ayer. Unlike the McCormick Buildings, the Ayer Building (cat. no. 264; more commonly called by its later name, the McClurg) was designed without major tenants lined up, but soon after completion A. C. McClurg and Company, booksellers, took over most of the space. This was entirely in keeping with the character of this part of Wabash. Whereas the street farther north by Washington and Randolph was dominated by the rear facades of the major department store complexes that extended across the alley from State, farther south, between Van Buren and Madison, Wabash provided a haven for smaller and more specialized retailers, especially those selling books and music. This character was due in part to the presence of the Loop elevated railroad, which made access easy but depressed rentals by darkening the sidewalks and periodically drowning out conversations with the roar of passing trains.

The interior arrangements of the Ayer Building were typical. Almost the entire space on most floors was open, interrupted only by a double row of columns. The space was lit only at the street front and the rear, meaning that although the windows were enormous, the central part must have remained fairly dark. The first floor, the area most frequented by customers, held showcases and a reading room as well as the old books department. Above this on the second floor were areas for clerks and salesmen and stock bins. On the third floor were sample tables. The McClurg Company probably rented out the floors above this but reserved the top floors for its offices, a lunchroom, and an area for engraving and printing. A small addition on the roof was occupied by the darkroom, print room, and other facilities of a photographer named Cox.

The facade of this small building has attracted attention quite out of proportion to its size. For example, Peter Bonnett Wight, Chicago's foremost critic at the turn of the century, wrote:

> In design the front is an illustration of what Holabird & Roche have so often done before,—showing that when windows much wider than their height set horizontal mass in opposition to vertical lines, the application of such a treatment in the high building problem gives more satisfaction to the eye than any other that has been attempted. The simplicity and refinement of detail in this street front is another illustration of the tendencies of architectural design at Chicago, especially where terra-cotta is used.[16]

11.12
*Ayer (McClurg) Building (264),
1898–99, 218–24 S. Wabash Avenue,
perspective drawing. Chicago Historical
Society Architectural Collections.*

11.13
*Ayer (McClurg)
Building, view of
building from east.
Photograph from
William T. Barnum
collection, Chicago
Historical Society
Prints and
Photographs
Department,
ICHi-23057.*

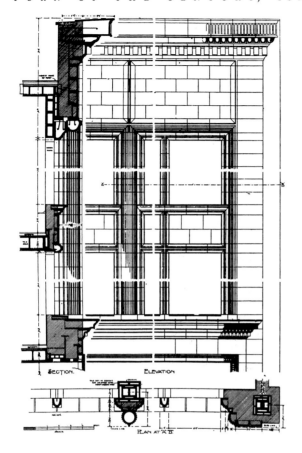

11.14

Ayer (McClurg) Building, elevation, section, and plan of wall details. From Brickbuilder, *February 1899.*

11.15

Ayer (McClurg) Building, detail of facade. Photograph by Robert Bruegmann, 1996.

Of all Holabird & Roche's simple loft buildings, this is the one that has been most consistently praised.[17] At first glance this is difficult to explain, since the Ayer facade, like that of the McCormick Buildings, is simplicity itself, hardly anything more than large windows and narrow piers and spandrels. Indeed, the desirability of lighting the very deep floors in this era before electric lighting was perfected and widely used made such a disposition necessary, and it can be seen on dozens of buildings of the era. As much as any building by Holabird & Roche, the Ayer might seem to be a case where the steel skeleton was covered as simply and with as little material as possible, revealing the underlying steel frame to a maximum extent. This was the opinion of at least one critic in the British magazine the *Brickbuilder*.[18]

A closer inspection reveals that, as with the nearly contemporary McCormick Buildings, it is not the simplicity that is most interesting but the effect of richness the architects were able to create with very little material. A glance at the drawings shows that in this case the terra cotta covering of the pier is quite complex in profile. It projects sharply forward, convex and fluted on both sides, culminating in the center in a sharp flat ridge. Although it is very thin, this fact is not obvious when the piers are viewed very obliquely, as they almost always must be on a street with so little space between the building and the elevated tracks.

Not only does the fluting create distinct shadows, giving the piers weight and solidity, but the profile creates the illusion that they are much wider than they really are, perhaps suggesting fully detached columns. Even without the rich cornice, which used to project sharply against the sky, the facade as a whole creates a feel completely different from the flat, repetitive appearance of many nearby buildings. Its success, like that of the Marquette, has undoubtedly been due to the fact that observers can see it as either a highly abstracted temple front or a simple abstract grid. Thus it has been able to please those who have read the facade as a classical building and also those who have chosen to see in it a prefiguration of minimal modernism.

Brooks Building

The Brooks Building (cat. no. 464), built in 1909–10 at the corner of Jackson and Franklin for the Brooks brothers of Boston, provides a fitting conclusion to the story of Holabird & Roche and the loft building. Although it was built nearly ten years after the examples discussed above and may well have seemed something of an anachronism at the time of its completion, it was almost interchangeable in its general lines with the loft buildings Holabird & Roche designed at the turn of the century. It was also very similar to many other structures in the loft district, and it garnered little special attention in its day.

It is nevertheless one of Holabird & Roche's most satisfying designs. Above the bottom two floors, clad in pale terra cotta and largely opened in expansive sheets of glass, are small colored terra cotta plaques that provide a preview of the ornamental scheme at the top of the building. Between these plaques and the upper portions of the structure, the middle section of the building is completely regular, each bay filled with three huge windows occupying all the space between the columns, which are treated like clustered colonnettes. One highly successful device used here was dividing the spandrel panel between windows into three parts, echoing the window arrangement and creating an insistent rhythm of verticals up the facade. The cladding used for

11.16

Brooks Building (464), 1909–10, 223 W. Jackson Boulevard, southeast corner of Franklin Street, exterior view.
Photograph from "Brooks Building—Chicago" rental brochure, ca. 1925. Chicago Historical Society Library.

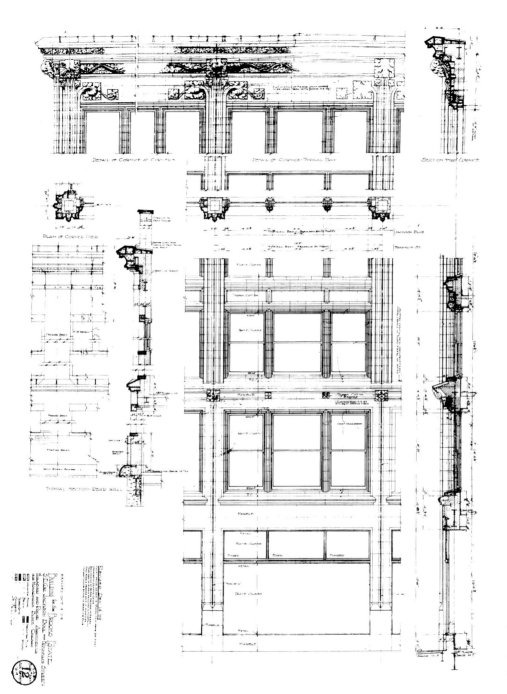

11.17
Brooks Building,
sections, elevations,
plans of terra cotta
cladding. Chicago
Historical Society
Architectural
Collections.

11.18

Aerial view of Chicago central business district looking from southwest showing the Brooks Building, labeled no. 1 in photograph. From "Brooks Building—Chicago," rental brochure, ca. 1925. Chicago Historical Society Library.

this section is a handsome buff terra cotta with darker speckles creating an appearance somewhere between granite and tortoise shell.

The great surprise in the Brooks Building comes at the very top. Just above the termination of the windows on the twelfth floor, the colonnettes split apart and flow into leafy forms in the frieze, recalling the work of Louis Sullivan at the McCormick

Buildings and elsewhere. This foliage is strictly contained in rectilinear blocks, however, creating a tension between the sinuous curves of the leaves and the rectilinear plaques within which they are constrained. All of this is juxtaposed with the rich dark green terra cotta used to form the background of the frieze. The result is like a series of stylized trees spreading their branches at the very top of the building but contained by the windows below and the cornice above. Whereas Sullivan allowed his organic forms to overflow their rectilinear frames, Holabird & Roche subordinated the foliage to the geometric discipline of the plaques. This hint of foliage, unexpected in a very businesslike corner of the Loop, must have been highly refreshing. As with many of its loft buildings, Holabird & Roche was able, with the most modest of means, to give the building a distinctly patrician image unique among the tightly serried ranks of the loft district.

This cityscape did not last long. By the 1920s, loft buildings in the city core had already started to become functionally obsolete as assembly lines and other adjacency requirements made lower buildings with larger floor plates more efficient. The land for these was available primarily away from the city center, preferably with easy access to the highways leading out of town. Because this development coincided with a boom in downtown office activity, many modest loft buildings on the west flank of the Loop were torn down or converted to office use. Its refined elegance made the Brooks Building particularly well suited to this transformation.

The switch from light manufacturing to office work allowed the district to persist well into the post–World War II era with relatively little change. As late as the 1960s entire blocks of Wells and Franklin Streets still maintained their early twentieth-century appearance. The demolitions required for vastly larger buildings since the 1960s, notably the Sears Tower, opened major holes in the rows of loft buildings, but even into the early 1980s the viewer looking south from the corner of Jackson and Franklin would have seen a strikingly intact set of loft buildings. It has been only in the past few years that many of these have come down, leaving the Brooks Building as a poignant reminder of the city's great loft era.[19]

TWELVE

TERRA COTTA ON STATE STREET:
THE DEPARTMENT STORE AND
THE TALL SHOPS BUILDING

In no part of Chicago has the cumulative effect of Holabird & Roche's work been stronger than along State Street, Chicago's major retail thoroughfare. After its initial experimentation in the 1890s,[1] Holabird & Roche was ready to become, starting in the early years of the twentieth century, the most important source of designs for the street. With millions of square feet of retail space to its credit by the outset of World War I, Holabird & Roche completed the transformation of the street begun in the 1890s. To this day a surprising amount of street frontage designed by the firm between 1900 and the First World War survives, and it is in large part these buildings that give State Street its distinctive appearance, so different from other streets in the Loop.

The Holabird & Roche buildings along State Street dating from 1900 to about 1915 can be seen as the culmination of earlier experiments. They represent, first, the final stage in the development of two main types of urban retail building: the horizontal palazzo-like department store with its acres of open display space and the high "arcade" shops building with its upper-floor sidewalks and show windows stacked on top of one another like streets in the sky. Second, they testify to the skill Holabird & Roche had developed in phased construction, which let buildings function and maintain a satisfactory appearance even during major remodeling and expansion so that they could stay competitive in an industry that was in constant flux. Third, they represent the climax of an attempt to fuse the inexpensive, highly flexible spaces of the loft type with the need for the elegant, ornamental exteriors demanded by the owners of the department store and the high-end tall shops building. Finally, they represent the most extensive use anywhere in the city of white glazed terra cotta.

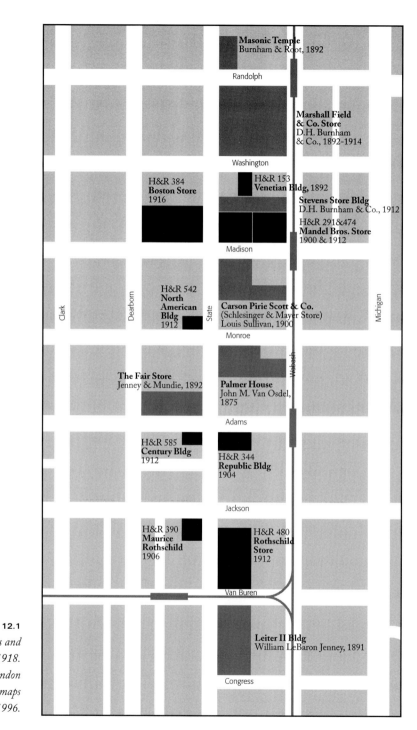

12.1

*Holabird & Roche department stores and
tall shops buildings on State Street, ca. 1918.
Map drawn by Dennis McClendon
from information on fire insurance maps
and other sources, 1996.*

The Department Store

As we have seen, the model for the State Street department store in the twentieth century had been set by Jenney's buildings for Siegel, Cooper and Company (Leiter II) and the Fair Store. Of the five largest stores erected between that time and World War I, the Burnham firm designed one, Marshall Field's; Louis Sullivan another, Schlesinger and Mayer (Carson Pirie Scott); and Holabird & Roche three, the Boston Store, Mandel Brothers, and the Rothschild Store. Although the Burnham and Sullivan stores are the best known in architectural histories—Marshall Field's because it was always the dominant retail operation in the Loop, Schlesinger and Mayer because of the highly personal, somewhat eccentric design—it is probably fair to say that the Holabird & Roche designs were more influential in setting the tone for the street and for Main Streets across the country.[2]

The Boston Store (cat. no. 384) provides a good introduction to the complexities of creating a department store on State Street. This establishment was the property of Charles Netcher and his wife Mollie. Netcher had gained his retail experience in the dry goods emporium of C. W. and E. Pardridges before buying out his employers and changing the name to the New Store, then to the Boston Store. In 1890 he met and soon married Mollie Alpiner, the store's chief underwear buyer, a woman who would become one of the city's best known and most dynamic personalities.[3] Edward A. Renwick has left an account of the match. Netcher, according to Renwick, was a "perfect slave driver" who slept on a store counter so he could keep an eye on the business at all times. His health was not good, however, "so he confined his slave driving to the first floor. One day he did get up to the third floor, so the story goes, and he said to the woman who became Mrs. Mollie Netcher, and was then the head of the millinery department, 'You've a good business head and you're a good looking woman, will you marry me?' He added, 'You needn't give me an answer now. I'll be back this afternoon.' They always said he got her out of stock."[4]

The store prospered, and the newlyweds started thinking about expansion. The store was in a good location on State Street just north of the corner of State and Madison Streets, according to Chicago legend the busiest corner in the world. To become a really important player in the Chicago retail scene, however, the Netchers needed more space. In the 1890s the couple started an intricate series of land transactions in the half block bounded by Madison, State, and Dearborn in what soon became a constantly escalating expansion scheme. These transactions were no doubt carried out in typical fashion, under conditions of complete secrecy by anonymous outside agents. Only after the land was assembled in 1901 was the news released to the press.

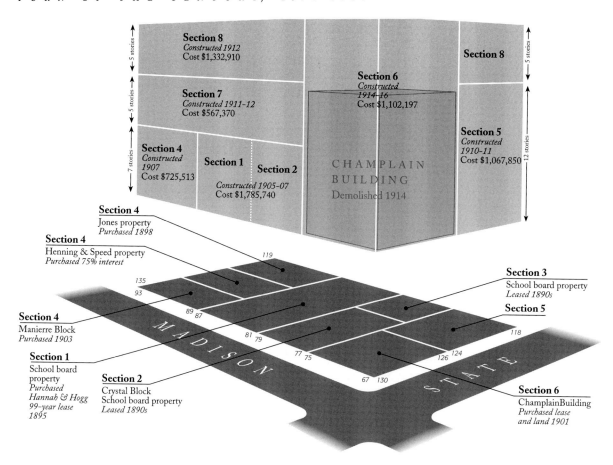

Section 8
Constructed 1912
Cost $1,332,910

Section 7
Constructed 1911–12
Cost $567,370

Section 4
Constructed 1907
Cost $725,513

Section 1

Section 2
Constructed 1905–07
Cost $1,785,740

Section 6
Constructed 1914–16
Cost $1,102,197

CHAMPLAIN
BUILDING
Demolished 1914

Section 8

Section 5
Constructed 1910–11
Cost $1,067,850

5 stories 5 stories 7 stories 5 stories 12 stories

Section 4
Jones property
Purchased 1898

Section 4
Henning & Speed property
Purchased 75% interest

Section 4
Manierre Block
Purchased 1903

Section 1
School board
property
*Purchased
Hannah & Hogg
99-year lease
1895*

Section 2
Crystal Block
School board property
Leased 1890s

Section 3
School board property
Leased 1890s

Section 5

Section 6
ChamplainBuilding
*Purchased lease
and land 1901*

119   135   93   89 87   81 79   77 75   67 130   118   126 124

MADISON   STATE

12.2

*Boston Store land assembly and building campaigns. Pre-1910 addresses. Diagram by Dennis McClendon
based on information in Holabird & Root records and on fire insurance maps, 1996.*

In a series of articles in 1901 the *Economist* revealed the story.[5] The original store building was at 118–20 State Street (for the sake of clarity, all addresses in this account are the old pre-1910 addresses). First the Netchers negotiated a lease for a School Board property at 77–79 Madison Street for $27,000 a year. Then in 1895 they bought out a ninety-nine-year lease on a property immediately to the west of this at 81–87 Madison. In 1898 came the Jones property at 119 Dearborn, which they purchased outright for $115,000. Then in 1901 they paid $827,000 for the leasehold on the key parcel in their land assembly, the lot at the corner of State and Madison (126–30 State). On this last site sat the Champlain Building, which had been designed by Holabird & Roche and finished a few years previously, in 1895.[6] Then they turned their attention to the Dearborn Street side of the block, for $550,000 buying the parcel at the northeast corner of Dearborn and Madison, a lot that contained the Manierre Block, a great post-Fire pile of masonry, then three-quarters interest in the Henning and Speed property just to the north along Dearborn at a cost of $360,000.[7] While they were assembling the land the Netchers started commissioning Holabird & Roche to design a series of renovations and modifications to expand the original store building at 118–24 State into the properties they were acquiring, first into the property at 77–79 Madison, creating an L-shaped store wrapped around the Champlain Building, then, once they had secured the Champlain leasehold, into the lower floors of that building as well. Not only was Holabird & Roche obliged to stitch together a set of buildings of different eras with varying floor heights, load-bearing capacities, and column spacings, but it had to accomplish this task while the store was operating.

While they were buying land and modifying the existing structures, the Netchers were also planning for a large new structure. They apparently first approached Jenney and Mundie, probably on the strength of that firm's experience with the Leiter II Building, but in the end they came back to Holabird & Roche, which had been working for them all along on the remodelings.[8] As soon as they had finished assembling the land, the Netchers announced they would build an immense new building from plans drawn for them by Holabird & Roche. According to the *Economist,* the store would be built in stages but would eventually cover the entire half block up to a height of fourteen stories, with sufficient foundation and steel structural capacity to add another four stories later.[9] Apparently the solution did not come easily, or the clients changed their minds frequently, because there are hundreds of drawings that vary considerably in number of stories, interior layouts, and details of exterior treatment. It is known, for example, that Mrs. Netcher at first wanted to build office space above the store, since she did not believe shoppers would go much above the seventh floor, but eventually she changed her mind.

According to the *Economist,* the most noteworthy aspects of the building were its deep basements and its escalators. As we have seen in the case of the Chicago Tribune Building, basements of significant depth were difficult in late nineteenth-century Chicago because the soft, spongy soil made it difficult to excavate without disturbing the adjacent properties, and the high water table made it hard to keep the excavations dry. In the case of the Boston Store the clients wanted three subsurface levels, the first a large sales floor fifteen feet high, the second a subbasement twelve feet high containing shipping rooms, and finally a second subbasement containing the boilers, generators, pumping plants, and other machinery. To keep the north party wall of the Champlain from sinking during the construction of the Boston Store basements, the architects had to replace the floating raft foundation under it with concrete caissons. This required holding up the wall with jackscrews while cutting through the floating foundations under it so the caissons could be sunk. This was an extraordinarily tricky maneuver.[10]

The use of escalators, the *Economist* claimed, was "much in vogue in the East," but the writer stated that the Boston Store would represent the most extensive use of this device ever attempted. Escalators allowed a much smoother circulation, eliminating the break in movement caused by the elevator and capitalizing on the great open floor plates of the big department store.

Construction of the new Boston Store turned out to be even more complicated than the land assembly or earlier renovations. Once again the Netchers could not

12.3
Boston Store (384), 1905–16, Madison Street between Dearborn and State Streets, view looking northeast showing construction of section 1 with old Boston Store building and the Champlain Building to the east (right) and the Manierre Block to the west (left). Photograph by Chicago Architectural Photography Company, 27 November 1905. Chicago Historical Society Prints and Photographs Department.

afford to close the store because they needed the continuing revenue to help pay the expenses they had incurred in obtaining the property and starting construction of the new building. Once again the architects not only had to devise a scheme in which the construction of the new building could go forward in stages with the store fully operational at every stage, but they had to accommodate constantly changing construction schedules, which were dependent on the cash flow of the store, and the design changes that inevitably occurred in a construction project that in the end took fifteen years to complete. Actual construction of the new building started in 1905 under the supervision of Mollie Netcher, who had taken over management of the store at the

12.4

Boston Store, view of sections 1–4 as finished, view looking northeast from Dearborn and Madison with the Champlain Building filling the block to State Street. Photograph ca. 1907–9. From John H. Jones, A Half Century of Chicago Building *(Chicago, 1910).*

death of her husband in 1904. Over the next several decades her active role in supervising the business and the construction, ordinarily a man's job, made her a Chicago legend.

The first work involved section one, a seven-story block at 81–87 Madison Street. This portion, with its rather plain fenestration and modest cornice, looked very similar to the loft buildings the firm was designing in the same years. In 1907 a seven-story section was added on each side at 77–79 and at 89–93 Madison Street to fill out the Madison Street side, and a new twelve-story piece at 118–24 filled out the State Street side. The twelve-story portion, perhaps because it fronted on State Street, was given a

12.5
Boston Store, view looking northwest of construction on section 5, with Champlain Building to the left. Photograph by Chicago Architectural Photography Company, 8 July 1910. Chicago Historical Society Prints and Photographs Department, ICHi-19927.

240

much more finished appearance by the creation of an elaborate top consisting of a three-story colonnade with recessed windows on floors nine through eleven surmounted by a terminal story with a substantial cornice. This treatment was apparently identical with the treatment intended for the top five floors of the completed seventeen-story building, and it is quite likely that the cladding was later removed and reused when the building was eventually raised to the full height. In 1911 work was started to bring all the sections except the Champlain Building up to the full seventeen stories. Finally the architects convinced Mrs. Netcher that the Champlain, even though it was less than twenty years old, could not be readily adapted to its new use, so she arranged to purchase the land, and the building was razed in 1915 to make way for the final section. At its completion the building covered the entire half block to a

12.6

Boston Store, perspective drawing looking northwest showing sections 1–5 and 6–8 completed wrapping around the old Champlain Building (demolished for construction of section 6 in 1914). Drawing ca. 1913.
Chicago Historical Society Prints and Photographs Department.

12.7
Boston Store, view of construction on section 6.
Photograph by Chicago Architectural
Photography Company, 16 September 1915.
Chicago Historical Society Prints and
Photographs Department.

uniform height of seventeen stories. In typical Chicago fashion, it was hailed as record-breaking, in this case claiming the distinction of being the tallest building in the world devoted exclusively to the retail business of a single concern.

Perhaps the most striking thing about the finished Boston Store was how simple and uniform it was. Although the two-story base and five-story cap provided some variety, the overwhelming impression was of large, regular bays marching from corner to corner. Curiously, this uniformity completely belied not only the ingenuity of the architects in designing for its phased construction but the complex uses that took place behind the regular facade. In addition to the retail floor areas, the building's upper floors contained areas for light manufacturing such as cigarmaking; food preparation areas for making candy, ice cream, and baked goods; chemical laboratories for making drugs and testing items sold by the store; a barber shop; Western Union offices; post

12.9

Mandel Brothers
Department Store
(474), 1909–12, 1–15
N. State Street,
northeast corner of
Madison Street,
advertisement
showing new store on
State Street (left) and
Central Trading
Company (Mandel
Annex) on the right.
From A Milestone at
57. *Pamphlet, Chicago*
Historical Society
Library.

office; emergency hospital; classrooms; lunchrooms; and a branch of the Chicago Public Library.[11] As was true in large hotels, the relatively simple urban fronts masked an entire teeming world. In fact, as at the hotels, it is possible the simplicity of the facade was meant to compensate for the astonishing complexity of the interior.

For many people the facade may have seemed too simple for an important downtown department store. The famous New York critic Montgomery Schuyler was certainly surprised. "Here is the architectural embodiment of the 'Chicago Idea' in architecture," he wrote. "Would anybody venture upon such extreme plainness in a like erection in New York or Boston? Evidently the essentials are supplied and evidently only the essentials."[12] In reality the building's facades comprised more than just the essentials. Like almost all of Holabird & Roche's commercial buildings, each street front had a distinct base, a well-defined middle section with the corner piers strengthened, and a distinct terminating feature, this last quite elaborate at the Boston Store. Compared with Holabird & Roche's earlier Mandel Annex, which was only a subsidiary space on Wabash, the Boston Store had a distinctly more elaborate terminating feature. Still, it appears that the Holabird & Roche architects themselves thought they might have gone too far in reducing the facade ornamentation at the Boston Store. In the firm's later department stores the loftlike quality receded and the palatial imagery for department stores started to regain ground.

Two department stores put up almost simultaneously between 1909 and 1912 demonstrate this process. The first was for the Mandel Brothers main building directly across State Street from the Boston Store. Holabird & Roche had already designed for them the large annex building on Wabash about 1900.[13] Asked to replace the main State Street building about ten years later, Holabird & Roche designed an imposing fifteen-story structure with an ornamental top enriched with arched openings and a fairly heavy garland below the substantial top cornice (cat. no. 474). In this building the architects apparently introduced for the first time a new method for integrating the sprinkler system into the building. Until that time pipes for sprinkler systems, which were used in many large buildings to protect them against fire and to secure lower fire insurance rates, had been left exposed and hanging near the ceiling. At the Mandel Building these pipes were routed through the floor so that only the ornamental heads extended below the ceiling. This method soon became nearly universal in American construction.[14]

12.10
Rothschild Department Store (480), 1909–12, 305–41 S. State, northeast corner of Van Buren Street, view of exterior looking northeast. Courtesy of Holabird & Root.

At the final building in this series, the Rothschild Department Store (cat. no. 480), the firm turned to an arcaded base and an enormous projecting cornice. This building, which replaced the older Rothschild store of 1895, was in many ways the most successful of the Holabird & Roche department stores. Like the Marquette, it managed to be as simple in its general lines as any building of its day, but the immediate visual response is not how plain it is but how rich. In it Holabird & Roche not only borrowed motifs from the Italian Renaissance palazzi but also managed to achieve something of their classical repose.

These buildings struck a balance. On the one hand, they were clearly less elaborate than earlier Chicago department stores or contemporary stores in New York. They never disguised the fact that, at base, the department store worked best as a series of stacked open floors. The architects' response was similar to the one they used in the office buildings. They removed the towers, turrets, and dormers, which were expensive and superfluous, in favor of manipulating a very thin cladding. However, because they were huge structures housing important stores on a major street, these buildings could not be as plain as the firm's loft structures or even its office buildings. The cornices, colonnades, and arcades in terra cotta resembled marble more than they did brick or dark stone. These stores can perhaps be best seen as lying halfway between the loft and office buildings on the one hand and the monumental public building on the other—that is to say, poised between the private and public realms, exactly the position they took in the city's life.

The Tall Shops Building

During the first years of work on the Boston Store Holabird & Roche also designed the first of its large terra cotta "arcade" buildings, the Republic (cat. no. 344). Situated at the southeast corner of State and Adams Streets, this building constituted a further development in the series of high retail and professional buildings that Holabird & Roche had begun in the 1890s with the Venetian Building. Whereas the Venetian and the Champlain housed large numbers of professional offices for doctors and dentists as well as shops, the Republic was almost entirely devoted to wholesale and retail sales.

The idea that lay behind the tall shops building was to take a rather small piece of expensive State Street frontage and multiply it many times by creating a kind of duplicate frontage on the upper floors. The *Economist* reported:

> It is the desire of the owner to have as tenants in the upper floors the business houses which wish to be on State Street and yet do not wish to pay

12.12
Republic Building, view of terra cotta upper floor and cornice, view to west along Adams Street. Photograph by Richard Nickel, November–December 1960. Courtesy of Historic American Building Survey, Library of Congress.

State Street store rents. Inasmuch as the tenants will wish, however, in many cases, to retail goods from the premises which they occupy, special provision will be made for this to those who desire it by lining the corridors with show windows similar to those in the street below and so providing opportunity for similar display of goods with the idea of so forming lighted and attractive arcades where shoppers will go as along the street below.[15]

In other words, the Republic acted like a retail equivalent of the speculative office building. It provided all the advantages single ownership could provide in the way of scale of operation, street-level advertising, excellent vertical communications, lunchrooms, and other amenities, but it made these advantages available to small shop owners.

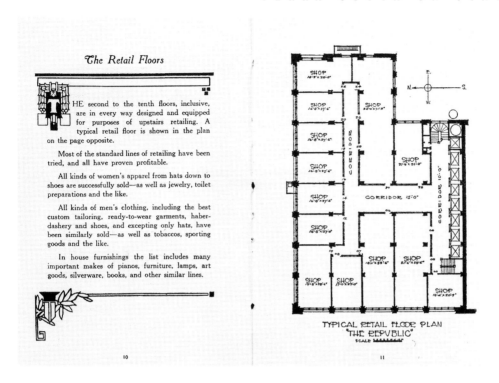

The Retail Floors

THE second to the tenth floors, inclusive, are in every way designed and equipped for purposes of upstairs retailing. A typical retail floor is shown in the plan on the page opposite.

Most of the standard lines of retailing have been tried, and all have proven profitable.

All kinds of women's apparel from hats down to shoes are successfully sold—as well as jewelry, toilet preparations and the like.

All kinds of men's clothing, including the best custom tailoring, ready-to-wear garments, haberdashery and shoes, and excepting only hats, have been similarly sold—as well as tobaccos, sporting goods and the like.

In house furnishings the list includes many important makes of pianos, furniture, lamps, art goods, silverware, books, and other similar lines.

TYPICAL RETAIL FLOOR PLAN
"THE REPUBLIC"
SCALE

12.13
Republic Building, plan of typical floor from building brochure, ca. 1915. Courtesy of Historic American Building Survey, Library of Congress.

Although the idea of the tall shops building was certainly not new, the use of arcades apparently was, if the commentary in a contemporary *Brickbuilder* article can be trusted.[16] The arcade device seems to have been the brainchild of the Republic's developer, General Henry Strong.[17] In the Republic an extensive arcade at the street level was lined with display windows announcing the tenants upstairs. Drawn into the building by these windows, the visitor would take the elevator to an upper floor where the hallway was lined with more shop windows, this time luring the visitors into the shops themselves. Shops originally occupied the first ten floors. Above this were the offices and display areas of wholesalers and manufacturers' representatives.

Like the roughly contemporary Boston Store, the Republic, in its simple rectangular configuration, regular facade treatment, and lack of elaborate ornamental detail, resembled the loft buildings the firm was doing in parts of the Loop where land was much less expensive. But again like the Boston Store, it would have been immediately apparent to any viewer of the day that this was not just a loft building. All the surfaces the visitor passed going in or out of the building—the terra cotta cladding around the exterior doorway, the paneled ceilings of the arcade, the checkerboard marble floor, the bronze elevator doors—were richly detailed. In addition to the shops, the Republic featured a number of other facilities for shoppers and for shop owners, including

12.14
*Republic Building,
view of arcade on
State Street.
Photograph by Richard
Nickel, 1960. Courtesy
of Historic American
Building Survey,
Library of Congress.*

a popular eating place, the States Restaurant, in the basement, a combined tearoom and social center on the eleventh floor, and a clubroom equipped with gymnasium equipment.

North American and Century Buildings

As Holabird & Roche developed the tall shops building type over the next decade and a half, it turned to more overt displays of building status. At the nineteen-story North American Building (cat. no. 542) of 1911–12, the windows of the base and the elaborate crowning feature were derived from "English perpendicular work of the fifteenth and sixteenth centuries."[18] This building was apparently aimed primarily at wholesale tenants, which is probably why it had no street-level arcade, but it did have a similar system of "streets in the air"—corridors lined with show windows. "The North American Building is a Great Exposition," the owners claimed, "where the world's foremost

The State Street Corridor Display Cases

O permit the upstairs merchants to display their goods not only upstairs but on the sidewalk level, the north wall of the State Street entrance corridor is to be lined with display cases—plate glass, polished bronze frames, mirrored backs and brilliant illumination.

The use of these display cases will be given to the upstairs merchants who have suitable goods to display—either in actual size or in miniature—and at a nominal rental to cover the cost of upkeep, and for periods based probably on the respective selling seasons.

Upstairs merchants, wherever located, will thereby have opportunity to display their goods, not only to those who enter the building for purpose of purchase, but also to those who pass through the corridors from one street to the other.

6

7

12.15

Republic Building, view of State Street corridor. Drawing from rental brochure, ca. 1915. Courtesy of Historic American Building Survey, Library of Congress.

The Retail Corridors

HE retail corridors of THE REPUBLIC were designed to accomplish two purposes—first, to attract the attention of the passer-by the display of the goods sold; second, to invite entering the shop by making the doorway rather like that of a public store than like that of a private office.

The character of the displays made by the many merchants of THE REPUBLIC determines to a considerable extent the interest and popularity of the retail corridors, and this character has steadily improved and the value of the corridors constantly increases.

To ensure this result, the management of the building carefully restrains any misuse of the display privileges of these corridors and co-operates wherever possible toward any betterment.

12

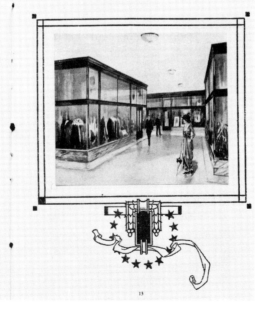

13

12.16

Republic Building, view of retail corridor on typical floor. From rental brochure, ca. 1915. Courtesy of Historic American Building Survey, Library of Congress.

12.17
*North American
Building (542),
1911–12, 36 S. State,
northwest corner of
Monroe Street, view
of exterior looking
northwest. Photograph
by Barnes-Crosby.
Chicago Historical
Society Prints and
Photographs
Department,
ICHi-19197.*

concerns maintain Permanent Display Rooms for the convenience of their customers—a towering Gothic structure in which the finest merchandise of the whole world is attractively displayed—located in the very center of Chicago's great retail and wholesale business district." In addition to the display rooms, the North American Building featured a lounge for women and a barbershop and smoking room for men.

A brochure issued before the building opened offers a particularly good description of the way the building owners hoped buyers would react:

> It will be the aim of both owners and architects to make the main hall
> and corridor representative in every respect of the tenancy of the building,
> and with this end in view no money or pains will be spared. One enters
> the vestibule through doors of chaste design. The walls of the vestibule
> will be lined with white statuary marble, the ceiling will be dome-shaped,
> lined with marble mosaic, and in the recesses will be bronze lighting fix-
> tures of ornate design.[19]

The final building in this series, the Century (cat. no. 585), was built in 1913–16. Here the facades were divided by a number of bands of low relief ornament that was described in a promotional booklet as a "modern translation of Spanish." In this case the lobby was particularly elegant, with white and colored marbles and dramatic lighting effects. It also contained twenty-two display cases for the use of the tenants on the upper floors.[20]

By 1915 State Street had reached its maximum development as a retail thoroughfare. Tightly packed with great department stores, high shops buildings, and other structures, it created one of the densest concentrations of people and goods ever seen in any city. The crush of foot traffic along the street, particularly at the famous intersection of State and Madison (where Holabird & Roche was responsible for three of the four corners), was one of the marvels of the city. The gleaming white facades of buildings erected in the twentieth century, many of them by Holabird & Roche, together with relics of earlier eras and the constant parade of patrons from all walks of life in all kinds of costumes, joined in creating a lively, constantly changing spectacle quite different from that seen on any other street in the Loop. Few people walking along the street in 1915 could have imagined that this world was then at its apogee and would start an inexorable decline after World War I. By the 1920s, however, the city had started to change. The development of North Michigan Avenue and of outlying retail centers would slowly sap the vitality of State Street as the uncontested center of Chicago's retail life. Although State Street continues to boast some very large retail establishments, substantial portions of the street have gradually been claimed for other uses,

12.18
Century Building (585), 1913–16, 202 S. State Street, southwest corner of Adams Street, view of exterior looking southwest. From Selected Photographs Illustrating the Work of Holabird & Roche, Architects, *1925.*

as offices and institutional spaces have taken over the buildings once occupied by shops, and it is possible that others may be converted for residential use. The Republic Building is gone, and many bright terra cotta facades have been hidden by later accretions. An ill-advised attempt to create a transit mall in the late 1970s further damaged the appearance of the street, as did the demolition in the early 1990s of virtually all of block 37, the block between Washington and Randolph from State to Dearborn. Still, the pre–World War I fabric of State Street has proved remarkably resilient, and with a little respect and careful restoration it could glow once again in all its terra cotta splendor.

THIRTEEN

GOLFING IN THE SUBURBS:
THE GLEN VIEW GOLF
AND POLO CLUB

One of the most striking aspects of late nineteenth-century Chicago, or any American city, for that matter, was the complex set of reciprocal relations that developed between the central city and its suburbs. Consider the case of the suburban country club. It is surely no coincidence that the increasingly dense central commercial districts of American cities were balanced by decreasing density in the elite suburbs at the metropolitan periphery. And it seems highly unlikely that it was by chance that these developments coincided almost exactly with a sudden interest in golfing.

Golf had been played in Britain since at least the fifteenth century. Although golfing did rise in popularity in Europe in the nineteenth century, nothing in Europe equaled the situation in the United States, where the number of golf courses skyrocketed from none in 1880 to some eighty by 1896 to nearly a thousand by 1900.[1] Why the sudden explosion of interest in America, and why the particular American form, the private suburban country club? The Glen View Golf and Polo Club (cat. no. 261), a country club on Chicago's North Shore designed by Holabird & Roche at the turn of the century and one of the Chicago area's pioneer golf clubs, provides excellent testimony on the early development of this peculiarly American institution.

The Glen View Club and Golf in America

According to traditional golf lore, the first full-fledged golf course anywhere in the United States appeared in 1888 in Yonkers, outside New York City. The name, the St. Andrew's Club, testified that it, like many early American clubs, was modeled on the famous Royal and Ancient Golf Club at St. Andrews, Scotland, the legendary birthplace and Holy of Holies of golf.[2] Although they looked to British precedent, the creators of the first American golf clubs developed a distinctive type of institution. Unlike the original Scottish links course, which used the natural sand and turf landscape of the seacoast, land that was often publicly owned, the American courses were most often created inland, at the edge of the expanding residential fringe of the major cities, since this is where easily accessible undeveloped land could be found. Also, more often than not, the American clubs were privately owned.[3]

If the East Coast led in introducing golf to America, the Midwest was not far behind. From all accounts, golf in Chicago was organized by Charles Blair Macdonald. A Chicagoan, Macdonald learned the game at St. Andrews, Scotland, while he attended the university there starting in 1872. Returning to Chicago in 1875, Macdonald tried to interest his friends in the game. At first there was little response, but in 1892 he set up an improvised course of seven holes weaving through the flower beds of a Lake Forest estate. By 1893 he had persuaded enough of his fellow members at the prestigious Chicago Club to contribute ten dollars each to acquire a farm west of the city in the Belmont area of Downers Grove, and build an eighteen-hole course, allegedly the first in the country. In 1894 the new Chicago Golf Club bought two thousand acres in Wheaton, built a new course, and with representatives from the four other leading American clubs, including St. Andrews in Yonkers, the Country Club

13.1
Shinnecock Hills Golf Clubhouse, Long Island, New York, McKim, Mead and White architects. Photograph by Robert Bruegmann, 1992

in Brookline, Massachusetts, Shinnecock Hills in Long Island, New York, and the Newport Golf Club in Rhode Island, founded the United States Golf Association.[4]

Following the Chicago Golf Club came a flood of new clubs in the Chicago area, including the Onwentsia in 1895, Edgewater in 1896, Exmoor in 1896, Evanston in 1897, and Glen View in 1897. Each catered to a specific social and geographic clientele. Whereas the Onwentsia, for example, was peopled by what was regarded in Chicago as the "old money," a socially prominent group residing primarily in Lake Forest, Glen View seems to have been a haven for rising businessmen living in a more scattered area in the city and along the North Shore.

According to club annals the Glen View Club was the inspiration of William Caldwell, a Scotsman who was a sociology professor at Northwestern University. It was necessary to find a location for the club convenient enough so that golfers from Evanston or Chicago could get there readily, but it had to be at least four miles from Northwestern University to escape laws prohibiting the sale of alcohol within that radius. Founding member Daniel Burnham has been credited with finding the 180 acre farm that became the club site. Quite likely Burnham could have taken on the commission of the clubhouse himself, but by the 1890s his office had its hands full with much larger jobs. He was undoubtedly quite happy to turn the job over to a friendly competitor who was also a neighbor, golfing enthusiast, and fellow founding member of the club. William Holabird, although his own office had become one of the most important in the city, was no doubt equally happy to get such a conspicuous commission.

Ossian C. Simonds, former partner of Holabird and another founding member of the Glen View Club, worked with Holabird & Roche in laying out the grounds. As was the case with most American inland courses, the soft, undulating lines of the fairways, gently extending across watercourses and around masses of trees and out of sight, came fairly directly from the tradition of the eighteenth-century British "landscape garden," where the intention was to create an idealized version of the pastoral landscape. British golfers had already exploited this tradition when they turned from the seacoasts toward the interior, where natural links sites were not available. The kind of wide, sweeping lawns found in the parks of British country estates of the eighteenth century turned out also to be ideal for the needs of golfers, particularly after the lawn mower, invented in the mid-nineteenth century, replaced sheep as the means of keeping the grass short.

Simonds shared with the British landscape gardeners the desire to make his designs look natural and indigenous, adapting these ideas to the American Midwest. According to the principles of the "prairie style" of landscape architecture, the natural

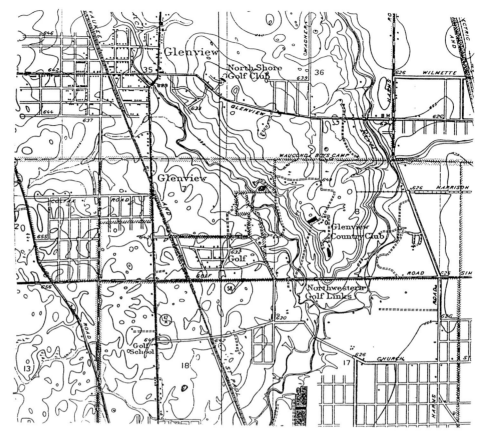

13.2
Glen View Club as seen in United States Geological Survey map, Highland Park Quadrangle, 1928, showing club in center right, the town of Golf and the Milwaukee Railroad to the west, and the North Shore and Western streetcar line along Harrison Street to the east.

landscape should be subtly enhanced using indigenous plants. A Glen View member recalled:

> Working with officers, architects, and golf experts, Simonds laid out the land, its forest, trees, and vistas, its roads and pathways. He said, "Let us here create a park to serve our pleasure, a thing of beauty; do not destroy it." His word became the law and was obeyed. When Simonds said, "Woodman, spare that tree," the tree remained. Wide lanes were cut through the forest, drained, planted, and transformed into fairways. Trees and shrubs appeared where he said they should be, and Nature responded to this artistic skill and guidance, producing a landscape whose beauty has increased with every year.[5]

With mature landscapes of the British picturesque sort it is often difficult to know exactly what changes have occurred naturally and which were induced by human de-

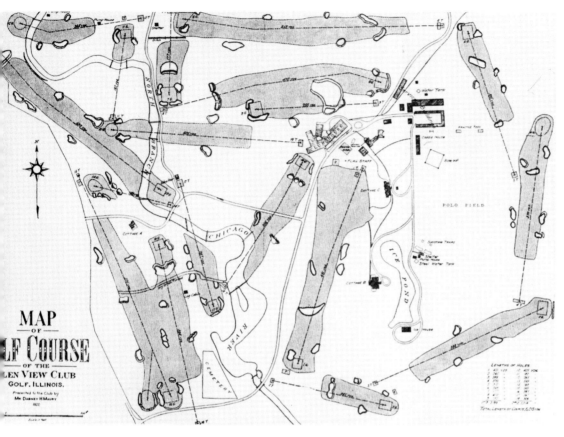

Glen View Club,
layout of golf course,
from Hotel Monthly,
October 1922.

sign, but the drive into the Glen View Club today, along a winding roadway first cross-
ing the North Branch of the Chicago River, then passing through a dense belt of
woodland, then skirting the manicured lawn of the first hole fairway before finally
arriving at an oblique angle at the clubhouse at the top of the hill, certainly must create
something like the same impression it did for viewers in the early twentieth century.

Selecting a style for the clubhouse was an interesting problem for Holabird &
Roche, as it had been for many American golf course architects. It would have logical
to follow the British examples, but most British clubhouses were too rudimentary to
suit American needs, while the few substantial examples, notably that at St. Andrew's,
were too monumental for the club's suburban setting. The major American prototype
was created in 1892 by Stanford White of the firm of McKim, Mead and White for
the golf club at Shinnecock Hills on Long Island. This long, low shingled affair looked
perfectly in place in the midst of the rolling Long Island countryside. It resembled the
kind of large seaside house or recreational building McKim, Mead and White had
specialized in, a type quite familiar to Chicagoans who frequented the major eastern

seaside resorts.[6] With its elegant clubhouse and exclusive membership, the Shinnecock Hills club was bound to be influential. When the Chicago Golf Club built its clubhouse, there was a strong resemblance.[7]

Perhaps because golf was a Scottish import or perhaps because the Glen View Club's nickname was "Leigh and Lang" (Long and Low), or perhaps merely to give it a distinctive appearance, Holabird & Roche decided to invoke the Scottish tradition for the clubhouse (cat. no. 274). Since there was so little precedent among Scottish golf courses, the firm turned to the Scottish baronial manor house. The result was some decorative "half-timbering" in the building's gables and small-paned leaded windows. Otherwise, however, it must be admitted, it more strongly resembled its illustrious predecessor on Long Island than it did a Scottish manor house and, like it, looked from the exterior much like a large single-family house set in particularly extensive grounds.

The entry was through a projecting bay, mostly glass, into the large wainscoted hall. To the left this led to a lounging room, and this in turn opened onto the large dining room, thirty by sixty feet, occupying an extension to the rear. The kitchen and servants' quarters were grouped into a wing off the dining room, effectively isolating them from the main structure. Upstairs were numerous bedrooms for "bachelors" and "families." All of this part of the building was clearly meant to resemble a house. Expensively and comfortably furnished, provided with a fireplace in each room, these areas constituted a kind of home away from home. A major difference, of course, was that turning right at the entrance door rather than left, the visitor would have found not a library but a large locker room.

At first access to the club was somewhat difficult. Members coming from Chicago could take the Chicago, Milwaukee and St. Paul line from Union Station and were met at a nearby depot at Morton Grove or Glenview by a carriage or horse-drawn bus.[8] According to legend, the name of what became the adjacent community derived from a more picturesque means of arriving at the club. Albert J. Earling, president of the railroad, could board his private railroad car in the Loop and ask to be dropped off at a siding about half a mile from the course. In time this spot came to be known as Golf. In 1928 the area was formally incorporated under that name.

In 1906 getting to the club from Evanston was made much simpler when the North Shore and Western Railroad was incorporated by George P. Merrick and several other club members. The route of this streetcar line began in north Evanston and ended at the golf club. Only members, caddies, and club employees were allowed to ride the train to its last stop. At first the railroad primarily served the Glen View Club, but in 1913 the Westmoreland Golf Club was opened and became a source of railroad business, along with traffic to the Memorial Park Cemetery and Harms Wood Forest

13.4
*Glen View Club
(261), 1897, view of
clubhouse. Photograph
from* Inland
Architect, *April
1899.*

Preserve. The line was subsidized by the clubs and cemetery until 1926, by which time members no longer needed the train, since most of them had automobiles and found it easier to drive.[9]

Holabird family members were frequent visitors to the club, using all available means to get there. In the early days they could take the horse-drawn bus from Avenue House, a hotel at Davis Street and Chicago Avenue in Evanston, or they could drive back and forth from Evanston themselves, leaving their horses in the stable at the club.[10] After the streetcar went into operation, it provided another option. More often than not, however, family members got to the club by bicycle. The club was a relatively short and enjoyable bicycle ride from Evanston, and for decades the numerous Holabird clan came and went primarily under their own power. Most of the adult male members of the family played golf, some of them very well. William Holabird's son William Jr. (Manny) was a runner-up in the National Open at age seventeen in 1901.

Both the immediate family and various relatives of William Holabird and of other members of the firm of Holabird & Roche maintained connections with the club for decades. William Holabird himself was for many years a director, and over the years the firm did quite a bit of additional work. There were designs for numerous outbuildings and club additions, and in 1921 a new clubhouse (cat. no. 809) when fire destroyed the old one. The new building had imagery similar to that in the earlier clubhouse. The structure was again long and low, punctuated with half-timbered gables. If any-

13.5
Glen View Club, clubhouse (809), 1920–22, view of exterior.
From Selected Photographs Illustrating the Work of Holabird & Roche, Architects, *1925.*

thing, however, the clubhouse may have looked older than the original building, since much of the visible material was salvaged from elsewhere. Many of the bricks came from a post-Fire commercial building in Chicago that had recently been demolished, much of the limestone from Old Trinity Church in Chicago, and some hewn timbers from the United States frigate *Constitution*, which was being rebuilt. This time, however, to help avoid another catastrophe, all the floors were of concrete, as well as the exposed beams, which were painted to resemble oak. The parts of the club were all arranged in roughly the same way as in the old building, but on a larger scale and with the latest heating, lighting, and food preparation equipment.[11] The building was the only Chicago example, and one of the few outside the seacoast states, to be illustrated in the definitive compendium of golf course designs of the 1920s, Clifford Wende-hack's *Golf and Country Clubs.*

The most impressive area of the 1921 building was certainly the main dining room, measuring approximately forty by thirty-two feet below a great beamed ceiling. By the 1920s the scale of many clubhouses had become quite grand, considerably more than domestic. In fact the Glen View dining room, particularly as shown in a perspective drawing prepared by the firm, might easily be mistaken, except for the dining tables, for the sanctuary of a large suburban church. One might even say the country club interior was a more careful and convincing medieval design than that seen in any church done by the firm.

Over the years, in addition to the rooms provided in the clubhouse itself, there was an increasing demand for lodgings at or near the club. About 1900, the club purchased a five-acre property adjoining the club's original tract that included the old homestead of the Dewes family. This was converted for use as a summer cottage for members and called cottage A. Holabird & Roche designed companion buildings known as cottage B (cat. no. 287), a two-story plus attic structure with large, mostly glazed projecting bays, and cottage C (cat. no. 380). All of these buildings stood near the "Ice Pond" south of the clubhouse.

13.6
Glen View Club, view of clubhouse dining room, 1920–22. From Selected Photographs Illustrating the Work of Holabird & Roche, Architects, *1925.*

263

The idea of living near the country club but in private quarters also appealed to some club members. Holabird & Roche designed a handful of residences close by, including one for steel agent Edwin S. Jackman and one for telephone company officer Angus Hibbard. In a book written in 1936 Hibbard devoted a whole chapter to the club, describing his own house as well: "Think of the joy of living just over the fence from such a lovely place: I did think of it, and bought land and built a house, and there we lived (with one intermission) for more than twenty years. Our house, which Martin Roche designed, was built to fit into some large lilac bushes at one end, and we called it 'Lilac Lodge.'"[12] The intimate marriage of golf club and residential neighborhood would become a common pattern in affluent suburbs across the country in the twentieth century as the clubhouse gradually became a major social center of middle-class as well as upper-middle-class American life.[13]

The story of the Glen View Club suggests some of the reasons for the dramatic rise in popularity of the golf course starting in late nineteenth-century America. The simplest explanation, of course, is that Americans learned to like the game. But the setting seems to have been at least as important as the game itself. Certainly for many golfers the walk through the beautifully maintained grounds was much more rewarding than trying to shave points off their scores. In fact the American country club from the beginning operated in many ways as the suburban equivalent of the public park in the city. In the mid-nineteenth century British and American urban reformers had established the idea of the public park as a place that would enhance the quality of urban air and water, give city dwellers a respite from the cares of daily living in an increasingly dense and brutal city, and provide a recreational outlet for city youths and increasingly sedentary office workers. Larger than most city parks and much better tended, the country clubs provided an equivalent system of green spaces and recreational facilities for outlying communities. Private ownership made it possible to control who was admitted.

Underpinning the urban park reformers' rhetoric was a deeply held belief in the beneficial and uplifting effects of nature. As the natural landscape in the vicinity of the great city started to disappear ever more quickly in the last decades of the century, many city dwellers developed an acute sense of loss. As the term "country club" implies, a major reason for the popularity of the institution was a desire to preserve natural landscape against the onslaught of the city. As golf course architect Clifford Wendehack put it in the 1920s: "It would seem as if there was a concerted effort in all our larger centers of population to preserve through the country club that touch with the open air of the country which progressive extension of our cities is making every day more difficult."[14] In a later passage Wendehack waxed rhapsodic about the value of exposure to nature. Although readers today may smile at his overheated prose, his conflation of pagan and Christian allusions, and his somewhat crude rendering of American Transcendentalism, he probably spoke for not a few of his fellow city dwellers:

> With the stress of modern business life, and the pull and tear of the city, it is becoming increasingly difficult to know our true selves in our daily surroundings. . . . The open country of the golf course increases our perspective, permits us to measure ourselves as well as our fellowmen by the yard stick of life. So in these oases of business activity, we are erecting in increasing numbers, modern temples of sport: shrines at which we worship and obtain a better understanding of the human side of our fellowmen, and perhaps more than suspected, God Himself through the glories of nature.[15]

More jaded observers of the time might have suggested that real estate issues were at least as important as the quest to find God. Many suburbanites had moved out of the city because they were unwilling to pay for city governments that they considered too large, too corrupt, and too easily dominated by bosses who gained power through what that many suburbanites believed was an appeal to the basest instincts of the least educated part of the urban population. Even when they lived in the city, many of the people who later moved to the suburbs were unwilling to pay for parks that they themselves did not use. On the other hand, public park development had for decades been used to enhance the value of real estate adjacent to it. For suburban communities, the country club, which was built and maintained at no cost to the taxpayers but provided a similar enhancement of property values, seemed an ideal substitute. Even a glance at a map from the late 1920s will show how integral the country club had become to the city's affluent suburbs. On maps that show wealthy communities like Glencoe or Lake Forest to the north of Chicago, Hinsdale and Wheaton to the west, or Olympia Fields and Flossmoor to the south, broad bands of green designating open spaces, golf clubs, cemeteries, and forests preserves thread their way through the patchwork of colors designating the various suburban municipal jurisdictions. These green spaces, although based on a crazy quilt of public and private ownership, brought carefully managed pieces of the countryside into intimate contact with a large number of residential neighborhoods.

The Glen View Club, for example, sat in the middle of one of the most extensive chains of green in the metropolitan area. Like many of the others, this chain followed the paths of streams because land there was often more expensive to develop for residential use and so could be obtained more cheaply for recreational purposes. Starting at the Deer Path Golf Club some eight miles north of the Glen View Club and follow-

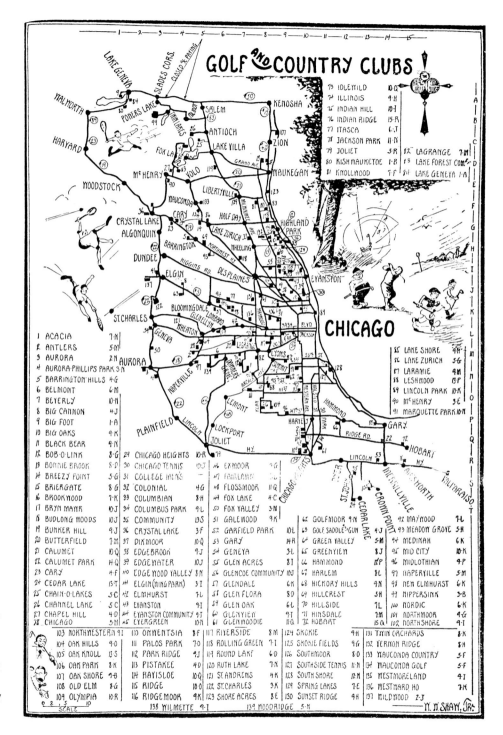

13.7

Diagram of country clubs in Chicago area. From Drake Blackstone Shopping List, *1929. Pamphlet, Chicago Historical Society. 1983.*

ing the Skokie River south through Lake Forest, Highland Park, Glencoe, Winnetka, and Glenview, the patches of green formed an almost continuous band as they linked the prestigious Onwentsia Club, the Old Elm Club, Exmoor Country Club, Highland Park's municipally owned Sunset Park, Sunset Valley Golf Club, Bob-o-link Golf Club, Northmore Country Club, Glencoe Golf Club, Cook County's Chewab Skokie Forest Preserve, Skokie Country Club, Skokie Playfield Golf Course, Northwestern University Golf Club, Cook County's Memorial Woods, Harm's Wood Forest Preserve, and North Shore Country Club before arriving at the Glen View Club near the confluence of the Skokie River with the north branch of the Chicago River. Continuing the band of green south from the club and following the north branch of the river through Morton Grove, Niles, and into the north edge of the city of Chicago were the Forest Preserve's Linne Woods, St. Paul Woods, and Miami Woods, Tam o'Shanter Country Club, Jane Miranda Reserve, Victoria Pothier Reserve, Billy Caldwell Reserve, the Sauganash and Labagh Woods of the Forest Preserve, Edgebrook Gold Club, Billy Caldwell Golf Club, Montrose and St. Lucas Cemetery, Bohemian National Cemetery, and then the city of Chicago's Gompers and Fields Parks, extending the band of green all the way to Foster Avenue, almost at the confluence of the north branch with the North Shore Channel.

So important were these oases of greenery to the suburban neighborhoods, and so important was the place of the country club in them, that one suspects suburbanites would have been obliged to invent something like the game of golf had it had not already existed. In addition to lowering density and providing green, open space for the community, the clubs also provided a kind of social and civic center for these neighborhoods, a perfect place for like-minded individuals to meet. Country clubs worked in great part for the same reasons the elite suburbs themselves worked. They provided formidable barriers to those parts of the metropolitan population who did not share their values.

In addition to providing a place to play golf and a setting for social activities, the clubs offered an excellent setting for making business contacts and a place where businessmen could meet more informally than in their clubs in the city. This was particularly true in the two most important all-male bastions of the country club, the locker room and the men's grill, which were usually adjacent to one another. At the Glen View Club, member and longtime director William Holabird would have rubbed shoulders with clients and potential clients in both of these places. Among members listed in 1898, to take just one year, W. B. Bogert, Charles Boynton, Angus Hibbard, and Edward F. Webster commissioned houses from Holabird & Roche. The number of commissions that came from firms via employees who belonged to Glen View is hard to reckon but is almost certainly substantial.

The Glen View Club, like other American country clubs, has faced major changes over the years. Particularly in the late 1960s and 1970s the institution came to seem somewhat anachronistic to many people, symbolizing discriminatory and repressive aspects of American society that had long since been abolished elsewhere in the life of the city. But the country club survived. Memberships have broadened, and club practices have been altered. Still, the clubs have shown remarkable resilience in maintaining their basic purposes. Nowhere is this more evident than in their landscape and buildings. The physical appearance of the Glen View Club, like that of many American country clubs, remains very similar to the way the club looked in the early twentieth century, despite changes that have fundamentally altered virtually every other part of the built environment. The continued success of the country club seems to stem from the delicate balance it has struck between business and pleasure, between upper-middle-class conservatism and social change, between the man-made and the natural, and between the city and its suburbs.

FOURTEEN

FISHING IN THE WILDERNESS:
THE COLEMAN LAKE CLUB

The appearance of the Tacoma, the Marquette, and other skyscrapers was symptomatic of a major transformation in the relation between city and countryside in the late nineteenth century. It is probable that in the city's early years most Chicagoans thought of the surrounding countryside primarily as a source of raw materials—grain to be traded, cattle to be slaughtered, logs to be cut up and made into houses.[1] For a while it appeared that everything was flowing to the city as the same mechanization that lowered the need for farmworkers also created the factory jobs that helped pull the inhabitants of rural areas into the city.

But as the city exerted ever more pull, its very intensity produced countervailing forces. As the metropolitan areas grew larger and more dense, many city dwellers wished to escape the increasing social, political, and environmental pressures, if only briefly. We have already seen this effect in the creation of the suburban country club. This was still too urban for many, however. Hunting and fishing became important recreations for city dwellers in part because it gave them a good excuse to leave the roar of traffic and the smoke of the factories for the serenity of forest and stream. In the process, the countryside took on a new meaning.

The Coleman Lake Club provides one of the most compelling as well as the most curious examples of this transformation. Here, in a rural area of northern Wisconsin, the same Chicago businessmen who had systematically exploited the countryside for the economic gain of their companies in the city found in the ravaged landscape a refuge from their business affairs and from the city these businesses had helped create. Like any resort, the new community provides a fascinating counterpoint and commentary on the city that spawned it.

Birth of the Club

As wonderfully situated as Chicago was for tapping the resources of the nation's heartland, it was rather limited when it came to picturesque environs. It could boast of very little to rival the seaside near Boston or the Catskills near New York. Chicagoans were obliged to fan out in all directions, often traveling enormous distances to reach areas they considered appropriate for rural recreation. William Holabird's diary for 1914 records trips to places as far-flung as Beebe Lake near Peoria, where he hunted ducks, and Dauphin Island, Alabama, where he fished. At the latter he planned to build a house for himself and also, apparently, some kind of resort development, suggesting that for Holabird escaping the city was not incompatible with business. By far the largest number of trips recorded in Holabird's diary, however, were to the Coleman Lake Club near Goodman in northern Wisconsin.

Coleman Lake was neither a suburban country club nor a luxurious rural resort. It totally lacked the amenities of fancier places such as Lake Geneva in Wisconsin or of Harbor Springs, Charlevoix, Petoskey, and Mackinac Island in Michigan. The Coleman Lake Club was for Chicagoans who wished to get far away from the city and who were really serious about fishing. Coleman Lake was part of a series of lakes, streams, and rivers in northern Wisconsin, about twenty-five miles south of Iron Mountain, Michigan. The area around the club had been heavily forested until the mid-nineteenth century when the massive logging operations that made Chicago the greatest lumber center in the world started the process that eventually led to the destruction of the forest throughout most of northern Wisconsin. In the brutal operations of that era, large trees were removed but their tops and trimmings were left. When these dried out, they became fuel for intensely hot fires that destroyed all the remaining plant and animal life.[2] In the case of the area immediately around Coleman Lake the timber was apparently harvested after it had been felled by a storm, but the result was the same.

Amazingly, it was this strange landscape—where rapidly dwindling forest alternated with a lunar vista of charred, cutover acres and with tracts where luxuriant new growth was already establishing itself—that was the setting for the Coleman Lake Club. The area now occupied by the club was initially owned by the T. W. Harvey Lumber Company of Chicago. It later came into the hands of the Kirby Lumber Company. Fred Stephenson, associated with the Kirby Company and an avid fisherman, provided the initial impetus for the club. As he traveled on business to the logging camp built by the Harvey Company, he experienced firsthand the excellent fishing. Eventually he brought friends from Chicago with him to the blasted landscape of the lumber camps.[3]

One of these Chicagoans, H. H. Gaylord, established and incorporated a non-profit organization called the Gaylord Club in 1888, one of the first fly-fishing organizations in the Midwest. The vice president was W. W. Augur, William Holabird's brother-in-law. During the first year the group, which boasted twenty-nine members, purchased a small tract of land. Gaylord left the club the next year, succeeded by Fred Stephenson, who served as president until 1918. The club leased six thousand acres of cutover land from the Kirby Company on condition that the club pay the taxes.[4] Gradually the landholdings were expanded and dams were built to create new ponds. Despite recurrent fires the trees eventually grew back, restoring the area's wooded appearance. Fish hatcheries were set up to ensure the supply of fish.

Club members were almost entirely from the Chicago area. In the early years travel to and from the club was long and arduous owing to its remote location. When the club was first established the only settled places in the area, Dunbar, five miles to the east, and Pembine, nine miles farther, were roaring lumber towns, filled with saloons catering to the lumberjacks. Farther still to the east were Menominee and Marinette, situated on either side of the Menominee River where it emptied into Green Bay and Lake Michigan. To the mills in these towns lumbermen floated logs from the area around Coleman Lake and a large area of northern Wisconsin and the Upper Peninsula of Michigan. As the area around the club was deforested, many of these

14.1

Coleman Lake Club, view of landscape. Photograph by Robert Bruegmann, 1983.

towns dwindled or disappeared. Goodman, the town closest to the club, was founded in 1908 and survived by processing logs that came from farther and farther away. It appears that on their travels to and from the club, members got to know the local businessmen, especially saloon keepers, in all the rough and ragged towns in the area.

For members from Chicago the most convenient way to get to the club was to take the Chicago, Milwaukee and St. Paul Railway night train on the Superior Division from Chicago to Pembine. According to published schedules, the train would leave Chicago at 10:00 P.M. and arrive at Pembine at 6:25 the next morning. Then, if everything went well, a Soo Line (Minneapolis, St. Paul and Sault Ste. Marie Railroad) train would arrive at 6:40 and leave them at Kirton at 7:10. From 1896 to 1911 the Dunbar Wausaukee Road served Coleman Lake siding and was the preferred means of arriving at the club, even though the train, which hauled cars loaded with logs, kept no schedule, and railroad employees stopped for meals at will. Once at Coleman Lake, the only transportation was a set of heavy wagons that lumbered slowly over muddy roads and rocky hills. In the early twentieth century the automobile revolutionized travel to the club, but even then it was a long trip over soft sand roads. An early drive from Evanston in 1911 was clocked at nineteen hours.

Despite the difficulties, Chicagoans kept coming back. One of the earliest and most frequent visitors was William Holabird. His name appears as the second member

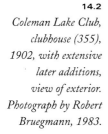

14.2
Coleman Lake Club, clubhouse (355), 1902, with extensive later additions, view of exterior. Photograph by Robert Bruegmann, 1983.

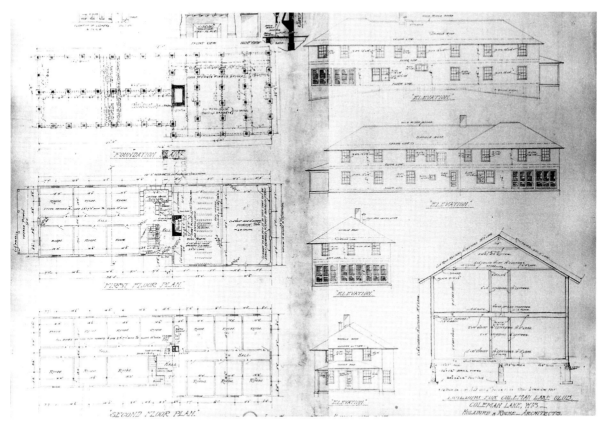

14.3
Coleman Lake Club, plans and elevations of clubhouse. Courtesy of Coleman Lake Club.

on the club register put into service with the opening of the new clubhouse in 1902. Various company records and personal papers reveal that Holabird made the trip to Coleman Lake as often as he could, often stretching a weekend from Thursday morning to Tuesday evening. Holabird family members and guests used their cabin, formerly a logging company building, for nearly fifty years before selling it to another club member in the 1940s.

The Holabird family's visit to the club was a highly organized affair, with the head of the household using his military training to run the operation as commander-in-chief. Family members recall how William Holabird presided from the front porch, telling everyone what to do, where to go fishing, what to wear. All members of the extended Holabird clan, even those with little interest in fishing, were obliged to learn to fly cast acceptably, and William Holabird's son John became one of the most accomplished fishermen at the club.[5]

In addition to the Holabirds, Martin Roche, Edward Renwick, and several other firm members belonged to the club, as well as many clients such as Alfred Cowles,

273

Byron Smith, and Ralph Otis. The Holabirds and other firm members would also have had the chance to meet distinguished guests including, around the turn of the century, Theodore Roosevelt and Herbert Hoover.

Membership at first was limited to thirty-five, but in 1891 it was increased to forty and in 1901 to fifty. The club extended its control over the land by a series of acquisitions and protective leases. The first clubhouse, probably one of the buildings constructed by the lumber company, was a simple six-room structure that was enlarged in 1897 to twelve rooms. It burned down in 1901. At this point the club, now a substantial, established organization, changed its name from the Gaylord Club to the Coleman Lake Club and decided to make a major land purchase of 2,860 acres, construct a fish hatchery, and build a new clubhouse.

The new clubhouse (cat. no. 355), built to the designs of Holabird & Roche, was a simple two-story shingled structure approximately 35 feet by 152. Downstairs was the large sitting room with its fireplace and adjoining porch, locker room, and six rooms for guests. Upstairs were thirteen more guest rooms. Across from the clubhouse was the "steward's quarters" or "superintendent's house" (cat. no. 356), a smaller, even simpler structure. The first floor was largely devoted to kitchen and dining room. Upstairs were four more rooms and a dormitory. Over the years Holabird & Roche designed a series of additional buildings including a dormitory, garage (cat. no. 986),

14.4
*Coleman Lake Club,
ice house (987), 1923,
view of exterior.
Photograph by Robert
Bruegmann, 1983.*

icehouse (cat. no. 987), pump house (cat. no. 1025), and simple cottages for members. All of these were minimal frame buildings. The earliest cottages are so poorly documented that it is not clear whether they had been houses or shelters for workmen and supervisors of the lumber company or were designed by Holabird & Roche for the club.

The Holabirds' own cottage (cat. no. 229) and the Campbell cottage (Scott Lodge), both built before 1900, are examples of the earliest dwellings at the club. The Holabird house was a log cabin of Norway pine with the bark left on. It was quite simple, though furnished with good Navajo rugs sent by Molly Holabird's brother, who was stationed in the West near Indian reservations. Photos of the interior of Scott Lodge show that it too was rustic. The wood floors were covered with braided rugs, and the rooms were furnished almost entirely with turned wood chairs and tables. A dining room was set off from the living room by curtains. A few pictures, two shelves of plates, two shelves of books, and several swords mounted high on the wall completed the embellishments. The interior looks like those seen in photographs of Adirondack camps, not surprisingly since the Adirondack camps were probably the inspiration for many rustic American resort areas. Nothing in the Midwest, of course, was as elaborate as the major wilderness camps of the East.[6]

14.5

Coleman Lake Club, Stephenson Campbell cottage (Scott Lodge) (68), 1889, view of exterior. Courtesy of Coleman Lake Club.

Stephenson Cabin

14.6
Coleman Lake Club, interior view of Campbell cottage. Courtesy of Coleman Lake Club.

Drawings exist for cottages starting about 1900, but they are always preliminary sketches. The earliest, dated 1900, was for Phil Mitchell (cat. no. 302). No one seems to remember the owner, but a famous trout fly bears his name.[7] In this and later cases, the rudimentary drawings were probably turned over to local craftsmen who worked directly from them. Some of the cottages were wood frame with siding. Others, like the Somerville cabin of 1919 (cat. no. 764), were constructed of logs. The style changed very little until the 1930s. The last house for which Holabird & Roche drawings exist was one built for Huntington B. Henry (cat. no. 1455) in 1935. By this time the size of the cabin had increased, and much of the overtly rustic character had disappeared; indeed, the colored elevation could easily have been drawn up for a suburban site. Only the boathouse door gives away its recreational use, and in the drawing even this could easily be mistaken for the front of a garage.

The presence of the Holabird family and several other firm members at the club apparently led to commissions for other buildings in that part of Wisconsin and nearby Michigan. For the Huron Mountain Club, an exclusive wilderness camp near Big Bay, Michigan, Holabird & Roche designed cottages for Judge George Carpenter (cat. no. 547) and A. L. Farwell (cat. no. 604). At Munising, Michigan, it drew up plans for a bank addition (cat. no. 1017). The best documented of these jobs is the bank building

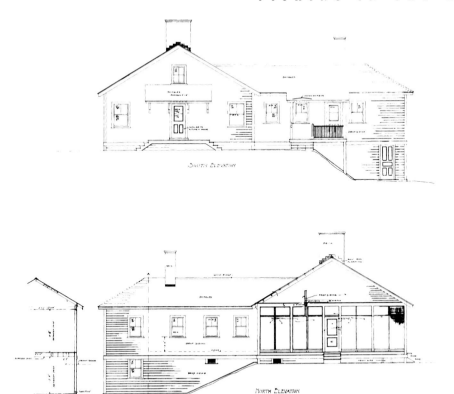

SOUTH ELEVATION

NORTH ELEVATION

.SCALE ¼IN.=1FT.

SUMMER COTTAGE
·FOR·
MR. PHIL MITCHELL

HOLABIRD AND ROCHE ARCHITECTS
1418 MONADNOCK BLOCK. CHICAGO.

14.7
*Coleman Lake Club,
Phil Mitchell cottage
(302), 1901, north
and south elevations.
Chicago Historical
Society Architectural
Collections.*

at Goodman in 1921 (cat. nos. 820, 882). It appears that the bank was originally intended for Pembine. One can imagine William Holabird and his son John discussing the matter over dinner with Coleman Lake Club members and the officers of the bank, who were also the owners of the Goodman Lumber Company, friends of the Holabirds, and probably club members as well. A rough scheme might have been worked out on the long train ride home. A sheet in the design folders with a sketch plan and elevation accompanied by notes and details overlaid by a large-scale profile looks like something that might have been produced by a recent graduate of the Ecole des Beaux-Arts like John Holabird, who had attended the famous French architecture school between 1910 and 1913 before joining his father's firm in 1919. The sheet might well be the one they brought back to the office on their return with instructions to the draftsmen to work up a plan and elevation.

Several schemes were probably produced and taken back up to the club the next weekend for approval. Perhaps the firm later prepared working drawings that have not

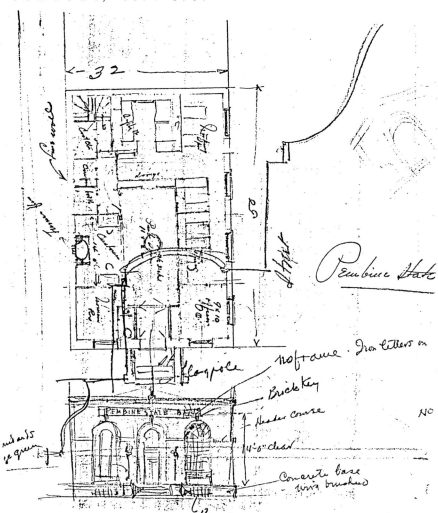

14.8

Pembine State Bank, Pembine, Wisconsin (820), 1920, sketch plan, elevation, and molding profile. Chicago Historical Society Architectural Collections.

survived, but it is just as likely that the rough drawings were handed over directly to local contractors. In any event the little bank was not erected in Pembine, but it, or one very similar to it, was built in Goodman, where it still stands, doing business at 502 Mill Street in pretty much its original state. With its brick construction, axial, symmetrical plan and academically correct facade incorporating three arched openings, it is about as formal and elaborate as a one-story structure measuring thirty-two feet by fifty can be.

It is a little hard today to imagine what compelled Chicagoans to go to Coleman Lake in the early years. The travel time was prodigious. Once there, they found the landscape ravaged. Conflicts between the club and local industry were inevitable even

14.10.

Coleman Lake Club, view of members sitting on porch, including William Holabird (seated, second from right) and his wife Maria Holabird (seated near the center of the photograph) with three children: William Holabird Jr. on his mother's lap, John Augur Holabird standing second from left, and daughter Jane Holabird (later Towne) standing to right behind her father. Courtesy of Coleman Lake Club.

though many of the businessmen involved in these industries were members. In 1924, for example, a wood alcohol plant set up at Goodman dumped acid waste into a brook that led to Coleman Lake, killing or driving out all the bass and trout. The pollution was so bad that Trout Lake Brook was renamed "Chemical Creek." It took club members several years and much negotiation to stop the practice. Even the appearance of club members in early photos, with their jackets, vests, ties, and shiny leather shoes, hardly looks conducive to relaxation.

Two explanations for the popularity of the club immediately come to mind. One was that good fishing exerted such an enormous pull that it outweighed all other considerations. The other is that by 1900 the pressures of urban life already provided an irresistible incentive to escape. Neither answer completely satisfies. The history of the Coleman Lake Club strongly suggests that a trip there was not an escape from the urban world. The very fact that the club was founded literally on the remains of Chicago companies' logging operations suggests a curious attraction to the very parts of the countryside that were most affected by the city. Once at the club, it was clearly an urban culture that prevailed, even though the setting was rural. In the case of William Holabird, the club probably offered just the distance he needed from the city of towers some three hundred miles to the south. From Coleman Lake he could contemplate, at some remove if never with perfect detachment, the frantic construction taking place over large areas of the metropolis, much of it to the designs of his own firm, all part of the ongoing transformation not just of the city itself, but of the vast American heartland around it.

Part

Four

FIFTEEN

THE   FIRM

1908–1910

By 1908 the amount of construction in Chicago, which had been rising slowly since the depression of the mid-1890s, surpassed for the first time the highest levels reached in the boom period of the late 1880s. Although this trend would reach a temporary crest in 1911, falling back slightly in the next few years and sharply during the war, it is perhaps accurate to see the 1908–10 spurt as the initial stage of Chicago's great building boom of the 1920s, which started in the 1910s and was interrupted, severely but only briefly, by the First World War.

In 1908 Chicago saw over $68 million worth of new construction, a figure that rose to over $105 million in 1911. Holabird & Roche's recorded commissions averaged over $6 million per year from 1908 to 1911 and reached a peak of $13 million in 1910, again keeping its share of construction in the city at a level of 5–10 percent. By this time Holabird & Roche was firmly established as one of the nation's leading firms. In 1909 the *Economist* reported that it had one hundred draftsmen in the office working on projects estimated at $30 million on the boards.[1] This may even have been a low estimate considering that the firm's known commissions finished between 1910 and 1912 totaled over $34 million, and there was undoubtedly other work for which no record exists. This volume of work means that Holabird & Roche had finally surpassed the level recorded by the firm of McKim, Mead and White in New York, which had been, during the late nineteenth century, the largest American architectural firm. Holabird & Roche's output probably still remained below that of Daniel Burnham's firm, known as D. H. Burnham and Company between 1891 and 1912 and Graham, Burnham and Company between 1912 and 1917. Already by 1910, however, Holabird & Roche was clearly starting to close in on the Burnham successor firm and would eventually surpass it in volume of commissions in the mid-1920s.[2]

In the office William Holabird remained the front man, bringing in most of the large commissions, but it is clear that other employees also performed this function. For example, Edward Renwick seems to have traveled around the Midwest drumming up hotel jobs. No matter what the source of the work, once the commissions arrived at the office they were distributed to several main designers, each specializing in one or more building types. By the turn of the century the volume of work had already reached the point where the partners themselves could not have designed or even closely supervised more than a few of the projects at a time. Although there is good evidence that Martin Roche himself had a large part in the design of every important commission, particularly those like the University Club in which he took a deep personal interest, other designers in the office played a major role in most of the other work. Although this division of labor can be inferred from the diverse designs coming out of the office, by the early twentieth century the ability of the Holabird & Roche office to control quality and maintain uniform drafting standards makes it all but impossible to guess who worked on which project. The partnership had attained a true corporate structure.

An excellent illustration of the way the firm worked can be found in the diaries of Maniere Dawson.[3] Dawson, who later became an important painter and one of the earliest American exponents of modernist abstraction, received an engineering degree in May 1909. Keen on ending any fanciful notions his son may have entertained about an artistic career, Dawson's father used his business connections to set up job interviews for him with engineers in the city. Unenthusiastic about taking a job with the Chicago Sanitary District, Dawson convinced his father to approach Frederick Atwood, owner of the Atwood Building, which had been built in 1895 to a design of Holabird & Roche. Through this connection Dawson came to have an interview with Martin Roche. The firm, Dawson reported in his diaries, had the reputation of doing more work than any other in Chicago.[4]

On 1 June, Dawson recorded, he met with Roche and was able to convince him that he could help in coordinating work with the engineers. This would involve checking design drawings against engineering drawings to make sure the designers at Holabird & Roche did not put doors or windows where consulting engineers Purdy and Henderson had located columns or wind bracing, for example, or to prevent the engineers from running a truss across an area the architects needed for a hallway. With any luck, he thought, he might get the chance to do some engineering design. Roche hired him and told Dawson to report to chief draftsman Frank B. Long in the firm's Monadnock roof penthouse the following Monday.[5]

Dawson reported on the meeting:

> I took with me two rulers with assorted scales, my slide rule, pencils,
> drawing tools, erasers, etc.—appearance 5 min. early. Long came in sharp
> 8:00 o'clock. I reported to his desk in front of the room and after two min-
> utes of silence he asked me if I could trace accurately.
>
> > I said Yes.
> > Can you understand plans? Yes
> > Can you relate plans to elevations? Yes
> > Take the left table in the rear. All right
> > I sat on a stool at the $4' \times 8'$ slab drawing board. After 20 minutes
> laying out tools and examining points of dividers and compasses and ma-
> nipulating a sliderule aimlessly, smiling in this direction and that as other
> draughtsmen looked my way, Mr. Long briskly slapped down an elevation
> on tracing paper of the lobby of the Sherman Hotel being planned.
> > Get tracing cloth from Brodhay [Holabird & Roche employee Louis
> Broadhay] and trace as quickly as you can. All blueprints have to go out
> in one month. Can you work 4 hours each evening this week? Yes.[6]

Several days later Dawson reported that his assignment had actually been a mistake.
Long had assumed that since Roche had hired him, rather than Holabird or one of
the engineers, Roche had hired Dawson as a designer. Dawson, because he wanted to
design rather than do engineering, was not inclined to point out the error. His description of the following days gives a good idea of what design development looked like
from the perspective of a draftsman:

> So far, my work has been tracing already formed designs and sometimes
> even rubbing out with erasers for hours in order to alter ink drawings
> ready for blue printing. Later the surprise of the week has been the assign-
> ment to me of Banquet Hall no. 2 [at the Sherman House] to be de-
> signed in Louis XVI style. I was too dumbfounded to say anything. Long
> marched away and left me. A week's observation of designers who had
> booths along two sides of the corner draughting room . . . indicated what
> to do. I went to Rebenbaum [apparently another Holabird & Roche em-
> ployee, the one responsible for maintaining the library].
> > Have you a Louis XVI folio?
> > Sure thing, here.

I looked at the floor plan on the small 1/8 scale paper layout Long had given me, one wall shown with one door. I tacked down my tracing paper and stared at the elevation of a French home in the folio. Long didn't show up again till next afternoon.

How much have you finished? Four elevations in 1/4.

Good, trace on cloth and send to printer.

After two weeks of tracing and getting pretty well acquainted with Rebenbaum, Smith Sutherland (both father and son) and others [other Holabird & Roche employees], I am drawing full size details of hollow tile cornice sections showing the steel hooks and heavier steel connections to the room beams, learning much about construction detail and fire-proofing ordinances.[7]

Finally on 7 August, Dawson reported, the blueprints for the Sherman House were all completed and bound together, and copies were sent to contractors for bids. With any luck, he reported, the Sherman would be ready to open in a year. He was given a day's vacation.[8]

It appears that during these years the firm made a major effort to obtain more work outside Chicago. In this effort they were perhaps influenced by the example of Daniel Burnham's firm, which by the turn of the century had created one of the country's first fully national rather than just regional practices. William Holabird made numerous trips to the East Coast in these years, and about 1910 the firm's ledgers record a sudden cluster of potential commissions from places scattered across the country. In New York City, for example, at least six or seven projects got as far as the preliminary drawing stage, although only a set of remodelings for the Royal Tailors, completed at a cost of about $60,000, and one new building materialized—a fairly unremarkable commission from Arthur Brisbane for a $400,000 building on West Thirty-eighth Street, apparently intended as a warehouse for Lane Bryant (cat. no. 687) and costing some $400,000.

It is interesting that the architect of record for the Lane Bryant job was Lucian Smith, a former Holabird & Roche employee who maintained close ties to the firm. It may have been that Holabird and Roche were simply lending Smith their expertise to help him set up a practice, but it seems more likely that these commissions, which were so unimportant that it is hard to understand why the firm was involved at all, were part of a strategy of gaining experience in building in New York. It seems most likely that Holabird & Roche was aspiring to open an office there, something every large regional firm outside that city must have contemplated, and that Daniel Burnham's firm had done about 1900.[9]

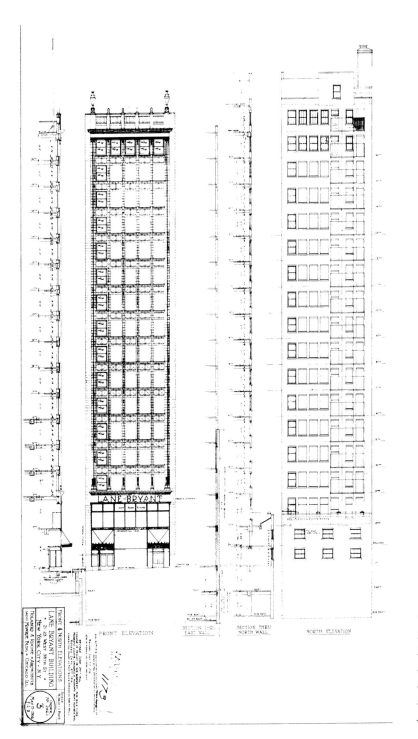

15.1

*Lane Bryant (Brisbane) Building,
New York City (687), 1916, Lucien Smith
architect, Holabird & Roche probably
associated architects, elevations and wall
sections. Chicago Historical Society
Architectural Collections.*

Though the firm was conspicuously unsuccessful in following Burnham's lead in getting major commissions in New York, Philadelphia, or any other of America's largest cities on the East Coast, it was eminently successful in establishing a substantial practice in large and small cities all across the Midwest. For small midwestern cities Holabird & Roche was often called in because of its reputation for turning out good work in the least time with the smallest possibility of unpleasant surprises. Some of these commissions involved unusual conditions. At the Deshler Hotel in Columbus, Ohio (cat. no. 657), the program consisted of providing as large and as good a hotel as possible using exactly as much money as had been left in a will. In this case, as in many others, the architects had done their cost estimating so carefully that the hotel came in almost to the penny, but they realized at the very last minute that this commission was unusual because it involved a bequest that had been invested and they had forgotten to figure in the interest earned during the time the hotel was under construction. They were obliged to work quickly to find an additional $6,000 to spend for decorations to

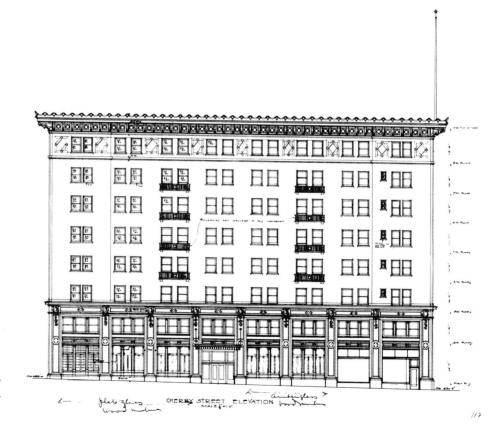

15.2
Hotel Deming, Terre Haute, Indiana (614), 1913–14, Cherry Street elevation. Chicago Historical Society Architectural Collections.

satisfy the terms of the program.[10] In a later case, in the 1920s, in Wausau, Wisconsin, they were asked to reproduce as closely as possible a hotel in Muncie, Indiana, because the brother of the owner there had been forced out of the business and wanted to run a hotel on his own.[11] From the 1910s the firm did numerous buildings in large cities like Milwaukee, Omaha, Kansas City, and Minneapolis. It is known that the firm actually did open a branch office in Kansas City but closed it after only a few years.[12] It is possible that this was only one of several such attempts.[13]

During 1908–10 the firm was responsible for five large first-class office buildings. The McCormick Building on South Michigan Avenue (cat. no. 442) in Chicago, completed in two phases between 1908 and 1912, was the largest and most expensive office building it had done to date but also the most unadorned. The Otis (cat. no. 477), although it lacked the visibility that came with Michigan Avenue frontage, occupied even more expensive real estate at the southwest corner of LaSalle and Madison

15.3

McCormick Building (442), 1908–12, 332 S. Michigan Avenue, northwest corner of Van Buren, view of completed building (center) with former Art Institute building (left), and Railway Exchange Building, D. H. Burnham & Company, 1904 (large structure at right). Chicago Historical Society Prints and Photographs Department, ICHi-14274.

Streets, at the very heart of the city's financial center, and was particularly robust in proportions. Owing to special circumstances, the other Chicago office structure, the Monroe Building (cat. no. 504), was an anomaly, a frothy confection in terra cotta comprising twisted colonnettes, blind arcades, and trefoil panels (figs. 19.11–19.13). It was the example of the stripped-down McCormick and Otis rather than the more elaborate Monroe that was influential in obtaining two Omaha clients. The City National Bank (cat. no. 492) and the Woodmen of the World Building (cat. no. 518) provide excellent examples of the kind of building clients in other midwestern cities expected from Chicago commercial architects. In fact it appears to be work of this era by Holabird & Roche and by the Burnham firm that set the standard for office building construction throughout the Midwest and western United States for at least the next decade.[14]

These years also witnessed substantial retail work on State Street, including two large department stores, the main building of Mandel Brothers (cat. no. 474) and the Rothschild and Company Store (cat. no. 480) just down the street (on the Mandel Brothers store see fig. 12.9; on the Rothschild store, fig. 12.10). This period also saw the final flowering of the standard Loop loft building, exemplified in the Brooks Building (cat. no. 464; figs. 11.16–11.18). At the Born Building (cat. no. 432) the firm used reinforced concrete construction on a large scale for the first time (fig. 11.6). Related to the loft buildings but larger in scale and designed for both production and administrative offices was a building Holabird & Roche designed for the Rand McNally Company in 1909 (cat. no. 478).

Among the commercial buildings the firm constructed in the years around 1910 were several clusters of commissions. The first was a group of no fewer than nine devoted to the sales, storage, and maintenance of automobiles, all situated on or near Michigan Avenue south of the Loop (figs. 18.7–18.14). The second was a power generating station for the Commonwealth Edison Company (cat. no. 494)—a company that would commission dozens of structures over the next few decades. Finally there was a group of buildings for the Chicago Telephone Company, again the first of dozens that the firm would ultimately do for this client (figs. 20.1–20.13). So important did the telephone company work become that during the Great Depression Illinois Bell, as it was then known, would sustain Holabird & Roche virtually single-handedly. The range of Holabird & Roche's institutional work during 1908–10 is suggested by the curious juxtaposition of the Industrial School for Girls at Park Ridge (cat. no. 458), a set of modest structures in the suburbs intended to house vagrant girls, and the University School for Girls (cat. no. 484), an elegant structure on a prime lakefront site on Chicago's Near North Side intended to house one of the city's most elegant educational institutions. For the University of Chicago the firm designed the Geology and

15.5

Woodmen of the World Building, Omaha, Nebraska (518), 1910–12, Fourteenth Street elevation. Chicago Historical Society Architectural Collections.

Geography Building (cat. no. 483). Here a simple, straightforward plan was matched with an equally simple exterior in the English Gothic style but embellished with an elaborate sculptural program. During these years the firm also did a good deal of work for Cook County's hospital system, perhaps because William Holabird acted for a time as county architect.[15] For the county's principal existing hospital complex on Chicago's Near West Side the firm did a series of projects, notably the Tuberculosis Hospital (cat. no. 441), a severely plain four- and five-story E-shaped structure. Holabird & Roche also planned an entirely new hospital to be built on an extensive 254 acre site at Oak Forest, on rich farming land twenty miles southwest of the Loop. On this site the new Cook County Poor Farm (cat. no. 444) was to replace the county's existing poor farm at Dunning. Of the forty or so planned buildings, Holabird & Roche saw about half through construction during 1908–10.

15.6
University School for Girls (484), 1909–10, 1106–14 N. Lake Shore Drive, view of exterior. From Selected Photographs Illustrating the Work of Holabird & Roche, Architects, *1925.*

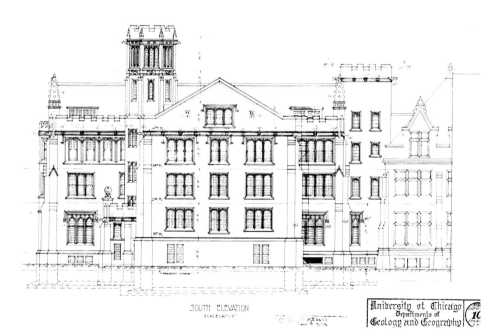

SOUTH ELEVATION
SCALE 1/8"=1'0"

University of Chicago
Departments of
Geology and Geography

15.7
University of Chicago Geology and Geography Building (483), 1909–14, 1011 E. Fifty-eighth Street, south elevation. Chicago Historical Society Architectural Collections.

The houses done by the firm in the first decade of the twentieth century were for the most part remarkably consistent. Whether large or small, they almost always followed the example set by the Slaughter house of 1894–96 (cat. no. 221) in the restrained symmetry of plan and classically ornamented masonry exteriors. The only real change was that the detailing became tighter and more abstract in the later years, prefiguring the remarkably simplified, stripped classical work of the 1920s. A good example from these years is a grand three-story house at Michigan Avenue and Thirty-seventh Street commissioned for Melville Rothschild by his mother, the wife of department store owner Maurice L. Rothschild (cat. no. 507).

1911–1914

The years 1911 to 1914 were relatively strong ones for Chicago construction generally, with the amount of construction averaging over $90 million each year. At Holabird & Roche these years saw solid billings for work that averaged over $3 million a year. In 1912 the firm announced a move from the Monadnock to larger quarters in the Monroe Building, at the corner of Michigan Boulevard and Monroe Street.[16] (See figs. 19.11–19.13.) For the first time the firm was lodged in a building of its own design.

15.8

Holabird & Roche employees with various members of the firm identified in ink on the print. Photograph labeled "1910—St. Paul, Minn. Courthouse." Chicago Historical Society Architectural Collections.

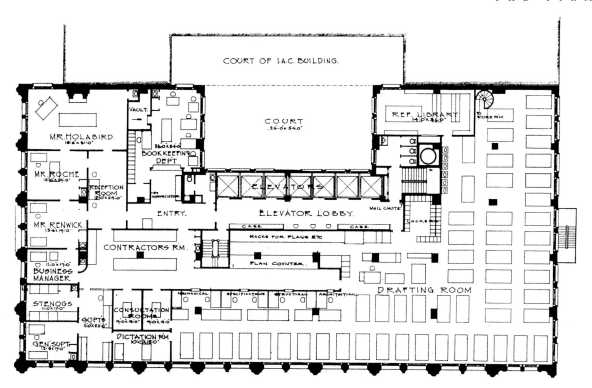

15.9

Holabird & Roche offices in Monroe Building, plan. The east (Michigan Avenue) frontage is to the left. A courtyard shared with the Illinois Athletic Club is to the south, and Monroe Street is to the north. From Architectural Record, *April 1912.*

The office took up an entire floor. The private offices in front overlooked the lake, with Holabird's large office in the corner and, next to him, Roche's and Renwick's in smaller spaces, then the business manager, stenographer, and general superintendent. Behind them were other offices, the elevator lobby, and the reference library. Wrapping around the north and west sides of the building was the large drafting room. Here the firm would remain until the late 1920s.

It was to this office that William Holabird's son John came to work in 1913. He had worked briefly in the office when it had still been in the Monadnock Building in 1909, but at that time he had no training as an architect, so he probably only did odd office jobs and some drafting. By 1913 he had graduated from West Point, gone to Paris, completed a program at the famous Ecole des Beaux-Arts there, and traveled extensively.[17] According to later testimony, when he returned to the office he was put to work on the Three Arts Club (cat. no. 601, figs. 21.1–21.5), where he did much of the stencil work for the wall decorations. The younger Holabird was soon joined by his Beaux-Arts classmate and fellow Chicagoan John Root, son of the famous architect John Wellborn Root, partner of Daniel Burnham. The two young men brought with them from Paris a new set of design ideas that appear to show up as exotic elements in the work of the firm during the years before World War I, when they were in the office but were not yet the major voices in day-to-day operations.

During these years Holabird & Roche did two large office buildings, an administrative building for the telephone company called the Bell Building (cat. no. 529) and a speculative structure on the southeast corner of LaSalle and Madison called the Lumber Exchange Building (cat. no. 596). Both followed the by now familiar formulas for buildings of this type, producing highly substantial but relatively simple structures with ornament concentrated around the base and top. In the case of the Bell Building this ornament was generically classical and consisted primarily of large pilasters on the top and bottom floors. At the Lumber Exchange, on the other hand, the ornamental treatment was entrusted to John Root, who had just joined the firm. Undoubtedly eager to display the design erudition he had acquired in Paris and wishing to create something novel, Root turned to more exotic sources. The story, as told years later by critic Russell Whitehead with a heavy dose of modernist moralizing, went as follows: "Root remembers the first big job that was assigned to him—the old Lumber Exchange in Chicago. . . . They operated on the then admitted principle that the man who could find the rarest book would do the most distinctive job. Root found a wonderful and little known book on Portuguese Gothic and had a circus with it."[18]

More interesting than either of the two buildings designed strictly for office use was the hybrid building housing the John Crerar Library and speculative office space (cat. no. 590). The Crerar Library, although privately funded, was open to the public and played a crucial role in Chicago's library system as defined by an agreement worked out with the Chicago Public Library and the private Newberry Library. Each of the three would specialize in a specific area, the Crerar devoting itself to the natural, physical, and social sciences. The trustees required a tall structure that would house the library and provide income, so they devised a program calling for retail space at grade level, four levels of rental office space directly above this, the library stacks above this, and the library public spaces at the very top of the building. This vertical organization is plainly visible in Holabird & Roche's design, in which the four upper stories, with their files of recessed, elaborately framed arched windows and corner sculptural elements, give the impression of being a separate four-story public building set on top of a typical Chicago speculative office building.

Closely related to the office buildings were two tall steel frame structures on State Street, the North American Building (cat. no. 542) and the Century Building (cat. no. 585). (See figs. 12.12–12.18.) These buildings followed the example of the Republic in having restaurants and shops at the lower levels with space on the upper floors primarily intended for shops and showrooms. They also followed the Republic in the choice of exterior cladding material—white terra cotta—but they were much more

15.10 (opposite)
John Crerar Library (590), 1913–20, 86 E. Randolph Street, northwest corner of Michigan Avenue, view to northwest. Photograph by Trowbridge. Chicago Historical Society Prints and Photographs Department.

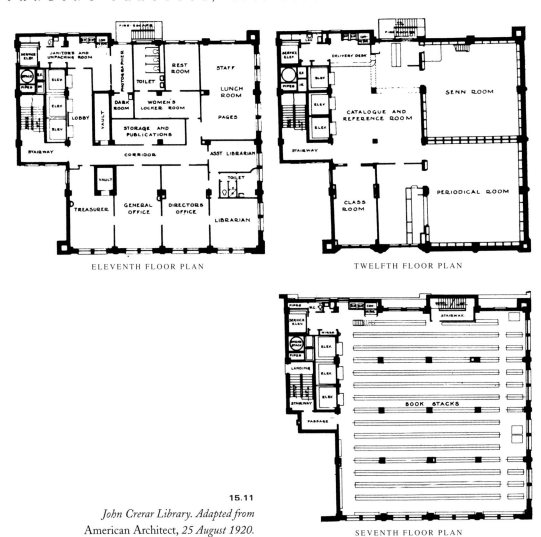

ELEVENTH FLOOR PLAN

TWELFTH FLOOR PLAN

15.11
John Crerar Library. Adapted from
American Architect, *25 August 1920.*

SEVENTH FLOOR PLAN

flamboyant in their use of the material. Not all of Holabird & Roche's commercial buildings were large structures in the Loop. A good example of a commercial structure for a neighborhood center is a building commissioned by Peter Brooks in 1913 (cat. no. 583) for a business center on the near Northwest Side where a major diagonal artery, Milwaukee Avenue, crossed two other important commercial streets, Damen Avenue and North Avenue.[19]

The firm continued its series of hotels with the Fort Dearborn in Chicago's south Loop (cat. no 564), the Deming in Terre Haute, Indiana (cat. no. 614), the Wisconsin in Milwaukee (cat. no 574), and the Muehlebach in Kansas City, Missouri (cat. no. 607). The first two were respectable efforts, if fairly modest in scale compared with earlier Holabird & Roche Chicago hotels like the LaSalle or the Sherman House. The Wisconsin, at its opening the largest hotel in Milwaukee, was somewhat more ambitious. It featured elaborately furnished public rooms with novel themes. The grill room, for example, was also known as the Indian Room because it had floor tiles set in a Navajo blanket pattern, lights fashioned from Indian baskets, and a large mural behind the bar painted by Theo Behr showing two Indians in birch bark canoes negotiating the rapids of the Wisconsin River. The Badger Room, intended as a tribute to the state, featured high on the walls a continuous mural of Wisconsin scenes such as the Dells, the state university, the Mississippi River, a frieze comprising an endless chain of dogs chasing badgers, and brackets, pillars, and lighting fixtures featuring leaf patterns in autumnal colors.

The firm's largest out-of-town hotel was the four hundred room Muehlebach of Kansas City, where the architects accommodated a sharply sloping site by arranging a set of public rooms on two levels, each entered from one of the streets, creating a complex but highly convenient circulation scheme that made full use of the split-level entry. A perspective section through this hotel perhaps conveys as well as any single

15.12
Hotel Muehlebach, Kansas City, Missouri (607), 1913–15, sectional perspective. From Hotel Monthly, *June 1915.*

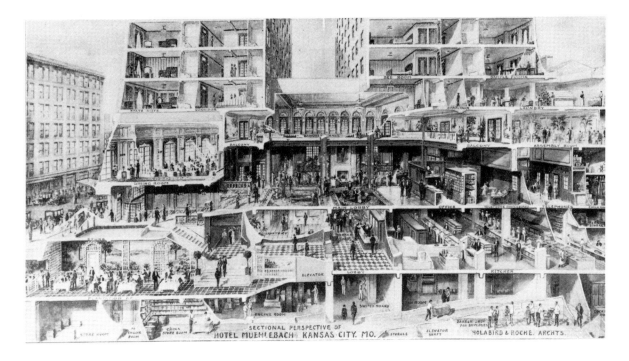

image the spatial complexity that resulted in trying to satisfy the adjacency requirements of lobbies, restaurants, meeting rooms, kitchens, and many other facilities, some of which had to be highly visible while others were supposed to remain all but invisible. Although every major Holabird & Roche hotel was the result of a collaboration between the architects, interior designers, mural painters, woodworkers, and many other skilled craftsmen, this hotel has been described as a model of harmonious effects.[20]

Among the institutional structures designed by the firm was the Three Arts Club (cat. no. 601), intended as a lodging and social setting for unmarried young women in the arts. Here Holabird & Roche provided a fortified brick box of a building with a whimsical interior (figs. 21.1–21.5). For the Chicago Nursery and Half Orphan Asylum (cat. no. 561), an organization devoted to the care of orphans, Holabird & Roche designed a set of informal buildings decorated with sprightly sculptural plaques by sculptor Alfonso Iannelli.

Over the years 1911–14 the firm did quite a number of residential structures in the agreeable classical style of the Rothschild house (cat. no. 507) of 1910. The Brandies house of 1911 at Bennett Avenue and Sixty-ninth Street in South Shore (cat. no. 527) and the Louis Ferguson house of 1912–15 in Evanston (cat. no. 580) were more modest versions of this type. For the large family of shoe manufacturer Joseph Tilt (cat. no. 602), the firm produced a Tudor-style house on a scale sufficient to contain twelve bedrooms and a gymnasium. Especially interesting from these years is the 1911 Rockwell house, a large dwelling shoehorned into a tight lot nineteen feet wide at 1260 N. Lake Shore Drive (cat. no. 543). Its restrained classical design contrasts with its neighbor to the south, the exuberant Arthur Aldis house (cat. no. 243), designed by Holabird & Roche and built in 1896. Certainly the most exotic house of this period was the Honolulu house built for C. W. Case Deering, a prominent Chicagoan who was a member of a family with exotic tastes in residential architecture (cat. no. 629).[21] Deering's house, on the beach at Waikiki, embodied an attempt to assimilate regional character. Constructed of concrete, the house contained high rooms with suspended ceilings, presumably to aid in ventilation, banks of casement windows opening to the outside, and a lanai, or sheltered porch, fronted by a portico of six concrete Doric columns. It is not known whether this house, which appears startlingly modern in the old photographs that remain, had any effect on architecture in Hawaii, but it appears to have provided someone in the Holabird & Roche office an interesting chance to experiment. It is tempting to venture that the young John Holabird and John Root were responsible for this commission. It seems to be related in feeling to the small studio the two men created for themselves during the same years (cat. no. 643, figs. 15.20–15.21). Both seem to reflect the progressive, but not avant-garde, European design of the early twentieth century.

15.13

Mrs. Lawrence D. Rockwell house (543), 1911, 1260 N. Lake Shore Drive, southwest corner of Goethe Street, view to the southwest with Rockwell House on the corner and the Aldis House by Holabird & Roche to the left. From Selected Photographs Illustrating the Work of Holabird & Roche, Architects, *1925.*

15.14

C. W. Case Deering House, Honolulu, Hawaii (629), 1914–17, perspective drawing. From Western Architect, *June 1915.*

1915–1918

The construction boom of the 1910s continued through 1916, reaching an all-time high exceeding $112 million in that year. Then, with America's entry into World War I, the figure plummeted to $64 million in 1917 and to $34 million in 1918, the lowest figure since the turn of the century. The work at Holabird & Roche followed the same pattern. Construction volume slid from $5.7 million to $1.2 million in 1917 to $700,000 in 1918. Beginning in 1915 the firm started a systematic recording of the amount of architectural commissions it collected, so from this point on there exists at least one set of accurate records compiled by the firm. Unfortunately the key figure, the actual construction cost total, is still not recorded, and the architectural commissions figure, though it rises and falls with construction costs as calculated from the known commissions, does not seem to have any direct relation to it. This is not surprising, since the fee could vary from commission to commission and the firm would have collected fees for planning and other work where no building was actually done. The fees collected were $236,000 for 1915, $169,000 for 1916, $157,000 for 1917, and $88,000 for 1918. By the end of the war the Holabird & Roche job log, started in 1902, numbered more than three thousand commissions.

America's entry into World War I had a major effect on the office as many of the young men left for military service. Among them were John Holabird and John Root,

15.15
Plankinton Arcade, Milwaukee, Wisconsin (661), 1915–16, interior view. Photograph by Robert Bruegmann, 1990.

who were both sent overseas in 1917. Both saw active combat during the Great War. Perhaps because of the presence of younger men, perhaps because of the onset of World War I, or perhaps just by chance, the years 1915–18 show a highly unusual mix of work at the firm. Conspicuously absent are the large-scale office or industrial buildings that dominated most previous periods.

Between 1915 and 1918 the firm completed only a single important retail commission. This project, the Plankinton Arcade, built along Grand (Wisconsin) Avenue, Milwaukee's most important commercial street (cat. no. 661), was an interesting mixed-use complex. At the street level a two-story base contained shops lined up on either side of an interior skylit pedestrian passage. Above the retail area and around the court over the skylight were five floors of offices. With its central fountain court, commemorative sculpture, and moving staircases, it functioned like an entire retail street encapsulated in a single building.[22]

During these years Holabird & Roche was also involved in other retail schemes of various types. At one end of the scale was the W. H. Taylor shopfront (cat. no. 652), a remodeling of the ground level of one of the old Gage Group Buildings (cat. no. 266) into an elegant and up-to-date shopfront with a nearly continuous glass wall interrupted only by the narrowest of mullions. This again appears to have been the work of the young John Holabird and John Root. At the other end of the scale was a study for the newly opened North Michigan Avenue done by the firm in collaboration with several other architects for the street's merchants association (cat. no. 705). The Hola-

15.16
Study for North Michigan Avenue (705), ca. 1917–18, perspective drawing. From American Architect, *11 December 1918.*

bird & Roche rendering, showing a huge triumphal colonnade leading to a great boulevard lined with substantial business blocks, is an eloquent testimony to the aspirations of the landowners and the power of City Beautiful ideals.[23] The gateway, however, was never built, and North Michigan Avenue, although it soon became a major rival to State Street as the city's premier shopping street, never achieved the unity the architects portrayed.[24]

If Holabird & Roche had comparatively few commercial commissions during the war years, it was busy with institutional work. The firm's entry in a 1916 competition for a new Cleveland public library (cat. no. 679) again strongly suggests the hand of the younger Holabird and John Root fresh from their Beaux-Arts training. Although the design has certain resemblance to the firm's earlier entry for the Cook County Courthouse, it is more academically correct, eliminating all the awkwardness of the earlier project, but perhaps also some of the vigor. Jurors did not place the Holabird & Roche submission among the finalists. During these years Holabird & Roche completed three projects on university campuses: the Education Building for the University of Illinois (cat. no. 689), a complex for the Wesley Foundation at the University

15.17

Garrett Biblical Institute, Evanston, Illinois (693), 1916–23, view to southeast with building C in foreground. Photograph by Trowbridge. Chicago Historical Society Prints and Photographs Department.

of Illinois (cat. no. 716), and four dormitories and a main building containing class-rooms, offices, library, and chapel for the Garrett Biblical Institute (cat. no. 693) at Northwestern University in Evanston. All three projects were Gothic in style. For the last two this style was chosen in part because they were for Methodist institutions and John Wesley had attended Oxford University. Probably more important was Martin Roche's desire to experiment further with the Gothic themes that had been so success-ful at the University Club. Still, in all three cases the viewer gets the impression that

15.18
Garrett Biblical Institute, chapel interior. Perspective drawing by Gilbert Hall. Photograph by Hedrich-Blessing.

devising a rational plan and maintaining economy of expression interested the architects more than the niceties of the Gothic facades, which, though perfectly respectable, can be thin and perfunctory in places. But on the interiors of the main Garrett building, more than in any other work of the firm except perhaps the great dining room of the University Club, the stone vaulting and the elaborate program of carved stone panels give the building something of the feel of a medieval structure.

One kind of commission conspicuously lacking in the firm's output after its earliest years was the church. Although there were projects, only one major building for religious worship seems to have been constructed, and it was a highly unorthodox one. For evangelical preacher Billy Sunday's ten-week Chicago campaign in 1918 the firm was involved, either as designer or as consulting architects, on a huge, temporary wood structure on the Near North Side at what is now the site of Northwestern University's Chicago campus at Lake Shore Drive and Chicago Avenue (cat. no. 708). Among the domestic commissions Holabird & Roche received during the war years, the building for Dr. Otto J. Stein at 514–22 Hawthorne Place (cat. no. 651) was remarkable for its severely simplified massing and moldings and trim pieces so reduced and stylized that

15.19
House for Dr. Otto J. Stein (651), 1915–17, 514–22 W. Hawthorne Place, view of exterior. Courtesy of Holabird & Root.

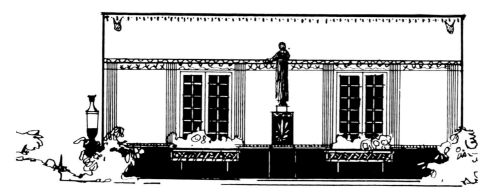

*Studio for John
Holabird and John
Root (643), 1915,
1114 N. Lake Shore
Drive, southwest
corner of Elm Street,
invitation with
elevation of studio.
Chicago Historical
Society Architectural
Collections.*

they looked almost like machined parts. This may well have been the work of the younger Holabird and Root.

One final building of these years deserves notice in passing. It appears that William Holabird at some point had some financial interest in a prime piece of Lake Shore Drive property between Division and Elm Streets. On the south part of this site the University School for Girls (cat. no. 484) was erected in 1910. Holabird apparently tried to develop the remaining parcel to the north of the school several times without success.[25] In 1915 the elder Holabird, probably not seeing any chance for making money on it at least in the short term, turned over use of the property to his son John and John Root. The two young men erected a small structure they called a "studio." It is probable that the building was ostensibly for business purposes, to provide a pied-à-terre for the younger Holabird, who was living with his wife at the family home in Evanston. After a long day at the office, he undoubtedly found it quicker and easier to return to the Near North Side than to Evanston, particularly if there were plans for evening meetings or social engagements in the Loop. It seems that from the first, however, its most important function was to serve as a place for both men to throw parties. Although the studio at 1114 N. Lake Shore Drive (cat. no. 643), was small and temporary and probably cost very little, its site would have made it conspicuous, as would its design, which was at once modest and raffishly monumental.

An account in a Minneapolis newspaper seems to have captured perfectly the flavor of this youthful, high-spirited enterprise. It described the building as a one-story structure with a "gaily colored cubist fresco" on three sides and a "graven image" in front.[26] Inside, a large bathtub occupied the center of the floor, surrounded by divans. When the structure was needed for large parties the tub would be drained and used as a pit for seating around a large central table. The entire enterprise strongly recalls the elaborate temporary settings created for the Beaux-Arts balls and other festivities both

15.21

Studio for John Holabird and John Root, view of interior. From Chicago Architecture Club Annual *(Chicago, 1916).*

men had experienced in Paris. It is likely that the studio was intended to evoke exactly this kind of slightly risqué and Bohemian atmosphere. It probably created something of a stir in Chicago, one that did nothing to hurt the firm's business.

Within a few years the two men would leave for another encounter with France, but of an entirely different kind. They would leave for the war as young men, several years out of school and with a few years of experience in a firm that was still tightly controlled by William Holabird and Martin Roche. At the time of their return home in 1919, even though they had been away only two years, everything would have changed. By 1919 their school days must have seemed far behind them and the studio like a relic from an era long past. Now in their mid-twenties, they both had matured quickly in the leadership roles they had been asked to play in the Great War. The elder Holabird and Roche, now in their sixties, were only too ready to leave some of the

15.22

Holabird & Roche office with various members of the firm identified: William Holabird and Martin Roche seated just right of center in second row, John Holabird and John Root Jr. in back row. Photograph labeled "1915 or 1916." Chicago Historical Society Architectural Collections.

demands of running a large practice to the younger men. After the constraints of a war economy eased, Chicago and America stood poised at the edge of an era of enormous growth. The task of guiding the firm through the years of the next generation would fall to the younger men. For Holabird & Roche 1918 decisively marked the end of an era.

SIXTEEN

PALACES   OF   DEMOCRACY:

THE   BUSINESS   HOTEL

No building type in the early twentieth-century American city was more important than the large business hotel, or more complex. These structures contained rooms of all shapes and sizes, from the small "sample" rooms used by traveling salesmen to the enormous banquet halls, ballrooms, and lobbies that served as settings for some of the city's most important civic events. Indeed, the privately owned large hotel provided some of the most important oases of calm and order in the often turbulent urban environment.

For the architect the task of designing a hotel was nothing less than accommodating many of the most disparate functions of the city in a single building on a restricted site. All the hotel's activities had to be orchestrated so that guests and employees, visitors and delivery people could each circulate freely without unduly impinging on one another. This caused endless difficulties in plan, equipment, and structure. The desire to put large public rooms on the lower floors for easy access from the streets, to cite just one example, posed major problems for the structural engineers, who had to find ways of supporting thousands of tons of walls, corridors, and furniture of the small guest rooms directly over the large, uninterrupted spans of the rooms on the lower floors. The answer was usually to create deep steel trusses, but in large hotels these trusses became so big that they took up the space of an entire floor or more. Height restrictions and material costs, however, made such a waste of space impractical, leading the architects and engineers to find ways to thread the rooms and corridors between the top and bottom chords and around the diagonal members of the trusses. This created quite a few odd-sized and nonstandard rooms, which was not entirely desirable but appeared to be the best solution available.

Another perennial hotel problem was the kitchen. For economy, kitchens had to be central, but for the convenience of the guests, the hotel's eating places were dispersed. Still, the food had to be warm by the time it reached every table. This led to the creation of large central kitchens, elaborate food-moving devices, and many smaller kitchens and serving pantries, all with special problems of fire prevention and ventilation. These conflicting structural and programmatic demands, together with constrained sites and building restrictions, resulted in schemes that in plan and section look like Chinese puzzles. (See, for example, fig. 15.12.)

After the functional requirements were met, other seemingly irreconcilable demands involved image and style. The hotel had to be intimate and homelike but at the same time grand enough to serve as the setting for some of the city's most important events. It had to seem luxurious but at the same time be efficient, easy to clean, and inexpensive to maintain. The decorations had to look up-to-date but at the same time feel comfortable and reassuring.

These were challenges ideally suited to a large and well-organized firm like Holabird & Roche. Shortly after their first venture into hotel design early in the century, the architects gained a national reputation as hotel experts. They were able to maintain this reputation for over half a century, producing along the way a remarkable number of major hotels, including some of the country's largest and most conspicuous.

The Congress

The firm's entry into the world of hotel design involved an addition, not an entirely new building, but it was a very large addition, and it provides an interesting illustration of a number of challenges presented by the city hotel. The existing hotel for which Holabird & Roche drew expansion plans in 1901 (cat. no. 335) was the Auditorium Annex. As the name implies, this building was itself an addition, or rather a freestanding annex, to the great Auditorium Hotel, one of Chicago's most famous landmarks. Occupying the Michigan Avenue frontage of a huge mixed-use building that covered half a city block and that also contained offices along the Wabash Avenue side and a theater with over four thousand seats in the center of the block, this first building in the complex, the Auditorium Hotel, was an instant landmark, a masterwork of Louis Sullivan and his partner Dankmar Adler and one of the largest and most opulent buildings west of the Atlantic seaboard. Its relatively simple exterior gave little indication of the almost barbaric splendor of the Sullivan interiors. With their gold leaf, murals, intricate patterns, rich materials, and sumptuous color, they conjured up

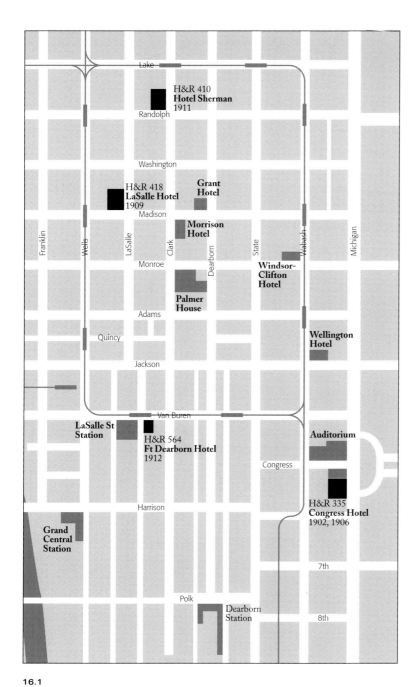

16.1

Locations of Holabird & Roche hotels and other buildings in the central business district, ca. 1914. Map drawn by Dennis McClendon using information from Holabird & Root records, fire insurance maps, and other sources, 1996.

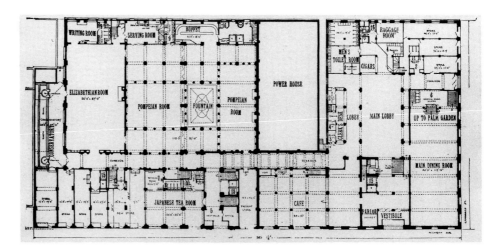

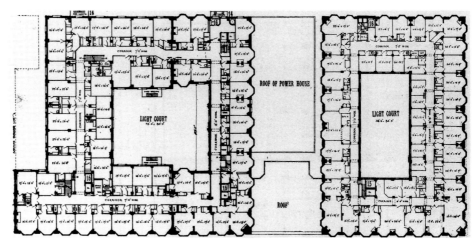

16.2

Congress Apartment (Hotel) Building (335), 1901–6, 518–36 S. Michigan Avenue, ground floor and typical floor plans after the completion of both the 1901 and 1906 building campaigns. The double row of columns to the left and the fountain in the Pompeiian Room mark the south edge of the 1901 building campaign. From Hotel Monthly, *January 1911.*

16.3

Congress Hotel, diagram of building campaigns drawn by Dennis McClendon, 1996.

Congress Hotel Company

The above picture shows the Auditorium Annex, Annex Apartments, Annex Extension and Auditorium Hotel, Chicago.

We offer the unsold portion of $850,000 First Mortgage 5 per cent Serial Gold Bonds on the southern extension, covering 130 feet frontage, at prices to yield approximately 5 per cent.

THE AMERCAN TRUST AND SAVINGS BANK
CHICAGO

E. H. ROLLINS & SONS
238 La Salle Street
CHICAGO

16.4

Congress Hotel, advertisement for bonds showing Studebaker (Fine Arts) Building (far right), original Auditorium Hotel by Adler and Sullivan (second from right), Auditorium Annex by Clinton Warren (eleven-story main building with four-story structure) and the thirteen-story Holabird & Roche addition to the left. From Economist, *21 July 1906.*

a darkly glowing magic kingdom far removed from the hustle and bustle of the city outside, overwhelming even the most jaded visitors by their originality and brilliance.

The second structure, the Auditorium Annex, at the southwest corner of Michigan Avenue and Congress Street, was built in 1893 to designs by Clinton J. Warren to serve as a companion structure to the Auditorium Hotel and was connected to it by a passageway that ran under Congress Street. In his design for the Annex Warren substituted a steel frame for the masonry bearing walls used by Adler and Sullivan but used the same materials and maintained the overall building configuration and many of the same design motifs, including the arched entryway, the projecting second-floor porch, and the mode of articulating the facade above the second-floor cornice. The continuity of materials and style was probably requested by the clients. Warren did make a number of changes, however, and those changes are telling. By making the bays narrower and having them project forward, he made his addition considerably simpler and more forthright. This may have been due in part to a desire not to upstage the original building, or it may have been due to the personality of Warren, whose buildings were more overtly practical and made fewer claims than Sullivan's to the status of art.

It was probably also due to a changing conception of hotels. Around the turn of the century a number of building types in Chicago veered sharply, but usually briefly, away from the palatial image that had been the norm in the post-Fire era. As we have seen, this was true of speculative office buildings and apartment buildings. It was also true, as we will see, in the case of the Cook County Courthouse–Chicago City Hall and other more pretentious building types. The same move from palatial to business-like was visible with hotels. The most famous of these newly sober structures was Burn-ham and Root's Great Northern, finished in 1891, which looked remarkably like any downtown business building (fig. 7.3). In fact the elevations of this building were so similar to those of an office building that one wonders if it may have been designed as one or with eventual conversion in mind.[1] It is possible that the Auditorium Annex and Great Northern each represented a special circumstance, but the result was that the visitor surveying the most important Chicago hotels built at the end of the century would have found them quite different in exterior appearance from their more monu-mental New York counterparts.[2]

No one was more influential in creating the new, simpler Chicago hotel than Clinton J. Warren, who was the most prolific designer of such buildings during the 1880s and 1890s.[3] For the Auditorium Annex, his most conspicuous work, Warren called for an eleven-story hollow rectangle extended twelve bays along Congress Street and eight bays along Michigan Avenue. There was also a small four-story, four-bay wing to the south along Michigan that masked the powerhouse at the back of the site. Warren retired from architecture soon after he finished work on the Auditorium Annex to devote himself to managing his hotel properties.

In 1901 Colonel Richard Southgate of the Congress Hotel Company, owners of the hotel, commissioned Holabird & Roche to extend Warren's Auditorium Annex some sixty feet farther along Michigan Avenue, displacing several old three-story houses. It is clear from Holabird & Roche's plan that this construction was conceived as the northernmost portion of a large new quadrangle that would eventually extend all the way to the southern edge of the block. Southgate called the new block the Congress Apartment Building, perhaps because he intended to use the new portion as apartments or because he intended to convert the entire Auditorium Annex, includ-ing both the Warren and the Holabird & Roche portions, into apartments. In fact the Annex was soon split off from its parent building, and the underground passage between the two was closed. In the end the Annex was not turned into apartments. It remained a hotel and, with the Holabird & Roche addition, was renamed the Congress.[4]

The planning problems inherent in creating an addition that had to defer to an older structure, had to operate as a self-contained unit, but also had to be designed so it could eventually function as a fragment of a much larger ensemble were familiar to the architects. They had faced similar challenges in the design of department stores, for example; but nowhere was a solution more difficult to execute than in a major hotel with its elaborate circulation patterns.

The architects, probably at the express instructions of the client and following Warren's example, maintained the materials and overall configuration of both earlier structures but, using the Warren building as the point of departure, provided further simplifications. Keeping the same rusticated street-level piers, cornice above the mezzanine floor, and projecting bays as in Warren's building, Holabird & Roche abandoned the arched entryway, the projecting second-story portico, the three-story upper zones, and the arched windows. In the Holabird & Roche scheme the projecting bays ran up to the twelfth floor, where they simply stopped. Above this two floors with windows in triplets and a cornice provided a simple visual termination. The result was a building in which virtually all traces of specific Romanesque detailing seen in Adler and Sullivan's facade and still visible in simplified form in the Warren addition were expunged in favor of a strictly businesslike facade that could easily have been mistaken for one of the simple, nominally classical office buildings that Holabird & Roche and other architects were putting up throughout the Loop at about the same time.

Certainly the sedate exterior offered no clue to the dazzling interiors. It suggests that the architects, like Sullivan before them, had been given so little room for artistic license on the exterior that they compensated with especially lavish interior spaces. At the Congress Holabird & Roche not only was called on to do designs for the main public rooms in the new portion but was also asked to extensively remodel the interiors of the original Warren section to make a unified whole out of the composition. With the precedent of the lavish Sullivan interiors in the original Auditorium Hotel before their eyes and a substantial budget, the architects had not only the means but a mandate to design interiors more elaborate than anything they had yet attempted.

They also had a chance to do something more archaeologically "correct" than any of their previous efforts. Although they had set a new standard in the city with their classical ornament in the Marquette lobby, there were undoubtedly elements of this composition that struck even Holabird & Roche as somewhat gauche and awkward a decade later. By this time classical ornament had become much more common, and Chicago architects had gained a good deal of sophistication in its use. In their designs for the new public rooms at the Congress, the architects decided to use a distinct theme and set of materials for each room. The great hallway running along the entire front of the building connecting the original portion and the new addition (later called Peacock Alley) was a sea of marble, with Italian statuary marble walls articulated by white marble pilasters and attached half columns and floors composed of a mosaic of black, red, and white marbles.[5] The French and English dining rooms were executed in eighteenth-century styles, with the English room paneled in mahogany while the French dining room sported bird's-eye maple woodwork with gilt ornaments and silk moiré wall panels.

The most remarkable of the rooms at the Congress and perhaps the most ambitious of all hotel period rooms in that era was the sixty by one hundred foot Pompeiian Room. Placed at the south edge of the addition so that part of the space would fall under a light well, the Pompeiian Room was an attempt to recreate part of the house of a wealthy Roman citizen from the first century A.D. Newspapers and journals contained elaborate descriptions of the room and the research that went into its creation.

At the south side of the room a pool, the "impluvium," dominated a mosaic-floored two-story space surrounded by a colonnade of Doric columns composed of verd antique and white marble with gilt capitals and moldings. At the center of the pool a jet of water shot into the air and then cascaded back over an elaborately colored and layered blue and green glass fountain. Designed by the Tiffany Company of New York, this fountain had reportedly been created for the Pan-American Exposition held in Buffalo in 1901. Exactly what it had to do with the antique Roman theme is some-

16.5
Congress Hotel,
Pompeiian Room.
Photograph by R. W.
Williams. From
Inland Architect,
January 1903.

16.6
*Congress Hotel,
Pompeiian Room.
Photograph by R. W.
Williams. From*
Inland Architect,
January 1903.

what hard to determine, since the artist's goal in this "weird and beautiful creation in myriad points of color, set by a most cunning craft in some kind of cement," had been to "interpret in his material the beauty of the geyser pools of Yellowstone," but it is probable that the hotel owners had obtained it at a good price and that it was too spectacular not to use.[6] Neither the architects nor the owners even attempted to explain its presence. Above the pool an elaborate Tiffany art glass skylight in shades of purple, amber, and green was used to give visitors the illusion of being under an arbor in the Campania.

In the spaces around the pool courtyard the architects confronted the problem of adapting Roman forms to modern usage. "Chicago businessmen are not accustomed to lounging on couches at their feasts in the manner of the Greeks or Romans," explained one journalist; "neither couches nor the stiff benches with turned legs, so common among the antique relics, would be serviceable." But, he continued, a little imagination, coupled with further research and the resources of the Marshall Field and Company furniture department, had solved the problem. Field's provided side chairs adapted from the Greek klismos and armchairs based on the Roman couch and settle, both upholstered in red plush and leather; a central table based on one found in the house of Cornelius Rufus at Pompeii; and bronze candelabra reproduced from originals in Naples but fitted with electric lights. Against the wall stood a series of "Ali Baba" jars six feet tall, with surfaces of a dark greenish color meant to resemble patinated bronze, their shapes based on classical amphorae. The jars were the product of the American Terra Cotta and Ceramic Company. The walls behind were decorated with panels painted with scenes of dancing figures, the work of artist Edward J. Holslag.[7]

The Pompeiian Room created a sensation. The British pre-Raphaelite painter Edward Burne-Jones was reported to have called it, without irony, the most beautiful room in America.[8] H. L. Mencken supposedly said that Chicago had only two things New York did not have: the Pompeiian Room and the Twentieth Century Limited back to New York.[9] Everyone who wrote about the hotel discussed it prominently, and it was included in every list of things visitors to Chicago should see.

The Pompeiian Room clearly stands as one of the foremost examples of late nineteenth-century "theme" architecture. The idea was not new. New York's Waldorf-Astoria, designed by Henry Janeway Hardenbergh and built in two stages in 1893 and 1897, for example, had a number of remarkably opulent period rooms.[10] Many Americans would also have seen period rooms of a somewhat different sort in Masonic lodges or as stage sets. It seems that the example of the national and theme buildings at the 1893 World's Fair in Jackson Park also had a major influence on both the cool white classicism of Peacock Alley and the more highly colored and exotic classicism of the Pompeiian Room.

It is difficult for us today to appreciate the reception accorded the Pompeiian Room. First of all, we cannot experience it ourselves because, like most of the most elaborate period rooms of the period, it has long since been remodeled out of existence. More fundamentally, having experienced Disneyland and Las Vegas, movies, television, and the color photographs in *National Geographic,* we have become somewhat jaded. It is important to realize that the decorations and furnishings that many observers in future generations would consider frivolous pastiches undoubtedly seemed scholarly and sophisticated to Chicagoans accustomed to the elaborately patterned fabrics and brightly colored carpets of the 1870s and 1880s that borrowed widely from the past but made no pretense of evoking a specific time or place. It seems likely that the designers at Holabird & Roche approached the task with the same mixture of amused detachment, genuine curiosity, and serious interest in the archaeological research and technical challenges that has always been necessary for creating any successful theme architecture.

Within a few years the hotel expanded again, filling out the entire half block bounded by Congress on the north, Michigan Avenue on the east, the midblock alley on the west, and Harrison on the south, with the exception of a single twenty-five-foot lot at the far south part of the property. Negotiations for this lot, occupied by an old three-story building, probably ended in one of those intense games of real estate poker that characterized Chicago. The hotel company clearly would have benefited by its purchase. Presumably the property owner, knowing its value to the company, held out for an enormous price. In this case the hotel owners pulled out. Even without the southernmost parcel the new addition, completed in 1906, brought the total number of rooms to sixteen hundred. This section, which at first glance seems identical in treatment to the earlier Holabird & Roche work, on closer examination turns out to have slightly larger bay windows, probably in response to requests for more daylight in the rooms. At about the same time the hotel commissioned from the architects a major new service wing across the alley from the hotel, fronting on Wabash Avenue and connected to the hotel by bridges. The owners claimed in typical Chicago fashion that the hotel was the largest in the world. The twenty-four-bay facade south of Congress, together with the ten wider bays of the original Auditorium Hotel across the street, formed a massive cliff of masonry along Michigan Avenue nearly two solid blocks long and half a block deep. It was the product of three separate architects and four building campaigns. All parts of the ensemble were similar in scale and materials, but each responded to new conditions and changing aesthetics. In its 1906 addition Holabird & Roche expanded considerably on the idea of the period room. In addition to enlarging the Pompeiian Room, they created a series of new rooms including the Louis XVI Dining Room and a Saxon Dining Room with murals portraying scenes from Norse mythology. The two most "authentic" of the period rooms were an elaborate Japanese Tea Room and the oak-paneled Elizabethan Room. The latter was modeled on Hatfield House in Britain and replicated it down to copies of the English portraits that hung on its walls. "The Elizabethan Room is a Tudor interior unsurpassed even in England," wrote an author in the *Fine Arts Journal.* "Surely it is Hatfield Hall itself, but glorified, larger, and a much more inhabitable, homelike and a more comfortably furnished room."[11]

An even more strenuous attempt to be faithful to historical sources was the Japanese Tea Room. Probably inspired by the tea houses built for the 1893 Fair, this room was described in an article in *International Studio* magazine as being based on Japanese temples of the Fujiwara and Ashikaga periods, that is, thirteenth to fifteenth century. For the room's striking black, red, and gold decorations the architects turned to the Kawabe Studios of New York. Not content merely to imitate Japanese designs, the designers imported much of the material for the room from Japan, including the hinoki wood for the elaborate carved beams, carvings, and frames. The panels depicting storks, peacocks, and chrysanthemums were carved by Professor K. Takouchi, an instructor at the College of Fine Arts in Tokyo. Other pieces of decoration, although

16.7
Congress Hotel, view of Elizabethan Room. From Architectural Review, *April 1908.*

16.8
Congress Hotel, view of Japanese Tea Room. From International Studio, *November 1907.*

16.9
Congress Hotel, view of Great Ballroom. From Selected Photographs Illustrating the Work of Holabird & Roche, Architects, *1925.*

distinctly American in manufacture, also had a Japanese theme. The stained glass panels were intended to suggest shoji screens.[12]

Finally, there was the enormous Great Ball Room or Gold Room. This room, fifty feet wide by ninety-four feet long and thirty-eight feet high, was one of the largest and, with its breche violet marble and gilt ornament, one of the most opulent hotel rooms in the country. The Gold Room is the sole surviving remnant of the original main rooms. Even in its current state, somewhat shabby and repainted, it continues to give some idea of the overwhelming impression Holabird & Roche's public spaces must have made.

The LaSalle Hotel and the Sherman House

The Congress was widely considered the most elegant large hotel in the city until the construction of a new set of hotels in the years around 1910. These large hotels reflected a distinct shift away from the relatively simple exteriors of the Congress and back to the palatial hotel popular in the third quarter of the nineteenth century. The model appears to have been a small group of New York establishments finished in the first years of the new century, including the Astor, the Knickerbocker, and the St. Regis, but particularly the St. Regis.[13] In Chicago the Blackstone, designed by Marshall and Fox and finished in 1909, occupied the upper end of the hotel hierarchy. Relatively small and without the elaborate set of meeting rooms of the Congress, it was more a luxury hotel than a business hotel.[14] The true successors to the Congress were two hotels designed by Holabird & Roche: the LaSalle Hotel, commissioned in 1907 and finished in 1909, and the Sherman House, commissioned in 1906 but not finished until 1911. The LaSalle and the Sherman, with their stylish designs and their locations at the heart of the Loop, set the standard for large business hotels in Chicago and the Midwest until well into the 1920s.

At twenty-two stories the LaSalle (cat. no. 418) claimed the distinction of being the tallest hotel in the country. Although its 1,150 rooms accommodated slightly fewer guests than the Congress, it did claim a hundred rooms more than the Waldorf-Astoria, making it, according to its owners, the largest in the country constructed all at one time. The LaSalle, like the Blackstone, was certainly more ornamental on the exterior than the Congress. With its red brick and heavily carved stone and its mansard roof, it was described as Louis XIV, a style chosen, according to accounts in the press, for its associations with the age of the French explorer La Salle, after whom the building was named. Clearly the building did not look like any known to seventeenth-century Parisians. Its mansards and ornamental details would have been quite at home in turn-of-the-century Paris, however.

On the exterior the LaSalle bore a striking resemblance to New York's St. Regis, which opened in 1904, built to the designs of Trowbridge and Livingston. Curiously, the St. Regis had marked a turn away from the florid designs of earlier New York hotels like the Waldorf toward a more refined and subdued style on both the exterior and the interior. In Chicago, on the other hand, the exteriors of the Blackstone and the LaSalle were somewhat more elaborate, less like office blocks than some of the best-known Chicago hotels of the 1880s and 1890s. The result is that by 1910 the practice in New York and that in Chicago had converged. Although this change was welcomed in many quarters, since it returned to Chicago hotels some of the distinctive character they had had in the nineteenth century, the most vocal advocates of a regional style were bitterly disappointed. Wrote Peter B. Wight:

Heretofore the Great Northern, the Auditorium and the Congress have been distinctively Chicago buildings, independent in plans, construction and design, adapted to the business requirements of the Middle West and eminently convenient, comfortable and profitable. But in the LaSalle, the

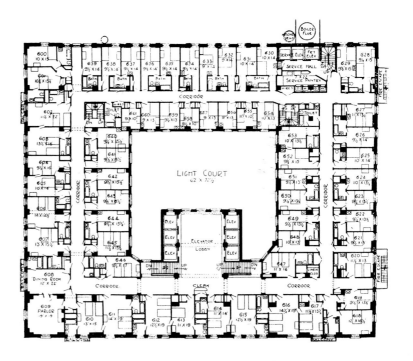

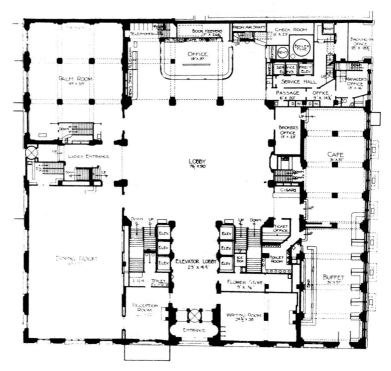

16.11
*LaSalle Hotel, first floor and typical floor
plans. From* Inland Architect,
March 1908.

Hotel LaSalle
CHICAGO'S FINEST HOTEL

On Summer Nights
THE ROOF GARDEN

FANNED by breezes from Lake Michigan, the Roof Garden of HOTEL LA SALLE on summer evenings is steeped in luxurious coolness. ❡ Fashionable people throng it nightly to beguile the hours with dainty refections, music and dancing. ❡ Its spacious floor in the rhythm of the dance presents a picture which in sparkle and color rivals some gay ball at Versailles in the sumptuous days of Le Grand Monarque. ❡ HOTEL LA SALLE throughout the summer is coolly comfortable. ❡ Its distinctive fame rests upon courtesy and service. Hospitality is its tradition.

HOTEL LA SALLE, *La Salle at Madison*
ERNEST J. STEVENS, Vice-President and Manager

Room Rates

Number of Rooms	Price per Day 1 Person	2 Persons
171	$2.50	$4.00
61	3.00	4.50
33	4.00	5.50
141	4.00	6.00
78	4.50	6.50
250	5.00	7.00
115	6.00	8.00
177	7.00	9.00

1026 guest rooms

Fixed-Price Meals
Breakfast   50c and 70c
Luncheon   85c
Dinner . . $1.25
A la carte service at sensible prices

HOTEL LA SALLE GARAGE
—*just around the corner*
For the convenience of its guests who motor to Chicago, HOTEL LA SALLE maintains the largest and finest garage in the city

16.12
LaSalle Hotel, advertisement.
From Hotel Monthly, *August 1923.*

Blackstone and the Sherman . . . we see the encroachment of those ideas in hotel building and architecture, recently prevalent in New York, as exemplified by the Knickerbocker and a few others.[15]

On the interior as well, the LaSalle resembled its New York contemporaries, particularly the Astor. In the interior decorations, however, both New York and Chicago hotels show evidence of the move already visible in the Congress and other hotels at the turn of the century, away from the grandiose, sometimes bombastic, public rooms of an earlier generation to ones that were meant to be rich but more refined and domestic.

Clearly the example of the New York hotels was very important in the creation of the LaSalle. The hotel's owner even imported a general manager from New York, hiring him away from the St. Regis. But the completion of the LaSalle marks a fundamental reordering of the relation between New York and Chicago in hotel design. By 1910 any lingering feeling that Chicago was provincial had been overcome. Chicago had already taken the lead in many branches of the hospitality business. Because of its central location, it was becoming the country's hub for salesmen and for business meetings. The Albert Pick Company, the country's largest supplier of hotel equipment and furnishings, and several other such businesses were based in Chicago, as was the most important trade journal, *Hotel Monthly*. Now, with the completion of the trio of big hotels around 1910, Chicago architects—Holabird & Roche at the forefront—were at least as likely as their New York counterparts to be the ones creating the largest and most widely known hotels in smaller American cities. From the 1910s through the early 1950s, Holabird & Roche was probably the country's most prolific designer of business hotels.

The LaSalle's public spaces were no less remarkable than those at the Congress. The architects intended the two-story lobby, at the center of the ground floor, to have a domestic feel. In reality the lack of natural light and the Circassian walnut paneling

16.13
LaSalle Hotel, view of Blue Fountain Room. From Selected Photographs Illustrating the Work of Holabird & Roche, Architects, *1925.*

must have made it somewhat dark. But most critics considered it an appropriate and handsome room. Also on the ground level were the main dining room, a "French creation in shades of green and gold," the bar and men's café, sturdily finished in carved oak and leather, and the Palm Room, a ubiquitous feature in the grander hotels of this era. With its walls and pilasters in Rookwood tile and pearl gray terra cotta and its central fountain "in a distinctly Italian manner," as in a courtyard of a Florentine palace, it was considered by some to be the city's most beautiful hotel dining room. Downstairs was the German Grill and the highly original Blue Fountain Room, with silver maple woodwork and highly decorated vaulted ceiling over a statue of the Venus de' Medici in the central fountain flooded with blue electric light. The grill room featured matte glazed tile, red brick, and Rookwood ornament, but its design was eclipsed by its reputation as the place where electric grilling was pioneered in Chicago. On the mezzanine level, galleries and a set of private dining rooms ringed the lobby.

Above the mezzanine level, floors two through eighteen housed the sleeping rooms. Laid out on a similar plan, these floors were arranged in a square doughnut with the guest rooms accessible from a double-loaded corridor around the central light well that extended from the top of the lobby to the top of the building. The rooms, typical of those in first-class hotels throughout the country in the 1910s and 1920s, each had a bathroom and were arranged in suites of paired rooms connected by a door.

16.14
LaSalle Hotel Grand Banquet Room, elevation. From New York Architect, *October 1918.*

·SIDE·ELEVATION·

Surprisingly enough, at the LaSalle the grand banquet hall was not in the lower portion of the building. Instead, as at the St. Regis, it was placed at the very top of the hotel, on the nineteenth floor, probably to eliminate major headaches involving food odors drifting upward from the base of the hotel into guest rooms and structural problems related to the need to span large open areas at the bottom of a tall building. This arrangement probably strained elevator capacity and worried fire officials, however, and it was not extensively copied. Said to be a reproduction of the ballroom in the Palace of Versailles, the LaSalle's banquet room was finished in gold and ivory with walls faced in Rookwood panels designed to match the color and texture of Caen stone, windows draped in red damask, and a trompe l'oeil ceiling representing the sky. Also on this floor, on the other side of the central light court, was the smaller Red Room, said to be in the style of Louis XVI, paneled in Circassian walnut and named for its crimson hangings.[16]

Holabird & Roche's Sherman House (cat. no. 410), built in 1909–11, was the fourth building to bear the name. The hotel had been a fixture in downtown Chicago since pioneer days. The new 757-bed structure designed by Holabird & Roche was similar in plan and style to the LaSalle, although slightly more modest and meant for a somewhat less affluent clientele. The main rooms were again lavishly decorated in period styles. The banquet rooms were on the second floor. The most notable room at the Sherman was the Celtic Bar. On the main floor facing Randolph Street, it was finished in American oak in imitation of Irish bog oak, painted with vivid colors and carved into forms resembling archaic sculpture. The highlight of the room was a mural by Maxfield Parrish, "Four and Twenty Blackbirds." The idea had, again, come from New York, where Parrish had created "Old King Cole" for the Knickerbocker. Even better known to many Chicagoans, however, was College Inn, an immense and extraordinarily busy dining room in the basement of the building.

One of the major obstacles to forming an opinion about these grand hotels of the early twentieth century is that they have largely disappeared. The LaSalle and the Sherman were both demolished. Although the Congress still stands, it has been repeatedly remodeled. More important, the entire place of the hotel in urban life has changed. The Sherman and the LaSalle were complex institutions. They had to please the captain of industry and the tobacco-chewing traveling businessman, the back-slapping Chicago booster and the businessman's wife. Many of the travelers from smaller towns were overwhelmed by the sheer size of the places. They were impressed by the kind of statistics that delighted the editors of the *Hotel Monthly*. The LaSalle, for example, incorporated 7,200 tons of steel, 4,500,000 bricks, and 22,000 electric lights. The dining rooms could seat 2,500 people at one time. The laundry could do 50,000 pieces daily. The hotel had its own branch telephone exchange. The general

china service, provided by the Albert Pick Company, numbered 43,506 pieces. The kitchen included sixty-eight feet of Van's French ranges and seventeen ovens. The wine inventory was valued at $40,000.[17]

More worldly travelers and Chicago citizens themselves were also impressed. Consider, for example, this description of the opening of the LaSalle:

> The LaSalle Hotel started out last night to get a history for itself. The LaSalle has everything else. While the invited guests of Manager George H. Gazley were assembling in the lobby before the banquet they lolled in chairs that were exact replicas of the great crown surmounted seats that graced the main state room of Louis at Fontainebleau. . . . Bankers, business and professional men and newspaper men sat around the fountain in the palm room on the Madison Street side of the ground floor beneath a Gobelin tapestry that took the grand gold medal at the Paris exposition, and felt proud that they were partaking of the first banquet spread in what they described as the finest hotel in the United States. The Gobelin, by the way, is nine by twenty feet, cost $10,000, is after a painting by Mazerolle, and kept many hands busy three years in the making. Aside from Alice Roosevelt Longworth's it is the only one in this country.
>
> The orchestra was playing and the waiters were deploying busily in the forest of flower-burdened tables when Homer A. Stillwell [Chicago businessman, vice president of Butler Brothers] was moved by the spell of all this magnificence to say something about it so that all could hear. The waiters and the music stopped and Mr. Stillwell raised his glass. "I propose a toast," he said "to the finest hotel in the world."[18]

Today it is a little difficult to read accounts like these without smiling. It would be easy to think that the LaSalle and Sherman House public rooms were a parody of upper-class environments of the past, a stage set for amusement of the American bourgeoisie. There were observers at the time who had similar sentiments. Peter B. Wight, who deplored the trend in Chicago hotels to follow the lead of New York, clearly saw this development as a threat to middle-American values. He described it as a "tendency to luxury and high life" that involved aping the habits of the very rich and described the results as part of the domain of fashion, which, he stated, "has no legitimate part in architectural evolution."[19]

But it is important to remember that the contemporary American city is vastly different from the city of 1910. In 1910 there were far fewer large public places that an average citizen could enter freely. The hotel of that era provided for many functions that were not adequately served otherwise. It was a common setting for important lectures and concerts. The art on the walls was more accessible to many citizens than that in the museum. Before television and color photographs in popular magazines overwhelmed readers with images of famous places from foreign lands or the country's museums had taken up in earnest the idea of the period room, interiors like the Pompeiian Room or Celtic Bar did manage to convey something of the feel of other times and places. The hotel, with some justification, felt it played a major educational and cultural role.

Even sophisticated observers of the day admired the skill with which technology and art were wedded in the LaSalle and other great hotels of the era and found in them a microcosm of what was best in the city as a whole. Montgomery Schuyler, dean of American architectural critics, for example, in a largely favorable review of the LaSalle in the *Architectural Record,* suggested that the hotel's large public rooms afforded a legitimate exercise in architectural effects. "This opportunity," Schuyler continued, "has been availed of, one may say, pounced upon, by an architect, commonly condemned to business skyscrapers, and, in the present instance, with impressive results."[20]

Other writers were still more enthusiastic. The popular American writer Elbert Hubbard dedicated an entire episode of his famous "Little Journeys" series to a visit to the Sherman. Hubbard noted that in the spacious lobby he had met "friends from Peoria, Macomb, Bloomington, Keokuk, Joplin, Kansas City, Danville and Decatur—bankers, merchants, statesmen, who had come to spend a day or so looking over the city." According to Hubbard these men had come from all over and from every station in life, yet suitable accommodations could be found for all of them in the hotel:

the Hotel Sherman is the last word in hotel building. I know of nothing in the world to equal it in the way of quiet magnificence and excellence, and yet the place is not gaudy or loud nor expressed in lavish fancy. . . . [It] has always been the home of earnest, active, intelligent people. If Thomas Jefferson were alive today and visited Chicago, he would stop at the Hotel Sherman. If Lincoln came to Chicago the Hotel Sherman would again be his home. The Hotel Sherman is the home of democracy, it is the best home of the people.[21]

SEVENTEEN

CIVIC GRANDEUR, CIVIC SQUALOR:
COOK COUNTY COURTHOUSE
AND CHICAGO CITY HALL

One of the oddest juxtapositions in Chicago's architectural history is the image of the soaring city hall found in the plates of Daniel Burnham's 1909 *Plan of Chicago* and the actual City Hall, designed by Holabird & Roche, that was under construction as the plan appeared. The dome of Burnham's ideal city hall, occupying the focal point of a grandiose civic center at what Burnham imagined would become the most important intersection of the city, would have floated serenely above the tops of Chicago's highest buildings, dominating the city. The building that was actually built to house the offices of the city of Chicago and the county of Cook, on the other hand, not only had no dome but was deeply embedded in the dense fabric of the city and could easily have been mistaken, at least at first glance, for a large bank or other commercial building.

Why would Burnham have published his scheme when he knew the city had already chosen a very different kind of building? Why, on the other hand, didn't the Holabird & Roche scheme look more like the building Burnham imagined, given that both partners were probably sympathetic with Burnham's political views and his architectural ideals? It appears that the answer lies in part with the circumstances behind each design and in part with the tensions within the camp of urban progressive reformers.

Moldering Grandeur

Even in a city long accustomed to political corruption, the saga of the twin pile that housed the Chicago City Hall and the Cook County Courthouse from the 1880s until the early twentieth century was remarkable. The building's history started with a competition held by the county in 1872–73 to design a structure for its half of Public

17.1
City hall study by Fernand Janin from Plan of Chicago *by Daniel Burnham and Edward Bennett, 1909. Courtesy of Art Institute of Chicago.*

17.2 (opposite)
Chicago City Hall and Cook County Courthouse (373), 1904–10, block bounded by Clark, Randolph, LaSalle, and Washington Streets, exterior view. Photograph by Kaufman and Fabry. Chicago Historical Society Prints and Photographs Department.

Square, the block bounded by LaSalle, Clark, Washington, and Randolph.[1] The result was a typical tale of bureaucratic bungling, probably involving considerable malfeasance as well. Competition winner Otto H. Matz did not get the commission. It went, rather, to third-place finisher Thomas Tilly, but he was obliged by the county to make modifications and ultimately withdrew in favor of James J. Eagan, who did not win a prize at all but, after being engaged to assist Tilly, made a deal to undercut him on the commission.[2]

Once construction started in August 1875, charges of corruption, favoritism, kickbacks, and poor building practices filled the air, continuing during the entire construction period, which lasted until 1882. Meanwhile, in a move designed to save on architects' fees, some officials in the city, which owned the other half of the block, proposed buying the county's plans and redrawing them in mirror image so they would fit there. In the end this was not practical, and John Van Osdel was engaged. The city did decide to mirror the county building on the exterior, but this was probably done

for economy. Any possibility that it was intended to ensure harmony between the two parts of the building was clearly dispelled by the City Council's decision to use stone of a different color—the result, almost certainly, of the political clout wielded by a stone supplier. In the long run, however, this decision probably made little difference, since Chicago's dirty air soon turned both halves of the complex black.[3]

By 1885, when the city's portion was finally finished, the total cost for the city and country had reached an astronomical $4 million, and the project had taken thirteen years to complete. The finished building was so large that it obliterated any trace of open space in what had been the public square in the initial plat of the city.[4] Because it had taken so long to finish, it was already overcrowded when it opened and its style was woefully out of date. Critics assailed its "barbarisms" and "cavernous shadows" and dubbed it "the Tombs." More immediately troubling than any aesthetic considerations were the structural problems that became increasingly obvious soon after construction and eventually became so serious they threatened the stability of the whole enormous

17.3

Chicago City Hall and Cook County Courthouse, 1873–82, John Van Osdel and James J. Egan, architects, respectively. Photograph by Barnes-Crosby. Chicago Historical Society Prints and Photographs Department, ICHi-19264.

pile. In short, the city-county building was a municipal disgrace. It became a perfect target for Progressive Era reformers. (See fig. 5.3 for site plan.)

The Image of Government

In the 1890s schemes to replace the building had already started to surface. Among these was a proposal by prominent Chicago architect Henry Ives Cobb, who suggested a skyscraper that would house government offices but would also contain excess space that could be rented out until government agencies needed it. This proposal had the virtue of recognizing that by the late nineteenth century, government had become a large bureaucracy and needed hundreds of offices of exactly the same kind used by business organizations. It failed to acknowledge the ceremonial and symbolic aspects of government, however, and was roundly condemned.[5]

At the other extreme were proposals for grandiose civic centers. Elaborate complexes to house government offices and cultural institutions were often advanced in the 1890s and continued into the new century.[6] The culmination of these was the civic center scheme in the famous 1909 *Plan of Chicago* by Daniel Burnham and Edward Bennett. In Burnham's plan the government center would occupy a spacious site south and west of the existing business center at a point that Burnham anticipated would soon become the new center of the downtown. The new city hall would dominate a Parisian-style ensemble of structures housing other government functions.[7]

The government center would, Burnham hoped, dominate the skyline, in this way reordering a city whose coherence had been compromised by nearly untrammeled private development. In his thinking about this problem and in his quest for a formal solution, Burnham brought his work at the 1893 Fair full circle. The buildings at the Fair represented a critique of the existing city order and a model for a new order. Burnham's civic center can be seen as an attempt to take the Court of Honor at the Fair and reinsert it into the city at an even larger scale. The new city hall at Congress Street would take the place of the Administration Building at the head of the formal basin at the Fair as the centerpiece in the plan.[8]

The building would do for Chicago what the cathedral and palace had done for medieval cities—provide a constant reminder of where the power lay. The major difference was that in democratic America the people were sovereign rather than the church or the king.

The Burnham scheme, like all the other grand civic center proposals, was no less problematic than "practical" proposals. In the first place, creating the proposed civic center would have demanded cooperation among all branches of the government. In fact, as the history of the previous city-county buildings had shown, the city and county had rarely been able to agree about anything, and even if they had there would still be the problem of housing the state and federal offices. A second problem was simply cost. The Burnham proposal would have been extremely expensive. Whereas the public square was already in the public domain, the new civic center would have required the purchase of a large chunk of urban real estate from private owners. This would have entailed raising a considerable amount of money through higher taxation or borrowing, neither of which was politically palatable.

The Burnham scheme also raised more basic issues, however. For many people the grandiose old city-county building expressed all that was wrong with government. It was too big, too isolated from the people and the life of the city. The Burnham building, even more than the existing one, would have set government apart from ordinary business, which many observers considered unwise. For them the proposed Burnham civic buildings, even more than the old ones, would have expressed primarily the ceremonial aspects of government. Many Chicagoans believed government in the twentieth century should be less ceremonial, more efficient, more businesslike.[9]

Even proponents of the Burnham scheme found themselves hard-pressed to defend its architectural expression. To dominate the business buildings of the city as Burnham wished, the dome of the main building would have had to rise to a height greater than a forty-story business building. Classical architecture had been invented for relatively low, horizontal buildings of only a few stories. To inflate a building to this height called into question the most basic assumptions about classical proportions.

The Competition

During all the debates about future government centers, the old city-county building, despite efforts to shore it up, continued to settle. Finally, in 1905 settlement in the basement had progressed so far that it severed a gas pipe, causing an explosion. Although repairs could have been made for $10,000, the building had become a symbol of inefficiency and greed, a grotesque reminder of the machine politics urban reformers were trying so hard to overcome.

A new building was clearly desirable, but true to form, the city and county could not bring themselves to cooperate. Once again the county went ahead on its own, deciding, apparently with no debate at all, to rebuild on the old site. It became clear that the commissioners had agreed early on that the only way to gain enough space for the burgeoning bureaucracy was to erect a structure that pretty much filled the county's half of the block, rising at least ten stories. Although this would necessarily give the building the same kind of massing as the business buildings surrounding it, the commissioners did not want it to look exactly like a business building.[10] Somehow the architects would have to find a set of design features that did not take up too much space or cost too much money yet would create an appropriate image.

The county authorized a bond issue and arranged a competition. This time the commissioners, probably acting on the recommendation of the American Institute of Architects, decided to take steps to avoid the charges of impropriety that had plagued the previous competition and many others elsewhere.[11] They appointed a professional panel of jurors including prominent Chicago businessmen such as Harry Selfridge of Marshall Field's and contractor John M. Ewen. For architectural advice, the county looked to New York, inviting Stanford White, partner in the famous New York firm of McKim, Mead and White. Finding White unavailable, the county replaced him with another prominent New York architect, William R. Ware. The jury was a distinguished one, giving every indication that all the projects would receive serious attention.[12]

Instead of the free-for-all of a completely open contest, the county invited seven of the country's most prominent architects and paid them for entering, guaranteeing that at least a few of the entries would be highly professional. The list from Chicago included D. H. Burnham and Company, Chicago's largest architectural firm; Holabird & Roche, by this time a close competitor; Frost and Granger; and Huehl and Schmid.[13] The county also invited Shepley, Rutan and Coolidge, a Boston firm that in the 1890s had been responsible for the design of Chicago's most impressive public buildings of that era, the Chicago Public Library and the Art Institute, and that had set up a Chicago office. From New York were the firm of Carrère and Hastings, architects of the splendid New York Public Library, and George B. Post, a major commercial firm with a reputation somewhat like that of Holabird & Roche.

Although this competition was better for the competitors than many such contests in which a large number of architects expended vast amounts of time and money to design buildings that were never built, it was still far from perfect. For one thing, although it was clear that the county would build a new building, there was no guarantee that it would use the winning entry. For another, in the case of the design that was built, the county specified a sliding fee scale that was less than the 5 percent recommended by the AIA. The three firms with the largest and most prestigious practices, including the two from New York and D. H. Burnham and Company, took the high moral ground and withdrew. For the rest, the lure of winning such a major prize outweighed any professional scruples they might have felt or their fear of being exploited.

The three firms that withdrew were replaced by three new competitors: from Chicago Louis Sullivan, by then a famous but troubled architect, and Jarvis Hunt; and from St. Louis the firm of Barnett, Haynes and Barnett, architects of the exotic Illinois Athletic Club on Michigan Avenue in Chicago. In the end Sullivan did not compete, but several uninvited firms sent in entries. Although some of the more famous architects had not participated, the thirteen sets of drawings received and exhibited in the public library represented a distinguished field. Because the projects were to be judged anonymously, each was marked with a number, the names to be revealed only after the judging. On 25 August 1905 the jury announced its verdict and identified the competitors:

1. Shepley, Rutan and Coolidge, Boston and Chicago
2. German and Lingell, Duluth, Minnesota
3. Henry Lord Gay, Chicago
4. P. J.and M. J. Morehouse, Chicago
5. Huehl and Schmid, Chicago
6. Holabird & Roche, Chicago
7. Frost and Granger, Chicago
8. James Gamble Rogers, Chicago
9. Herbert C. Shivers, St. Louis
10. Wm. H. Pruyn Jr. and Company, Chicago
11. J. J. Flanders, Chicago
12. Jarvis Hunt, Chicago
13. Barnett, Haynes and Barnett, St. Louis and Chicago

Then came the recommendation of the jury:

To the Special Committee on the New Court House, of the Board of Commissioners of Cook County:

After a careful and detailed examination of all these drawings we are unanimously of the opinion that the design and plan marked by the commissioners with the number thirteen [Barnett, Haynes and Barnett] present, as they stand, the best combination of plan and elevation, although some of the others offer more convenient plans, and others present, in our judgment, more satisfactory elevations. We accordingly recommend the design and plan numbered 13 for the first prize of five thousand dollars.

We find that the design and plan numbered six [Holabird & Roche] has similar merits, although this also is not entirely satisfactory in respect either of elevation or of plan. We recommend it for the second prize of twenty-five hundred dollars.

17.4

Cook County Courthouse competition, Shepley, Rutan and Coolidge perspective. From Western Architect, *September 1905.*

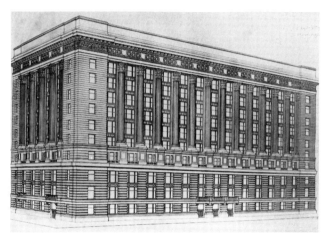

17.5

Cook County Courthouse competition, Holabird & Roche perspective. From Western Architect, *September 1905.*

17.6

Cook County Courthouse competition, Barnett, Haynes and Barnett perspective. From Western Architect, *September 1905.*

We find, however, that the drawings numbered five [Huehl and Schmid] and six [Holabird & Roche] offer more convenient interior arrangements of plan than any of the others, although the accompanying elevation of number five seems to us to be better adapted to a building occupied by private offices than to one occupied by public offices.

We therefore recommend that inasmuch as the design numbered one [Shepley, Rutan and Coolidge] presents the most attractive exterior and the plans numbered five [Huehl and Schmid] and six [Holabird & Roche] the most convenient interiors, the Commissioners entrust the work to the authors of one of these two designs, conjointly with the author of number one, making such arrangements as to the share of each, in the work, as shall be acceptable to them and to the County Commissioners.[14]

This announcement probably confounded nearly everyone. The winners, Barnett, Haynes and Barnett, were undoubtedly happy to have been awarded first prize, but without the commission the victory was somewhat hollow. Among the three competitors singled out for a role in the new building (Holabird & Roche; Shepley, Rutan and Coolidge; and Huehl and Schmid), there were probably high hopes mixed with more than a little annoyance.

What is most striking about the winning entries is how similar they all were. Each consisted of a large rectangular solid completely filling the site out to the street line, with offices laid out around interior light courts. This is not really surprising, since county officials had told the press their expectations of what the building should be like. And given the tight site constraints, the height limits specified in the building code, and the enormous amount of office space required, the building would almost of necessity be laid out like an office building. There was simply no room for the great halls, stair towers, rotundas, and domes that had given earlier public buildings their imposing silhouettes.

At first glance more surprising was the similarity in facades. Each consisted of a more or less pronounced base, rows of regularly spaced windows in the middle section, and a great colonnade running across the upper floors. On reflection, this similarity was not unexpected either. All the entrants must have quickly realized they needed to find a feature that would elevate their designs above the status of a speculative office building, and among the possibilities only the colonnade, because it could be made very shallow, could produce a fairly grand effect without usurping needed floor area.

This formula had developed over the previous decade as the preferred way of making buildings look important without sacrificing efficiency. Earlier city halls and

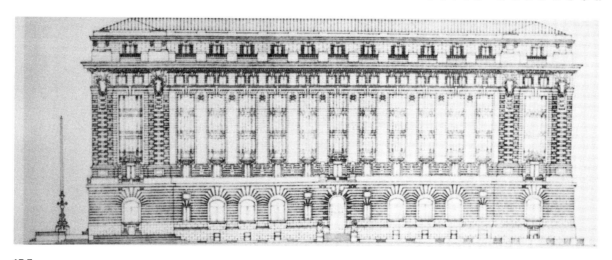

17.7

United States Customs House competition, New York City, 1899, Carrère and Hastings, architects, elevation. From Inland Architect, *February 1900.*

other government buildings had tended to rely on vertical elements like towers, cupolas, and domes that rose above the main mass. As buildings in the city got larger and higher, these crowning features became monstrous in size—witness the towers at the city halls of Philadelphia, Detroit, Buffalo, and St. Louis or the dome at Baltimore. Although the giant colonnade had been used on some public buildings throughout the nineteenth century, it became ever more common as the picturesque, often vertically disposed buildings of the late nineteenth century yielded to the more horizontal classical ones of the early twentieth. The most important prototype seems to have been the set of competition schemes produced for the New York Customs House. Eventually built to designs by Cass Gilbert, this was architecturally the most conspicuous new public building in America in the first years of the century.[15] The solutions seen in the winning Customs House designs were soon used on a enormous number of buildings around the country, not just for public structures, but for banks and other pretentious private ones as well.[16]

The Shepley, Rutan and Coolidge facade appears to have followed very closely the Carrère and Hastings scheme for the Customs House. Shepley, Rutan and Coolidge certainly produced the most expansive and stylish facade of the lot. It was bold in relief and heavily ornamented with sculpture, and its weighty basement, great end pavilions, and ponderous entablature were also a logical continuation of this same firm's earlier efforts at the Art Institute of Chicago and the Chicago Public Library. The plan, like the Barnett, Hayes and Barnett scheme, faltered when the attempt to offer a correspondingly grand set of interior public spaces required sacrificing convenience in lighting and circulation for the rest of the building, which of necessity would be devoted primarily to offices.

Of the schemes in contention, that of Holabird & Roche stands at the opposite pole. By comparison, the facades here offered no sweeping civic gestures. Despite the colonnade and the attempts to give the building monumentality, the designers seem to have been reluctant to break the relentless succession of large windows and minimal intervening wall surfaces. Not even the entrance doors were allowed to break the grid. A minimal balcony was virtually all that alerted viewers to the entrance. It is hard to believe that this facade was the result of timidity. In previous public commissions— for example, the Evanston city hall—the firm had been willing to create a civic building very different from a commercial structure. Nor was the firm opposed to the use of richly developed classical architecture for public buildings. It is known, for example, that in 1910 Martin Roche hired a special train so the entire office could see the Minnesota State Capitol, designed by Cass Gilbert, under construction. This edifice, along with Gilbert's earlier New York Customs House, was a brilliant exercise in the classical style and one of the most opulent monuments of the American Renaissance. It was finished in 1905 just before the Cook County Courthouse competition.[17]

It is likely that Holabird and Roche intended the building as a polemic gesture. The partners probably did not wish to compete with Shepley, Rutan and Coolidge on the famous Boston firm's own turf. Primarily designers of office buildings, they may have reasoned that since the site and program dictated that the structure would be primarily an office building, they could accentuate this fact to make their scheme stand out to the jury, which they knew included several hardheaded Chicago businessmen. Certainly the published plans for the eighth, ninth, and tenth floors show very straightforward double-loaded corridor schemes that would be instantly familiar to any businessmen.

The scheme by Barnett, Haynes and Barnett, finally, seems to have fallen somewhere between that of Holabird & Roche and that of Shepley, Rutan and Coolidge. It had neither the grandeur of facade of the Shepley scheme nor Holabird & Roche's simplicity of plan. Although it was awarded the prize, it seems to represent a compromise and evoked little enthusiasm from anyone.

Final Plans and Construction

Once the jury's recommendations were made public, informed opinion in Chicago would probably have considered it virtually a foregone conclusion that Holabird & Roche would be named architects. Not only was its scheme considered the most efficient of the three, but Holabird & Roche alone among the three prizewinners was based in Chicago, and it already had an unshakable reputation for honesty and dependability. Perhaps knowing the firm had the inside track, Holabird made it clear that he did not wish to collaborate with any other office. The firm lost no opportunity to ensure its victory, however. Edward Renwick later recalled the means by which Holabird & Roche had already built a constituency. Immediately after the competition was announced, Holabird & Roche employees had gone over to the county offices and interviewed all the department heads about their requirements. Then, according to Renwick, after the awarding of the prizes they

> induced the County Board to call in the heads of departments and have them examine the competition drawings, which were still hanging in the Board room and not marked in any way to identify the competitors. We suggested that the heads of departments examine them to see which set of drawings most nearly met their requirements.
>
> Inasmuch as we had made a personal study of the question with these heads of departments they picked our drawings as being those most nearly complying. A meeting of the County Board was held, and two or three competing architects were called in to explain their drawings. With this meeting in mind we had taken off in our office answers to all the questions which we thought likely to be asked; tonnage of steel, cubic yards of concrete, cubic feet of stone, number of thousands of brick, number of yards of plastering, and a good many other items on which we thought they might be disposed to ask questions. Holabird, before going to the meeting, memorized all these items.
>
> The first architect to be called was the first prize winner. Some of these questions were asked and his answer invariably was, "I'll look it up and let you know." Holabird was called in next. As there were several contractors on the County Board the questions were rather explicit. The first was "What is the cubic content of the building?" Immediately Holabird gave his answer. A number of other questions on which Holabird had prepared himself, followed. At the end of the examination one of the commissioners arose and made a motion that the County Board employ Holabird and Roche as architects. The result was a vote of twelve for Holabird and Roche, and three scattering.[18]

Although this account from a member of the firm must be read with some skepticism, the *Tribune* did confirm the results. The tally went twelve for Holabird & Roche, two for Barnett, Haynes and Barnett, and one for Huehl and Schmid. There were no votes for Shepley, Rutan and Coolidge. The commissioners were probably quite pleased with themselves. They might well have feared that the jury would have opted for expensive architectural effects rather than economy and efficiency and would have suggested the commission be given to Shepley, Rutan and Coolidge. This choice might have set off a touchy political debate, but the unorthodox report of the jury allowed them to get the no-nonsense building they probably wanted and let them give the commission to a Chicago firm they trusted without compromising their obligation to art or a fair competition.

A subsequent editorial in the *Chicago Tribune,* measured in tone but unmistakably tinged with local pride, probably reflected the sentiments of most commissioners and of Chicagoans:

> The work of pulling down the courthouse has begun. That relic of a day when Chicagoans believed that the exterior of a public building was the only thing to be considered soon will disappear. They have broken the fetters of custom and tradition. It has dawned on them that a public building should be primarily a place for doing work and that a copy of a Grecian temple or a medieval cathedral does not furnish the condition which workers need.
>
> In 1875 it would have been deemed a sin against the laws of decency and fitness to propose the erection of a business county building. The one wanted was the one which would make the most show. Economy of space and comfort of occupants were not considered. The public has learned much in thirty years. It now gives the business architect the preference over the florid and ornate brethren of the profession.
>
> The new county building, which is to be built for business purposes in accordance with business methods, will be an object lesson for other cities. They had to come here to learn how to build skyscrapers. They will come here to learn how to build city halls and courthouses. Space is becoming so valuable in the center of great cities that public buildings must go up in the air. The activities of a modern city are so multifarious and its employees so numerous that the buildings which are to house them must begin to emulate the skyscrapers. After Chicago has shown how municipal edifices should be constructed other cities will imitate the example, timidly at first, but with increasing courage.[19]

The *Economist* also lauded the decision but gave another reason less flattering to the city and country:

*Cook County
Courthouse,
perspective of final
scheme. Chicago
Historical Society
Prints and
Photographs
Department,
ICHi-16101.*

It is not necessary to speak in praise of Holabird & Roche. They have many monuments in this city and elsewhere. Doubtless the selection was made with less reference to their high reputation as architects than to the excellence of their plan. But even more important than any difference in the plans that were submitted is the certainty that so long as Holabird & Roche have charge of the undertaking it will be free from the one evil that has so often marred local governmental work of all sorts. There will be no graft, if it is in human ingenuity and determination to prevent it. That the county is obliged to have a new building within less than thirty years of the completion of a structure that had cost a great deal of money, and which structure has been in a dangerous condition for a decade past, is evidence of what local government has been in the past. It is to the credit of the present county commissioners that they have taken every precaution against a repetition of the old abuses.[20]

Not everyone was pleased, of course. Not surprisingly, Barnett, Haynes and Barnett protested, but the rules had been clearly established. True to the nature of local politics, charges of corruption promptly appeared. A statement was reported that the commissioners were swayed by the lobbying efforts of a limestone quarry operator, but this charge was promptly refuted and dropped. The way was clear for Holabird & Roche to draw up final plans.

In making the final design scheme, Holabird & Roche apparently did exactly as the jury recommended. It studied the Shepley, Rutan and Coolidge elevations. The Boston architects had produced a scheme with the clearly delineated masses of a free-standing public building on an ample site. The problem was that their composition necessarily implied a series of rooms of graduated size inside to correspond with the differentiated window spacing seen on the exterior. This did not fit the county's program, which required vast amounts of standard office space to house the large bureaucracy. Holabird & Roche, on the other hand, coming from a commercial practice, had provided for hundreds of nearly identical interior rooms that fit the county's space needs, but because of this the elevations lacked the large-scale ordering gestures seen in the Shepley, Rutan and Coolidge scheme. In fact Holabird & Roche's competition elevations, except for the giant attached columns, look surprisingly similar to those of the Marquette Building.

At first glance the changes Holabird & Roche made appear minor. In the revised elevations the lower three floors, which had appeared in the competition scheme as a two-story block sitting on a one-story base that had been sunk partially into the ground, were greatly strengthened by raising the height of the first floor and consolidating the two floors above it into a single block beneath a weighty cornice. Likewise the end pavilions, although they remained nearly identical in plan, were heavily re-

17.9
Cook County Courthouse, lettering at corner of building. Photograph by Robert Bruegmann, 1996.

Phone Monroe 928   Phone Monroe 929

Wm. J. Newman
CONTRACTOR
Wrecking, Excavating and Caisson Work

General Offices: **Old 50 S. Curtis St. New 19 N. Curtis St.**

Material and Storage Yards:

Van Buren and Desplaines Sts.   **46th and Chicago Aves.**
Phone Monroe 3812   Phone Austin 116

Down Town Disposal Station:
Fulton Street and the River. Phone Main 3393

THE RECORD BREAKER — Old City Hall. The wrecking of this building and the sinking of the caissons for the new structure was performed by W. J. NEWMAN in record time, 230 days being required for the entire work, while contract allowed 260 days.

FIRST PUBLIC WORK ACCOMPLISHED AHEAD OF TIME

17.10
Cook County Courthouse. advertisement showing demolition of the old Chicago City Hall and the last stages of construction on the new courthouse. From Jones, A Half Century of Chicago Building, *1910.*

inforced by the addition of pilasters running up along each side, echoing the giant Corinthian order of the central bays. The result was a compromise between efficiency of plan and dignity of elevation. It was the same kind of compromise that had led to the Marquette elevations, but here both the scale and the effect were grander.

Once plans were complete, work went fairly smoothly. Demolition of the old structure started even before plans were finished. The cornerstone was laid in September 1906, and by July 1908 the building was completely furnished and the books were closed. The *Economist* reported, with obvious amazement, that there had been no scandal at all:

> Settlement was made this week by the county and Holabird & Roche, architects, on the one side, and William Grace Company contractors, when the latter were given their final check of $500,000 for the construction of the county building, the contract price for which was $3,284,000. The

353

contractors receive $3,282,000, the building having been completed $1,657 less than the contract price, a highly creditable record, probably unlike that of any in connection with any great public work in this country, and it reflects much credit upon all who are connected with it.[21]

Monumental Efficiency

The finished building, the largest county building in the country, was well received by the public and the critics. The Holabird & Roche structure, though very large, did its best not to appear intimidating. It was planned in a forthright way. The offices frequented by the public, such as those dealing with taxes and property ownership, occupied the lower floors. The courts and administrative offices were above, with a good deal of unfinished space at the top of the building reserved for expansion. There was also ample provision for storage vaults, with nearly two acres of space set aside for this purpose in the basement and on a mezzanine above the third floor.

The exterior, likewise, was grand but not ostentatious. Most of the sculptural embellishment of the facades was practical rather than decorative. Along each facade, for example, one of the enormous corner blocks of stone at about eye level carried the

17.11

Cook County Courthouse, sculptural group by Hermon MacNeil by main entrance, Photograph by Robert Bruegmann, 1995.

names of the streets the building faced, chiseled in fine Roman lettering. The major artistic effort was concentrated at the Clark Street entrance. Here, on either side of the doors four large relief panels by New York sculptor Hermon MacNeil represented Justice, Labor on Land, Labor on the Sea, and Law. On other public buildings these might have been freestanding, but here no space could be spared and instead they were done in relief in the wall.

Sophisticated critics might have complained that the panels followed Michelangelo and other famous sculptors of the past rather too literally. Others might have been somewhat perplexed by the iconography, especially the relation between the abstract themes and the somewhat odd poses of the voluptuously developed and scantily clothed male youths the sculptor used to personify them. For most observers, however, the use of allegorical sculpture on public buildings was so commonplace that few really looked very carefully. It showed that this was a public building; it provided a little curvilinear contrast to an otherwise rectilinear facade; and like almost all allegorical sculpture since the classical era, it reminded those citizens who did make the effort to

17.12

Cook County Courthouse, view of ground floor corridor. Photograph by Barnes-Crosby.
Chicago Historical Society Prints and Photographs Department, ICHi-19286.

study the figures of the ideals supposedly honored within. MacNeil's composition also gave them a chance to revel without guilt in the glories of beautifully formed, nearly nude young bodies.[22]

Inside the doors the visitor would have found a hallway thirty-six feet wide and twenty-one feet high connecting the entrance with elevators and a cross hall running from Washington to Randolph Streets. This T-shaped arrangement of hallways was so ample in scale and so richly finished in blocks of gleaming Botticini marble, mosaic panels, and bronze hardware that most viewers would not have commented on the fact that there was no lobby or rotunda at the center of the building—or anywhere else for that matter—and that the plan was more like that of an office building than a great public structure. Almost every floor was laid out in a similar fashion with the large, wainscoted corridors providing access to a regular succession of rooms. All in all, it was useful and grand and apparently, to everyone's amazement, just what the commissioners had wanted.

Chicago City Hall

Meanwhile, city officials had been watching with interest from their own offices in the truncated half block to the east of the large new county building. Since they had delayed so long and the county had already decided on a scheme, the city had ample incentive to go along with it and build their half of the block in a similar design. To construct a building of a different design would have been more expensive and would have given the block an unfortunate, even bizarre aspect. (See fig. 5.4 for the site plan.) Besides, Holabird had a good many friends among the city's officials. But common sense and civility have never been much in evidence in the Chicago City Council.

One contention was that the county had sacrificed utility for the sake of monumentality. The *Economist* reported that there was some discussion of making the La-Salle Street side of the city building even more like a standard office building to afford more light. In the midst of this argument, according to the *Economist*, one of the amateur Chicago architecture "experts," apparently as numerous then as now, presented the results of his own detailed analysis of the county building, comparing it with the Marquette and several other fairly recent office buildings. His study showed, to the considerable amazement of many, that the county building, despite the colonnade, compared favorably with any office in the city in terms of the percentage of window to wall. This silenced the critics.[23]

At least one alderman tried to gain space in the press by suggesting that the city proceed as it had threatened to do in the old city hall and merely duplicate all the

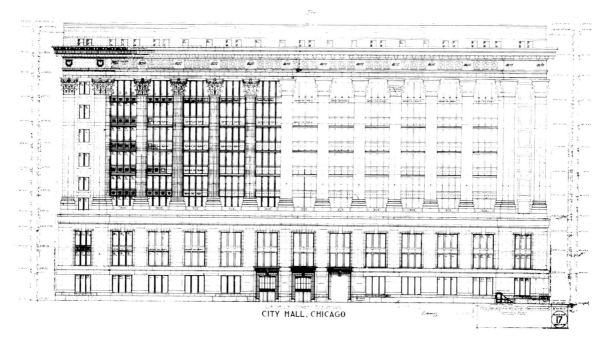

17.13

Chicago City Hall, LaSalle Street elevation. Chicago Historical Society Architectural Collections.

county's plans in reverse. Several newspapers trumpeted his assertion that the city clerks could copy the drawings in forty minutes, thus avoiding the architect's fee of 5 percent on the first million, 4 percent on the second million, and 3 percent on the remainder or, according to the newspapers, $4,500 per minute. In reality, of course, almost all reasonable city officials knew that a large amount of work was required to fit the city's program into the same envelope as the county building, and that someone would have to supervise construction. A vote was finally taken on 17 June 1907 to give the commission to Holabird & Roche.

The old city building was promptly demolished and work started. The construction job included some novel features. One was the necessity of getting the huge sixty-five-foot built-up girders needed to support the floors above the council chamber from the steel works on the north branch of the Chicago River to the construction site. H. L. Marsh, Holabird & Roche's superintendent on the job, recalled:

> Probably no such load ever has been put upon a wagon as was that 88,000 pound girder which overhangs the council chamber. . . . We could hope

to move it only in the night, after the last of traffic virtually was gone from the streets. Rush Street Bridge was the only bridge on which we could cross, and then only after we had laid steel tracks for the wheels.

At the building, one engine hoist has been used on every other piece of steel. On this 88,000 pound girder, as on the 75,000 and the two 70,000 pound girders, two engines were set and the steel grappled at each end. With the council chamber on the second floor, two floors in height to the ceiling, and each of these big girders to clear the ceiling of the chamber and rising a full floor space to the level of the vault floor, you can imagine how I sat there with cold chills and hot feverishness alternating, hoping that no accident would occur in either engine to stop the steady, even rising of those loads. Yet there wasn't a kink in the handling of any of them.[24]

The engineering problems proved minor compared with the political ones. There were, first of all, a good many labor problems. Then came changes of corruption in building construction. Many observers in the city believed these were aimed at incumbent mayor William Busse, since they erupted just before election time. Edward A. Renwick later recalled that these were ultimately found to be the work of a disgruntled former workman who had unsuccessfully tried to blackmail the president of the construction company. An investigative committee was set up and a panel of experts convened. Renwick recalled the results:

It seems that the blackmailer had submitted a list of twenty nine defects in the building and Mr. Noel [president of the construction company] and ourselves agreed to see that spaces were opened up for a proper investigation of these places. The charge was that the concrete around the steel columns had been omitted. We explained that the steel columns were amply protected by the four inch brick work, that the concrete was merely an added insurance against rusting or any other corrosion, so that even if concrete had been omitted in some places it was not of great importance. But the twenty-nine places were opened up. Out of them all one space was found where a few inches of concrete a space as big as my two fists perhaps—was missing. . . .

The findings were that on the five million dollar building the amount of skimping which they were able to locate amounted to just $129. They made the further comment that the building was the most perfect of any building they had ever examined. During the investigation it developed that this blackmailer who had been employed as a mason was actually in the pay of a politically opposed Chicago newspaper for the purpose of finding something in this building from which to make political capital. He had even attempted, being a mason, to so lay the bricks surrounding the columns that the concrete, which was rather thin and was according to specifications poured in every three feet, would not be able to go through. The only trouble was the poor fellow had no memory and out of twenty-nine places he had fixed he could only find one of them.[25]

The problems did not end here. The death of the contractor led to further construction problems. The contract for movable furniture had to be settled in court. An error in the spelling of LaSalle on one corner of the building held up a $400,000 contract. Two men were killed in the demolition of the old building, two more in erecting the new structure. But finally, in late 1910 the building was ready. The finished structure continued on the exterior the lines of the county building, creating a gigantic single edifice filling the whole block. On the inside the general office layout was very similar to that of the county building. The major new features were the large office of the mayor on the fifth floor and the oak-paneled council chamber on the second floor, both embellished with murals by Frederic Clay Bartlett.[26]

Critical opinion on the joint structure was again largely positive. One thing everyone agreed on was the impressiveness of the building's scale. The columns of the great colonnade had shafts seventy-five feet high and over nine feet in diameter at the base. Just outside the upper windows loomed capitals twelve and a half feet high, which the local press reported were larger than those of St. Peter's in Rome. City Hall alone had nearly thirteen acres of floor space, 21,000,000 pounds of steel, 162,000 rivets aggregating fourteen miles of rivet, 180,000 cubic feet of granite, and nearly 4,000,000 bricks.

The more reflective critics inevitably had to deal with the problem of the modern government building. How can a building that is composed primarily of an endless series of office cubicles be made suitably monumental? Or conversely, how can the monumental classical tradition be adapted for modern purposes when the space needs, the materials, even the function of civic buildings have changed so radically? Montgomery Schuyler, the most distinguished of American critics at the time, best addressed these questions:

The work of Messrs. Holabird & Roche which puts them most in view and gives them their rank among American architects, is the huge twin monster of the Cook County Court House and Chicago City Hall. With

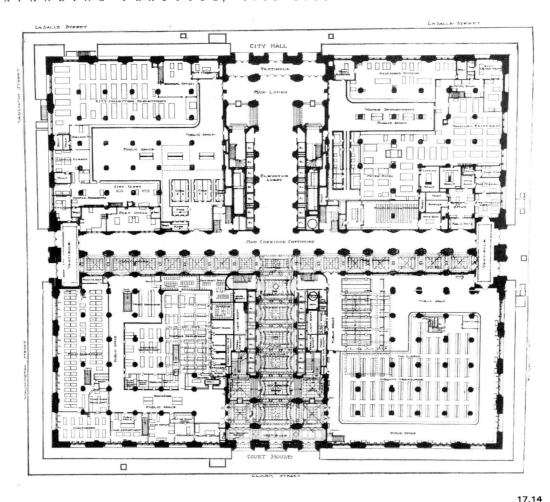

17.14

Chicago City Hall and Cook County Courthouse, plan of first floor. LaSalle Street at top. From Architectural Record, *April 1912.*

this they have supplanted a similar double erection which was for a generation a political, social and architectural scandal to Chicago. This is strictly
an academic study. Nobody can pretend that there is any future in this,
anything but the reminiscences of an immemorial past. Even, unlike its
classical predecessors, it is a contradiction in terms. In fact it is a steel-
frame ten-story building of similar and equal cells, like the common skyscraper. Necessarily its apartments differ from one another in magnitude,
importance and function, but there is no pretense of expressing these
differences in the exterior architecture. What is asserted is that the divi-

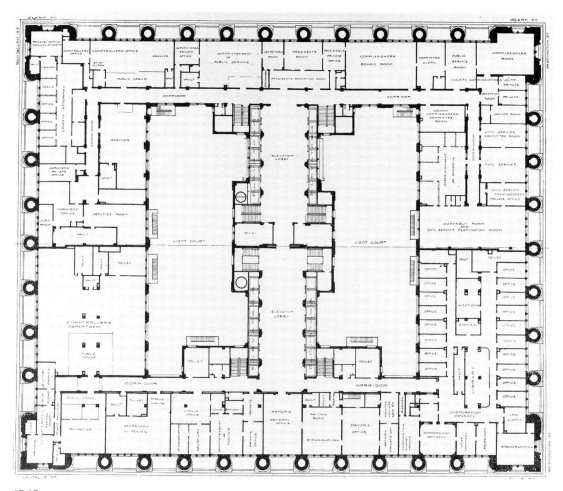

17.15

Chicago City Hall and Cook County Courthouse, plan of fifth floor. LaSalle Street at bottom. From New York Architect, *October 1909*

sion denoted by the great columns is superior in importance to the lower divisions from which the order is omitted, and this is distinctly "not so." The real inequalities are suppressed, and inequalities which do not exist are asserted.[27]

In this analysis, as was the case throughout his work, Schuyler took as his point of departure a moral position about structural and programmatic honesty in the tradition of the great English critic John Ruskin.[28] This led him to criticize most severely just those facade-ordering devices that Holabird & Roche borrowed from Shepley,

17.16
Chicago City Hall,
view of council
chamber. From
Architectural
Record, *April 1912.*

Rutan and Coolidge, devices that had no necessary relation to plan but were necessary if the building was to have a suitably monumental exterior. It is interesting that Schuyler seems to have realized his position did not fully address the fact that modern requirements and modern urban scale made demands on the appearance of buildings that simply could not be satisfied using any existing vocabulary. He continued:

> Of course, this is the contradiction which we always encounter in modern examples of monumental classic, and, of course, having once noted them, we have to ignore them and to admit that it makes all the difference how they are done. The present example is very well done. There is undoubtedly an awkwardness in the infringement of the solidity of the terminal pavilion, caused by the interposition of a big window between the capitals of the pilasters, and indeed by the general scale of the openings in this pavilion, which should manifestly have been kept as solid as possible. Nevertheless, the thing is greatly impressive. In "scale" the order exceeds anything west of Albany, and is about twice that of Isaiah Rogers's old

Custom House in New York. This would, of itself, make a building noteworthy anywhere, but it is also to be said that it has been well and faith-
fully studied in mass, in scale, and in detail. It is not only much the most
impressive thing of its own kind that Chicago has to show, but one of the
most impressive in the United States.[29]

The questions posed in this passage clearly set forth the arguments over the
proper form of civic buildings that were heard in the debate that led to the selection of
the Holabird & Roche scheme rather than one closer to the vision set out by Daniel
Burnham in his 1909 plan, and the arguments would erupt again and again over the
next decades. It is interesting to see how subsequent events in the history of the city-
county building illustrate the continuing struggle. The story might be said to start
soon after the completion of the building. From the vantage point of the 1990s we
can only smile at the advice given by Holabird & Roche to the city's statistician and
municipal librarian:

DEAR SIR:

We are in receipt of your favor of May 25th requesting an estimate of the
natural or probable life of the Chicago City Hall or the time it is likely to
suffice for the city's executive and administrative departments.

Our estimate of the probable life of the building, from a structural
standpoint, is 100 to 150 years. From the standpoint of its adequacy for
the city executive and administrative departments we would say that it
would be fully adequate for 50 to 75 years. . . .

It is also within the limits of possibility that fifty years hence the
County and City administrations may be combined under one government, thus dispensing with a duplication of departments which now exists and that the entire County and City Hall may be combined for City
Hall purposes.

Very truly yours,
HOLABIRD & ROCHE, Architects[30]

Reality soon intervened. A joint city-county government was not a politically
viable option. Nor was it possible to restrain the growth of government bureaucracy.
Already by the 1920s existing space in the new city-county building was completely
occupied, and the two government bodies started to rent additional space nearby. In
1926 Holabird & Roche proposed an extraordinary solution to the problem: a twenty-
three-story, $13 million office tower addition to be erected on top of the old building

and carried on new caissons sunk into the area of the existing courtyards. The new tower would have been even more obviously an office building than the original competition design. It looks, in perspective rendering, as if it would have been nearly indistinguishable from the office towers going up around it at that time.

This was apparently the last Holabird & Roche involvement with the building, but soon the city and county were considering even more grandiose schemes. In 1926 Eric Hall, county architect, made public a plan for an addition composed of two huge fifty-story structures on the north side of Washington Street, flanking the existing city-county building, to cost $32 million. This was too much even for Chicagoans with a taste for superlatives, and little was done over the next several decades. After World War II there were further schemes, including a huge civic center proposal for the west

17.17
Chicago City Hall and Cook County Courthouse, proposed addition, 1922. Perspective drawing by Gilbert Hall. Chicago Historical Society Architectural Collections.

17.18

*Cook County Courthouse and
Richard J. Daley Center, view from
Daley Center Plaza. Photograph by
Robert Bruegmann, 1996.*

side of the Loop that would have created a Burnham-scaled government complex but
using buildings distinctly in the postwar modernist style.[31] Interestingly enough, in all
these cases there seems to have been little hesitation about the form the buildings
should take. These were merely administrative annexes. They could and should be
exactly like contemporary office buildings.

The next "final solution" to the space problem brought Schuyler's issues back into
clear focus. In 1963 construction started on the Civic Center, later renamed the Richard J. Daley Center, a thirty-one-story skyscraper containing both offices and new
courtrooms, on the block east of the city-county building. The architectural firm of
C. F. Murphy Associates, under the supervision of Jacques Brownson, followed Holabird & Roche's lead in creating a structure that in general configuration resembled a
straightforward business building. Rather than the colonnades Holabird & Roche used
to distinguish the Cook County Courthouse from the surrounding commercial buildings, the architects at the Daley Center counted on a large plaza out front and the
elegant refinement of the structural steel.

Heavily indebted to the work of Ludwig Mies van der Rohe but in many ways a more convincing large building than anything Mies himself ever designed, the Daley Center was a masterpiece of mid-twentieth-century modernism. In some ways it represented the furthest possible development in the movement that had led away from the monumental classicism seen in the 1885 city-county building to the minimal classical details of the Holabird & Roche building and then to postwar abstract modernism. One might think that the two buildings, sitting side by side—one low and massive, filling its site to the limit and adorned with figurative sculpture and a huge colonnade, the other a narrow, completely unornamented slab sitting freely on a flat, paved plaza—might make an incongruous ensemble. But the Daley Center, with its simple forms, dark Cor-Ten steel exterior, and huge seventy-eight foot structural bays, shares the same tough-minded, unsentimental approach Holabird & Roche used a half century earlier. Both of them are quite different from the monumental classical buildings that went before, or from the Burnham civic center design, or from the more recent civic buildings in which architects have turned back to the nineteenth century for classical elements that they believe can recapture the legibility and grandeur of another era.

The two buildings complement each other very well. If the city-county building had remained completely surrounded by others like itself, filling out the surrounding blocks, it would not have the striking presence it now possesses viewed from across the Daley Center Plaza. The Daley Center, likewise, can be best appreciated in the context of the earlier city in which dense masonry-clad buildings form tightly serried walls at the perimeter of their blocks. In this setting the Daley Center's open plaza and soaring vertical lines achieve their greatest effect. The two buildings form a striking pair visually bracketing fifty years of Chicago architecture and creating a compellingly simple and orderly stage set for the daily dramas of Chicago's still chaotic political life.

EIGHTEEN

Today Michigan Avenue south of the Loop is a backwater. As buses and cars roar past empty lots and boarded-up buildings, they deposit a little more soot on already grimy facades. At first glance the area looks largely derelict. Actually, behind their poorly remodeled and badly neglected fronts, these buildings house considerable activity. The low rents have attracted an intriguing collection of entrepreneurs at the margins of the city's economic life. The nightclubs that occupy a number of old commercial buildings along the strip, for example, appear to constitute a center of bohemian life for the South Side black community. Equally bohemian are the young artists and others who now occupy the loft space above the ground floors of many buildings.

Although much of this activity is almost invisible, often because it is not quite legal, the careful viewer will notice telltale signs: new sets of buzzers at the doorways, a fresh coat of paint on a door, small but highly designed graphics. For the observer of the city fabric, moreover, it is precisely the years of neglect that make Michigan Avenue between Sixteenth and Thirty-fourth Streets so fascinating. Like other pieces of Chicago that time seems to have forgotten, it offers remarkable evidence of previous eras in the life of the city.

In this case Michigan Avenue provides a vivid example of a classic American urban development pattern. As waves of invasive growth can transform a pasture into a thicket of bushes and saplings, then a stand of softwood trees, and finally a great oak climax forest, which may then be destroyed by a fire that starts the entire succession over again,[1] so this portion of Michigan Avenue started life as farmland, was developed as an affluent residential neighborhood, and was then invaded by retail users and finally by light manufacturing and warehouses before losing most of its economic vigor, and with it many of its buildings, to revert in places to bare land. In the past few years the area has seen a variety of small-scale new enterprises, but it appears to be marking time, waiting for the next big development push that will start the cycle once more.

For the moment, in spite of demolitions, remodelings, and the thick layer of dirt, a surprising amount of evidence—a delicate white cornice here, an unexpectedly bright checkerboard facade there, an exuberant Corinthian colonnade above a remodeled first-floor shop—survives to testify to one of the most dramatic and unexpected developments in its earlier history. At the turn of the century this stretch of Michigan Avenue was transformed virtually overnight from a substantial neighborhood of heavy masonry houses and churches into a brash terra cotta–fronted showplace for the newly emerging automobile industry. It was Chicago's early twentieth-century "automobile row," and no firm played a larger part in its creation than Holabird & Roche.

The Rise and Fall of the Gold Coast

As happened all across the country, when Chicago's central business district expanded in the late nineteenth century, many of the city's more affluent citizens chose to live farther and farther from the commercial center. In Chicago this was most pronounced on the South Side, where every year new rows of grand stone-fronted palaces pushed southward along Michigan, Prairie, Indiana, and the other broad avenues that run parallel to each other south from the business district. Along with the houses came fashionable clubs and churches.

Chicago's wealthiest families, once they reached the area around Twentieth Street in the years just before the Great Fire, paused for a few years, creating the city's late nineteenth-century "Gold Coast." Holabird & Roche's Walker house of 1891–93 in the 1700 block of South Prairie Avenue, the most palatial of all the streets, provides a good example of a substantial, but by no means baronial, house of that period in this affluent area (see fig. 4.4).[2] Although Michigan Avenue did not have the largest houses, it served as the chief thoroughfare. Of the scene along this road in the 1890s, the author of the *Standard Guide* penned this description:

> I don't care what people may say about other streets and avenues—about Prairie, Calumet, Lake, Ellis, Grand, the Lake Shore Drive or Ashland— Michigan is the finest of them all. What a magnificent stretch of perfect roadway lies before us! How stately and how elegant the graceful residences of the boulevard with their handsome lawns and their wide-spreading shade trees, rising on either side. . . . The roadway is as level as

18.1

Michigan Avenue, view looking north from Twenty-fourth Street showing the Standard Club in the left foreground, the Immanuel Baptist Church in the middle distance, and the Second Presbyterian Church (at Twentieth Street) in the background, with Christ Episcopal Church on the right. Photograph ca. 1891. Chicago Historical Society Prints and Photographs Department, ICHi-26162.

the top of a billiard table, and the clickety-clack of the horse's feet over the well-kept pavement is music to our ears.[3]

From the appearance of the buildings along Michigan, one would assume that their owners felt they were building if not for all time, then at least for well beyond their own generation. In other times and places this might have been true, but not in late nineteenth-century Chicago. There were many causes for the early decline of the South Side's most elegant neighborhood. One was that the Illinois Central Railway's wide swath of tracks cut the enclave off from the lakefront and brought roaring locomotives practically into the residents' backyards. Another was the proximity of some of Chicago's poorest citizens just to the west and the specter of labor violence in an era of increasingly strained relations between factory owners and workers.[4] A final blow was the rapid and continuing expansion of commerce south from the Loop.

In another pattern seen in cities across the United States, the retail trade tended to move closer and closer to the homes of its preferred clientele along the principal routes out of town, bringing increased traffic and noise and pushing the wealthy residents still farther out. The most famous examples of this were Broadway and Fifth Avenue in New York, but the same transition could be seen on Broad Street in Philadelphia, Euclid Avenue in Cleveland, Peachtree Street in Atlanta, Van Ness Avenue in San Francisco, Figueroa Street in Los Angeles, and South Michigan Avenue in Chicago.[5]

On South Michigan Avenue by far the most aggressive retailing was related to automobiles,[6] and the building that may well have started the trend was a small, innocuous structure designed by Holabird & Roche in 1902. Although the story remains sketchy, it is known that about 1902 the firm was asked by the Mandel brothers to design a one-story commercial building at the corner of Fourteenth Street and Michigan Avenue (cat. no. 338). The Mandel brothers were major Holabird & Roche clients at the turn of the century. In addition to work on their large department store complex in the Loop, the brothers commissioned a number of smaller buildings, some of them warehouses, garages, and small store buildings they used themselves, others apparently speculative real estate investments.[7]

From the sketchy evidence available it appears that the building at Michigan and Fourteenth was of this latter kind and that the brothers already had a tenant in hand—the American Locomobile Company, an automobile manufacturer.[8] It further appears that this automobile showroom was run by a man named Barney Sykes and that with this building Sykes became the first automobile entrepreneur to venture south of the Loop.[9]

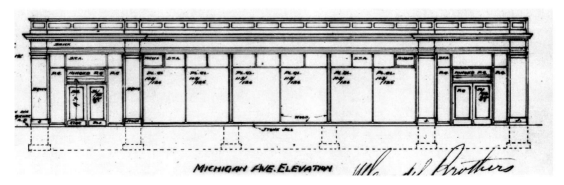

18.2

Store building for Mandel Brothers (338), 1902, northwest corner of Michigan Avenue and Fourteenth Street, Michigan Avenue elevation. Chicago Historical Society Architectural Collections.

A modest edifice, it was built for slightly less than $12,000. Like many other commercial buildings of its day, it was a one-story structure with brick walls at the rear and a front consisting almost entirely of enormous sheets of plate glass extending from the sidewalk up to a sheet metal cornice and held in place by the narrowest of wood frames. The interior was divided into two parts, a large, open room in front and a "repair shop" in back. The building itself would have attracted little notice. What would have drawn considerable attention was the nearly uninterrupted view of gleaming new automobiles through the great windows.

Architecture of the "Strip"

The type of one-story plate glass–fronted building that Holabird & Roche designed at Fourteenth and Michigan appears to have been developed in the 1880s. In this decade the extremely rapid rise in land prices in the Loop and its immediate vicinity encouraged structures that were simple and inexpensive to build but could help defray costs for the owner while the land appreciated to the point where it would support more intensive use. Holabird & Roche designed such a building in 1884 for Francis Bartlett for a site on Dearborn Street (cat. no. 7) on the southern edge of the downtown area. This little structure seems to have aroused considerable interest among contemporary observers. The Kirklands, in their history of Chicago, reported that the building was the first in the city of so temporary a nature where "slow-burning construction" was used and that the building, which made extensive use of glass, rented well.[10]

It is likely that the location of this building within the central business district justified the latest in building materials, notably the great sheets of plate glass that were then coming into use for downtown retail spaces.[11] Edward Renwick described Bartlett's building as a "taxpayer," suggesting that its main purpose was to cover the cost of taxes and ensure some income flow while the land was being held for future development.[12] In this case the building was indeed torn down within ten years so that Bartlett could erect the Old Colony Building, also designed by Holabird & Roche.

It appears that no drawings or photographs of the 1884 taxpayer survive, but a building commissioned in 1886 by Wirt D. Walker for a site on South Wabash Avenue (cat. no. 23) probably gives us a good idea. The interior of Walker's building, commissioned almost simultaneously with his Tacoma Building, consisted of an almost entirely open floor space for shops, interrupted only by the wood columns that carried the wood beams and joists. The rear elevations were constructed of brick.

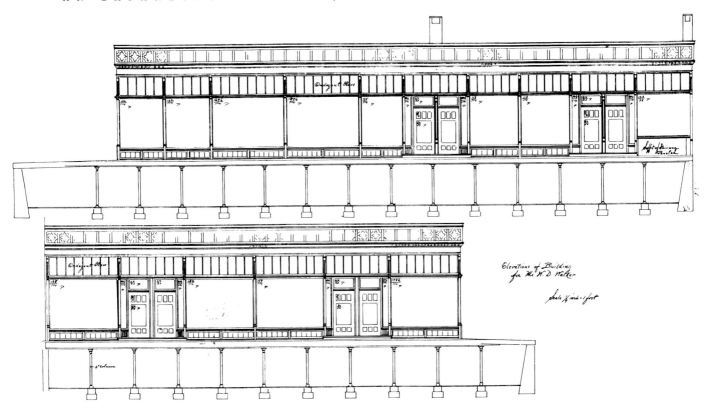

18.3

Wirt D. Walker Building (23), 1886, 400–408 S. Wabash Avenue, southwest corner of Van Buren Street, elevations.
Chicago Historical Society Architectural Collections.

The only place where any design ingenuity was expended was the street fronts. The major goal, it is obvious, was to produce as open a facade as possible, presumably to allow passersby a good view of the merchandise on sale within. An elevation drawing of this building shows that contemporary construction techniques allowed the architects to go remarkably far. The drawing shows a facade consisting of enormous plate glass windows divided by the narrowest of iron mullions. Notations show that the glass sheets ranged in size up to a full $9\frac{1}{2}$ by 14 feet. Even the doors to the shops have large glass panels and are topped with glass transoms. Above the plate glass are panels of "Ondoyant Glass," undoubtedly some kind of prismatic glass intended to diffuse the light and to throw it farther into the deep shop spaces. The facade is capped by a decorative but inexpensive metal cornice.

By the turn of the century there were probably hundreds of buildings of this kind, particularly along major roads leading out of the central area that were used by the streetcars and elevated railways. It was the most advanced "strip" architecture of its day. It was also a logical prototype for architects who were starting to design spaces for the newly emerging automobile trade.

Arrival of the Automobile

In 1902, the year the Mandel brothers commissioned the building on South Michigan Avenue tenanted by Barney Sykes, the impact of the automobile was just starting to be felt. Although the first automobile had appeared on Chicago streets as early as 1892, and though Chicago played a major role in the early development of the industry, for a number of years automobiles remained, as elsewhere, primarily playthings for the wealthy. As late as 1902 it was estimated that there were only six hundred in use in Chicago.[13]

There were numerous obstacles to widespread car ownership. Although the bicycle craze in the 1890s had created a strong lobby for improved roads, the condition of city streets and country lanes was still far from adequate. Writers from the early days of automobiles spun endless yarns about knee-deep mud, misplaced road markers, and the speed traps and other deliberate obstacles some communities placed in the way of motorists. Another major problem was a nearly total lack of traffic laws. Although Chicago's first automobile fatality did not occur until 1899, it was apparent well before this that the new form of transportation was creating major circulation problems.

Finally, before automobiles could reach a mass market, more efficient ways had to be found to sell, service, fuel, and house them. In the earliest years cars were usually bought in cash transactions. Many were sold through existing bicycle dealerships, which had established a mass distribution system in the last decade of the nineteenth century, others by carriage makers who also had showrooms. The first dealers to devote themselves solely to automobile sales appeared about 1900.[14] In these years repairs were frequent, expensive, and difficult, in part because so many of the parts had to be specially manufactured by boiler repairmen, coach makers, or anyone else who had suitable tools. Lodging the new machines was perhaps the easiest task, since in many cases stables could be pressed into service without any trouble.

Most automobile showrooms at the turn of the century shared space with bicycle and carriage dealers on the basement and ground floors of existing buildings in the central business district. In Chicago they were located in the south part of the Loop, especially along Wabash and Michigan Avenues.[15] The most famous structures associated with the carriage and automobile trade were the two successive Studebaker Buildings, both designed by Solon S. Beman. The first, on Michigan Avenue, opened in

18.4

Studebaker Building (Wabash Avenue), 1895, 625 S. Wabash Avenue, Solon Spencer Beman, architect, view of exterior. Photograph by Barnes-Crosby. Chicago Historical Society Prints and Photographs Department, ICHi-19179.

1885.[16] Beman's design appears to have been an attempt to reconcile two conflicting demands—to open the walls in enormous windows so as to provide maximum light to the showroom and factory work spaces behind, and to ensure that the building would be in harmony with its august neighbors, notably the Auditorium Theater immediately to the south. The result is a building that was open and glassy on the lower levels and massive on the upper floors, appearing to defy structural logic. This probably also reflected the status of the carriage and later the automobile, which were luxury items but also bulky and, in the case of the early automobile, often rather crude pieces of machinery. (See fig. 16.4.)

With the second Studebaker Building, opened in 1895 on Wabash Avenue, Beman was under fewer restraints. It featured a nearly continuous glazed facade that permitted dealers to show off machines to their best advantage.[17] It can perhaps be considered a ten-story version of the one-story taxpayer, since it had the repetitive simplicity and nearly continuous glazing of the taxpayer rather than the monumentality of most office buildings. The second Studebaker Building almost immediately became the center of the Chicago auto trade as dealers moved into the area, accompanied by parts manufacturers and distributors. From these showrooms the dealers and their prospective buyers would drive the same routes taken by the carriages of the wealthy— that is, down Michigan Avenue and along the grand tree-lined boulevards parallel to it, perhaps traveling as far as Hyde Park for lunch.

If the automobile had remained the plaything of the wealthy, the auto trade might well have remained in the Loop indefinitely. Instead the machines became more reliable, prices dropped, financing became available, and the car quickly became a mass market item. Within a few years an entire network of sales, service, and storage facilities was on its way to maturity. One sign of this was the founding in Chicago in 1902 of the American Automobile Association, and in 1906 of the Chicago Motor Club.[18] Chicago's Automobile Blue Book of 1906–7 provides a list of over 4,500 automobile owners in Chicago, not including those who had electric cars. It took five tightly packed pages to record the city ordinances passed in 1904 pertaining to automobiles, including the original speed limit—ten miles an hour when traveling straight along the street and four miles an hour when turning. It also carried an illustration of the elegant new home of the Chicago Automobile Club on Plymouth Place between Jackson and Van Buren, designed by prominent Chicago architects Marshall and Fox. At the back of the book, however, the remarkably crude maps showing the few main roads out of town are reminders of how little the automobile had yet affected the fabric of the city.[19]

The Automobile Invasion

The small Holabird & Roche building at Fourteenth and Michigan served as the beachhead for what soon became an automobile invasion of Chicago's most elegant residential neighborhood. How this toehold was gained is not known. Up until this time the stone-fronted houses, churches, schools, and clubs that lined this part of the boulevard formed a coherent streetscape. The buildings were compatible in style and materials and were almost all uniformly set back twenty feet from the sidewalk. This may have been due to an informal agreement among property owners, or it may have been contained in deed covenants.[20] Any landowner selling a lot to a commercial developer would have brought down on himself the censure of all his neighbors, if not legal challenges, but for at least one owner the profit to be made overcame any qualms.

The Mandel brothers' building and those that immediately followed systematically violated all the customary expectations about building on the avenue. These buildings typically occupied every inch of the site, extending from lot line to lot line on the sides and from the sidewalk in front to the alley behind. The contrast between the sober, heavily built masonry houses and churches and the shiny new facades, blatantly commercial advertisements, and enormous glass windows of the automobile buildings could not have been greater.

The objections to the building were not just aesthetic. Running automobiles involved a number of dangerous and flammable substances. Because the first structures were far from fireproof and because they were often built only a few feet from the adjacent houses, the roar of a gasoline engine next door would have been viewed by any head of the family as more than just a noise nuisance. The neighbors probably could have lived with a single intruder. What they feared most was that, once the breach had been made, they would have little power to prevent others from following. Zoning restrictions designed to stop this kind of development were still far in the future.[21]

18.5
Michigan Avenue looking north from Fifteenth Street, 1908. Chicago Historical Society Prints and Photographs Department, ICHi-24762.

By 1905 any formal agreements either had expired or were no longer enforced, and the new automobile buildings started to rip into the urban fabric with a vengeance. The earliest of these clustered around Fourteenth and Michigan. Henry Ford's decision to locate his dealership at 1444–46 S. Michigan Avenue influenced other automotive concerns. The Ford dealership was soon joined by a factory branch of the Firestone Rubber and Tire Company that had formerly been on Wabash near Harrison Street.[22] Once established, the automobile industry expanded very rapidly to the south. As architect Peter Bonnett Wight reported a few years later:

> It was not easy at first to procure building sites. The property had been
> held at a high price always for residence purposes; but owners soon
> yielded to the demand at a higher price than formerly and some tore
> down their houses and built stores, which were quickly rented. The "auto"
> people from all over the city then began to besiege the property owners
> for more sites and buildings and the natural consequence was a "boom" in
> the price of lots. Now nearly all the property for two miles is "for sale" at
> boom prices: many of the old families are in a panic to get away from the
> street; some because they want to sell at high prices and others because
> they are sensitive to the association with trade. This state of affairs exists
> from Twelfth Street south to Twenty-sixth Street, and scattering prop-
> erties have been sold along the Boulevard as far south as Thirty-ninth
> Street, four miles from the business centre of the city where a large store
> and factory combined is to be erected.[23]

Creating a Building Type

Although the automobile buildings that went up in the years between the Mandels' pioneer effort in 1902 and the end of the decade were quite varied, most of them had a number of traits in common, since they all housed showrooms, garages, repair shops, and offices in a variety of combinations. Most were two to five stories high with huge show windows opening onto the salesroom on the ground floor and smaller windows in the floors above where cars were repaired and stored. Automobile buildings usually sported facades in glazed brick or terra cotta.[24]

This kind of design obviously was heavily indebted to earlier taxpayers. In their large, often arched, ground-floor openings and open interior spaces, some of the early buildings also had quite a bit in common with stables, which were often used as garages and repair shops in the auto's earliest years.[25] To create a successful automobile showroom, however, something more was needed. Neither the taxpayer shops building nor the stable provided the visual stimulation dealers felt was necessary to convey the excitement of the rapidly changing new technology. But this had to be done within a strict budget, because these buildings were basically utilitarian. The stakes were high enough for the automobile dealers to enlist the services of some of the most important designers in the city, notably Christian Eckstorm, William Le Baron Jenney, Mundie and Jensen, Howard Van Doren Shaw, and Jarvis Hunt. There was also at least one building by Detroit's great industrial architect, Albert Khan.[26]

Holabird & Roche was among the earliest and most prolific of all of the designers of auto showrooms, and from the existing evidence it appears to have produced the most varied and interesting set. After the building for the Mandel brothers at Michigan and Fourteenth, Holabird & Roche designed two other buildings for the same clients, one in the 1400 block of Michigan, one in the 1700 block, both built in 1907. On the drawings one of these was labeled Mandel Brothers Store (cat. no. 421), the other Mandel Brothers Warehouse (cat. no. 423), but both appear to have been intended from the start as automobile buildings. The latter, a three-story brick structure, already shows the new formula. Very simple in plan with large, open floors interrupted only by rows of columns, it was distinguished on the outside by a festive facade of brick and galvanized iron. By 1911 virtually the entire stretch of Michigan and Wabash in the blocks between Fourteenth and Twenty-fifth Streets was turning commercial. Fire insurance maps show only about ten houses remaining between Thirteenth and Fifteenth Streets on Michigan and Wabash, and some of these had obviously been converted to clubs, boardinghouses, or other uses. Two churches remained, the Wabash Avenue Methodist Episcopal Church and Grace Episcopal Church. Otherwise all the buildings were commercial structures, almost all erected within the previous few years. The most prominent single buildings were furniture wholesale stores and warehouses, but in sheer numbers the street was dominated by buildings used for automobile sales, storage, and repair.

Farther south the process had not advanced as much. In the 2300 and 2400 blocks, for example, commercial buildings had usurped about half of the lots formerly occupied by houses. The result was a landscape in turbulent transition. In this stretch of road, between 1909 and 1915 Holabird & Roche designed at least ten automobile buildings, making it the ideal place to study the work of the firm on this building type. Although some of the buildings in these blocks are gone, particularly south of Twenty-fourth Street on Michigan, where a wide swath was demolished to make way for the construction of the Stevenson Expressway, a surprisingly large number survive, including almost all the Holabird & Roche buildings, especially on the east side of Michigan between Twenty-third and Twenty-fourth Streets. Here virtually the entire street front

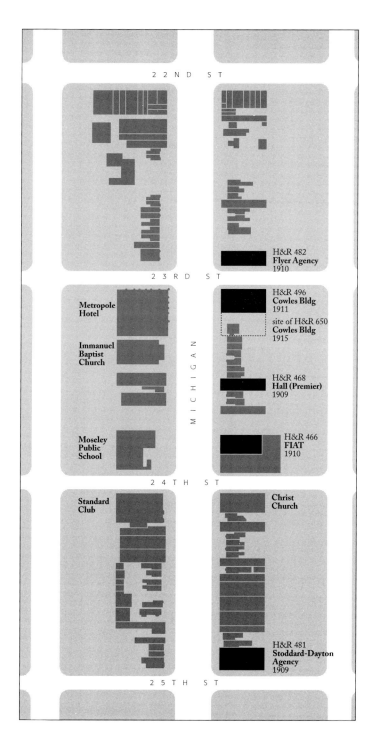

18.6

Holabird & Roche on Automobile Row, ca. 1911.
Drawn by Dennis McClendon, 1996, from
information on fire insurance maps and
Holabird & Root records.

was built to designs of Holabird & Roche, and though obscured, it remains, miraculously, almost intact.

A good example of a typical auto building in this block is the Hall (Premier Auto Cab Company) Building (cat. no. 468) at 2329–31 S. Michigan. Commissioned in 1909 by Florence Lathrop Page, a relative of real estate agent and Holabird & Roche client Bryan Lathrop, the three-story structure replaced a row house that had probably stood on the site since the 1880s. Completely covering its 34 by 160 foot lot, it had a simple facade on Michigan Avenue in which the middle section was almost completely opened in windows, with only small bands of green terra cotta for the mullions and spandrel panels. Around this middle section a narrow band of terra cotta at the sides and top formed a kind of picture frame. It must have looked even lighter and more open in contrast with the old row houses on either side. There was no confusion about the use of the building. The name Premier appeared in jaunty script on three large terra cotta plaques, one above each floor.

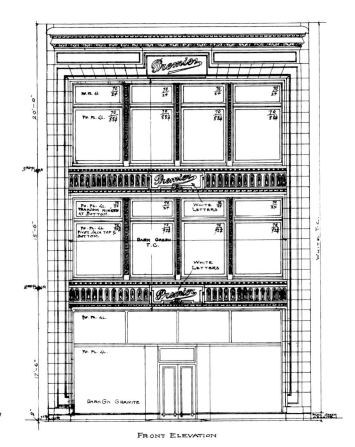

18.7

Hall (Premier) Building (468), 1909, 2329–31 S. Michigan Avenue, elevation. Chicago Historical Society Architectural Collections.

Through the plate glass windows on the ground floor, customers approaching the building would have seen automobiles displayed. Entering by a recessed door in the center, they would have found themselves in the double-height showroom with a "tutti-colori" tile floor edged in black. To make transactions easier, the offices and cashier were directly behind the showroom. Forming a balcony to the rear was a "retiring room." These rooms constituted the front, public part of the building. The rear was devoted to service and storage.

The ground floor was open except for a wash rack and combination turntable and wash rack. Cars from the storage areas above would be brought down by elevator, turned on the turntable, and driven out the rear door into the alley to reach the city streets. All the upper floors were primarily open. Some of the space was probably used for the storage and sale of parts, the rest for the storage and repair of automobiles.[27] The Premier, at a cost of $41,407, was frankly utilitarian. It was also designed for a relatively short life span. Styles changed quickly in most retail buildings, but in the automobile business what was adequate one year might be functionally and aesthetically obsolete the next. This was clearly reflected in the Premier lease, which was for only twenty years rather than the fifty- or ninety-nine-year terms common for large commercial structures downtown.

The Premier would have been an arresting building by itself, but it sat in a whole row of such buildings designed by Holabird & Roche. Several doors to the south was the building for the Italian company FIAT at 2347–53 S. Michigan (cat. no. 466). Here a gabled roof ran parallel to the street, and the central, heavily glazed portion

18.8
FIAT Building (Fauch-Lang-Baker Company) (466), 1909–10, 2347–53 S. Michigan Avenue, elevation and section. Chicago Historical Society Architectural Collections.

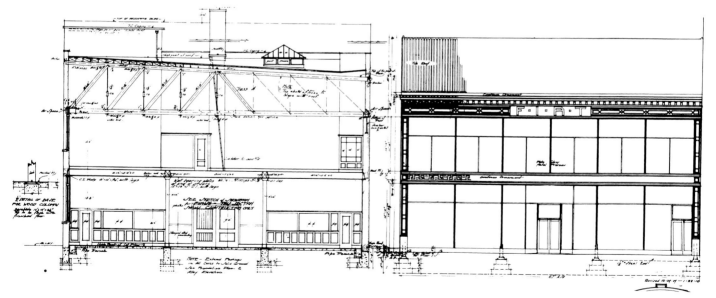

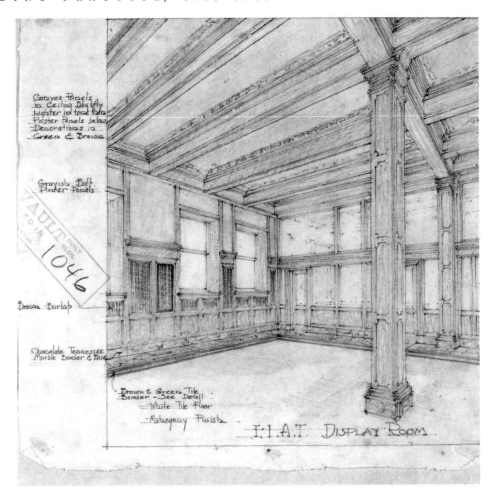

The text annotations on the drawing read:

Canvas Panels
in Ceiling Slightly
Lighter in tone than
Plaster Panels below
Decorations in
Green & Brown

Grayish Buff
Plaster Panels

Brown Burlap

Chocolate Tennessee
Marble Border & Base

Brown & Green Tile
Border – See Detail
White Tile Floor
Mahogany Finish

F.I.A.T. DISPLAY ROOM

18.9
FIAT Building,
perspective drawing of
display room. Chicago
Historical Society
Architectural
Collections.

was surrounded by a frame of white terra cotta with an intricate buff and green pattern. A rare surviving Holabird & Roche interior perspective drawing of this building shows what the customer would have seen after entering. The wood and burlap paneled walls and the ceiling with borders of tile and marble might have given the room the feel of one of the firm's hotel lobbies, but this would have been offset by the flood of light entering the space from the huge windows and reflecting off the white tile floor.

To the north stood the Franklin Motor Car Company (cat. no. 641), a jewellike building of about 1915 with its white terra cotta panels extravagantly festooned with classical wreaths and medallions. Farther north still were two commissions for Alfred Cowles. The northernmost, at the corner of Twenty-third Street, was a relatively sober five-story building in white glazed terra cotta with minimal classical detail. It was built

18.10

Cowles Buildings. Two buildings to right: (650), 1915, 2309–13 S. Michigan Avenue; building on left (496), 1910–11, for Cadillac Automobile Company, southeast corner of Twenty-third Street and Michigan Avenue. Photograph by Robert Boettcher, 1986. Chicago Historical Society Architectural Collections.

in 1910–11 as a Cadillac showroom (cat. no. 496). As if to make up for its sobriety, the two adjacent buildings, at 2309–13 S. Michigan (cat. no. 650), commissioned by Cowles four years later, each had its own elaborate decorative scheme. To the north diamonds of white accented blind Romanesque arches in a stepped gable of dark brick. Next door brilliant patterns in buff, white, and green covered the entire terra cotta surface. Immediately across the street at 2255–59 S. Michigan stood the E. P. Thomas Flyer garage (cat. no. 482), a three-story building that was again enlivened with terra cotta ornament.

The most remarkable of the Holabird & Roche showrooms, unfortunately demolished for the construction of the Stevenson Expressway, was the four-story McDuffee Automobile Company, or Stoddard-Dayton Building, at the northeast cor-

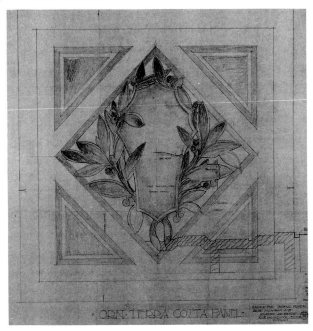

18.11

E. P. Thomas (Flyer) garage (482), 1909–10, 2255–59 S. Michigan Avenue, terra cotta panel detail drawing. Chicago Historical Society Architectural Collections.

18.13 (opposite page) *Stoddard-Dayton Building, plan. Chicago Historical Society Architectural Collections.*

ner of Michigan Avenue and Twenty-fifth Street (cat. no. 481). At a cost of just over $100,000, this was the largest and most elaborate of Holabird & Roche automobile buildings before World War I. Following the usual formula, huge windows along the shorter Michigan Avenue and the longer Twenty-fifth Street frontages allowed an unimpeded view into the showroom at the front. Behind and above were the floors for storing and servicing the automobiles.

In this building Holabird & Roche produced one of its most unorthodox designs. The walls were of brick with terra cotta quoins and cornices, but these were treated in a most unclassical way. Colonnettes ran up the quoins, giving an impression of verticality, and raised ornamental blocks formed an unorthodox cornice. At the corners caricature figures of race car drivers holding steering wheels served visually as substitutes for capitals. Even more unusual were the windows. Instead of the individual rectangular openings common in most automobile buildings, the windows at the Stoddard-Dayton Building were set back to form unified vertical groupings four stories high. At the grade level, where unimpeded vision was important, virtually the entire bay was opened up in a huge sheet of glass. Above this were movable transoms for ventilation. At the second-and third-floor levels, where the view into the building was less important, smaller and less expensive sheets of glass were set in wood frames with slightly arched tops. Above this an eruption of decorative members resembling English perpendicular tracery filled the top of the round arches of the fourth-floor

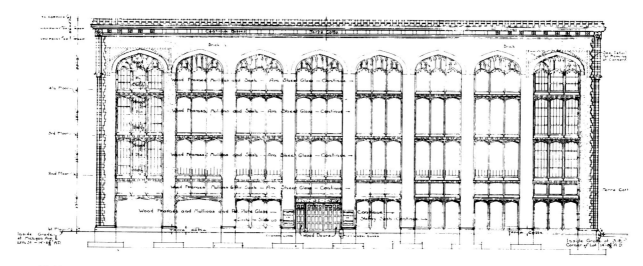

18.12

Stoddard-Dayton Building (481), 1909, 2453 S. Michigan Avenue, northeast corner of Twenty-fifth Street, elevation. Chicago Historical Society Architectural Collections.

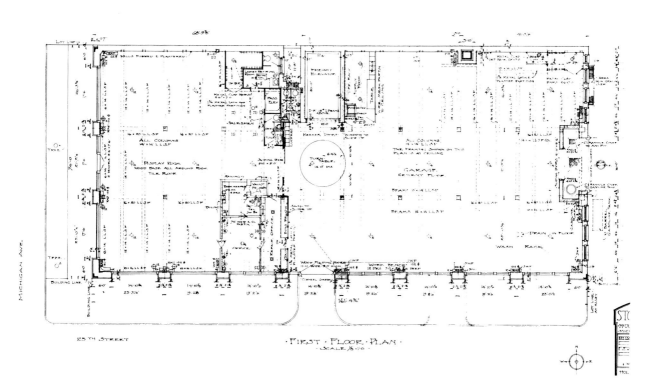

18.14
Stoddard-Dayton Building, view of exterior. From Architectural Record, *April 1912.*

windows. Between the windows the spandrel areas were faced with wood meant to resemble English linenfold paneling. The contrast between the boxy overall form and large, almost industrial glazing, on the one hand, and the intricate window tracery and unusual combination of wall materials produced an effect that might be called industrial Gothic. It was as novel as anything on the street.

Peter B. Wight terminated his discussion of automobile buildings with a description of the Stoddard-Dayton:

It is of gray pressed brick and white terra-cotta. It should not be called Gothic, for it is not like any building ever erected in the Gothic period. The treatment of the corners and the cornice which serves to unite all the angles of the building, is very effective. It may have been suggested by Italian models and yet it is not Italian. The cornice is more English than Italian. The brick work it will be noticed is one unvaried surface serving to make the window tracery all the more effective by contrast, and this tracery is not copied from any English model. The plainness of the window openings also serves by contrast to accentuate the tracery. It will be noticed that all the windows run from floor to ceiling, leaving no room for the transoms.[28]

Wight concluded that the building was the "most original and attractive" on auto row. Although none of these buildings could be called outstanding works of art, he argued, they were interesting as examples of the way architects were trying to create a new building type. He commented that they almost all had come to a similar solution: the basic utilitarian box behind and the ornamental terra cotta facade in front.

Indeed, what seems most striking about auto row, even in its current tattered state, is the diversity the architects managed to create. Terra cotta was perfect for the purpose. It was inexpensive and by 1905 could be obtained in a wide range of colors. Because it was a new material there were few precedents for using it, and the architects were free to experiment. Sometimes they reproduced classical moldings and details—for example, at 2317 S. Michigan—but increasingly the material was used in ways less dependent on stone detailing. Multiple panels and mosaiclike frames started to appear, relying on the color and light relief rather than the higher relief and the play of light and shadow characteristic of stone detailing. The glossy appearance of terra cotta was also appropriate because it looked shiny and new, a perfect frame for the modern machines inside.

This stretch of roadway in its heyday must have been quite a spectacle. Peter B. Wight reported in 1910:

> Michigan Boulevard, since the "auto" came into extensive use, with traffic teams forbidden and its splendid bitulithic pavement, has been the largest and best automobile course in any city of this country. . . . What with the use of the roadway by the thousands who now go up and down town between house and office or store, the shopping crowd that is too dainty to put its feet on the pavements, and the "auto" dealers "showing off" their machines, the Boulevard is a lively street with a continuous stream of machines going both ways at all hours: sometimes two abreast and at all speeds.[29]

In their pristine, original state the arresting facades, with their bright terra cotta, varied patterns, and wide range of colors, must have formed a vibrant and constantly changing environment. Even today the remnants document the heady moment between the time the machines began to be accessible to the middle class and the time they started to transform and, some might say, overwhelm the city, a transformation in which automobile row was itself left far behind.[30]

NINETEEN

AT THE CORNER OF
MICHIGAN AND MONROE:
THE UNIVERSITY CLUB AND
THE MONROE BUILDING

For generations of Chicagoans the view back toward the Loop from Lake Michigan has been a favorite representative image of their city. In this view the wall of buildings along Michigan Avenue, rising sheer from the park and the avenue like a great masonry cliff, forms Chicago's front facade. The initial impression is one of exceptional uniformity. On closer inspection, it becomes apparent that this wall is hardly uniform. Massive stone blocks rub shoulders with narrow terra cotta slivers and the occasional postwar metal-skinned building. Vertical projections like the ziggurat atop the massive Straus Building at 310 South Michigan Avenue contrast with the flat, low silhouette of buildings such as the Chicago Public Library (now the Cultural Center). Still, the fairly consistent height, usually sixteen to twenty-four stories, the constant repetition of fenestration patterns, and the widespread use of masonry exteriors give this street facade a remarkable consistency.

The building wall and the formal park in front of it together constitute one of the country's most conspicuous demonstrations of the power of the City Beautiful ideal. This example is all the more remarkable since this is not a group of public buildings that could be designed and built as a unit but a piece of the commercial city, erected by many developers and institutions over a long period. The ensemble achieves exactly the kind of coherence sought after in the most famous document of that movement, Daniel Burnham and Edward Bennett's famous 1909 *Plan of Chicago*. At the time Burnham started assembling the plan, Michigan Avenue, like most of the Loop, was very uneven in its architectural development, with huge and opulent new hotels looming above modest loft buildings and old row houses. As we have seen, Holabird & Roche had played a significant role along the avenue at both ends of the architectural scale with relatively small loft structures like the McCormick Buildings (Gage Group) at one extreme and the giant Congress Hotel (Auditorium Annex) at the other.

In the illustrations accompanying the 1909 plan, Michigan Avenue was depicted as a set of huge buildings, completely filling the block between Michigan and Wabash and rising as high as the city's height limit allowed. In much of the literature about the plan since that date, writers have charged that Burnham advocated a monotonous, unending series of classical buildings extending to the horizon. It is highly unlikely that Burnham intended any such thing. What Michigan Avenue actually became probably better suggests what he anticipated. The goal of the illustrations was not to prescribe the exact appearance of buildings but to suggest their general character and massing (see fig. 7.15). With a few municipal regulations, notably the height limit first put into effect in 1893, market forces would do the rest, as the work of Burnham's own firm on Michigan Avenue suggests. The heavily textured Peoples Gas Company building of 1911, the rippling white terra cotta bays of the Railway Exchange of 1904, and the chaste brick with stone trim of Orchestra Hall of 1905 showed clearly that consistency need not entail sacrificing visual interest (see fig. 15.3). The power of the Burnham vision is well illustrated by two Holabird & Roche buildings at the corner of Michigan Avenue and Monroe Street. These buildings also illustrate the deeply intertwined nature of public and private space in the city.

The University Club

The University Club was founded in 1887, its purpose the "promotion of literature and art." Although its ranks included relatively few of the Pullmans, Fields, Potters, and other giants of Chicago industry and commerce, most of whom belonged to more exclusive organizations, notably the Chicago Club, it did number many successful Chicago businessman.[1] One newspaper reporter suggested that membership in the club was so desirable that some fathers sent their sons to college expressly so they would qualify. He reassured his readers that this was the exception, however.[2]

In its early years the club occupied two floors of the Henning and Speed Building at 21 W. Madison Street. By 1890 club members were affluent enough to buy a building of their own, the Hansen Block, at 30 N. Dearborn. By the early years of the twentieth century this building in turn proved inadequate for the club's membership, now totaling 525. Members selected a building committee and charged it with starting negotiations for a site on or near Michigan Avenue. This area was considered a prime location for the club, since it was adjacent to the business district but not immediately in it. Directly across from the Art Institute and the other cultural institutions, and near

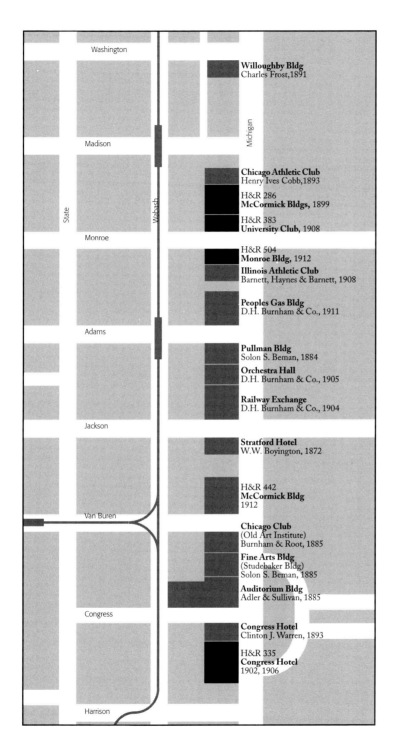

Washington

Willoughby Bldg
Charles Frost,1891

Madison

Michigan

Chicago Athletic Club
Henry Ives Cobb,1893

H&R 286
McCormick Bldgs, 1899

H&R 383
University Club, 1908

Monroe

H&R 504
Monroe Bldg, 1912

Illinois Athletic Club
Barnett, Haynes & Barnett, 1908

Peoples Gas Bldg
D.H. Burnham & Co., 1911

Adams

Pullman Bldg
Solon S. Beman, 1884

Orchestra Hall
D.H. Burnham & Co., 1905

Railway Exchange
D.H. Burnham & Co., 1904

Jackson

Stratford Hotel
W.W. Boyington, 1872

H&R 442
McCormick Bldg
1912

Van Buren

Chicago Club
(Old Art Institute)
Burnham & Root, 1885

Fine Arts Bldg
(Studebaker Bldg)
Solon S. Beman, 1885

Auditorium Bldg
Adler & Sullivan, 1885

Congress

Congress Hotel
Clinton J. Warren, 1893

H&R 335
Congress Hotel
1902, 1906

Harrison

State

Wabash

19.1

*Michigan Avenue map showing University
Club, Monroe Building, and other structures,
ca. 1918. Drawn by Dennis McClendon, 1996,
based on information from Holabird & Root
records, fire insurance maps, and other sources.*

many other clubs, it was a prestigious address, but land prices were lower than in the heart of the Loop.[3] Michigan Avenue itself also held another attraction, one that helped draw many of the other clubs there. It provided an unimpeded view out over Lake Michigan, and from the lakefront it gave the club maximum exposure. Eventually it would also look out on the formal gardens of Grant Park, which was still in the process of emerging from the landfill.

Even before the site was secured, probably as early as 1904, Holabird & Roche started working informally with the club on site selection and preliminary planning. This was not surprising. Holabird had been a founding member in 1887, and the building committee was composed of friends and clients including Arthur Aldis, Alfred Cowles, and Bryan Lathrop. It appears that no other firm was seriously considered, even though club rosters contained several well-known architects, including Howard Van Doren Shaw, who was on the committee to plan the new clubhouse. Edward Renwick later reported that some members found Holabird & Roche's design of the Venetian Building particularly suggestive in trying to imagine what the new clubhouse should look like.[4] At first glance this seems odd, since the Venetian had been constructed quite a few years earlier, was decidedly commercial in character, and was rather exotic in the firm's oeuvre. Perhaps it was the exotic quality that appealed to members, or it may simply have been the Venetian's pitched roof that gave it a slightly less mercantile aspect (see fig. 10.4).

Eventually the club chose an expensive and desirable piece of property at the northwest corner of Michigan Avenue and Monroe Street, leased it for 196 years, and secured financing by creating a separate real estate entity that floated a stock issue (see fig. 11.8).[5] The location selected already functioned as a kind of club row. Several doors to the north, separated from the University Club's property by Holabird & Roche's McCormick Buildings (Gage Group), was the florid Venetian facade of the Chicago Athletic Club at 12 S. Michigan, finished in 1893 to designs of Henry Ives Cobb.[6] A little to the south, across Monroe Street, was the proposed site of the Illinois Athletic Club at 112 S. Michigan. University Club members and the architects would have known about a preliminary design by Barnett, Haynes and Barnett of St. Louis (at this same period competing with Holabird & Roche for the Cook County Courthouse) for an ornate eight-story building costing between $600,000 and $800,000.[7] Given the rather forceful designs of nearby clubs, University Club members undoubtedly felt under some pressure to have a building with an equally distinctive character.

Martin Roche must have decided at an early stage on the medieval English university tradition as his source of inspiration, because as soon as the site was fixed he traveled to England to study the colleges at Oxford. This decision must have seemed logical enough to club members, since the British colleges were the prime image many

19.2

Crosby Hall, London, view of vaulted ceiling,
From Architectural Review, *July 1910.*

Americans had of the way an institution of higher education should look. The Gothic also seems to have been Roche's own favorite style.[8]

In Britain he was impressed by Magdalen College at Oxford. What apparently interested him even more, however, was Crosby Hall, a late medieval banqueting hall that had been built in the Bishopsgate section of London for a wealthy wool merchant in the fifteenth century. In the path of new development, it had been pulled down, but at the time of Roche's trip it was being reinstalled in Chelsea as a dining hall for a residential college complex.[9] The most remarkable feature of this interior was an extraordinary paneled wood ceiling with elaborate pierced arched ribs and pendants. Roche returned to Chicago and presented to the building committee a scheme that used as its centerpiece an adaptation of this impressive room.

Two accounts survive of what happened at Roche's meeting with the committee. Although they basically tell the same story, the variations are most interesting because they provide, from two different points of view, some telling insights into the problem of clubhouse design. What should a club look like? How could all the functions be accommodated on the small site? Both accounts also show clearly how, in matters artistic, Chicagoans were obsessed with New York, betraying a simultaneous desire for approbation and need to assert independence. The main point of reference was, logically enough, the University Club of New York, a splendid urban palace on Fifth Avenue designed by McKim, Mead and White and recently finished.[10] This building would probably have been known to a large number of club members, since many of them made frequent trips to New York on business.

The first account is a fictionalized skit put on at the club in the 1930s titled the "Reading of the Minutes":

[Scene: A small room, with chairs for all. On a small table, center, are architect's sketches. Five or six members of the Plans Committee are listening to Mr. Roche.]

ROCHE: This is the front elevation. . . . Here, we have a drawing of the Michigan Avenue front and the entire Monroe Street side.

ALDIS: Just a minute, Mr. Roche, please. . . . Do I correctly understand you to mean, and to make this Committee believe, we are to put up a fifteen story club house?

ROCHE: That's correct, Mr. Aldis.

ALDIS: I never heard anybody suggest anything of the sort. Who ever heard of a skyscraper club building?

ISHAM: Nobody! . . . Why, when the New York University Club decided to build five stories high, they disguised their building so that it looks to be only three stories high.

ALDIS: Mr. Roche, I entirely agree with Dr. Isham.

ROCHE: Had it ever occurred to you that we have a rather small plot of land and that on it we must construct a building large enough to care for the needs of more than one thousand members? You can't have the facilities you want unless you get more ground, or else you must build high. Fifteen stories is the minimum, in my judgment. Actually, there are twelve separate floors and a basement in my plan.

ISHAM: There's something in that, of course.

ALDIS: Possibly. . . . Now, did I understand you to say this is Gothic architecture?

ROCHE: It's a Gothic adaptation to a tall building, Mr. Aldis.

ALDIS: That's something new, isn't it?

ROCHE: Entirely so.

ALDIS: I thought as much. A Gothic skyscraper! No wonder New York calls us the wild and woolly west!

ROCHE: I grant the idea may shock the traditions of some people.

ISHAM: To my eye, that building savors more of a hotel than of the domesticity which we associate with a social club.

ALDIS: Again I concur, Dr. Isham. And, may I add, if a fifteen-story club house is an anomaly, what shall we say about a fifteen-story club house in the—er—Gothic style?

ROCHE: Gentlemen, are there any well-established, universally conceded ideas or principles as to what is right in architecture? It's good Gothic.

ISHAM: It's not ugly, I'll concede, but I'm afraid we'll be the laughing stock of the country if we build such a hybrid.

ROCHE: I hope not, and I'm staking my reputation on my hope.

ALDIS: Sorry, Mr. Roche, but I don't believe I can ever vote to approve your plans. I had rather expected an Italian Renaissance structure —something on the order of the New York University Club.

ISHAM: Only much finer.

ALDIS: Yes, of course. . . . Have you any other or alternate design to offer?

ROCHE: No, this is all. . . . Do the other members of the Plans Committee feel the same way?

[The others say they do.]

Well, gentlemen, I am bitterly disappointed. Your judgment, of course, controls. Before you take a vote, however, I wonder if you'll do me, personally, a favor.

ALDIS: Certainly. What is it?

ROCHE: Ralph Adams Cram is in the city. Are you willing to hear his opinion about my plans?

ALDIS: By all means. Cram's opinion may change mine. I count him the greatest living authority on Gothic architecture.

ROCHE: That's his reputation. Howard Shaw showed my sketches to him and he's waiting outside, if you care to see him.

ALDIS: Let's have him at once.

[Roche produces Cram.]

How do you do, Mr. Cram. It's very good of you to drop in.

CRAM: I consider it a great privilege, gentlemen, because it affords me the opportunity to tell you what I think about Martin Roche's design for your new building.

ALDIS: Have you seen these sketches?

CRAM: I have sir, this morning, and it was one of the memorable moments in my life. If I had not seen them, I would not have believed it possible for any man to make a beautiful Gothic skyscraper.

Martin Roche, you have designed the most notable new building in America. You have pioneered in the development of our art. Put up that building, and you will mark the beginning of new beauty in high buildings. Gentlemen of the Committee, if you fail to approve those plans, you can never be forgiven, because you will have rejected the product of sheer genius.

[Curtain][11]

It is likely that the author of this account had no firsthand information about the designing of the club, and that he relied on published sources and thirty-year-old recollections, probably poorly remembered and heavily embroidered, of some event that did take place.[12] It is also quite likely that parts of the story came directly from members of the Holabird & Roche office. A variant of this tale, less dramatic but from someone who was surely privy to the actual events, came from the pen of Holabird & Roche partner Edward A. Renwick. Also writing much later, in the 1930s, Renwick told the tale this way:

> The University Club building committee decided to choose the architects without any competition or before any public announcement had been made, to avoid undue pressure being brought to bear. They chose us perhaps because we were building more buildings than anybody else at that time, and I think the design of the Venetian Building had some influence. They felt they couldn't afford an elaborate building and Mr. Roche's first design which was Gothic was objected to by Mr. Aldis and several others on the ground that a brick front couldn't be used with the Gothic. It took many sessions before it was decided to make it of stone. The sketches were changed two or three times to try to use brick, we tried everything else—O there were weeks of it!
>
> The rivalry between Chicago and New York has always been amusingly evident, it was evident to me in an incident which occurred during the planning of the club. We had the plans almost made, a fine watercolor perspective was finished, when Mr. Ralph Adams Cram, the greatest expert on Gothic architecture in this country, happened to be in Chicago. The committee of the University Club thought it would be a good idea for him to criticize the drawings and offered to pay him, of course, for his services.
>
> Mr. Holabird was in Europe at the time and Mr. Roche was in New York so it was left for me to meet Mr. Cram and show him the drawings. I can see him now as he came in, the expression on his face said as plainly as day, "O, do I have to see what these barbarians have been trying to do? It will be wild and woolly stuff, a painful job, etc." Well, I asked him to come into the library and as we approached it I opened the door. The water color perspective was on an easel against the opposite wall. As he reached the door Mr. Cram, looking at the perspective and stopping stock still, fairly breathed out "O—beautiful!" I told him it was a little early to

be reaching a decision, but he said "If I studied it a thousand years I could not say otherwise."

After he had examined all the drawings he said "There is just one criticism I'll make, a trivial one and I hate to even say that. I think there should be a couple of pilasters on the gable, it is a little too plain." I called for the sketch Roche had made of the gable on which there were two pilasters exactly as he had described them. He said, "Just the very thing. I should have known that the man that had designed this building would see that too." His final verdict to the committee was more than generous. He said "Gentlemen, you're going to have one of the notable buildings of the United States when that is done. If the commission had been given to me I couldn't have done better or as well."[13]

The watercolor perspective Renwick mentioned may well have been a drawing published in *Inland Architect* in April 1908 while the building was under construction. In any case, it appears that once the design was approved, the process of entering contracts and building the structure went forward during 1907–8 without incident. The finished structure received a good deal of favorable attention in architectural journals. *Inland Architect* reported that the building represented "substantial evidence of a culture not generally credited to Chicago."[14] The longest and most thoughtful review was an extensive piece in the *Architectural Record* accompanied by thirty-five illustrations. The piece was unsigned but similar in style and content to the work of Montgomery Schuyler, America's foremost architectural critic.[15]

The building, the author asserted, was likely to become one of the architectural "lions" of Chicago. He disapproved of the storefronts on the ground floor, feeling that these intrusions were probably tolerated because of the revenue they generated, but otherwise he had little but praise for the building. The bulk of the arguments made in the piece were essentially on moral grounds, having to do with the honesty of expression of the program requirements. He explicitly compared the club with its New York counterpart, remarking that whereas the latter rose only five stories and disguised these to appear as three in order to minimize the deviation from classical proportions, the Chicago building made no effort to dissemble the fact that land costs forced it up to fifteen stories. The author, while reserving judgment on the conditions that made such a situation necessary, found the frank admission of the "facts of the case" admirable. He then focused on the way, although it was a private club that most people would never enter, the building had a certain legibility even to casual viewers. The location of the two most important spaces, the lounging room on the second floor and the main

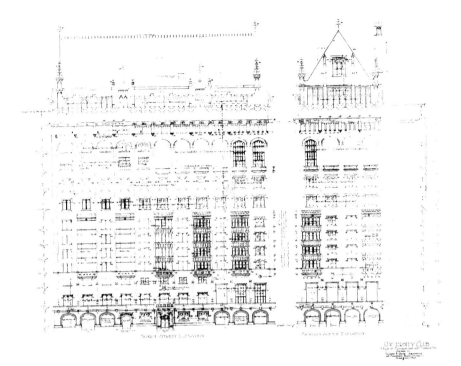

19.4
*University Club,
elevations and wall
section. Chicago
Historical Society
Architectural
Collections.*

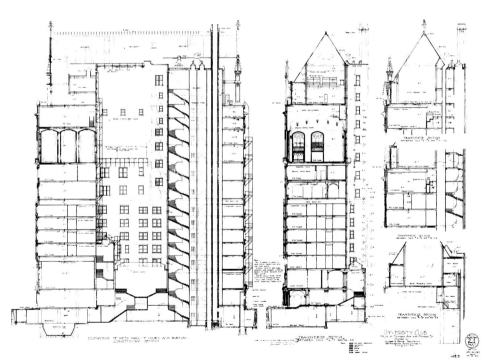

19.5
*University Club,
sections. Chicago
Historical Society
Architectural
Collections.*

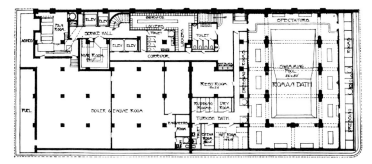

BASEMENT PLAN

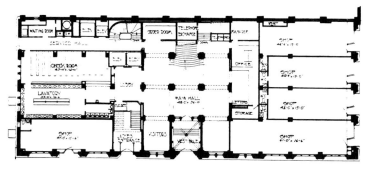

FIRST FLOOR PLAN

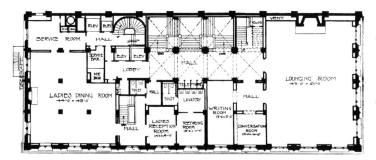

SECOND FLOOR PLAN

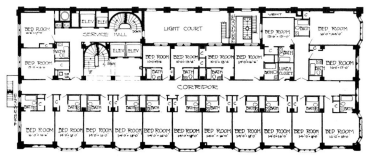

THIRD, FOURTH, AND FIFTH FLOOR PLAN

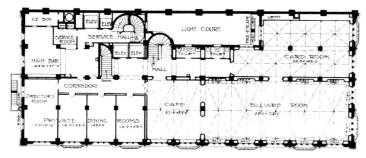

SEVENTH FLOOR PLAN

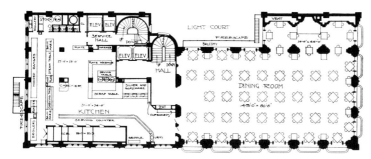

NINTH FLOOR PLAN

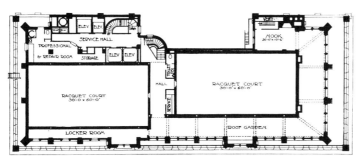

RACQUET-COURT

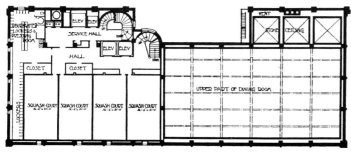

SQUASH-COURT PLAN

19.6

University Club, plans. From
University Club of Chicago,
booklet, 1908.

dining room on the ninth, could be clearly read from the exterior, as could the lesser public spaces of the seventh and eighth floors and the simple guest rooms on floors three through six.

This focus on the symbolic expression of the public exterior serves as a reminder of the complex relations between the public and private worlds even in an institution as intensely private as the club. City clubs, even those that are primarily social and artistic, necessarily have an intimate relation to the larger city around them. In addition to its already large membership, the club welcomes thousands of other individuals into its spaces every year as guests of the members. Activities of the club, from lectures by invited guests to art exhibitions, necessarily engage with the outside world in even more direct fashion.

Architecturally, one of the most interesting things about the University Club, as at many prominent clubs, is the way the building simultaneously asserts and obscures this public role. As we have seen, the entire building, based as it is on associations with British collegiate architecture, suggests its identity to a knowledgeable viewer. The huge arched windows of the main dining room give an indication of the character of the great hall that can be found within. How many thousands of Chicagoans, before ever entering the building, have imagined what lay behind the traceried windows and aspired to an invitation from a friend or business associate?

At the same time the University Club, like many such clubs, refuses to identify itself in any explicit way. The front entrance, fairly small and situated on Monroe Street, around the corner from the main facade, carries no identifying sign. Anyone who does not know what the institution is has no business there. The privacy of the place is underscored by the contrast between the rather forbidding opacity of the street level, where an outsider might peer in, and the extravagant openness of the second floor lounging room or the great dining room where members can easily see the public on the sidewalk through the windows but can be seen only with great difficulty.

The Private Realm

Well mannered but discreet, the exterior of the University Club is a lesson in cool, dignified restraint. Once inside the building, however, in its purely private spaces, one finds the atmosphere considerably warmer and more personal. It is here that the talents of Martin Roche were allowed free reign. The clubhouse was a nearly perfect commission for him. Freed of many of the restraints imposed by strictly business buildings, he was able to devote more time than usual to working out details and coordinating the work with artist Frederic Clay Bartlett, another club member, who designed the stained glass, painted decorations, and other embellishments.[16]

A male visitor to the building at the time of its opening would have entered by a door in the middle of the Monroe Street facade. A woman, although she would not have been admitted as a member, would, on certain occasions, have been allowed into some parts of the building, but she would have been obliged to enter by another doorway farther down the facade that communicated with a secondary staircase leading directly to the ladies' dining room on the second floor. Our male visitor would have proceeded through a vaulted vestibule to the main hall. A large but relatively low room with stone piers holding up oak beams, a plaster roof between the beams, and oak paneled walls, the hall was described by a club handbook as departing from the "pure Gothic" seen on the exterior and employing instead English Renaissance or Elizabethan style.

The hall gave access to club offices on the east and to a checkroom, a lavatory, and an elevator lobby on the west. The chief feature of the hall, however, was the immense staircase with massive oak balustrade directly in front of the vestibule, leading up to the second floor. The first-time visitor might well have been startled by the way the horizontal amplitude of the room and the sweeping grandeur of the staircase belied the building's narrow site.

Before going up the stairs, the visitor might have first wished to go downstairs by a smaller staircase, to the side of the main one. The basement contained the "Roman bath," or swimming pool, various dressing rooms, a "hot room," steam room, and "Turkish bath," toilets, and—out of sight—fans, the building's heating plant, and wine storage. Returning to the first floor and mounting the main staircase, the visitor would climb three flights of stairs interrupted by a landing to arrive at the second floor. The hall in front of him led to the west to the Ladies' Annex, an area containing the ladies' dining room and various auxiliary spaces for the use of women visiting the club. To the east of the staircase was the first of the building's two great interior spaces, the lounging room (also called the assembly room, and later the Michigan Room). Here was an excellent place for the visitor to sample the results of the collaboration of Roche and Bartlett. Two stories high, it resembled some of the firm's hotel lobbies, except that it was more elegantly finished in architectural detail and more intimate and casual in its furnishings. On three sides the walls were entirely covered in paneling, in simple large rectangles at the bottom, with blind arcades in the next tier of panels, then with moldings forming intricately subdivided panels above, followed by the visual respite of a kind of cornice composed of simple flat and convex moldings, and finally a frieze with pierced quatrefoils at the top, the whole a tour de force in rich dark English oak. At

19.7

University Club, view of lounging room (later Michigan Room). From Selected Photographs Illustrating the Work of Holabird & Roche, Architects, *1925.*

the center of the north wall an enormous stone fireplace, also decorated with quatre-foils and tracery, dominated the room.

To the east the large windows contained clear glass at the bottom, but at the top had splendid stained glass designed by Bartlett incorporating medieval motifs like crowns, flowers, and medallions with legends of the saints. Through the brilliantly colored glass warm light flooded the room. The chief ornament of the lounging room, however, was the magnificent coffered oak ceiling whose inset panels Bartlett had decorated with painted scenes from a medieval chase and feast. Like the leaded glass, these were executed in a consciously archaic way, in this case to resemble the miniatures in a slightly faded medieval tapestry. With their elaborate painted frames of gold and green and their simple, mostly frontal figures in shades of green, red, and blue, they produced a warm, highly decorative effect.[17]

To get to floors three to six, which contained mainly bedrooms, our guest would have taken the elevator, since the main staircase stopped at the second floor. The space occupied by the staircase on the first two floors became, on the upper floors, an open light court, allowing for an efficient double-loaded corridor plan on these floors. Although the rooms were not luxurious, they were sufficient for short stays by members and guests, and the rooms in front enjoyed spectacular views over Lake Michigan.

Above the guest rooms, floors seven and eight contained larger public areas, including on seven a large billiard room, a card room, a café, and several private dining rooms, and on eight the library and "College Hall," another interesting room with ceiling decoration by Bartlett. From floors seven and eight a new staircase led up to the ninth. The visitor arriving at the ninth floor would have found himself in a small entry hall. Turning left, he would have entered directly into the largest and most impressive space in the club, the main dining room (later Cathedral Hall), a stone-walled room measuring forty-three by eighty-seven feet and rising two stories or some thirty-six feet to the great trusses of the wooden ceiling. Seating about two hundred on most

19.8

University Club, view of main dining room (later Cathedral Hall). From Selected Photographs Illustrating the Work of Holabird & Roche, Architects, *1925.*

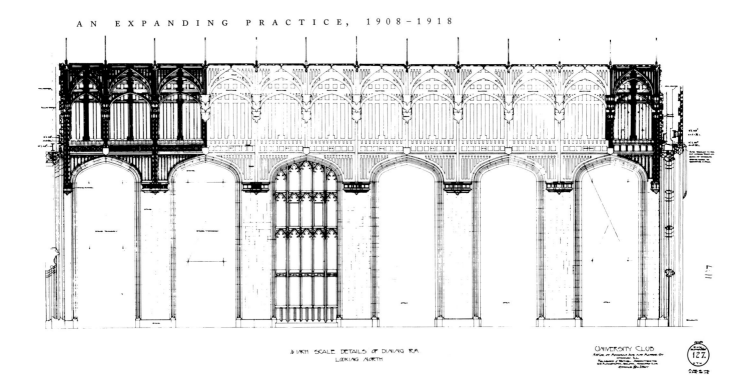

University Club, elevations of main dining room. Chicago Historical Society Architectural Collections.

19.9

occasions, the room could accommodate twice that number for banquets. As in the lounging room on the second floor, the Gothic details of this space might at first glance have reminded our visitor of many lobbies, dining rooms, and ballrooms in hotels of the period in which a nominal historical theme was used primarily to set a mood but did not bear close scrutiny. On close examination, it would have become apparent that Martin Roche and Frederic Bartlett took their Gothic quite seriously.

The room represented a re-creation rather than a copy of Crosby Hall. An expansion from three to five rows of pendants was necessary because the University Club dining room was substantially larger than its prototype. In addition, to provide more seating and to fill out the Michigan Avenue frontage, the architects added an adjoining alcove measuring fourteen feet by forty-four, with stone vaulting and a great carved stone fireplace occupying the north wall.

Carefully cut Bedford stone was used for the piers, the walls, and the corbels carrying the ceiling arches. The wooden ceiling was meticulously worked into intricate ribs, arches, and pendants. The twelve great banks of traceried and leaded windows contained clear panels at the bottom so as not to obstruct the view, and at the top had splendid stained glass fabricated by the Heinigke and Bowen Company of New York to designs by Bartlett. The windows exhibited a rather complex iconography that included elements from both medieval and modern times. The underlying framework of each was a stylized "Tree of Knowledge." Seven of the windows represented the disciplines studied at five of the sixty-five universities members had attended.[18]

So convincingly Gothic was the effect of the main dining hall that it would have been easy to forget this room was a product of the twentieth century on the ninth floor of a steel frame building in the Chicago business district with squash and racquetball players pounding courts directly above the diners' heads, and with several more floors containing the kitchen, service areas, and a roof garden above that. No one appreciated this aspect of refuge better than the shy and retiring Martin Roche. A small stone plaque on the wall near the first pier on the left as one enters the room marks the table where Roche habitually lunched in later life. Although he had not attended a university, Roche was admitted to membership in 1906 as one of a limited number of "director's members."[19] From Roche's table the outside world would have produced only a faint echo. Instead his eye would have rested on the substantial stone walls, heavy wood beams, and Bartlett's brilliant stained glass. All in all, it was a soothing, comforting world. It was also as faithful a re-creation of a previous era as Holabird & Roche ever accomplished.

To a considerable extent Roche and Bartlett were pleasing themselves. Club members would probably have been quite content with a considerably less scholarly result, but they appreciated what the architects and artists had given them, and the small plaque they erected on the pier provides the most fitting monument to the architectural career of Martin Roche. From the very first the room has served the club splendidly. Recalling, years later, the festivities that marked the opening of the clubhouse, club member Angus Hibbard gave a vivid impression of the room as backdrop for ceremonial events:

> Who of the thousand members who participated will ever forget the opening on April 3, 1909: the gathering at the old Club House, where we sang the splendid song, "Farewell to the Old, Hail to the New," written for us by Chancellor Jenks; the march to the new building, flooded with light as we approached; the donning of caps and gowns and the assembling in college groups in our great dining hall?
>
> Through this gathering marched the officers, directors, and other dignitaries, led by the Glee Club, in crimson gowns, singing to the music of Gounod's great chorale:
>
> Domine salvam fac patriam nostram Americam, et exaudi nos in die qua invocaverimus te!

Reaching the front, the procession turned and, accompanied by the orchestra and organ and with everyone saluting, sang the National Anthem, at which from the high balcony the Flag was unfurled. Then came "Fair Harvard" and the Harvard flag; "Bright College Days" and Yale's blue banner; "Old Nassau" and the Princeton flag. One by one they came: Chicago, Michigan, Northwestern, Amherst, Wisconsin, and the rest, the college song and then the flag. The balcony and the wall around it blazed with color.

About a week before, with this program all set up and known to one or two, I asked a fellow member to go to the gallery with me, look down into this great hall, and see a picture in the coming event. It was John T.

19.10

University Club, drawing by John T. McCutcheon of festivities at the opening of the new building. From University Club News.

408

McCutcheon, than whom we know of no more talented cartoonist. I told him of the college groups, the singing, the marching, the banners, and the rest. He said, "I see it!"

And so at midnight when the festivities were at the peak, a dozen newsboys invaded the hall with raucous cries of "Extra! Extra!" and distributed McCutcheon's picture of ourselves and what we were doing at that very moment. With this University Club News "Extra" in hand, we sang a new marching song to celebrate the moving in. We began it with a rollicking, roaring, turning, twisting serpentine of capped and gowned and otherwise caparisoned men, old and young, who "made the welkin ring" and shook the rafters of our replica of classic Crosby Hall. The last line ran, "There'll be a hot time in the new Club tonight!" It was the truth. I have never led such a joyous band in all my life.[20]

The Monroe Building

In 1910 Shepherd Brooks asked Holabird & Roche to design a building for him on the southwest corner of Michigan Avenue and Monroe Street directly across Monroe from the University Club. One might have expected that Brooks, a speculative developer who did not live in Chicago and who had long been famous for producing no-nonsense money machines, would have commissioned a large, regular box filling the site up to the city's height limit, at the time 260 feet.

Brooks did not pursue this course of action. Some years later William Holabird recalled:

> An illustration of how an owner sacrificed his own interests for the benefit of the community is in the Monroe Building. . . . The owner, Shepherd Brooks of Boston, stated that he would in no way injure the effect of the University Club opposite; that consequently he would not go to the limit of height and insisted upon a silhouette in keeping with that of the club-house.[21]

It is interesting to speculate on Brooks's motives. Such delicate concern for purely aesthetic issues has never been the hallmark of real estate developers. One important factor may have been that Arthur and Owen Aldis, his Chicago agents, and both Holabird and Roche, his architects, were longtime University Club members. It is also likely that Brooks felt certain obligations in building on Michigan Avenue that he

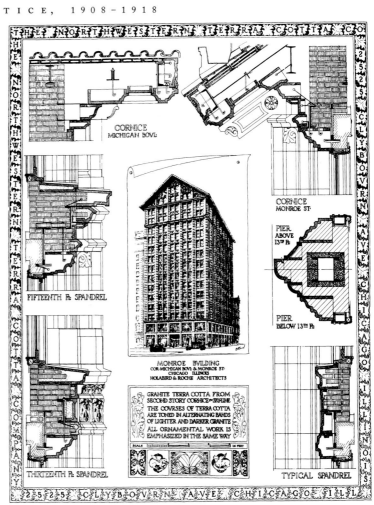

19.11
Monroe Building (504), 1910–12, 104 S. Michigan Avenue, southwest corner of Monroe Street, advertisement for Northwestern Terra Cotta Company. From Brickbuilder, *November 1915.*

would not have even considered when it came to his loft properties on Franklin Street. The *Economist* probably mirrored a general satisfaction with the scheme when it announced:

> Plans have been drawn by Holabird & Roche and accepted. These plans show a building fourteen stories and an attic with a gabled roof. It will thus balance nicely with the University Club on the opposite corner. The exterior of the lower two floors will be polished granite and the upper floors of gray terra cotta. The design is somewhat Gothic in style and it is hoped that the building will be harmonious in every way with its surroundings and particularly with the University Club on the opposite

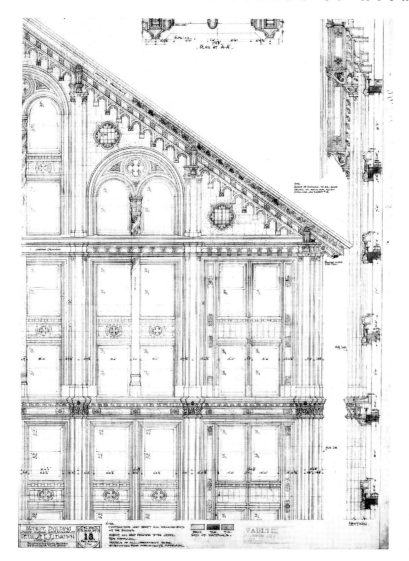

19.12
Monroe Building, elevation detail of terra cotta cladding at top of building. Chicago Historical Society Architectural Collections.

corner and the Illinois Athletic Club adjoining it on the south. It seems fortunate and appropriate that the same architects who designed the University Club should now have the opportunity to design the building for the opposite corner.[22]

The contract for the Monroe Building (cat. no. 504) was signed with the George A. Fuller Company in February 1911, and the building opened on 1 May 1912. On the interior this was a standard office building, distinguished only by the vaulted en-

tryway, which was sheathed in Rookwood tile. On the exterior the gray and pink walls and the fanciful ornamentation would have seemed frivolous on LaSalle Street, but opposite the University Club on Michigan Avenue it looks entirely appropriate. Comments on the finished building were mostly favorable.[23]

Today, from the vantage point of the Monroe Street bridge over the railroad tracks in Grant Park, it is clear that the Monroe Building and the University Club still function visually as a gateway to the Loop. They read as a pair, flanking the street with their twin gables and channeling the traffic through the narrow passage between them. What is remarkable, on closer examination, is how dissimilar the buildings actually are. The Monroe, because it is an office building, is wider and more regular in fenestration. In part this is offset by the use of pink and gray terra cotta, which allows a much more fanciful and decorative effect than the monochromatic stone of the University Club where only the pattern of leaded glass windows relieves the starkness of the wall surfaces.

As the visitor walks closer the differences in detailing become more pronounced. Where the Monroe Building is opened at the base in large plate glass shop windows, the architect tried to maintain the solidity of the stone facades of the University Club by making the base as solid as possible and recessing the shopfronts deep into the mass of the walls. Where the Monroe Building invites one with an entry in the center of the Michigan Avenue front, the University Club's entry is tucked away on the Monroe Street side of the building. At the top, where the Monroe Building has a wide, low gable enlivened with twisting colonnettes, leaded windows in arched openings, and quatrefoils, the University Club's gable is much higher and punctuated by vertical crockets and a pair of pilasters on the gable face, crockets at the corner, and a high brick chimney.

The two buildings form a small but important part of the Michigan Avenue street wall, one of the most successful urban compositions in America. William Holabird and Martin Roche were undoubtedly proud of their role in creating this cityscape, something they would have had ample opportunity to savor, since from their drafting room in the Monroe Building the partners would have had an excellent view across Monroe Street to the University Club. Likewise, from the main dining room of the University Club they could look back at the Monroe Building and the offices of Holabird & Roche.

19.13 (opposite)
University Club (right) and Monroe Building (left), looking east on Monroe Street with
McCormick Buildings (Gage Group) to right. Photograph by Trowbridge. Chicago Historical Society
Prints and Photographs Department.

TWENTY

THE ARCHITECTURE

OF COMMUNICATIONS:

BUILDINGS FOR THE

CHICAGO TELEPHONE COMPANY

Within a year of Alexander Graham Bell's demonstrations of the telephone at the Philadelphia Centennial Exposition in 1876, two machines went into service in Chicago. Over the next several decades technical innovations and service expansions followed one another in breathless succession. For example, Chicago's first exchange opened in June 1878 to serve seventy-five instruments within two months after the first exchange started to operate in New Haven, Connecticut. Within two years some four hundred machines were in operation in Chicago, and by the end of 1882 there were nearly three thousand.[1] By 1892 long distance service started between Chicago and New York.

As we have seen, William Holabird was not among the enthusiasts. He did not like the new machines and allowed one into the office only in the mid-1880s. It is therefore somewhat ironic that within a few years after getting the first commission from the Chicago Telephone Company in 1908 Holabird & Roche had become the company's favored designers and would remain so for decades, along the way overseeing the construction of telephone buildings in neighborhoods throughout the entire Chicago metropolitan area.[2]

The Chicago Telephone Company

Like many other infant industries, the telephone industry started amid bitter rivalries. In this case the combatants included the company created to exploit Bell's patent versus the Western Union Telegraph Company, which had hired Thomas Edison to make substantial improvements in Bell's invention. Amid fierce warfare among East Coast

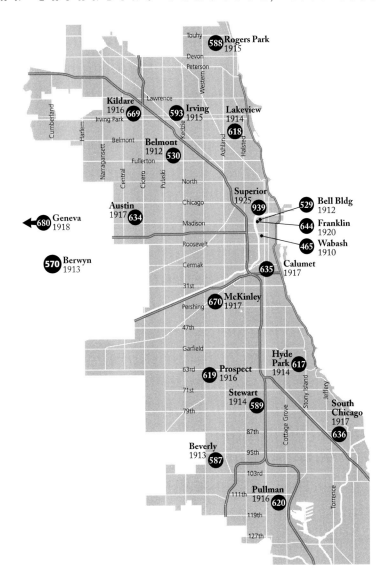

Touhy
588 **Rogers Park**
1915

Devon

Peterson

Western

Cumberland

Harlem

Lawrence

Kildare
1916 669

Irving Park

593 **Irving**
1915

Lakeview
1914
618

Belmont

Narragansett

Central

Cicero

Pulaski

Kedzie

Ashland

Halsted

Belmont
1912 530

Fullerton

North

Chicago

Superior
1925 939

529 **Bell Bldg**
1912

Austin
1917 634

Madison

644 **Franklin**
1920

680 **Geneva**
1918

Roosevelt

465 **Wabash**
1910

570 **Berwyn**
1913

Cermak

31st

635 **Calumet**
1917

670 **McKinley**
1917

Pershing

47th

Garfield

63rd

**Hyde
Park**
1914 617

619 **Prospect**
1916

Stony Island

Jeffery

71st

Stewart
1914 589

79th

**South
Chicago**
1917
636

Cottage Grove

87th

Beverly
1913 587

95th

103rd

Pullman
1916
111th 620

Torrence

119th

127th

20.1

Some Chicago area telephone buildings designed by Holabird & Roche, ca. 1920. Drawn by Dennis McClendon based on information from Holabird & Root records, fire insurance maps, and records of Illinois Bell Telephone Company.

capitalists, Western Union capitulated, and in 1880 the Bell patent holders reorganized as the American Bell Telephone Company.[3] In Chicago the combatants in the struggle were the Bell Telephone Company of Illinois under the leadership of G. S. Hubbard, father-in-law of Alexander Graham Bell, and the American District Telegraph Company, subsidiary of the Western Union Telegraph Company. After the Bell group triumphed, the Chicago Telephone Company was incorporated in 1881 to operate the property of the two competing systems. After some technical problems were

THE ARCHITECTURE OF COMMUNICATIONS

resolved, the company grew very quickly. The number of phones leaped from some 3,000 in 1880 to nearly 8,000 in 1890 to over 34,000 in 1900 to 239,000 in 1910.[4]

The company was still growing fast when Holabird & Roche appeared on the scene at the end of the first decade of the twentieth century. Little evidence appears to survive about the first commission for the phone company, an exchange building in the Lawndale section of Chicago's West Side (cat. no. 435), but the client was obviously satisfied, since by the early 1910s Holabird & Roche had become virtual house architects for Chicago Bell Telephone. The Holabird & Roche buildings ranged in scale from simple barns, garages, and warehouses for the company's equipment and a house for its summer camp to the Bell Building, a twenty-story administration building at the heart of the Loop (cat. no. 529).[5] None of these buildings gave much indication that they were the property of the phone company, however. They all functioned and looked like any other buildings of their type.

The most important new building type spawned by the invention of the telephone was the exchange. The exchange functioned as the nerve center of the entire system, the place where every incoming call was connected by operators to the line that would take it to its final destination. The earliest Chicago exchange, built in 1878, was at what is now 17 N. LaSalle Street in the heart of the financial district. It apparently consisted of several banks of crude switching consoles operated by teenage boys in a single room.

This facility soon proved inadequate, and the company started a building campaign that would continue for decades as it raced to keep up with demand. As the system grew, so did the complexity of the electronic installations and the specifications for the buildings that housed them. Because all the wiring and circuitry had to be absolutely reliable, the buildings were designed to be extremely substantial, require very little maintenance, and provide maximum protection against unexpected disasters like floods and fires.

Holabird & Roche designed one major downtown exchange, the eleven-story Franklin Exchange (cat. no. 644) of 1915. This building, which occupied a site in the west Loop, was U-shaped, with corridors, staircases, elevators, offices, and rest rooms occupying the short crossbar of the U along the street front and large operating rooms where workers staffed the switchboards occupying the long arms. Like most of the early phone exchange buildings, it did not look different from the buildings around it. From the outside it could easily have passed for a simple speculative office building. Clad in red brick with Bedford stone trim, it had a relatively sparse decorative treatment, nominally in the Venetian Renaissance style. From street level some of the building's special protective devices—for example, the metal window frames and wire glass in all the windows—would hardly have been noticeable, and the rolling steel

Franklin Exchange, Chicago Telephone Company (644), 1915–20, 311–27 W. Washington Street, view of exterior.
From Selected Photographs Illustrating the Work of Holabird & Roche, Architects, *1925.*

shutters that would close in case of fire were entirely out of sight, concealed behind the spandrel panels.

The Neighborhood Exchange

The tall exchange building not only was a necessity downtown but was probably considered an entirely appropriate expression of the company's services to business clients. As the phone ceased to be primarily an instrument of business and started to reach into every home in the city, the telephone company needed to build exchanges in the city's neighborhoods and to find a new and appropriate image. This is where Holabird & Roche made its mark.

Early neighborhood exchanges, built before Holabird & Roche became involved with the phone company, were almost always quite small, usually two to three stories high and two to five bays wide. It appears that most were in neighborhood commercial strips along the major streetcar lines and looked exactly like other business buildings along these streets. When exchanges were within the residential districts themselves, they usually closely resembled small houses or apartment buildings. In both cases the goal was apparently to blend in.

From the first the Holabird & Roche neighborhood exchange buildings, whether they were on commercial strips or in neighborhoods, all looked more like small public buildings than like either houses or shops. Exactly how Holabird & Roche arrived at this design solution is not known, but it is likely that the impetus came from within the telephone company. Although there were almost certainly a number of factors, the most important appears to have been a practical matter, the need to attract and retain the best employees possible.

The teenage boys who were the original operators, although they demanded very few amenities, were considered far from ideal employees. They often did not stay long in the job, and company officials found them lacking in patience, precision, and tact. They were soon replaced by what company literature at the time called "pleasant voiced girls."[6] Actually these were women of various ages, who often made the switchboard their lifework. They were crucial to the telephone company. No matter how up-to-date the equipment, service was only as good as the operators in the exchanges. They were also the company employees who had the most frequent contact with the public.

To attract and retain its new labor force, the company found that pleasant working conditions were important. Not only did the operating rooms themselves have to be clean and well lit, but the buildings had to satisfy other needs. Because the work tended to be demanding and repetitive, the company felt obliged to provide areas in

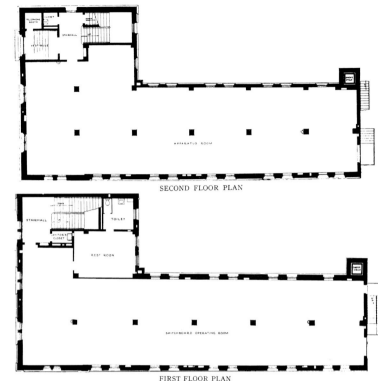

SECOND FLOOR PLAN

FIRST FLOOR PLAN

20.3

McKinley Exchange, Chicago Telephone Company (670), 1916–17, 2240 W. Thirty-seventh Street, plans of initial phase. Ultimate structure would have two additional bays on other side of stair. From American Architect, *August 1920.*

the building where employees could exercise, take breaks, prepare food, and have refreshments. To build morale and boost loyalty to the organization, the company found it in its own interest to provide places for committee meetings, club activities, musical and dramatic performances, and all kinds of social events. In good weather outdoor areas allowed active recreation and quiet contemplation. To make all these pursuits possible the company needed to provide lockers, showers, and dressing rooms. Although many of these features would have appealed to employees of either sex, most employers did not feel that men demanded them. They were specifically aimed at the women, who constituted the bulk of the company's employees in the exchanges. In many ways the telephone exchange became a woman's building.

In Holabird & Roche the company found the perfect architects. The firm seems to have hit on an acceptable prototype almost immediately and reproduced it with endless variations for decades. As in the loft building, the main plan and massing features of the telephone exchange were largely determined by functional requirements. The exchange building program, as it was eventually codified by the company, called for construction to take up no more than half of the ground area, with the rest of the space given over to gardens and recreation areas for the employees. Photographs of the

Beverly Office (cat. no. 587), for example, show carefully landscaped grounds, well-tended tennis courts, and roof gardens used by the switchboard operators. Not building out to the lot lines also provided space for carefully tended landscape features that helped connect the building visually to its residential neighbors and enhanced the appearance of the neighborhood.

In plan almost all the exchanges were simple rectangular, L-shaped, or U-shaped structures. The longer wings housed the large, well-lit, uninterrupted space of the operating rooms. The administrative offices, utility rooms, and common areas were housed in the shorter crosspiece that also provided the frontispiece to the street and buffered the operating wings from street noise. Because all these buildings had ample fenestration and none of the wings were very wide, all the spaces enjoyed ample light and air.

Most of the buildings were constructed of reinforced concrete because this provided maximum stability, durability, and ease of maintenance. They ranged from three to five stories and were clad in brick, terra cotta, or stone. They were usually designed so they could be built in stages yet always present a finished appearance. This was accomplished by making them regular and cellular, with only modest ornamentation at the edges and tops that could easily be removed and installed elsewhere at the time of expansion. At the McKinley Exchange (cat. no. 670), for example, the initial three-story structure contained one long wing for switchboard operations and a three-bay front block housing entry, toilets, staircases, and rest rooms (lounges). It looked and

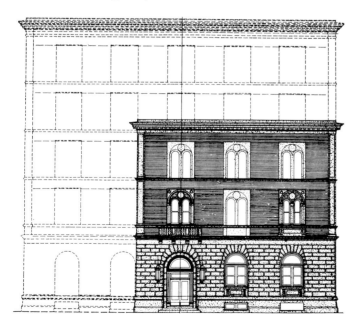

20.4
McKinley Exchange, Chicago Telephone Company, elevation indicating phases of construction. From American Architect, *August 1920.*

20.5
*McKinley Exchange,
Chicago Telephone
Company, view of
exterior. From*
American Architect,
August 1920.

functioned at this stage as if this were the completed building, but it was designed so that with minimal disruption its size could be nearly doubled, as eventually happened. In this expansion one wall and the cornice were removed, and the building was expanded to four stories and five bays, probably reusing many of the decorative elements from the original structure and without disrupting service.

The insides as well as the outsides of most of the buildings were quite similar. The basement held the boiler room, storage batteries, and vaults containing the cables, which usually entered at the rear of the structure. The first floor housed the major mechanical apparatus—the distributing frame along with power machinery and testing apparatus—and several offices. The heart of the switching operation was on the upper floors in the operating rooms, the large open areas that contained the switchboards. The Hyde Park Exchange (cat. no. 617) can serve as an example. This large switching office handled nearly 100,000 calls a day from 25,000 telephones—more, the *Bell Telephone News* proudly noted, than the entire city of New Orleans or Jersey City and more than Greece, Portugal, Serbia, and Bulgaria combined.[7] Photographs show the cables entering and running through the cable vault to the terminal room and the operating rooms on the second and fourth floors. In the latter, in front of a massive switchboard, dozens of young women wearing identical uniforms—long dark skirts and white blouses—sit in regimented rows with a series of supervisors identically dressed standing at regular intervals behind them. The spartan decor, consisting of a regular row of fans and of ceiling light fixtures, perfectly matches the regimentation of the women.

This scene was obviously staged. The company photographer, in his desire to create a sense of order and technical mastery, provided a scene that was almost a caricature of the company management style. The same is true of a second view that appeared on the same page of *Bell Telephone News*. This scene, of employees in the operators' rest room on the third floor during a break, was clearly intended as a contrast. The floor plan is obviously the same as that of the switchboard, only fitted out differently. Here some of the women are reading, others sewing. A small group is gathered around the piano. It was intended as the very image of female contentment and good labor relations. Although we are not obliged to believe the scene was always as harmo-

20.6
Hyde Park Exchange, Chicago Telephone Company (617), 1914, 6045 S. Kenwood Avenue, view of cable vault. From Bell Telephone News, *January 1916.*

20.7
*Hyde Park Exchange,
Chicago Telephone
Company, view of "A"
switchboard. From*
Bell Telephone
News, *January 1916.*

20.8
*Hyde Park Exchange,
Chicago Telephone
Company, view of
operators' room. From*
Bell Telephone
News, *January 1916.*

nious as it appears here, it is interesting to note how a few elements make the same space look completely different. Comfortable armchairs and rocking chairs scattered about in a loose, informal manner, curtains and drapes at the windows, carpets covering the floor, and paintings adorning the walls make it as homelike and inviting as the operating room was efficient and businesslike.

In addition to all the other constraints the architects faced, there was the pressure of time. Because the telephone company was growing so quickly and because any delay in the cutover from one exchange to a new one caused great additional expense, the buildings had to go up very quickly and absolutely on schedule. At the Stewart Exchange (cat. no. 589) on the South Side, for example, officials broke ground on 29 May 1913. The building was completed that same year on 4 October. The switchboard installation started that very day, and the cutover took place at midnight on 14 March. Less than ten months from the time of groundbreaking, an operator completed the first call, from Stewart 9550 to Edgewater 8340 on the North Side.[8]

Community Relations and Company Image

Beyond their functional aspects, the exchanges seem to have satisfied several less easily identified but equally important needs of the company. One was a desire for good relations with the general public. The phone company liked to think of itself as part of each community where it operated. Indeed, company employees, even if they did not live in the immediate vicinity of the exchange, soon came to know intimately the communities they served, as the frequent accounts of operators' intervening in local emergencies make clear.[9] In part to foster this sense of community, the exchanges were designed to be compatible with other neighborhood structures. Although larger than the residential buildings around them, they consistently displayed similar elements. Doorways and windows, for example, though they may have been executed at larger than domestic scale, had the same proportions as those of houses and apartment buildings. Landscaping likewise was designed to resemble that of domestic buildings.

In some cases the style of the building seems to have some direct connection with the neighborhood. The Geneva Central Office (cat. no. 680), for example, seems to nod toward the Federal and Greek Revival buildings in town.[10] In most cases, however, the connection was tenuous at best. All the buildings are basically similar, relatively simple boxes with regular windows. They were adorned with a little decoration, but this decoration was never more than skin deep, and the style chosen was apparently somewhat arbitrary. Looking at any one of the buildings, one can easily imagine it with other stylistic treatments or in a different neighborhood.

425

At the McKinley Exchange the rusticated base, the two lanterns by the arched doorway, the shallow balcony above the door, the paired window openings subsumed within a larger arch, and the projecting cornice all proclaimed a derivation from the Italian High Renaissance. Also Renaissance were the exchanges at Pullman (cat. no. 620) and Austin (cat. no. 634). Certainly very few of the residential buildings in any of these neighborhoods could be labeled High Renaissance in style. At Beverly and at Rogers Park (cat. no. 588), on the other hand, very similar buildings were fitted out with pedimented doors, fanlights, and brick voussoirs borrowed from American Georgian and Federal era houses. This may have been a little closer to the style of houses and apartment buildings in those areas, but no direct connection appears to have been intended. The Kildare Exchange (cat. no. 669), with its pointed arches and delicate trim derived from Venetian Gothic, was certainly intended to be exotic.

The explanation for the exterior appearance of Holabird & Roche's exchanges can perhaps best be understood by considering the peculiar status of the telephone company. By the time Holabird & Roche started designing for it, the phone company was no longer just another business competing with others. It had become an enormous, government-regulated monopoly and increasingly enjoyed powers usually reserved for government. Because the exchange building was the most tangible symbol

20.9
Geneva Exchange, Chicago Telephone Company, Geneva, Illinois (680), 1916–18, 127 S. First Street, view of exterior. Courtesy of Illinois Bell Telephone Company Archives.

426

20.10

*Austin Exchange, Chicago Telephone Company
(634), 1915–17, 5055 W. Fulton Street at
LeClaire Avenue, view of exterior. Courtesy of
Illinois Bell Telephone Company Archives.*

20.11

*Rogers Park
Exchange, Chicago
Telephone Company
(588), 1913–15,
1622 W. Pratt
Avenue, view of
exterior. Photograph
taken 11 December
1914. Courtesy of
Illinois Bell Telephone
Company Archives.*

20.12

Kildare Exchange, Chicago Telephone Company (669), 1916–17, 4923 W. Warner Avenue, view of exterior. Photograph taken 7 July 1920. Courtesy of Illinois Bell Telephone Archives.

of the company's ability to affect lives in every neighborhood, it had to reflect this important position in the American business firmament. It could not look like a house or an apartment or a mere business office. It needed to have a more public, institutional character. In fact the Holabird & Roche buildings, although fairly small, used axial symmetry and architectural detailing and landscaping to make them appear monumental. In this way they came to resemble rather closely branch libraries, post offices, and other neighborhood public and civic buildings.

The phone company also wanted to sell more telephone service. For this the buildings served as excellent advertising. Located in every corner of the city, their reassuringly simple and sober designs were a constant reminder that the phone company was a careful steward of the community communications network and that it had domesticated technology, making it fit into the existing patterns of life and the fabric of the city. The faintly exotic designs, whether Georgian or Venetian, may also have alluded to the wider world that could be reached through the new technology. More important than the exotic variations were the reassuring similarities. As different as their nominal styles may have appeared, all exhibit certain characteristics that made them immediately recognizable as the buildings of a single client. They provided what we might today call a "corporate identity."[11]

This aspect of the Holabird & Roche building program is perfectly captured by an illustration published in a phone company history that appeared in 1928 in which the artist created a composite "Telephone City" by combining in one image a number of phone buildings owned by the company but scattered around the metropolitan area. The Franklin Exchange at center right, for example, stands in front of the Kildare, Stewart, and Austin exchanges, all by Holabird & Roche. The illustration is too small and impressionistic to allow the viewer to determine whether all of the buildings were modeled directly after actual phone company buildings, but this seems to have been the impression the artist wished to create. Most of the structures shown are typical exchange buildings of the kind Holabird & Roche produced.[12]

Although the buildings are diverse in their details, they fit together in a coherent way because of the similarities in massing and materials and form a plausible downtown—in fact, a more coherent and orderly downtown than could been seen in any real city. The setting for this ideal city is both generic and specific. It is obviously a flat riverside site. No Chicago viewer could have failed to see similarities between this image, with its two-level street and classically ornamented bridge, and Chicago's riverfront, Wacker Drive, and Michigan Avenue Bridge. But it is an idealized Chicago, a Chicago with more trees, more open space, and a more consistent architecture. The implication is that the building program of the telephone company was intended to create a City Beautiful downtown, like the one seen in the image, but a downtown that in actuality was dispersed into the neighborhoods to bring the company closer to its customers.

20.13
"Telephone City" drawing by H. M. Pettit prepared for Illinois Bell Telephone Company, A Golden Anniversary, 1878–1928, *1928.*

All evidence suggests that the Holabird & Roche designs worked almost perfectly for the company's purposes. Still, considering how quickly the phone company had grown between 1880 and the 1910s and how quickly the scale of the exchanges had increased, one might have expected that the prototype worked out by Holabird & Roche would have had a short life. Unexpected technical developments intervened. Although the number of telephones in Chicago surged dramatically through the mid-1920s, various automated devices started to replace humans in switching operations and cut down on space needs. The result was that Holabird & Roche continued to produce somewhat similar buildings, slightly updated in exterior style, throughout the interwar years and into the postwar era.

A by-product of this development has been a remarkably high preservation rate for Holabird & Roche's exchanges. Because many of the buildings were simply refitted for automated operations and because the telephone company has always had an excellent maintenance program, in many cases it appears from the outside that virtually nothing has changed in over three-quarters of a century. In neighborhoods that have gentrified and neighborhoods that have fallen on hard times, the telephone exchange buildings have stood as anchors of stability and graceful neighbors in a constantly changing world.[13]

TWENTY ONE

BY WAY OF CONCLUSION:
THE THREE ARTS CLUB,
HOLABIRD & ROCHE, AND
THE AMERICAN CITY

The Three Arts Club, a modest three-story brick building at the northwest corner of Dearborn and Goethe Streets on Chicago's Near North Side, might seem an odd choice with which to conclude this account of the work of Holabird & Roche before 1918. It was, after all, neither particularly large nor especially conspicuous. The site, while a fairly prominent one in an affluent neighborhood, was not exceptional. The same could be said for the client and the program. If the object of this book were to select the best or most influential works of the firm, this building would certainly not merit a prominent place here. But since this study is primarily about the operation of the firm as a whole and its impact on the built environment of the city, a building like the Three Arts Club perhaps provides as suitable a point of departure as any of the firm's most prominent works.

The Client, the Club, and the Neighborhood

In founding the Three Arts Club (cat. no. 601), socially prominent Chicagoan Gwenthalyn Jones intended to provide a secure place for young women who wanted to live on their own in the city while pursuing careers in music, drama, and the pictorial arts.[1] After the club received its charter in 1912, it moved into a house in the 1500 block of North LaSalle Street. From the first this was considered a temporary measure, and Jones prevailed on her father, zinc magnate David B. Jones, to bear the cost of constructing a new clubhouse on a lot he owned in the elegant Gold Coast district of Chicago's Near North Side, successor to the South Side Gold Coast of the late nine-

21.1

Three Arts Club (601), 1913–14, 1300 N. Dearborn Street, northwest corner of Goethe Street, exterior view looking to the northwest. From Selected Photographs Illustrating the Work of Holabird & Roche, Architects, *1925.*

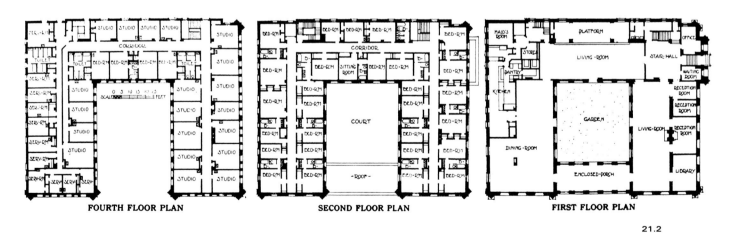

FOURTH FLOOR PLAN

SECOND FLOOR PLAN

FIRST FLOOR PLAN

21.2

Three Arts Club, plans. From Brickbuilder, *August 1915.*

21.3
*Three Arts Club, view of courtyard.
From* Brickbuilder, *August 1915.*

teenth century.[2] Commissioned in 1913 and finished in 1914 at a cost of just under $200,000, the building was a birthday gift from Jones to his daughter. She in turn deeded it over to a newly created board of trustees.

The building had a straightforward reinforced concrete interior frame with solid brick exterior walls. In plan it was arranged in a square-doughnut configuration with three-story blocks to the east, west, and north and a glazed one-story passageway on the south, together enclosing a raised, paved courtyard with a fountain at its center. The public rooms of the club occupied the ground floor of the three-story blocks, with the entrance, living room, and library to the east, a second living room or ballroom to the north, equipped with a raised platform for theatrical events, and a dining room to the west. The three-story blocks were connected via the one-story glazed corridor along the south, which was fitted up as a tearoom. Above the ground level, bedrooms and baths occupied the second and third floors, with studios and servants' quarters above them on the top floor.

21.4
Three Arts Club, view of dining room with glazed corridor containing tearoom beyond. Chicago Historical Society Prints and Photographs Department, ICHi-19906.

Compared with much of Holabird & Roche's work, this was a relatively small and inexpensive structure. If anything distinguished the building it was the lively, if somewhat eccentric, exterior ornamental scheme and decorations of the public rooms. They were reportedly the work of John Holabird, twenty-seven years old and newly returned from his years in Europe, where he had studied at the Ecole des Beaux-Arts in Paris and traveled around the Continent. He, or whoever else in the firm was responsible, obviously lavished considerable attention on the decoration, finding room for a virtual catalog of motifs from European art history. For the twisted columns and the fine brickwork encrusted with ornament, the inspiration obviously came from Byzantine models, particularly the churches of Ravenna and Bologna, but the exterior was also, more than a little incongruously, enlivened with plaques of Greek sculpture, reliefs based on the designs of old English bookmarks, and most prominently, casts of female figures from the famous sixteenth-century Fontaine des Innocents in Paris by Jean Goujon.

In contrast with the exterior, the interiors were for the most part as plain as those in any college sorority or dormitory, but the public areas were enlivened by a few decorative flourishes that managed to convey some whiff of the exotic. One wall of the dining room was painted in trompe l'oeil to resemble tapestries. In the dining room the beams were stenciled in a manner reminiscent of the early French Renaissance decorations at the château of Blois. Glazed tiles were used on the lobby floor to imitate carpet, and fountains, apparently ordered from catalogs and perhaps not quite in keeping with the rest of the ornamental scheme, graced several of the rooms.

The building elicited only a few comments in the architectural press. The magazine *Brickbuilder,* understandably enthusiastic about the elaborate exterior brickwork, carried a short description along with a set of plans and a few photographs in the August 1915 issue. Otherwise the building was not much reviewed, at least in the national architectural magazines. This is not surprising. The club was not meant to be a major artistic statement.

Not everyone in the world of American architecture would have been happy with the design of the Three Arts Club. It is likely, for example, that some conservative architects would have been offended on aesthetic grounds. They would probably have considered the obviously playful mixture of ornamental styles arbitrary or simply frivolous. They would have preferred, if not a more academically correct version of a single historical style, at least an approach in which historical models were more systematically adapted to programmatic needs or regional influences.[3]

For other conservatively inclined American architects, on the other hand, particularly those who followed the tenets of nineteenth-century British architectural writers like A. W. N. Pugin and John Ruskin, moral and religious issues would probably have outweighed aesthetic ones. They might well have criticized the use of wall painting to imitate tapestries as dissimulation or deplored using imagery drawn from Byzantine religious architecture on a clearly secular structure as a mockery of medieval Christian devotion. They probably would also have condemned the use of mechanical reproductions of famous pieces of sculpture as trivializing work that originally had embodied the labor and faith of the craftsman's hand. Socially conscious critics might further have protested that using such reproductions took work away from contemporary sculptors and craftsmen.

On the other end of the artistic and political spectrum were individuals who would have considered themselves more progressive than Holabird & Roche. For Frank Lloyd Wright, for example, or many European avant-garde modernists, the Three Arts Club might well have seemed like an ill-assorted and irrelevant collection of historical elements on an otherwise unremarkable brick box. The building made no effort to overturn existing aesthetic norms and certainly did not try to upset the social and political order. It is easy to understand how individuals concerned with ill-housed factory workers, poorly fed families, and a looming world war might not have been sympathetic to the club's purpose, the delicate task of lodging artistically inclined seventeen- to thirty-year-old American women from middle-class American families who "upon discovering a talent within themselves, yearned to pursue it in cities where conservatories, museums and dramatic schools were equipped with well trained teaching staffs."[4]

The Three Arts Club, like virtually all the work of Holabird & Roche, fell solidly between extreme points of view. This was apparently exactly what the client wanted. From all reports Gwenthalyn Jones was delighted with the building, as were subsequent board members and inhabitants. Most Chicagoans, likewise, would probably have heartily applauded the structure, and for good reason. Substantially built of durable and easily maintained materials, the building provided a perfect backdrop for the pursuits of its residents. Regular and handsome in its general lines, its decoration was clearly related to its purpose. The central door of the entrance, with its mosaic depictions of lyre, palette, and mask labeled "musica," "pictura," and "fabula," announced the function of the club, while the rest of the ornament, especially the Jean Goujon figures, alluded in a more general way not only to a reverence for the great artistic tradition of Europe but also to an idealized vision of the young womanhood residing within. Although it is likely this imagery seemed a little sentimental, perhaps even hackneyed, to the more sophisticated residents of the club, and though it may have been done somewhat tongue-in-cheek at the Holabird & Roche offices, where it must have seemed like a deliberately anachronistic exercise, it was at least direct and refreshingly optimistic.

The building was also a good neighbor. The architects carefully avoided overpowering adjacent structures. The building's large scale was broken down by the use of the wing plan and by the fine texture of the masonry. Viewed obliquely, as the trees planted along the street would soon make necessary, the irregular rhythm of windows, the lively pattern of the twisted columns and cornice at the top, and the projecting buttresses at the corners gave the building a texture and cadence similar to that of its elegant townhouse neighbors.

On the interior the handsome public spaces had just enough decoration to make them look finished and to provide, for the more sophisticated, visual quotations from monuments of the great artistic periods of the past. The stenciled decorations derived from the château at Blois, for example, evoked the elegantly attenuated art of the rarefied court of François I of France. Yet the decoration was unobtrusive and sturdy enough to permit continually changing uses and furnishings. The arrangement of public rooms, raised above the level of the street and buffered from it but opening generously on the interior courtyard, created a sheltered, almost monastic refuge in the city. On the whole, assuming one was sympathetic to the goals of the club and to the aes-

21.5

Three Arts Club, view of mosaic decorations in arches above doors. From Brickbuilder, *August 1915.*

thetic aspirations of its upper-middle-class urban neighbors, it would have been hard to imagine a more successful building, one that contributed more to the streetscape or more gracefully sheltered its residents, all this with economy and restraint.

Time has not diminished the charm of the Three Arts Club. The structure has aged well. Despite continuous hard use by generations of constantly changing residents, the building is virtually intact and in good condition, thanks in great part to a highly practical design. On the exterior, the robust proportions and substantial masonry exterior have allowed it to hold its own against the recent high-rises that have sprung up along the street. Even though the needs of the residents have changed, and many of the proprieties considered necessary for artistic young ladies of the pre–World War I era have long since been swept away, the building still offers security and calm in the heart of the city and remains a dignified and pleasant place to live.

That the Three Arts Club did not and does not set in motion the complex emotional reactions inspired by certain works of challenging new architecture or that it was not considered a masterpiece would not have troubled its creators. Primarily commercial architects, they were first of all concerned with creating good serviceable buildings that added to the utility and beauty of the city. If they were also judged artistic successes, so much the better.

In fact, a very large number of Holabird & Roche's buildings over the decades were considered aesthetic successes, both by the general public and by members of the architectural profession. If relatively modest popular success in a given building like the Three Arts Club seems no great feat, it is important to remember that Holabird & Roche managed to repeat this performance hundreds of times over an entire range of building types, decade after decade. And despite the legions of other architects who would have been only too happy to topple the firm from the position it occupied, Holabird & Roche continued to reign at the pinnacle of the Chicago architectural world for well over half a century.

The achievement of Holabird & Roche was very different in kind from that of a Louis Sullivan or the other single creators whose work has traditionally dominated American architectural history, but it was every bit as impressive. It required striking a balance among a wide range of conflicting demands: how to decide between tradition and innovation, for example, or how to weigh the competing claims of business and art; whether to strive for an architecture that expressed the building's structure and program or one that was specifically about Chicago or about America; whether to create a set of coherent stylist elements applicable to all the firm's work that could be refined from building to building over time or to allow each structure to reflect its particular client, site, and program. Perhaps the greatest success of the firm lies in the fact that when we look at the work we hardly think about these often incompatible goals. The buildings look so reasonable, so devoid of conflict or strain, that we assume they are the entirely logical outcome of the various requirements placed on the architects rather than what we know was actually the case—that they were the result of hundreds of conscious, often difficult decisions.

Assessing the Work

Looking back across the work today, perhaps the first thing that strikes any viewer is the variety. What, for example, does the rustic frame church at Lake Linden, Michigan, have in common with the colossal order of the Cook County Courthouse? Or the simple brick corbeling of a loft building with the mansarded roof of the LaSalle Hotel? How is it possible that the same partners who created the blunt and unelaborated St. Mark's Church in Evanston could have designed the Venetian fantasy at the Aldis house on Lake Shore Drive? How did it come about that the same firm was responsible for the completely midwestern appearance of the Boynton house in Evanston and the exotic concrete forms of the Deering house in Honolulu?

Some of this variety is, of course, due to the very different kinds of building involved, the different needs of the clients, and the different sites. It is conspicuous that buildings designed years apart within a similar program or for a given client or in a particular location often bear a closer relation than buildings built simultaneously for very different sites or programs. The relation between programs, clients, and sites was very complex, moreover, and constantly changing. As we have seen, for example, around 1890 the State Street department store, with its huge open floors and simple facades, started to converge in appearance with the more expensive decorated loft buildings. On the other hand, by 1905 the city hotel, which had previously shared many traits with the office building, started to take on a completely different, more monumental character. Likewise, the needs of clients could change, as the firm's work for the Chicago Telephone Company clearly shows. Within a single geographic area, finally, the firm sometimes created buildings of very different character, as the contrast between the rustic cabins of the Coleman Club and the studied, if diminutive, classical embellishment of the Goodman Bank makes clear.

But even allowing for all these differences, the variety in the Holabird & Roche buildings is still striking. One explanation is that these buildings were the work of many hands. Although the founding partners remained at the head of the firm, there was, over the decades, considerable turnover among the rest of the personnel. From the beginning Holabird & Roche attracted many of the brightest young designers and draftsmen, some of them remaining at the firm for years, others moving on to other firms or leaving to start their own practices.

It is easy to imagine how a bright young architect might have taken initial sketches by Martin Roche for a loft building and developed its ornamental program into something quite different from anything Roche had intended. If the ideas were good, they were probably accepted and further refined. It is likely, in other cases, that houses and other small buildings were simply turned over to junior architects, who were allowed to design them under the supervision of more senior personnel.

Considering all the factors that encouraged variety, what is probably more surprising is the unity in the work of the firm. Even a cursory study shows that there existed a kind of internal consistency among buildings of a given type. The firm's loft buildings, for example, differed from one another only in minor, superficial ways. With the work on public and institutional buildings, on the other hand, although there was much more room to maneuver and the buildings did differ considerably in appearance, there are still fairly strong family resemblances. In all these building types, once a successful solution to a problem was found, the firm was not adverse to reusing it, making only minor changes to accommodate the site and program and to provide a little variety.

A more careful study shows that even across the building types there was considerable unity in feeling. This was not the kind of unity seen in the work of Frank Lloyd Wright or Louis Sullivan, where specific stylistic traits set their creations apart, but a unity of a different sort. At the most basic level the common thread that seems to run through the work of Holabird & Roche involves an economy of means. The basic layout and volumetric configuration are almost always simple and straightforward. In most cases the buildings exhibit clear and largely symmetrical plans, a regularity of massing and fenestration, and a forthright use of materials. The decorative treatment, which at first seems more varied and less restrained, appears on closer examination to have similar characteristics. Even at its most elaborate, there is a kind of measure and regularity and a judicious economy that dictates exactly how much decoration a given facade or room should receive. One never has the impression, as one often does with some of the most famous art architects, that individual expression has become more important than the program. With Holabird & Roche the decorative treatment always remains well within the boundaries of what was considered appropriate for a building of a given type at a given place in a given era.

These characteristics did limit the firm. Holabird & Roche was clearly more at home with some types of building than with others. Although it did designs for churches, for example, this was clearly not its strong suit. The churches often look stiff and uncomfortable. The main dining room of the University Club and that in the Glen View Club are more convincing efforts in Gothic than any the firm produced for a religious institution. The same might be said for the firm's public buildings. From the Science Building at Northwestern University to the giant Cook County Courthouse, these designs can be called sound and satisfying, but they typically do not inspire in the way that work by the most brilliant monumental architects like Carrère and Hastings or Cass Gilbert sometimes does.

It is probable that the monumental building allowed too much room for artistic expression. Holabird & Roche had based its practice on building programs that stringently restricted any display of art not in direct service to utility, and it was difficult to change this mind-set. Where Chicago commercial architects, and Holabird & Roche in particular, really excelled was in the buildings that seemed to allow the least scope for art. Although as commercial architects they were bound to take clients' desires seriously, they also had standards and aspirations of their own. This required the most delicate balance between art and business.

In matters of business the partners at Holabird & Roche were as adventurous as any architects in the city. When advances in building programs, changing technology, or new materials allowed them to produce better buildings for less money, they were among the boldest experimenters in Chicago. The firm led the profession in developing the metal frame, riveted construction, deep basements, and integrated sprinkling systems. It was among the first to turn to the general contractor to construct its buildings. It was also quite willing to explore the aesthetic possibilities that might flow from these building practices, as the preliminary aluminum-skinned project for the Champlain Building demonstrates.

But innovation was never an end in itself. Maniere Dawson, who worked in the firm from 1908 to 1912, writes in his diary that he tried to convince Martin Roche to adapt a more experimental style, one more in line with the European avant-garde, about which Dawson had become enthusiastic. In an entry in his diaries for 2 April 1911 Dawson recorded the results:

> My efforts to convince Roche that a style can be developed for the elevations of our present day skyscrapers that would indicate the true structure of these buildings, are not meeting with any success. In fact he will not spend more than a few seconds either looking at designs or discussing the idea that a breakaway from the accepted conventions would be progressive. Once he said, Progress! Holabird will get a new job for the firm. That's progress.[5]

Neither William Holabird nor Martin Roche ever deliberately set himself against accepted notions of how buildings should look for the sake of experiment. There is no evidence that either was interested in overturning traditions unless they stood in the way of business necessity. Although they were keenly interested in all the advances in business and technology around them and probably believed these would eventually be the basis of a new architecture, they saw no reason for radical change until some clear need arose. In this as in most matters concerning the art of architecture, they were fundamentally conservative.

In fact, as we have seen, the call for a new architecture, like the call for a distinctively regional literature, came most frequently not from busy practitioners like Holabird & Roche but from the academies. The quest for an architecture particularly suited to the modern world was a fixture at the Ecole des Beaux-Arts in Paris. The most conspicuous American champions of a new American art, one that would grow out of the conditions of the American soil, were, moreover, just those architects and critics who had the greatest exposure to academic architectural education on the East Coast and in Europe. This included men like Montgomery Schuyler in New York and, in the Midwest, like Henry Van Brunt and Louis Sullivan, who had been raised and educated in the East and were never quite at home elsewhere.[6] William Holabird and Martin Roche, with their limited exposure to such ideas, were more typical of the Chicago architects of their day. It is characteristic that the only recorded instance in which Holabird or Roche spoke about the possibility of a new American architecture was in connection with the unseen reinforced concrete subbasement of the distinctly conservative Chicago Tribune Building.

In no commission or statement did the partners ever leave behind the conservative business-oriented clientele that was the mainstay of their practice. A review of their work suggests that this stance was not a studied response to business demands but a position congenial to them. Rather than a handicap, the constraints involved in commercial architecture turned out to be a blessing. Of all its work, the firm's lofts and the simplest of the office buildings, some of the automobile showrooms, and the telephone switching stations are among the most satisfying. Where art demanded of the firm the least conscious attention, it was best served.

This conclusion in turn suggests that in the end it is futile to try to evaluate the work of Holabird & Roche in the ways usually employed by architectural historians for either the great Beaux-Arts masters of the nineteenth century or the European avant-garde figures of the twentieth. In most cases this evaluation has been confined to the role of the architect in the history of style. Did the architect create buildings that were beautiful or at least a consistent and interesting expression of an individual personality? Did the buildings break significant new ground in stylistic expression and become important influences on later work?

With Holabird & Roche, as with the vast majority of architects, these questions seem largely irrelevant. Although no firm in Chicago was held in higher esteem over such a long period or could count so many handsome and useful interventions in the city, what is interesting in the work of Holabird & Roche is not any set of progressive refinements in a personal style or the expression of the personalities of the designers. There were many styles and many paths of development going on simultaneously, and even if we knew more biographical details about the architects, these details would probably tell us less of importance than the study of the complex outside factors that went into each building. Nor can the firm's architects be seen as stylistic pathbreakers whose importance can be judged by the extent of their influence. Although the work of Holabird & Roche was reviewed a great deal and was known and admired by many in the profession, its influence is difficult to measure. Since the partners at Holabird & Roche were working within accepted artistic ideas of the day, their work generally resembled that of many other architects practicing at about the same time. It is probably as unimportant as it is futile to try to determine who was influencing whom, since the influence of Holabird & Roche, while at least as important as that of a Louis

Sullivan or Frank Lloyd Wright, was broader and more diffuse and is less immediately apparent visually. It also involved things that are more difficult to measure but perhaps more basic: the firm's way of conducting business, for example, or general attitudes about buildings' massing, structure, organization, and equipment.

If this study of the work of Holabird & Roche has done little to further the traditional narratives of architectural history, it has perhaps suggested some of the ways the architects operated in the development of the city. Traditional architectural history has tended to see the city less as a process than as a product, a collection of high art architectural objects in a setting dominated by mundane buildings of little interest. This has tended to perpetuate a destructive and divisive attitude about the built environment, suggesting that only a few buildings are worthy of careful study and preservation while all the others are mere backdrop. I hope that these explorations into the work of Holabird & Roche have shed light on parts of the city rarely visited by the architectural historian and on some little explored aspects of its history. If so, perhaps it has achieved its most basic goal: providing an insight into the city as the ultimate human artifact, our most complex and prodigious social creation, and the most tangible result of the actions over time of all of its citizens.

This list includes commissions for new buildings and significant additions completed by the firm as well as a few exceptional unbuilt projects designed before 1918. The information has been extracted from Robert Bruegmann, *Holabird & Roche/Holabird & Root: An Illustrated Catalog of Works, 1880–1940*, 3 vols. (New York: Garland, 1991), updated and corrected where necessary. For any real study the three Garland volumes remain indispensable, since they contain considerably more information and more detailed instructions for using the catalog.

Notes on the Entries

Entry Number The number assigned in the Garland catalog for easy reference.

Name The first name given is the name by which the project was known at the time of the commission. Later names are given in parentheses. In some cases this means that a building familiarly known by a later name will be listed under a less common original name, but all the names are included in the index.

City The city is Chicago unless otherwise noted.

Address The address listed is the current address whenever this is known. Fre-quently, to locate a building as precisely as possible, a range of numbers is given. The actual address used at any given time might vary.

Date Unless otherwise indicated, the first date given is the date of the commission and the last is the date of completion of the building.

Status The first part of the entry tells whether the building was built, the second whether it was still standing at the time of my last visit to the site.

Architect After 1883 the architect is usually Holabird & Roche, but occasionally one or another of the firm's partners did jobs on their own or the firm was associated with another architect. In most cases this involved a commission where Holabird & Roche was responsible for the design and the associated architect handled administrative aspects and made working drawings. In a few cases Holabird & Roche acted as associated architect for out-of-town firms. If no architect is listed, Holabird & Roche was alone responsible for design and execution.

H&R Commission Number A continuous set of numbers was assigned to com-missions by the firm after 1902. If no number is listed, none is available.

Description Where drawings exist, the description is taken from the latest and most complete set of drawings. Where no drawings are available the description has been compiled from written and graphic evidence and from an examination of the existing building.

2. Graceland Cemetery—Cemetery Office and Station
ADDRESS Near Seminary and Buena Sts.
DATE ca. 1881–83
STATUS Built. Not standing 1983
ARCHITECT Holabird, Simonds & Roche
DESCRIPTION One-and-a-half-story L-shaped station

6. Robert H. Taggert Residential Building
ADDRESS 3972 S. Drexel Blvd.
DATE 1883–84
STATUS Built. Standing 1984, not standing 1996
DESCRIPTION Three-story brick row residential building

7. Francis Bartlett Building
ADDRESS 407 S. Dearborn St.
DATE 1884–86

STATUS Probably built. Not standing 1983
DESCRIPTION "One-story taxpayer"

11. Webster Building
ADDRESS NE corner Madison St. and Ogden Ave.
DATE ca. 1884–85
STATUS Built. Not standing 1983
DESCRIPTION Four-story brick building

12. South Evanston (Second) Presbyterian Church
CITY Evanston, Illinois
ADDRESS NE corner Hinman and Main Sts.
DATE 1884–85
STATUS Built. Not standing 1983
DESCRIPTION Frame church

13. Fort Sheridan General Planning
CITY Fort Sheridan, Illinois (Highwood)
DATE ca. 1884–89
ARCHITECT Holabird & Roche? United States Army officials?
DESCRIPTION Military installation with numerous buildings (see various entries for specific buildings)

14. Brooks Estate Building
ADDRESS NE corner Harrison and Dearborn Sts.
DATE ca. 1885
STATUS Built. Not standing 1983
DESCRIPTION Six-story brick building

20. Edward Funk Residence
ADDRESS 5848 W. Midway Pk.
DATE ca. 1886
STATUS Built. Standing 1996
DESCRIPTION Frame house

22. Tacoma Building
ADDRESS NE corner LaSalle and Madison Sts.
DATE 1886–89; constructed 1888–89
STATUS Built. Not standing 1983
DESCRIPTION Twelve-story partially metal frame L-shaped office building

23. W. D. Walker Building
ADDRESS 400–408 S. Wabash Ave.
DATE 1886
STATUS Probably built. Not standing 1983

DESCRIPTION One- or two-story (?) brick building

24. T. F. Wheeler Factory
ADDRESS Twenty-fourth and Normal Sts.
DATE 1886
STATUS Built. Not standing 1985
DESCRIPTION Three-story and basement brick (?) building

25. First Congregational Church
CITY Lake Linden, Michigan
ADDRESS First and Tunnel Sts.
DATE 1886–87
STATUS Built. Standing 1985
DESCRIPTION Shingled rectangular frame structure

29. Northwestern University Science Hall (Fayerweather Hall)
CITY Evanston, Illinois
ADDRESS North of Sheridan Rd. on axis with Hinman Ave.
DATE 1886–87
STATUS Built. Not standing 1983
DESCRIPTION U-shaped classroom and laboratory building

37. Charles Spoehr Residence
CITY Chicago (Lakeview, Illinois)
ADDRESS 4321 N. Broadway
DATE 1887
STATUS Built. Not standing 1985
DESCRIPTION Two-story frame residence

39. Taylor Apartment House
ADDRESS 1412 W. Congress St.
DATE ca. 1887
STATUS Probably built. Not standing 1984
DESCRIPTION Three-story brick row apartment house

40. Uebele Factory
ADDRESS 1661 S. Clark St.
DATE ca. 1887
STATUS Probably built. Not standing 1984
DESCRIPTION Three-story brick factory building

43. Brooks Estate Store Building
ADDRESS NE corner Ashland Ave. and Madison St.

DATE 1888
STATUS Built. Not standing 1984
DESCRIPTION One- and two-story glass and iron store and office building

49. Graceland Cemetery—Chapel and Mortuary Crypt
ADDRESS Graceland Cemetery
DATE 1888
STATUS Built. Standing 1996
DESCRIPTION One-story granite chapel and adjacent mortuary crypt

53. John Tait Residence
ADDRESS 3614 S. Martin Luther King Dr.
DATE 1888
STATUS Built. Standing 1996
DESCRIPTION Three-story brick residence

54. Wirt D. Walker Commercial Building (Dearborn Building)
ADDRESS 33–37 W. Harrison St.
DATE 1888
STATUS Probably built. Not standing 1983
DESCRIPTION Six-story brick building

55. Evanston Country Club ("Old Shelter")
CITY Evanston, Illinois
ADDRESS Hinman and Clark Sts.
DATE ca. 1888
STATUS Built. Not standing 1983
DESCRIPTION One-room building

56. J. D. Allen Residence
ADDRESS Unknown
DATE 1889
STATUS Built. Standing (?)
DESCRIPTION Three-story stone row house

58. Charles F. Dwight Houses
CITY Chicago or Evanston
ADDRESS Unknown
DATE 1889
STATUS Built. Standing (?)
DESCRIPTION Four detached two-story frame residences

61. Pontiac Building
ADDRESS 542 S. Dearborn St.
DATE 1884–91
STATUS Built. Standing 1996

DESCRIPTION Fourteen-story partly steel frame structure

63. William B. Bogert House
CITY Evanston, Illinois
ADDRESS 1818 Sheridan Rd.
DATE 1889
STATUS Built. Not standing 1983
DESCRIPTION Two-and-a-half-story frame house

64. C. T. Boynton Residence
CITY Evanston, Illinois
ADDRESS 1007 Greenwood St.
DATE 1889
STATUS Built. Not standing 1983
DESCRIPTION Two-story frame house

65. Evanston Club
CITY Evanston, Illinois
ADDRESS NW corner Chicago Ave. and Grove St.
DATE 1889
STATUS Built. Not standing 1983
DESCRIPTION One-story red brick structure

66. St. Mark's Episcopal Church
CITY Evanston, Illinois
ADDRESS 1509 Ridge Ave.
DATE 1889–91
STATUS Built. Standing 1996
DESCRIPTION Stone church with tapering tower

67. Dr. E. H. Webster Residence
CITY Evanston, Illinois
ADDRESS 1332 Chicago Ave.
DATE 1889
STATUS Built. Not standing 1985
DESCRIPTION Frame and stone residence

68. Coleman Lake Club—Campbell Cottage (Stephenson Cottage, "Baltullo," "Sko-Kel-Kins," Scott Lodge)
CITY Near Goodman, Wisconsin
DATE 1889
STATUS Built. Standing 1983
ARCHITECT Holabird & Roche (?)
DESCRIPTION One-story log structure

72. Brinks Express Barn
ADDRESS 711–19 W. Monroe

DATE 1890
STATUS Built. Not standing 1983
DESCRIPTION Two-story brick structure

74. Sam Brown Residence
CITY Chicago (Sheridan Park)
ADDRESS 4608 N. Beacon St.
DATE 1890
STATUS Built. Not standing 1983

75. Caxton Building (Bryan Lathrop Building)
ADDRESS 508 S. Dearborn St.
DATE 1889–90
STATUS Built. Demolished 1947
DESCRIPTION Twelve-story steel frame building

78. Everett and Post Factory
ADDRESS 400 block of W. Illinois St.
DATE 1890
STATUS Apparently built. Not standing 1983
DESCRIPTION One-story wood frame building

94. F. H. Prince Residence
ADDRESS 1845 N. Orleans St.
DATE ca. 1890
STATUS Built. Standing 1996
DESCRIPTION Two-story brick row house

100. Servite Sisters' Mausoleum
ADDRESS In block bounded by Van Buren, Kedzie, Congress, and Albany
DATE ca. 1890
STATUS Built. Not standing 1983
DESCRIPTION Low cruciform structure of concrete and brick

106. Nellie Woods Residence
ADDRESS 5809 S. Blackstone Ave.
DATE ca. 1890
STATUS Built. Not standing 1985
DESCRIPTION Two-story brick residence

110. Hollister Residence
CITY Grand Rapids, Michigan
ADDRESS Unknown
DATE ca. 1890
STATUS Built. Standing (?)
DESCRIPTION Two-story frame structure

112. Mrs. C. D. Paine Residence
CITY Oak Park, Illinois
ADDRESS 543 N. Oak Park Ave.
DATE ca. 1890
STATUS Built. Standing 1984
DESCRIPTION Two-story frame house

115. Robert S. Clark House
CITY Evanston, Illinois
ADDRESS 1100 or 1110 Michigan Ave.
DATE 1890
STATUS Built. Standing 1996

116. E. A. Dawson Residence
CITY Evanston, Illinois
ADDRESS 1225 Judson St.
DATE 1890
STATUS Built. Standing 1996
DESCRIPTION Two-and-a-half-story clapboard-covered frame building

119. Arthur Little Residence
CITY Castine, Maine
ADDRESS Battle Ave.
DATE 1895–96
STATUS Built. Standing 1985
DESCRIPTION Two-story frame house

127. Frank Stevens House
CITY Evanston, Illinois
ADDRESS 1422 Judson Ave.
DATE 1890
STATUS Probably built. Standing (?)

128. Fort Sheridan Lieutenants' Quarters (Fort Sheridan Building Numbers 3, 4, 5, 6, 7, 15, 16, 17, 21, 22, 23, 24, 25, 26, 27, and 56)
CITY Fort Sheridan, Illinois
DATE 1890
STATUS Built. Standing 1983
DESCRIPTION Two-and-a-half-story rectangular brick buildings

129. Fort Sheridan Field Officers' Quarters Number 2 (Fort Sheridan Building Number 8)
CITY Fort Sheridan, Illinois
DATE 1890
STATUS Built. Standing 1983
DESCRIPTION Two-and-a-half-story brick building

130. Fort Sheridan Field Officers' Quarters (Post Commandant's Residence) (Fort Sheridan Building Number 9)
CITY Fort Sheridan, Illinois
DATE 1890
STATUS Built. Standing 1983
DESCRIPTION Two-and-a-half-story brick building

131. Fort Sheridan Captains' Quarters (Fort Sheridan Building Numbers 10, 11, 12, 13, 18, 19, 20, 53, 54, 73, 74, 75, 76)
CITY Fort Sheridan, Illinois
DATE 1890
STATUS Built. Standing 1983
DESCRIPTION Two-and-a-half-story rectangular brick buildings

132. Fort Sheridan Pumping Station (Fort Sheridan Building Number 29)
CITY Fort Sheridan, Illinois
DATE 1890
STATUS Built. Standing 1983
DESCRIPTION One-story brick building

133. Fort Sheridan Guardhouse (Fort Sheridan Building Number 33)
CITY Fort Sheridan, Illinois
DATE 1890
STATUS Built. Standing 1983
DESCRIPTION One-story brick building

134. Fort Sheridan Bakery (Fort Sheridan Building Number 34)
CITY Fort Sheridan, Illinois
DATE 1890
STATUS Built. Standing 1983
DESCRIPTION One-story structure

135. Fort Sheridan Quartermaster and Commissary Storehouses (Fort Sheridan Building Number 35)
CITY Fort Sheridan, Illinois
DATE 1890
STATUS Built. Standing 1983
DESCRIPTION Large rectangular brick building

136. Fort Sheridan Workshops (Fort Sheridan Building Number 36)
CITY Fort Sheridan, Illinois
DATE 1890
STATUS Built. Standing 1983
DESCRIPTION Long rectangular brick building

137. Fort Sheridan Quartermaster's Stables (Veterinary Hospital) (Fort Sheridan Building Number 38)
CITY Fort Sheridan, Illinois
DATE 1890
STATUS Built. Standing 1983
DESCRIPTION One-and-a-half-story brick building

139. Fort Sheridan Cavalry Stables (Fort Sheridan Building Numbers 42, 43, 62, 63, 65)
CITY Fort Sheridan, Illinois
DATE 1890
STATUS Built. Standing 1983
DESCRIPTION One-and-a-half-story rectangular brick building

140. Fort Sheridan Noncommisssioned Officers' Quarters (Fort Sheridan Building Number 46)
CITY Fort Sheridan, Illinois
DATE 1890
STATUS Built. Standing 1983
DESCRIPTION One-and-a-half-story brick double house

141. Fort Sheridan Infantry Barracks (Fort Sheridan Building Number 48)
CITY Fort Sheridan, Illinois
DATE 1890
STATUS Built. Standing 1983
DESCRIPTION Two and-a-half-story brick building

142. Fort Sheridan Water Tower (Fort Sheridan Building Number 49)
CITY Fort Sheridan, Illinois
DATE 1890
STATUS Built. Standing 1983
DESCRIPTION Brick and stone water tower

143. Fort Sheridan Cavalry Barracks (Fort Sheridan Building Number 50)
CITY Fort Sheridan, Illinois
DATE 1890
STATUS Built. Standing 1983
DESCRIPTION Two-and-a-half-story brick building

144. Fort Sheridan Stable Guardhouse (Fort Sheridan Building Number 44)
CITY Fort Sheridan, Illinois
DATE ca. 1890
STATUS Built. Standing 1983

146. John Berry, Esq., Store Building
ADDRESS NE corner Madison St. and Ashland Ave.
DATE 1891
STATUS Built. Not standing 1983
DESCRIPTION Two-story brick store building

150. Monadnock Block Addition (Katahdin and Wachusetts Building)
ADDRESS 54 W. Van Buren St.
DATE 1891–93
STATUS Built. Standing, 1996
DESCRIPTION Sixteen-story partly steel frame office building

151. Sheridan Drive Station
ADDRESS East of Clifton Ave., north of Wilson Ave.
DATE 1891
STATUS Built. Not standing 1983
DESCRIPTION One-story stone railroad station

153. Venetian Building
ADDRESS 15 E. Washington St.
DATE 1891–92
STATUS Built. Not standing 1983
DESCRIPTION Twelve-story steel frame structure

154. James R. Walker Residence
ADDRESS 1726 S. Prairie Ave.
DATE 1891–93

STATUS Built. Not standing 1983

DESCRIPTION Two-and-a-half-story brick house

156. Racetrack for Corrigan and Burke (Hawthorne Racetrack)

CITY Cicero, Illinois

ADDRESS 3501 S. Laramie St.

DATE 1891

STATUS Built. Not standing 1983

DESCRIPTION Grandstand, betting stand, carriage entrance, main entrance, judge's stand, and foreman's cottage

157. Lieutenant Augur Residence

CITY Dixon, Illinois

ADDRESS Unknown

DATE 1891

STATUS Built. Standing (?)

159. Mrs. P. N. Fox Residence

CITY Evanston, Illinois

ADDRESS Unknown

DATE 1891

STATUS Built. Standing (?)

160. House for Mrs. Graham

CITY Evanston, Illinois

ADDRESS Unknown

DATE 1891

STATUS Built. Standing (?)

161. Holmes Hoge House

CITY Evanston, Illinois

ADDRESS Unknown

DATE 1891

STATUS Built. Standing (?)

162. Store and Flat Building for John Witt

CITY Evanston, Illinois

ADDRESS 1581 Wesley Ave.

DATE 1891

STATUS Built. Standing 1996

DESCRIPTION Two-story brick building

163. Fort Sheridan Forage Warehouse (Fort Sheridan Building Number 39)

CITY Fort Sheridan, Illinois

DATE 1891

STATUS Built. Standing 1983

DESCRIPTION Two-story brick building

164. Fort Sheridan Mess Hall, Kitchen, and Heating Plant (Fort Sheridan Building Number 47)

CITY Fort Sheridan, Illinois

DATE 1891

STATUS Built. Standing 1983

DESCRIPTION Long one-story brick building

165. Bryan Lathrop Residence (Fortnightly Club)

ADDRESS 120 E. Bellevue Pl.

DATE 1892

STATUS Built. Standing 1996

ARCHITECT McKim, Mead and White; Holabird & Roche, supervising architects

DESCRIPTION Three-story brick residence

167. James F. O'Brien Residence

ADDRESS 4018 S. Martin Luther King Dr.

DATE 1892

STATUS Built. Standing 1996

DESCRIPTION Three-story brick row house

170. St. Bartholomew's Church (True Vine Missionary Baptist Church)

CITY Chicago (formerly Englewood)

ADDRESS NW corner Stewart Ave. and Normal Pkwy.

DATE 1892

STATUS Built. Standing 1996

DESCRIPTION Stone church

171. Matthew J. Swatek Flat Building and Lodge Hall

ADDRESS 1504 N. Clark St.

DATE 1892

STATUS Built. Not standing 1983

DESCRIPTION Four-story brick building

172. World's Columbian Exposition— Boone and Crockett Club Exhibit

ADDRESS Fairgrounds at Jackson Park

DATE 1892–93

STATUS Built. Not standing 1983

DESCRIPTION One-story log cabin

178. World's Columbian Exposition— Livestock Pavilion

ADDRESS Jackson Park

DATE ca. 1892

STATUS Built. Not standing 1983

DESCRIPTION Exposition arena in the shape of a Roman circus

179. World's Columbian Exposition— New South Wales Building

ADDRESS Jackson Park

DATE ca. 1892

STATUS Built. Probably demolished ca. 1894

DESCRIPTION Square hall with porch

183. World's Columbian Exposition— Proctor Steel Tower

ADDRESS Jackson Park

DATE ca. 1892

STATUS Unbuilt

ARCHITECT Holabird & Roche; Corydon Purdy, Engineer

DESCRIPTION Very tall (1,110 feet) steel tower

188. Evanston Country Club

CITY Evanston, Illinois

ADDRESS NW corner Lake and Oak Sts.

DATE 1892

STATUS Built. Not standing 1983

DESCRIPTION Large two-story frame structure

190. Fort Sheridan Bachelor Officers' Quarters and Open Mess (Fort Sheridan Building Number 31)

CITY Fort Sheridan, Illinois

DATE 1892

STATUS Built. Standing 1983

DESCRIPTION Two-and-a-half-story rectangular brick building

190A. Fort Sheridan Quartermaster Stables Guardhouse (Fort Sheridan Building Number 37)

CITY Fort Sheridan, Illinois

DATE 1892

STATUS Built. Standing 1983

DESCRIPTION One-story brick building

191. Fort Sheridan Magazine (Fort Sheridan Building Number 57A)
CITY Fort Sheridan, Illinois
DATE 1892
STATUS Built. Standing 1983
DESCRIPTION One-story brick building

193. Fort Sheridan Ordnance Storehouse (Fort Sheridan Building Number 59)
CITY Fort Sheridan, Illinois
DATE 1892
STATUS Built. Standing 1983
DESCRIPTION One-story brick residential building

194. Fort Sheridan Stable Sergeant's Quarters (Saddler's and Stable Sergeant's Building Numbers 72, 78)
CITY Fort Sheridan, Illinois
DATE 1892
STATUS Built. Standing 1983
DESCRIPTION One-story nearly square building

195. Fort Sheridan Blacksmith Shop (Fort Sheridan Building Number 77)
CITY Fort Sheridan, Illinois
DATE 1892
STATUS Built. Standing 1983
DESCRIPTION One-story brick building

196. Fort Sheridan Oil Storage (Fort Sheridan Building Number 88)
CITY Fort Sheridan, Illinois
DATE 1892–93
STATUS Built. Standing 1983
DESCRIPTION Small one-story building

197. Fort Sheridan Gun Shed (Fort Sheridan Building Number 89)
CITY Fort Sheridan, Illinois
DATE 1892
STATUS Built. Standing 1983
DESCRIPTION One-story rectangular building

199. The Cristoval Apartments
ADDRESS 3980 S. Cottage Grove Ave.
DATE 1893
STATUS Built. Not standing 1983
DESCRIPTION Four-story rectangular brick building

200. Marquette Building
ADDRESS 140 S. Dearborn St.
DATE 1891–95
STATUS Built. Standing 1996
DESCRIPTION Sixteen-story U-shaped steel frame building

201. Old Colony Building
ADDRESS 407 S. Dearborn St.
DATE 1893–94
STATUS Built. Standing 1996
DESCRIPTION Seventeen-story rectangular steel frame building

202. Williams Memorial Chapel
ADDRESS Site where Orchard St. and Scott St. intersected
DATE 1893
STATUS Probably built. Not standing 1983
DESCRIPTION Brick church with wood and stone trim

203. Byron L. Smith Residence ("Briar Lodge")
CITY Lake Forest, Illinois
ADDRESS 1133–61 Lake St.
DATE 1893–94
STATUS Built. Not standing 1983
DESCRIPTION Two-and-a-half-story brick residence with terra cotta trim

206. Blanchard Houses
CITY Evanston, Illinois
ADDRESS 1209–17 N. Maple St.
DATE ca. 1893
STATUS Built. Standing 1996
DESCRIPTION Five attached two-and-a-half-story brick houses

207. Evanston City Hall
CITY Evanston, Illinois
ADDRESS NW corner Davis St. and Sherman Ave.
DATE 1891–93
STATUS Built. Not standing 1983
DESCRIPTION Three-story buff brick building

208. Fort Sheridan Infantry Drill Hall (Fort Sheridan Building Number 60)
CITY Fort Sheridan, Illinois
DATE 1893
STATUS Built. Standing 1983
DESCRIPTION Large one-story brick building

210. Fort Sheridan Dead House (Fort Sheridan Building Number 87)
CITY Fort Sheridan, Illinois
DATE 1893
STATUS Built. Standing 1983
DESCRIPTION Small one-story structure

211. Fort Sheridan Noncommissioned Officers' Quarters (Fort Sheridan Building Numbers 90 and 91)
CITY Fort Sheridan, Illinois
DATE 1893
STATUS Built. Standing 1983
DESCRIPTION Two-story, two-family residences

212. Owen Aldis Store Building
ADDRESS NW corner Milwaukee Ave. and Bloomingdale Rd.
DATE 1894
STATUS Built. Not standing 1983
DESCRIPTION One-story triangular stone store building

213. Auger Building
ADDRESS NW corner Larrabee and Crosby Sts.
DATE 1894
STATUS Built. Not standing 1983
DESCRIPTION Two-story brick store and flat building

214. Arthur P. Brink Residence
CITY Chicago (formerly Buena Park)
ADDRESS Approximately 4635 N. Sheridan Rd.
DATE 1894
STATUS Built. Not standing 1983
DESCRIPTION Two-and-a-half-story brick house

215. Champlain Building
ADDRESS NW corner State and Madison Sts.

DATE 1894–95

STATUS Built. Demolished 1915

DESCRIPTION Fifteen-story steel frame building

216. Ingals Flat Building

ADDRESS 1445 W. Van Buren St.

DATE ca. 1894

STATUS Built. Not standing 1985

217. George W. Meeker Residence (Edward L. Ryerson Jr. House)

ADDRESS 1431 N. Astor St.

DATE 1894

STATUS Built. Standing 1996

DESCRIPTION Three-story brick residence

218. W. D. O'Brien Residence

ADDRESS 3634 S. Martin Luther King Dr.

DATE 1894–95

STATUS Built. Not standing 1985

DESCRIPTION Two-and-a-half-story brick residence

220. State Safety Building (A. M. Rothschild Building)

ADDRESS 337 S. State St.

DATE 1894–95

STATUS Built. Demolished ca. 1909

DESCRIPTION Seven-story metal and wood frame mercantile building

221. A. O. Slaughter Residence

ADDRESS 4548 S. Drexel Blvd.

DATE 1894–96

STATUS Built. Not standing 1984

DESCRIPTION Three-story brick and terra cotta residence

222. D. S. Morgan Building

CITY Buffalo, New York

ADDRESS Franklin, Eagle, Niagara, and Pearl Sts.

DATE 1894

STATUS Built. Not standing 1983

ARCHITECT Green and Wicks, Holabird & Roche consulting architects

DESCRIPTION Twelve-story steel frame brick- and terra cotta–clad pentagonal building

223. N. A. Fletcher House

CITY Grand Rapids, Michigan

ADDRESS Unknown

DATE 1894–95

STATUS Built. Standing (?)

224. C. H. Fitzhugh Residence (Insley)

CITY Lake Forest, Illinois

ADDRESS 360 Mayflower Rd.

DATE 1894

STATUS Built. Standing 1984

DESCRIPTION Two-story brick residence

225. P. Noud House

CITY Manistee, Michigan

ADDRESS Unknown

DATE 1894

STATUS Built. Apparently standing 1985

228. G. W. Whitefield House

CITY Evanston, Illinois

ADDRESS 1518 Hinman

STATUS Built. Standing (?)

DESCRIPTION Two-story and attic house

230. Atwood Building (6 North Clark, Straus, H. O. Stone Building)

ADDRESS 6 N. Clark St.

DATE 1895

STATUS Built. Not standing 1983

DESCRIPTION Ten-story steel frame building

232. Dr. E. Fletcher Ingals Residence

ADDRESS 4757 S. Martin Luther King Dr.

DATE 1895

STATUS Built. Not standing 1984

DESCRIPTION Two-story brick residence

235. G. W. Shannon Residence

ADDRESS 4130 S. Martin Luther King Dr.

DATE 1895

STATUS Built. Standing 1996

DESCRIPTION Two-and-a-half-story brick house

236. S. and O. Sollitt Houses

ADDRESS Forrestville Ave. near Forty-ninth St.

DATE 1895–96

STATUS Built. Apparently not standing 1983

DESCRIPTION Three brick row houses

241. R. R. Blacker Stable

CITY Manistee, Michigan

ADDRESS Unknown

DATE 1895

STATUS Built. Standing (?)

DESCRIPTION One-and-a-half-story wood stable

242. Fort Sheridan Range House on Target Range (Fort Sheridan Building Number 68)

CITY Fort Sheridan, Illinois

DATE ca. 1895

STATUS Built. Not standing 1983

DESCRIPTION One-story frame building

243. Arthur T. Aldis Residence

ADDRESS 1258 N. Lake Shore Dr.

DATE 1896

STATUS Built. Standing 1996

DESCRIPTION Three-story brick and stone building

244. Graceland Cemetery—Office Building

ADDRESS Clark St. North of Irving Park Rd.

DATE 1896

STATUS Built. Standing 1996

DESCRIPTION One-story stone-faced brick structure

245. Graceland Cemetery—Waiting Room Building

ADDRESS Clark St. north of Irving Park Rd.

DATE 1896

STATUS Built. Standing 1996

DESCRIPTION One-story L-shaped brick and stone structure

246. Graceland Cemetery—Fence and Gates

ADDRESS Clark St. and Irving Park Rd.

DATE 1896

STATUS Built. Standing 1996

DESCRIPTION brick cemetery wall, ornamental metal gate

248. M. Naughton Flat Building

ADDRESS 2801 N. Seminary Ave.

DATE 1896

STATUS Built. Standing 1996
DESCRIPTION Four-story brick apartment
building

249. Richard Tyson Apartment Building (Windham Apartment House)

ADDRESS 20 E. Goethe St.
DATE 1896
STATUS Built. Standing 1996
DESCRIPTION Six-story steel frame
apartment building

250. Updike Apartment Building

ADDRESS Forty-seventh St. (?)
DATE 1896
STATUS Apparently built. Standing (?)

253. Dupuy (DuPrey) Residence

CITY Chicago (formerly Ravenswood)
ADDRESS 4526 N. Paulina St.
DATE 1897
STATUS Built. Not standing 1983
DESCRIPTION Two-story brick and frame
structure

255. Hart, Schaffner and Marx (Price) Building

ADDRESS 319–35 W. Van Buren St.
DATE 1897
STATUS Built. Not standing 1983
DESCRIPTION Eight-story steel frame
structure

256. Robert Leesley Residence

ADDRESS 4701 N. Beacon St.
DATE 1897–98
STATUS Built. Not standing 1983
DESCRIPTION Two-and-a-half-story brick
residence

257. McConnell Apartments

ADDRESS 1210 N. Astor St.
DATE 1897
STATUS Built. Standing 1996
DESCRIPTION seven-story steel frame
apartment building

258. Watson Store Building

ADDRESS 119 N. Wabash Ave.
DATE 1897

STATUS Built. Not standing 1984
DESCRIPTION Seven-story store building

259. Lewis D. Webster Building

ADDRESS NW corner Ogden Ave. and
Madison St.
DATE 1897
STATUS Built. Standing (?)
DESCRIPTION Three-story building

260. Williams Building

ADDRESS 205 W. Monroe St.
DATE 1897–98
STATUS Built. Standing 1996
DESCRIPTION Ten-story steel frame
commercial building

261. Glen View Golf and Polo Club— Golf and Polo Clubhouse

CITY Golf, Illinois
ADDRESS Golf Rd.
DATE 1897
STATUS Built. Not standing 1983
DESCRIPTION Two-and-a-half-story frame
building

262. Glen View Golf and Polo Club— Stable Complex

CITY Golf, Illinois
ADDRESS Golf Rd.
DATE 1897
STATUS Built. Not standing 1985
DESCRIPTION Frame buildings on brick
piers (stalls, shed, and living
quarters)

263. Young Men's Christian Association (Lord's Department Store)

CITY Evanston, Illinois
ADDRESS 1611–21 Orrington Ave.
DATE 1897–98
STATUS Built. Not standing 1983
DESCRIPTION Three-story structure, brick
with steel interior frame

264. Ayer Building (McClurg, Crown, Pakula)

ADDRESS 218–24 S. Wabash Ave.
DATE 1898–99
STATUS Built. Standing 1996

DESCRIPTION Nine-story steel frame
mercantile building

265. Bailey Building (Carter Estate— North Section)

ADDRESS 529 S. Franklin St.
DATE 1898
STATUS Built. Not standing 1983
DESCRIPTION Ten-story commercial
building

266. McCormick Buildings (Gage Group: Gage, Edson Keith, and Ascher Buildings)

ADDRESS 18–28 S. Michigan Ave.
DATE 1898–99
STATUS Built. Standing 1996
ARCHITECT Holabird & Roche; Louis
Sullivan for facade detail of 18 S.
Michigan Avenue
DESCRIPTION Three rectangular, steel frame
loft buildings

267. P. H. McNulty House

CITY Chicago (formerly Edgewater)
ADDRESS 5453 N. Lakewood Ave.
DATE 1898
STATUS Built. Standing 1996
DESCRIPTION Two-and-a-half-story
stuccoed building

268. Poole Building (Wells Building)

ADDRESS SE corner Clark and Harrison
Sts.
DATE 1898
STATUS Built. Not standing 1983
DESCRIPTION Six-story brick-clad structure

269. Sollitt Apartment Building

ADDRESS 4729–31 S. Indiana Ave.
DATE 1898
STATUS Built. Not standing 1984
DESCRIPTION Four-story brick- and stone-
faced courtyard apartment building

270. Henry Strong Building

ADDRESS 320–22 S. Franklin St.
DATE 1898
STATUS Built. Not standing 1983
DESCRIPTION Ten-story steel frame
commercial building

272. Store Building for Tait and Roche
ADDRESS Calumet Ave. at Forty-seventh St.
DATE 1898
STATUS Built. Standing (?)

273. Yukon Building
ADDRESS SW corner Clark and Van Buren Sts.
DATE 1898
STATUS Built. Standing 1996
DESCRIPTION Two-story building

275. Henry Dibblee Residence ("Green Gables")
CITY Rye Beach, New Hampshire
ADDRESS South side of South St.
DATE 1898–99
STATUS Built. Standing 1984
DESCRIPTION Two-and-a-half-story shingled frame house

277. W. G. Miller House
CITY Evanston, Illinois
ADDRESS Unknown
DATE 1898
STATUS Apparently built. Standing (?)

278. Elgin, Joliet, and Eastern Railroad Depot
CITY Fort Sheridan, Illinois
DATE 1898
STATUS Built. Not standing 1983

279. Cable (Hoops, 57 East Jackson) Building
ADDRESS 57 E. Jackson Blvd.
DATE 1899
STATUS Built. Not standing 1983
DESCRIPTION Ten-story steel frame building

281. Home for Missionaries' Children
ADDRESS Morgan Park area (street address unknown)
DATE 1899
STATUS Apparently built. Standing (?)

282. P. H. Rice Malting Company
ADDRESS Appriximately 4500 block W. Cortland Ave.
DATE 1899
STATUS Built. Not standing 1983
DESCRIPTION Six-story brick malt house

284. Store and Office Building for Martin Ryerson
ADDRESS 1400–1416 S. Michigan Ave.
DATE 1899
STATUS Built. Not standing 1983
DESCRIPTION Five brick structures

285. Bauer and Black—Unit One
ADDRESS SE corner Twenty-fifth and Federal Sts.
DATE 1899
STATUS Built. Not standing 1984
DESCRIPTION Three-story brick commercial building

287. Glen View Golf and Polo Club—Cottage B
CITY Golf, Illinois
ADDRESS Golf Rd.
DATE 1899 (?)
STATUS Built. Not standing 1985
DESCRIPTION Two-story frame building

290. Brink and Simonds Barn
ADDRESS Unknown
DATE 1900
STATUS Built. Standing (?)

291. Central Trading Company (Mandel Brothers Annex, Wieboldt's Annex)
ADDRESS NW corner Wabash Ave. and Madison St.
DATE 1900–1901
STATUS Built. Standing 1996
DESCRIPTION Nine-story steel frame building

293. Joseph P. Hubbard Manufacturing Building
ADDRESS SW corner Lake and Carpenter Sts.
DATE 1900–1901
STATUS Built. Standing 1996
DESCRIPTION Three-story brick building

294. LeMoyne Warehouse (Park Fireproof Warehouse, Werner-Kennelly Warehouse)
ADDRESS 1742–50 N. Clark St.
DATE 1900
STATUS Built. Standing 1996, greatly altered
DESCRIPTION Nine-story brick warehouse

295. M. Naughton Stable
ADDRESS Wolfram and Seminary Sts.
DATE 1900
STATUS Built. Standing (?)
DESCRIPTION One-and-a-half-story brick structure

298. Old National Bank
CITY Grand Rapids, Michigan
ADDRESS Unknown
DATE 1900
STATUS Probably built. Standing (?)
DESCRIPTION Eight-story hotel and bank building

304. Eagle Building
ADDRESS 729–31 S. Dearborn St.
DATE 1901
STATUS Built. Not standing 1983
DESCRIPTION Two-story building

306. George M. Hill Company (Automatic Electric Company)
ADDRESS SW corner Morgan and Van Buren Sts.
DATE 1901–2
STATUS Built. Standing 1996
DESCRIPTION Six-story building of mill construction

307. Sidney A. Kent Estate Building (Brock and Rankin Building)
ADDRESS 515–17 S. LaSalle St.
DATE 1901–2
STATUS Built. Standing 1996
DESCRIPTION Seven-story structure

308. Chicago Tribune (Tribune Building III, Union Trust, First Federal Savings, Citicorp Savings, Citibank)

453

ADDRESS SE corner Dearborn and
Madison Sts.

DATE 1901–2

STATUS Built. Standing 1996

DESCRIPTION Seventeen-story steel frame
building

309. Chicago Yacht Club

ADDRESS On Lake Michigan east of
Monroe St.

DATE 1901–2

STATUS Built. Not standing 1983

ARCHITECT Holabird & Roche; Jarvis
Hunt, associated architects

DESCRIPTION Three-story brick building

**310. Clow Building (Mandel
Brothers Warehouse)**

ADDRESS NW corner Franklin and
Harrison Sts.

DATE 1901–2

STATUS Built. Not standing 1983

DESCRIPTION Seven-story steel frame
structure

**311. McCorkle Building (Janeway
and Carpenter Building)**

ADDRESS 520–24 S. Canal St.

DATE 1901–2

STATUS Built. Not standing 1983

DESCRIPTION Eight-story warehouse of mill
construction

312. Mandel Brothers Stable

ADDRESS 4812–14 S. Cottage Grove Ave.

DATE 1901–2

STATUS Built. Standing 1996

DESCRIPTION Three-story stable

313. Leon Mandel Store Building

ADDRESS Sixty-third St. and Rhodes Ave.
or University Ave.

DATE 1901

STATUS Built. Not standing 1996

DESCRIPTION One-story building

**314. Building for Newberry Library
(Turner Brass Company)**

ADDRESS SE corner Franklin and Hubbard
Sts.

DATE 1901

STATUS Built. Apparently standing 1996

DESCRIPTION Six-story mill construction
building

**315. Orthodox Aged Jews Home
(Beth Moshav Z'Keinim)**

ADDRESS 1648 S. Albany Ave.

DATE 1901–3

STATUS Built. Not standing 1983

DESCRIPTION Three-story classical structure
of pressed brick

316. Paulson Flat Building

ADDRESS 1249 W. Argyle St.

DATE 1901

STATUS Built. Standing 1996

DESCRIPTION Two-story frame structure

**317. Powers (Champlain, Monroe)
Building**

ADDRESS 58 S. Wabash Ave.

DATE 1901–3

STATUS Built. Standing 1996

DESCRIPTION Thirteen-story steel frame
office building

318. H. G. Reynolds Building

ADDRESS SE corner Milwaukee and
Ashland Aves. (?)

DATE 1901

STATUS Built. Standing (?)

DESCRIPTION Triangular two-story brick
structure

319. Ida Richardson Building

ADDRESS NE corner Madison and Canal
Sts.

DATE 1901

STATUS Built. Not standing 1983

DESCRIPTION Five-story brick structure

321. Angus Hibbard House and Stable

CITY Near Golf, Illinois

DATE 1901

STATUS Built. Standing (?)

322. Indiana Harbor Cottages

CITY East Chicago, Indiana

ADDRESS Unknown

DATE 1901

STATUS Apparently built. Not standing
1984

DESCRIPTION Eight frame structures

**323. Glen View Golf and Polo Club—
Servants' Quarters**

CITY Golf, Illinois

ADDRESS Golf Rd.

DATE 1901

STATUS Built. Not standing 1985

DESCRIPTION One-story frame structure

**326. American Cycle Company
Building**

ADDRESS Institute Pl. and Franklin St.

DATE 1902

STATUS Built. Present status unknown

327. American Cycle

ADDRESS Schiller and Wells Sts. (?)

DATE 1902

STATUS Built. Exact location and present
status unknown

**328. American Medical Association
Building (Building A)**

ADDRESS 537–39 N. Dearborn

DATE 1902–3

STATUS Built. Not standing 1983

DESCRIPTION Three-story brick building

**329. David M. Bernstein Flat and
Shops Building**

ADDRESS 1243 N. Milwaukee Ave.

DATE 1902

STATUS Built. Probably standing

DESCRIPTION Three-story building (?)

**330. Chapman and Smith Company
Building (Acorn Lofts)**

ADDRESS SE corner Washington and
Carpenter Sts.

DATE 1902–4

STATUS Built. Apparently standing 1996

DESCRIPTION Six-story structure of mill
construction

**333. Children's Memorial Hospital—
Maurice Porter Hospital Pavilion**

ADDRESS Fullerton Ave. west of Orchard
St.

DATE 1902–8

STATUS Built. Not standing 1983

DESCRIPTION Two-story brick building

335. Congress Apartment Building (Congress Hotel, Auditorium Annex, Pick-Congress, Pick-Americana) Additions and Alterations
ADDRESS 518–36 S. Michigan Ave.
DATE 1901–2
STATUS Built. Standing 1996
ARCHITECT Clinton J. Warren, original 1893 building; Holabird & Roche, subsequent additions
H&R. COMM. NO. 1901 addition, none; 1905–6 addition, 333
DESCRIPTION Steel frame structure of various heights

336. Liquid Carbonic Acid Manufacturing Company (Carpenter Building)
ADDRESS 430–40 N. Wells St.
DATE 1902–3
STATUS Built. Standing 1996
H&R. COMM. NO. 12
DESCRIPTION Eight-story mill construction commercial building

338. Mandel Brothers Building
ADDRESS NW corner Michigan Ave. and Fourteenth St.
DATE 1902
STATUS Built. Standing 1996, altered
DESCRIPTION One-story brick building

340. Emanuel Mandel Store Building
ADDRESS SW corner Forty-seventh St. and Evans Ave.
DATE 1902
STATUS Built. Standing 1983, not standing 1996
DESCRIPTION One-story brick building

342. Patent Vulcanite Roofing Company
ADDRESS NW corner Ogden and Campbell Aves.
DATE 1902
STATUS Built. Not standing 1996
DESCRIPTION One-story brick structure

344. Republic Building (Strong Building, Adams Building)
ADDRESS 201–11 S. State

DATE 1902–4
STATUS Built. Not standing 1983
H&R. COMM. NO. 56
DESCRIPTION Twelve-story steel frame commercial building

346. Battle Creek City Bank
CITY Battle Creek, Michigan
ADDRESS Unknown
DATE 1902
STATUS Built. Standing (?)
H&R. COMM. NO. 45

347. Calumet Gas and Electric Company Purifying House
CITY Blue Island, Illinois
ADDRESS Unknown
DATE 1902
STATUS Built. Standing (?)
H&R. COMM. NO. Original, none; addition, 23
DESCRIPTION One-story brick building

348. Calumet Gas and Electric Company (Northwestern Light and Coke Company) Power House (Gas House?)
CITY Blue Island, Illinois
ADDRESS Unknown
DATE 1902
STATUS Built. Standing (?)
H&R. COMM. NO. Original, none; addition, 40
DESCRIPTION One- and two-story brick building

349. Grandstand, Hawthorne Racetrack
CITY Cicero, Illinois
ADDRESS 3501 S. Laramie Ave.
DATE 1902
STATUS Built. Not standing 1983
DESCRIPTION Three-story grandstand

351. McHie Building (Hammond Building)
CITY Hammond, Indiana
ADDRESS NE corner Hohman and Fayette Aves.
DATE 1902–3
STATUS Built. Standing 1985

H&R. COMM. NO. 2
DESCRIPTION Five-story brick and terra cotta office building

353. Westward Ho Golf Clubhouse
CITY Oak Park (Mont Clare, Illinois, on drawings)
ADDRESS Unknown
DATE 1902
STATUS Built. Not standing 1983
DESCRIPTION Two-story frame building

354. First State Bank
CITY Petoskey, Michigan
ADDRESS 300 Howard St.
DATE 1902–7
STATUS Built. Standing 1985
H&R. COMM. NO. 25

355. Coleman Lake Club—Clubhouse
CITY Near Goodman, Wisconsin
DATE 1902
STATUS Built. Standing 1984
DESCRIPTION Two-story shingled structure

356. Coleman Lake Club—Steward's Quarters (Superintendent's Quarters, Dining Hall and Kitchen)
CITY Near Goodman, Wisconsin
DATE 1902
STATUS Built. Standing 1984
DESCRIPTION Two-story shingle-covered frame house

357. American Radiator Company Building
ADDRESS 820 (?) S. Michigan Ave.
DATE 1903–4
STATUS Built. Not standing 1984
DESCRIPTION Small commercial building (?)

359. Chicago Savings Bank Building (Chicago Building)
ADDRESS SW corner State and Madison Sts.
DATE 1903–4
STATUS Built. Standing 1996
H&R. COMM. NO. 65
DESCRIPTION Fifteen-story steel frame commercial building

360. Hamilton Building (formerly Weber Department Store)
ADDRESS SE corner Clark and Van Buren Sts.
DATE 1903
STATUS Built. Not standing 1983
H&R. COMM. NO. 73
DESCRIPTION Five-story steel frame building

363. McNeill Building (325 W. Jackson Blvd. Building)
ADDRESS 325 W. Jackson Blvd.
DATE 1903–4 (original); 1910–11 (addition)
STATUS Built. Standing 1983, not standing 1996
H&R. COMM. NO. Original, 135; 1910–11 addition, 1044
DESCRIPTION Ten-story steel frame building

365. Mandel Brothers Warehouse
ADDRESS 3254–58 N. Halsted St.
DATE 1903
STATUS Built. Standing 1996
H&R. COMM. NO. 58
DESCRIPTION Two-story brick structure

366. Ryerson Building (Union Terminals, Palmer Building)
ADDRESS 367 W. Adams St.
DATE 1903–4
STATUS Built. Not standing 1983
H&R. COMM. NO. 198, 239
DESCRIPTION Ten-story building

368. Edwin S. Jackman Residence and Stable
CITY Golf, Illinois
ADDRESS 57 Overlook Dr.
DATE 1903–4
STATUS Built. Standing 1983
H&R. COMM. NO. House, 150; stable, 161
DESCRIPTION Two-story residence, one-story stable

369. First National Exchange Bank (Port Huron Bank)
CITY Port Huron, Michigan
ADDRESS SW corner Huron Ave. and Quay St.

DATE 1903
STATUS Built. Standing (?)
H&R. COMM. NO. 27
DESCRIPTION Two-story office and bank building

370. Union Station Power House
CITY St. Louis, Missouri
ADDRESS 421–25 S. Eighteenth St.
DATE 1903
STATUS Built. Not standing 1987
DESCRIPTION Brick powerhouse with two-hundred-foot stack

371. Farmers' State Bank (D. K. Peterson Building)
CITY Wausa, Nebraska
ADDRESS 522 E. Broadway
DATE 1903
STATUS Built. Standing 1984
H&R. COMM. NO. 34
DESCRIPTION Two-story brick building

373. Cook County Courthouse–Chicago City Hall
ADDRESS Block bounded by Washington, LaSalle, Randolph, and Clark Sts.
DATE 1904–10
STATUS Built. Standing 1996
H&R. COMM. NO. Courthouse, 395; city hall, 605
DESCRIPTION Eleven-story steel frame building

374. Lowney Chocolate Company Building (Meyer Meystel Wholesale Clothing)
ADDRESS 1222–24 S. Wabash Ave.
DATE 1904
STATUS Built. Standing 1996
H&R. COMM. NO. 217
DESCRIPTION Three-story mill construction building

375. Building for Leon Mandel
ADDRESS SW corner Sixty-third St. and Ingleside Ave.
DATE 1904
STATUS Built. Apparently not standing
DESCRIPTION Seven-story building (?)

377. Ryerson Building
ADDRESS 1110–12 W. Lake St.
DATE 1904
STATUS Built. Standing 1996
H&R. COMM. NO. 151
DESCRIPTION Two-story brick manufacturing building

378. Joseph Schaffner Residence
ADDRESS 4819 S. Greenwood Ave.
DATE 1904–5
STATUS Built. Standing 1996
H&R. COMM. NO. 159
DESCRIPTION Two-and-a-half-story brick building

379. Building for Henry Strong
ADDRESS Armitage and Milwaukee Aves.
DATE 1904
STATUS Built. Present status unknown
DESCRIPTION Two-story store and flat building

380. Glen View Club—Cottage C
CITY Golf, Illinois
ADDRESS Golf Rd.
DATE ca. 1904
STATUS Probably built. Not standing 1985
ARCHITECT Holabird & Roche (?)
H&R. COMM. NO. 186 (?)

381. Schipper and Block Building (Jefferson Trust and Savings Bank, Block and Kuhl Department Store)
CITY Peoria, Illinois
ADDRESS 122–26 SW Adams St.
DATE 1904
STATUS Built. Standing 1983
H&R. COMM. NO. 200
DESCRIPTION Seven-story steel frame commercial building

382. Coleman Lake Club—Stearns House (Armour Cottage)
CITY Near Goodman, Wisconsin
DATE 1904
STATUS Built. Standing 1985

383. University Club
ADDRESS 76 E. Monroe St.
DATE 1904–8

STATUS Built. Standing 1996
H&R. COMM. NO. 392
DESCRIPTION Fourteen-story steel frame structure

384. Boston Store (Charles Netcher Building, State-Madison Building)

ADDRESS Madison St. between Dearborn and State Sts.
DATE 1905–7; 1910–12; 1913–16
STATUS Built. Standing 1996
H&R. COMM. NO. 1905, 293; 1911, 1291; 1913, 1865
DESCRIPTION Seventeen-story steel frame department store

385. Delaware Building

ADDRESS 508–16 E. Sixty-third St.
DATE 1905
STATUS Apparently built. Standing (?)

386. Dr. E. Fletcher Ingals Residence and Stable (Brent House)

ADDRESS 5534–40 S. Woodlawn Ave.
DATE 1905–6
STATUS Built. Standing 1996
H&R. COMM. NO. 375
DESCRIPTION Two-story brick residence

387. Kresge Building (Mercantile Building)

ADDRESS 10–14 S. State St.
DATE 1905
STATUS Built. Standing 1983, not standing 1996
H&R. COMM. NO. 229
DESCRIPTION Six-story steel frame building

390. Maurice L. Rothschild Building (Building for Isham Estate)

ADDRESS SW corner State St. and Jackson Blvd.
DATE 1905–6
STATUS Built. Standing 1996
H&R. COMM. NO. 197
DESCRIPTION Eight-story steel frame mercantile building

391. M. A. Ryerson Livery Stable

ADDRESS 38–39 E. Fourteenth St.

DATE 1905
STATUS Probably built. Not standing 1983
DESCRIPTION One- and two-story brick building

392. Lucius Teter Residence

ADDRESS 5637 S. Woodlawn Ave.
DATE 1905
STATUS Built. Standing 1996
H&R. COMM. NO. 408
DESCRIPTION Three-story brick building

393. Bass Estate Building

ADDRESS 2320–39 S. Wabash Ave.
DATE 1905
STATUS Built. Not standing 1983
H&R. COMM. NO. 429
DESCRIPTION One- and two-story mill construction, brick building

395. Masonic Temple

CITY Kewanee, Illinois
ADDRESS Unknown
DATE 1905–6
STATUS Built. Apparently standing
DESCRIPTION Pressed brick and stone building

397. Boston Store West Side Stable

ADDRESS 978–80 W. Madison St.
DATE 1906
STATUS Built. Apparently not standing 1985
H&R. COMM. NO. 483
DESCRIPTION Brick stable

398. Boston Store South Side Stable (Greater Chicago Elks Lodge No. 954)

ADDRESS 4330 S. Vernon Ave.
DATE 1906
STATUS Built. Standing 1996
H&R. COMM. NO. 434
DESCRIPTION Three-story brick stable

399. Chicago Portrait Company Building (Ohio Building)

ADDRESS SE corner Wabash Ave. and Congress Pkwy.
DATE 1906–7
STATUS Built. Not standing 1983

H&R. COMM. NO. 459
DESCRIPTION Four-story brick and terra cotta building

400. Fairbanks, Morse and Company (Fairbanks Lofts)

ADDRESS SW corner Wabash Ave. and Ninth St.
DATE ca. 1906
STATUS Built. Standing 1996
ARCHITECT Christian Eckstorm (with Holabird & Roche?)
DESCRIPTION Eight-story brick building

401. Kohn Building (Brooks Building, Oxford Building)

ADDRESS SE corner Franklin St. and Congress Pkwy.
DATE 1906–7
STATUS Built. Not standing 1983
H&R. COMM. NO. 610
DESCRIPTION Ten-story steel frame building

403. Children's Memorial Hospital— Cribside Pavilion

ADDRESS Orchard St. south of Fullerton Ave.
DATE 1906–8
STATUS Built. Not standing 1983
H&R. COMM. NO. 582
DESCRIPTION Two-story brick structure

404. Congress Hotel Service Building

ADDRESS 63–67 E. Congress Pkwy.
DATE 1906–7
STATUS Built. Not standing 1983
H&R. COMM. NO. 464
DESCRIPTION Two-story brick building

405. Mandel Brothers Store

ADDRESS SE corner Sixty-third St. and Greenwood Ave.
DATE 1906
STATUS Built. Standing 1996 (?)
H&R. COMM. NO. 493
DESCRIPTION Brick store building

406. Mandel Mausoleum

ADDRESS Rosehill Cemetery
DATE 1906
STATUS Built. Standing (?)

407. Store Building for Newberry Library

ADDRESS 705–13 N. Wells St.

DATE 1906

STATUS Built. Standing (?)

H&R. COMM. NO. 399

DESCRIPTION One-story brick shop building

408. Oliver Typewriter Building

ADDRESS 159 N. Dearborn St.

DATE 1906

STATUS Built. Standing 1996

H&R. COMM. NO. 524

DESCRIPTION Five-story steel frame building

409. Plamondon Building

ADDRESS NW corner Clinton and Monroe Sts.

DATE 1906

STATUS Built. Not standing 1983

ARCHITECT Holabird & Roche? Leon E. Stanhope?

DESCRIPTION Seven-story reinforced concrete structure

410. Hotel Sherman (Sherman Hotel IV)

ADDRESS SW corner Randolph and Clark Sts.

DATE 1906–11

STATUS Built. Not standing 1984

H&R. COMM. NO. 533

DESCRIPTION Fifteen-story steel frame structure

411. Arthur Walter (Walker?) Building

ADDRESS NW corner Sixty-third St. and Cottage Grove Ave.

DATE 1906

STATUS Built. Not standing 1985

H&R. COMM. NO. 521

DESCRIPTION One-story brick building

412. Fitzhugh Luther Company Shop Building

CITY Hammond, Indiana

ADDRESS Unknown

DATE 1906

STATUS Built. Standing (?)

H&R. COMM. NO. 510

DESCRIPTION One-story brick shop building

413. J. A. Jameson Residence

CITY Winnetka, Illinois

ADDRESS SW corner of Sheridan Rd. and private road

DATE 1906

STATUS Built. Not standing 1983

H&R. COMM. NO. 373

DESCRIPTION Two-and-a-half-story frame building

415. Harvester Building (Fairbanks-Morse, Columbia College)

ADDRESS SW corner Michigan Ave. and Harrison St.

DATE 1907

STATUS Built. Standing 1996

ARCHITECT C. A. Eckstorm, architect; Holabird & Roche consulting architects

DESCRIPTION Fifteen-story office building

416. Joseph Husser Carriage Garage

ADDRESS 730 W. Buena Ave.

DATE 1907

STATUS Built. Not standing 1983

417. Children's Memorial Hospital— Heating Plant and Laundry House

ADDRESS In block bounded by Fullerton and Lincoln Aves. and Orchard St.

DATE 1907–8

STATUS Built. Not standing 1983

H&R. COMM. NO. 587

DESCRIPTION One-story brick structure

418. Hotel LaSalle

ADDRESS NW corner LaSalle and Madison Sts.

DATE 1907–9

STATUS Built. Not standing 1983

H&R. COMM. NO. 566

DESCRIPTION Twenty-two-story steel frame structure

419. Lincoln Park Comfort House

ADDRESS Near North Ave.

DATE 1907

STATUS Built. Not standing 1983

420. Lincoln Park Bridge

ADDRESS Over lagoon south of Fullerton Ave.

DATE 1907–8

STATUS Built. Not standing 1984

H&R. COMM. NO. 541

DESCRIPTION Reinforced concrete arch bridge

421. Mandel Brothers Store

ADDRESS 1462–64 S. Michigan Ave.

DATE 1907

STATUS Built. Apparently standing 1996

H&R. COMM. NO. 535

DESCRIPTION Three-story brick building

422. Mandel Brothers Stable

ADDRESS SE corner Van Buren St. and Washtenaw Ave.

DATE 1907

STATUS Built. Not standing

H&R. COMM. NO. 609

DESCRIPTION Two-story brick stable

423. Mandel Brothers Warehouse

ADDRESS 1712–14 S. Michigan Ave.

DATE 1907

STATUS Built. Standing 1996, altered

H&R. COMM. NO. 559

DESCRIPTION Three-story brick warehouse building

427. Glen View Club—Caddie and Chauffeur House

CITY Golf, Illinois

ADDRESS Golf Rd.

DATE 1907

STATUS Built. Not standing 1985

H&R. COMM. NO. 561

DESCRIPTION Two-story frame structure

428. Fitzhugh (Frederick?) Luther Residence (Factory Building?)

CITY Hammond, Indiana

ADDRESS Unknown

DATE 1907

STATUS Probably built. Standing (?)

430. Iredale Warehouse (Vance Fireproof Warehouse)

CITY Evanston, Illinois

ADDRESS 1719–25 Benson Ave.

DATE 1907–8
STATUS Built. Standing 1996
H&R. COMM. NO. 554

431. Bauer and Black Unit Two
ADDRESS SW corner Twenty-fifth and
Dearborn Sts.
DATE 1908–9
STATUS Built. Not standing 1984
H&R. COMM. NO. 766
DESCRIPTION Three-story reinforced
concrete factory building

432. Born Building
ADDRESS 540 S. Wells St.
DATE 1908
STATUS Built. Not standing 1996
H&R. COMM. NO. 687
DESCRIPTION Twelve-story reinforced
concrete commercial building

433. Boston Store North Side Stable
ADDRESS 4858 N. Clark St.
DATE 1908
STATUS Built. Standing 1996
H&R. COMM. NO. 736
DESCRIPTION Two-story brick stable

435. Chicago Telephone Company—
Lawndale Exchange
ADDRESS 3608 W. Ogden Ave.
DATE 1908–9
STATUS Built. Not standing 1985
H&R. COMM. NO. 758
DESCRIPTION Three-story fireproof
exchange building

437. Hart, Schaffner, and Marx
Building
ADDRESS NE corner Franklin and Monroe
St.
DATE 1908–10
STATUS Built. Not standing 1983
H&R. COMM. NO. 726
DESCRIPTION Twelve-story steel frame
structure

438. S. Krug Stable and Flat Building
ADDRESS Wentworth Ave. and Twenty-
ninth St.
DATE 1908
STATUS Built. Not standing 1985

H&R. COMM. NO. 735
DESCRIPTION Two-story brick building

439. Cook County Detention Hospital
Airing Yards
ADDRESS NW corner Polk and Wood Sts.
DATE 1908
STATUS Built. Not standing 1985
H&R. COMM. NO. 746

440. Cook County Hospital Stable and
Workshop
ADDRESS 736–38 S. Wolcott St.
DATE 1908
STATUS Built. Not standing 1985
H&R. COMM. NO. 745
DESCRIPTION Two-story brick building

441. Cook County Tuberculosis
Hospital
ADDRESS NE corner Polk and Wolcott Sts.
DATE 1908–9
STATUS Built. Standing 1996
H&R. COMM. NO. 740
DESCRIPTION Four-story structure

442. McCormick Building
ADDRESS NW corner Michigan Ave. and
Van Buren St.
DATE 1908–10 (original ten bays);
1911–12 (additional eight bays)
STATUS Built. Standing 1996
H&R. COMM. NO. Original, 11; addition,
1116
DESCRIPTION Twenty-story office building

444. Cook County Poor Farm
(Cook County Poor House,
Oak Forest Hospital)
CITY Oak Forest, Illinois
ADDRESS SE corner Cicero Ave. and 159th
St.
DATE 1908–10
STATUS Built. Standing 1983
H&R. COMM. NO. 701, 846, 1016, 1021,
1022, and 1033
DESCRIPTION Two-story brick buildings

445. Cook County Poor Farm—
Infirmary Laundry
CITY Oak Forest, Illinois
ADDRESS SE corner Cicero Ave. and
159th St.

DATE 1908–9
STATUS Built. Standing 1983
H&R. COMM. NO. 701
DESCRIPTION One-story brick-clad building

446. Cook County Poor Farm—
Infirmary Power House
and Water Tower
CITY Oak Forest, Illinois
ADDRESS SE corner Cicero Ave. and
159th St.
DATE 1908–10
STATUS Built. Power House standing 1983;
Water Tower not standing
H&R. COMM. NO. 701
DESCRIPTION Brick-clad two-story house

447. Cook County Poor Farm—
Administration Building
CITY Oak Forest, Illinois
ADDRESS SE corner Cicero Ave. and
159th St.
DATE 1908–9
STATUS Built. Standing 1985
H&R. COMM. NO. 701
DESCRIPTION Three-story brick-clad
building

448. Cook County Poor Farm—
General Hospital
CITY Oak Forest, Illinois
ADDRESS SE corner Cicero Ave. and
159th St.
DATE 1908–9
STATUS Built. Standing 1983
H&R. COMM. NO. 701
DESCRIPTION Two-story hospital structure

449. Cook County Poor Farm—
Infirmary Workshop
CITY Oak Forest, Illinois
ADDRESS SE corner Cicero Ave. and
159th St.
DATE 1908–9
STATUS Built. standing 1983
H&R. COMM. NO. 701
DESCRIPTION Two-story brick structure

450. Cook County Poor Farm—
Receiving Building
CITY Oak Forest, Illinois
ADDRESS SE corner Cicero Ave. and
159th St.

DATE 1908–9
STATUS Built. Standing 1983
H&R. COMM. NO. 701
DESCRIPTION Two-story brick building

**452. Cook County Poor Farm—
Recreation Hall and Bathhouse**
CITY Oak Forest, Illinois
ADDRESS SE corner Cicero Ave. and
159th St.
DATE 1908–10
STATUS Built. Apparently standing 1983
H&R. COMM. NO. 701
DESCRIPTION One-story brick building

**453. Cook County Poor Farm—
Building for Aged Couples**
CITY Oak Forest, Illinois
ADDRESS SE corner Cicero Ave. and
159th St.
DATE 1908
STATUS Built. Standing 1983
H&R. COMM. NO. 701
DESCRIPTION Two-story brick building

**454. Cook County Poor Farm—
Ward Buildings**
CITY Oak Forest, Illinois
ADDRESS SE corner Cicero Ave. and
159th St.
DATE 1908–9
STATUS Built. Standing 1983
ARCHITECT Holabird & Roche; Schmidt,
Garden and Martin for addition
H&R. COMM. NO. 701
DESCRIPTION Two-story brick building

**455. Cook County Poor Farm—
Nurses' Home**
CITY Oak Forest, Illinois
ADDRESS SE corner Cicero Ave. and
159th St.
DATE 1908–9
STATUS Built. Standing 1983
H&R. COMM. NO. 701
DESCRIPTION Brick dormitory

**456. Cook County Poor Farm—
Isolation Hospital, Mortuary
Chapel, and Morgue**
CITY Oak Forest, Illinois

ADDRESS SE corner Cicero Ave. and
159th St.
DATE 1908–9
STATUS Built. Standing 1983
H&R. COMM. NO. 701
DESCRIPTION One-story brick building

**457. Illinois Industrial School for
Girls (Park Ridge School
for Girls, Park Ridge Youth
Campus)—Detention Cottage
(Hannah G. Solomon Cottage)**
CITY Park Ridge, Illinois
ADDRESS 733 N. Prospect Ave.
DATE 1908
STATUS Built. Standing 1983
H&R. COMM. NO. 754
DESCRIPTION One-story brick building

**458. Illinois Industrial School for
Girls (Park Ridge School
for Girls, Park Ridge Youth
Campus)—Patten, Talcott, and
Chicago Women's Club Cottages**
CITY Park Ridge, Illinois
ADDRESS 733 N. Prospect Ave.
DATE 1908–10
STATUS Built. Standing 1983
H&R. COMM. NO. 707
DESCRIPTION Brick cottages

**459. Evanston Water Works—
Boiler Room**
CITY Evanston, Illinois
ADDRESS Lincoln St. at Lake Michigan (?)
DATE 1908
STATUS Built. Standing (?)

**460. Coleman Lake Club—
R. W. Cox Cottage**
CITY Near Goodman, Wisconsin
DATE 1908
STATUS Built. Standing 1983
H&R. COMM. NO. 753

**460A. American Medical Association
Building (Building B)**
ADDRESS NE corner Dearborn St. and
Grand Ave.
DATE 1909–10

STATUS Built. Standing 1983, not standing
1996
H&R. COMM. NO. 807
DESCRIPTION Six-story steel frame structure

**464. Brooks Estate Building (Brooks
Building)**
ADDRESS SE corner Jackson Blvd. and
Franklin St.
DATE 1909–10
STATUS Built. Standing 1996
H&R. COMM. NO. 1000
DESCRIPTION Twelve-story steel frame
mercantile structure

**465. Chicago Telephone Company—
Wabash Exchange (Office)**
ADDRESS 514 S. Federal St.
DATE 1909–10
STATUS Built. Standing 1996, reclad
H&R. COMM. NO. Original, 870; 1928
addition, 4957
DESCRIPTION Seven-story steel frame
structure

**466. FIAT Auto Company Building
(Fauch-Lang-Baker Company)**
ADDRESS 2347–53 S. Michigan Ave.
DATE 1909–10
STATUS Built. Standing 1996
H&R. COMM. NO. 907
DESCRIPTION Two-story brick building

467. Goldenberg Brothers Store
CITY Chicago
ADDRESS 1829–31 S. State St.
DATE 1909
STATUS Built. Standing 1996, refaced
H&R. COMM. NO. 831
DESCRIPTION Two-story brick building

**468. Hall Building (Premier Auto Cab
Company)**
ADDRESS 2329–31 S. Michigan Ave.
DATE 1909
STATUS Built. Standing 1996
H&R. COMM. NO. 859
DESCRIPTION Three-story garage

469. Charles J. Happel Building
ADDRESS 4474–4518 N. Broadway (?)
DATE 1909

STATUS Built. Not standing 1985

DESCRIPTION One-story store building

471. Kissel Motor Company

ADDRESS 2515 S. Michigan Ave.

DATE 1909–10

STATUS Built. Not standing 1984

H&R. COMM. NO. 914

DESCRIPTION Three-story garage

473. City Motor Cab Company (Newberry Library Garage)

ADDRESS NE corner Huron St. and Fairbanks Ct.

DATE 1909 (original building); 1910 (addition)

STATUS Built. Not standing 1985

H&R. COMM. NO. Original, 833, addition, 942

DESCRIPTION One-story brick building

474. Mandel Brothers Store (Wieboldt's Department Store, One North State)

ADDRESS NE corner State and Madison Sts.

DATE 1909–12

STATUS Built. Standing 1996

H&R. COMM. NO. 747

DESCRIPTION Fifteen-story steel frame structure

476. Moser Paper Company Building

ADDRESS 621–31 S. Plymouth Ct.

DATE 1909

STATUS Built. Standing 1996

H&R. COMM. NO. 602

DESCRIPTION Nine-story reinforced concrete commercial building

477. Otis Building

ADDRESS SW corner Madison and LaSalle Sts.

DATE 1909–12

STATUS Built. Only lower floor walls standing 1996

H&R. COMM. NO. 801

DESCRIPTION Sixteen-story granite and brick-clad office building

478. Rand McNally Building

ADDRESS Block bounded by Clark, LaSalle, and Harrison Sts. and Congress Pkwy.

DATE 1909–12

STATUS Built. Standing 1996

H&R. COMM. NO. 815

DESCRIPTION Ten-story steel frame building

480. Rothschild and Company Store (Davis Store, Goldblatt's, De Paul Center)

ADDRESS NE corner State and Van Buren Sts.

DATE 1909–12

STATUS Built. Standing 1996

H&R. COMM. NO. 835

DESCRIPTION Ten-story steel frame mercantile building

481. Stoddard-Dayton Building (McDuffee Automobile Company)

ADDRESS NE corner Michigan Ave. and Twenty-fifth St.

DATE 1909

STATUS Built. Not standing 1983

H&R. COMM. NO. 881

DESCRIPTION Four-story brick garage

482. E. P. Thomas Garage (Flyer, Flynn [?], Chalmers Garage)

ADDRESS 2255–59 S. Michigan Ave.

DATE 1909–10

STATUS Built. Standing 1996

H&R. COMM. NO. 894

DESCRIPTION Three-story reinforced concrete building

483. University of Chicago— Departments of Geology and Geography (Julius Rosenwald Hall; School of Business)

ADDRESS 1011 E. Fifty-eighth St.

DATE 1909–14; 1909 (preliminary scheme); 1913–14 (new scheme and construction)

STATUS Built. Standing 1996

H&R. COMM. NO. 1909 preliminary scheme, 840; version dated 1914, 1856

DESCRIPTION Four-story structure with six-story tower

484. University School for Girls

ADDRESS 1106–14 N. Lake Shore Dr.

DATE 1909–10

STATUS Built. Not standing 1983

H&R. COMM. NO. 848

DESCRIPTION Four-story building

489. Cook County Poor Farm— Infirmary Buildings for Irresponsibles

CITY Oak Forest, Illinois

ADDRESS SE corner Cicero Ave. and 159th St.

DATE 1909

STATUS Built. Standing 1983

ARCHITECT Holabird & Roche; Schmidt, Garden and Martin

H&R. COMM. NO. 846

DESCRIPTION One-story brick-clad wards

490. Cook County Poor Farm— Farmhouse

CITY Oak Forest, Illinois

ADDRESS SE corner Cicero Ave. and 159th St.

DATE 1909–10

STATUS Built. Not standing 1983

H&R. COMM. NO. 1016

DESCRIPTION Two-story brick farmhouse

492. City National Bank

CITY Omaha, Nebraska

ADDRESS SE corner Sixteenth and Harvey Sts.

DATE 1909–10

STATUS Built. Standing 1983

H&R. COMM. NO. 885

DESCRIPTION Sixteen-floor office and bank building

493. Leland Hotel

CITY Springfield, Illinois

ADDRESS NW corner Sixth and Capitol Sts.

DATE 1909–11

STATUS Built. Standing 1983

H&R. COMM. NO. 893

DESCRIPTION Nine-story brick-clad, reinforced concrete structure

**494. Commonwealth Edison—
Northwest Station**
ADDRESS NW corner California Ave. and
Roscoe St.
DATE 1910–15
STATUS Built. Partially standing 1983, not
standing 1996
H&R. COMM. NO. 946; 1743
DESCRIPTION Two- and three-story
buildings including a substation

**496. Automobile Building for A.
Cowles (Cadillac Building)**
ADDRESS SE corner Twenty-third St. and
S. Michigan Ave.
DATE 1910–11
STATUS Built. Standing 1996
H&R. COMM. NO. 980
DESCRIPTION Five-story automobile
showroom building

**497. Crane Manufacturing Company
Building**
ADDRESS Unknown
DATE ca. 1910
STATUS Probably built. Standing (?)

498. Great Lakes Building
ADDRESS SW corner Lake St. and Wacker
Dr.
DATE 1910–12
STATUS Built. Standing 1996
H&R. COMM. NO. 1125
DESCRIPTION Six-story trapezoidal brick-
clad commercial structure

499. H. G. Hart House
ADDRESS 5036–38 S. Ellis Ave.
DATE 1910–11
STATUS Built. Standing 1996
H&R. COMM. NO. 988
DESCRIPTION Two-and-a-half-story brick
structure

**500. Chicago Telephone Company
(Illinois Bell Telephone)
Central Division Barn**
ADDRESS 1531–39 W. Harrison St.
DATE 1910
STATUS Built. Not standing 1985
H&R. COMM. NO. 1885

504. Monroe Building
ADDRESS SW corner Michigan Ave. and
Monroe St.
DATE 1910–12
STATUS Built. Standing 1996
H&R. COMM. NO. 789
DESCRIPTION Fourteen-story steel frame
office structure

507. M. N. Rothschild Residence
ADDRESS NE corner Michigan Ave. and
Thirty-ninth St.
DATE 1910
STATUS Built. Not standing 1984
H&R. COMM. NO. 817
DESCRIPTION Three-story stone and brick
residence

**508. Building for Martin Ryerson
(Ryerson Warehouse)**
ADDRESS 1132–34 S. Wabash Ave.
DATE 1910
STATUS Built. Standing 1996
H&R. COMM. NO. 1059
DESCRIPTION Six-story brick-clad building

511. Building for J. Tait and M. Roche
ADDRESS 715–19 E. Forth-seventh St.
DATE 1910
STATUS Built. Standing 1983, not standing
1996
DESCRIPTION One-story building

**514. Cook County Poor Farm—
Chapel**
CITY Oak Forest, Illinois
ADDRESS SE corner Cicero Ave. and
159th St.
DATE 1910
STATUS Built. Standing 1983
H&R. COMM. NO. 846
DESCRIPTION Cross-shaped chapel

**515. Cook County Poor Farm—Ward
Building for Tubercular Inmates**
CITY Oak Forest, Illinois
ADDRESS SE corner Cicero Ave. and
159th St.
DATE 1910
STATUS Built. Standing 1983
H&R. COMM. NO. 1106

DESCRIPTION Two-story brick ward
building

**516. Cook County Poor Farm—
Medical and General
Superintendents' Houses**
CITY Oak Forest, Illinois
ADDRESS SE corner Cicero Ave. and
159th St.
DATE 1910
STATUS Built. General Superintendent's
house only standing 1983
H&R. COMM. NO. 846
DESCRIPTION Two identical residences

**517. Cook County Poor Farm—
Service Buildings**
CITY Oak Forest, Illinois
ADDRESS SE corner Cicero Ave. and
159th St.
DATE 1910–11
STATUS Built. Standing 1983
H&R. COMM. NO. 1021
DESCRIPTION Food service and dining
facilities

518. Woodmen of the World Building
CITY Omaha, Nebraska
ADDRESS SE corner Farnam and
Fourteenth Sts.
DATE 1910–12
STATUS Built. Not standing 1983
ARCHITECT Holabird & Roche; Fisher and
Lawrie, associate architects,
Omaha, Nebraska
H&R. COMM. NO. 897
DESCRIPTION Eighteen-story steel frame
building

**519. Illinois Industrial School for
Girls (Park Ridge School
for Girls, Park Ridge Youth
Campus)—Household Economics
Building (Straut School)**
CITY Park Ridge, Illinois
ADDRESS 733 N. Prospect Ave.
DATE 1910
STATUS Built. Standing 1983
H&R. COMM. NO. 764
DESCRIPTION Two-story brick building

520. Illinois Industrial School for Girls (Park Ridge School for Girls, Park Ridge Campus) Ida Noyes Cottage

CITY Park Ridge, Illinois
ADDRESS 733 N. Prospect Ave.
DATE 1910
STATUS Built. Standing 1983
H&R. COMM. NO. 1065
DESCRIPTION Two-story brick building

521. Illinois Industrial School for Girls (Park Ridge School for Girls, Park Ridge Youth Campus)—Shelter

CITY Park Ridge, Illinois
ADDRESS 733 N. Prospect Ave.
DATE 1910
STATUS Built. Not standing 1983
H&R. COMM. NO. 844
DESCRIPTION One-story square frame building

523. Anderson Carriage Company (Bland Garage, Northwestern University Garage, Detroit Electric Company Service Station)

CITY Evanston, Illinois
ADDRESS SE corner Clark and Benson Sts.
DATE 1910
STATUS Built. Standing 1985, not standing 1996
H&R. COMM. NO. 989
DESCRIPTION One-story garage

527. Brandies Residence and Garage

ADDRESS 6854 S. Bennett Ave.
DATE 1911
STATUS Built. Standing 1996
H&R. COMM. NO. 1315
DESCRIPTION Two-story stucco-covered frame residence

529. Chicago Telephone Company— Bell Building

ADDRESS 212–16 W. Washington St.
DATE 1911–12
STATUS Built. Standing 1996
H&R. COMM. NO. 966

DESCRIPTION Twenty-story steel frame building

530. Chicago Telephone Company— Belmont Office

ADDRESS SW corner Central Park Ave. and Cortland St.
DATE 1911–12
STATUS Built. Standing 1996
H&R. COMM. NO. 1071
DESCRIPTION One-story and part two-story building

531. Children's Memorial Hospital— Observation Ward Building (Agnes Wilson Memorial Pavilion)

ADDRESS South side Fullerton Ave. west of Orchard St.
DATE 1911–12
STATUS Built. Not standing 1983
H&R. COMM. NO. 1244
DESCRIPTION Three-story building with one- and two-story wings

534. Crane Company Office Building

ADDRESS SE corner Canal and Maxwell Sts.
DATE 1911
STATUS Built. Not standing 1983
H&R. COMM. NO. 1298
DESCRIPTION Six-story brick office building

535. Arthur Dixon Transfer Company Barn

ADDRESS 1321–29 S. State St.
DATE 1911
STATUS Built. Not standing 1985
H&R. COMM. NO. 1300
DESCRIPTION Four-story brick building

538. Madison Terminal Building

ADDRESS SE corner Madison and Clinton Sts.
DATE 1911–12
STATUS Built. Not standing 1983
H&R. COMM. NO. 1370
DESCRIPTION Eight-story structure

542. North American Building

ADDRESS NW corner State and Monroe Sts.

DATE 1911–12
STATUS Built. Standing 1996
H&R. COMM. NO. 998
DESCRIPTION Nineteen-story steel frame structure

543. Mrs. Lawrence D. Rockwell Residence

ADDRESS SW corner Lake Shore Dr. and Goethe Sts.
DATE 1911
STATUS Built. Standing 1996
H&R. COMM. NO. 1104
DESCRIPTION Four-story residence

547. Huron Mountain Club—Judge George A. Carpenter Cabin

CITY Near Big Bay, Michigan
DATE 1911–12
STATUS Built. Standing 1985
H&R. COMM. NO. 1333
DESCRIPTION T-shaped log house

548. Marlowe (Marlo in Holabird & Roche Records) Exchange

CITY Lakewood, Ohio
ADDRESS NE corner Detroit and Marlowe Sts.
DATE 1911–12
STATUS Built. Standing 1985
H&R. COMM. NO. 1287
DESCRIPTION Three-story structure

549. Chicago Telephone Company Building Number 2

CITY Gary, Indiana
ADDRESS 225 Madison St.
DATE 1911
STATUS Built. Apparently standing 1985
H&R. COMM. NO. 1273
DESCRIPTION Two-story brick- and terra cotta–faced building

551. Mount Prospect National Bank

CITY Mount Prospect, Illinois
ADDRESS NE corner Main and Busse Sts.
DATE 1911
STATUS Built. Apparently not standing
H&R. COMM. NO. Unknown
DESCRIPTION One-story bank building

556. Chicago Telephone Company— River Forest Barn
CITY River Forest, Illinois
ADDRESS Unknown
DATE 1911
STATUS Built. Standing (?)
DESCRIPTION Two-story brick barn

557. Dr. D. R. Brower Residence
CITY Wilmette, Illinois
ADDRESS SE corner Washington Ct. and Fifth St.
DATE 1911–12
STATUS Built. Standing 1984
H&R. COMM. NO. 1398
DESCRIPTION Three-story brick house

559. Allegretti Chocolate Cream Company Store
ADDRESS McCormick Bldg., NW corner Michigan Ave. and Van Buren St.
DATE 1912
STATUS Built. Not standing 1983
H&R. COMM. NO. 1460
DESCRIPTION One-story store interior

560. Beckley Ralston Company Building
ADDRESS SE corner Michigan Ave. and Eighteenth St.
DATE 1912–13
STATUS Built. Standing 1996
H&R. COMM. NO. 1624
DESCRIPTION Six-story structure of mill construction

561. Chicago Nursery and Half Orphan Asylum (Chapin Hall)
ADDRESS SW corner California and Foster Aves.
DATE 1912–16
STATUS Built. Standing 1984, not standing 1996
H&R. COMM. NO. 1439
DESCRIPTION Main building and small outbuildings

562. Commonwealth Edison Company—Ravenswood Station
ADDRESS 4646 N. Lincoln Ave.
DATE 1912–13
STATUS Built. Standing 1996
H&R. COMM. NO. 1594
DESCRIPTION One-story substation

563. Crane Company Building
ADDRESS NW corner Michigan Ave. and Ninth St.
DATE 1912–13
STATUS Built. Standing 1996
H&R. COMM. NO. 1429
DESCRIPTION Twelve-story structure

564. Fort Dearborn Hotel (LaSalle Atrium Building)
ADDRESS SE corner LaSalle and Van Buren Sts.
DATE 1912
STATUS Built. Standing 1996
H&R. COMM. NO. 1346
DESCRIPTION Seventeen-story steel frame construction hotel

570. Chicago Telephone Company— Berwyn Exchange
CITY Berwyn, Illinois
ADDRESS Harlem Ave.
DATE 1912–13
STATUS Built. Apparently not standing 1985
H&R. COMM. NO. 1641

571. M. L. Barrett and Company Factory—New Building
CITY Cicero, Illinois
ADDRESS NE corner Fifty-first Ave. and Sixteenth St.
DATE 1912–13
STATUS Built. Standing 1985
H&R. COMM. NO. 1606
DESCRIPTION Three-story reinforced concrete structure

574. Hotel Wisconsin
CITY Milwaukee, Wisconsin
ADDRESS 172–76 Third St.
DATE 1912–13
STATUS Built. Standing 1984
H&R. COMM. NO. 1585
DESCRIPTION Eleven-story steel frame structure

575A. Evangelical Lutheran Church
CITY Mount Prospect, Illinois
ADDRESS NE corner Elm and Busse Sts.
DATE 1912–13
STATUS Built. Not standing 1984
H&R. COMM. NO. 157
DESCRIPTION Cross-shaped brick church

580. Louis A. Ferguson Residence
CITY Evanston, Illinois
ADDRESS NE corner Wesley Ave. and Davis St.
DATE 1912–15
STATUS Built. Standing 1996
H&R. COMM. NO. 1416; garage, 2322
DESCRIPTION Two-story house

583. Building for Peter C. Brooks
ADDRESS SE corner Milwaukee and North Aves.
DATE 1913
STATUS Built. Standing 1996
H&R. COMM. NO. 1617
DESCRIPTION Three-story triangular store and office building

585. Century (State and Adams, Buck and Rayner) Building
ADDRESS SW corner State and Adams Sts.
DATE 1913–16
STATUS Built. Standing 1996
H&R. COMM. NO. 1803
DESCRIPTION Sixteen-story steel frame structure

587. Chicago Telephone Company— Beverly Office Building
ADDRESS 1620 W. Ninety-ninth St.
DATE 1913
STATUS Built. Standing 1996
H&R. COMM. NO. 1786
DESCRIPTION Three-story building

588. Chicago Telephone Company— Rogers Park Office Building
ADDRESS 1622 W. Pratt Blvd.
DATE 1913–15
STATUS Built. Standing 1996
H&R. COMM. NO. 1933
DESCRIPTION Three-story reinforced concrete structure

**589. Chicago Telephone Company—
Stewart Office Building
(Toll Building Number 3)**

ADDRESS NE corner Eggleston Ave. and
Seventy-sixth St.

DATE 1913–14

STATUS Built. Standing 1996

H&R. COMM. NO. 1700

DESCRIPTION Three-story structure

590. John Crerar Library

ADDRESS NW corner Michigan Ave. and
Randolph St.

DATE 1913–20

STATUS Built. Not standing 1985

H&R. COMM. NO. 1989

DESCRIPTION Sixteen-story steel frame
building

591. Graceland Cemetery—Barn

ADDRESS West side of Clark St. north of
Irving Park Rd.

DATE 1913–15

STATUS Built. Standing 1996

H&R. COMM. NO. 1728; shelter, 2305; fence,
2015

DESCRIPTION Trapezoidal complex

**593. Chicago Telephone Company
(Illinois Bell Telephone)—Irving
Office (now residential building)**

ADDRESS 3312 W. Belle Plaine Ave.

DATE 1913–15

STATUS Built. Standing 1996

H&R. COMM. NO. 1847

DESCRIPTION Three-story reinforced
concrete structure

594. Building for Roy D. Keehn

ADDRESS 634–46 N. Western Ave.

DATE 1913

STATUS Built. Standing 1996 (?)

H&R. COMM. NO. 1672

DESCRIPTION Two-story brick-walled
structure

**595. Lakeview Trust and Savings
Bank Building**

ADDRESS 3201–5 N. Ashland Ave.

DATE 1913–14

STATUS Built. Standing 1996, altered

H&R. COMM. NO. 1904

DESCRIPTION Two-story brick building with
terra cotta facing

**596. Lumber Exchange Building
(Roanoke Building)**

ADDRESS SE corner LaSalle and Madison
Sts.

DATE 1913–15 (original sixteen stories);
1922 (additional stories); 1925
(tower addition)

STATUS Built. Standing 1996

ARCHITECT Holabird & Roche (Rebori,
Wentworth, Dewey, and
McCormick Inc., associated
architects for 1925 addition)

H&R. COMM. NO. Original sixteen stories,
1869; five additional stories, 3490;
tower addition, 3925

DESCRIPTION Sixteen-story building (five
stories added 1922, thirty-six-story
tower addition 1925)

**597. Cigar Factory Building for
Newberry Library**

ADDRESS 215–17 W. Chicago Ave.

DATE 1913

STATUS Built. Standing 1996

H&R. COMM. NO. 1687

DESCRIPTION Two-story mill construction
building

**598. Store Building for Newberry
Library**

ADDRESS 1010 N. State St.

DATE 1913

STATUS Built. Not standing 1983

H&R. COMM. NO. 1280

**600. Building for Rothschild and
Company**

ADDRESS 324–28 S. Wabash Ave.

DATE 1913

STATUS Built. Not standing 1985

H&R. COMM. NO. 1726

DESCRIPTION Three-story mill construction
building

601. Three Arts Club

ADDRESS NW corner Dearborn and
Goethe Sts.

DATE 1913–14

STATUS Built. Standing 1996

H&R. COMM. NO. 1915

DESCRIPTION Four-story U-shaped brick
residential clubhouse

**602. Joseph E. Tilt Residence
(Salvation Army dormitory)**

ADDRESS 700 W. Brompton Ave.

DATE 1913

STATUS Built. Standing 1996

H&R. COMM. NO. 1754

DESCRIPTION Three-story house

**604. Huron Mountain Club—
A. L. Farwell Log Cabin**

CITY Near Big Bay, Michigan

DATE 1913

STATUS Built. Standing 1985

H&R. COMM. NO. 1765

607. Hotel Muehlebach

CITY Kansas City, Missouri

ADDRESS SW corner Baltimore Ave. and
Twelfth St.

DATE 1913–15

STATUS Built. Standing 1984, not standing
1996

ARCHITECT Holabird & Roche; Baird and
Huselton, associated architects (?)

H&R. COMM. NO. 1727

DESCRIPTION Ten-story brick- and terra
cotta–clad hotel

610. John Taylor Dry Goods Store

CITY Kansas City, Missouri

ADDRESS 1034–40 Main Street

DATE 1913–15

STATUS Built. Standing 1983

H&R. COMM. NO. 1707

DESCRIPTION Six-story steel frame building

611. Terminal Arcade Building

CITY Kansas City, Missouri

ADDRESS Unknown

DATE 1913

STATUS Probably built. Standing (?)

H&R. COMM. NO. Unknown

612. BPOE Clubhouse

CITY Muskegon, Michigan

ADDRESS SW corner Western Ave. and Second St.
DATE 1913–14
STATUS Built. Not standing 1983
H&R COMM. NO. 1719
DESCRIPTION Three-story reinforced concrete building

614. Hotel Deming
CITY Terre Haute, Indiana
ADDRESS Cherry and Sixth Sts.
DATE 1913–14
STATUS Built. Standing 1982
H&R COMM. NO. 1816
DESCRIPTION Eight-story reinforced concrete construction hotel

615. Central Union Telephone (Central Union Telegraph? Illinois Bell Telephone Company)—Rock Island Exchange
CITY Rock Island, Illinois
ADDRESS 635 Eighteenth St.
DATE 1913–14
STATUS Built. Apparently standing 1983
H&R COMM. NO. 1804
DESCRIPTION Two-story structure

617. Chicago Telephone Company— Hyde Park Office Building
ADDRESS 6045 S. Kenwood Ave.
DATE 1914
STATUS Built. Standing 1996
H&R COMM. NO. 1920
DESCRIPTION Four-story structure

618. Chicago Telephone Company— Lakeview Office
ADDRESS 3528–36 N. Sheffield Ave.
DATE 1914
STATUS Built. Standing 1996
H&R COMM. NO. 2072
DESCRIPTION Four-story brick-clad structure

619. Chicago Telephone Company— Prospect Office
ADDRESS 6316–22 S. Claremont Ave.
DATE 1914–16
STATUS Built. Standing 1996
H&R COMM. NO. 2021 (?)
DESCRIPTION Three-story structure

620. Chicago Telephone Company— Pullman Central Office
ADDRESS 165 W. 113th Pl.
DATE 1914–16
STATUS Built. Standing 1996
H&R COMM. NO. 2099
DESCRIPTION Two-story structure

622. S. I. Frank Building
ADDRESS 2412–16 W. North Ave.
DATE 1914
STATUS Built. Standing 1996
H&R COMM. NO. 1713
DESCRIPTION Four-story brick and mill construction building

624. State and Harrison Building
ADDRESS SE coirner State and Harrison Sts.
DATE 1914
STATUS Built. Not standing 1983
H&R COMM. NO. 1967
DESCRIPTION Two-story U-shaped brick structure

626. University of Chicago— Laboratory Building (Ricketts Lab)
ADDRESS 5724 S. Ellis Ave.
DATE 1914
STATUS Built. Demolished 1983
H&R COMM. NO. 2110
DESCRIPTION One-story E-shaped brick laboratory

629. C. W. Case Deering Residence
CITY Honolulu, Hawaii
ADDRESS Waikiki Beach
DATE 1914–17
STATUS Built. Not standing 1983
H&R COMM. NO. 2085
DESCRIPTION One-story rectangular concrete residence

634. Chicago Telephone Company— Austin Office Building
ADDRESS 5155 W. Fulton St.
DATE 1915–17
STATUS Built. Standing 1996
H&R COMM. NO. 2315
DESCRIPTION Three-story brick building

635. Chicago Telephone Company— Calumet Office Building
ADDRESS 2215 S. Wabash Ave.
DATE 1915–17
STATUS Built. Standing 1996
H&R COMM. NO. 2234
DESCRIPTION Four-story building

636. Chicago Telephone Company— South Chicago Central Office
ADDRESS NW corner Marquette Ave. and Eighty-ninth St.
DATE 1915–17
STATUS Built. Standing 1996
H&R COMM. NO. 2344
DESCRIPTION Three-story structure

640. Elite Garage
ADDRESS Unknown
DATE 1915
STATUS Probably built. Standing (?)

641. Franklin Motor Car Company
ADDRESS 2315–17 S. Michigan Ave.
DATE ca. 1915
STATUS Built. Standing (?)
DESCRIPTION Two-story white terra cotta–clad building (?)

643. Studio for John Holabird and John Root
ADDRESS SW corner Lake Shore Dr. and Elm St.
DATE 1915
STATUS Built. Not standing 1983
H&R COMM. NO. 2355
DESCRIPTION One-story tile-walled building

644. Chicago Telephone Company (Illinois Bell Telephone)— Franklin Exchange
ADDRESS 311–27 W. Washington St.
DATE 1915–20
STATUS Built. Standing 1996
H&R COMM. NO. 2429
DESCRIPTION Eleven-story building faced in brick and stone

645. Garage Building for Dr. E. Fletcher Ingals
ADDRESS Harper Ave. at Fifty-sixth St.
DATE 1915

STATUS Built. Not standing 1985
DESCRIPTION One-story garage building

646. W. Gifford Jones House
CITY Evanston, Illinois
ADDRESS 2878 Sheridan Pl.
DATE 1915
STATUS Built. Standing 1996
H&R. COMM. NO. 2204
DESCRIPTION Two-story brick house

647. W. G. Jones Factory
CITY Evanston, Illinois
ADDRESS Unknown
DATE 1915–16
STATUS Built. Standing(?)
H&R. COMM. NO. 2349

**650. A. Cowles Automobile Buildings
(Saxon Building—Southern)**
ADDRESS 2309–13 S. Michigan Ave.
DATE 1915
STATUS Built. Standing 1996
H&R. COMM. NO. 2258
DESCRIPTION Two adjacent three-story
brick automobile buildings

651. Dr. Otto J. Stein Residence
ADDRESS 514–22 W. Hawthorne Pl.
DATE 1915–17
STATUS Built. Not standing 1984
H&R. COMM. NO. 2310
DESCRIPTION Two-story brick house with
stone trim

**653. Chicago Tribune Color Press
Building**
ADDRESS 427–39 E. Ontario St.
DATE 1915–16
STATUS Built. Not standing 1985
H&R. COMM. NO. 2255
DESCRIPTION One-story brick structure

657. Deshler Hotel
CITY Columbus, Ohio
ADDRESS Broad, High, and Wall Sts.
DATE 1915–16
STATUS Built. Not standing 1983
H&R. COMM. NO. 1591
DESCRIPTION Twelve-story steel frame hotel

**660. Chicago Telephone
Company Barn**
CITY Harvey, Illinois
ADDRESS Unknown
DATE 1915
STATUS Probably built. Standing (?)
H&R. COMM. NO. 2308
DESCRIPTION One-story brick-clad building

**661. Plankinton Arcade
(Grand Avenue Arcade)**
CITY Milwaukee, Wisconsin
ADDRESS 161 W. Wisconsin Ave.
DATE 1915–16 (original); 1924 (five-story
addition)
STATUS Built. Standing 1996 (as part of
Grand Avenue Mall)
H&R. COMM. NO. Original, 2089, 2572;
addition, 3142
DESCRIPTION Terra cotta–clad commercial
arcade

663. Fred J. Thielbar Residence
CITY River Forest, Illinois
ADDRESS 246 Keystone Ave.
DATE 1915–16
STATUS Probably built. Standing (?)
H&R. COMM. NO. 2376
DESCRIPTION Two-story brick veneer frame
house

**666. Margaret Mackin Hall (Illinois
Bell Telephone) Camp**
CITY Warrenville, Illinois
DATE 1915–16
STATUS Built. Standing (?)
H&R. COMM. NO. 2343
DESCRIPTION Numerous buildings

**669. Chicago Telephone Company—
Kildare Exchange (Warner
Avenue Building)**
ADDRESS 4923 W. Warner Ave.
DATE 1916–17
STATUS Built. Not standing 1983
H&R. COMM. NO. 2462
DESCRIPTION Three-story building

**670. Chicago Telephone Company—
McKinley Exchange (Lafayette)**
ADDRESS 2240 W. Thirty-seventh St.
DATE 1916–17

STATUS Built. Standing 1996
H&R. COMM. NO. 2469
DESCRIPTION Three-story reinforced
concrete building

**672. First Cavalry Armory
(Second Artillery Armory)**
ADDRESS Chicago Ave. east of Seneca St.
DATE 1916–17
STATUS Built. Standing 1984, demolished
1994
H&R. COMM. NO. 2154
DESCRIPTION Six-story reinforced concrete
structure

673. George W. Griffiths Residence
ADDRESS 6011 N. Sheridan Rd.
DATE 1916
STATUS Built. Not standing 1985
H&R. COMM. NO. 2446
DESCRIPTION Two-and-a-half-story
colonial-style brick house

**674. Nestor Johnson Manufacturing
Company**
ADDRESS NE corner California Ave. and
Crystal St.
DATE 1916
STATUS Built. Standing 1996
H&R. COMM. NO. 2438
DESCRIPTION Two-story brick building

**675. LaSalle Garage
(Washington Warehouse)**
ADDRESS 217–19 W. Washington St.
DATE 1916–18
STATUS Built. Standing 1996
H&R. COMM. NO. 2629
DESCRIPTION Five-story reinforced concrete
structure

**676. Francis W. Parker School—
Gymnasium**
ADDRESS 330 W. Webster St.
DATE 1916–17
STATUS Built. Not standing 1983
DESCRIPTION One- and two-story brick
structure

**678. Illinois Bell Telephone—
Warehouse and Garage**
CITY Aurora, Illinois
ADDRESS Second Ave. and CB&Q railroad

467

DATE 1916–17

STATUS Built. Apparently not standing 1986

680. Chicago Telephone Company— Geneva Central Office

CITY Geneva, Illinois

ADDRESS 127 S. First St.

DATE 1916–18

STATUS Built. Standing 1983

DESCRIPTION Two-story brick- and stone-clad structure

681. Illinois Bell Telephone Company—Warehouse and Garage

CITY Hammond, Indiana

ADDRESS Hudson St. and Chicago Ave.

DATE 1916–17

STATUS Built. Standing (?)

H&R. COMM. NO. 2513

DESCRIPTION One-story warehouse and garage building

682. Illinois Bell Telephone Company—Garage and Storehouse

CITY Joliet, Illinois

ADDRESS De Kalb and Water Sts.

DATE 1916–17

STATUS Built. Standing (?)

683. Dibble Building

CITY Kansas City, Missouri

ADDRESS 1009–17 McGee St.

DATE 1916

STATUS Built. Standing 1983

ARCHITECT S. E. Edwards; Holabird & Roche, associate architects (?)

684. Wheeler Convalescent House— Laundry Building

CITY Lake Bluff, Illinois

ADDRESS Unknown

DATE 1916–17

STATUS Apparently built. Standing (?)

H&R. COMM. NO. 2599

685. J. C. Mechem Residence

CITY Lake Forest, Illinois

ADDRESS 436 Woodland Rd.

DATE 1916–17

STATUS Built. Standing 1984

H&R. COMM. NO. 2495

DESCRIPTION Clapboard-covered frame house

687. Lane Bryant Building (Brisbane Building)

CITY New York, New York

ADDRESS 21–23 W. Thirty-eighth St.

DATE 1916

STATUS Built. Standing 1984

ARCHITECT Lucien Smith; Holabird & Roche probably associated architects

H&R. COMM. NO. 2461

DESCRIPTION Sixteen-story commercial and studio building

688. Michigan Children's Hospital (Child and Family Services of Michigan)

CITY St. Joseph, Michigan

ADDRESS 2000 S. State St.

DATE 1916

STATUS Built. Standing 1985

H&R. COMM. NO. 2182

DESCRIPTION Three-story brick-walled building with interior concrete frame

689. University of Illinois— Educational Building (University High School)

CITY Urbana, Illinois

ADDRESS Springfield and Matthew Aves. and Stoughton St.

DATE 1916–20

STATUS Built. Standing 1983

ARCHITECT Holabird & Roche and James M. White, university supervising architect

H&R. COMM. NO. 2430

DESCRIPTION Three-story building

690. Chicago Telephone Company— Waukegan Barn

CITY Waukegan, Illinois

ADDRESS Unknown

DATE 1916–17

STATUS Built. Standing (?)

H&R. COMM. NO. 2453

DESCRIPTION One-story brick structure

691. Accounting Devices Building

CITY Evanston, Illinois

ADDRESS Benson Ave. and Emerson St.

DATE 1916

STATUS Built. Not standing 1985

DESCRIPTION One-story structure

693. Garrett Biblical Institute (Garrett Evangelical Theological Institute)

CITY Evanston, Illinois

ADDRESS Sheridan Rd. at Garrett St.

DATE 1916–23 (dormitories commissioned 1916, constructed 1916–17; recitation hall commissioned 1917, constructed 1922–23)

STATUS Built. Standing 1996

H&R. COMM. NO. dormitories, 2418; recitation hall, 2730

DESCRIPTION Four-story recitation hall flanked by three-story dormitories

695. Bauer and Black Unit Nine

ADDRESS SW corner Twenty-fifth and Federal Sts.

DATE 1917–18

STATUS Built. Not standing 1984

H&R. COMM. NO. 2736, 2899

DESCRIPTION Three-story mill construction factory building

697. Garage for P. C. Brooks

ADDRESS 1923–29 W. North Ave.

DATE 1917

STATUS Built. Standing 1996

DESCRIPTION One-story structure

701. R. J. Ederer Company Building

ADDRESS SW corner Orleans and Ohio Sts.

DATE 1917–18

STATUS Built. Not standing 1983

H&R. COMM. NO. 2721

DESCRIPTION Four-story mill construction factory building

703. Illinois Training School for Nurses—Laundry Building

ADDRESS 590 S. Monroe St.

DATE 1917

STATUS Built. Not standing 1983

H&R. COMM. NO. 2794

DESCRIPTION One-story brick building

708. Billy Sunday Tabernacle
ADDRESS Block bounded by Fairbanks Ct., Chicago Ave., Superior St., and Lake Shore Dr.
DATE 1917–18
STATUS Built. Not standing 1983
ARCHITECT J. H. Speisce; Jess Henderson, associate architect; Holabird & Roche, consulting architects
H&R. COMM. NO. 2703
DESCRIPTION Temporary all-wood tabernacle

716. Wesley Foundation Social Center Building
CITY Urbana, Illinois
ADDRESS SW corner Green and Goodwin Sts.
DATE 1917–21
STATUS Built. Standing 1984
H&R. COMM. NO. 2685
DESCRIPTION Two-story U-shaped building

Chapter One

1. The story of the founding of the firm is given in Charles E. Jenkins, "A Review of the Work of Holabird & Roche," *Architectural Reviewer* 3 (June 1897): 1–41. This account is retold nearly verbatim in all later histories.

2. Probably the best introduction to Chicago's physical development is Harold M. Mayer and Richard C. Wade's *Chicago: Growth of a Metropolis* (Chicago, 1969), a prodigious work of scholarship to which this book is deeply indebted. On visitors' reactions, see Bessie Louise Pierce, *As Others See Chicago: Impressions of Visitors, 1873–1933* (Chicago, 1933).

3. For an account of the economic interdependence of Chicago and its vast hinterland, see the masterly study by William Cronon, *Nature's Metropolis: Chicago and the Great West* (New York, 1991).

4. Adna Ferrin Weber, *Growth of Cities in the Nineteenth Century* (New York, 1899), 174. For some excellent observations on the "booster" nature of this kind of passage see Cronon, *Nature's Metropolis*, 34–41.

5. On the train as symbol of the city's modernity, see Carl S. Smith, *Chicago and the American Literary Imagination, 1880–1920* (Chicago, 1984), 10–11, 106–17.

6. See, for example, Hamlin Garland's description in *Rose of Dutcher's Coolly* (New York, 1899), 56: "Rose looked—far to the southeast a gigantic smoke-cloud soared above the low horizon line, in shape like an eagle, whose hovering wings extended from south to east, trailing mysterious shadows upon the earth. The sun lighted its mighty crest with crimson light, and its gloom and glow became each moment more sharply contrasted. Toward this portentous presence the train rushed, uttering an occasional shrill neigh, like a stallion's defiance."

7. Remarkably little has been written on American real estate history for any period. Perhaps the most revealing of the existing studies is Marc A. Weiss, *The Rise of the Community Builders: The American Real Estate Industry and Urban Land Planning* (New York, 1987). For Chicago there is Ann Durkin Keating, *Building Chicago: Suburban Developers and the Creation of a Divided Metropolis* (Columbus, Ohio, 1988).

8. Garland, *Rose of Dutcher's Coolly*, 156.

9. Quoted in Mayer and Wade, *Chicago*, 134.

10. The best source on Holabird's early career is the entry by Thomas Tallmadge in *Dictionary of American Biography* (New York, 1932), 9:127–28. See also Henry F. Withey and

Elsie Rathburn Withey, *Biographical Dictionary of American Architects (Deceased)* (Los Angeles, 1956), 293–94.

11. Good accounts of Samuel Beckley Holabird's career can be found in George W. Cullum's *Biographical Register of the Officers and Graduates of the U.S. Military Academy at West Point, N.Y.* (Boston, 1891), 2:393–94, and an obituary in the U.S. Military Academy's *Annual Report,* 1909, 48–49.

12. Letter from John A. Holabird Jr. to the author, 3 October 1983. Samuel Beckley Holabird's diaries are in the manuscript collection of the Chicago Historical Society.

13. Letter from John A. Holabird Jr. to the author, 3 October 1983.

14. The former story came from Holabird's friend Thomas Tallmadge and is found in *Dictionary of American Biography,* 9:127. The latter account is found in John Root, "John Augur Holabird—an Appreciation," Inland Society of Architects *Monthly Bulletin,* August–September 1945.

15. We have only a few fragments of evidence on William Holabird's abrupt departure from West Point and his marriage. The most important is a letter from Samuel Beckley Holabird to Maria Augur's father, C. C. Augur, written on 13 November 1875, in which Holabird urged Augur to give his consent to the marriage of William and Maria. The elder Holabird noted that he had hoped William would graduate but that this was impossible given his "current frame of mind." Letter in the Chicago Historical Society Architecture Collections.

16. Manuscript obituary notice in the National Archives. Thereafter Samuel Beckley Holabird went to California, where he served as head of the Pacific Department between 1878 and 1879, and in 1879 he arrived in Washington, D.C. Family memory connects him with the Holabird home in Evanston, but no documentation seems to exist to confirm this except papers issued on his retirement, where he listed his home as Evanston. He did not return there, however. He spent the rest of his life in Washington, and no Evanston directory lists him.

17. Edward A. Renwick, in his manuscript volume titled "Recollections" (1932), 149, recounts a story in which William Holabird, newly arrived in Chicago, asked advice on getting a job from a friend who had been a military engineer and had moved to Chicago. The friend suggested he apply at Jenney's office. According to this version of events, Holabird thought Jenney was an engineer, not an architect, and by this accident he became an architect rather than an engineer.

18. On the professional training of Chicago architects see Sibel Bozdogan Dostoglu, "Toward Professional Legitimacy and Power; An Inquiry into the Struggle, Achievements and Dilemmas of the Architectural Profession through an Analysis of Chicago, 1871–1909" (Ph.D. diss., University of Pennsylvania, 1982).

19. The fullest treatment of Jenney is in Theodore Turak, "William Le Baron Jenney: A Nineteenth Century Architect" (Ph.D. diss., University of Michigan, 1966). See also Carl Condit, *The Chicago School of Architecture: A History of Commercial and Public Building in the Chicago Area, 1875–1925* (Chicago, 1964), 79–94. There is also some excellent material in David Van Zanten, "The Nineteenth Century: The Projecting of Chicago as a Commercial City and the Rationalization of Design and Construction," in *Chicago and New York: Architectural Interactions,* ed. John Zukowsky (Chicago, 1984), 30–49.

20. *Industrial Chicago* (Chicago, 1891), vols. 1–2, *The Building Interests,* 1:62.

21. The Portland Block also played a key role in bringing to Chicago one of Holabird & Roche's chief clients, the Brooks brothers. On this see chapter 5.

22. Edward Renwick recorded in his "Recollections," 149, that Holabird also worked for a time with Daniel Burnham as a construction engineer, but no other source mentions this.

23. On Simonds see Wilhelm Miller, "The Prairie Spirit in Landscape Gardening" (Urbana, Ill., 1955); Mara Gelbloom, "Ossian Simonds: Prairie Spirit in Landscape Gardening," *Prairie School Review* 2, no. 2 (1975): 5–18; Robert E. Grese, "Ossian Cole Simonds," in *American Landscape Architecture: Designers and Places,* ed. William H. Tishler (Washington, D.C., 1989), 74–75; and Charles A. Birnbaum and Lisa E. Crowder, *Pioneers of American Landscape Design: An Annotated Bibliography* (Washington, D.C., 1993), 113–17. The Simonds family records are in the Chicago Historical Society, Manuscripts Department.

24. Bryan Lathrop was born in Virginia in 1844. He studied in the East and in Europe before coming to Chicago at the end of the Civil War. In Chicago he went into the real estate business with his uncle, Thomas B. Bryan, who was involved with Graceland Cemetery. Lathrop eventually became president of the cemetery company. In 1875 he married Helen Lynde Aldis of Washington, D.C., the sister of Owen Aldis, who was to become a major figure in Chicago real estate. On Aldis see chapter 6 below on the Marquette Building. Lathrop also represented other investors, notably Francis Bartlett of Boston, who also became a major Holabird & Roche client. Lathrop was heavily involved in the Chicago real estate community and in numerous Chicago area charities. On Lathrop see Chicago Historical Society, *Annual Report,* 1916, 173–74, and John Leonard, ed., *The Book of Chicagoans* (Chicago, 1905), 348.

25. Renwick, "Recollections," 28.

26. Renwick, "Recollections," 26. This midwestern tradition supposedly broke with the formal beds and axial allées of European prototypes by incorporating native midwestern plants into its designs, especially horizontal or "stratified" ones like thorn apple, witch hazel, and pepperidge. This claim, similar to the one made about Chicago school architects, considerably exaggerates the novelty of using indigenous

plants in informal, natural-looking settings. The creation of apparently natural but idealized landscapes had, after all, been the basis of much of the work of eighteenth-century British landscape gardeners such as Capability Brown and Humphrey Repton, and it was revived in the work of William Robinson in the mid-nineteenth century. Many of the same ideas would also have been espoused by Frederick Law Olmsted, America's most famous nineteenth-century landscape designer, with whom Simonds apparently had corresponded a great deal. It is true that Simonds was a pioneer in adapting this tradition to the Midwest, and he started a movement whose most famous figure would be the landscape architect Jens Jensen. Simonds served as landscape architect at Graceland Cemetery until 1898, then he became a member of the cemetery's board of managers. He subsequently founded O. C. Simonds and Company in 1903, which became Simonds and West in 1925. Simonds was a founding member of the American Society of Landscape Architects and was elected president in 1913, and he belonged to numerous midwestern landscape groups. He taught at the University of Michigan starting in 1908 and published *Landscape Gardening* in 1920. Among other Simonds designs are schemes for Washington Park, Springfield; Frick Park, Pittsburgh; and grounds for the Universities of Maryland and Iowa, Fort Sheridan near Chicago, and the Nichols and Morton Arboretums. Simonds died in 1931 at age seventy-six. For an obituary see *Chicago Tribune,* 22 October 1931, 16.

27. The Major Block was designed by Dixon and Hamilton in 1872; see Frank A. Randall, *History of the Development of Building Construction in Chicago* (Urbana, Ill., 1949), 62. For more discussion about typical business blocks after the Fire, see chapter 5.

28. Renwick, "Recollections," 29.

29. Unfortunately, there are few good biographical sources on Roche. The fullest is Withey and Withey, *Biographical Dictionary,* 518,

but unfortunately this compilation is often inaccurate, and in the case of Roche there are pieces of information that seem to be in error (for example, that Roche studied part time at the Art Institute), but it also appears to contain plausible information not available elsewhere. See also the obituary by Lucian E. Smith in *Architecture,* August 1927, 84.

30. Turak, "William Le Baron Jenney," 249–50. Both the Holmes Estate and Leiter I buildings were influential in the work Holabird & Roche would later do. On this, see chapter 11.

31. Renwick, "Recollections," 30.

32. The old address was 115 Monroe Street. Under the new address scheme, put in place about 1910, this would be 56 W. Monroe.

33. The First National Bank II stood from 1882 to 1902, when it was replaced by a new building. Randall, *Building Construction in Chicago,* 48.

34. A full account of Renwick's earlier life is contained in his manuscript volume "Recollections."

35. Ibid., 30. For a very similar story, see the account by Maniere Dawson in chapter 15.

36. Ibid., 30–32.

37. Ibid., 33.

38. Information on the firm's offices is taken from the Lakeside and other Chicago directories. Renwick, "Recollections," 52, puts the move to the Montauk in May 1884, but the directories show the firm already there in 1883.

39. On the Montauk see Randall, *Building Construction in Chicago,* 95; Condit, *Chicago School of Architecture,* 53–57; and Donald Hoffmann, *The Architecture of John Wellborn Root* (Chicago, 1973), 24–27. On the history of the skyscraper there is a large and largely unsatisfactory literature. Perhaps the best account is the few lines devoted to the subject in Gerald Larson, "The Iron Skeleton Frame," in *Chicago Architecture, 1872–1922: Reconfiguration of an American Metropolis,* ed. John Zukowsky (Chicago, 1993), 50–51.

40. On the career of the Brookses, see the material in chapters 5 and 6.

Chapter Two

1. Edward A. Renwick, "Recollections" (1932), 148–51.

2. Renwick, "Recollections," 149.

3. Interview with author, 20 August 1980.

4. See chapter 8 on William Holabird's Evanston.

5. See chapter 13 on the Glen View Golf and Polo Club and chapter 14 on the Coleman Lake Club.

6. Letter of 16 October 1929 from John A. Holabird to W. J. Hamilton, president of the Evanston Historical Society. The only intimate glimpse into William's private life comes in a few remarks recorded in his father's diaries. On one page dated 23 August 1885 Samuel Beckley Holabird wrote that he visited William in Evanston: "William evidently worried about his business. His great family expenses must [?] tell on him a good deal. Hope I can be help —." On 24 June 1889 he wrote: "For the first time had a written statement of W. H.'s bad habits as to liquor drinking — He cuts church etc — stays from home days at a time. Have had hints before of these . . . [rest illegible]." Although there is no further evidence on most of William's "bad habits," there is ample evidence that hard drinking became a tradition in the firm. In this it seems to have been exactly like many other architectural firms. The "bad habits," apparently, were not in any case major enough to merit attention from anyone outside his own family. For the world at large, and probably most of the time to his own family, Holabird was a model business and family man.

7. Renwick, "Recollections," 176. The best documentation of Holabird's role in the office is found in a diary that he kept during the year

1914 preserved at the Chicago Historical Society.

8. Renwick, "Recollections," 151.

9. *Economist*, 28 July 1923, 207.

10. Renwick, "Recollections," 152. Interview with Mrs. John A. Holabird Sr., 20 August 1980.

11. Renwick, "Recollections," 152.

12. The neighborhood was obviously very modest. The building Roche lived in was just a block from the Armour Mission, a philanthropic institution providing schooling and health care for poor children in the area. The house no longer stands.

13. Interview, 20 August 1980.

14. Martin Roche's diaries are preserved at the Chicago Historical Society.

15. Renwick, "Recollections," 153–54.

16. On MacNeil's sculpture see chapter 17 on the Cook County Courthouse and Chicago City Hall.

17. Renwick, "Recollections," 68.

18. See Robert Craik McLean, "Martin Roche, FAIA: An Obituary," *Western Architect*, July 1927, 119, and Lucian E. Smith's obituary in *Architecture* 56 (August 1927): 84. McLean relates that Roche took the entire office staff to St. Paul to see the newly completed Minnesota State Capitol, designed by Cass Gilbert.

19. Roche joined the Western Association of Architects at the time of its organization in 1884 and became a fellow of the American Institute of Architects in 1889 when the two groups merged.

Chapter Three

1. All figures for Chicago annual construction costs in this book are taken from Frank A. Randall, *History of the Development of Building Construction in Chicago* (Urbana, Ill., 1949), 294–95, who compiled them from Homer Hoyt, *One Hundred Years of Land Values in Chicago* (Chicago, 1933).

2. On the arrival of trained architects in Chicago see John Zukowsky and Pauline Saliga, *Chicago Architects Design: A Century of Architectural Drawings from the Art Institute of Chicago* (New York, 1982), 40–63.

3. The Chicago chapter of the American Institute of Architects was founded in 1869. As late as the 1880s, however, there were only some thirty members, even though census records show over one hundred people calling themselves architects, according to Sibel Bozdogan Dostoglu, "Toward Professional Legitimacy and Power: An Inquiry into the Struggle, Achievements and Dilemmas of the Architectural Profession through an Analysis of Chicago, 1871–1909" (Ph.D. diss., University of Pennsylvania, 1982), 43–45. Dostoglu also has excellent comments on the rivalry between the building profession and architects.

4. Figures for the stenographer's salary are taken from Lisa M. Fine, *The Souls of the Skyscraper: Female Clerical Workers in Chicago, 1870–1930* (Philadelphia, 1990), 43; those for the executive are from Olivier Zunz, *Making America Corporate* (Chicago, 1990), 43.

5. Reconstructing office practice for the years before 1890 is difficult because the evidence is so fragmentary. There are hundreds of drawings and quite a lot of financial data, but much of the information does not match up. Also, the compensation of architects demands considerably more research. In general the firm tried to charge a fee of 6 percent of the total construction cost as its compensation, but it is clear from numerous cases that this figure was not invariable. Sometimes the firm donated services; sometimes, particularly for the largest jobs, an alternative fee schedule was established. In some cases the firm took an equity position in the development or accepted securities in lieu of payment.

6. Edward A. Renwick, "Recollections" (1932), 55, 68. Renwick was made a partner in 1896.

7. For more on Francis Bartlett see catalog volumes, Old Colony Building, cat. no. 201.

8. For more on Aldis see chapter 6 on the Marquette Building.

9. According to Renwick, "Recollections," 33, this was the Merchant's Building which was at the northeast corner of Wabash Avenue and the river. Nothing else is known about this commission. On Owen Aldis see Earle Schultz and Walter Simmons, *Offices in the Sky* (Indianapolis, 1959), 20, and chapter 6 on the Marquette Building.

10. For this building, called the Pontiac (1888–89), see below.

11. Renwick, "Recollections," 176.

12. Not all the "rustic" designs were for outlying towns. The Nellie Wood house in Hyde Park (cat. no. 106) is similar.

13. Unfortunately, very little is known about the business of architecture generally in the late nineteenth century, and comparative figures are almost completely lacking. By this period McKim, Mead and White had construction totals of over $3 million per year, according to Leland M. Roth, *The Architecture of McKim, Mead and White, 1870–1920: A Building List* (New York, 1978), 178.

14. Renwick, "Recollections," 80.

15. Office directories give the old address, 115 Monroe. Street addresses in the Loop were changed in 1910 to bring them into line with the numbering system used throughout the city.

16. The Monadnock was another project of the Brooks brothers. The original, north half was designed by Burnham and Root and built in 1890–92. It gained instant fame for being even more severely unornamented than the Montauk, commissioned by the same client and designed by the same architects. It also marked the southernmost march of prestige office buildings, in fact touching the south edge of the Loop proper—that is, reaching Van Buren Street, where the elevated tracks ran. At the time the firm moved into the north end, plans had been drawn for the south end, but no construction had started. *Economist,* 26 March 1892; *Inland Architect,* April 1892.

17. Renwick, "Recollections," 80.

18. Ibid., 79.

19. Ibid., 80; Randall, *Building Construction in Chicago* , 32.

20. On the reasons for this switch see chapter 6 on the Marquette Building; Donald Hoffmann, *The Architecture of John Wellborn Root* (Chicago, 1973), 165; and Renwick, "Recollections," 77.

21. The old Gold Coast had been on the South Side. For more on the move of the city's elite to the North Side see chapter 18 on Automobile Row.

22. As this book was in press a substantial article on the New South Wales building has come to light courtesy of Robert Freestone of the University of New South Wales. According to *Australian Builder and Contractors' News,* 29 July 1893, 54–56, the building was an adaptation of the old General Post Office in Sydney of 1848.

23. Since the Holabird & Roche catalog was written new information on the Proctor Tower has appeared in Gerald R. Larson, "The Iron Skeleton Frame: Interactions between Europe and the United States," in *Chicago Architecture, 1872–1922: Reconfiguration of an American Metropolis,* ed. John Zukowsky (Chicago, 1993), 53, and in Robert Jay, "Taller Than Eiffel's Tower: The London and Chicago Tower Projects, 1884–1894," *Journal of the Society of Architectural Historians* 46 (June 1987): 144–56. It is difficult to know what to make of the tower. It is likely that in the office it was considered more an engineering challenge than a serious architectural composition.

Chapter Four

1. An alternative route would have taken the traveler north on Sheridan Road, an artery laid out to connect the city with its northern suburbs. On this route see Perry R. Duis, "The

Scenic Route to the Suburbs," *Chicago,* March 1984, 120–24, and Michael Ebner, *Creating Chicago's North Shore: A Suburban History* (Chicago, 1988), 106–13.

2. On Fort Sheridan the best single source is Martha E. Sorenson and Douglas A. Martz, *View from the Tower: A History of Fort Sheridan, Illinois* (Highwood, Ill., 1985). Surprisingly little has been written on America's nineteenth-century military architecture. From the scant literature it appears that many army bases were very casual in appearance, the result of gradual accretions of buildings. See, for example, Herbert M. Hart, *Old Forts of the Far West* (New York, 1965), for comparative site plans. The most monumental military complexes were fortifications like those at Fort Point in San Francisco or great arsenals like the ones at Rock Island, Illinois, and Benicia, California.

3. On the 1877 railroad strike see Robert V. Bruce, *1877, Year of Violence* (1959; reprinted Chicago, 1989). There is an excellent analysis of late nineteenth-century class dissension and an architectural response in Robert M. Fogelson, *America's Armories: Architecture, Society, and Public Order* (Cambridge, Mass., 1989).

4. On this see chapter 5 on the Tacoma.

5. On the early history of Fort Sheridan see Ebner, *Creating Chicago's North Shore,* 140–42, Sorenson and Martz, *View from the Tower,* and Robert Schall, "The History of Fort Sheridan, Illinois," 1944, typescript prepared for Public Relations Office, found in the former Fort Sheridan Museum. On the role of the Commercial Club see Nina B. Smith, "This Bleak Situation: The Founding of Fort Sheridan Illinois," unpublished paper at Chicago Historical Society, and Vilas Johnson, *A History of the Commercial Club of Chicago* (Chicago, 1977), 49, 125, 126.

6. The 1884 starting date, as unlikely as it seems, appears unequivocally in the Holabird & Roche building lists. "In 1884 H&R were commissioned to develop plans for a military post be-

tween Highwood and Lake Forest. . . . First appearance on record was November 25th 1884."

7. On this subject see the inconclusive evidence in Suzanne Carter Meldman, "O. C. Simonds and Fort Sheridan's Historic Landscape," in "Cultural Resource Studies relating to Fort Sheridan, Illinois: Supplemental Research," ed. Andrew Bohnert et al., manuscript report prepared for United States Army Corps of Engineers, Louisville District, 1995, 40–71.

8. The one original building not designed by the firm was the hospital. Constructed in 1893 from designs supplied by the office of the surgeon general, this high mansarded block with a one-story wing on each side was quite different from the Holabird & Roche buildings and must have looked old-fashioned by the 1890s. A firm employee writing later about the fort recalled: "The Hospital at the post was later designed by the Army doctors and erected by the government without Holabird & Roche's services. It was entirely out of character and marred the landscape." Manuscript notes in the firm's scrapbooks, Chicago Historical Society.

9. Quotation from manuscript sheets in Holabird & Roche scrapbooks in the collections of the Chicago Historical Society. Ample evidence of this process survives in a large set of drawings preserved at the National Archives. These drawings, apparently submitted to Washington, D.C., by the architects, probably were consigned to the Archives after they were not approved by the army and were therefore no longer needed. Presumably the approved drawings and any subsequent working drawings for the approved designs remained in Chicago and Fort Sheridan and were then lost or destroyed.

10. Charles E. Jenkins, "A Review of the Work of Holabird & Roche," *Architectural Reviewer* 3 (June 1897): 1–41.

11. Good examples of large, towered main buildings can be seen, for example, at the United States Arsenal in Indianapolis, built in 1863–64, or at the Arsenal at Rock Island, built in 1865.

12. On this, see chapter 8 on William Holabird's Evanston.

13. Jenkins, "Review," 29.

14. Anonymous Holabird & Roche employee. MS sheets in Holabird & Roche scrapbook, Chicago Historical Society.

15. Samuel Beckley Holabird Diary, Chicago Historical Society. He was not as charitable about the post administration: "The grounds have been neglected. The roads are not well preserved. [Post Commander] MacCauley is incapable. . . . The day a trying one."

16. Jenkins, "Review," 34.

17. Quoted in Schall, "History of Fort Sheridan, Illinois."

18. See Ebner, *Creating Chicago's North Shore*, 145.

19. The current status of Fort Sheridan is uncertain. Deactivated as a military base, it has been the subject of a major tug-of-war between competing interests.

Chapter Five

1. As this work was in the final stages of preparation, but too late to aid in the preparation of this volume, two important books on commercial architecture appeared: Carol Willis, *Form Follows Finance: Skyscrapers and Skylines in New York and Chicago* (New York, 1995), and Sarah Bradford Landau and Carl Condit, *Rise of the New York Skyscraper* (New Haven, Conn., 1996).

2. On the development of the managerial class see the classic study of Alfred D. Chandler Jr., *The Visible Hand: The Managerial Revolution in American Business* (Cambridge, Mass., 1977). There is also excellent material in Olivier Zunz, *Making America Corporate* (Chicago, 1990), a book filled with information that could be used to great effect by architectural historians, and in Lisa M. Fine, *The Souls of the Skyscraper: Female Clerical Workers in Chicago, 1870–1930* (Philadelphia, 1990). There are some useful figures in Daniel Bluestone, *Constructing Chicago* (New

Haven, Conn., 1991), 108–9, on the number of workers in various classes.

3. On London, for example, see the material in Francis Sheppard, *London, 1808–1870: The Infernal Wen* (Berkeley, Calif., 1971), 198–201. The great monument among the insurance companies was the enormous structure designed by Alfred Waterhouse and built by the Prudential Mutual Assurance Company. For excellent general remarks on the development of the office building district, see Larry Ford, *Cities and Buildings: Skyscrapers, Skid Rows and Suburbs* (Baltimore, 1994), 13–40.

4. Two good examples are the large building the First National Bank built for itself in 1881–82 to house both the place where money was changed and the offices of workers who managed these transactions, and the offices of the Chicago, Burlington and Quincy Railroad, finished in 1883. See Donald Hoffmann, *The Architecture of John Wellborn Root* (Chicago, 1973), 30–32, and Zunz, *Making Corporate America*, 37–66.

5. On the development of the office building see Nikolaus Pevsner, *History of Building Types* (Princeton, N.J., 1975), 213–24. Two excellent texts from this period are George Hill, "Office Building," in *Dictionary of Architecture and Building: Biographical, Historical, and Descriptive*, ed. Russell Sturgis (New York, 1901–2), 3:11–18, and George Hill, "Some Practical Limiting Conditions in the Design of the Modern Office Building," *Architectural Record*, April–June 1893. There are some excellent observations in the chapter "Inside the Skyscraper," in Zunz, *Making America Corporate*, and in *Constructing Chicago* Daniel Bluestone has made excellent use of McCormick Company records to trace office use in the case of a major Chicago manufacturing firm.

6. In London, for example, Sir John Summerson reports, a speculative office building was constructed as early as 1825. John N. Sum-

merson, *The Architecture of Victorian London* (Charlottesville, Va., 1976), 20–21. The most conspicuous example of a speculative office building at midcentury was the Royal Exchange Chambers of 1848. On this see Pevsner, *History of Building Types,* 214–15, and Henry-Russell Hitchcock, *Early Victorian Architecture in Britain* (New Haven, Conn., 1954), 381–82.

7. Good testimony on the rise of the building strictly for office use can be found in the John J. Flinn, *Standard Guide to Chicago for the Year 1891* (Chicago, 1891), 129, where the author writes, "Fifteen years ago there was no such thing as an office building known in Chicago. The Howland Block on the southwest corner of Dearborn and Monroe streets, the Kentucky Block on the northeast corner of Clark and Adams streets, and the Ashland Block on the northeast corner of Clark and Randolph streets, come nearer the requirements of office buildings than any in the city. Strictly, they were what insurance men would have denominated omnibus blocks." These latter are presumably buildings that housed, in addition to offices, some light construction, wholesaling operations, showrooms, and so forth. The Howland, originally named the Honore, was finished in 1869 to designs of Otis Wheelock; see Frank A. Randall, *History of the Development of Building Construction in Chicago* (Urbana, Ill., 1949), 65. The Kentucky dated to 1873 (Randall, 230). The Ashland Block was built in 1872 to designs of F. and E. Baumann (Randall, 131).

8. A very expensive building that was as much civic venture as business building was the Chamber of Commerce Building of 1865, which cost $495,000. Gerald Wade Kuhn, "History of the Financing of Commercial Structures in the Chicago Loop, 1868–1934" (Ph.D. diss., University of Indiana Business School, 1969).

9. On the post-Fire blocks see Commission on Chicago Landmarks, *1870s Commercial Building in the Loop* (Chicago, 1989).

10. In the late nineteenth century most people used the word "skyscraper" to refer to something very tall. See Gerald Larson, "The Iron Skeleton Frame: Interactions between Europe and the United States," in *Chicago Architecture, 1872–1922: Reconfiguration of an American Metropolis,* ed. John Zukowsky (Chicago, 1993), 47. According to Larson the Equitable Life Insurance Company's Kendall Building, designed in 1871 and under construction at the time of the Great Fire, would have been the first really tall building in Chicago, but the Fire halted construction. During the heyday of modernist architectural history the term took on a quite different meaning as historians attempted to redefine it as a steel-frame building, for reasons of civic pride and to make the skyscraper fall more neatly into modernist structural history. For a remarkable, if not entirely convincing, example of this kind of attempt see Carson Webster, "The Skyscraper: Logical and Historical Considerations," *Journal of the Society of Architectural Historians,* December 1959, 126–39.

11. An interesting study of building in Chicago during these years is Kenneth Turney Gibbs, *Business Architectural Imagery in America, 1870–1930* (Ann Arbor, Mich., 1984). His data on real estate business are somewhat impressionistic, however. See also David Van Zanten, "The Nineteenth Century: The Projecting of Chicago as a Commercial City and the Rationalization of Design and Construction," in *Chicago and New York: Architectural Interactions,* ed. John Zukowsky (Chicago, 1984).

12. Cleveland Amory, *The Proper Bostonians* (New York, 1947), 41, 65. Unfortunately, relatively little is known about the Brooks brothers. Intensely private, they spent their adult lives quietly in and around Boston at their houses on Beacon Hill and at the family estate in West Medford. On Shepherd Brooks see obituary in *Boston Evening Transcript,* 24 February 1922, 6. On Peter Chardon Brooks, see *Who's Who in*

New England (Boston, 1916), 164. Characteristically there appears to be no mention of Chicago real estate in any of the notices on either of the brothers.

13. On the business methods of the Brooks brothers there is interesting information in Miles Berger, *They Built Chicago: Entrepreneurs Who Shaped a Great City's Architecture* (Chicago, 1992), 29–38, but unfortunately there are no notes, so it is difficult to use. See also Earle Schultz and Walter Simmons, *Offices in the Sky* (Indianapolis, 1959), 20. On the post-Fire Portland Block see chapter 1.

14. The Montauk briefly housed the offices of Holabird & Roche. See chapter 3.

15. On the passenger elevator see Carl Condit, *Chicago School of Architecture: A History of Commercial and Public Building in the Chicago Area, 1875–1925* (Chicago, 1964), 21.

16. In Chicago bedrock lay some 80 to 120 feet below grade, too deep to be used to support the foundations of large buildings using any practical known techniques. The only firm layer between grade and bedrock was a stiff blue-and-yellow clay crust called hardpan. The problem arose because this layer was very thin. The spread foundation, a pyramidal arrangement of stone courses, was used to distribute the load of the walls and interior columns over the largest possible surface of the hardpan. The crucial advance came in 1873 with the publication of a pamphlet by Frederick Baumann titled *The Art of Preparing Foundations* (Chicago, 1873). In this publication Baumann described how to proportion the foundations to the load carried by each pier or column above. As buildings got heavier, the bulk of these pyramids increased until they usurped practically the entire basement of the buildings just at the moment when basement space was becoming more valuable than ever before. At the Montauk Burnham and Root reduced the weight and bulk of the spread footing by using iron rails embedded in concrete that stiffened the horizontal slabs sufficiently so that

the concentrated weight of the wall above would not crack them. On foundations see Ralph Peck, "History of Building Foundations in Chicago," *University of Illinois Engineering Experiment Station Bulletin,* no. 393, 2 January 1948.

17. On metal framing see Larson, "Iron Skeleton Frame."

18. On fireproofing see Larson, "Iron Skeleton Frame."

19. On some of these building services see Walter Nashert, *America's Builders* (Los Angeles, 1975), 118–28.

20. On the appearance of the Montauk see Donald Hoffmann, *The Architecture of John Wellborn Root* (Baltimore, 1973), 24–28.

21. On the Home Insurance see Theodore Turak, "Remembrances of the Home Insurance Building," *Journal of the Society of Architectural Historians,* March 1985, 60–65, and Gerald Larson and Roula Geraniotis, "Toward a Better Understanding of the Evolution of the Iron Skeleton Frame in Chicago," *Journal of the Society of Architectural Historians* 46 (March 1987): 39–48.

22. A photograph in Paul T. Gilbert, *Chicago and Its Makers* (Chicago, 1929), 247, gives a good idea of the architecture of Chicago insurance companies from the time of the Fire through the 1880s. The great bulk of the Home Insurance Building dwarfs the adjacent buildings of the Merchant's, Phoenix, and Aetna Insurance Companies.

23. On the Leiter I see chapter 11 on lofts.

24. According to Jenney's own words in his famous article "The Construction of a Heavy Fireproof Building on a Compressible Soil," "A square iron column was built into each of the piers in the street fronts" (*Sanitary Engineer,* 10 December 1885, 32–33). Jenney's experiment was noted by other Chicagoans but not copied.

25. On the Rookery see Hoffmann, *Architecture of John Wellborn Root,* 65–83, and Robert Bruegmann, "Touchstone of Preservation," *Inland Architect,* July–August 1992, 50–55.

26. This story is told by an individual who

would have been in a position to know—Jenney's partner, William Mundie. See William Mundie, "Skeleton Construction, Its Origin and Development as Applied to Architecture" (1932), 43, manuscript preserved on microfilm, Burnham Library, Art Institute of Chicago. It is unlikely that the interior courtyard walls of the Rookery were influenced by the structural experiments at the Home Insurance. It is more likely that they owed something to the example of the Produce Exchange in New York, designed by George B. Post, and to other buildings in which light glazed brick coverings were applied directly to metal frames. One piece of interesting testimony that has apparently never been followed up is an assertion by Edward Renwick that the angle irons that held up much of the masonry on the Home Insurance Building were actually added as an afterthought on the drawings. Renwick noted that they were the suggestion of Erastus Foote, who made the castings. Herbert Stewart Leonard, "History of Architecture in Chicago" (Ph.D. diss., University of Chicago, 1934).

27. Edward C. Kirkland, *A History of American Economic Life since 1860* (New York, 1971), 311–12; Alfred Chandler, *The Visible Hand: The Managerial Revolution in American Business* (Cambridge, Mass., 1977), 28, 36–37; Alan Trachtenberg, *The Incorporation of America: Culture and Society in the Gilded Age* (New York, 1982), 3–5, 84–86.

28. On the rise of real estate bonds see Schultz and Simmons, *Offices in the Sky,* 144–45; Kuhn, *Financing of Commercial Structures,* 43–60.

29. The concept of limited liability was developed at much the same time in the United States and Britain, but because American corporation law was regulated by the states, practices differed dramatically from state to state. Through much of the third and fourth quarters of the nineteenth century large companies relied on the trust mechanism rather than the corporation. General acceptance of limited liability

corporations did not come until the very end of the century.

30. I am indebted to Katherine Solomonson for alerting me to the legislation restricting real estate investments by limited liability corporations in the 1880s, notably "Act concerning Corporations," Public Laws of the State of Illinois, 27th General Assembly, 298. This prohibition limiting corporations to the construction of only that space they needed for themselves continued in force until 1915 but was widely circumvented by various means. Solomonson cites the case of the Pullman Palace Car Company's successful contention that it should be permitted to lease three-quarters of the space in the Loop office building because this space was needed for future expansion. In a set of manuscript notes supplied to me, Solomonson cites the legal decisions in this and similar cases, including one lost by a safety-deposit corporation in 1902.

31. In the case of the "Massachusetts trust" Illinois corporations law was no obstacle, but it was never clear that a Massachusetts trust had the right to develop real estate in Illinois. On this question see Kuhn, "History of the Financing of Commercial Structures," 104, Berger, *They Built Chicago,* 26, and chapter 12 below on terra cotta on State Street. The Massachusetts trust was apparently first used in 1888 as a way of avoiding Massachusetts restrictions on corporate real estate development and a way to minimize taxes. On the history and operation of the Massachusetts trust see Blake Snyder and Wilmot Lippincott, *Real Estate Handbook* (New York, 1925), 148–55; Nelson L. North, De Witt van Buren, and C. Elliott Smith, *Real Estate Financing* (New York, 1928), 126–28; Robert F. Bingham and Elmore L. Andrews, *Financing Real Estate* (Cleveland, 1924), 80–87. The Massachusetts trust was a model for the real estate investment trusts (REITs) of the 1960s.

32. On the subject of real estate financing there is a great deal of material in Kuhn, "His-

tory of the Financing of Commercial Structures."

33. Real estate bonds generally paid between 5 and 6 percent in this period. Presumably, because real estate was always somewhat risky, this represented a point or two premium above an alternative high-grade investment.

34. Kuhn, "History of the Financing of Commercial Structures," 256.

35. On the creation of the Chicago Real Estate Board in 1883 and the rise of the title insurance companies see Bessie Louise Pierce, *A History of Chicago,* vol. 3 (Chicago, 1957), 207–9. Holabird & Roche client Bryan Lathrop was very active in local real estate organizations. On the creation of the National Real Estate Association in 1891 see Pearl Janet Davies, *Real Estate in American History* (Washington, D.C., 1928), 43. By the 1890s Chicago had become a relatively mature real estate market and the real speculative fever moved to less developed places farther west.

36. On the financing of the Auditorium see Kuhn, "History of the Financing of Commercial Structures," 51–52.

37. On the rivalry of LaSalle and Dearborn Streets see Gerald Larson, "Chicago's Loop, 1830–1890: A Tale of Two Grids," in *Fragments of Chicago's Past: The Collection of Architectural Fragments at the Art Institute of Chicago,* ed. Pauline Saliga (Chicago, 1990), 72–75.

38. On the idea of the taxpayer see Chester H. Liebs, *Main Street to Miracle Mile: American Roadside Architecture* (Boston, 1985), 10–13, and chapter 18 below.

39. The best documentation of the genesis of the project comes from Edward Renwick writing in his "Recollections" (1932).

40. Renwick, "Recollections," 55.

41. On Loring the best source is seven pages of typewritten notes by Ralph Renwick with cover letter to a Mr. Lucas dated 10 July 1947, found in papers in the possession of Holabird & Roche and now at the Chicago Historical Society. According to Renwick, Loring had been a draftsman with Van Osdel in the 1860s. In the late 1860s he practiced for several years with William Le Baron Jenney as a senior partner, but he left apparently to found his own architectural practice and became involved in the Chicago Terra Cotta Company, of which he was president by 1872. See also Larson, "Iron Skeleton Frame," 47.

42. According to the much later, but highly plausible, testimony of Thomas E. Tallmadge, Loring had offered the same idea to Adler and Sullivan for use on the Auditorium, but the scheme was not adopted. See his *Architecture in Old Chicago* (Chicago, 1941), 198.

43. On the use of metal columns and terra cotta for storefronts see the comments by Chicago engineer H. J. Burt in his "Growth of Steel Frame Buildings: Origins and Some Problems of the Skyscraper," *Engineering News Record,* 17 April 1924.

44. See the discussion of the State Safety Building in chapter 10. Designers of cast iron fronted buildings, very common in the warehouse districts of New York, Chicago, and elsewhere, had long since explored the use of cladding panels that supported only their own weight and were bolted back to a bearing wall or to a metal frame. See Margot Gayle and Edmund V. Gillon Jr., *Cast-Iron Architecture in New York* (New York, 1974), and her "A Heritage Forgotten: Chicago's First Cast Iron Buildings," *Chicago History,* summer 1978, 98–108.

45. On the revival of terra cotta in Chicago in the nineteenth century, see the Landmarks Preservation Council of Illinois publication by Nancy D. Berryman, *Terra Cotta* (Chicago, 1984).

46. On the Mallers Building see letter of 5 December 1930 from W. Carbys Zimmerman to William B. Mundie, in Mundie, "Skeleton Construction," 41. According to Zimmerman the terra cotta was attached to the floors by iron struts.

47. For a discussion of Root's unwillingness to use a skeletal system for the street facades of the Rookery see Mundie, *Skeleton Construction*, 43.

48. The rental figure I have used was derived in part from Kuhn, *Financing of Commercial Structures*, 235. Kuhn estimated a figure of $1.50 to $2 for first-class office space in 1893. As we will see, the Tacoma charged $1.45, presumably representing the highest rents in the market in the late 1880s. It is possible that $1 per square foot would be more likely for the old building. Unfortunately, there has been almost no study of rental rates in this period. The best source is still the pages of the *Economist*.

49. Renwick, "Recollections," 57; Burt, "Growth of Steel Frame Buildings," 682.

50. On this subject see Corydon Purdy, "The Skeletal Type of High Building," *Engineering News* 26 (26 December 1891): 608. Some sense of the state of research on the subject can be gained by consulting the *Annual Report of the Department of Buildings to the Mayor and Council*, 1894, 10, in which tests were made on the deflection of the Monadnock Building during high winds.

51. See discussion of the building height limits in chapter 6 on the Marquette Building.

52. *Economist*, 29 December 1888, 7.

53. On Hale see Hoffmann, *Architecture of John Wellborn Root*, 177–78, and Berger, *They Built Chicago*, 49–58.

54. Renwick, "Recollections," 58.

55. It is odd that only two sources mention the name Seiffert in connection with the Tacoma Building. One is Renwick in his manuscript "Recollections." It is unlikely that Renwick would have been wrong about the name of the person who had worked on the Tacoma, but he was often vague in his descriptions, and it is troubling that no account published at the time of the building mentions Seiffert. The most logical assumption would be that Seiffert was in the employ of an engineering firm such as Wade and Purdy. This would be consistent with several other descriptions, notably that of Colonel W. A. Starrett, *Skyscrapers and the Men Who Build Them* (New York, 1928), 32, that Purdy and Henderson were the engineers, and the "Report on the Tacoma Building" of an AIA committee reported that the engineers were Wade and Purdy. If Seiffert was an employee of Wade and Purdy at the time of the Tacoma it would explain all the various accounts. The second source on Seiffert's role at the Tacoma, however, was William Mundie. In his manuscript "Skeletal Construction," 73–74, Mundie stated emphatically that Seiffert was the engineer and not the Purdy firm. The evidence of Mundie, although like all these individuals he wrote long after the fact, must be given considerable weight.

56. The name Tacoma was originally used to designate a lake in Maine, but in his well-known *The Canoe and the Saddle* of 1863 Theodore Winthrop used the term to designate Mount Rainier and all covered peaks, according to George Stewart, *American Place Names* (New York, 1970), 470.

57. The Brooks brothers appear to have started this trend with the Montauk, although it is unclear whether it was the place itself at the tip of Long Island or the association with American Indians that was uppermost in their minds. If the latter is true, the name reflected the widespread enthusiasm for things related to the American Indians that followed their gradual elimination from most of the eastern United states. The most conspicuous marker of this enthusiasm was the appearance of Henry Wadsworth Longfellow's poem *Hiawatha* in 1855. It also anticipated the use of mountain names exemplified most strikingly in the four buildings—the Monadnock, Wachusetts, Kearsarge, and Katahdin—now collectively known as the Monadnock.

58. Pierce, *History of Chicago*, 212; Kuhn, "History of the Financing of Commercial Structures," 48. Slaughter later commissioned a house from Holabird & Roche (cat. no. 221).

59. Safes were mentioned in the rental brochure issued at the time of completion. Every office had one, and there was a large safe in the basement. Wardrobes in the offices and the letter chute received as much attention, however.

60. Renwick, "Recollections," 60.

61. On the methods of George A. Fuller see the information below.

62. On the rise of the general contractor see Sibel Bozdogan Dostoglu, "Toward Professional Legitimacy and Power: An Inquiry into the Struggle, Achievements and Dilemmas of the Architectural Profession through an Analysis of Chicago, 1871–1909" (Ph.D. diss., University of Pennsylvania, 1982), 95–103.

63. Fuller started his career as an architect working in Worcester, Massachusetts; in Boston, where he was in charge of the office of the distinguished architects Peabody and Stearns; and in the latters' New York office before setting up his own firm in 1880. He came to Chicago in 1883. He appears to have pioneered some aspects of his "cost-plus" basis doing contract work on the Chicago Opera House, built in 1885 to designs by Cobb and Frost, and on the Union League Club, designed by Jenney and constructed in 1886. After the Tacoma, Fuller was involved with virtually every large office building in Chcago. By the turn of the century the capital of his firm had increased to $750,000 and it had become a national business. Fuller died in 1900. Information on Fuller seems surprisingly sketchy. The account here is drawn from an article "Large Construction in Chicago," *Economist*, 31 December 1894, 750; Paul Starrett, *Changing the Skyline* (New York, 1938), 70; Renwick, "Recollections," 59–61; Henry Ericsson, *Sixty Years a Builder* (Chicago, 1942), 220; Starrett, *Skyscrapers*, 32–34; Chad Wallin, *The Builders' Story* (Chicago, 1966), 5–6; a notice in *New York Architect*, October 1907; and Walter Nashert, *America's Builders* (Los Angeles, 1975), 145–47.

64. Fuller probably had a great deal to do with the experimental aluminum facade proposed for the Champlain Building, for example. On this see chapter 10.

65. A good description of the structural system can be found in a report by a committee of the American Institute of Architects when the building was demolished in 1929. See "Report on the Tacoma Building," *Monthly Bulletin of the Illinois Society of Architects*, February 1930, 3. For a good summary of late nineteenth-century practice generally, consult the article "Iron Construction," in *A Dictionary of Architecture and Building: Biographical, Historical, and Descriptive*, ed. Russell Sturgis (New York, 1901–2), 2:502–19.

66. Peck, "History of Building Foundations," 23; *Industrial Chicago* (Chicago, 1891), 1:471.

67. *Chicago Tribune*, 13 January 1899, 2.

68. Renwick, "Recollections," 64.

69. Carl Condit, for example, in his *American Building Art: The Nineteenth Century* (New York, 1960), 52, writes: "No building in the United States has been investigated more thoroughly than it [the Home Insurance] because no building has had a more decisive effect on the building techniques of our time." More recently Gerald Larson has reexamined the issue and returned to the conclusion that the Home Insurance was not a skeletal building. See Larson and Geraniotis, "Toward a Better Understanding of the Evolution of the Iron Skeleton Frame," 39–48, and Larson, "Iron Skeleton Frame," 39–56. But Larson's conclusions merely restate the most authoritative earlier studies, notably the one conducted by the Western Society of Engineers in December 1931 and published in the *Journal of the Western Society of Engineers*, March 1932.

70. Wallin, *Builders' Story*, 6; Renwick, "Recollections," 64. An excellent illustration of what the Tacoma must have looked like under construction is seen in a construction photograph of the Pontiac Building. See chapter 3.

71. Tallmadge, *Architecture in Old Chicago*, 197–99.

72. An important article in *Northwest Architect* in March 1888 and another in *Inland Architect* in July 1888 by William Buffington of Minneapolis described some of the possibilities of the new construction.

73. Excellent testimony on this subject can be found in the entry "United States" by Montgomery Schuyler in Sturgis, *Dictionary of Architecture and Building*, 3:929.

74. The exact chronology of the first metal frame buildings has never been adequately determined because so few of the chief contenders, which include Baumann and Huehl's Chamber of Commerce Building, Burnham and Root's Rand McNally Building, and Jenney's Leiter and Manhattan Buildings, have been thoroughly studied. See, for example, Condit, *Chicago School*, chap. 4.

75. Condit, *American Building Art*, 47–48.

76. Condit, *American Building Art*, 48–50.

77. On this story see Robert Bruegmann, "The Home Insurance, the Tacoma, and the Myth of the First Skyscraper," forthcoming in *Journal of the Society of Architectural Historians*.

78. Structural expression had been at the foundation of the work of Eugène-Emmanuel Viollet-le-Duc in France. His ideas were well known in America, but in their more dogmatic forms they were more likely to be held by eastern critics than by western practitioners. See, for example, G. Twose, "Steel and Terra Cotta Buildings in Chicago: Some Deductions," *Brickbuilder*, January 1894.

79. Construction costs were expressed in cents per cubic foot well into the twentieth century. Although this system probably more accurately conveyed unit costs than the current system of dollars per square foot, it does make it hard to relate construction costs to rentals that in the late nineteenth century were listed in dollars per square foot.

80. Flinn, *Standard Guide*, 493.

81. Provisions permitting bays had been in force for a great many years by the 1880s. They were originally drafted to encourage flexibility and diversity in houses. Some sample wording from the ordinances as they appeared in the 1890s: "The walls of all bay and oriel windows shall be constructed entirely of incombustible materials. . . . No such bay or oriel window shall be at a less distance than 12 feet from the sidewalk grade. No such bay or oriel windows shall project more than 3 feet over the street line of any building. . . . No such bay or oriel window shall have a greater street frontage than 15 feet." J. W. Ritchie, *Building Inspector's Handbook of Chicago* (Chicago, 1897), 107. It appears that the provision making these projecting bays possible was deleted for the first time in the ordinance passed on 18 March 1905. See *An Ordinance relating to the Department of Buildings and Governing the Erection of Building, etc. in the City of Chicago* (Chicago, 1905). The last known Holabird & Roche building with projecting bays appears to be the Chicago Building of 1904. A chart giving the provisions of various cities for projections beyond the building line can be found in *American Architect and Building News*, 11 February 1893, 90. See also Schultz and Simmons, *Offices in the Sky*, 128.

82. Meredith Clausen, "Frank Lloyd Wright, Vertical Space and the Chicago School's Quest for Light," *Journal of the Society of Architectural Historians* 44 (March 1985): 66–74.

83. On this see Hill, "Office Building," 16: "Generally about 35 per cent of windows surface in the wall gives a very efficient light. Very large glass surfaces should be avoided in cold climates as the glass radiates externally the heat of the interior producing the effect of a draught which is difficult to neutralize."

84. *Chicago Tribune*, 12 May 1889.

85. William Gray Purcell, "First Skyscraper," *Northwest Architect*, January–February 1953, 4.

86. Renwick, "Recollections," 85–88.

87. Julian Ralph, "Chicago—the Main Exhibit," *Harper's Magazine* 84 (February 1892): 426.

88. According to Hill, "Office Building," 15, the corridors were most often four to six feet wide and the offices from nine by fifteen feet to fifteen by twenty-five.

89. Hill, "Office Building," 17–18. See also *Industrial Chicago,* 1:191, and Schultz and Simmons, *Offices in the Sky,* 128–35.

90. *Chicago Tribune,* 12 May 1989.

91. Purcell, "First Skyscraper," 5.

92. On building services see Bluestone, *Constructing Chicago,* 132. The Durham system is described in *Industrial Chicago,* 2:73.

93. On rent levels at various heights see Richard M. Hurd, *Principles of City Land Values* (New York, 1905), 101.

94. *Chicago Tribune,* 12 May 1889.

95. Henry B. Fuller, *The Cliff-Dwellers* (1893), 4–5. In his description of the skyscrapers of Chicago Fuller mentions two by name, the Tacoma and the Monadnock.

96. On the role of the building as city in itself see the excellent passages in Bluestone, *Constructing Chicago,* 104–51.

97. John J. Flinn, *Handbook of Chicago Biography* (Chicago, 1893), 375.

98. The Tacoma has had a curious life in architectural history. Virtually all the earliest serious historians of American architecture mentioned it, but they all discussed it solely in the context of its structural advances; for example, Thomas Tallmadge, *Story of Architecture in America* (New York, 1927), 179; Fisk Kimball, *American Architecture* (Indianapolis, 1928), 144; Charles Whitaker, *From Ramses to Rockefeller* (New York, 1934). Only Lewis Mumford, in his *Sticks and Stones: A Study of American Architecture and Civilization* (New York, 1924) and *Brown Decades: A Study of the Arts in America, 1865–1895* (New York, 1931), failed to mention Holabird & Roche or the Tacoma. In 1929 Henry-Russell Hitchcock inaugurated what would be-

come the modernist view of Chicago architecture. In his *Modern Architecture* (New York, 1929) he tried to make the case for the Tacoma based on structural morality, something neither Holabird & Roche nor the early American writers were likely to have done: "With all its awkwardness and its ornament—which was second rate Richardsonian Romanesque—this first real skyscraper has never been equalled as frank expression of functional structure: all the way that skyscraper design has traveled since then has been from the point of view of rationalism along a false route." Hitchcock judged the work of Holabird & Roche to be much more important than that of Sullivan in creating the skyscraper. The moral position that an obviously thin cladding was more honest than one that emphasized a building's weight was maintained in all subsequent modernist histories, notably Sigfried Giedion, *Space, Time and Architecture: The Growth of a New Tradition* (Cambridge, Mass., 1941), 295–96; John E. Burchard and Albert Bush-Brown, *The Architecture of America: A Social and Cultural History* (Boston, 1961), 251; Pevsner, *History of Building Types,* 218–21; Manfredo Tafuri and Francesco Dal Co, *Modern Architecture* (New York, 1979), 66.

Chapter Six

1. Carl Condit, *Chicago, 1930–70: Building, Planning, and Urban Technology* (Chicago: University of Chicago Press, 1974), table 2, 284–85.

2. Data on building heights compiled from Frank A. Randall, *History of the Development of Building Construction in Chicago* (Urbana, Ill., 1949).

3. *American Architect and Building News,* 25 February 1888.

4. The process by which man-made objects in the landscape come to appear "natural" is beautifully evoked in William Cronon, *Nature's Metropolis: Chicago and the Great West* (New York, 1991), xvii and elsewhere.

5. Henry B. Fuller, *The Cliff-Dwellers* (1893), 1–2. On the subject of the *Cliff-Dwellers* as a response to the 1893 World's Fair see Kenneth Scambray, *A Varied Harvest: The Life and Works of Henry Blake Fuller* (Pittsburgh, 1987), 82–91.

6. Among the many examples that could be cited see "A Pen Picture of Chicago Street Scenes," in George E. Moran, *Moran's Dictionary of Chicago and Its Vicinity* (Chicago, 1909).

7. On Fuller's attitude toward the city see Scambray, *Varied Harvest.*

8. Joseph Kirkland and Caroline Kirkland, *The Story of Chicago* (Chicago, 1892–94), 2:357.

9. *Builder,* 9 July 1892, 25.

10. A large literature grew up on the subject of building regulations. See, for example, *Chicago Tribune,* 7 July 1889, part 2, 9, or a series of articles in *Engineering Magazine,* including John Beverley Robinson, "What Is the Use of Building Laws," August 1890, 656–62; Edward Henry, "What Is the Use of Building Laws," November 1890, 239, 251; Henry A. Goetz, "Dangers from Tall Buildings," March 1892, 792–818. Perry Duis, "The Sky's the Limit?" in *Chicago,* April 1984, has an excellent short summary on this problem. See also the discussion in Daniel Bluestone, *Constructing Chicago* (New Haven, Conn., 1991), 150. A discussion of height limit legislation will be a prominent part of a forthcoming book on downtowns by Robert Fogelson.

11. On the question of interpreting the reaction of Americans to the rise of big business, see the introductory pages in Louis Galambos, *The Public Image of Big Business in America: A Quantitative Study in Social Change* (Baltimore, 1975), 15–20, and William J. Lloyd, "Understanding Late Nineteenth Century American Cities," *Geographical Review,* October 1981. See also several excellent passages in Richard Hofstadter's classic *The Age of Reform: From Bryan to F. D. R.* (New York, 1955), for example, 140–41.

12. Kenneth Turney Gibbs, *Business Architectural Imagery in America, 1870–1930* (Ann Arbor, Mich., 1984), 113–67.

13. Interesting observations on anti-skyscraper sentiment can be found in Bluestone, *Constructing Chicago,* 150, with good sources in note 115.

14. Henry B. Fuller, "The Upward Movement in Chicago," *Atlantic Monthly,* October 1897, 537. On Fuller's antagonistic relationship with Chicago capitalism, see the discussion in Scambray, *Varied Harvest,* 77–97.

15. On this issue, see the stance against height limits taken by the editors of *Inland Architect,* October 1891, 26. See also the discussion of the issue in *Chicago Sunday Tribune,* 7 July 1889, 9, "More Cloud Scrapers."

16. Hamlin Garland, *Rose of Dutcher's Coolly* (New York, 1899), 82.

17. On this topic and the "beautification" movement see Timothy J. Garvey, *Public Sculptor: Lorado Taft and the Beautification of Chicago* (Urbana, Ill., 1988), 20–25.

18. *Real Estate and Building Journal,* 8 March 1884, 114.

19. Montgomery Schuyler, for example, who was generally admiring of the work of Burnham and Root, had little good to say about the Masonic Temple in his article "D. H. Burnham & Co.," *Architectural Record,* February 1896, 49–69.

20. *Economist,* 25 February 1893, 262.

21. On this point there is considerable contradictory evidence. According to Edward Renwick, "Recollections" (1932), 77, the switch was due in great part to the experience at the Monadnock where, according to Renwick, Holabird & Roche provided a design that cost 15 percent less but provided 15 percent more space. Miles Berger in *They Built Chicago: Entrepreneurs Who Shaped a Great City's Architecture* (Chicago, 1992), 46, has suggested that Aldis was more comfortable with Root than with Burnham so that after Root died in 1891 Aldis felt little loyalty.

22. On Owen Aldis see John Leonard, ed., *The Book of Chicagoans* (Chicago, 1905), 17; *Economist*, 26 July 1924, 223; and an obituary in *Economist*, 8 August 1925, 369. Unfortunately the large correspondence between the Brooks brothers and Aldis was thrown away in the 1960s. See Donald Hoffmann, *The Architecture of John Wellborn Root* (Chicago, 1973), 19. Some interesting glimpses into their operations are offered by quotations in a number of books cited in Gibbs, *Business Architectural Imagery*, 61. There are also scattered surviving letters, for example, some at the Chicago Historical Society relating to the Pontiac Building. These letters were preserved by the Brookses' heirs, the Saltonstall family. By the end of the nineteenth century the firm of Aldis, Aldis, and Northcote, established by Owen Aldis and his brother in 1888, was widely considered the most important single player in Chicago real estate. By 1902 he had either produced or managed one-fifth of Chicago's office space, according to Earle Schultz and Walter Simmons, *Offices in the Sky* (Indianapolis, 1959), 33.

23. Among many other buildings involving most of these players were the Venetian and Champlain (see chapter 13), and the Pontiac, Brooks, and Kohn (chapter 11).

24. *Economist*, 25 February 1893, 262.

25. On the Honore Building see chapter 4. Some confusion exists about the Honore, apparently because the building was erected just before the Fire and reconstructed just after. The information in Randall, *Building Construction in Chicago*, 65, and in the captions to illustrations on 51 and 63 is apparently contradictory. In any event, it was one of the most lavishly ornamented structures of its day.

26. Renwick, "Recollections," 70–71.

27. Renwick, "Recollections," 71–72.

28. *Economist*, 28 November 1891, 893.

29. A bill passed in February 1892 limiting buildings to 150 feet, but this was vetoed by Mayor Hempstead Washburne. See Duis, "Sky's the Limit?" 105. An even more stringent measure limiting buildings to 130 feet was passed in 1893 and again vetoed by the mayor, but the veto was overridden forty-nine to two. *Engineering News*, 1 June 1893, 521.

30. Although many citizens were undoubtedly delighted with this outcome, most business interests and most architects felt its provisions were unnecessarily restrictive, since the market would regulate the problem by itself. According to some owners and developers, the owners of high buildings, simply to protect their own interests, had to arrange matters so they controlled the developments around their own. Otherwise they would find their windows blocked by adjacent buildings. On this see Richard M. Hurd, *Principles of City Land Values* (New York, 1903), 99–100. Some observers have even suggested that one of the reasons for New York's rejuvenation as a business center in the 1920s was the inability of Chicago developers to compete owing to the height restrictions. See Schultz and Simmons, *Offices in the Sky*, 274–89. There is little reason to believe the height limits had any major effect on business generally. In fact, as often as not they were at or above the level that permitted maximum return on investment.

31. *Builder*, 9 July 1892, 25.

32. The movement of commercial activities in fast changing cities is treated at length in Hurd, *Principles of City Land Values*.

33. On the investigation of metal deterioration in tall office buildings see Randall, *Building Construction in Chicago*, 15–16. An important study was conducted in 1929 on the Tacoma Building at the time of its demolition. The report by Paul E. Holcomb, research engineer for the National Association of Building Owners and Managers, titled "Depreciation and Obsolescence in the Tacoma Building," has apparently not survived, but an account was published in *Engineering News Record*, 26 December 1929, 1003–4.

34. It is difficult to determine when depre-

ciation calculations started to be systematically used. Although the idea seems to have been known in the middle of the nineteenth century, its use almost certainly was greatly expanded in the building boom of the late nineteenth century. By the end of the century depreciation calculations were a common feature in bookkeeping for buildings, at least in the largest cities, as the language at the beginning of Hurd, *Principles of City Land Values,* 1–2, makes clear. See also Richard P. Brief, ed., *The Late Nineteenth Century Debate over Depreciation, Capital and Income* (New York, 1976).

35. It is tempting to see the comparison between early pre-Fire buildings like the Honore Block, with its elaborate sculptural facade, and the Tacoma or the initial design for the Marquette as demonstrations of this process. We must approach this kind of conclusion with care, however, since it is hard to find any observers at the time who stated that this was the case. Perhaps the change that took place was a subconscious reaction to new economic realities whose influence would become clear only later. Perhaps no such cause-and-effect relation was involved at all. It is possible that any increased awareness of rapid obsolescence was countered by a reduction in the cost of mass-produced ornament, making it economically feasible to create temporary buildings just as elaborate as any earlier building that had been considered permanent.

36. The Chicago Real Estate Board, for example, was founded in 1883 as a way of protecting the reputation of established real estate firms like Baird and Bradley and W. D. Kerfoot and Company and separating them from unscrupulous or unorthodox brokers and property managers. On this organization see Betty Pegg, *Dreams, Money, and Ambition: A History of Real Estate in Chicago* (Chicago, 1983). The board's first agenda items involved regulating commissions and devising standard lease forms.

37. George W. Steevens, *Lord of the Dollar* (New York, 1897), 149.

38. Burnham and Root had designed the Art Institute, but this was a relatively modest structure. Adler and Sullivan had been responsible for the Auditorium Theater, but the theater part of this building was encased in a hotel and office block, and it was these private, commercial aspects that dominated the exterior expression. In fact Chicago in the late nineteenth century was often perceived as lacking in its public buildings. On this subject see "Architecture in Chicago, Adler and Sullivan," *Architectural Record,* February 1896, and Daniel Bluestone's chapter "Less of Pork and More of Culture," in *Constructing Chicago,* 152–81. When the two most significant cultural buildings of the era, the Chicago Public Library and the first section of the current Art Institute, were commissioned in the early 1890s, it is conspicuous that these commissions were given not to Chicagoans but to Shepley, Rutan and Coolidge of Boston.

39. Montgomery Schuyler, "Architecture in Chicago: Adler and Sullivan," *Architectural Record,* February 1896; reprinted in Schuyler, *American Architecture, and Other Writings,* ed. William H. Jordy and Ralph Coe (Cambridge, Mass., 1961), 383.

40. On the creation of architectural corporations see Thomas J. Holleman and James P. Gallagher, *Smith, Hinchman and Grylls, 125 Years of Architecture and Engineering, 1853–1978* (Detroit, 1978), 61.

41. According to the testimony of a writer in the *Architectural Record,* December 1895, 9, "Chicago architects are different in that they have frankly accepted the conditions imposed by the speculator. . . . there is no getting away from these conditions if one would win and keep the reputation of a 'practical architect.'"

42. On the role of the Western Association of Architects there are some very good comments in Andrew Saint, *The Image of the Architect* (New Haven, Conn., 1983), 89–91, and Sibel Bozdogan Dostoglu, "Toward Professional Legitimacy and Power: An Inquiry into the Strug-

gle, Achievements and Dilemmas of the Architectural Profession through an Analysis of Chicago, 1871–1909" (Ph.D. diss., University of Pennsylvania, 1982), 44–46. On the differences between eastern and Chicago architects see also the comments in chapter 7 on the Marquette.

43. Dmitri Tselos in his article "The Chicago Fair and the Myth of the Lost Cause," *Journal of the Society of Architectural Historians*, December 1967, clearly demonstrated how the classical impulse had affected Sullivan in the 1890s.

44. On the Women's Temple see Hoffman, *John Wellborn Root*, 192–95.

45. On the Monadnock see ibid., 155–76.

46. The major critical voice lauding the Monadnock was Montgomery Schuyler. Following critics like Ruskin, Schuyler insisted on the truthfulness of buildings and by that standard found the Monadnock the least deceptive of any in the city. Montgomery Schuyler, *American Architecture and Other Writings*, ed. William H. Jordy and Ralph Coe (New York, 1964), 410–12. Schuyler, however, was not a Chicagoan. He was a pillar of the New York architectural establishment. His sentiments are perfectly in line with those of another New York establishment figure, William Dean Howells, who championed the more naturalistic western novels of Henry Blake Fuller and others against their more genteel eastern counterparts. For a discussion of these polemical positions see Robert Bruegmann, "The Marquette and the Myth of the Chicago School," *Threshold* 5–6 (fall 1991): 6–23.

47. *Industrial Chicago* (Chicago, 1891), 70.

48. My analysis of the Burnham and Root and Holabird & Roche versions of the Monadnock is indebted to the presentation of this subject by Stuart E. Cohen in *Chicago Architects: Documenting the Exhibition of the Same Name* (Chicago, 1976), 14. According to Renwick, "Recollections," 77, when the Monadnock addition was completed "Mr Aldis stated, in our office, that the new building cost 15% less than the north, contained 15 to 16% more available renting space and that space 15% lighter than the space of the north half. 'This makes me decide,' he said, 'that I can no longer afford to employ another architect.'"

49. Contrary to what has usually been written about the Monadnock, there was no simple division between the masonry bearing wall north end and the steel frame southern end. Although the north end did in fact use load-bearing walls throughout, the structural system of the southern half, by Holabird & Roche, was a hybrid. On this see the catalog entry for the Monadnock (no. 150) in Bruegmann, *Holabird & Roche/Holabird & Root*.

Chapter Seven

1. Letter preserved in materials donated to the Chicago Historical Society by Holabird & Root.

2. *Economist*, 14 October 1893, 405.

3. *Brickbuilder*, June 1895, 132–33.

4. On the increasing use of the steel frame see chapter 5.

5. A good exposition of this matter, written by longtime Holabird & Roche employee Edward Renwick, can be found in his article "Office Buildings as an Investment," *Economist*, 29 June 1918, 1176.

6. In traditional classical architecture it was widely believed that the cornice had a function in throwing water away from the building walls, thus preventing unsightly streaking and in some cases damage to the stone. By 1900 it had become clear that in skyscrapers the cornice could never be large enough to serve this function adequately. Where classical cornices had usually been corbeled out in solid stone and were thus reasonably stable, in many large nineteenth-century commercial buildings, particularly in metal frame structures, these cornices were made of pressed metal or terra cotta and attached to the building by metal ties. When these ties

rusted, the cornices could come crashing down. By the last part of the century this problem had become apparent, and owners started removing cornices on many buildings. Better constructed than many, the Marquette's cornice survived until well into the twentieth century. On cornices and their problems see *Architectural Record,* May 1910, 431, and Peter B. Wight, Additions to Chicago's Skyline, a Few Recent Skyscrapers," *Architectural Record,* July 1910, 6–18.

7. For a fuller treatment of the classical impulses in the Marquette Building see Robert Bruegmann, "The Marquette and the Myth of the Chicago School," *Threshold* 5–6 (fall 1991); 6–23.

8. It is not clear whether the Marquette owners removed the portico because they were obliged to by the city or whether they simply had it removed the first time repairs were necessary on the assumption that it was superfluous and the building was cheaper to maintain without it.

9. Edward Renwick, in his "Recollections" (1932), 224, offered an explanation for the odd proportions of the columns: "Mr. Roche had designed them as fluted columns, and the concave surface, polished must have a little more than a double entasis. But George Fuller, the contractor, who was a one-third owner of the Marquette Building, when he found out that the fluting was going to cost $6,000 ordered them turned. They were smooth and polished so that you get the curves two ways and they impressed your eye as being much bigger than they were."

10. On the sculptural program of the Marquette, see Ira J. Bach and Mary Lackritz Gray, *A Guide to Chicago's Public Sculpture* (Chicago, 1983), 58–59, and James L. Riedy, *Chicago Sculpture* (Urbana, Ill., 1981), 26–27.

11. Very few interior public spaces in late nineteenth-century office buildings were much larger than that of the Marquette, the great exception being the enormous atrium at the Rookery Building.

12. The lighting of the Marquette lobby was greatly altered when the open elevator cages were removed. It was further changed during a recent renovation with the addition of rather strident lighting that shines directly on the murals. They can certainly be seen more clearly now, but the effect of the thousands of glass pieces shimmering in what was probably a relatively dark space is gone.

13. Bach and Gray, *Chicago's Public Sculpture,* 58.

14. On the N. W. Harris and Company offices see *Economist,* 4 May 1895.

15. Although the upper floors had started to become as valuable as the lowest in many buildings, the men's toilet took up nearly the entire top floor at the Marquette, showing that this idea had not completely taken hold. At the turn of the century it was apparently the middle floors—from three to eight, for example—that were the least sought after. Richard M. Hurd, *Principles of City Land Values* (New York, 1903), 101.

16. The planning of office floors so that spaces could be configured by the tenant when the space was leased is noted by Joseph K. Freitag, *Architectural Engineering,* 2d ed. (New York, 1907), 34, who writes: "Many of the floors in the larger office building are never subdivided until rented, in order that the arrangements of the partitions may be made to suit tenants."

17. Late nineteenth-century office buildings had washbasins in each office in part because the largest ones had restrooms only on a single floor, often at the very top of the building. It would have been very inconvenient to take the elevator all the way up merely to wash one's hands before lunch, for example.

18. *Engineering News,* 17 October 1895.

19. The differences between building conditions in Chicago and New York are the subject of an interesting commentary in Kenneth Turney Gibbs, *Business Architectural Imagery in America, 1870–1930* (Ann Arbor, Mich., 1984). A good example of the way Chicagoans saw this

difference can be found in an article by F. W. Fitzpatrick in *Inland Architect,* June 1905: "In New York one type has served as a model for all that city's architecture. As soon as one of the profession secures a commission for a tall building he sets himself to work designing a wonderfully ornate Greek temple cocked up on a basement of sixteen or seventeen stories, and that in turn resting upon a supposed plinth of a couple or more stories wonderfully tortured with ornament. Up and down Broadway, and crosswise, do you get that same thing, it stares you in the face at every turn. In Chicago the architects when confronted with a tall building proposition accepted it as a new form, and proceeded to build their structures of few architectural features, of simple lines and dignified masses. In the most part good square fronts pierced with unlabored fenestration."

20. The building housing the Mills and Gibb Company, importers of lace, embroidery, and dry goods at 462–70 Broadway, at the northeast corner of Grand Street, for example, has the same forthright rectangular massing, the same regular array of large rectangular windows, the same even cornice line. According to the Manhattan docket books, the Mill and Gibb Building was constructed in 1879 to designs by John Correja. Dozens of other loft buildings not unlike the Marquette in their regularity of massing and window treatment appear on the pages of *Both Sides of Broadway,* compiled by the De Leeuw Riehl Publishing Company (New York, 1910), or in the illustrations to Moses King, *King's Views of New York 1896–1915, and Brooklyn, 1905* (Boston, 1894–95; reprinted New York, 1974).

21. A. C. David, "The New Architecture: The First American Type of Real Value," *Architectural Record* 28 (December 1910).

22. The Mills Building was on Broad Street between Wall Street and Exchange Place. It is visible in Moses King, *King's Handbook of New York City* (Boston, 1895), 771. See also Russell Sturgis, "The Work of George B. Post," *Architectural Record,* June 1898, 3–102.

23. Unfortunately, little is yet known about New York's "bread and butter" commercial architects. A good start was made by Robert A. M. Stern et al., *New York Nineteen Hundred: Metropolitan Architecture and Urbanism, 1890–1915* (New York, 1983), which tackled the problem from the standpoint of position in the block, a very fruitful new way to approach these buildings. A forthcoming volume on New York commercial architecture by Carl Condit and Sarah Bradford Landau promises to shed more light on this important subject.

24. *Industrial Chicago,* 1:70.

25. Louis Sullivan, "Ornament in Architecture," *Engineering Magazine* 3 (August 1892), reprinted in Robert Twombly, *Louis Sullivan: The Public Papers* (Chicago, 1988), 80.

26. One of the best ways to appreciate this phenomenon is to look at collections of pictures of major streets in American cities in the early twentieth century. Unfortunately these are hardly ever found in architectural history books, though, curiously, they often appear in works on other subjects, notably transit systems. See, for example, the view of Seattle's Madison Street on page 46, Denver on page 96, Olive Street in St. Louis, page 152, or Eleventh Street, Tacoma, on page 166 of George Woodman Hilton, *The Cable Car in America,* 2d ed. (San Diego, Calif., 1982).

27. On this see chapter 5 on the Tacoma Building.

28. On the discussion of the metal frame of the Tacoma and Home Insurance Buildings see chapter 5 on the Tacoma Building.

29. On the coining of the term "Chicago school" see Robert Bruegmann, "The Marquette Building and the Myth of the Chicago School," *Threshold* 5–6 (fall 1991): 6–23.

30. Sigfried Giedion, *Space, Time and Architecture: The Growth of a New Tradition* (Cambridge, Mass., 1941), 298–99.

31. Carl Condit, *Chicago School of Architecture: A History of Commercial and Public Building in the Chicago Area, 1875–1925* (Chicago, 1964), 121–22.

32. On the influence of architectural history and preservation on postwar Chicago architecture see the excellent commentary by Daniel Bluestone in *Journal of Education* 47 (May 1994): 210–23.

Chapter Eight

1. In the vast literature about the city, the contrast between the elite residential neighborhoods and the tenement districts of the poorest citizens was stressed over and over. Most of the average middle-class neighborhoods were ignored. William J. Lloyd, "Understanding Late Nineteenth-Century American Cities," *Geographical Review,* October 1981. On the history of American suburbs generally the best source is Kenneth T. Jackson, *Crabgrass Frontier: The Suburbanization of America* (New York, 1985). On Chicago's North Shore communities see Michael H. Ebner, *Creating Chicago's North Shore: A Suburban History* (Chicago, 1988).

2. William Archer, *America To-day* (1900), 103.

3. This system was still under construction at the end of the nineteenth century. There is an excellent description of it in Daniel Bluestone, "Landscape and Culture in Nineteenth Century Chicago" (Ph.D. diss., University of Chicago, 1984), and his *Constructing Chicago* (New Haven, Conn., 1991), chap. 2.

4. For example in John J. Flinn, *Standard Guide to Chicago* (Chicago, 1891), the reader would find good descriptions of Kenwood on pages 398–99, of the boulevards of the South Side on pages 530–32, or of the North Side on pages 541–42.

5. On Evanston, see Ebner, *Creating Chicago's North Shore,* 91–94, and Margery Blair Perkins, *Evanstoniana: An Informal History of Evanston and Its Architecture* (Chicago, 1984).

6. Flinn, *Standard Guide to Chicago,* 389.

7. On the Burnham house see Perkins, *Evanstoniana,* 98.

8. William Holabird's daughter-in-law, Mrs. John A. Holabird Sr., was a frequent visitor in the 1910s and early 1920s. She recalled that the house was large and very comfortable, with four bedrooms on the second floor and more on the third. She remembered a big stone horse block at the curb and the Evanston Country Club, for which the firm did the design, across the street. Also within a few hundred feet was St. Mark's Episcopal Church. Interview with Mrs. John A. Holabird Sr. 20 August 1980.

9. Although McKim, Mead and White's Newport Casino in Newport, Rhode Island, constructed in 1879–80, may not have been a specific model for the Holabird & Roche structure, it is very likely that they had just such a building in mind when designing it. On the Newport building see Leland M. Roth, *The Architecture of McKim, Mead and White, 1870–1920: A Building List* (New York, 1978), cat. no. 612.

Chapter Nine

1. By comparison the firm of McKim, Mead and White in New York recorded over $3 million during these years. Leland M. Roth, *The Architecture of McKim, Mead and White, 1870–1920: A Building List* (New York, 1978), 178–79.

2. Charles E. Fox went on to an illustrious career in partnership with Benjamin Marshall. Marshall and Fox created some of the most elegant apartment buildings in the Chicago area. Frank B. Long was a longtime chief draftsman in the firm.

3. In his "Recollections" (1932), 93, Edward Renwick stated that he paid $2,000 for his share. He also relates that during 1896, because of the continuing business downturn, his share of losses in the firm was $12,000, suggesting that the firm lost $60,000 as a whole for the year.

4. The apogee of this development would

come at the McConnell Apartments a few years later. On this see below.

5. This institution was founded in 1859 and folded in 1886. See Harold M. Mayer and Richard D. Wade, *Chicago: Growth of a Metropolis* (Chicago, 1969), 102.

6. Charles E. Jenkins, "A Review of the Work of Holabird & Roche," *Architectural Reviewer* 3 (June 1897): 1–41.

7. On the rise of tall apartment buildings for the affluent see William Westfall, "From Homes to Towers: A Century of Chicago's Best Hotels and Apartment Buildings," in *Chicago Architecture, 1872–1922: Reconfiguration of an American Metropolis*, ed. John Zukowsky (Chicago, 1993), 266–89. See also George Hill, "Apartment House," in *A Dictionary of Architecture and Building: Biographical, Historical, and Descriptive*, ed. Russell Sturgis (New York, 1901–2), 1:82–89.

8. On the construction workers' strike see Sibel Bozdogan Dostoglu, "Toward Professional Legitimacy and Power: An Inquiry into the Struggle, Achievements and Dilemmas of the Architectural Profession through an Analysis of Chicago, 1871–1909" (Ph.D. diss., University of Pennsylvania, 1982), 100.

9. Roth, *McKim, Mead and White*, 178–79.

10. By the time of the Tribune Building windows were definitely becoming smaller. Some scholars have believed this was due primarily to the improved performance of electric lighting. It is just as likely that the improved lighting simply made possible changes based on aesthetic ideals. On this subject, see George Hill, "Office Building," in Sturgis, *Dictionary of Architecture and Building*, 3:15.

11. "A New Era of Building in Chicago," *Harper's Weekly*, 7 September 1901, 892–93.

12. On the construction of the Tribune basement see Renwick, "Recollections," 97–100.

13. William Holabird in *Inland Architect*, September 1902, 112–13.

Chapter Ten

1. On downtown shopping see the chapter on the department store in Gunther Barth, *City People: The Rise of Modern City Culture in Nineteenth-Century America* (New York, 1980), and Neil Harris, "Shopping—Chicago Style," in *Chicago Architecture, 1872–1922: Reconfiguration of an American Metropolis*, ed. John Zukowsky (Chicago, 1993), 137–56. On State Street land prices see Homer Hoyt, *One Hundred Years of Land Values in Chicago* (Chicago, 1933), 89–90, 188, 211.

2. See, for example, the caption to an old photograph reproduced in Paul T. Gilbert, *Chicago and Its Makers* (Chicago, 1929), 262.

3. There is no adequate study of Jenney's State Street stores. Some information can be found in Carl Condit, *Chicago School of Architecture: A History of Commercial and Public Building in the Chicago Area, 1875–1925* (Chicago, 1964), 90–91. One of the most important questions is why Jenney was able to design his Chicago department stores in a way that was much more dependent on the tradition of the warehouse and wholesale store than was true in the other cities. Certainly one of the most intriguing similarities is between the Leiter I and Leiter II Buildings, structures whose programs might have suggested they be very different. Whether this was a matter of business or of architectural aesthetics is impossible to decide. The correlations between department stores' clientele and their design is likewise obscure, although Robert A. M. Stern, Gregory Gilmartin, and John Montague Massengale, *New York Nineteen Hundred: Metropolitan Architecture and Urbanism, 1890–1915* (New York, 1983), 192–96, has some interesting comments.

4. Unfortunately, despite all that has been written about Chicago's department stores, there is still a great deal that has not been studied. The relation between Chicago's stores and those of Paris and New York remains problematic, for

example. On the development of department stores generally see Meredith L. Clausen, "The Department Store," in *Encyclopedia of Architecture, Design, Engineering and Construction,* ed. Joseph A. Wilkes (New York, 1988–89), 2:204–22. On Chicago's department stores see the excellent piece by Neil Harris, "Shopping Chicago Style," in Zukowsky, *Chicago Architecture,* 137–55.

5. On the Massachusetts trust see chapter 5 on the Tacoma and Miles Berger, *They Built Chicago: Entrepreneurs Who Shaped a Great City's Architecture* (Chicago, 1992), 43–44.

6. On the Chicago Real Estate Trustees see Gerald Wade Kuhn, "History of the Financing of Commercial Structures in the Chicago Loop, 1868–1934" (Ph.D. diss., University of Indiana Business School, 1969), 100, who states that this was a Massachusetts Trust, and Berger, *They Built Chicago,* 43, who calls it the first of the Chicago general real estate trusts. According to Berger the trust remained active until 1979. See also Earle Schultz and Walter Simmons, *Offices in the Sky* (Indianapolis, 1959), 26.

7. *Inland Architect,* June 1891.

8. On the influence of theories of disease transmission on architectural form see Robert Bruegmann, "The Architecture of the Hospital, 1770–1870" (Ph.D. diss., University of Pennsylvania, 1976), 175–80.

9. According to Kuhn, "History of the Financing of Commercial Structures," 100, this was a Massachusetts trust. Berger, *They Built Chicago,* 44, seems to believe it was a Chicago trust. See also Schultz and Simmons, *Offices in the Sky,* 32.

10. *Brickbuilder,* June 1995, 132.

11. Robert C. Mack, "Manufacture and Use of Architectural Terra Cotta in the United States," in *Technology of Historic American Buildings: Studies of the Materials, Craft Processes, and Mechanization of Building Construction,* ed. Ward Jandl (Washington, D.C., 1983), 118–37.

12. Donald Hoffmann, *The Architecture of John Wellborn Root* (Baltimore, 1973), 177–91.

13. Not only were many of the claims made for it inaccurate, but the material had a number of other major problems. The most serious was the difficulty of marrying terra cotta to the underlying steel frame. Because the terra cotta expanded and contracted with temperature changes much less readily than the steel frames it was attached to, and because it was brittle, severe cracking often occurred over the years. This in turn allowed water to penetrate behind the terra cotta, rusting out the metal pieces that tied the cladding to the frame. If this deterioration went unchecked, the terra cotta panels eventually would fall off the building, posing a major safety hazard.

14. Today, with these windows mostly covered up, the effect is entirely lost, and it is hard to judge how well this feature might have worked.

15. Sullivan's building was announced in 1898 but not finished until 1903. On Carson Pirie Scott see the excellent monograph by Joseph Siry, *Carson Pirie Scott: Louis Sullivan and the Chicago Department Store* (Chicago, 1988).

16. For an excellent analysis of the way the terra cotta was detailed so it resembled stone, see Siry, *Carson Pirie Scott,* 98–99.

Chapter Eleven

1. In the late nineteenth century the demand for architectural photography increased dramatically as architectural firms found they needed clear, large-negative record shots of their buildings under construction to help them in construction supervision and also good-quality, well-composed shots of the finished buildings to submit to architectural periodicals. This led to the founding of a number of important architectural photography firms, the Barnes-Crosby enterprise among them. On this firm see Larry Viskochil, *Chicago at the Turn of the Century in Photographs* (New York, 1984).

2. Theodore Dreiser, *Sister Carrie* (New York, 1900), 14.

3. Ibid., 17.

4. Generations of European writers have described all of Chicago's commercial architecture in this way. See, for example, Heinrich Klotz, "The Chicago Multistory as a Design Problem," in *Chicago Architecture, 1872–1922: Birth of a Metropolis,* ed. John Zukowsky (Chicago, 1987), 57–76. In fact, as we have seen, between the least expensive loft and the most prestigious office building there was an enormous range of possibilities in imagery, structure, use of materials, and class of tenants.

5. For a discussion of Chicago's height limits, see chapter 6 on the Marquette Building.

6. Too little is known about loft buildings in any city. It is conspicuous that many buildings of essentially the loft type in London, Manchester, and Liverpool had such elaborate facades that they looked more like hotels. The best-known and best-documented loft district in the United States is Manhattan's Soho, or "cast iron" district, the area adjacent to lower Broadway roughly between Canal and Houston Streets. In Soho the visitor can still get a good idea of what a midcentury loft district would have been like. Block after block of loft buildings, typically six or seven stories high, line the streets, with their brick, stone, or cast iron facades marked by a regular succession of large windows lighting the open interior spaces. Whereas the simplest buildings consist of nothing more than large sheets of glass filling the spaces between minimal iron panels, on the more elaborate examples highly ornamental decorative features such as Italianate window surrounds or ponderous cornices, all in cast iron, provide a note of fantasy in an otherwise austere streetscape. On Soho see the extensive report of the New York Landmarks Commission, "Soho Cast Iron Historic District Designation Report" (1973), and Margot Gayle and Edmund V. Gillon Jr., *Cast-Iron Architecture in New York* (New York, 1974).

7. On State Street and the segregating of Chicago's uses see Harold M. Mayer and Richard C. Wade, *Chicago: Growth of a Metropolis* (Chicago, 1969).

8. On the development of the metal skeleton framing system see chapter 5 on the Tacoma.

9. On the Turner system and others see Carl Condit, *American Building Art: The Nineteenth Century* (New York, 1960), 167–68, 353–54.

10. On the framing of the Leiter I Building see chapter 5 on the Tacoma Building.

11. An example of a slightly earlier New York example that uses a similar vocabulary is the Eberhard Faber factory at Greenpoint, Long Island, built in 1872 and illustrated in Moses King, *King's Handbook of New York City* (Boston, 1895), 899. A later example is 83–85 White Street, designed by J. Morgan Slade in 1881. An illustration of this building can be seen in Gayle and Gillon, *Cast Iron Architecture in New York,* 31.

12. Jeffrey Karl Ochsner, *H. H. Richardson, Complete Architectural Works* (Cambridge, Mass., 1982), 380–84.

13. Some of these buildings include the Bailey (1898) at 529 S. Franklin, the Clow (1901–2) at the northwest corner of Franklin and West Harrison, the McNeil (1903–4) at 325 W. Jackson, the Ryerson (1903–4) at 367 W. Adams, the Kohn (1906–7) at 501–9 S. Franklin, the Hart Schaffner and Marx (1908–10) at 36 S. Franklin, and the Born (1908) at 540 S. Wells. On comparable lofts in New York see "Loft Buildings," *Architect's and Builder's Magazine,* February 1908.

14. Joseph Siry, in his book on Sullivan's Carson Pirie Scott Building, clearly shows that for Sullivan terra cotta and marble were related. See *Carson Pirie Scott,* 97–98.

15. According to Edward Renwick in his "Recollections" (1932), 182, in the Holabird & Roche facades the windows were as large as possible. To enhance the artistic effect of his facades,

Renwick claimed, Sullivan sacrificed four feet of window space by filling the top of each with ornamentation. Renwick obviously was not an unbiased observer, but it seems likely that his comments would have been seconded by others in the profession.

16. Peter B. Wight, "Fire-Proofing: Recent Improvements in Fire-Proof Construction at Chicago," *Brickbuilder*, February 1899, 34.

17. Recently, for example, Stuart Cohen called this facade more handsome than Sullivan's Carson Pirie Scott and perhaps the finest work of its day. Stuart E. Cohen, *Chicago Architects: Documenting the Exhibition of the Same Name* (Chicago, 1976), 12–13.

18. G. Twose, "Steel and Terra Cotta Buildings in Chicago: Some Deductions," *Brickbuilder*, January 1894, 1–5.

19. The fate of many lofts, including those of Holabird & Roche, is ironic. Although many have been bulldozed, the very marginality of others saved them. Because the income stream was so small, their owners had little ability to alter them over the years. Most loft buildings merely became dirtier as owners collected rent checks but did little else. Meanwhile, new construction in the city bypassed them. Then, just when things looked least promising, artists discovered New York's Soho and started to colonize the half-abandoned loft districts. Where artists, homosexuals, and other groups marginal to the economy pioneered, others followed. Since the 1960s particularly, in cities across the country, former factories have become discotheques, law offices, seafood restaurants, and condominiums. In the process, buildings that once represented the most laissez-faire attitudes are now protected by municipal preservation laws, and the building hierarchy of the nineteenth century has been almost completely inverted.

Chapter Twelve

1. See chapter 10.

2. For an excellent survey of Chicago department stores at the turn of the century see "The State Street Stores," *Economist*, 13 June 1896, 728–29. On Carson Pirie Scott see Joseph Siry's superb "The Carson Pirie Scott Building in Chicago" (Ph.D. diss., MIT, 1984) and his subsequent book, *Carson Pirie Scott: Louis Sullivan and the Chicago Department Store* (Chicago, 1988). For bibliography on the department store generally see the notes to chapter 10.

3. Margaret Corwin, "Mollie Netcher Newbury: The Merchant Princess," *Chicago History*, spring 1977, 4–43.

4. Edward Renwick, "Recollections" (1932), 115.

5. *Economist*, 22 June 1901, 755, and 1 July 1901, 655. For the earlier history of the store properties see *Economist*, 13 June 1896, 728–29.

6. On the Champlain see chapter 10 on State Street in the 1890s.

7. These purchases are outlined in the *Economist* of 22 June 1901, 755, and 1 July 1901, 655.

8. Renwick, "Recollections," 116.

9. *Economist*, 1 July 1901, 655.

10. The architects had been faced with a somewhat similar problem before when they were obliged to put caissons under the Old Colony foundations. On the foundation problems at the Boston Store see Renwick, "Recollections," 118.

11. The Mandel Brothers Store boasted a laundry capable of processing three thousand pieces a day and an ice plant that could produce eighty tons of ice daily. The Rothschild Store had piano demonstration rooms and a two-story fur storage area.

12. Franz Winkler (pseud. Montgomery Schuyler), "Some Chicago Buildings Represented by the Work of Holabird & Roche," *Architectural Record* 31 (April 1912): 318.

13. On the Mandel Annex, see chapter 10 on State Street in the 1890s.

14. The information about the sprinkler system is contained in a manuscript at the Evanston Historical Society titled "Memorandum

for Evanston Historical Society." The document was obviously written at the time of William Holabird's death.

15. *Economist,* 5 December 1903, 741.

16. *Brickbuilder,* September 1904, 191–92.

17. Strong was a major figure in Chicago real estate. Born in 1829 in Scotland while his father was serving as consul general for the United States, he attended the University of Rochester and Albany Law College. Strong practiced law in Iowa, retiring in 1876 with a large fortune and extensive real estate holdings in Chicago and Washington, D.C., which he continued to develop until his death in 1911. His work was carried on by his son, Colonel Gordon Strong. On Strong see Henry Hall, *America's Successful Men of Affairs: An Encyclopedia of Contemporaneous Biography* (New York, 1895–96), 2:773, and *Economist,* 28 October 1911, 748.

18. These descriptions were contained in the building's house magazine, the *North American,* in 1923.

19. Caption for "Main Corridor" from North American Building brochure, Chicago Historical Society.

20. In addition to the Holabird & Roche buildings there were other tall shops buildings, notably the Stevens Building by Graham, Burnham and Company, built in 1912–13. On the Stevens Building see Sally A. Kitt Chappell, *Architecture and Planning of Graham, Anderson, Probst and White, 1912–1936: Transforming Tradition* (Chicago, 1992), 113–14.

Chapter Thirteen

1. On the history of the golf club see the classic volume by architect Clifford Wendehack, *Golf and Country Clubs* (New York, 1929), and more recently, Geoffrey S. Cornish and Ronald E. Whitten, *The Golf Course* (New York, 1981).

2. Cornish and Whitten, *Golf Course,* 44.

3. Ibid., 36–41.

4. Herbert Warren Wind, "Golfing in and around Chicago," *Chicago History,* winter 1975–

76; idem, *The Story of American Golf,* 3d ed. (New York, 1975).

5. This quotation comes from Angus Hibbard in a chapter titled "Golf and the Glen View Club" from a book of memoirs, Angus Hibbard, *Associations by Choice* (Chicago, 1936).

6. On Shinnecock Hills, a design by Stanford White, see Leland M. Roth, *The Architecture of McKim, Mead and White, 1870–1920: A Building List* (New York, 1978), 142, and Wind, *Story of American Golf,* 23–25.

7. On the Chicago Golf Club see *Chicago Golf Club Jubilee, 1892–1967* (Chicago, 1967).

8. Information about access can be found in a pamphlet issued by the club, titled "Glen View Club, 1897–1982," in the club's collection.

9. James Buckley, *The Evanston Railway Company* (Chicago, 1958).

10. "Glen View Club, 1897–1982."

11. For descriptions of the 1921 clubhouse see "Glen View Club, 1897–1982" and *Hotel Monthly,* October 1922, 44–47.

12. Hibbard, *Associations by Choice.*

13. Holabird & Roche was involved with only a few other country club residential districts, but Chicago was a leader in developing this concept. Perhaps the best example was the giant Olympia Fields Club in Flossmoor. Founded in 1916, the club was an immediate success. By 1925 it had four eighteen-hole courses and an eighty-acre practice course. Reputed to be the world's largest club, it boasted a total of 1,348 players on the grounds on a single day. The English Tudor clubhouse designed by George C. Nimmons was two and a half city blocks long. On the Olympia Fields Club, see *Hotel Monthly,* July 1925.

14. Wendehack, *Golf and Country Clubs,* 1.

15. Ibid., xix–xx.

Chapter Fourteen

1. For an excellent evocation of the relation between timber interests in Chicago and the timber lands of northern Wisconsin see William

Cronon, *Nature's Metropolis: Chicago and the Great West* (New York, 1991).

2. See Cronon, *Nature's Metropolis*, 202, and the manuscript "History of the Coleman Lake Club" (1938), in the possession of the club.

3. On lumber camps see Cronon, *Nature's Metropolis*, 155–56.

4. Edward Renwick, "Recollections" (1932), 207.

5. Interview with John A. Holabird Jr., 13 January 1983, and John Root, "John Augur Holabird—an Appreciation," Illinois Society of Architects *Monthly Bulletin,* August–September 1945.

6. On the Adirondack camps see Harvey Kaiser, *The Great Camps of the Adirondacks* (Boston, 1982).

7. Information courtesy of club member Corwith Hammill.

Chapter Fifteen

1. *Economist,* 24 July 1909, 132. By contrast the New York firm of McKim, Mead and White had, at the point of its greatest expansion, one hundred employees in 1902, according to Leland M. Roth, *The Architecture of McKim, Mead and White, 1870–1920: A Building List* (New York, 1978), xxxv.

2. Figures on the dollar volume of work for McKim, Mead and White are given in Roth, *Architecture of McKim, Mead and White,* 178–79. No similar figures appear to exist for Daniel Burnham's firm, but it is known that in 1912 it reached a peak payroll roster of 180, nearly twice as large as that of Holabird & Roche. On this see Thomas S. Hines, *Burnham of Chicago: Architect and Planner* (Chicago, 1979), 269.

3. A microfilm copy of the Dawson diaries is held in the Archives of American Art. The notes that follow refer to the page numbers in the ledger into which the diary entries were copied. I am grateful to Randy Ploog of Pennsylvania State University for alerting me to these documents.

4. Dawson diaries, 2.

5. Ibid.

6. Ibid., 2–3.

7. Ibid.

8. Ibid., 4.

9. Hines, *Burnham of Chicago,* 269.

10. Edward Renwick, "Recollections" (1932), 181.

11. That the Hotel Wausau in Wausau, Wisconsin (cat. no. 1022), was modeled on a hotel in Muncie, Indiana, was reported by Theodore Young, an employee at Holabird & Roche in the 1920s. Interview with the author, 1984.

12. There are only a few shreds of evidence in the Holabird & Roche papers on the existence of this office. I am grateful to George Ehrlich of the University of Missouri at Kansas City for reviewing Kansas City directories to confirm its presence. The work of the firm in the city is marked by a handful of commissions executed between 1913 and 1915, the most substantial of which was the Hotel Muehlebach (cat. no. 607).

13. Edward Renwick, for example, reported to the *Economist,* 11 July 1914, 86, that much promotional work was going on and that he expected considerable new commissions from the West and South.

14. Probably most of the buildings labeled "Chicago school" in guidebooks to various cities are of this era and derive from buildings like Holabird & Roche's Tribune, Otis, and McCormick and comparable buildings of the D. H. Burnham Company rather than buildings like the Marquette or the works of Louis Sullivan in the 1890s, which would have faded into obscurity by this time. The R. A. Long Building in Kansas City, built in 1906 to plans of architects Howe, Hoit and Cutler and pictured in George Ehrlich, *Kansas City, Missouri: An Architectural History, 1826–1990,* rev. and enl. ed. (Columbia, Mo., 1992), 58, is just one example taken virtually at random. Similar designs can be seen in the tall bank buildings at the main intersections of hun-

dreds of small American cities, particularly in the Midwest and West.

15. Holabird is given this title in *Report of the Special New County Hospital Commission,* dated 20 September 1910, for example.

16. *Economist,* 10 February 1912, 318, announced that Holabird & Roche would move into the Monroe Building on 1 May.

17. John Holabird was born in 1886. He attended the Hill School in Pottstown, Pennsylvania, and West Point, from which he graduated in 1907. After two years at the Engineers' School at Washington Barracks he returned to Chicago and worked briefly for his father's firm before setting out for the Ecole des Beaux-Arts in Paris in 1911. Returning to Chicago in 1913, he again entered the Holabird & Roche office and served as a captain in the Illinois National Guard. John Wellborn Root Jr. was born in Chicago in 1887, the son of the architect John Wellborn Root and Dora Louise Monroe. He attended the Chicago Latin School and Cornell University, from which he graduated in 1909, and studied at the Ecole des Beaux-Arts in Paris until 1913. On his return in 1914 he joined his friend John Holabird at Holabird & Roche. For a full account of the early careers of Holabird and Root see the forthcoming volume 2 of this work.

18. Russell F. Whitehead, "Holabird & Root: Masters of Design," *Pencil Points,* February 1938, 68.

19. On these outlying commercial nodes see Robert Bruegmann, "Schaumburg, Oak Brook, Rosemont, and the Recentering of the Chicago Metropolitan Area," in *Chicago Architecture and Design, 1923–1993,* ed. John Zukowsky (Munich, 1993), 159–78, and Malcolm Proudfoot, "The Major Outlying Business Centers of Chicago" (Ph.D. diss., University of Chicago, 1936).

20. The Muehlebach was sometimes compared to the Blackstone of Chicago, built in 1909 to designs by Benjamin Marshall. The Blackstone was smaller and slightly more opulent than the larger Holabird & Roche hotels like the LaSalle and the Sherman House, which were geared more to large business events.

21. Deering's grandfather, William, had founded Deering Harvester, and his father, Charles, was for years chairman of International Harvester. Although he lived in Evanston, C. W. Case's father always maintained an interest in the sea that began with his years in the navy, and in his later years he withdrew to his "castle" at Sitges, Spain, and his house in Florida. Charles's brother James, C. W. Case Deering's uncle, maintained a house in Paris and built Vizcaya, one of the country's most fabulous estates, in Miami. Walter Dill Scott and Robert B. Harshe, *Charles Deering: An Appreciation* (Boston, 1929).

22. On arcades see Johann Friedrich Geist, *Arcades: The History of a Building Type* (Cambridge, Mass., 1985).

23. On the City Beautiful see William H. Wilson, *The City Beautiful Movement* (Baltimore, 1989).

24. On this commission see John W. Stamper, *Chicago's North Michigan Avenue: Planning and Development, 1900–1930* (Chicago, 1991), and Miles Berger, *They Built Chicago: Entrepreneurs Who Shaped a Great City's Architecture* (Chicago, 1992), 179–82.

25. One such attempt is recorded in a scheme for the Holabird apartment building (cat. no. 470).

26. *Minneapolis Journal,* 1 November 1915. This clipping can be found in a scrapbook donated by Holabird & Root to the Chicago Historical Society.

Chapter Sixteen

1. Donald Hoffmann, in *The Architecture of John Wellborn Root* (Chicago, 1973), 153–54, reports that the owners of the site originally intended to build an office building. It is conceiv-

able that Burnham and Root merely modified existing plans slightly when the switch to a hotel was made.

2. See Robert A. M. Stern, Gregory Gilmartin, and John Montague Massengale, *New York Nineteen Hundred: Metropolitan Architecture and Urbanism, 1890–1915* (New York, 1983), 252–305.

3. On Clinton J. Warren see William Westfall, "From Homes to Towers: A Century of Chicago's Best Hotels and Tall Apartment Buildings," in *Chicago Architecture, 1872–1922: Reconfiguration of an American Metropolis,* ed. John Zukowsky (Chicago, 1993). See also Carl Condit, *Chicago School of Architecture: A History of Commercial and Public Building in the Chicago Area, 1875–1925* (Chicago, 1964), 150–56.

4. The building was called the Auditorium Apartments on drawings by Holabird & Roche. The change in name to the Congress Hotel apparently took place about 1911.

5. The original Peacock Alley was the tunnel connecting the Auditorium Hotel with the Annex. Later, after the tunnel was closed, the new corridor connecting the Warren and Holabird & Roche portions became known as Peacock Alley. The name derived from the corridor of the same name at New York's Waldorf-Astoria, designed by Henry Janeway Hardenbergh in 1897. It is possible that the design of Peacock Alley was done by Clinton J. Warren and merely extended by Holabird & Roche.

6. "New Auditorium Annex," *Inland Architect,* January 1903, 51.

7. The role of Holslag at the Congress is not entirely clear. According to Chicago directories and the 1911 edition of Marquis's *Book of Chicagoans* (Chicago, 1911), Holslag was born in 1870 and was trained at the Art Institute of Detroit, at the Academy of Design in New York, and in Europe. He had come to Chicago in 1889 and was president of his own firm, Holslag and Company. Holslag apparently had a wide range

of commissions in Chicago and elsewhere and seems to have worked at the Congress during the 1901 and 1905 additions and later in the 1910s.

8. Evelyn Marie Stuart, "Public Palaces and Their Art Treasures," *Fine Arts Journal,* October 1917.

9. Mencken quoted in David Lowe, *Chicago Interiors: Views of a Splendid World* (Chicago, 1979), 7.

10. On the Waldorf see Stern, Gilmartin, and Massengale, *New York Nineteen Hundred,* 257.

11. Stuart, "Public Palaces and Their Art Treasures," 37.

12. "The Japanese Tea Room of the Auditorium Annex, Chicago," *International Studio,* November 1907, xxxiv–xxxviii. I am indebted to Richard Joncas for this reference, which was found by Mary Woolover at the Burnham Library at the Art Institute of Chicago.

13. On New York hotels of this period see Stern, Gilmartin, and Massengale, *New York Nineteen Hundred,* 253–72.

14. On the Blackstone see Westfall, "From Homes to Towers," 279.

15. Peter B. Wight, "Additions to Chicago's Skyline," *Architectural Record,* July 1910, 18.

16. Martin Roche, "Recent and Current Work by Holabird & Roche, Chicago," *New York Architect* 3 (October 1909).

17. These statistics are taken from "Chicago's New Hotel LaSalle," *Hotel Monthly,* March 1910, 38–59.

18. "$6,500,000 LaSalle Hotel Thrown Open," *Chicago Tribune,* 9 September 1909.

19. Wight, "Additions to Chicago's Skyline," 18.

20. Franz Winkler (pseud. Montgomery Schuyler), "Some Chicago Buildings Represented by the Work of Holabird & Roche," *Architectural Record* 31 (April 1912): 330–31.

21. Elbert Hubbard, *A Little Journey to Hotel Sherman* (East Aurora, N. Y., 1911), 9–10.

The purpose of this pamphlet is unclear. Unlike the other "journeys," this work was not widely distributed or reprinted in collections of Hubbard's work. It is possible that it was produced as a kind of paid endorsement by Hubbard. The only copy I have found is in the Chicago Historical Society.

Chapter Seventeen

1. The previous city hall–county building had burned in the Great Fire of 1871.

2. Tilly ultimately appealed all the way to the United States Supreme Court, but without success.

3. On the 1885 building see Daniel Bluestone, *Constructing Chicago* (New Haven, Conn., 1991), 159–62.

4. In the 1830s this had been a park with a small courthouse in it. By the time of the Fire the city had joined the county, and their buildings occupied much of the site.

5. Bluestone, *Constructing Chicago*, 172.

6. On various schemes for a government center see the discussion in Bluestone, *Constructing Chicago*, 183–91.

7. Daniel H. Burnham and Edward Bennett, *Plan of Chicago* (Chicago, 1909; reprinted New York, 1993), chap. 7, "The Heart of Chicago."

8. Bluestone, *Constructing Chicago*, 195–97. For an excellent analysis of the essentially conservative nature of such City Beautiful schemes, see also Daniel Bluestone, "Detroit's City Beautiful and the Problem of Commerce," *Journal of the Society of Architectural Historians* 47 (September 1988): 245–62. For a broader context of Progressive movements see the classic volume by Richard Hofstadter, *The Age of Reform* (New York, 1955). An excellent example of Burnham's planning can be found in Paul Boyer, *Urban Masses and Moral Order in America, 1820–1920* (Cambridge, Mass., 1978), 261–76.

9. On this subject see the interesting comments of the important but today too little appreciated critic Barr Ferree in "The City Hall in America," *Engineering* 4 (1892): 201–20. Ferree, after complaining about the pomposity of many recent city halls in large American cities, writes (210): "Our cities are so rapidly becoming examples of commercial architecture that it seems not unreasonable to ask that in one type of building at least some monumental feeling be permitted, into which the ornamental shall be allowed to enter to a greater extent than into a business building. But the large buildings have failed so often to fulfill this public feeling that it would seem to be better, in the end, to treat our city buildings as business buildings, which, in very truth, they are."

10. *Chicago Tribune*, 11 April 1905.

11. On nineteenth-century competitions see Helene Lipstadt, ed., *The Experimental Tradition: Essays on Competitions in Architecture* (New York, 1989).

12. The complete jury consisted of John G. Shedd, William R. Ware, David B. Jones, and William McLaren, with John M. Ewen as chairman.

13. Frost and Granger had been founded in 1898. At the time of the county competition its major work had been the new LaSalle Street Station (1901–3). During the construction of the county building it would be awarded its largest and best-known work, the North Western Railroad Station. See John Zukowsky and Pauline Saliga, *Chicago Architects Design: A Century of Architectural Drawings from the Art Institute of Chicago* (New York, 1982), 76. The firm of Huehl and Schmid was founded in 1890. Huehl had been involved, with Edward Baumann, in the design of the well-known Chamber of Commerce Building of that year. See Roula Geraniotis, "An Early German Contribution to Chicago's Modernism," in *Chicago Architecture, 1872–1922: Reconfiguration of an American Metropolis,* ed. John Zukowsky (Chicago, 1993), 97.

14. *Proceedings, Cook County Commissioners,* 28 August 1905, 658–59. Excerpts also published in "Competition, Cook County Courthouse, Chicago," *Inland Architect* 46 (September 1905): 24.

15. The Customs House was the result of a major competition won by a relatively young midwestern architect, Cass Gilbert. Robert A. M. Stern, Gregory Gilmartin, and John Montague Massengale, *New York Nineteen Hundred: Metropolitan Architecture and Urbanism, 1890–1915* (New York, 1983), 74–75.

16. Among the many banks with similar facades are the Union Trust and Savings Bank by Wood, Donn and Deming, architects in Washington, D.C. (photograph in *Architectural Record,* January 1909, 19); the Northwestern Mutual Life Insurance Company, built in Milwaukee by Chicago architects Marshall and Fox (illustrated in Landscape Research, *Built in Milwaukee: An Architectural View of the City* [Milwaukee, n.d.], 86); and the Importers' and Traders' National Bank in New York by Joseph W. Freedlander (illustrated in Stern, Gilmartin, and Massengale, *New York Nineteen Hundred,* 185).

17. On the trip to Minneapolis see the obituary of Roche by Robert Craik McLean, *Western Architect,* July 1927, 120. According to McLean: "[Roche's] regard for the education of his draftsmen was evidenced when the Capitol of Minnesota was completed over twenty years ago. His firm chartered a special train and took the entire office force to Saint Paul to see Cass Gilbert's symphony in form and material." Although the characterization of the building is not specifically ascribed to Roche, McLean knew the architect well for many years and would certainly not have inserted a phrase like this in an obituary if it had been at odds with Roche's own ideas. On the Minnesota State Capitol, see Henry-Russell Hitchcock and William Seale, *Temples of Democracy: The State Capitols of the U.S.A.* (New York, 1976), 206–26.

18. Edward Renwick, "Recollections" (1932), 107–8.

19. *Chicago Tribune,* 30 August 1905, 8.

20. *Economist,* 2 September 1905, 332.

21. *Economist,* 4 July 1908, 30.

22. The panel to the north, for example, ostensibly represents Law. There are emblems that do relate to this theme, specifically a book under the seal of Cook County, a set of papers held by the youth on the left, and a sword held by the one to the right. But these symbolic props are not nearly as prominent as the spectacular musculature of the two nearly identical figures who hold them. Nor does the legal theme explain why they are apparently locking fingers above the county seal, or the prominence of the bulbous head and spiraling shaft of the sword handle. It is hard today to imagine that these panels were not viewed, at least by part of the Chicago population, as deliberately and provocatively homoerotic, but if so the viewers seem to have left us no tangible evidence. On these panels see also James L. Riedy, *Chicago Sculpture* (Urbana, Ill., 1981), 132–34.

23. *Economist,* 13 April 1907, 720.

24. Franz Winkler (pseud. Montgomery Schuyler), "Some Chicago Buildings Represented by the Work of Holabird & Roche," *Architectural Record* 31 (April 1912): 374.

25. Renwick, "Recollections," 112–13.

26. Unfortunately a fire in 1957 severely damaged the council chamber, and it was totally rebuilt in the style of the day.

27. Winkler, "Some Chicago Buildings," 370.

28. On Schuyler see the introduction by William H. Jordy and Ralph Coe to Montgomery Schuyler, *American Architecture and Other Writings* (New York, 1964).

29. Winkler, "Some Chicago Buildings," 370.

30. *Chicago City Manual, 1910,* 12.

31. On the civic center scheme, see pam-

phlet issued by the Chicago Plan Commission, "Chicago Civic Center" (1949).

Chapter Eighteen

1. This metaphor from biology has frequently been used by urban historians and others to describe the transformations of the city. See, for example, F. Stuart Chapin and Edward J. Kaiser, *Urban Land Use Planning*, 2d ed. (Urbana, Ill., 1965), 27–29.

2. On this house see the discussion in chapter 4 on Fort Sheridan.

3. John J. Flinn, *Standard Guide to Chicago for the Year 1891* (Chicago, 1891), 531.

4. On the juxtaposition of wealth and poverty and Chicago labor violence in the 1870s and 1880s, see chapter 4 on Fort Sheridan.

5. On the commercial invasions of Manhattan neighborhoods see Charles Lockwood, *Manhattan Moves Uptown: An Illustrated History* (Boston, 1976), and Christine Boyer, *Manhattan Manners: Architecture and Style* (New York, 1985), chap. 3 on Ladies Mile, 43–130.

6. There is no good study on the development of American automobile rows. Information for many cities can be gleaned from insurance maps used in conjunction with city directories. In other cases good photographs exist. For New York, for example, a good pictorial source is the set of photographs of Broadway in *Both Sides of Broadway*, compiled by the De Leeuw Riehl Publishing Company (New York, 1910). This can be correlated with the pages in E. Belcher Hyde, *Miniature Atlas Borough of Manhattan* (New York, 1912), to locate automobile buildings, which clustered along Broadway north of Times Square. On other cities there is just beginning to be a secondary literature. On Van Ness Avenue in San Francisco, for example, see San Francisco City Planning Department, *Van Ness Avenue Plan* (San Francisco, 1983). On Jefferson Avenue in Detroit see Allan Nevins, *Ford: The Times, the Man, the Company* (New

York, 1954), 254. For the automobile showroom there is even less published information. Richard Longstreth is working on automobile showrooms, particularly those of Washington, D.C. He was kind enough to share his extensive clipping file with me. See also Peter H. Phillips, "Walking in and Driving Out: A Brief Architectural History of Automobile Dealerships," *Society of Commercial Archaeology Journal*, spring–summer 1993.

7. Among these investment buildings were a building at Fourteenth and Wabash (cat. no. 339) and a store at Forty-seventh and Evans (cat. no. 340), also of 1902. It is interesting how similar all these buildings were.

8. It is also possible that this building was actually intended as a branch of the main Mandel Brothers Department Store and was devoted to the store's car sales. See, for example, the testimony in James J. Flink, *America Adopts the Automobile, 1885–1910* (Cambridge, Mass., 1970), 220, on the Wanamaker's garages in New York and Philadelphia.

9. The story of the earliest auto showroom south of the Loop is told in an anecdotal way in James Braden, "Chicago's Automobile Row: Once a Pygmy, Now a Giant," *Chicago Daily News*, 24 June 1929.

10. Joseph Kirkland and Caroline Kirkland, *The Story of Chicago* (Chicago, 1892–94), 2:348.

11. On the subject of the renovation of the ground floors of Loop office buildings to create large window spaces, see chapter 5 on the Tacoma.

12. On the development of taxpayers there is interesting information in Chester H. Liebs, *Main Street to Miracle Mile: American Roadside Architecture* (Boston, 1985), 1–14. Liebs uses "taxpayer" to mean any of the low commercial buildings found along commercial strips. According to Liebs, real estate operators believed these strips would all eventually be replaced by

taller buildings. Usage in Chicago at the turn of the century seems to suggest that the term was applied in a much more specific way and designated buildings in areas where the neighbors were already developed to a much higher density. It is hard to believe that developers along Forty-seventh Street or Sixty-third Street ever really expected their land to be developed with tall buildings.

13. Perry Duis and Glen Holt, "Boon for the Environment—the Car," *Chicago,* May 1977. Figures for the number of automobiles and garages in Chicago are from *Automobile,* 21 June 1902, as quoted in Flink, *America Adopts the Automobile,* 220. See also Stephen Sennott, "Chicago Architects and the Automobile, 1906–26," in *Roadside America: The Automobile in Design and Culture,* ed. Jan Jennings (Ames, Iowa, 1990), 157–69, and Louis S. Schafer, "Yesterday's City: Chicago's Horseless Carriages," *Chicago History,* winter 1994–95, 52–64.

14. See "Motor Row," in George E. Moran, *Moran's Dictionary of Chicago and Its Vicinity* (Chicago, 1909), 176–68: "Eleven years ago Chicago did not have a single automobile agent; ten years ago the first one put up his shingle, and at the present time there are 99 different makes of car represented in the city and many more clamoring to get in."

15. Henry Ericsson, *Sixty Years a Builder* (Chicago, 1942), 271–72.

16. On the first Studebaker (later Fine Arts) Building, see Pauline A. Saliga, ed., *The Sky's the Limit: A Century of Chicago Skyscrapers* (New York, 1990), 18–21.

17. The Studebaker Building at 629 S. Wabash was built in 1895. Frank A. Randall, *History of the Development of Building Construction in Chicago* (Urbana, Ill., 1949), 142. Carl Condit, *Chicago School of Architecture: A History of Commercial and Public Building in the Chicago Area, 1875–1925* (Chicago, 1964), 145; Saliga, *Sky's the Limit,* 18–21; Thomas Schlereth, "Be-

man, Pullman, and the European Influence," in *Chicago Architecture, 1872–1922: Reconfiguration of an American Metropolis,* ed. John Zukowsky (Chicago, 1993), 183–84.

18. *Motor News,* September–October 1986.

19. In the Blue Book there were dozens of pages of advertisements for garages, "auto stations," and other facilities. C. A. Coey and Company, for example, served notice that its "Main Office, Salesroom, Repair station and Livery Depot" at 1424–26 S. Michigan and its one hundred car capacity garage at 1710–18 Indiana Avenue were the largest in the West. See also George Moran, "Automobiles," in *Moran's Dictionary of Chicago,* 21–22.

20. On the use of deed covenants in residential neighborhoods see Marc A. Weiss, *Rise of the Community Builders: The American Real Estate Industry and Urban Land Planning* (New York, 1987).

21. Chicago's first comprehensive zoning law was passed in 1923.

22. The Ford dealership, whose building was designed by Chicago architect Christian Eckstorm, is discussed in Ericsson, *Sixty Years a Builder,* 273–74, and Braden, "Chicago's Automobile Row."

23. Peter B. Wight, "The Transmutation of a Residence Street, Resulting in Another Solution of a Utilitarian Problem by Architects," *Architectural Record,* April 1910, 286–87.

24. Illustrations and descriptions of some of these automobile buildings can be found in Wight, "Transmutation," and in J. L. Snow, "Automobile Sales and Service Building and Public Garage," *Brickbuilder,* March 1913. I am grateful to Suzanne Carter Meldman for calling my attention to the latter article. See also page on automobile buildings in Wells Brothers, *Buildings of Distinction* (Chicago, n.d.).

25. According to the recollection of builder Ericsson, the first specially constructed automobile "garage" in Chicago was built at 1217–20

Sheridan Road in 1905 to the plans of Christian Eckstorm. Ericsson, *Sixty Years a Builder,* 270–71, illustration after 148.

26. Wight, "Transmutation."

27. For a good description of a typical dealership see Nevins, *Ford: The Times, the Man, the Company,* 402–3.

28. Wight, "Transmutation," 293.

29. Wight, "Transmutation," 287.

30. Holabird & Roche would later design dozens of additional car-related buildings, including a number that are far more ambitious aesthetically than the modest ones on Michigan Avenue, notably the elegant fifteen-story headquarters of the Chicago Motor Club (cat. no. 1154) built in 1927–28 in the Loop, a set of extraordinarily modern-looking prototype designs for the Texaco station (cat. no. 1380) in 1932, and the highly acclaimed Chrysler Building (cat. no. 1383) at the 1933 Century of Progress fair. On South Michigan Avenue itself a second generation of automobile buildings in the 1920s, particularly the buildings of Alfred Alschuler, would be larger and more sophisticated than anything produced in the years 1900 to 1915. All these buildings date to a different era, one in which the car had become a fixture in everyday life.

Chapter Nineteen

1. On the University Club and its building the best source is Franz Schulze, *A Heritage: University Club of Chicago, 1887–1987* (Chicago, 1987). On club memberships see Dalton Potter, *Some Aspects of the Social Organization of the Elite of Chicago* (Chicago, 1949), and Dan Rottenberg, "The Right Club," *Chicago,* October 1978, 113 ff.

2. *Economist,* 14 August 1915.

3. The price for a front foot of land along Michigan Avenue between Monroe and Madison (assuming it extended back a half block) was about $15,000 in 1910. For a front foot in the same block of Clark or LaSalle the price would have been $20,000 and for State Street $31,000. Homer Hoyt, *One Hundred Years of Land Values in Chicago* (Chicago, 1933), 341.

4. See Edward Renwick, "Recollections" (1932), 130.

5. Some details of this interesting transaction are sketched in the *Economist,* 10 March 1906, 1482, and in Schulze, *University Club,* 51. According to these accounts, the land was leased by the International Harvester Company for $30,000 for the first year, $35,000 for the next five, $40,000 for ten years, and $45,000 for 178 years to a separate entity, the University Auxiliary Association, which was set up to own the leasehold and erect the clubhouse with $1,100,000 raised from the sale of stock. The club would in turn pay the association $100,000 a year, of which $45,000 went to the Harvester Company for the lease and $55,000 to the Auxiliary Company to provide 5 percent dividends on the stock.

6. Literature on the Chicago Athletic Club is cited in Frank A. Randall, *History of the Development of Building Construction in Chicago* (Urbana, Ill., 1949), 136.

7. On the Illinois Athletic Club see Randall, *Building Construction in Chicago,* 232, and *Chicago Tribune,* 19 March 1906.

8. Testimony on Roche's preference for Gothic can be found in an obituary of Roche by former Holabird & Roche employee Lucian Smith in *Architecture,* August 1927, 84.

9. On Crosby Hall see Nikolaus Pevsner, *London,* vol. 2 (Baltimore, 1952), 93. On the reconstruction see "The Rebuilding of Crosby Hall at Chelsea," *Architectural Review,* July 1910, 14–16.

10. On the New York University Club see Leland M. Roth, *McKim, Mead and White, Architects* (New York, 1983), 119–23.

11. Manuscript in the University Club archives.

12. What makes the "Reading of the Minutes" seem authentic is its verisimilitude—the

way much of the language really does recall the first decade of the twentieth century. On closer examination it becomes apparent that several of the most interesting phrases were lifted from a review of the building in the *Architectural Record* of July 1909, 1–23.

13. Renwick, "Recollections," 130–33.

14. *Inland Architect,* April 1908, 30.

15. *Architectural Record,* July 1909, 1–23.

16. Frederic Clay Bartlett also worked with Holabird & Roche on the Cook County Court-house–Chicago City Hall. On Bartlett, see Schulze, *University Club,* 39–41.

17. A description of the fifty-six panels can be found in *Architectural Record,* July 1909, 6.

18. The dining room windows are described in a series of columns, "Archivist's Corner," by University Club archivist Francis Weeks in the club's monthly newsletter, *Seventy Six,* starting in 1976. The library of the club has an index to these articles. The October 1982 issue of the magazine, also reprinted as a separate folder, carried a diagram identifying each of the windows.

19. Information on Roche's membership was provided by Francis Weeks.

20. Angus Hibbard, *Associations by Choice* (Chicago, 1936), 15–16.

21. This was contained in a speech Holabird gave in 1921. See also Renwick, "Recollections," 182.

22. *Economist,* 19 November 1910, 22. The author also revealed that a movement was afoot to have a suburban station of the Illinois Central Railroad built at Michigan and Monroe. Opined the writer: "If the station is put there, the effect of two handsome and thoroughly harmonious buildings upon the two corners of Michigan avenue and Monroe street will lend dignity and beauty to this entrance to the business portion of the city."

23. The most extensive notice appeared in *Architectural Record,* April 1912. Under the pseudonym Franz Winkler critic Montgomery

Schuyler wrote that he liked the building, and he commented on the way it failed to fully exploit the building envelope: "Whether, simply as the administrator of an investment, the architect is justified in a gable roof instead of continuing his walls to the usual uncouth parallelopiped may be questionable, but at any rate the sensitive spectator will thank him for having found the variation permissible." The building also appeared in *Wasmuths Monatshafte,* 1909.

Chapter Twenty

1. Illinois Bell Telephone Company, *A Golden Anniversary, 1878–1928: The Story of Fifty Years of the Bell Telephone in Chicago* (Chicago, 1928), 1–11. See also William Eugene Dickerson, "Organization and Control of the Illinois Bell Telephone Company" (Ph.D. diss., University of Chicago, 1926).

2. According to one hoary piece of Holabird & Roche firm lore, Martin Roche took stock in the telephone company in lieu of his share of the commissions and made a very large amount of money. Although it is quite possible this happened, there appears to be no confirmation of it.

3. On the battle between the telegraph and telephone companies see Alfred D. Chandler Jr., *The Visible Hand: The Managerial Revolution in American Business* (Cambridge, Mass., 1977), 200. A subsidiary of the American Bell Telephone Company, the American Telephone and Telegraph Company, was formed in 1885 to handle long distance calls. In 1900 AT&T became the parent company, absorbing the ABTC.

4. Illinois Bell Telephone Company, *Golden Anniversary,* 14.

5. Among the simple utilitarian structures was the Central Division Barn of 1910 (cat. no. 500). The camp designed by the firm was Margaret Mackin Hall in Warrenville (cat. no. 666).

6. Illinois Bell Telephone Company, *Golden Anniversary,* 17.

7. *Bell Telephone News,* September 1915.

8. *Bell Telephone News*, May 1914.

9. See, for example, Illinois Bell Telephone Company, *Golden Anniversary*, 26–27.

10. "Cut-over at Geneva," *Bell Telephone News*, January 1918, stated that the style was "colonial," but the fine distinctions between various late eighteenth- and early nineteenth-century styles were often not made by architects, let alone by writers of company magazines.

11. On the idea of a corporate identity see "Bell System Buildings: An Interpretation," *Bell Telephone News*, July 1928.

12. Illinois Bell Telephone Company, *Golden Anniversary*, 12–13.

13. See also Michael J. P. Smith, "Switching and Changing," *Inland Architect*, November–December 1990.

Chapter Twenty-one

1. The club was founded in 1911 and included a group of prominent Chicago women such as Jane Addams, Mrs. Ogden Armour, Mrs. Martin Ryerson, and Mrs. Harold McCormick. Although the three arts originally contemplated were music, drama, and the visual arts (painting and sculpture), the designation was soon changed to encompass architecture, photography, and design as well. A discussion of the aims of the club and its early history can be found in Harry Malm, "The Three Arts Club—70 Years of Service," *Townsfolk*, May 1981, "Three Arts Club Fact Sheet," undated sheets in the collection of the club, and an untitled history of the club by Frances Grace, compiled in 1967.

2. On the old South Side Gold Coast see chapter 18 on automobile row.

3. Eclecticism, in the hands of some of the most scholarly French architects, involved a rigorous intellectual analysis in which the style or combination of styles used in a building was the product of geographical, historical, and programmatic aspects of the proposed building. See, for example, the discussion of the Paris Opera by Charles Garnier in Christopher Curtis Mead, *Charles Garnier's Paris Opera: Architectural Empathy and the Renaissance of French Classicism* (Cambridge, Mass., 1991), and that of the Marseilles cathedral in Arthur Drexler, ed., *The Architecture of the Ecole des Beaux-Arts* (Cambridge, Mass., 1977), 424–27, and in Barry Bergdoll, *Leon Vaudoyer: Historicism in the Age of Industry* (Cambridge, Mass., 1994), 68–79. For American importations of this kind of idea see Richard Longstreth, "Academic Eclecticism in American Architecture," *Winterthur Portfolio*, spring 1982, 55–82.

4. Malm, "Three Arts Club," 17.

5. Diaries of Maniere Dawson, 30, from microfilm in the Archives of American Art.

6. On Van Brunt see "Architecture in the West," in *Architecture and Society: Selected Essays by Henry Van Brunt*, ed. William A. Coles (Cambridge, Mass., 1961), 180–94.

For those seeking specific information on a given building by the firm of Holabird & Roche/Holabird & Root, the most comprehensive listing can be found in my three-volume catalog *Holabird & Roche/Holabird & Root: An Illustrated Catalog of Works, 1880–1940* (New York: Garland, 1991). There is also a short introduction to the firm at the beginning of that work. Another concise account of the firm and its work is an essay titled "Holabird & Roche and Holabird & Root: The First Two Generations" that I wrote for *Chicago History,* fall 1980, 130–65. A somewhat different approach to the work of the firm from its founding through the present can be found in Werner Blaser's *Chicago Architecture: Holabird & Root, 1880–1992* (Cambridge, Mass.: Birk-hauser, 1992).

For those wishing to do further research on the firm's work before 1919, the place to start is the set of materials it has issued over the years. Although it never published a complete monograph as many other architectural offices did, Holabird & Roche did issue a publication shortly after 1925 titled *Selected Photographs Illustrating the Work of Holabird & Roche Architects.* There is also a volume titled *Hotels Designed by and Erected under the Supervision of Holabird & Roche,* issued in the 1910s. Both of these are rather rare. *Selected Photos* can be found in several libraries including that of the Art Institute of Chicago; *Hotels* is also in the Art Institute's collection. The firm also published, after World War II, various promotional materials that contain illustrations of early work—for example, *Holabird & Root: A Record of Practice since 1882.*

The most important general discussions of the firm's work published during 1880–1918 include Charles E. Jenkins, "A Review of the Work of Holabird & Roche," *Architectural Reviewer* 3 (June 1897): 1–41; Martin Roche, "Recent and Current Work of Holabird & Roche, Chicago," *New York Architect* 3 (October 1909); and the most substantial and insightful of all the early articles, Franz Winkler (pseudonym for Montgomery Schuyler), "Some Chicago Buildings Represented by the Work of Holabird & Roche," *Architectural Record* 31 (April 1912): 312–86.

Italic numbers refer to page numbers of illustrations. Maps 1-5 are found on pages 542-44. Buildings for which no location is given are in Chicago.

Barnes-Crosby Company, 207, 495n. 1

Barnett, Haynes and Barnett: Cook County Courthouse competition, 343–50, *345*, 351; Illinois Athletic Club, 343, *391*, 392

Barrett, M. L., and Company Factory—New Building (Cicero, Ill.) (cat. no. 571), 464

Bartlett, Francis, 31, 40, 473n. 24

Bartlett, Francis, Building (cat. no. 7), 31, 371, 445

Bartlett, Frederic Clay: City Council murals, 359; University Club interiors, 403, 404, 405, 406, 407

Bartlett Building (Kansas City, Mo.) (cat. no. 111), 40

basements: Boston Store, 237–38; Chicago Tribune Building, 178; English basement, 74; neighborhood telephone exchanges, 422; University Club, 403

Bass Estate Building (cat. no. 393), 457

Battle Creek City Bank (Battle Creek, Mich.) (cat. no. 346), 455

Bauer, Augustus, 29

Bauer and Black Unit One (cat. no. 285), 453

Bauer and Black Unit Two (cat. no. 431), 459

Bauer and Black Unit Nine (cat. no. 695), 468

Baumann, Edward: Ashland Block, 479n. 7; Chamber of Commerce Building, *75, 89,* 485n. 74; and Huehl, 502n. 13

Baumann, Frederick: *The Art of Preparing Foundations,* 480n. 16; Ashland Block, 479n. 7

bay windows: benefits of, 91, 127; Chicago Building, 485n. 81; code provisions on, 485n. 81; Marquette Building preliminary scheme, 111, 124; problems with, 91, 127; Tacoma Building, 91

Beaux-Arts style: Cleveland Public Library competition, 306; and eastern architects, 116; and John Holabird, 277, 297; ornament in, 139; and John Root Jr., 297; and Sullivan, 178

Beckley Ralson Company Building (cat. no. 560), 464, map 5

Behr, Theo, 301

Bell, Alexander Graham, 415

Bell Building (cat. no. 529), 298, *416,* 417, 463, map 3

Bell Telephone Company of Illinois, 416. *See also* Chicago Telephone Company

Belmont Country Club (Downers Grove, Ill.), 256, *266*

Belmont Office (Chicago Telephone Company) (cat. no. 530), *416,* 463, map 1

Beman, Solon Spencer: Chicago architects of 1880s, 30; first Studebaker Building, 373–74, *391;* Pullman Building, *391;* second Studebaker Building, *374,* 374–75

Bennett, Edward, 140, 337, *338,* 341–42, 363, 389, 390

Bernstein, David M., Flat and Shops Building (cat. no. 329), 454, map 1

Berry, C. B., 7

Berry, John, Esq., Store Building (cat. no. 146), 448

Berwyn Exchange (Berwyn, Ill.) (cat. no. 570), *416,* 464

Beth Moshav Z'Keinim (Orthodox Aged Jews Home) (cat. no. 315), 454

Beverly Office (Chicago Telephone Company) (cat. no. 587), *416,* 421, 426, 464, map 2

Blacker, R. R., Stable (Manistee, Mich.) (cat. no. 241), 451

Blackstone Hotel, 326, 329, 500n. 20

Blanchard Houses (Evanston, Ill.) (cat. no. 206), *149,* 450

Bland Garage (Anderson Carriage Company; Northwestern University Garage; Detroit Electric Company Service Station) (Evanston, Ill.) (cat. no. 523), 463

Block and Kuhl Department Store (Schipper and Block Building; Jefferson Trust and Savings Bank) (Peoria, Ill.) (cat. no. 381), 456

block 37, 256

Blue Book, 375, 505n. 19

Bogert, William B., House (Evanston, Ill.) (cat. no. 63), *149,* 267, 447

bonds, real estate, 482n. 33

Boone and Crockett Club (World's Co-

lumbian Exposition) (cat. no. 172), *47,* 449

Boone Building, *74*

Borg-Warner Building, 389

Born Building (cat. no. 432), *214,* 215, *215,* 292, 459, 496n. 13

Boston, Mass., 37

Boston Store (Charles Netcher Building; State-Madison Building) (cat. no. 384), 235–44; basements, 237–38; catalog of works, 457; central business district location, map 3; and Champlain Building, 236, 237, *238, 239,* 240, *240;* completed complex, *243;* complex uses, 242, 244; construction, 238–41; *Economist* on, 236, 237, 238; escalators, 238; as Holabird & Roche's first large department store, 181; land acquisition, 235–37, *236;* original buildings, *196;* perspective drawing of sections 1–5 and 6–8, *241;* Schuyler on, 244; section 1 under construction, *238;* sections 1–4 as finished, *239;* section 5 under construction, *240;* section 6 under construction, *242;* simplicity and uniformity of, 242; staged construction, 239; State Street map, *234;* street fronts, 244

Boston Store North Side Stable (cat. no. 433), 459

Boston Store South Side Stable (Greater Chicago Elks Lodge No. 954) (cat. no. 398), 457, map 2

Boston Store West Side Stable (cat. no. 397), 457

boulevards, 4, 145–46, 493n. 3

Boyington, W. W.: Columbus Memorial Building, *186, 188;* pre-Fire Chicago architects, 8, 29, 30; Schlesinger and Mayer Store, *186;* Stratford Hotel, *391*

Boynton, C. T., Residence (Evanston, Ill.) (cat. no. 64), *149,* 151–52, *152,* 267, 447

BPOE Clubhouse (Muskegon, Mich.) (cat. no. 612), 465

Bradley, Amis Aldis, 130, 133

Brandies Residence (cat. no. 527), 302, 463, map 2

Brent House (Dr. E. Fletcher Ingals Resi-

True Vine Missionary Baptist Church
(St. Bartholomew's Church) (cat. no.
170), 449, map 2
trusts. *See* real estate trusts
Tudor style, 302, 323
Turner Brass Company (Building for
Newberry Library) (cat. no. 314),
454, map 3
Tyson, Richard, Apartment Building
(Windham Apartment House) (cat.
no. 249), 452, map 4

Uebele Factory (cat. no. 40), 446
Union League Club, 484n. 63
Union Station Power House (St. Louis,
Mo.) (cat. no. 370), 456
Union Terminals (Ryerson Building;
Palmer Building) (cat. no. 366), 178,
456, 496n. 13
United States Customs House competi-
tion, 347, *347,* 503nn. 15, 16
Unity Building, *136*
universities. *See* Northwestern University;
University of Chicago; University of
Illinois
University Apartments, 165–66, *166, 167*
University Club (cat. no. 383), 390–409;
Architectural Record on, 398, 402;
Bartlett's decorations, 403, 404, 405,
406, 407; basement, 403; bedrooms,
405; catalog of works, 456; central
business district location, map 3;
College Hall, 405; Crosby Hall as
model, 393, 406; dining room (Cathedral Hall), 402, 405–7, *405, 406,*
507n. 18; earlier locations, 390; elevations, *399;* entrance, 402, 403,
413; founding, 390; gable, 398, 413;
Gothic style, 392–93, 394–95, 396,
403, 406, 407; Holabird as founding
member, 392; *Inland Architect* on,
398; Ladies' Annex, 403; leasehold,
506n. 5; light court, *400, 401,* 405;
lounging room (Michigan Room),
398, 403–5, *404;* main hall, 403;
Michigan Avenue location, *391;* and
Monroe Building, 409, 410–11, *412,*
413, 507n. 22; newsletter, 507n. 18;
opening ceremonies, 407–9, *408;*
perspective drawing, 396, *397,* 398;
plans, *400, 401;* private realm of,

402–9; Roche as member, 407; as
Roche's most accomplished work,
181; Roche's meeting with building
committee, 393–96, 398; Roche's
plaque, 407; Roche's special interest
in, 286; Roche's table in dining
room, 407; sections, *399;* shops on
ground floor, 398, 413; stained glass
windows, 404–5, 406–7; staircase,
403; Venetian Building influence,
392, 396; women's entrance, 403
University Club of New York, 393, 394,
395, 396, 398
University of Chicago: Geology and Geography Building (cat. no. 483), 292,
294, *295,* 461, map 2; Ricketts Lab
(cat. no. 626), 466
University of Illinois (Urbana, Ill.): Education Building (cat. no. 689), 306,
468; Wesley Foundation complex
(cat. no. 716), 306, 469
University School for Girls (cat. no. 484),
292, *295,* 461
Updike Apartment Building (cat. no.
250), 452
Urbana, Ill. *See* University of Illinois
urban history, xi—xii

Van Brunt, Henry, 441
Van Buren Street: Fort Dearborn Hotel,
300, *315,* 464, map 3; Hart, Schaffner & Marx Building, 171, 452; La-
Salle Street Station, *315,* 502n. 13;
Leiter Building II, 136, 183, 184,
185, 186, 234, 494n. 3; Rothschild
and Company Department Store,
234, 245, 246, 461, 497n. 11, map 3;
Wirt D. Walker Building, 73, 371–
72, *372,* 446; Yukon Building, 453,
map 3. *See also* McCormick Building; Monadnock Block Addition;
Old Colony Building; State Safety
Building
Vance Fireproof Warehouse (Iredale
Warehouse) (Evanston, Ill.) (cat. no.
430), 458
Van Osdel, John, 338, 340: Jenney contrasted with, 8; Palmer House, 183,
186, 234; as traditional builder, 29,
30
Van Zanten, Ann, x

Venetian Building (cat. no. 153), 187–90;
brickwork, 187; catalog of works,
448; cladding, 187; demolition, 199;
exterior view, *188;* location, *186,*
187, *234;* Massachusetts Trust for,
72, 187; medical offices, 187; nam-
ing, 187; natural light, 187; perspective, *189;* pitched roof, 190; plans of
first and typical floors, *190,* in securing reputation of firm, 40; signage,
189; terra cotta, 187, 198; top, 190;
and University Club, 392, 396; windows, 187, 189
Viollet-le-Duc, Eugène-Emmanuel,
485n. 78

Wabash Avenue: automobile showrooms,
373; book and music dealers, 223;
Cable Building, 453; commercializa-
tion south of Fourteenth Street, 378;
elevated tracks, 223; Grace Episcopal Church, 378; Lowney Chocolate
Company Building, 456, map 3;
Marshall Field Annex, *186,* 195;
Merchant's Building, 31, 476n. 9;
Palmer House, *315;* Powers Build-
ing, 454, map 3; rear facades of de-
partment stores, 223; Ryerson Building,
462, map 3; Studebaker
Building, *374,* 374–75; Wellington
Hotel, *315;* Windsor-Clifton Hotel,
315; Wirt D. Walker Building, 73,
371–72, *372,* 446. *See also* Auditorium
Building; Ayer Building; Cen-
tral Trading Company
Wabash Avenue Methodist Episcopal
Church, 378
Wabash Exchange (cat. no. 465), *416,*
460, map 3
Wacker Drive: Great Lakes Building,
462, map 3; Sears Tower, 231
Wade and Purdy, 80, 483n. 55
Waid, D. Everett, 122
Wainwright Building (St. Louis, Mo.),
136
Waldorf-Astoria (New York City), 322,
326, 501n. 5
Walker, James R., Residence (cat. no.
154), 52, *53,* 368, 448
Walker, Wirt D., 73; and Auditorium
Building, 73; death of, 99; first plan

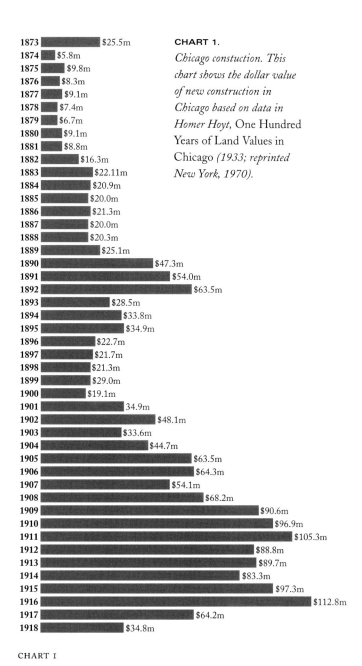

Year	Value
1873	$25.5m
1874	$5.8m
1875	$9.8m
1876	$8.3m
1877	$9.1m
1878	$7.4m
1879	$6.7m
1880	$9.1m
1881	$8.8m
1882	$16.3m
1883	$22.11m
1884	$20.9m
1885	$20.0m
1886	$21.3m
1887	$20.0m
1888	$20.3m
1889	$25.1m
1890	$47.3m
1891	$54.0m
1892	$63.5m
1893	$28.5m
1894	$33.8m
1895	$34.9m
1896	$22.7m
1897	$21.7m
1898	$21.3m
1899	$29.0m
1900	$19.1m
1901	34.9m
1902	$48.1m
1903	$33.6m
1904	$44.7m
1905	$63.5m
1906	$64.3m
1907	$54.1m
1908	$68.2m
1909	$90.6m
1910	$96.9m
1911	$105.3m
1912	$88.8m
1913	$89.7m
1914	$83.3m
1915	$97.3m
1916	$112.8m
1917	$64.2m
1918	$34.8m

CHART 1.

Chicago constuction. This chart shows the dollar value of new construction in Chicago based on data in Homer Hoyt, One Hundred Years of Land Values in Chicago *(1933; reprinted New York, 1970).*

CHART I

MAPS 1–5.

Holabird & Roche buildings in Chicago. These maps show all known substantial commissions by Holabird & Roche in the city of Chicago built between 1880 and 1918 and still standing in reasonably intact condition. The numbers refer to the entries in Robert Bruegmann, Holabird & Roche/Holabird & Root: An Illustrated Catalog of Works, 1880–1950 *(New York: Garland, 1991).*

94

90

588
Chicago Tel. Co.
Rogers Park Office

Pratt

Devon

Peterson

Bryn Mawr

Lincoln

Foster

McNulty
House **267**

Lawrence

316 Paulson
Flat Bldg.

562 Commonwealth
Edison
Ravenswood
Station

Montrose

593 Chicago Tel. Co.
Irving Office

Irving Park

Graceland
Cemetery
structures

49
244-6

Addison

Chicago
Tel. Co.
Lakeview **618**
Office

602 Tilt
House

Belmont

365

Mandel Bros.
Warehouse

Diversey

248
Naughton
Flats

Fullerton

Armitage

530
Chicago Tel. Co.
Belmont Office

S. I. Frank
Bldg. **622**

P. C.
Brooks
Bldg.

94 Prince
House

North

583 **697**
P. C. Brooks
Garage

329

SEE
NEAR
NORTH
MAP

Division

674
Nestor
Johnson
Mfg.

Bernstein
Flats and Shops

Chicago

20 Funk
House

Joseph P.
Hubbard
Mfg. Bldg.

Lake

634
Chicago Tel. Co.
Austin Office   Madison

293
330

Chapman
& Smith Bldg.

SEE
DOWNTOWN
MAP

306

290

George
M. Hill
Co. Bldg.

Roosevelt

441
Cook Co.
Tuberculosis
Hospital

L A K E   M I C H I G A N

Austin

Central

Laramie

Cicero

Pulaski

Central Park

Kedzie

California

Western

Damen

Ashland

Halsted

Broadway

Clark

Elston

Clybourn

Milwaukee

Grand

Ogden

Ridge

Broadway

MAP I

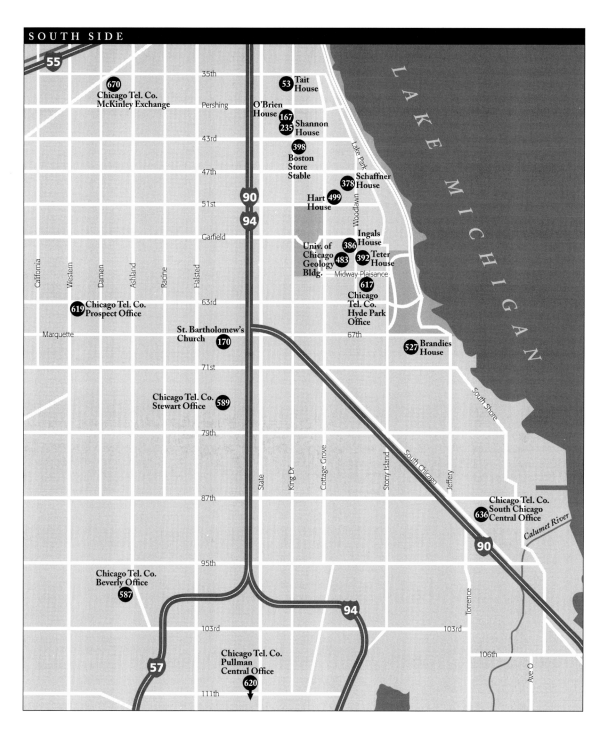

55

670 Chicago Tel. Co.
McKinley Exchange

35th

Pershing

53 Tait
House

O'Brien
House

43rd

167
235 Shannon
House

398
Boston
Store
Stable

47th

378 Schaffner
House

Hart **499**
House

51st

90

94

Garfield

Ingals
House

Univ. of **386**
Chicago
Geology **483** **392** Teter
Bldg. House

Midway Plaisance

617
Chicago
Tel. Co.
Hyde Park
Office

619 Chicago Tel. Co.
Prospect Office

63rd

Marquette

St. Bartholomew's
Church
170

67th

527 Brandies
House

71st

Chicago Tel. Co.
Stewart Office **589**

79th

LAKE MICHIGAN

Lake Park

Woodlawn

California

Western

Damen

Ashland

Racine

Halsted

State

King Dr

Cottage Grove

Stony Island

South Chicago

Jeffery

South Shore

87th

Chicago Tel. Co.
South Chicago
636 Central Office

Calumet River

90

Chicago Tel. Co.
Beverly Office

95th

587

94

103rd

103rd

106th

Torrence

Ave O

57

Chicago Tel. Co.
Pullman
Central Office

111th

620

MAP 2

MAP 4

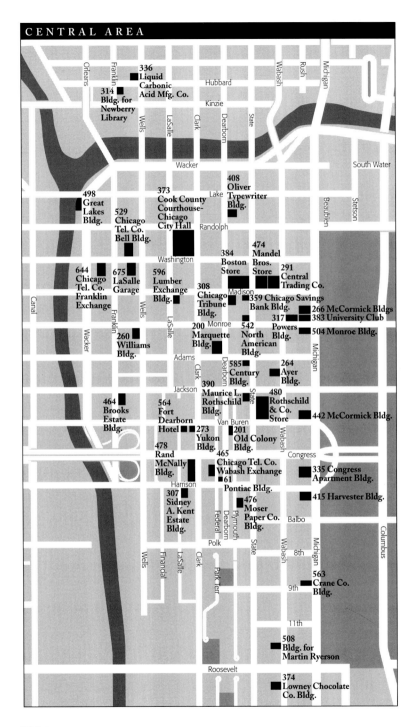

CENTRAL AREA

336 Liquid Carbonic Acid Mfg. Co.
314 Bldg. for Newberry Library
498 Great Lakes Bldg.
529 Chicago Tel. Co. Bell Bldg.
373 Cook County Courthouse-Chicago City Hall
408 Oliver Typewriter Bldg.
474 Mandel Bros. Store
384 Boston Store
291 Central Trading Co.
644 Chicago Tel. Co. Franklin Exchange
675 LaSalle Garage
596 Lumber Exchange Bldg.
308 Chicago Tribune Bldg.
359 Chicago Savings Bank Bldg.
266 McCormick Bldgs
383 University Club
317 Powers Bldg.
504 Monroe Bldg.
260 Williams Bldg.
200 Marquette Bldg.
542 North American Bldg.
585 Century Bldg.
264 Ayer Bldg.
390 Maurice L. Rothschild Bldg.
480 Rothschild & Co. Store
442 McCormick Bldg.
464 Brooks Estate Bldg.
564 Fort Dearborn Hotel
273 Yukon Bldg.
201 Old Colony Bldg.
478 Rand McNally Bldg.
465 Chicago Tel. Co. Wabash Exchange
61 Pontiac Bldg.
335 Congress Apartment Bldg.
307 Sidney A. Kent Estate Bldg.
476 Moser Paper Co. Bldg.
415 Harvester Bldg.
563 Crane Co. Bldg.
508 Bldg. for Martin Ryerson
374 Lowney Chocolate Co. Bldg.

Orleans, Franklin, Wells, LaSalle, Clark, Dearborn, State, Hubbard, Kinzie, Rush, Wabash, Michigan, Wacker, South Water, Lake, Randolph, Washington, Madison, Monroe, Adams, Jackson, Van Buren, Congress, Harrison, Balbo, Polk, Roosevelt, Canal, Franklin, Wacker, Financial, Wells, Clark, Park Ter, Federal, Plymouth, Dearborn, State, Wabash, 8th, 9th, 11th, Michigan, Columbus, Beaubien, Stetson

MAP 3

NEAR NORTH SIDE

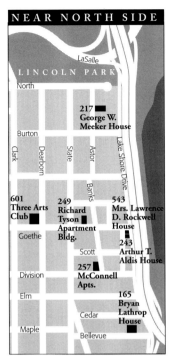

LINCOLN PARK
217 George W. Meeker House
601 Three Arts Club
249 Richard Tyson Apartment Bldg.
543 Mrs. Lawrence D. Rockwell House
243 Arthur T. Aldis House
257 McConnell Apts.
165 Bryan Lathrop House

LaSalle, North, Burton, Clark, Dearborn, State, Astor, Banks, Lake Shore Drive, Goethe, Scott, Division, Elm, Cedar, Maple, Bellevue

NEAR SOUTH SIDE

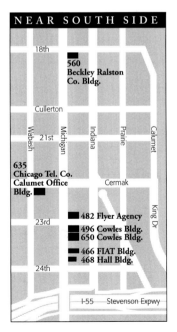

560 Beckley Ralston Co. Bldg.
635 Chicago Tel. Co. Calumet Office Bldg.
482 Flyer Agency
496 Cowles Bldg.
650 Cowles Bldg.
466 FIAT Bldg.
468 Hall Bldg.

18th, Cullerton, 21st, 23rd, 24th, Wabash, Michigan, Indiana, Prairie, Calumet, King Dr, Cermak, I-55, Stevenson Expwy

MAP 5